POLICING
for the
21st CENTURY

Realizing the Vision of Police in a Free Society

Kendall Hunt
publishing company

Christine L. Gardiner
California State University, Fullerton

Matthew J. Hickman
Seattle University

Cover image © Shutterstock.com

Kendall Hunt
publishing company

www.kendallhunt.com
Send all inquiries to:
4050 Westmark Drive
Dubuque, IA 52004-1840
Copyright © 2017 by Kendall Hunt Publishing Company

ISBN 978-1-4652-9112-7

Printed in the United States of America

DEDICATION

Christie Gardiner:

To Steve, Allie, Mackenzie, Cara and Brian: You are the light of my life and the reason for my perseverance.

Matt Hickman:

To Orit and Emerson: The time I spend on these projects is time I can't spend with you, but it makes the time we share all the more wonderful. You get that, and we are stronger for it. Like everything that I do, this one's for you.

BRIEF TABLE OF CONTENTS

TABLE OF CONTENTS

PART 1   BACKGROUND

PART 4   MAINTAINING PUBLIC TRUST

PREFACE

Author's note: When we proposed this book in 2013 policing was not a national discussion point. Except for a few academics, police leaders, students, and the occasional journalist—no one was really talking much about the state of policing. That changed during the summer of 2014 when Eric Garner and Michael Brown died while being taken into police custody. The deaths of these two men (both Black) led to serious questions about police use of force practices and public protests across the country. These protests revealed the serious lack of trust that still exists between many communities and the police. Although President Obama convened a Presidential Task Force in December 2014 to investigate the matter and offer recommendations, little has changed. As this book goes to press in July 2016, there has been a new round of questionable police shootings involving men of color that has captured the nation's attention and outrage. This time, however, seems to be different as individual police officers have become the targets of public anger and killed for retaliatory purposes. These events make the text within these pages more important and timely than perhaps they were when we began this project. We hope that this book will inspire the next generation of police leaders.

Law enforcement is one of the core functions of the criminal justice system. It is also the function most visible to members of the public. This function has changed remarkably through the ages and reflects changes in society. One constant, however, is that the police in a democratic society must be accountable to the public in order to ensure that police activity reflects democratic ideals. Too often, and too easily, members of the public, the police, elected officials, and others forget this simple fundamental proposition. The intent of this text is to provide a thematic overview of policing and its role in American society. It examines the history and basic functions of law enforcement, highlights the role of police within a democratic society, and discusses the importance of legitimacy for the system and society at large.

The book is divided into four thematic areas: 1) the background of policing; 2) fundamentals of policing; 3) controlling crime and 4) maintaining the public trust.

THE BACKGROUND OF POLICING

The introductory section of this book highlights the current state of policing in a democratic society and provides the history of policing up to the present day.

Chapter 1, *democratic policing*, focuses on three common themes in discussions of democratic policing: transparency, accountability, and fairness. The chapter frames democratic policing as a process, rather than an end in and of itself, in which agencies must stay constantly engaged. To a large extent, this requires some acknowledgment that the principal concern of democratic policing is not the behavior of citizens; it is the behavior of the police. The precept also requires some investment in data collection that permits evaluation of the extent to which these democratic ideals (transparency, accountability, and fairness) are being satisfied as part of the process of democratic policing. This foundational chapter "sets the tone" for the other chapters.

Chapter 2, *history of policing: ancient roots and early policing*, focuses on historical aspects of the police role in society. It traces the roots of policing from the state police in Egypt, the Praefectus Urbi in Rome, and kin policing in Greece to frankpledge, the constable system, the Bow Street Runners, and the London Metropolitan Police in England, and to the night watches, slave patrols, and vigilance committees in the United States.

The history of policing continues in chapter 3 with *modern policing in America*, which traces the history of American policing from the first official police departments in the 1800s through to present day. It follows Kelling and Moore's three eras of American policing (political, reform/professional, and community) and proposes that we are now in a new, fourth, era which we term the intelligence era in recognition of the emphasis that is now placed on using crime and criminal intelligence and technology to guide policing tactics and reduce crime.

FUNDAMENTALS OF POLICING

The second section presents students with the rudimentary facts about the structure and organization of law enforcement as well as characteristics of the job and officers that students need to possess to move deeper into the topics in subsequent chapters.

Chapter 4, *the law enforcement industry*, examines the structure of law enforcement in the United States. Specifically, it introduces students to the unique functions of law enforcement at the federal, state, and local level. It also explains the function and purpose of private police. This chapter includes lists of the main agencies at each level along with counts of personnel.

Chapter 5, *local agency structure and organization*, provides an overview of organizational theory, describes the most common management structures found in law enforcement agencies, and explains the importance of agency from a democratic policing perspective. In addition, the chapter examines organizational structure from the lens of community policing to identify the organizational components that are needed to support and truly achieve this type of policing. It also looks at some of the special functions and units found in law enforcement agencies as well as multi-jurisdictional task forces.

Chapter 6, *police officers*, focuses on the characteristics of police officers and the impact that the job has on officers. Specifically, it begins with a discussion of the recruitment and selection of police officers and continues with discussions about police subculture, diversity, education and training, and the stresses of the job. It pays particular attention to these topics as they relate to democratic policing and the increasing desire of agencies to hire and train guardians rather than warriors.

Chapter 7, *police discretion*, examines the importance of discretion in a police officer's daily job. It starts with an introduction to the concept of discretion and explains some of the limits on officers' discretion. It also examines the use of discretion within the context of street level bureaucracy and highlights the importance of using discretion to balance the constitutional rights of the public with the need to protect the public. It concludes with a discussion of the potential negative consequences of discretion (corruption, racial profiling, etc.).

CRIME CONTROL

The third section represents the majority of the material pertaining to how law enforcement officers control and prevent crime. It includes chapters on the most popular policing strategies as well as policing special populations and situations, legal issues, and investigations and interrogations.

Chapter 8, *basic functions*, presents an overview of the basic functions that law enforcement officers perform (order maintenance, service, and law enforcement) and explains how dispatchers manage calls for service. The chapter also describes the patrol function, the traffic function, and the history and controversy of police paramilitary units. It discusses the classic research studies on patrol practices and presents our current state of knowledge on the topic. The chapter incorporates discussions of public perceptions of police during traffic stops and other encounters and the implications for police legitimacy

Chapter 9, *identifying problems*, explains how police officers and supervisors decide where to focus their efforts and deploy their resources to most efficiently and effectively reduce crime or community problems. The chapter emphasizes intelligence-led policing as a commitment by police agencies to use data to support their crime reduction strategies and practices. It includes introductions to crime mapping, crime analysis, COMPSTAT, real-time crime centers, and fusion centers. These tools, their benefits and potential consequences, are discussed within a democratic policing framework.

Chapter 10, *responding to problems*, describes a variety of the most popular police philosophies and strategies in use throughout the United States to reduce crime and community problems. It explains community oriented policing, problem-oriented policing, order maintenance policing according to the broken windows theory, and zero tolerance policing. It also depicts "Stop and Frisk" and civil "no trespass" orders in use in some cities. All of these strategies and philosophies are framed and discussed within the context of democratic policing, legitimacy, and the struggle for due process and public safety.

Chapter 11, *policing special populations*, describes unique strategies and tactics used to combat specific, re-occurring issues with discrete populations such as gangs, homeless individuals, mentally ill individuals, and juveniles. The democratic policing theme is carried through each sub-topic. For example, the role of police officers in beats with a high concentration of individuals experiencing homelessness (and often mental illness) is quite complex and has implications for police legitimacy for all users of public space within the area (and beyond).

Chapter 12, *investigations and interrogations*, traces the history of investigations and explains what investigators do and how they solve crimes, including through the use of science, technology, and community support. It explains the research on investigations and interrogations and describes recent approaches and policies aimed at improving both. Finally, it illuminates the consequences of improper interrogation tactics for the entire criminal justice system and society from a democratic policing perspective.

MAINTAINING PUBLIC TRUST

The fourth section concludes the text with a discussion of police behavior, legitimacy, and accountability. It also includes a chapter about emerging issues and the future of policing.

Chapter 13, *police behavior*, discusses the police behaviors that most often defy public trust and describe how police behavior affects public cooperation and ultimately public safety. It examines legal constraints on police behavior, corruption and ethics violations, as well as use of force and policing crowds. Importantly, it discusses the dual role of democratic police in crowd situations to protect demonstrators' right to free speech while maintaining public peace and safety and enforcing applicable laws.

Chapter 14, *legitimacy and accountability*, describes the mechanisms for achieving democratic policing goals. It revisits the ideas presented in chapter 1, expands the discussion, and takes it to a much deeper level. Finally, it proposes new measures of ascertaining public satisfaction with police officer job performance, discusses citizen oversight committees, federal pattern and practice suits, and police community relations, including media relations.

The final chapter of the book, chapter 15- *future issues in policing*, discusses emerging issues that currently, or will in the future, pose challenges for police and the criminal justice system. It discusses issues that have become dominate due to the global economy and accessibility of information across the world through the internet (human trafficking, sex tourism, child pornography, financial scams). Additionally, it touches on new crimes that have emerged (or proliferated) with the advent of the internet (cyber bullying, copyright infringement) and how policing has (or will need to) adapt to these new categories of crime.

FEATURES

This book contains several pedagogical features to enhance student learning of the material. Specifically, each chapter includes *learning objectives* at the beginning of each chapter to draw the readers' attention to important concepts and ideas, *key terms* italicized and defined throughout the chapter, and *discussion questions* at the conclusion of each chapter to encourage critical thinking by the students and conversations on the material presented. In addition, each chapter contains special topic boxes that highlight key concepts/themes and special interest material. These opportunities allow students to connect their reading from this text to real world examples to enhance skills. Numerous charts, tables, and graphics also enhance students' learning experience. Instructor-related resources such as a test-bank, lecture outlines, or PowerPoint slides are also available.

ACKNOWLEDGMENTS

Writing this book has been a labor of passion and persistence. It exists because we both are passionate about the policing profession and hopeful that the positive changes now underway will continue to develop into greater accountability, transparency, and fundamental fairness for all. Despite this passion, this book would not have come to fruition without the assistance of a few key people.

We would first like to thank Paul Carty at Kendall-Hunt for suggesting the project and working with us from inception to completion, Angela Willenbring for her patience and hard work on our behalf, and the many others at Kendall Hunt who made this book better than it was when it left our hands.

We would also like to thank the reviewers for providing honest and valuable comments that improved the final product: Vaughn Crichlow (Florida Atlantic University), Phillip Kopp (California State University, Fullerton), and Joseph Schafer (Southern Illinois University)—this book is better because of you.

We also owe a debt of gratitude to each of the contributors who took the time to write about their experiences in the field: James Bueermann, Joel Davis, William Donoghue, Brian Meux, Timothy Miller, Sue Rahr, and Michael Scott.

Also Timothy Smith (California State University, Fullerton), our undergraduate research assistant, deserves a special shout-out for his efforts and contributions.

Finally, we owe more gratitude than we can express in a few sentences to our families (Steve, Allie, and Mackenzie; Orit and Emerson) who had to suffer the pains and pick up the slack when we were in the throes of this project. We sincerely appreciate your willingness to put up with us, your consideration when we were under deadlines, and your patience during the entire process. We couldn't have done it without you!

PART 1

BACKGROUND

1 DEMOCRATIC POLICING

LEARNING OBJECTIVES

After reading this chapter, students should be able to:

1 Explain/discuss the core function of police in a democratic society.

2 Demonstrate understanding of key elements of democratic policing, such as transparency, accountability, and fundamental fairness.

3 Explain/discuss the idea of police legitimacy.

4 Explain/discuss the role of coercion in policing.

KEY TERMS

Democratic policing	Police power	Transparency
Police legitimacy	Bill of Rights	Accountability
Natural rights	Rule of law	Fairness

OVERVIEW

In this chapter, we tackle the "why" question: why do we need the police? In order to answer this question, we will explore ideas about the origins of the police in the United States. We will do so through the lens of **democratic policing**, a loosely-defined but critically important concept, especially in light of contemporary questions about the increasing militarization of police, recent federal civil rights investigations focused on the behavior of law enforcement agencies (including racially-biased policing and the use of excessive force), tragedies such as the recent events in Ferguson, MO, and New York, NY (see A Crisis of Police Legitimacy box), and an increasing focus on what can be done to enhance **police legitimacy**—the extent to which we recognize and are willing to defer to the authority of the police to regulate behavior. By the end of the chapter, the reader should have a firm grasp of the origins and core vision of police in a free society.

"A CRISIS OF POLICE LEGITIMACY?"

A recent newspaper headline summarizes a large part of the current controversy surrounding policing and legitimacy in the United States: "Why do small police departments need 18-ton armor-plated assault vehicles?" (Martin, 2014). While there were a variety of issues surrounding both the Michael Brown case in Ferguson, MO and the Eric Garner case in New York, (including but not limited to race relations, police use of force, and prosecutorial discretion in the grand jury process), concerns over the increasing militarization of the police came out strongly at the national level during the police response to citizen protests in Ferguson. On August 9, 2014, Michael Brown was shot and killed by Ferguson police officer Darren Wilson. Brown had robbed a convenience store and Officer Wilson responded to the robbery call. Wilson encountered Brown in the street while seated in his cruiser, at which point an altercation ensued in which Brown allegedly grabbed for Wilson's gun, which discharged. Brown fled and Wilson pursued, shooting at Brown several times. Brown was unarmed, and there were conflicting witness accounts as to his actions (and those of Officer Wilson) as well as physical evidence. Brown was an African-American teenager, while Officer Wilson is white. Race was an immediate issue in a town that is largely black but policed by a predominately white police force, and protests and rioting ensued. The entire nation (and indeed the world) watched as the police in Ferguson deployed military-like personnel and equipment, including officers dressed in camouflage and carrying automatic weapons and armor-plated assault vehicles. This incident focused attention on the Department of Defense "1033" program, by which surplus military equipment is transferred to state and local law enforcement agencies, and has led to ongoing debate about whether police departments (particularly small town departments) actually need such equipment. The Michael Brown case heated up even further on November 24, 2014 when it was announced that a grand jury had voted not to return an indictment in the case. This decision resulted in destructive rioting in Ferguson and additional protests (though largely peaceful) for several weeks across the United States and abroad. A common protest slogan being chanted and appearing on picket signs was, "Black lives matter!"

On July 17, 2014, 43-year-old Eric Garner was arrested for selling cigarettes illegally, in that they were "loose" and from packs without tax stamps. However, he had apparently just broken up a fight, which may have been what drew officers' attention. Garner was also known to officers and had been previously arrested some 30 times. When officers tried to handcuff Garner, he pulled away and then Officer Daniel Pantaleo placed Garner in a chokehold. Garner was heard to say, "I can't breathe!" several times during the arrest, lost consciousness, and was taken to a hospital where he was pronounced dead. Garner was African-American, while Officer Pantaleo is white. On December 3, 2014, shortly after the announcement of the grand jury decision in the Michael Brown case, it was announced that a grand jury in New York voted not to indict Officer Pantaleo. Protests ensued in New York and many other cities, and common protest slogans included both, "I can't breathe!" and "Black lives matter!"

In response to these high-profile incidents, President Obama on December 18, 2014 signed an Executive Order creating a Task Force on 21st Century Policing. The task force was empaneled with several notable police leaders, academics, community leaders, and others. A major purpose of the task force was to examine how to strengthen public trust in the police and foster strong relationships between local law enforcement agencies and the communities that they protect. In a series of meetings, they heard testimony from invited speakers and took public comment. The task force report with recommendations was released in May 2015. It can be found on the internet at http://www.cops.usdoj.gov/pdf/taskforce/TaskForce_FinalReport.pdf; the recommendations are contained in Chapter 3.

LIFE, LIBERTY, AND PROPERTY

If nothing else, one core value shared by most citizens of the United States is individual freedom, an idea that we often use synonymously with *liberty*. Perhaps it's something we tend to take for granted these days, or maybe we value it on a more abstract level, yet we certainly exercise our liberty on a regular basis. But what does this concept mean? Most would probably agree with the general idea that we ought to be able to live our lives as we see fit, free from oppressive governmental rule, provided we don't infringe on anyone else's equal right to do the same. This idea was certainly embraced by American colonists when they formally declared separation from Great Britain, and in many ways, this idea succinctly summarizes who we are as a people.

This is not a political science textbook, and we will leave much of the details to that discipline. However, it is necessary to review some of the basics in order to properly situate the origins and evolving role of the police in the United States. First and foremost are the ideas of **natural rights**—particularly those of life, liberty, and property—and of the need for order, and a system for protecting these natural rights. Although the writings of philosopher John Locke were a particularly strong influence on the early colonists, Thomas Hobbes and others also provided the intellectual roots of *social contract* that we find interwoven in our Nation's foundational documents. This is the idea that order naturally emerges from the fact that humans are reasoning and self-interested creatures, and they recognize that it is in their interests to establish a system of governance for the purpose of ensuring order. Some persons may choose to violate the natural rights of others, thus the benefit of forming a system of governance with each other in order to protect those natural rights.

The citizens of the United States value individual freedom.

© Mike Flippo/Shutterstock.com

One needs look no further than the Declaration of Independence:

> We hold these truths to be self-evident, that all men are created equal, that they are endowed by their Creator with certain unalienable rights, that among these are life, liberty, and the pursuit of happiness. That to secure these rights, governments are instituted among men, deriving their just powers from the consent of the governed ....

A major purpose—if not *the* purpose of government—as envisioned by Locke (and important because Locke's work so heavily influenced the early colonists and subsequent framers of the Constitution), is to protect these core natural rights of life, liberty, and property. Although the Declaration of Independence states "pursuit of happiness" rather than property, and it is a far from settled matter what Thomas Jefferson intended with that particular phrase, it is widely believed that property rights (the right to own, use, and transfer property) underlie the pursuit of happiness.

The key mechanism for protecting these natural rights, then, is a government imbued with **police power**, deriving its authority from the people. Where the Declaration of Independence expresses the ideals of government, the Constitution provides the framework for a government charged with protecting those ideals, and the first 10 Amendments (or the **Bill of Rights**) establish the rights of individuals within the context of governance. A primary concern of the Founders was the need to limit the power of those so entrusted by decentralizing authority within and across levels of government, separating powers, and providing a system of checks and balances (thus the Constitution establishes the three branches of government, where the Legislative makes the laws, the Judicial interprets the laws, and the Executive enforces the laws). Another primary concern was that those entrusted with power would tend to abuse their power, and so the **rule of law** was central to the structure of government.

In the context of law enforcement, we therefore place importance not only on the substantive laws being enforced, but perhaps even greater importance on the procedural laws that govern enforcement, which are rooted in the Bill of Rights (see box). This need to balance the concern for order with the concern for procedure, often referred to as a tension between crime control and due process, is a perennial source of conflict for law enforcement.

"THE BILL OF RIGHTS"

The first 10 amendments to the Constitution, called the Bill of Rights, guarantee certain basic individual rights and freedoms. The Constitution was ratified by the required nine states on June 21, 1788; remaining states refused to ratify the Constitution until these 10 amendments were added. The Bill of Rights was ratified on December 15, 1791. The fourth and fifth amendments are particularly important from the perspective of police procedure.

First Amendment	Guarantees freedom of religion, speech, and the press, and the rights to peaceably assemble and to petition the government.
Second Amendment	Guarantees the right to keep and bear arms.
Third Amendment	Protects citizens against forced quartering of soldiers.
Fourth Amendment	Protects citizens against unreasonable searches and seizures of their person, houses, papers, and effects; specifies that warrants require probable cause and must be specific with regard to the places to be searched and the persons or things to be seized.
Fifth Amendment	Requires a grand jury indictment for serious crimes; protects citizens against double jeopardy (being tried twice for the same offense) and self-incrimination; requires that no person be deprived of their life, liberty, or property without "due process of law"; and forbids the taking of private property for public use (eminent domain) without fair compensation.

Sixth Amendment	Guarantees the right to a speedy and public trial by jury; to be told of the charges against him/her; to be confronted with the witnesses against him/her; be permitted to introduce his/her own witnesses; and to have legal counsel.
Seventh Amendment	Guarantees the right to jury trial in civil cases.
Eighth Amendment	Prohibits courts from requiring excessive bail, imposing excessive fines, and forbids cruel and unusual punishment.
Ninth Amendment	Makes clear that these first eight amendments are not an exhaustive list of the rights of citizens, and that the people retain any rights not specifically listed.
Tenth Amendment	Makes clear that the individual states and the people retain any powers not specifically delegated to the United States.

DEMOCRATIC POLICING: WHAT IS IT?

Perhaps it is a cliché, but it can be useful to begin this type of discussion by examining the etymology of these words, *democratic* and *policing*. The word democratic comes from the Greek *demokratikos* (of or for democracy), and democracy comes from the Greek *demos* (the common people) and *kratos* (rule, power). Democracy then, at a basic level, refers to a system of governance by the people. We have already been discussing this idea in the context of creating the structure of government. To put some finer points on it, ours is a republic (a government without a monarch) and a type of representative democracy where individuals are elected to public office in order to govern on our behalf. In theory (if not in practice), power resides with the people and is exercised through our elected representatives (i.e., with the consent of the governed).

The word *police* is a little more difficult, but is often traced to the Latin *politia* (citizenship, government, the state), the Greek *polis* and *politen* (a city and its citizens), and later to the French *policier* (civil organization, administration of public order). Police then, at a basic level, refers to governmental regulation, control, and order but also has some traces of the citizen—those whose behavior is being regulated. *Policing* can then be taken as the act or system of regulation, control, and order, but those loose traces of the citizen are important, and perhaps made more clear in a core principle of policing expressed by a pivotal figure in the history of policing, Sir Robert Peel (who founded the Metropolitan Police in London and whom you'll be reading about in the next chapter on the history of policing):

> *Police, at all times, should maintain a relationship with the public that gives reality to the historic tradition that the police are the public and the public are the police; the police being only members of the public who are paid to give full-time attention to duties which are incumbent on every citizen in the interests of community welfare and existence.*

What comes to mind when you think of democratic policing?

This principle is often referred to as a key part of the foundation for what we today call *community policing*, but it also captures something about the idea that policing is part of the social contract, and the underlying authority and legitimacy of the police derives from the people.

So what do we learn from this? At its most basic level, democratic policing is a model of policing that is consistent with—and supports—the basic tenets of a democratic government. We generally take that to refer to our particular type of democracy, and this means that the police derive their authority from the people and are therefore accountable to the people for fulfilling the important role of protecting life, liberty, and property, and doing so by enforcing the laws while also obeying the laws.

Democratic policing, as we've defined it so far, is still a little vague. So we are going to offer another way to approach democratic policing, what one might call a "behavioral" approach. Consider the following questions: How often do police in the United States use force upon its citizens? How about *excessive* force? How about *deadly* force? It seems like we ought to know the answers to these basic questions, since (as we will discuss later) they actually go to the very core of policing in a free society. But the embarrassing reality is that we simply do not know the answers to these questions, and we are unfortunately a long way from having them. We will return to this important point later in the chapter.

Democratic policing is currently a topic of much discussion in law enforcement circles; unfortunately, it tends to be a somewhat abused buzz-phrase. Law enforcement administrators will often say they are "doing" democratic policing, and the United States actively advocates democratic policing abroad. But what does this really mean? Well, if you listen carefully you will find that these executive utterances, as well as our foreign policy on democratic policing, are generally organized around three core themes: **transparency**, **accountability**, and fundamental **fairness** in policing.

These three core themes are important. Police agencies in a democracy should be *transparent* to the public about police activity, which we generally understand to mean that the police should be accessible and open to public scrutiny. We recognize that there are some things that must be kept secret for operational purposes (the details of an investigation, for example), but outside of these particular domains, the last thing we want to see is a button-lipped, stonewalling, secretive police. Ultimately, the people want to understand how decisions were made and with what results, and this requires transparency.

Agencies should also be *accountable* to the public for police activity. This means that when the public and/or its elected representatives identify a problem, the police need to first acknowledge the behaviors that the public views as a violation of their trust, and then the

The public expects police to be accessible and open to scrutiny.

police should seek to either explain or correct the identified problems in a timely manner. Law enforcement agencies in the United States, through their chief executive, typically report to an elected body, such as a town council, and/or an elected official of some sort, such as a mayor. And, in some cases, the chief executive may himself be an elected official, as is common among county sheriffs.

Finally, agencies should strive for fundamental *fairness* in the distribution of justice. Equality under the law is a core tenet of democracy. As Yale law and psychology professor Tom Tyler has noted, the police need to constantly ask whether what they are doing is objective, unbiased, and consistent, and whether citizens are being treated with dignity, politeness, and respect. This idea of fairness, combined with transparency and accountability, tends to drive our understanding of *police legitimacy*— the extent to which we recognize and are willing to defer to the authority of the police to regulate behavior. Research on police legitimacy has emphasized the role of procedural justice,

An early cartoon highlights police corruption.

particularly procedural fairness, on individual's willingness to obey the law, defer to police authority, comply with police requests, and assist the police in investigations, and this holds true regardless of the outcome for the individual. Funny thing—it turns out people are OK with negative outcomes, such as being arrested, provided they believe the process was fair, that they were heard, respected, and the police explained their decision-making. When the police are viewed as a legitimate authority, it can also result in safer encounters for officers and less need to resort to use of force.

A significant problem in delivering on these core themes of transparency, accountability, and fairness is the tendency of law enforcement administrators to treat democratic policing as if it is an achievable end in itself, like a box that can be checked off on a police chief's list of "Things to Do Today." This is a serious problem because viewing democratic policing as an achievable end in itself misses the point. Democratic policing is best viewed as a *process*—it's something that can never really be achieved, but something that we should constantly strive to demonstrate. This requires a process of constant evaluation to determine whether policing is working toward the goals of transparency, accountability, and fairness. But a key challenge that we face in the process of democratic policing is a lack of adequate information. We can't evaluate whether these democratic ideals are being satisfied without systematic information on, for example, the use of force by the police.

COERCION AS THE CORE FUNCTION OF THE POLICE

One of the most important academic works on policing is Egon Bittner's (1970) monograph *The Functions of the Police in Modern Society*. Bittner probably did more than any other scholar to date in terms of advancing theory about the role of police in society, and understanding policing in terms of what the police actually *do* as opposed to the idealized visions of the police as "crime fighters" and "keepers of the peace." Bittner carefully draws the reader to the notion that,

... whatever the substance of the task at hand, whether it involves protection against an undesired imposition, caring for those who cannot care for themselves, attempting to solve a crime, helping to save a life, abating a nuisance, or settling an explosive dispute, police intervention means above all making use of the capacity and authority to overpower resistance to an attempted solution in the native habitat of the problem.

Bittner is often summarized by scholars for his suggestion that "... the role of the police is best understood as a mechanism for the distribution of non-negotiably coercive force employed in accordance with the dictates of an intuitive grasp of situational exigencies." That's quite a mouthful, isn't it? The bottom line is that no matter what the police are doing, what makes them distinctive is their capacity to verbally or physically coerce individuals to do things that they are not otherwise inclined to do—individuals who are not following the rules. This use of coercion tends to stand in direct contradiction to our strong preference for individual liberty, and this can create a substantial dilemma. But if we can agree on the idea that coercion is the core function of the police, then it might logically follow that *liberty* should be the core organizing principle of policing in the United States. To be more specific, the challenge is in how best to use (or "distribute") coercion as part of the process of democratic policing.

Of course the police, both individually and as an organizational entity, do more than just exercise coercive authority. They also arguably provide needed social services and have a much more complex role in modern society. But in this chapter we are focusing on the core vision of policing in a free society, and we will delve into these other more expansive areas in later chapters.

LIBERTY AS THE CORE ORGANIZING PRINCIPLE OF POLICING: THE INTELLIGENT USE OF COERCION

A model of policing with liberty as the core organizing principle requires a determined shift in focus from the behavior of citizens toward the behavior of the police. This may be an uncomfortable idea for some—particularly for the police—and it sounds like a significant challenge, but it might not be as hard as one would think. We are already seeing the beginnings of a trend toward undermining the model of the police as "warriors" fighting a "war" on crime or drugs, with the attendant quasi-military model of training and organization. It is unfortunate that it often takes events such as those highlighted in the box on Ferguson, MO, where we see first-hand the deleterious effects of the warrior model, to reinvigorate these movements. One current example of this shift is in the training occurring at the criminal justice academy in Washington State, where the executive director, former King County Sheriff Sue Rahr, has implemented a transitional program she calls "Warriors to Guardians" (see box). This model explicitly rejects the quasi-military warrior model and emphasizes a service role for police as protectors, as the guardians of democracy and Constitutional rights.

"FROM WARRIORS TO GUARDIANS"

Sue Rahr is the Executive Director of the Washington State Criminal Justice Training Academy, where basic law enforcement training is provided for all agencies within the state (with the exception of the Washington State Patrol). Rahr has over 30 years of experience in law enforcement, including 7 years as the elected Sheriff of King County, WA. Following the national reaction to grand jury decisions in the Michael Brown (Ferguson, MO) and Eric Garner (New York, NY) cases, President Obama announced the creation of a Task Force on 21st Century Policing; Rahr was appointed to this important panel in December 2014.

Courtesy Criminal Justice Training Commission

Sue Rahr

When Sue Rahr took over as director of the state's centralized law enforcement training academy in 2012, she already knew that American policing had strayed from the ideal image of the police officer as community guardian, toward the image of police officer as "... an urban warrior trained for battle and equipped with the accoutrements and weaponry of modern warfare." Rahr had recently developed new in-service training for the King County Sheriff's Office based on principles of procedural justice (a program called LEED, for *L*isten and *E*xplain with *E*quity and *D*ignity), and carried this with her to the academy. But there was still a strong disconnect between the types of officers that police chiefs and sheriffs said they wanted (officers who were engaging, respectful, effective at de-escalation, and had good critical thinking and independent decision-making skills) and the training environment at the academy. The academy had a quasi-military "boot camp" style and emphasized physical control tactics, firearms, and obedience, while providing very little training related to human interaction skills.

Combined with a desire to return the culture of policing to its democratic origins, several significant changes were made to the training model at the academy. These changes were aimed at replacing those elements of training that tended to reinforce the "warrior" mentality with a greater emphasis on the police as guardians of democracy:

- **No more "bracing"**—When encountering academy staff members on campus, recruits were required to salute and remain silent; now recruits are required to respectfully initiate a conversation when they come into contact with staff members.

- **Modifying the "tune up"**—During the orientation phase, training officers would berate recruits in the style of a military boot camp, complete with physical drills and deliberately impossible tasks designed to invoke fear and respect, and emphasize physical fitness; this physical humiliation process was replaced with coaching to encourage recruits to push themselves physically, and to build a sense of team/camaraderie.

- **Modifying the symbols and rituals**—The main lobby was previously dominated by trophy cases including displays of policing equipment; this was replaced with a mural of the Constitution and in large letters, the phrase: "In these Halls ... Training the Guardians of Democracy." Wall posters emphasizing officer safety have been augmented with posters about the honor and nobility of policing. Recruits are given a pocket Declaration of Independence and Constitution and reminded that their mission is to protect civil rights. Patriotism is reinforced through flag ceremonies and marching. Graduation speeches emphasize the distinction between warriors and guardians.

- **Curriculum changes**—Six behavioral and social science programs were added to the curriculum, including:
  - *Justice based policing* (principles of procedural justice through the LEED model);
  - *Fair and impartial policing* (covers the neuroscience of implicit bias and strategies to ensure biases don't influence decision-making);
  - *Blue Courage* (a motivational program about the nobility of policing and the importance of physical, emotional, and spiritual health);
  - *Crisis Intervention Training* (responding to the mentally ill and those experiencing mental health crises; a large portion of mock scenario training has been modified to include crisis intervention techniques as an alternative to physical force);
  - *The "Respect Effect"* (the entire academy organization completed this program developed by Paul Meshanko, and lessons about the neuroscience of human interaction were integrated into the curriculum); and
  - *Tactical Social Interaction* (in partnership with the Defense Advanced Research Projects Administration, a program was created to teach recruits specific actions that increase rapport between strangers).

Rahr is careful to caution that these changes do not mean that training at the academy has become "soft." Recruits still learn defensive tactics and firearms skills, and discipline standards have not been relaxed. Rahr has commissioned a 5-year, longitudinal study of the "Warriors to Guardians" model to help determine whether it positively influences recruits' attitudes about policing and the public, and whether it leads to better outcomes in the field.

For greater detail, see, Rahr, S., & Rice, S. (2015). *From warriors to guardians: Returning American police culture to democratic ideals.* Harvard Executive Session.

A model of policing with liberty as its core organizing principle would recognize that coercion is the core function of the police, but that this core function is necessary and serves to protect natural rights to life, liberty, and property. We shouldn't necessarily fear this essential coercive mechanism; we just need to be certain that the police are adequately trained to intelligently exercise discretion in their use of coercion (and in Rahr & Rice's (2015) terms, seek voluntary compliance first and reserve physical control as a last resort for those who cannot be managed in any other way), and that its use is adequately monitored and systematically reported upon. This highlights the importance of effective citizen oversight mechanisms, something that we will take up in later chapters.

To take it a step further, a model of policing organized around liberty would generally restrict the focus of the police to combating those acts of force or fraud that threaten individual life, liberty, and property. This actually wouldn't require much change in what the police are already doing, but it would mean some changes, such as getting out of low-level drug enforcement and reinvesting those resources. We are seeing some movement in that direction, particularly with recent legislation legalizing possession of marijuana for medical and/or personal recreational use in several states, active law enforcement advocacy groups such as Law Enforcement Against Prohibition (LEAP), and growing recognition of drugs as a public health problem rather than a law enforcement problem (see Policing and Social Change box). But there's a long way to go in resolving these issues, particularly with regard to the conflicts between federal and state laws, as well as local ordinances within states.

"POLICING AND SOCIAL CHANGE: MARIJUANA ENFORCEMENT"

As of this writing, the citizens of four states (Alaska, Colorado, Oregon, and Washington) have voted to legalize marijuana. Citizens of the District of Columbia have also voted to legalize marijuana, but due to the unique relationship between DC and the federal government (the U.S. Congress controls the budget for DC), marijuana legalization in DC is presently being blocked by Congress. Twenty-four states have either or both medical marijuana and decriminalization laws (with nine states having legalized medical marijuana only, and five states having decriminalized possession only). Twenty-two states still absolutely prohibit marijuana, medical or otherwise. Federal law (in the form of the Controlled Substances Act of 1970) still prohibits marijuana as a Schedule I controlled substance (meaning that it has a high potential for abuse and no accepted or safe medical use), and the Drug Enforcement Administration (DEA) still enforces the law. While the "Supremacy Clause" of the U.S. Constitution (Article VI) establishes that federal law takes precedence over state laws, the U.S. Department of Justice under Attorney General Eric Holder stated that it will not seek to block those laws, provided there is an adequate regulatory system in place, and instructed all U.S. Attorneys about drug enforcement priorities. It remains to be seen whether Holder's successor, Loretta Lynch, will continue or revise these policies.

Law Enforcement Against Prohibition (LEAP), founded in 2002, is an organization of current and former members of law enforcement and other justice agencies who speak out about the failure of U.S. drug policies and the "war on drugs." LEAP advocates the replacement of drug prohibition with a policy of drug control and regulation. According to the LEAP Web site:

> *The mission of LEAP is to reduce the multitude of harmful consequences resulting from fighting the war on drugs and to lessen the incidence of death, disease, crime, and addiction by ending drug prohibition.*

LEAP's goals are: (1) To educate the public, the media and policy makers about the failure of current drug policy by presenting a true picture of the history, causes and effects of drug use and the elevated crime rates more properly related to drug prohibition than to drug pharmacology and (2) To restore the public's respect for police, which has been greatly diminished by law enforcements involvement in imposing drug prohibition.

LEAP's main strategy for accomplishing these goals is to create a constantly growing speakers bureau staffed with knowledgeable and articulate current and former drug-warriors who describe the impact of current drug policies on: police/community relations; the safety of law enforcement officers and suspects; police corruption and misconduct; and the excessive financial and human costs associated with current drug policies.

For more information on LEAP, see their Web site at www.leap.cc.

THE LACK OF ADEQUATE INFORMATION ABOUT POLICE COERCION

If we can agree that coercion is the core function of the police, and that liberty should be the core organizing principle for policing, then what we really require is adequate information about coercion in order to fulfill the promise of democratic policing. This should be the primary concern of the citizens living in a free society who recognize the need for a police entrusted with coercive authority for purposes of protecting life, liberty, and property. But we have a rather sad state of affairs in that the world's leading global advocate of democracy, the United States, cannot claim that its own agents of state authority are truly engaged in democratic policing using these criteria.

Back to those questions we asked before: How often do police in the United States use force upon its citizens? How about *excessive* force? How about *deadly* force? Why don't we know the answers to these questions? Back in 1994, when Congress passed the Violent Crime Control and Law Enforcement Act (also known as the Clinton Crime Bill), the package included a very important provision (found at 42 USC 14142) that specifically required the U.S. Attorney General to "acquire data about the use of excessive force by law enforcement officers" and to "publish an annual summary of the data acquired under this section." So, where are these annual summaries?

A long series of Attorneys General over the years since the 1994 Crime Act was passed have failed to act in a meaningful way on this requirement. To give some credit where credit is due, important research and development on police use of force has been supported by the Department of Justice, particularly under Attorney General Janet Reno. In stark contrast, the Department of Justice under Attorney General John Ashcroft actively tried to suppress findings from the very same studies (see Politics box). This provides a very real demonstration of the politics of information.

"THE POLITICS OF RACE, ETHNICITY, AND POLICING

The Police Public Contact Survey (PPCS), administered by the Bureau of Justice Statistics (BJS), has consistently documented no difference in the rates with which drivers of different races are stopped by police. Once stopped, however, the PPCS has consistently documented that blacks and Hispanics are more likely to have their person and/or vehicles searched, and are more likely to experience the use or threat of force by police. In 2005, when the PPCS results were ready, a formal press release was prepared and submitted by the BJS Director to higher administrators for review. The reviewing official, acting in the political interests of the Administration, did not want the secondary finding (regarding racial inequality in searches and the distribution of force) to be mentioned. The *New York Times* reporter Eric Lichtblau publicly broke the ensuing story in August 2005, about four months after it occurred (Lichtblau, 2005a):

> *The planned announcement noted that the rate at which whites, blacks and Hispanics were stopped was 'about the same,' but the references in the draft to higher rates of searches and use of force for blacks and Hispanics were crossed out by hand ... A note affixed to the edited draft, which the officials said was written by Ms. Henke, read 'Make the changes,' and it was signed 'Tracy.' That led to a fierce dispute after Mr. Greenfeld refused to delete the references, officials said.*

The BJS Director was subsequently forced out of BJS due to his insistence that these important findings not be tampered with or otherwise "spun" by Justice Department political appointees. As Lichtblau reported, the Director was formally asked to resign but invoked personnel rules requiring that he be placed elsewhere. In a letter to Attorney General Alberto Gonzales, Representative John Conyers Jr. (D-Mich.) and other House colleagues formally requested that the Attorney General "immediately reinstate" the Director. Representative Conyers also separately requested an investigation into these matters by the Government Accountability Office. The *Washington Post* jumped into the fray with coverage of the episode as well as an editorial piece decrying the political interference in justice statistics (Eggen, 2005; Lichtblau, 2005b; Washington Post, 2005).

Numerous popular authors, news commentators, and journalists have alleged that the second Bush Administration in general, and the Bush Justice Department in particular, are unique in the degree of information control and secrecy they have exercised (e.g., Lichtblau, 2008). Despite the unquestionable impact of September 11, 2001, on the Justice Department and government broadly, it is unclear whether this was an uncharacteristic political climate—at least not uncharacteristic of other periods in history dominated by conservative politics. For example, political pressure and the creative management of crime statistics during the Nixon Administration have been well documented (Seidman & Couzens, 1974). At the very least, these types of incidents reinforce the idea that politics and government data are simply inseparable.

There are some periodic data collections that we can point to, such as the PPCS, a supplement to the National Crime Victimization Survey, in which a sample of U.S. households is asked roughly every 3 years to report whether they had any contact with the police during the previous year. They are also asked if the police used force, and whether the respondent thought that the force used was excessive. We will discuss this study in much greater detail in a later chapter; suffice to say that it produces some useful information, such as the finding that police rarely use force in the context of all police-public interactions, and that while minorities are no more likely than non-minorities to be stopped by the police, once they are stopped, minorities are more likely to have their vehicles searched and have force used upon them (this latter finding is what the Ashcroft Justice Department preferred not to discuss, as discussed in the box). But there are also substantial limitations to these types of studies, and to be clear, it is not a simple task. Government and academic researchers have struggled for years to define, measure, and collect data on police use of force.

The bottom line is this: we don't have any idea how often the police in our country use force upon its citizens. How can we possibly be fully engaged in the *process* of democratic policing if we can't even begin to evaluate whether the police are fundamentally fair in the distribution of coercive force? The use of physical force is, admittedly, the most extreme form of police coercive authority, but is also arguably the most important. Unfortunately, it sometimes takes high-profile tragedies like what occurred in Ferguson, MO, to spur action and free up federal resources to address an issue that has been neglected for decades. The President's Task Force is a step in the right direction, and as of this writing, BJS is planning new use of force data collections. It remains to be seen whether Congress will allocate the resources necessary to undertake this important work.

CONCLUSION

In this chapter, we have suggested that the core function of the police in democratic society is to protect life, liberty, and property, and that coercion is the fundamental means by which they achieve those democratic goals. In order to do so efficiently and effectively, they must be seen as a legitimate authority by the citizenry. This legitimacy stems from transparency, accountability, and fairness, values which also tend to structure our understanding of democratic policing. We suggested that democratic policing, as a process, requires adequate information in order to determine whether these democratic ideals are being satisfied. The most important task to improve the quality of policing in the United States is to systematically collect and report data on police activity, particularly the use of force.

The purpose of this chapter was to provide an overview of the origins and core vision of police in a free society through the lens of democratic policing. In the next two chapters, we round out the background material with a detailed review of the history of policing in the United States. We then turn to the fundamentals, including chapters discussing the nature and scope of the law enforcement industry, police organizations and officers, and the nature of police discretion. A section on controlling crime includes chapters on basic law enforcement functions, problem identification and response, special populations, and investigations. Finally, we return to some of the core issues discussed in this chapter, with a section on maintaining the public trust. Chapter topics in this last section include police behavior, legitimacy and accountability, and future directions.

REVIEW QUESTIONS

1. Do you think democratic policing is an achievable end or is it an ongoing process? Is it a relative and situational concept (e.g., consider democratic policing in an emerging democracy versus an established democracy)? What do you think are the minimum criteria?

2. Consider Sir Robert Peel's principle that "Police, at all times, should maintain a relationship with the public that gives reality to the historic tradition that the police are the public and the public are the police." Do you believe that the police in the United States are adhering to this principle, or are they becoming more detached from the public?

GLOSSARY

Accountability a condition that exists when the police acknowledge behaviors that the public views as a violation of their trust, and the police seek to either explain or correct the identified problems in a timely manner.

Bill of Rights the first 10 Amendments to the Constitution of the United States of America.

Democratic policing a model of policing that is consistent with, and supports, the basic tenets of a democratic government; recognizes that the police derive their authority from the people and are therefore accountable to the people for fulfilling the important role of protecting life, liberty, and property, and doing so by enforcing the laws while also obeying the laws; best viewed as an ongoing process (rather than an achievable end) in which law enforcement agencies constantly strive to demonstrate transparency, accountability, and fundamental fairness.

Fairness referring to fairness in the distribution of justice; policing that is objective, unbiased, and consistent.

Natural rights rights imbued to individuals as part of their personhood, generally life, liberty, and property.

Police legitimacy the extent to which we recognize and are willing to defer to the authority of the police to regulate behavior.

Police power the power to regulate behavior through the enactment and enforcement of laws.

Rule of law the idea that laws should govern behavior and decision-making; addresses the behavior of citizens as well as those in power.

Transparency the idea that the police should be accessible and open to public scrutiny, and that they should make clear how decisions are made and with what results.

REFERENCES

Bittner, E. (1970). *The functions of the police in modern society.* NIMH.

Eggen, D. (2005). Official in racial profiling study demoted. *The Washington Post*, August 25.

Lichtblau, E. (2008). *Bush's law: The remaking of American Justice.* Pantheon.

Lichtblau, E. (2005a). Profiling report leads to a demotion. *The New York Times*, August 24.

Lichtblau, E. (2005b). Democrats want official to be reinstated over report on profiling. *The New York Times*, August 26.

Martin, J. (2014). Why do small police departments need 18-ton armor-plated assault vehicles? *The Seattle Times*, December 8.

Rahr, S., & Rice, S. (2015). *From warriors to guardians: Returning American police culture to democratic ideals.* Harvard Executive Session.

Seidman, D., & Couzens, M. (1974). Getting the crime rate down: Political pressure and crime reporting. *Law and Society*, (Spring), 457–493.

The Washington Post. (2005). Lowering profiling's profile. August 26.

2 THE HISTORY OF POLICING: ANCIENT ROOTS AND EARLY POLICING

LEARNING OBJECTIVES

After reading this chapter, students should be able to:

1 Explain how the law enforcement function was achieved in early civilizations.

2 Describe early policing in England.

3 Give an account of 18th century attempts to reform and formalize policing in England.

4 Describe the history and evolution of policing in the United States in each region of the country.

KEY TERMS

Code of Hammurabi	Hundred	Slave Patrols
Medjay	Community constable	Vigilante justice
Kin policing	Shire	Posse comitatus
Praetorian Guard	Shire reeve	Vigilance committees
Prafectus Urbi	Parish constable system	Constable
Vigiles	Stipendiary policing	Sheriff
Frankpledge	Thief-takers	
Tything	Bow Street Runners	

With the abundance and sophistication of today's technology, it can be hard to envision a time when police officers were anything other than the professional law enforcer of today. For most of our history, however, law enforcement officers had few tools and little, if any, training. For example, portable radios, which are used by probably every patrol officer in America today, were not readily available until the early 1960s. Moreover, "prevention of crime" was not really a consideration or objective until the mid-19th century (or later). In this chapter, we will learn about the history of policing, starting with ancient policing so that we may better understand and appreciate modern policing. After reviewing ancient policing, we will learn about policing in medieval England, then 19th century England, and finally, early policing in America.

EARLY ROOTS

Policing developed in concert with society. As populations grew and societies evolved, law enforcement became more formalized—little, by little. The first recorded civilization is commonly thought to have been established in Mesopotamia around 3500 BC. It was many years, however, before codified laws were established and even more before "law enforcer" became a job title. Keep in mind that, in order for police to exist, a society must have developed to the point where there is an organized government (political structure), a formal legal system, social differentiation (social hierarchy), as well as a surplus of material resources.

© ileana_bt/Shutterstock.com

The Code of Hammurabi is one of the oldest sets of law known to exist.

The **Code of Hammurabi**, a set of laws written by Hammurabi, the King of Babylon, around 1750 BC is commonly thought to be the oldest existing set of laws. With 252 separate laws and prescribed punishments, it may be the most comprehensive set of ancient laws; however, it is not actually the oldest. There are several sets of laws which are thought to predate the code, including the Code of Ur-Nammu (circa 2050 BC), Laws of Eshunna (circa 1930 BC), and the Laws of Lipit-Ishtar (circa 1870 BC), all of which are from city-states within Mesopotamia (Barton, 2009). Formalized policing was not established in Mesopotamia until much later, when city-states became politically organized and the distribution of wealth between different social strata necessitated the protection of property (a pattern we see repeated throughout world history).

Nearby in Ancient Egypt, civilization developed simultaneously but separately. While it is highly probable that Egypt had its own set of established laws, no legal codes exist to confirm this belief. Judicial records, however, indicate that ancient Egypt had a sophisticated government as well as a judicial system whereby legal disputes between individuals (and/or the state) were resolved in court. According to Egyptologists, several police groups existed in ancient Egypt (Bagnall, 2012; Bunson, 2002; David, 2003). In every era, there were units of border police stationed along the frontiers to protect Egypt from invaders as well as to regulate trade and maintain order (Bunson, 2002). Additionally, state police kept peace in the capitol and served the king during the second intermediate period (1640–1550 BC) and temple police protected the temple and ensured that worshippers abided by religious customs and rituals (Bunson, 2002). Starting in the 18th

Dynasty (1543–1292 BC), the Medjay, a paramilitary police force that had previously been trained as warriors, protected Egyptian towns as well as valuable areas, such as royal palaces and tombs (David, 2003; Wilkinson, 2005). It is unknown whether any of these "police" survived Egypt's collapse in the mid-12th century.

Meanwhile, in Greece, a system of kin policing was in place from the end of the Dark Age (approximately 800 BC). Kin policing refers to the practice whereby a family, clan, or tribe enforced customary rules and socially defined norms of behavior. Families were responsible for investigating crimes and bringing suspects to justice. This system lasted for a couple hundred years until the dictator Peisistratus seized control of Athens in 560 BC and began using publicly owned slaves as police. These "Scythian foot-archers" kept order at public meetings, controlled crowds, and performed other duties (Hunter, 1994). This dedicated police system spread to Egypt and eventually to Rome.

The first Roman Emperor, Augustus, established the Praetorian Guard in 27 BC and the Praefectus Urbi shortly thereafter (around 13 BC). The Praetorian Guard, which consisted of nine cohorts of 500 men (later 1000), existed to protect the emperor and the city of Rome (Dunstan, 2010; Nippel, 1995). The guards were not uniformed but did carry swords; they patrolled Rome as well as other Italian cities, accompanied the emperor when he travelled, and supplemented the military when necessary (Dunstan, 2010). The Praefectus Urbi, which consisted of three cohorts of 500 men (later 1000) were also known as the *urban cohorts*. They patrolled the streets of Rome during the day to keep the peace. Whereas the Praetorian Guard was associated with the military (and eventually was absorbed into the military), the Praefectus Urbi was not and is closer to what we would consider to be the first paid police force (Nippel, 1995). After a fire in 6 AD, Augustus added six cohorts of vigiles to fight fires and keep watch during the night but they did not have a full policing role (Nippel, 1995). This idea of separate day and night watches appears in English and American police history also.

EARLY POLICING IN ENGLAND

Modern (western) policing originated in England. Prior to the industrial revolution, policing was primarily a collective social responsibility. During the reign of Alfred the Great (870–901 AD), citizens were expected to help their neighbors and apprehend outlaws (Uchida, 2004). The state granted individual citizens' power to maintain order through the necessary use of force (Uchida, 2004). There was no formal system; what existed could best be described as informal social control based on customs and norms rather than actual laws. It is another example of *kin policing*.

FRANKPLEDGE

This eventually developed into a more formal, communitarian system of law enforcement called frankpledge after the Norman Conquest in 1066. The system was based on geographical boundaries and individuals were organized into three levels: tythings, hundreds, and shires. Every male over the age of 12 was required to participate in a tything—a group of men from 10 families living near each other who were sworn to uphold justice (apprehend suspects, escort suspects to court, hold defendants in custody during trial, appear in court and provide testimony) (Uchida, 2004). Tythingmen were mandated "volunteers"—they weren't paid but if one person failed to carry out his responsibilities, everyone in the tything could be fined. A respected elder of the group was selected to be the "leader."

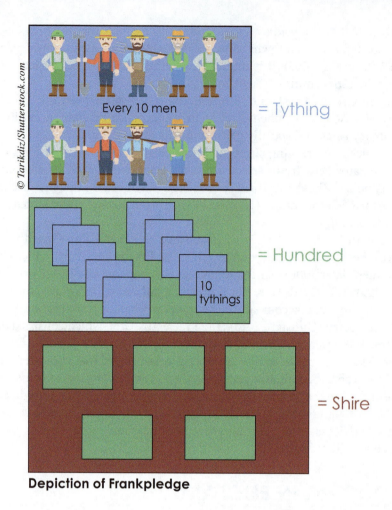

© Tarikdiz/Shutterstock.com

Every 10 men = Tything

10 tythings = Hundred

= Shire

Depiction of Frankpledge

Ten tythings formed a **hundred**, and each hundred was supervised by a **community constable** who was appointed by a nobleman (Uchida, 2004). Several hundreds were then organized into a **shire**, which is equivalent to a modern-day county and overseen by a **shire reeve** (precursor to **sheriff**) who was appointed by the King of England.[1] The shire reeve's job was to maintain order and enforce law throughout the shire, and also to collect taxes. This last duty was very lucrative since the shire reeves were allowed to keep a portion of the taxes they collected. The shire reeve was not a popular position but because of its income generating potential, it was an esteemed position which was held by wealthy friends of the king.

THE WATCH SYSTEM

The frankpledge system began to break down in the 13th century. In 1285, Edward I drew up the Statute of Winchester which created the **parish constable system**. Under this system, every parish[2] had a *volunteer* constable who served a 1-year term on a rotating basis (Emsley, 1991). His

---

1   A tything could be considered the medieval version of a community or neighborhood and, although not technically "the same," a hundred could be thought of as a city (without the political structure).

2   A parish at this time in history was the territory associated with the local church. It was not an official arm of government but was legally mandated to perform many of the roles of local government, such as public works, public safety, and care of the poor.

job was to organize a group of watchmen to protect the city during the night (some parishes had more than 300 watchmen). If a serious disturbance arose, the constable (or whichever watchman was on duty at that time) would raise the *hue and cry* to summon men in the parish to assist with regaining order. On top of organizing the night watch, the constable was also expected to investigate crimes, serve summonses and warrants, arrest law breakers, take charge of prisoners, as well as other duties (Reynolds, 1998). This was a large job and took much of the constable's time (remember that the constable was a volunteer and had his own business or farm to run). For this reason, it eventually became commonplace for wealthy farmers and businessmen to pay someone else (often someone unemployable) to take their turn as constable, as well as night watchman. Eventually, constables had assistants to help them perform their duties. Beadles, who were paid parish officers, assisted constables with supervising the night watch, patrolling the streets during the day, and calling roll. They also had other parish duties such as town crier and assistant to the overseer of the poor (Reynolds, 1998). In addition, watch-house keepers guarded prisoners and issued equipment to the watchmen.

The locally implemented watch system worked well for roughly 400 years but it started to crumble in the 1500s. Although watches were notorious for being ineffectual and many parishes were troubled by incompetent, idle, and/or drunk watchmen, not all of them could be so categorized. Some parishes had watches that would be properly characterized as honorable and proficient (Emsley, 1991; Reynolds, 1998). Also, politicians in many parishes improved their watch systems over the years by instituting standards, rules, expectations, and consequences to suit local needs as those parishes grew and changed. Some parishes eventually paid their constables a small stipend, which helped control crime in that parish (Reynolds, 1998). All of the watches were eventually replaced with professional police forces in the 1800s.

STIPENDIARY POLICING

These early forms of informal social control were relatively effective in small, homogenous (and predominately agrarian) societies. As cities grew larger, more diverse, and more lawless, however, there was a need for more formalized police. By the early 1500s, parts of England had been overtaken by thieves and robbers (Samaha, 1974). Merchants, traders, insurers, and others often hired private individuals to protect (or retrieve) their property and policing became a service available to anyone who could afford it (Emsley, 1991). The practice became so common that, eventually, standard fees were established for the apprehension and conviction of suspects and the return of stolen property (McMullan, 1996). This practice was called **stipendiary policing** (today we might call it private policing) and the men who did the job were called **thief-takers** (they were more akin to bounty hunters than actual policemen). Stipendiary policing supplemented the watch system, it did not supplant it (Reynolds, 1998).

The government condoned the practice and passed the *Highwaymen Act* in 1692 which stipulated that ordinary citizens who helped apprehend criminals would be paid a reward (House of Commons, 2014). Regrettably, it also led to false accusations and blackmail (McMullan, 1996). Jonathan Wild, who was London's most famous thief-taker, fence, and possibly the first iteration of a mob boss, ran London's underground criminal network for several years and became wealthy by working the system. He arranged for thieves to steal items from homes and then got paid by victims to retrieve the stolen property; any thieves who did not give him a portion of their booty were turned into the authorities (Emsley, 1991).

For the first time in 1735, George II recognized the problems with a volunteer constable system and allowed parish councils to collect taxes in order to provide a paid watchman system (Reynolds, 1998). This was the first recorded tax initiated for the purpose of providing law enforcement services (Reynolds, 1998) and it marks the shift toward publicly funded, government-controlled police. It did not, unfortunately, stop constables and watchmen from taking bribes to "look the other way" when individuals were found to be breaking the law; nor did it end the practice of stipendiary policing. At this time in history, however, corruption was ingrained in England's political system as well as its justice system.

CORRUPTION IN 18TH CENTURY ENGLAND

Although there were honest thief-takers in 18th Century England, there were also plenty of corrupt thief-takers at this time. The following excerpts from McMullan (1996) provide vivid accounts of law enforcement in 18th Century London. Read the accounts and compare them to accounts of police in 21st Century America. How do the complaints differ? Are we better off today? Do any of our laws incentivize corruption, like the Highwaymen Act did in 17th and 18th Century England?

"These Thief-Catchers will do anything for money. They live by nothing but taking men's lives away" (quoted from Linebaugh, 1991, P. 59). In the mid-eighteenth century, there were between 30 and 40 active thief-takers in London. They were drawn largely from the ranks of skilled artisans or those with jobs that formally associated them with the forces of law and order (as prison turnkeys, constables, bailiffs, or minor court officers). They also brought with them strong and enduring ranks to the world of London crime. "In general one is looking at men with a clear and unambiguous history of involvement in the world of professional crime" (quoted from Paley, 1989, p. 304). The monied police often relieved their prisoners of money and stolen goods, and made more income by accepting hush money, giving perjured evidence, swearing false oaths, blackmailing the innocent, the vulnerable, and the guilty, and operating extortion rackets. By the mid-eighteenth century, private policing was booming and thief-taking was essentially a freelance business, organized through numerous informal networks.

The market for private gain in crime control was extensive, innovative, and elastic. It was driven by the provision of rewards, immunities, and exemptions, whether made under state statutes or offered privately, and the opportunities for extortion, blackmail, and conspiracy produced by the private policing process itself. The McDaniel case is illustrative. On 29 July, 1754, Peter Kelly, John Ellis, and a third man robbed James Salmon on the highway near Deptford. Within a few days, the youths were caught and arrested by the London thief-taker Stephen McDaniel after they had sold the stolen goods to a man named James Egan. Salmon's property was easily identified and Egan further identified Kelly and Ellis as the felons. It looked a clear-cut case. Kelly and Ellis did not deny the charges and they were committed to Maidstone goal. But they implicated a third person named Thomas Blee whom they said planned the robbery, recruited them, led the assault on Salmon, and advised them to sell the goods to Egan. At court on the evening of 15 August 1754, there was also a man named John Berry. He had been a thief-taker for over 25 years and he had apparently come to see justice done.

Sergeant, the constable who had been told of the suspicious involvement of Blee in the robbery, made some inquiries before the trial and reported his findings to Joseph Cox, High Constable of Blackheath. Cox then travelled to London, interviewed Salmon who confirmed the facts of the robbery, and said that he could recognize Blee if he saw him again. Through careful investigation, Cox discovered that Blee was living in lodging with McDaniel who, of course, had arrested Ellis and Kelly. Cox grasped the truth at once and tracked Blee down. Blee confirmed all of Cox's suspicions and agreed to turn King's Evidence.

It was in the evening when the trial proceeded. Cox, fearing that Berry might leave the area, arrested him and then returned to court. The jury gave in their verdicts. Kelly and Ellis, as expected, were found guilty largely on the testimony of McDaniel, Egan, and Salmon. Then there occurred the event that caused the sensation of the sessions. Before sentence could be pronounced, Cox announced that he had just arrested Berry, McDaniel, Salmon, and Egan as accessories before the fact. Kelly and Ellis, it now transpired, were the victims of a blood money conspiracy. The robbery had been entirely stage-managed. Thomas Blee, the accomplice whose escape had seemed to be so fortunate was implicated in the plot. He had recruited the two men in order to commit the robbery on Salmon, who was only too willing a victim having been provided by Blee with the goods to be stolen in the first place. Blee had carefully led Kelly and Ellis to a prearranged meeting with Egan to dispose of the stolen goods. The entire conspiracy had been organized by McDaniel and Berry in order to profit share in the parliamentary reward of £40 [more than the annual salary of a local artesian] that was payable for prosecuting a highwayman to conviction. So careful were their arrangements that they chose the place of the robbery, knowing that there was an extra local reward in addition to the statutory one. Altogether, the McDaniel gang stood to gain £120 from the success of their fit-up.

18TH CENTURY ATTEMPTS TO REFORM AND FORMALIZE POLICING

In 1750, crime was out of control in London; and while society was not ready for a professional police force, something had to be done to regain control of the city. *Henry Fielding* (novelist and magistrate of Middlesex and Westminster) personally recruited six of the most trustworthy thief-takers to serve as paid constables (McMullan, 1996). These plain-clothed men, the **Bow Street Runners**, investigated crimes, served warrants, and performed other tasks for the Bow Street Magistrates. They were well respected and quite successful (Reynolds, 1998). Henry's brother *Sir John Fielding* helped lead the group, which was small for most of its existence but grew to approximately 70 officers on foot and another 44 on horseback after several decades. The Bow Street Runners are noteworthy for three reasons. First, they were the first group to focus on crime prevention. Drawing on Jeremy Bentham's deterrence theory, they aimed to increase the certainty that criminals would be apprehended and prosecuted. They did this by intensifying the surveillance of Londoners (McMullan, 1996). Second, they were the first detective unit. They went to great lengths to solve crimes by collecting and linking bits of information about unsolved crimes and suspected criminals together. Finally, as the forerunners of the London police department, they represent the first experiment with a semiprofessional, albeit very small, police force (Reynolds, 1998).

The Fieldings were important for their innovations and attempts to reform policing. For example, they believed that communication about crime and criminals would improve detection and apprehension (thereby deterring would-be criminals and decreasing crime). They made the Bow Street station a clearinghouse of information on everything crime related in Westminster—descriptions of stolen items and suspects, wanted criminals, information about recent crimes, etc. They then published this information in London newspapers and circulated it to other metropolitan London law enforcement officials (magistrates and constables) (McMullan, 1996; Reynolds, 1998).

Another big move forward came in 1798 when the West Indies merchants who operated on the River Thames (the largest port in the world), tired of losing £500,000 in cash and cargo annually to thieves, financed the first preventative policing department—the Thames River Police (Emsley, 1991; Paterson, n.d.; Reynolds, 1998). The force, conceptualized by Justice of the Peace John Harriott, and founded by Scottish Economist and London Magistrate *Patrick Colquhoun,* started with 50 men to police 33,000 river workers (of whom, 11,000 were suspected of being "on the take") (Paterson, n.d.; Reynolds, 1998). Unlike watchmen of the time, these officers were full-time, paid, and prohibited from taking stipends (payments for solving a crime, apprehending a suspect, or returning property). In later years, the force was increased to 80 full-time staff and 1000 "on call" staff to help with major incidents (Paterson, n.d.). Crime decreased tremendously and in 1800, Parliament passed the Marine Police Bill which made the department a publicly funded entity.

Despite the success of the Bow Street Runners and Thames River Police, however, English society was still not interested in having a full-time, centralized police force. Not only would a full-time police department require a great deal of public monies, which would have meant an increase in taxes; it would also have required citizens to give up some freedom in exchange for protection. This was something most citizens were unwilling to do, as they distrusted the government and viewed the crime and disorder problems to be unique to certain parts of London.

Nevertheless, as London's population nearly doubled between 1750 and 1820, so too did the crime, disorder, and public health problems. The informal, locally governed, and fragmented law enforcement system that existed was ineffective in most areas and simply could not be sustained. Once the problems spread to other large cities in the country and riots became routine occurrences, citizens began to support the idea of a professional, civil police force capable of providing public safety.

METROPOLITAN POLICE

Since at least 1770s, fears of crime put pressure on local and central authorities to improve policing in London (Reynolds, 1998). Reformers such as Henry and John Fielding, Patrick Colquhoun, and philosopher Jeremy Bentham advocated for a structured, but politically neutral, police force focused on crime prevention. Legislative attempts to establish a centralized, professional police force in London go back to at least 1785 (Reynolds, 1998). Historians conclude that the main controversy in London was not whether a professional police force was needed but whether a *centralized* (government-run) police force was consistent with English liberty and whether it could be trusted[3] (Emsley, 1983; Lyman, 1964; Reynolds, 1998).

Despite years of riots and hotly debated hearings to bandage the watch system that the country had outgrown, as well as numerous failed attempts to pass legislation on the matter, reformers finally found favor with politicians in 1820s (Emsley, 1983; Reynolds, 1998; Taylor, 1998). *Sir Robert Peel* became the Home Secretary in 1822 and went to work reforming the criminal code (as a precursor to reforming the police). In April 1829, Peel introduced "A Bill for Improving the Police in and Near the Metropolis," taking care to carefully define boundaries and to not increase costs to residents or businesses. After much political wrangling and public dialogue, the Metropolitan Police Act was signed on June 19, 1829, creating England's first centralized, full-time, uniformed, paid civil police force (Lyman, 1964; Reynolds, 1998; Taylor, 1998). The legislation created a single police department that had authority over a 7 mile radius from the city center. The initial force comprised approximately 3000 civilian men wearing blue uniforms, armed with wooden truncheons (batons), and carrying rattles to summon assistance. Additionally, each officer was issued an identification number so that he could be held accountable for his actions. The officers were nicknamed "Bobbies" in honor of Sir

---

3   British politicians were keenly aware of the tyranny by which French police forces operated and did not want to open the door to such a model in England.

Robert Peel. The Metropolitan Police Act rationalized and extended the concept of policing and the benefits of centralization, but it did not change existing practices (Reynolds, 1998). In fact, there was as much continuity in policing at this time as there was change.

Peel appointed *Richard Mayne,* a young lawyer, and *Charles Rowan,* a former army colonel, as the first commissioners of the London Metropolitan Police Department. It was their responsibility to develop the organization and hire "a sufficient number of fit and able men" to serve as officers. Together, Mayne and Rowan developed a civilian police force arranged in a hierarchal, paramilitary structure. They split metropolitan London into 17 districts based on crime data and appointed a supervisor, 4 inspectors, 16 sergeants, and 144 constables to each district (Reynolds, 1998). Constables (officers) were assigned a small permanent beat within the district so that they could get to know the residents and become part of the community. Eight constables walked the beats in 12-hour shifts; originally half were assigned to day shift and half to night shift, but after many complaints of inefficiency from both the officers and the public, the majority of constables were reassigned to night shift (Reynolds, 1998). Officers were on call 24 hours per day, 7 days per week, and were paid a measly 19 shillings per week (Emsley, 1983).

Some of the first recruits were working-class Londoners, but many came from the countryside; some were ex-military servicemen and many applied to work during a period of unemployment (usually due to inclement weather) (Smith, 1985). Mayne and Rowan intentionally hired civilians, specifically physically fit, young (less than 35 years old) men of strong and admirable character, to quiet public fears that the police would become an occupying military force (Emsley, 1983). Even so, they met with major resistance and many officers were ill-equipped to handle the pressure. Although hiring standards were said to be high—only one-third of applicants were accepted—turnover was great during the first decade. "Of the 2800 constables serving in May 1830 there were only 562 still with the force four years later" (Emsley, 1983, p. 63). Hundreds of constables had been dismissed for disciplinary reasons (often drunkenness on the job) and more than 1000 resigned to "better" themselves (in other words, the pay was not worth the sacrifice) (Emsley, 1983).

THINK ABOUT IT

*Note to students: In 1829, concerned citizens wrote a letter to the editor of the newspaper to express their views. This section of the paper was quite long and facilitated public discourse about current events. Letters to the Editor in the 1820s could be equated to today's blogs and social media posts.

Editorial which appeared in the London Times on April 23, 1829

We have received many letters on the subject of Mr. Peel's Police Bill, but they are so voluminous, and some of them so intemperate, that insertion cannot be given to them.

"A case is reported from Lambeth street, as having happened yesterday, which proves—if any proof had been necessary—the absolute want of a central and controlling power in the metropolitan police. Here were a gang of robbers pursued by one set of watchmen, and actually suffered to escape by another set, who would not stir foot beyond their own boundary line, to cross and turn the flying villains. It is impossible without a spirited and cordial co-operation throughout the police in all its departments, to afford protection to property, or to punish crime.

There is another report, and from a different office—namely, Bow-street,—which will tell its own story, and place in a proper point of view the lamentations of those wiseacres who are so extremely apprehensive touching the military principles of Mr. Peel's new bill. The ruffian Beazeley—the keeper of a brothel—the tyrannical persecutor of unhappy women who failed, or were unable, to bribe him—and the brutal assailant of a peaceful passenger whom he "suspected of ringing" a door bell in St. Martin's court,—this vagabond, who had on a former occasion been suspended by Mr. Halls for general bad character, or specific transgression, was restored, it seems, by the precious parish authorities to his forfeited post of watchman, and again commissioned to insult and knock down all such of the liege subjects of His Majesty as might be deemed fit matter for experiment on their purses to the profit of this worshipful peace-officer. The advocates for parish patronage in the nomination of watchmen can scarcely be ignorant of the peculiar talents for which these ancient, reverend, and most "constitutional" guardians of life and property had been celebrated. From Shakespeare down to Fielding [Westminster Magistrate] and Sheridan, your watchman was the standing jest [joke]. Night-constable Dogberry might be famed for his wisdom, but of Fielding's watchmen, drowsiness seems to have been the characteristic. In his description of the hour which precedes the dawn, he describes it as that period when highwaymen are awake and "honest watchmen fast asleep." So when Puff is asked, whether certain of his dramatis personae were supposed "to be asleep all this time?" the answer supplied by Sheridan is, "fast as watchmen!" So much for the protectors furnished to us by the "ancient constitution of England!"—more ancient, confessedly, than that of eighty-eight. Alas! that the Duke of Wellington's Ministry [the head of Parliament at this time] should make such deadly war on constitutions!"

Imagine you lived in London at this time. Crime had increased 55% in the previous 7 years, riots were regular occurrences. The watchmen were completely ineffectual at controlling crowds or crime. Would you support the police bill? How would you react to the police—with the power to limit your movements and arrest you? While we have grown up with the police and the idea that they have power to control our movements, citizens at this time had not.

There was much animosity toward the new officers. Few citizens trusted the police since they were agents of the government; most viewed them as infringing on their individual rights. The public questioned whether the officers (who were considered to be semiskilled labor, at best) had the power to affect their movements (Smith, 1985). Some members of the public ignored constable's instructions, others jeered them or worse.

PEEL'S PRINCIPLES

Peel guided the early development of the police force by drawing on the ideas proposed by the Fieldings, Colquhoun, Bentham, and others. Given the public's trepidation toward a public police force, Peel felt strongly that the police would only succeed if they had approval from the public (note that we are having a similar discussion today with regard to the legitimacy of the police in the United States) and that could only happen if the quality of officers improved from the standards of the day (which were very low and typified by stipendiary police). Toward this end, Peel established a set of nine tenets to guide the London Metropolitan Police. These are known as *Peel's Principles* and were given to each officer upon hire[4] (UK Home Office, 2012):

---

4   There is no evidence Peel, himself, wrote these and it is quite likely that the first commissioners, Charles Rowan and Richard Mayne, wrote the principles based on conversations they had with Peel regarding his philosophy (UK Home Office, 2012).

1. The mission of the police is to prevent crime and disorder (so that military force and severe legal sanctions are not necessary).

2. The ability of the police to perform their duties depends on the public's approval of their existence, actions, and behavior as well as earning (and keeping) the public's respect. (Notice the importance he places on legitimacy!)

3. Earning the public's respect and approval includes gaining their cooperation in observing all laws.

4. High levels of public cooperation result in low levels of physical force by police.

5. Police strive for and sustain public favor not by catering to public opinion but by constantly demonstrating absolute impartial service to the law and to all members of the public, regardless of social standing. (Today we call this procedural justice.)

6. Use physical force only when persuasion, advice, and warning have failed to induce compliance or restore order; use only the minimum amount of force necessary to achieve the police objective.

7. At all times, police should maintain a relationship with the public that honors the historic tradition that the police are the public and the public are the police, the police being only members of the public who are paid to give full-time attention to duties which are incumbent on every citizen in the interests of community welfare and existence. (In other words, public safety is everyone's responsibility.)

8. Police should strictly adhere to their function and never appear to usurp the powers of the judiciary to avenge individuals or the State, judge guilt, and impose punishment.

9. The test of police efficiency is the absence of crime and disorder, not the police action in dealing with it.

In addition to the principles above, Peel championed other ideas that were instrumental in shaping the development of the Metropolitan Police Department, including[5]:

1. The police must be stable, efficient, and militarily organized under government control.

2. The absence of crime will best prove the efficiency of the police.

3. Crime news must be widely distributed.

4. Territorial distribution of the force by hours and shifts must be accomplished.

5. No quality is more indispensable to an officer than a perfect command of his temper; a quiet, determined action has more effect than violent action.

6. Good appearance commands respect.

7. Proper securing and training of personnel lies at the root of police efficiency.

8. Public safety requires that a policeman be given a number.

9. Police headquarters should be centrally located and easily accessible to all the people.

10. Policemen should be appointed on a probationary basis.

11. Police records are necessary for the correct distribution of police strength.

12. The best way to select men is to size them up and then find out what their neighbors think of them.

---

5   Some history books refer to these as Peel's Principles. There is no authoritative document which answers conclusively which list is actually "Peel's Principles."

Peel's policing philosophy was profoundly different from anything that existed at the time. According to police history scholar Charles Reith, it was the first time in history that policing "derived not from fear but almost exclusively from public cooperation with the police" (UK Home Office, 2012, para. 2). Peel focused on preventing crime by working with the community and gaining the public's support. Although the ideas are noble and obviously very similar to community policing (which we will discuss briefly later in this chapter and more thoroughly in Chapter 9), there was a practical reason for this emphasis—the police needed the public to give them legitimacy.

Eventually the public hostility quieted, disorder and crime declined, and the success of the metropolitan police department spread to other parts of England and elsewhere. In 1835, the Municipal Corporations Act mandated all incorporated boroughs to establish police forces under the control of a watch committee; however, it was not until 1856 that Parliament required provinces to found independent police departments (Emsley, 1983, 1991; Reynolds, 1998).

EARLY POLICING IN AMERICA

Like so many of our customs and traditions, American policing is modeled after English policing. When emigrating to the new world, English settlers brought with them the ideas and solutions they were accustomed to back home. This included ideas about justice and law enforcement.

17TH AND 18TH CENTURY COLONIAL AMERICA

Although it would be easy to say that the United States has a single, shared history of policing, that would be inaccurate. Policing developed uniquely in different parts of the country at different times.

North

In the North, 17th and 18th century colonists transplanted the English watch system. The county sheriff, appointed by the Governor, was the most important law enforcement post in rural America at this time. His duties, which were similar to his counterparts in England, included apprehending criminals, serving warrants and subpoenas, appearing in court, supervising elections, collecting taxes, as well as other justice-related functions. Sheriffs were paid on a per-task basis and although apprehending suspects paid money, collecting taxes paid more money. Naturally, tax collection superseded other tasks, including apprehending criminals.

In addition to county sheriffs, law enforcement in colonial America included volunteer constables and night watches. Constables were the chief law enforcement officers in Colonial America (Vila & Morris, 1999). Volunteer night watchmen maintained the street lamps, reported fires, walked around the village, raised the hue and cry when a disturbance broke out, and arrested suspects. The first night watch was established in Boston in 1631 (Vila & Morris, 1999). New York followed with a

Source: NYPD Museum

Rules of the Rattle Watch

1. Watchmen to be on duty before bell-ringing, under penalty of 6 stivers.
2. Whoever stays away without sending a substitute, to be fined two guilders.
3. 1 guilder fine for drunkenness.
4. 10 stivers fine for sleeping on post.
5. If any arms are stolen through negligence of the watch, the watchman will have to pay for the arms and be fined 1 guilder for the 1st, 2 guilders for the 2nd, and the fine for the 3rd offense to be discretionary with the court.
6. A fine of 2 guilders for going away from the watch, and 1 guilder for missing turn.
7. The Watch is to call the hour at all corners from 9am until reveille, for which they received an additional compensation of 18 guilders per month.

RULES OF THE RATTLE WATCH

rattle watch (a form of night watch that involved alerting citizens to disturbances) in 1658, and Philadelphia started a night watch in 1700. Night watchmen were notorious for sleeping and drinking on the job (Emsley, 1983). By and large, American watches consisted of men who (1) volunteered to keep watch in lieu of military service, (2) were working it as punishment, or (3) were paid substitutes for wealthy citizens (Emsley, 1983). The substitutes were generally drawn from society's unemployables—idles, drunkards, idiots. Like watches in England, watches in American cities also varied greatly in quality. Eventually, night watches evolved into formal police departments by the mid-19th century.

American constables, like their counterparts in England, were usually volunteers who

A policeman leads a protestor away from a woman's suffrage demonstration at the White House in 1918.

served rotating terms. They organized the night watch, arrested suspicious persons, took suspects to court, and undertook many other random duties. In the beginning, colonists did not mind taking their turn on the night watch or as constables; however, as villages grew and the time devoted to law enforcement tasks became a burden, more and more colonists paid others to do the job for them (Vila & Morris, 1999).

Just as with England, the Industrial Revolution brought on tensions resulting from mass immigration and cultural change that erupted into riots and presented problems in cities across America that night watchers were unable to handle. The military was called in as necessary but it became obvious that an organized, full-time police force was required.

South

Meanwhile, the population in the south during the 18th century was significantly smaller and more spread out than in the north. Just as in England, law enforcement was seen as every citizen's responsibility. Instead of a voluntary constable system, however, a mix of kin policing and **slave patrols** was used. When a crime not involving a slave or the slave trade had been committed in the south, individuals generally took matters into their own hands, thereby establishing an American tradition of **vigilante justice**. There was no established night watch or constable system focused on white on white crime (Hadden, 2005). There was, however, a formal system of social control created to protect the white population from slaves (and to protect their investment).

The slave patrol working in New Orleans, circa 1863.

Slave patrols existed to catch runaway slaves, to prevent slave insurrection, and generally to protect whites from slaves. They also helped enforce laws against slave literacy, trade, and gambling. The patrols varied in size but were typically small, about three to five heavily armed men on horseback. Some patrols checked plantations within their district only periodically for evidence of law-breaking while other patrols had more traditional policing functions, such as those found in urban watches (Hadden, 2001).

Slave patrols were the precursor to modern policing in the South and were the first example of the patrol function (Vila & Morris, 1999). According to Roth (2005), "the evolution of the southern slave patrols in the early 1700s marked the first real advances in American policing" (p. 64). The first recorded slave patrol was established in 1704 in the colony of South Carolina (Hadden, 2001). In 1727, Virginia became the second colony to establish a slave patrol, but they chose to enlist the militia on special occasions (usually holidays) to protect against uprising rather than create a separate, regular patrol (Hadden, 2001). While cities in the south eventually developed watches (called patrols) similar to their northern counterparts in the 1800s, their primary purpose was to prevent slave gatherings and reduce urban (slave) crime (Hadden, 2001). Southern watches went through a similar evolution as those in England and the north—towns became so large and the task of law enforcement so burdensome that the townspeople felt it better to hire a permanent group of men to patrol, rather than rely on volunteers (Hadden, 2001). Southern patrols, just like northern watches, varied in quality (Hadden, 2001). Legal slave patrols disappeared after 1865—some patrols became police and others became vigilante groups (most notably, the Ku Klux Klan) (Hadden, 2001).

Frontier

The U.S. Frontier was known as the Wild West for a reason—it was dangerous. While the eastern and southern parts of North America had established systems of law enforcement, the West was up for grabs in the 18th and 19th centuries. It was a potpourri of law enforcement that mainly consisted of five separate groups: (1) U.S. Marshals, (2) town marshals and county sheriffs, (3) state police agencies, (4) private citizens and businessmen, and (5) private police.

Prior to the establishment of municipal, county, and state law enforcement agencies, U.S. Marshals (who were established in 1789 for precisely this purpose) enforced laws throughout the west. However, they only had jurisdiction over federal crimes, such as mail theft, crimes against railroad property, and murder on federal lands. They had no jurisdiction over nonfederal matters. As a result, many crimes went unpunished by the authorities. Federal marshals were politically appointed stipendiary police—they received no salary, just fees and rewards. In fact, they didn't earn an annual salary until 1896, more than 100 years after their inception (U.S. Marshals Service, n.d.).

In addition to U.S. Marshals, county sheriffs and town marshals also enforced law on the frontier. Like their counterparts in the colonies and in England, frontier sheriffs spent most of their time collecting taxes. If a dangerous criminal was in the vicinity or a crime spree occurred, the sheriff would summon the **posse comitatus** (men aged 15 and above) to help regain order or catch the suspect. *Posse comitatus* literally means "power of the county" in Latin; it derived from the hue and cry and evolved into an accepted form of vigilantism. Lynching and other forms of vigilante justice were commonplace in the west because of the lack of professional policing on the frontier. Some of the most famous marshals and sheriffs in the Old West were of questionable character and background (Wyatt Earp and Wild Bill Hickok, for example) which made differentiating the good guys from the bad guys challenging.

Some states and territories created their own agencies when it was thought necessary to protect property or capture dangerous criminals. Texas was the first state to create a state-wide police force in 1823 (22 years before it officially became a state). Stephen Austin (father of Texas) paid 10–12 men to protect his colony from Native Americans and Mexicans. They were called the Texas

Rangers. Another state that felt it necessary to create a state-wide police agency was California. The California legislature created the California Rangers in 1853 with one purpose: to "capture the party or gang of robbers commanded by the five Juaquin" (Military Museum, n.d., paragraph 6). The agency was disbanded after they caught their subjects and brought them to justice, a mere three months after inception. State police agencies did not generally play a large role in law enforcement in the west.

Private citizens participated in law enforcement efforts through vigilance committees and by hiring private police to protect their businesses. **Vigilance committees** were groups of individuals who administered justice on their own. They were established by citizens when they felt the government was unable, or unwilling, to administer law and order on their behalf (due to corruption or incompetence). The first vigilance committee in California was formed in Pueblo de Los Angeles in 1836 (Gardiner & Williams, 2014). Merchants and traders hired private individuals to protect their property and person on trade routes and in ports and other sultry neighborhoods. One of the first examples of private policing (stipendiary policing) in the West was the San Francisco Patrol Special Police, which was established in 1847 when local merchants hired men to protect their interests from outlaws in the seedy and crime-ridden Barbary Coast section of the city[6] (Gardiner & Williams, 2014). Wells Fargo is another example of private policing. The company, started in 1852, operated banks as well as mail-carrying and stagecoach services throughout the West (Vila & Morris, 1999). In order to protect their money and other valuable cargo, they created a security division to accompany the stagecoaches to prevent robberies and also to apprehend criminals who had stolen from them.

St. Louis traffic policeman in 1918, using 4th Liberty Loan fans for signals.

CONCLUSION

As you can see, policing developed uniquely in different parts of the world. The evolution of policing in England was incremental. It began as an informal system of social control and slowly became more formalized as populations grew and societies became more industrialized. Kin policing matured into Frankpledge which developed into the night watch system. When the part-time watch system crumbled, stipendiary policing filled the gaps until a full-time centralized police force was eventually established. Policing in the United States, which was modeled after English policing, developed in a similar incremental fashion, though not as uniformly as it did in England. The distinctive characteristics of early U.S. colonies and territories meant that law enforcement in these regions was unique and varied. Legitimacy and power, the issues of paramount importance when the idea of formalized policing was being debated, are still major concerns today—almost 200 years later.

---

6   This department still exists and is unique because it is the oldest, continually-operating, private police force in the state of California (and possibly the country); it was the pre-cursor to the San Francisco Police Department (first public police department in the state), and also because its existence is written into the city charter (Gardiner & Williams, 2014).

REVIEW QUESTIONS

1. When and where were the first instances of "law enforcement" observed in the world?
2. What is Kin Policing? Can you explain it?
3. What is Frankpledge? Can you explain it?
4. Can you describe the Constable watch system in place in England? How did the watch system in America differ?
5. Who was Robert Peel and why is he important to the history of policing? Why was he "the right man at the right time?"
6. How did policing develop in the southern part of the United States? How did this differ from the North? And the West?

GLOSSARY

Bow Street Runners paid constables who investigated crimes, served warrants, and performed other tasks for the Bow Street magistrates.

Code of Hammurabi a set of laws written by the King of Babylon around 1750.

Community constable a man, appointed by a nobleman, who supervised the volunteer tythings-men in a hundred.

Constable a local law enforcement officer who was responsible for collecting taxes and enforcing ordinances in the colonial and post-colonial period United States, similar to sheriff; constables today are typically law enforcement officers in small towns.

Frankpledge a communitarian system of law enforcement in England between 1066 and 1285.

Hundred a geographic grouping that consisted of ten tythings in ancient England.

Kin policing practice in which a family, clan, or tribe enforces customary rules and socially defined norms of behavior.

Medjay paramilitary police force in ancient Egypt that protected Egyptian towns and other valuable areas.

Parish constable system system of English law enforcement created by the Statute of Winchester in 1285.

Posse comitatus townsmen who were summoned by the sheriff to help regain order during the colonial period; in Latin, "power of the county."

Praefectus Urbi also known as urban cohorts, three cohorts of 500 men that patrolled the streets of Rome during the day to keep the peace starting in 13 BC.

Praetorian Guard nine cohorts of 500 men that protected the city of Rome and the emperor starting around 27 BC.

Shire geographic area roughly equivalent to a county in the United States.

Shire reeve a man, appointed by the King of England, to maintain order, enforce laws, and collect taxes within a shire.

Sheriff a local law enforcement officer who was responsible for collecting taxes and enforcing ordinances in the colonial and post-colonial period United States, similar to a constable; sheriffs today serve as law enforcement officers at the county level.

Slave patrols police-like groups in the South in the colonial era that focused on regulating the activities of slaves. Vigilante justice—the taking on of law enforcement responsibilities and the dispensing of punishment by private citizens; the precursor to modern policing in the south.

Stipendiary policing the early practice of private policing in England.

Thief-takers men who were paid to recover stolen property, identify and capture criminals in the middle ages in England.

Tything a volunteer group of men from 10 families living near each other who were sworn to uphold justice.

Vigilance committees groups of individual citizens who administered justice on their own during the colonial period.

Vigiles individuals who fought fires and kept watch during the night in Rome starting in 6 AD.

REFERENCES

Bagnall, R. (2012). Police, Pharaonic Egypt. *Encyclopedia of ancient history.* Maldan, MA: Wiley-Blackwell.

Barton, G. A. (2009). *Archaeology and the Bible.* University of Michigan Library (originally published in 1916 by American Sunday-School Union), p. 406.

Bunson, M. (2002). Police in ancient Egypt. *Encyclopedia of ancient Egypt, Revised.* New York, NY: Facts on File, Inc. Ancient and Medieval History Online. Retrieved from http://www.fofweb.com

David, R. (2003). Police in ancient Egypt. *Handbook to life in ancient Rome, Updated Edition.* New York, NY: Facts on File, Inc. Ancient and Medieval History Online. Retrieved from http://www.fofweb.com

Dunstan, W. (2010). *Ancient Rome.* New York, NY: Rowman and Littlefield.

Emsley, C. (1983). *Policing and its context 1750–1870.* New York, NY: Schocken Books.

Emsley, C. (1991). *The English police: A political and social history.* New York, NY: St. Martin's Press.

Gardiner, C., & Williams, S. (2014). Policing in California. In C. L. Gardiner & P. Fiber-Ostrow (Eds.), *California's criminal justice system.* Durham, NC: Carolina Academic Press.

Hadden, S. E. (2001). *Slave patrols: Law and violence in Virginia and the Carolinas.* Cambridge, MA: Harvard University Press.

House of Commons. (2014). *House of Commons Journal, Volume 10, 1688–1693.* London: University of London School of Advanced Study, Institute of Historical Research.

Hunter, V. J. (1994). *Policing Athens: Social control in the Attic lawsuits, 420–320 B.C.,* Princeton, NJ: Princeton University Press.

Los Angeles Police Department (LAPD). (n.d.a). *History of the LAPD.* Retrieved from http://www.lapdonline.org/history_of_the_lapd

Los Angeles Police Department (LAPD). (n.d.b). *Women in the LAPD.* http://www.lapdonline.org/join_the_team/content_basic_view/833

Lyman, J. L. (1964). The Metropolitan Police Act of 1829. *Journal of Criminal Law and Criminology, 55*(1), 141–154.

McMullan, J. T. (1996). The new improved monied police: Reform, crime control, and the commodification of policing in London. *The British Journal of Criminology, 36*(1), 85–108.

Military Museum. (n.d.). *California State Militia and National Guard unit histories: California State Rangers.* http://www.militarymuseum.org/CaliforniaStateRangers.html

Mosse, G. L. (1975). *Police forces in history.* SAGE Readers in 20th Century History Volume 2. Beverly Hills, CA: SAGE Publications.

Nippel, W. (1995). *Public order in ancient Rome.* Cambridge, England: Cambridge University Press.

Patterson, D. (n.d.). *Thames Police: History.* London, England: Thames Police Museum. Retrieved from http://www.thamespolicemuseum.org.uk/history.html

Reynolds, E. A. (1998). *Before the bobbies: The night watch and police reform in metropolitan London, 1720–1830.* Palo Alto, CA: Stanford University Press.

Roth, M. P. (2005). *Crime and punishment: A history of the criminal justice system.* Belmont, CA: Thomspon-Wadsworth.

Samaha, J. (1974). *Law and order in historical perspective.* New York, NY: Academic Press.

Smith, P. T. (1985). *Policing Victorian London: Political policing, public order, and the London Metropolitan Police.* Westport, CT: Greenwood Press.

Taylor, D. (1998). *Crime, policing and punishment in England, 1750–1914.* New York, NY: St. Martin's Press, Inc.

Uchida, C. (2004). The development of the American police: An historical overview. In Roger Dunham & Geoffrey P. Alpert (Eds.), *Critical Issues in Policing: Contemporary Readings.* Waveland Press, Inc. Retrieved from http://storage.globalcitizen.net/data/topic/knowledge/uploads/2009042815114290.pdf

UK Home Office. (2012, December 10). *Policing by consent.* Retrieved from: https://www.gov.uk/government/publications/policing-by-consent

U.S. Marshals Service. (n.d.). *Historical timeline.* Retrieved from http://www.usmarshals.gov/history/timeline.html

Vila, B., & Morris, C. (1999). *The role of police in society: A documentary history.* Westport, CT: Greenwood Press.

Wilkinson, T. (2005). *Dictionary of ancient Egypt.* New York, NY: Thames & Hudson Ltd.

3

THE HISTORY OF POLICING: MODERN POLICING IN AMERICA

LEARNING OBJECTIVES

After reading this chapter, students should be able to

1 Describe the defining characteristics for each of the four eras of modern policing in America.

2 Explain why politics was an issue in policing during the 19th and early 20th centuries.

3 Name some of the major police reformers and list their contributions to policing.

4 Describe how technology influenced policing during each of the eras.

5 Explain how the 1960s race riots and research conducted during the 1970s contributed to the community era.

6 Explain why the intelligence era began when it did.

KEY TERMS

Lexow Committee

Volstead Act of 1919

Wickersham Commission

Kerner Commission

President's Commission on Law Enforcement

Omnibus Safe Streets and Crime Control Act of 1968

Team policing

Problem-oriented policing

Community-oriented policing

Broken windows theory

Violent Crime Control and Law Enforcement Act of 1994

Zero tolerance policing

Stop and frisk

Compstat

USA Patriot Act

Militarization

President's Task Force on 21st Century Policing

Evidence-based policing

Police Foundation

Police Executive Research Foundation

International Association of Police Chiefs

Law Enforcement Assistance Administration

The different policing histories introduced in Chapter 2 eventually evolved into very similar law enforcement experiences throughout the country. While policing in America evolved similarly to policing in England, there were some unique differences that allowed policing in America to become very political, especially in the 19th and early 20th centuries. This chapter details the development of policing in America since the first police departments in the mid-19th century until today. It follows Kelling & Moore's (1988) classification of modern American police history into three eras: The Political Era (1845–1920s), The Reform Era (1920s–1980s), and The Community Problem Solving Era (1980s–2000s). Using their analytic framework, we introduce a new, fourth era: The Intelligence Era (post–2001).

THE POLITICAL ERA, 1845–1920s

Chaos and crime brought on by the Industrial Revolution pushed politicians, who were aware of the developments in England, to closely examine their crime control efforts in the 1830s and 1840s. However, similar to the story in London, most American cities were not keen to establish professional police forces, instead preferring to rely on informal social control based on the common belief that law enforcement was everyone's responsibility. Thus, cities were slow to act. Philadelphia was the first city to establish a day watch in 1833, but it was disbanded in 1836 (Peak, 2008). Boston also experimented with a day watch in 1838 but policing reform truly started in New York in 1845 when the state legislature passed a law mandating the creation of a preventative police department in New York City (Vila & Morris, 1999). This is where the modern era begins.

THE JOB

The New York City Police Department (NYPD) started with 800 salaried, full-time officers who patrolled the city during the day and night. Although understaffed by today's standards, this was a very large department for the time. Like the watchmen before them, NYPD constables (and their counterparts in other cities) lit the streetlamps, walked a beat, and arrested lawbreakers; but unlike most watchmen, they also investigated crimes, regulated traffic, and provided a variety of social services (Vila & Morris, 1999). Some departments operated ambulances or housed indigents, others provided basic healthcare services or ran soup kitchens.

Courtesy of Library of Congress

Police give relief to citizens in the 1930s.

Boston police, for example, cleaned the streets and checked every house for signs of cholera during outbreaks.

Being a police officer in 19th century America was a desirable job because it paid well, typically about twice as much as other unskilled jobs. On paper New York City police were not allowed to accept money or other rewards without the mayor's permission; yet bribing officers to "look the other way" was commonplace in New York and other places. Unlike their British counterparts, American officers in most departments did not wear uniforms in the early days. Many officers adamantly opposed wearing uniforms stating they were demeaning and unmanly, and that wearing them would eliminate their anonymity, making their job more difficult and dangerous (Vila & Morris, 1999). Officers in San Francisco objected on the belief that uniforms made them appear to be servants (Ackerson & Tully, n.d.). Eventually, in 1853, New York police officers were forced to sign a new employment contract agreeing to wear a uniform or lose their job. A similar technique was used in San Francisco in 1856 to get officers there to wear uniforms (Ackerson & Tully, n.d.). Other large cities quickly followed suit requiring uniforms, though not always with the loud grumbling by officers. While British police only carried a truncheon, American officers were outfitted with a firearm from the beginning; a choice that was made in response to America's long-standing history of a right to bear arms. It was felt that the police should be at least as well armed as the criminals they were expected to protect the public from and apprehend. By 1880, nearly every large city in America had a police department modeled on the London Metropolitan Police (Monkkonen, 1981).

Whereas many night watches were spoiled by incompetent men enforcing order erratically and inefficiently, the new police forces were instead spoiled by systematic corruption. At this period of time politics influenced every aspect of policing—who was hired, who worked each beat, who was promoted, who supervised each district, as well as who ran the department. Even arrest decisions were sometimes political. As with other aspects of public life, political entrepreneurs used the police to control their adversaries and establish their power and position within the city's social and political hierarchy. Police historian Samuel Walker (1980), concluded that "officers were primarily tools of local politicians" (p. 61). This is very different from London which was known for impartial and detached policing (at least as far as politics were concerned).

TABLE 3.1 Important Historical Events in American Policing

1631	First night watch—Boston, MA
1704	First slave patrol—South Carolina
1789	First federal law enforcement agency—U.S. Marshal's
1791	Bill of Rights adopted
1823	First state-wide law enforcement agency—Texas Rangers
1829	First full-time, centralized, "modern," police force established by Sir Robert Peel London Metropolitan Police
1845	First unified, "prevention-focused" police department in U.S.—New York City, NY
1847	First private police force established—San Francisco Special Police Patrol, CA
1853	First U.S. department to require uniforms—New York City Police Department
1867	First African American police commissioner & police officers hired in New Orleans, LA
1871	First National Police Convention held in St. Louis, MO
1874	First Indian police force—Apache reservation in San Carlos, AZ
1878	First police matrons hired by departments
1891	First female police detective, Marie Owens, hired by Chicago PD
1894	Lexow Committee formed to investigate corruption within NYPD

continued

TABLE 3.1   Important Historical Events in American Policing *(continued)*

1899	First electric police car used in Akron, OH
1905	Lola Baldwin hired by Portland PD to work with women and children
1910	First official female police officer with arrest powers, Alice Stebbins Wells, hired by Los Angeles PD
1911	Berkley (CA) Police Chief, August Vollmer, puts entire patrol division on bicycle
1912	Berkley (CA) Police Chief, August Vollmer, begins motorcycle patrol
1914	*Weeks v. United States* establishes the exclusionary rule
1919	Boston police officers strike for better wages and working conditions
1921	Berkley (CA) Police Chief, August Vollmer, first to install and use radio in patrol car; also uses first lie detector in police laboratory
1924	J. Edgar Hoover appointed director of Department of Justice's Bureau of Investigation (later renamed Federal Bureau of Investigation)
1928	Detroit (MI) police department develops improved radio system & has first police dispatcher.
1930	Legislation creates first crime data collection effort—Uniform Crime Reports
1935	FBI's National Police Academy established
1950	O.W. Wilson publishes "Police Administration" William H. Parker appointed Chief of Los Angeles P.D. after corruption scandal
1961	*Mapp v. Ohio* establishes the "fruit of the poisonous tree" doctrine
1966	*Miranda v. Arizona*—police must inform suspects of their rights before questioning
1967	President's Commission on Law Enforcement and Administration of Justice report
1968	Kerner Commission report with causes and solutions of race riots issued *Terry v. Ohio*—establishes officer's legal right to stop, question, and frisk a suspicious person Congress passes Omnibus Crime Control and Safe Streets Act, establishes the Law Enforcement Assistance Administration James Q. Wilson publishes "Varieties of Police Behavior" study findings
1972	Knapp Commission report detailing widespread corruption within NYPD released
1974	George L. Kelling and colleagues publish findings of Kansas City Preventative Patrol Experiment
1979	Herman Goldstein introduces the concept of "Problem Oriented Policing."
1982	James Q. Wilson & George L. Kelling advance the idea of "Broken Windows"
1985	*Tennessee v. Garner* establishes "defense of life" standard for when police can use deadly force
1991	Los Angeles police officers are videotaped beating Rodney King; the Christopher Commission investigates the incident and issues a report recommending the department adopt a community policing approach.
1994	Congress passed the Violent Crime Control & Safe Streets Act, among other things the law intended to hire 100,000 new community policing officers

continued

TABLE 3.1   Important Historical Events in American Policing *(continued)*

2001	New York City's Twin Towers are taken down by terrorists, starting a new era in policing
2012	*U.S. v. Jones*—established that police attaching a GPS monitoring device to a suspect's car constitutes a search
2014	Michael Brown, Eric Garner, and Tamir Rice are killed by police in separate incidents. Numerous public protests against police violence erupt around the country. The movement #BlackLivesMatter (born in 2012 after the death of Trayvon Martin by Neighborhood Watch member George Zimmerman) gains momentum. *Riley v. California*—establishes that police must have warrant to search cell phone
2015	Videos showing the deaths of Freddie Gray, Walter Scott and several other black men by police keep the public focused on police use of force President's Task Force on 21st Century Policing releases final report

THE POLITICS

Although the New York City Police Department was modeled on the London Metropolitan Police, there were key differences that caused the NYPD and other American departments to be highly political (a couple of which were mentioned—uniforms and firearms). The main issue was that whereas the London police were accountable to England's Home Secretary, New York City police were accountable to the politicians in each ward (Vila & Morris, 1999). In other words, while English police derived their central authority from the Crown, early American police derived their authority and resources from local politicians; this made the two entities (police and politicians) inexorably intertwined (at least for the first half-century). In London, constables were hired by the commissioners for indefinite terms; provided he did not break the rules, a constable could keep his job as long as he wanted. In New York, however, constables were selected by the mayor (after their name had been nominated by the alderman or assistant alderman of the district); they were appointed to one-year terms (later extended to four-year terms) and could be re-appointed if the appropriate politicians were satisfied with their work (Richardson, 1970, reprinted in Vila & Morris, 1999). The New York police chief was similarly appointed and had no supervisory power over the hiring, firing, or promotion of constables in his department (Richardson, 1970, reprinted in Vila & Morris, 1999). This was not atypical. Many American officers served at the whim of the executive (marshal, chief, or sheriff), or more appropriately the politicians, and were replaced when the chief was replaced (Ackerson & Tully, n.d.; Vila & Morris, 1999).

This system assured that local men were hired—those familiar with the ways of the neighborhood, of proper ethnic stock, and willing to support and take direction from their political leaders. It was opposite of the philosophy in England, which was to hire officers not familiar with the neighborhood so as to encourage impartiality. Politics pervaded policing until the 1930s. Starting with the Lexow Committee in 1894, however, a small group of reformers worked to reduce the influence it had on policing, one department at a time.

EARLY EFFORTS TO REFORM

The **Lexow Committee,** led by future US President Theodore Roosevelt, was formed to investigate allegations of corruption within the NYPD; what it found was shocking—rampant and pervasive corruption which included officers buying their positions and blackmailing criminals and the general public alike. For example, the "going rate" to become a patrolman was $200–$300 (roughly $6,000 today) and the going rate for promotion to captain was $12,000–$15,000 (a whopping, and conservative, $333,000 in 2014 dollars) (Roosevelt, 1897, reprinted in Vila & Morris, 1999). In Roosevelt's own words:

> *The money was reimbursed to those who paid it by an elaborate system of blackmail. This was chiefly carried on at the expense of gamblers, liquor sellers, and keepers of disorderly houses; but every form of vice and crime contributed more or less, and a great many respectable people who were ignorant or timid were blackmailed under pretense [original spelling] of forbidding or allowing them to violate obscure ordinances and the like. (Roosevelt, 1897, reprinted in Vila & Morris, 1999, p. 64).*

Fortunately, Roosevelt and his committee found that

> *In spite of the wide-spread corruption which had obtained the New York police department, the bulk of the men were heartily desirous of being honest. There were some who were incurably dishonest, just as there were some who had remained decent in spite of terrific temptation and pressure; but the great mass came in between (Roosevelt, 1897, reprinted in Vila & Morris, 1999, p. 64).*

Courtesy Library of Congress

Roosevelt served as police commissioner.

As a result of their investigation, the committee fired 200 officers (they wanted to fire more but could not), promoted 130, and hired about 1,700 in an attempt to reset the department's moral code (Roosevelt, 1897, reprinted in Vila & Morris, 1999). Because elections officers had been used to enable fraud at the polls, ensuring honest elections was another main priority for the committee. After rejecting more than 1,000 men recommended by politicians to oversee the elections, the committee had to train the new officers to understand that "their sole duty was to guarantee an honest election" (Roosevelt, 1897, reprinted in Vila & Morris, 1999, p. 65). After a couple of years the committee achieved its goals, and noted a dramatic increase in the integrity of the force as well as its efficiency.

Unfortunately, history books suggest that things went "back to normal" after the committee disbanded and the corrupt Tammany Hall politicians regained office in 1898 (Richardson, 1970). Still, the Lexow Commission was important, not only for the corruption it uncovered but also because it represented the first efforts to expose the ugly underbelly of policing and change the culture. It was part of the larger progressive era movement that aimed to remove politics from government and reform all aspects of American society.

AFRICAN AMERICANS IN POLICING[1]

This era also saw the first major introduction of African Americans into policing. Even before the advent of modern police departments, there is evidence that a small number of "free men of color" served in the city guard in New Orleans as early as 1805 (Dulaney, 1996). As in other cities, keeping the peace (and in the south, controlling slaves) was not a job many men wanted. This opened the door, so to speak, for "free men of color" to demonstrate their abilities and prove their loyalty and trustworthiness to powerful whites (Dulaney, 1996). Regrettably, their time on the city guard was rather short-lived and in 1822 the New Orleans city council mandated hiring only white city workers. By 1830 all "free persons of color" had been removed from the city guard (Dulaney, 1996). It would be another 37 years before another African American worked as a police officer in New Orleans (or any other city in the United States).

What was the reason for this? Politics. New Orleans was no different than any other urban city in this regard. Recognizing the power of the office, different factions (ethnic groups) fought to control the police and rewarded their supporters with jobs within the police department. Since no ethnic group sought their support, "free men of color"

Courtesy Library of Congress

Police portrayed as blackmailers.

were left without jobs or political appointments (Dulaney, 1996). After 1820, racial tensions grew at a fever pitch due to immigration and other social facts of the time. Segregation laws, which applied to all "persons of color" regardless of status (free or slave), were passed to restrict the rights and movements of black individuals. After the end of the civil war, blacks gained (or regained) some rights which whites attempted to remove through the passage of "Black codes." This struggle for power erupted into violent race riots in 1866, and white police were unable and unwilling to protect blacks from white hostility and even instigated some of the harassment and violence against blacks. After much criticism by the *New Orleans Tribune* (the first daily African American newspaper in the United States) and the African American community, the military governor of Louisiana ordered the mayor to reorganize the police force and appoint former Union Army soldiers to be one-half its members (Dulaney, 1996).

As a result, in 1867, New Orleans appointed the first African American police commissioner (Charles Courcelle) in the nation and hired more than a dozen African American police officers (the first two were Dusseau Picou and Emile Farrar) (Rousey, 1987). Thought to be the first police department in the nation to integrate, New Orleans Police Department (NOPD) also had the largest contingent of black officers in 1870 (182 out of 647 officers) (Rousey, 1987).

Historians estimate that there were probably about 350 black men working as police officers in the South in 1870, of which more than half worked for NOPD (Rousey, 1987). Some of these African American officers were able to enforce the law and perform their job duties in the same manner as their white counterparts (including carrying a firearm, wearing a uniform, and arresting white offenders), but many others were relegated to administering law enforcement in only black communities. In the most egalitarian departments, African Americans could, and did, hold administrative and command positions. Still, there is much evidence that whites resented

---

[1] For a remarkable accounting of the history of black police officers in America, check out *Black Police in America* by W. Marvin Dulaney (1996).

African American police officers and would not obey them. According to historians, "the exercise of police powers by African Americans [was] one of the most hated features of the Reconstruction governments" (Dulaney, 1996, p. 13). White southerners strongly fought against racial equality, and by 1877 most southern states had "redeemed" their governments by voting out Republicans (white and black). This, in turn, resulted in the removal of African Americans from the police

TABLE 3.2	African-American Representation in Selected Southern Police Departments			

City	1st Reconstruction Hire	1st Post-Reconstruction Hire	1st Promotion to Sergeant	1st Promotion to Captain
New Orleans, LA	1867	1950		
Selma, AL	1867	?		
Mobile, AL	1867	1954		
Montgomery, AL	1868	1954		
Raleigh, NC	1868	1942		
Washington, DC	1869	?		1965
Houston, TX	1870	(continuous)	1974	
Austin, TX	1872	(continuous)	1969	
Chattanooga, TN	1872	1948		
Jacksonville, FL	1873	?		
Memphis, TN	1878	1948	1950	
Louisville, KY		1923	1944	
Baltimore, MD		1937	1947	
Charlotte, NC		1941	1956	
Little Rock, AR		1942		
Durham, NC		1944		
Miami, FL		1944	1955	
Norfolk, VA		1945		
Richmond, VA		1946	1952	
Dallas, TX		1947	1966	
Savannah, GA		1947		
Atlanta, GA		1948	1956	1968
Macon, GA		1948		
Nashville, TN		1948		
Columbia, SC		1949		
Charleston, SC		1950	1971	
Fort Worth, TX		1953		
Jackson, MS		1963		

Adapted from Dulaney, W.M. (1996). Black police officers in America. Bloomington, IN: Indiana University Press.

force such that by 1910 there were only 576 African American police officers in the nation, most of whom worked in northern cities (Dulaney, 1996).

Like many other facets of American life, the history of African Americans in policing is divided by geography. Ironically, police departments in the south were quicker to integrate than those in the north. While at least 12 southern departments had black police officers in 1870, there is no indication that any northern departments had black officers at that time (Dulaney, 1996; Rousey, 1987). Chicago Police Department was likely the first northern police department to hire an African American officer in 1872, followed by Pittsburgh (PA) in 1875 and Indianapolis (IN) in 1876 (Dulaney, 1996).

Similar to in the south, black men in the north had to rely on the political patronage system to gain access to lucrative police positions. In Chicago, African Americans secured 260 police appointments between 1872 and 1930 through deals made with powerful politicians and parties which sought the support of the African American community on specific issues (Dulaney, 1996). The situation was similar in other northern cities. African Americans were most successful in gaining police appointments in cities, such as Philadelphia, that were dominated by the Republican Party. Eventually, civil service procedures played a larger role than politics in obtaining employment in the police department (unfortunately this led to fewer African Americans serving as police officers, not more). In most places, African American police officers had to wear

TABLE 3.3	African-American Representation in Selected Northern Police Departments		
City	1st Hire	1st Promotion to Sergeant*	1st Promotion to Captain
Chicago, IL	1872	1897	1940
Pittsburgh, PA	1875		
Indianapolis, IN	1876		
Boston, MA	1878	1895 (1937)	
Cleveland, OH	1881	1949	1960
Philadelphia, PA	1881	1929 (1943)	1954
Columbus, OH	1885	1943 (1946)	1952
Los Angeles, CA	1886	1917 (1943)	1969
Cincinnati, OH	1886	1949	
Detroit, MI	1890	1918	
Brooklyn, NW (before consolidation)	1891		
St. Louis, MO	1901	1923 (1948)	1956
New York City, NY (after consolidation)	1911	1923 (1926)	1952

* Dates in parentheses represent when African-American were appointed to a sergeant position with supervisory responsibilities.

Adapted from Dulaney, W.M. (1996). Black police officers in America. Bloomington, IN: Indiana University Press.

plainclothes, rather than a uniform, so that they would not stand out nor incite a riot and were prohibited from arresting white persons.

While African Americans remained a part of policing in the north from their first inception in 1872, that was not the case for African Americans in the south. Southern blacks disappeared almost entirely from policing after Redemption. In fact, "up to the 1940s, not a single African American held a police position in the Deep South states of Georgia, Alabama, South Carolina, Mississippi, and Louisiana" despite the fact that "these five states contained a majority of the black population in the United States" (Dulaney, 1996, p. 30). Only a few southern cities (for example, Houston, Austin, and Galveston, Texas) retained black officers during this period. For the rest of the south, regaining black representation on the city police force was a very long and hard-fought battle.

Residents of some cities fought for decades before they saw the appointment (or reappointment) of black police officers. Dallas residents, for example, fought for more than 60 years before they gained black police representation in 1947 (Dulaney, 1996). Supporters in Atlanta provided politicians a list of five "reasons for employing Negro officers" in 1933, including: "(1) to reduce Atlanta's high homicide rate; (2) to relieve white police of the burden of policing black areas; (3) to keep order in black communities, (4) to improve the morale of the black community; and (5) because other southern cities were employing them with much success" (Dulaney, 1996, p. 40). However, it was not until 1948 that Atlanta hired its first black police officers under the leadership of police Chief Herbert Jenkins and only after considerable controversy and protests (from both blacks and whites).

Change happened in a very piecemeal fashion and was highly determined by each city's political leader and the ability of blacks to organize politically and to impact the political process through voting. For example, Violet Hill Whyte, who holds the distinction of being the first African American appointed to the Baltimore Police Department as well as the first African American women to hold a police appointment before African American men, was appointed in December 1937, only after a new police commissioner took office (Dulaney, 1996). In some cases, blacks had to file lawsuits to be allowed to take the civil service exam to become a police officer. More often than not blacks who became police officers, especially in the south, were severely limited in their powers to enforce law; they were treated as second-class officers and more accurately described as quasi-law enforcement, often ineligible for promotion beyond patrol officer.

Still, "race officers" were an important step forward in policing and race relations. Not only did blacks fight for representation on the police force as a matter of principle, they also fought for better policing of their neighborhoods. As previously discussed, it is important to have officers who can empathize with and gain the support of minority populations in increasingly diverse communities. African Americans wanted fair, equitable, and unbiased law enforcement which they believed only black officers would provide. They didn't want white officers taking bribes to ignore the vice and other crimes occurring in their neighborhoods on a daily basis. They wanted crime control. African American officers were recognized for their success at reducing and solving crime in black neighborhoods.

Even though the history of African American police officers is long, their numbers had until recently not amounted to anything more than tokenism until recently. Prior to the 1950s, only two African Americans had achieved the rank of captain (Octave Rey of New Orleans from 1868 to 1877 and John Scott of Chicago from 1940 to 1946) (Dulaney, 1996). This situation began to change in the 1950s and 1960s when more opportunities for promotion were created by progressive leaders and as a result of black representation in politics. Prior to the 1970s, a few African Americans did achieve the status of chief; however, this occurred mostly in small cities that had few African American residents (Dulaney, 1996). In 1970, Cleveland, Ohio, became the first major city in America to appoint a black police chief, beating out Gary, Indiana, by a matter of months.[2] By the end of the 1980s, more than 130 African Americans had served as their jurisdiction's top administrator.

There was a push to increase the number of officers of minority status (race and gender) in the 1970s. This was really the beginning of diversity in policing and was instigated by the passage of the Civil Rights Act, which prohibited discrimination on the basis of race or sex, among other things. The Civil Rights Act and the multitude of lawsuits that followed essentially forced law enforcement to diversify. Black women, who were often subjected to double-racism, benefitted greatly from these diversification efforts. For example, whereas 15% of all officers in 1990 were black, 35% of female police officers were black (Dulaney, 1996).

PROGRESSIVE ERA

The years between 1900 and 1930 represented a period of intense social change in America. Not only were the demographics of the United States shifting, so too were the philosophies and values. Women gained the right to vote, industrial workers saw improved working conditions, alcohol was banned, wealthy citizens formed philanthropic societies to help (some say control) the less fortunate, the US economy grew considerably, then collapsed and initiated the Great Depression the country fought in WWI, and technological innovations such as the automobile, telegraph, and electricity changed society profoundly.

Not surprisingly, this period also had a great effect on policing. Several police leaders along with some concerned and outspoken citizens advocated for higher standards, better training, and other improvements. Specifically, reformers wanted to define policing as a profession. In order to do that, they needed to get politics out of policing (which was easier said than done). It involved reorganizing departments so that the chief was no longer just a figurehead (unable to make decisions about personnel or operations) and removing power from the precinct captains (who did call the shots and were beholden to local politicians). To do this, chiefs hired mid-level managers to help monitor officers, as well as develop and institute new operational plans and policies. Chiefs also reorganized police districts so that they no longer coincided with political boundaries, thereby diminishing (or diffusing) the power of the politicians and shifting power for operations to the chief and his management staff (where it belonged). Finally, chiefs instituted centralized special units (such as detectives, traffic, vice, and juveniles) which had powers of arrest throughout the entire jurisdiction—not just one precinct.

Raising the personnel standards was another key piece to creating a professionalized police force. Police chiefs and other reformers wanted minimum hiring standards, training for recruits, and promotions based on testing (not favoritism). Given the arduous hiring process new recruits go through today, it seems hard to believe that most cities did not have any hiring standards (other than political patronage) until the early part of the 20th century. Some of the new standards included minimum requirements for intelligence, health, and moral character. In terms of training, the New York City and San Francisco police departments both established police academies in 1895 (Ackerson & Tully, n.d.). These were the first attempts to offer recruits instruction on the job (but offered very little training in comparison to today's academies).

---

[2] Portsmouth, Ohio, had an African American.

Other important changes that occurred around this time and that had important and lasting effects on law enforcement included: technological innovations, the introduction of women to policing, and attempts to unionize.

TECHNOLOGICAL INNOVATIONS

Technology was rapidly developing at this time and police leaders experimented with a variety of innovations that improved the efficiency of officers as well as perceptions of police professionalism. Call boxes were one such innovation; they provided more communication between headquarters and beat officers as well as better accountability.

Courtesy of Library of Congress

Metro police officer uses call box.

The first callbox was installed in Albany, NY, in 1877; the year after Alexander Graham Bell invented the device (Police Museum, Fl). Callboxes went through several iterations over the next couple decades—original devices were a one-way system from headquarters to the call box, later models allowed officers to "check in," receive and provide crime information, and request assistance or a paddy wagon. Callboxes were the main method of communication between beat officers and the station until two-way radios were installed in patrol cars in the 1930s, 1940s, or 1950s (depending on the area) and even later for officers assigned to foot patrols.

Police cars are the innovation that most changed policing and the relationship between officers and the public. The first police car was introduced in Akron, OH, in 1899; it was electric, needed charging every 30 miles, and could go up to 18 MPH (Akron, n.d.). It was only in service a few years, but by 1908 there were nine large departments using automobiles and by the 1920s automobiles were common in police departments across the country; first as paddy wagons, then as patrol vehicles (Vila & Morris, 1999). Motorcycles were also common starting in the 1910s. All of these allowed officers to cover more distance in less time than foot or bicycle patrol and appear more efficient. Still, foot patrol remained the primary method of patrolling for quite some time in most cities.

Courtesy of Library of Congress

State troopers stand next to their patrol car.

WOMEN IN POLICING

This time period also saw the introduction of women to policing, mainly to work with women and juveniles. *Marie Owens* became the first female detective sergeant in the nation when she was transferred from Chicago's health department to the police department in 1891 (Mastony, 2010). As a health inspector, she enforced child labor and compulsory education laws in the factories, but inspectors did not have the power to enter businesses without a warrant. Public outrage against sweatshop conditions grew and Owens was transferred to the police department, given powers of

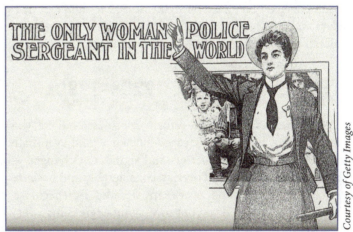

Courtesy of Getty Images

Photo illustration of Marie Owens from the Chicago Daily Tribune on August 7, 1904.

arrest, a police star, and the title of police detective to continue her work enforcing labor laws for another 32 years[3] (Mastony, 2010). Notice that the impetus for her move to the police department was the powers of the office (the ability that detectives had to go into warehouses without a warrant). She was hired in spite of the fact that she was a woman, not because of it; still, she must have been good at her job and must have had substantial support to break into this completely male organization and profession.

The next woman to be hired was *Lola Baldwin*. She was hired by the Portland (OR) Police Department in 1908 to prevent young women from getting involved in prostitution (Vila & Morris, 1999). It is important to note that she was hired as an "operative," not a police officer. *Alice Stebbins Wells,* hired by the Los Angeles Police Department in 1910 to patrol penny arcades,

---

[3] Chicago had a very well-established "Child Savers" movement that helped found the nation's first juvenile court in 1899, and female health inspectors working to help children would have been in line with their overall purpose.

Courtesy of Library of Congress

Women police practice with guns.

skating rinks, movie theaters, dance halls, and other public entertainment spots and to work with juveniles, women, and families with corrupted children, could be considered the nation's first female special patrol officer (Vila & Morris, 1999).

BOSTON POLICE STRIKE

Like other blue collar workers, police officers struggled under moderate–high inflation and stagnating wages during the early part of the century. At the same time, they watched the working conditions and wages of factory workers improve after unionization. The officers formed a union (masquerading as a social club) to protest poor wages and working conditions, but the police commissioner forbade officers from being members of the union/social club and then prosecuted 19 newly elected leaders (Vila & Morris, 1999). In response to the commissioner's actions, three-quarters of Boston's police officers went on strike in 1919 to fight for the right to unionize. The strike lasted three days and failed miserably. All of the officers were fired and attempts to unionize law enforcement all but died for at least the following 40 years.

THE REFORM ERA, 1920s–1980s

The next era, called the reform or professional era, was characterized by the adoption of a law enforcement function, increased efficiency, and eventually a professional crime fighter model. It is punctuated with numerous and significant changes —both good and bad. The political and reform/professional eras overlap considerably and because politics was so entrenched in policing, reform efforts took root over many decades. Furthermore, not all corruption was rooted out and some areas remained corrupt to varying degrees for a very long time into the professional era.

While progressive reformers were attempting to increase police professionalism, prohibition derailed (or at least delayed) reform efforts in many cities and presented new and difficult challenges for police throughout the country. Prior to prohibition, officers allowed local norms and values to dictate enforcement of moral crimes such as vice and public drunkenness. After the **Volstead Act of 1919** (Prohibition) was passed police officers were, for the first time, required to proactively enforce a moral law that was actively resisted by members of the public. This was a big change and meant that, for essentially the first time, police were performing a law enforcement function; and they were doing so against the wishes of the social majority. It spawned citizen contempt of law enforcement and magnified corruption amongst rank and file officers.

Another major event that forced officers to prioritize law enforcement over order maintenance was the Great Depression and resulting crime waves brought on by personal desperation. There were many civil uprisings and protests, as well as a large number of transients, homeless encampments, and altercations at soup kitchens during the 1930s. Police officers were tested by having to contain large, frequent, and often violent riots. At the same time, many police departments in the nation served as "reluctant relief agencies" (Starr, 1996, p. 227), providing food and shelter to unemployed men and families during the Great Depression.

Attempts to reform and professionalize the police continued. Officials began studying policing practices in an effort to make officers more efficient, to legitimize the profession, and to change the public's poor perception of the police. The **Wickersham Commission**, for example, was appointed by President Hoover in 1929 to conduct the first national study of the US criminal justice system, and more specifically law enforcement's concerns about prohibition. The commission issued its official report (all 14 volumes) in 1931 and 1932. It was highly critical of prohibition, stating that it was unenforceable. It was also highly critical of police officers— portraying them as incompetent, racist, dishonest, and brutal. The report condemned officers for extensively using the "third degree" when interrogating suspects (a practice that had already been denounced by the International Association of Chiefs of Police in 1910 yet was obviously still in practice 20 years later). It condemned the industry for not providing adequate training, education, and discipline to officers. The report concluded with 10 recommendations for professional police departments, including selection criteria for chiefs as well as officers, improved work conditions and salaries, better training, more police women, better communication between patrol officers and headquarters, as well as between law enforcement agencies, and a suggestion that states should create agencies to share information and aid in investigations. Most of these recommendations were, eventually, voluntarily implemented by most police departments in the nation (Vila & Morris, 1999).

As should be apparent by now, police reform was a slow process that evolved over a long period of time, and like any other change, was punctuated with successes and failures. Thankfully, reform-minded police chiefs were relentless in their pursuit to professionalize policing. These reformers were driven by a vision of professional police departments in which (1) officers were trained and educated experts, not inept puppets of politicians; (2) police leaders, not politicians, were in control of police personnel and operations; and finally, (3) modern technology was used to improve business practices and efficiency (Uchida, 2004).

REFORMERS

Some of the most important police reformers of the early 20th century were August Vollmer, O.W. Wilson, and William H. Parker. *August Vollmer* was the police chief of the Berkley Police Department (CA) from 1905 to 1932 and is considered the "father of modern policing" due to his many innovations and achievements. Not only was he one of the first to use bicycles, then motorcycles, then automobiles for patrol, he created a system of red lights hung on intersections to notify patrol officers of calls before radios and was the first to put a radio in a patrol car. He developed a centralized records system, created the first crime lab, was one of the first to categorize fingerprints and handwriting samples, was the first to use a lie detector in a police lab, interviewed criminals and trained officers on the importance of identifying and using a criminal's *modus operandi* to solve crimes. He also established entrance exams for police applicants, including intelligence, psychological, and neurological tests and was the first police chief to actively recruit college graduates (Uchida, 2004).

Although he, himself, did not have a college degree, Vollmer strongly advocated for educated police officers and helped establish police programs at three different colleges. He founded a law enforcement training program at the University of California at Berkeley (UCB) in 1916 and taught in the program from 1931 to 1937 (Gardiner & Williams, 2014; Vila & Morris, 1999). Vollmer also helped establish a criminology program at the University of Chicago and has the distinction of being the first professor of police administration in the nation (Vila & Morris, 1999). Finally, he convinced T. W. MacQuarrie, President of State Teachers College at San Jose (now known as San Jose State University [SJSU]), of the need for a police training school. In 1930, SJSU became the first university in the nation to offer a two-year college police program that led to an A.A. degree in Police Training (San Jose State University, 2005).

Continuing Vollmer's tradition of excellence and influence, *O.W. Wilson*, mentee of August Vollmer, Police Chief of Fullerton Police Department (CA) and Dean of University of California at Berkeley's School of Criminology (among other esteemed positions) shaped policing in the professional model. Although he was the first person to conduct a systematic study of one-person patrol cars, arguing that they were more efficient than two-person patrol cars (Uchida, 2004); he is most well-known for his 1943 book, *Police Administration,* which revolutionized police administration throughout the United States. Under his system, law enforcement agencies were to be organized along military lines with a distinct chain of command that allowed for close supervision of line officers. He advocated using motor patrols, rather than foot patrols, to reduce police–citizen contact and the opportunity for corruption. These suggestions, which were implemented in most police departments, essentially shaped policing in the professional mold.

FIELD PERSPECTIVES: WALKING A BEAT IS REAL COMMUNITY POLICING

By Sgt. William J. Donoghue (Ret.)

Courtesy of William Donoghue

William Donoghue

I began my long police career, graduating from the St. Louis Police Academy in September of 1956. At that time, the city of my birth, had been undertaking some changes that would require addressing a long tradition of segregation of the races. I believe we were the first integrated academy classes, the eighteenth and nineteenth classes. The St. Louis Metropolitan Police Department was, and probably still is, administered by a Board of Police Commissioners, appointed by The Governor of The State of Missouri. The short story for this lack of home rule is that, in the war between the states in the mid-1800s the local St. Louis police had joined with The Confederacy, whereupon federal troops from Jefferson Barracks occupied the city and patterned a reconstructed department after the state-of-the-art model of the time, The London Metropolitan Police Department, and had removed local control back in the day.

With the above history in mind, the appointed leadership of the St. Louis Metropolitan Police Department began the integration of the department with the eighteenth and nineteenth academy classes in 1956. The leadership had the two combined classes remain separated from the existing districts and precincts for an extended period after academy graduation, during which time we were described as a "Mobile Unit" and were assigned month after month to the district and precincts that had experienced the highest incidence of crime for the previous month. We were instructed to be aware; that even in the most crime ridden districts, there would be good and bad elements; that it would be our responsibility to identify and protect the good; that if we arrested anyone, we would not have the advantage of squad car, radio, and shotgun; and that we would most likely be waiting at the police call box for the "Paddy wagon" to arrive, with an unruly subject in tow! All of this emphasized the necessity for having friends in the neighborhood, and as soon as possible. We, obviously, would be somewhat vulnerable and dependent on the community.

I partnered up with Larry Crusoe, a black Air Force Veteran and fellow mobile unit stalwart, as my first involvement in the historic integration of St. Louis Metro. I remember a particular night, walking my beat alone in a tenement area on Franklin Avenue, for "whatever" reason Larry wasn't with me on that night. Someone began firing at me, with what sounded like a rifle from the upper floors of a flat across the avenue. I stepped into the brick and stone doorway of a flat on my side of the street, and began praying that someone in the neighborhood would call the police. I was relieved to hear a police siren, after what seemed a very long wait. The squad car pulled up to the curb in front of me and the lone officer (unusual then, probably just the start of one man car cut backs) yelled out to me "What's going' on?" "Get up here in the doorway, somebody's shooting from up there!" I said, pointing up. Whereupon he jumps out of the car with his shotgun, cranks in a round and says: "Let's go" and starts running across the street. That didn't seem wise to me but I had no choice, being a rookie. We ended up back in the rear of the tenements, where outdoor stairs connect to all the floors. We ran up to the second or third floor, where the shots had come from and where lights were on. It must have been warm weather, because the windows were open, with no screen and just light drapes. My "follow-up" pulled the drapes aside and exposed an African American Woman, lying on a bed with a bottle of booze and a rifle (ticked off at her man, or any man she'd see). My "follow-up" then said at the top of his voice: "All right N-----, drop that gun!" I then looked around and saw that most of the residents of the adjacent flats had been awakened and were now standing down in the courtyard. My follow-up could now take the woman into custody and call for the "Paddy wagon" with his radio. And I would return to walking Franklin Avenue in the neighborhood alone. No Way! I then said, loud and clear: "Hey Man! Don't you be using that kind of language in *my neighborhood*." As I walked down those stairs, I heard cheers from the crowd and repeatedly I heard the comment "You're some bad ass!," which I knew was a big compliment in the neighborhood.

I gave Larry Crusoe bad points for not being with me that night, but he just laughed it off and reminded me that, I probably would never get another "follow-up" from that same source. But he did say: "Welcome to the neighborhood Bad Ass!," Which I appreciate. Law enforcement has evolved in this country, from a tradition of cops (especially in large cities) beginning by walking a beat to get to know neighborhoods and how to be truly "Guardians of The Peace," to now sometimes being isolated in a one man car and only responding to calls from people who are complete strangers. Even as an experienced police officer from St. Louis, MO and Downey, CA, I was required to "walk the beat" on Center Street, shake door knobs at night and meet the people in Anaheim, before being allowed to isolate in a patrol car or motorcycle. I can see the need for police officers to gain that neighborhood involvement and sensitivity, it's very evident in places like Ferguson and Baltimore. There is an art and a science that develops whilst surviving on the beat. A sensitivity and even compassion develop; while becoming friendly and helpful are indispensable.

William J. Donoghue is a retired police sergeant. He began his career in 1956 with the St. Louis Police Department. In 1958 he moved to California and was hired by Downey PD and then later called to Anaheim PD the same year (for higher pay). During his 28-year career with Anaheim, he served on foot patrol, in a squad car, and on a motorcycle. He worked as a Crime Scene Investigator, a traffic officer, a hostage negotiator, SWAT team sergeant, the stadium and convention liaison, and the reserve officer coordinator.

Another Californian who made a permanent mark on law enforcement in the United States was *William H. Parker*, Chief of LAPD from 1950 to 1966. Parker, a controversial leader who took over the department after a corruption scandal, coined the term *"thin blue line"* to indicate the integral role police play in sustaining order over chaos. Determined to eliminate corruption and professionalize the LAPD, he reorganized and simplified the agency's organizational structure from the bottom up. He focused on administrative oversight (rather than political oversight) and initiated a positive public relations campaign (including allowing film studios access to LAPD to produce television shows; a move that worked very much in his favor). He also increased the requirements for trainees, implemented a standardized police academy, encouraged proactive law enforcement tactics, reduced foot patrols, and reassigned officers to motor patrol in correspondence with Wilson's ideas (LAPD, n.d.; Vila & Morris, 1999). As a result of these efforts, he remade the image and job of a police officer to be that of a professional crime fighter; an image that resonates with us today. He also turned the LAPD into a model agency for reform (Uchida, 2004; Vila & Morris, 1999).

Law enforcement departments during the professional era valued officers for their ability to follow orders rather than their ability to think. This led to a generation of officers who could not reason in a professional capacity, either because they were not trained to do so or because doing so threatened their job security. As you will see, this became problematic as agencies entered the community era and were expected to become good problem solvers rather than good soldiers.

1960s CRIME & RACE RIOTS

The 1960s were a time of chaos and upheaval in the United States. The crime rate doubled and the robbery rate tripled between 1960 and 1970. Anti-war sentiment was high as was anti-police sentiment, especially in America's inner cities. Between 1964 and 1968 more than 50 race riots erupted in urban ghettos, some lasting as many as five days and killing dozens; the most famous were in Watts, Detroit, Newark, and New York. Many of these occurred after routine encounters between police and citizens (Uchida, 2004); minorities did not feel they were being treated fairly by police. Frequent and numerous civil rights protests also taxed police resources, particularly in the south. As Uchida noted, "police became the symbol of a society that denied blacks equal justice under law" (2004, p. 22).

After the Detroit riot in 1967, President Lyndon Johnson appointed a National Advisory Commission on Civil Disorders (**The Kerner Commission**) to investigate the causes of the urban riots (Vila & Morris, 1999). The Kerner Commission report, issued in 1968, concluded that structural, and deep-seated, racism was the main cause of the riots but that other societal problems such as unemployment, discriminatory housing and employment practices, inadequate social services, and unequal justice contributed to the riots; and that police response exacerbated underlying tensions and triggered the protests (Uchida, 2004). The Kerner Commission described the relationship between police and ghetto communities at this time as "deeply hostile" (Vila & Morris, 1999).

Part of the problem, as pointed out by the earlier **President's Commission on Law Enforcement and Administration of Justice** report (published in 1967), was that professional era police practices created significant distance and distrust between police and the community. Namely, police agencies lacked community relations programs, acceptable citizen complaint procedures, appropriate officer discipline strategies, and an adequate number of minority officers (Vila & Morris, 1999). As the most "visible representatives of society," the commission recommended that police communicate more openly with the public and made it clear that the situation was at a critical level and needed to be addressed immediately because "police-community relations have a direct bearing on the character of life in our cities, and the community's ability to maintain stability and to solve its problems" and "the police department's capacity to deal with crime depends to a large extent upon its relationship with the citizenry" (President's Commission on Law Enforcement and Administration of Justice, 1967, reprinted in Vila & Morris, 1999, p.183). The main point made by both of these reports to police was clear: improve your relationships with the communities you serve.

The police did not appreciate the criticism in the two reports, nor then recent U.S. Supreme Court decisions that limited police powers; they took matters into their own hands at the 1968 Democratic National Convention in Chicago—they covered their badges and descended into the crowd with night sticks.

RESEARCH AND EDUCATION

The President's Commission on Law Enforcement and the Administration of Justice (1967) advocated for college-educated officers and criminal justice research as solutions to the growing crisis of confidence in policing. In response, Congress passed the **Omnibus Crime Control and Safe Streets Act of 1968** (OCCSSA) which created the Law Enforcement Assistance Administration (LEAA) (and within it the Law Enforcement Education Program [LEEP] and the National Institute of Law Enforcement and Criminal Justice [NILECJ], the precursor to the current National Institute of Justice [NIJ]). LEAA, the lead agency, provided grants to law enforcement agencies to improve public safety (most often to purchase new equipment and personnel) and LEEP provided funding to increase the number of college-educated police officers. NILECJ was the research center of the LEAA (Gardiner, 2014).

As a result of newly available federal funding, the number of colleges offering police science or criminal justice degree programs increased exponentially; unfortunately, the quality of the programs was not uniform and many early programs were non-rigorous extensions of police academies (Roberg & Bonn, 2004; Sherman & the National Advisory Commission on Higher Education for Police Officers; 1978). It was also the first time efforts were made to produce and fund criminal justice research on a wide scale. OCCSSA was instrumental in prompting permanent changes in policing and criminal justice and is probably the reason you are reading this book (the research and education it funded instigated the creation of criminal justice as a discipline separate and distinct from sociology) (Gardiner, 2014).

The funding provided by OCCSSA allowed us to expand our knowledge about crime control strategies and policing practices—more precisely, we learned which practices were effective and which were ineffective. A few studies funded as a result of this Act that will be discussed in later chapters include: Kansas City Preventative Patrol Experiment, Flint and Newark foot patrol experiments, as well as studies on neighborhood watch programs, team policing strategies, fingerprinting, investigations, and crime prevention through environmental design (LEAA, 1979). Unfortunately the money being thrown at criminal justice programs (and research) did not have any effect on the rising crime rates at the time; so most of the grant money disappeared by about 1982 (Vila & Morris, 1999). Some of the early programs funded by the 1968 OCCSSA, many of which were focused on improving police—community relations, are still in existence today (Barker, 2010).

For all the good that arose from the professionalization movement, there were two specific unintended consequences that resulted: the emergence of a distinct police subculture and poor police–community relations. The subculture developed out of two separate, but complementary, paths. First, as training improved, officers grew into the image of a professional ("Just the facts ma'am. I'm the expert") crime fighter. This led to an "us vs them" mentality that was further solidified through the extensive use of automobiles that served to separate officers from the people they served. At the same time that officers were disengaging from the public, they were feeling alienated by the media, the public, and their supervisors (Uchida, 2004). It was a very rare occasion when officers were portrayed in the media in a positive light. This, combined with what seemed to be widespread public antipathy, made officers feel like they were unappreciated and disliked. These incidents served to confirm their identity as separate from the public (Uchida, 2004).

Police-community relations suffered greatly during the later part of the professional era—partly because of social issues that were affecting society in general and partly due to technological innovations that served to simultaneously increase the public's expectations of officers and distance officers from the pro-social public. For example, telephones, and eventually the 911 system, allowed more citizens to summon the police and expect them to respond rapidly. The use of patrol cars similarly allowed officers to cover more distance in less time and to be visible to more people. The downside was (and is) that officers in cars (especially those with the windows rolled up) are barricaded from the public, which means that they have fewer positive encounters with the general public and more negative encounters with suspected law breakers. The same situation arises for citizens—as more officers use automobiles on patrol, rather than walking a beat, citizens have fewer positive contacts with officers and more negative encounters. This adversely affects both officers and citizens.

THE COMMUNITY PROBLEM SOLVING ERA, 1980s–2000s

Just as the professional era was a response to the politics that were destroying policing during the political era, the community problem solving era was a direct attempt to remedy the negative effects of the professional/reform era, as well as to address research that called into question the validity of the general response model. While the reform era improved police efficiency, recruitment, level of service, and professionalized the police, some problems still existed, namely: (1) devolving relationships between the police and the public, (2) concerns about violations of civil rights by police officers, (3) over-dependence on a professional (scientific) style that emphasized efficiency and effectiveness (over community relations or problem solving), (4) seclusion of officers in patrol cars, (5) use of high-tech gadgets that diminished human interactions, (6) restricting of police purpose to crime fighting only, and (7) police administrators who were shielded from public scrutiny and input (Gaines & Kappeler, 2008). Researchers, after finding that many standard police strategies (rapid response to calls for service, random patrolling, collecting evidence rather than witness statements, etc.) did not improve criminal detection or apprehension rates, urged police professionals to ditch the reactive model of the professional era and instead adopt a proactive model that emphasized community partnerships and holistic thinking about the crime problem.

One of the first efforts to improve police–community relations was **team policing** in the 1970s. The concept was developed in Coventry, England, in 1966 and was recommended for adoption by the 1967 President's Crime Commission. Essentially, it involved a team of officers assigned semi-permanently to a specific neighborhood so the officers could get to know the residents and vice versa and develop legitimate liaisons. The main components of team policing were: geographic stability as achieved by the long-term assignment of officers to a single area, maximum interaction between team members, and maximum communication amongst team members and citizens of the community (Sherman et al., 1973). This worked in some areas but allowed corruption to exist in other jurisdictions. Although team policing failed for several reasons, most of which were related to implementation, many components developed during this time lent themselves to community policing.

Another strategy developed to improve police community relations and reduce crime was **Problem-oriented Policing** (POP). Developed in 1979 by University of Wisconsin policing scholar Herman Goldstein, POP expanded the role of police to include quality of life, not just crime stats. It called on police to focus on a single problem and identify the root cause/s of the problem in order to reduce crime and improve quality of life (Goldstein, 1979). This strategy has had a lasting effect on policing but because it is labor intensive, broadens the purview of police, and requires officers who can think critically and problem solve, it has been slow to be adopted in its purest form. Over time, the problem-solving approach became a main component of community-oriented policing. It will be discussed in detail in chapter 10.

Community-oriented policing (COP) was the trademark philosophy of the era. There was no "founder" per se, but it evolved from three distinct but related sets of work: (1) research conducted by Robert Trojanowicz and other scholars at Michigan State University on foot patrols and their findings that fear of crime was just as important as incidence of crime to community members, (2) Herman Goldstein's 1979 call for a problem-solving approach, and (3) James Q. Wilson and George L. Kelling's broken windows thesis. The philosophy is based on forging a relationship between police and the public so they can work together to solve problems, reduce fear of crime, crime, and disorder; thereby improving the quality of life in a neighborhood. Unlike the other strategies mentioned above, true COP requires changing the entire organization's operating philosophy not just adding a specialized unit. Like POP, community policing continues to be a central strategy and guiding philosophy today and will be discussed in much further detail in Chapter 10.

While there were a few "early adopters" in the mid-late 1980s, most police agencies had not implemented anything that resembled community-oriented policing until the mid-late 1990s. Keep in mind that during the 1980s, American police were embroiled in a "war on drugs" and in the early 1990s they were fighting to get a grip on crime, in particular gang violence (both of which were at all-time highs). It wasn't until the federal government provided grant money to implement community policing that a swell of agencies began to focus their attention on this emerging philosophy. Federal funding was crucial to gaining organizational support for the philosophy because the main tenets of community policing, particularly forming partnerships with community stakeholders, are antithetical to the traditional police culture. The **Violent Crime Control and Law Enforcement Act of 1994** expanded community policing exponentially. Amongst the law's other provisions, it allocated $1.3 billion in 1995 ($8.8 billion over 6 years) to assist municipalities across the country put "100,000 more cops on the beat" in community policing roles and created a Community-oriented Policing Services office (COPS) in the Department of Justice to oversee the massive undertaking (Boettcher, 1995). This was the largest anti-crime legislation in the history of the United States and one of President Bill Clinton's crowning achievements.

As it turned out, the funding was not adequate to achieve the lofty "100,000 officers" goal, and many of the officers funded through the program returned to traditional patrol units after their agency's funding went away. Still, the bill was important for the monumental shift in attitudes it helped push during the mid-1990s. Federal funding for community policing continues today, although at a dramatically reduced level in the years following the September 11, 2001, terrorist attacks. While most departments declare they abide by a community policing philosophy, evidence suggests that it is often more rhetoric than reality.

In truth, officers in the community era were in a sort of tug-of-war between being the idealized, empathetic beat cop who knew the neighbors and the neighborhood and being a warrior fighting crime. Remember, the "war on drugs" started in the mid-1980s and developed into a full-fledged "war on crime" by the late 1980s/early 1990s. This warrior mentality was simply not congruent with community policing. Agencies that tried to reconcile and fulfill both roles usually did so by relegating "community policing" to a few officers in a single division or instituted a foot patrol program. Most agencies did not infuse community policing throughout the organization. There were of course some notable exceptions, such as Santa Ana Police Department in California (Boettcher, 1995; Skolnick & Bayley, 1985).

FIELD PERSPECTIVES: HOW POLICING HAS CHANGED SINCE I WAS A ROOKIE POLICE OFFICER IN 1980

By: Sgt. Joel Davis (Ret.)

Joel Davis

This is the time to be a police officer. I say so after reflecting on the many changes in the profession during my 31-year career (1980–2011), and in considering the climate of law enforcement today.

After completing a bachelor's degree in criminal justice in 1980, I started my career the next week as a rookie police officer. After riding with a training officer for just three weeks, I was cleared to go to work on my own. And at that time, because I had a bachelor's degree, I did not have to attend a basic training academy, which is unheard of today as officers have to complete a 24-week academy and then work with a training officer for another 12 weeks minimum. I look back today and laugh at how little I knew when I was entrusted with such power and authority.

Technology changed so fast and so often that it was challenging and exciting. For many years, we wrote everything down. Your pen was your computer, and our patrol units came with a mounted scratch pad so you could write down information being relayed to you over the radio. You carried a map of the city to find your way around, and reports with arrests or suspect information had to be typed out on a typewriter. There was no 911 emergency telephone system and most officers carried a dime taped on the inside of your handcuff case for an emergency phone call if you didn't have a radio.

Today we have 911, computers in the units, smart cell phones that allow you to send and receive so much information, GPS maps, video cameras in the cars and on the officers, automatic license plate readers, OnStar and LoJack, 800 MHz radios that are encrypted, traffic cameras, and so on. It was incredible to have a computer in the unit—with all call information, the history of the location in question, and a map to show you how to get there with turn-by-turn directions. When you stopped a person, you could find out almost everything about him or her in seconds, including a photo. However, it's critical that officers today still develop and practice the skill of talking to people and obtaining information through interview techniques rather than only relying on a computer to do the police work.

The officer's personal equipment saw many changes during my career as well. When I first started, revolvers were the standard weapon with speedy loaders. You had a baton, tear gas, and handcuffs on your belt. Today, officers have semi-auto handguns with high capacity magazines, and it is not uncommon to see officers carrying at least four magazines. In the early 1980s, most officers did not wear body armor (bullet proof vests) as it was heavy and stiff. If you did own one, you had to purchase it yourself—and then it mostly hung in your locker. Today the vests are much lighter and more pliable, and most departments issue and require their officers to wear them at all times while working patrol. Today, your belt will hold pepper spray, a Taser, a camera or audio recorder, a high illumination compact flashlight, an impact weapon, and radio. I know some small-waisted officers have a difficult time getting all of the equipment on their belts.

The access to information and level of equipment are incomparable, yet officers today do have many challenges. The lack of public support can be disheartening, as it seems an officer's word is no longer trusted or believed without video or independent evidence. Many believe this feeling of distrust will lead to officer hesitation that could cost lives. I tell everyone: Remember police officers are human like the rest of us, but carry tremendous responsibility. May God bless them and keep them safe!

Joel Davis started his career with the Grand Junction Police Department in Colorado in 1980. He transferred to the San Marino Police Department in Southern California for 6 years, before completing 25 years of service with the Irvine Police Department. His worked a variety of assignments including field training officer, background investigator, SWAT team negotiator, and the department's use of force expert. As a California-certified master instructor through the Peace Officer Standards and Training (POST), most of Davis' career centered on training. Davis holds a bachelor's degree from California State University, Los Angeles, and a master's degree in public administration from the University of Southern California.

RHETORIC VERSUS REALITY

While academics firmly supported and advocated community policing, most practitioners did not embrace the idea wholeheartedly and instead adapted the philosophy to fit their world-view and experience. Wilson and Kelling's 1982 article Broken Windows served their purpose well and became very popular in police departments across the country. In the article Wilson and Kelling hypothesized that disorder invites criminal activity by sending messages to law-abiding citizens and potential criminals about the safety of a neighborhood, such that law-abiding citizens retreat and criminals take over the space. The general premise was that removing disorder (panhandlers, homeless persons and belongings, trash, etc.) would reduce crime and that police should work *with* communities to reduce disorder (more on this in Chapter 10). This strategy, which helped initiate the push toward community policing, is neither inherently aggressive nor inherently community oriented. Although many theorists (including Wilson and Kelling) place it within the community policing paradigm, as history illustrates, it is open to interpretation and was adopted by departments across the nation in a form that was more consistent with police culture than the originally intended community policing philosophy.

One of the first agencies to adopt the broken windows strategy was New York City Transit Police Department (NYCTPD) in 1984. Within six years they were able to rid the subway trains of graffiti after instituting a program whereby tagged trains were taken out of service and cleaned immediately. In 1990, William Bratton became chief of NYCTPD and, with George Kelling's assistance, implemented a zero tolerance approach to fare evasion, public urination, public drunkenness, and other quality of life crimes in the subway based on the broken windows theory (Bratton & Knobler, 1998). When Bratton became chief of NYPD in 1994, he brought this strategy with him to reduce crime. His version of broken windows entailed NYPD officers aggressively targeting offenders committing low level "quality of life" offences, usually through arrest.

By the late 1990s/early 2000s academics, reporters, and police leaders were talking about the crime decline happening across the nation. New York City was soon in the spotlight (partly because they had a remarkable story to tell and partly because Bratton is a marketing genius) and the nation was learning about zero tolerance policing, Bratton's version of broken windows. As a result, cities (and schools) across the country began implementing similar zero tolerance policies. These programs, including a later iteration NYPD called "stop and frisk" after zero tolerance received bad press, have been found to be net widening and have alienated the public, increased civil rights violations, and caused some serious police–community relations problems (in particular disenfranchising young men of color) in New York City as well as other cities which adopted similar practices (Fagan *et al.*, 2010). The way broken windows was adopted in most agencies reflects the fact that making arrests is more congruent with police culture than is forming community partnerships. Focusing on low-level misdemeanor arrests as a way to reduce crime became synonymous with broken windows in the late 1990s/early 2000s. Unfortunately it did so at the expense of the community partnerships that broken windows also advocated.

Broken windows was not the only thing that Bratton changed upon taking over the NYPD. His other hallmark policing initiative was Compstat, an intelligence-led approach that entailed holding middle managers responsible for crime in their area. Bratton's management style is best described as "measuring what matters" then holding managers accountable for those measures (crime and other performance indicators). Compstat, which was introduced in late 1996, was a first-class attempt at integrating crime analysis throughout the organization at a time when very few agencies employed crime analysts. NYPD's Compstat was ahead of its time and when combined with the change in federal funding priorities, the technological revolution, the trend to reinterpret broken windows as arrest-oriented, and sentinel social events, helped move policing into a new era.

TALK ABOUT IT: ARE WE REALLY IN A NEW POLICING ERA?

There is much debate about whether the changes that are occurring within policing now represent a new era or whether the changes are simply refinements of the community era. Before debating the issue, it's useful to know a little about how the "eras" came to be.

THE ORIGINAL PAPER

Highly respected and established scholars George Kelling and Mark Moore presented these three eras (political, reform, community problem-solving) in a 1988 paper they wrote for the first Executive Session on Policing (1985–1991) convened by the John F. Kennedy School of Government at Harvard University. This executive session, which was comprised of approximately 30 police executives and academic experts, was tasked with examining the state of policing at the time and making recommendations for improvement (Bayley & Nixon, 2010). During the session, various experts would take the lead on producing "essays" on specific topics that were then heavily debated by the invited leaders. Authors refined their essays in accordance with the discussions that ensued; then the National Institute of Justice, in conjunction with Harvard University, published the papers as part of the "Perspectives on Policing" series associated with the executive session. These reports were intended to share the "information and perspectives that were part of the [Session's] extensive debates" so that "police officials and other policymakers who affect the course of policing will debate and challenge their beliefs just as those [experts] in the Executive Session [had] done" (Stewart & Moore in Hartman, 1988, p.1).

In their paper, Kelling & Moore (1988) presented "an interpretation of police history" that they hoped would "help police executives considering alternative future strategies of policing" (p.1). This was not just a historical piece, it was an advocacy piece! And it was hotly debated (see Hartmann, 1988 for the partial transcript that accompanied Kelling & Moore's paper). Keep in mind that "policing in the mid-1980s was perceived to be in crisis and there was a strong sense that fundamental changes were needed in the way that [policing] was delivered" (Bayley & Nixon, 2010; p.1).

One of the major points of contention was whether policing was in a third era, and if so what to call it. Kelling and Moore wanted to call it the "community" era but others proposed calling it "problem oriented" or "strategic policing" instead because they felt that using the term "community policing" was too inhibiting and did not fully capture the variety or nature of the changes that were taking place (Hartmann, 1988, p.5). Attorney General Edwin Meese, for example, agreed that community policing was an important aspect of the new era but he took issue with community policing being *the defining feature* of the new era (Hartmann, 1988; Stone & Travis, 2011). Responding to Meese's concerns, Moore agreed that community policing was one of several important aspects shaping policing at that time but argued that the other innovations would take hold rather easily, without any help from the Executive Session; community partnerships on the other hand would be very uncomfortable for police and therefore required assistance to be accepted and inculcated in police agencies. Moore concluded that "labeling the entire package of innovations as community policing would give special prominence to the very aspect that would be most difficult for the police to adopt" (Stone & Travis, 2011, p.10). According to Stone & Travis, "the name was a dare" (2011, p.10). If it was, it worked; and community policing was successfully marketed with the help of President Bill Clinton's 1994 crime bill. However, Meese and others were correct in pointing out that community policing was only one part of the larger, systemic changes that were occurring and needed to be captured (Stone & Travis, 2011).

Thanks in part to the name choice and the decision to advocate for a profoundly different style of policing, we sit here today debating whether we are in "phase two of the community era" or whether we are in a completely new, fourth era of policing—a situation we probably would not be in, had the authors named the third era "strategic" back in 1988. The name "community era" does, however, allow us to consider whether the practice of policing looks the same today as it would have if a different name had been selected. Would President Clinton have chosen to make community policing a major part of his crime bill if the Executive Session had not highlighted it in such dramatic fashion? Would police executives have embraced and implemented community policing if there was no money attached to it? Did the name make any difference in the policing strategies that developed and took hold during the 1990s? Are we as a society better off today because the era was titled "community"? **What do you think? We invite and encourage you to have this discussion with your professor and classmates during this course.**

READ THE ORIGINAL DOCUMENTS. Kelling and Moore's paper can be found here: https://www.ncjrs.gov/pdffiles1/ nij/114213.pdf . Hartmann's edited debate can be found here: https://www.ncjrs.gov/pdffiles1/nij/114214.pdf

WHAT OTHER EXPERTS SAY

Stone and Travis (2011) argue in a paper presented as part of the second Executive Session on Policing and Public Safety (2008–present) at Harvard's Kennedy School that we are in an era they term "new professionalism." Rather than suggesting that the "new professionalism" era follows the community era, they propose that it replaces the community era and provides a more encompassing organizing framework than the name "community" allows. They define the new professionalism era in terms of four principles: accountability, legitimacy, innovation, and coherence. In their view, the new professionalism era encapsulates the community era within it, as a precursor or transition period between the two "professional" eras. They use the term "new" to distinguish this era of true professionalism from the preceding era which began the work of professionalizing the police.

Others argue that new tools (technological innovations) do not equate to a new era. Some experts, such as Kenneth Peak (police scholar) and Ronald Glensor (police executive), contend that we are still in the community era because there is nothing fundamentally different about policing now (Glensor & Peak, 2012). They point out that while technology has improved policing, it has not changed policing. According to Glensor and Peak, "policing is indeed in an information 'age' but not in an information 'era'" (2012, p.11). In their view, "intelligence-led policing and predictive policing will advance the evolution of community oriented policing and problem solving to address 21st century challenges of crime and disorder" (p.14).

OUR RATIONALE

Although much of the confusion, it seems, stems from the name chosen more than 25 years ago, we find it useful to go back to the original framework used by Kelling and Moore to classify police history into the three distinct eras we know today. They used a "corporate strategy" framework to describe police organizations along seven interconnected dimensions (1988, p.1):

1. The sources from which the police construct the legitimacy and continuing power to act on society

2. The definition of the police function or role in society

3. The organizational design of police departments

4. The relationships the police create with the external environment

5. The nature of police efforts to market or manage the demand for their services

6. The principal activities, programs, and tactics on which police agencies rely to fulfill their mission or achieve operational success, and

7. The concrete measures the police use to define operational success or failure.

We have attempted to assess the current state of policing along these dimensions (see Table 3.4) and concluded that policing changed in the early 2000s. Our argument is laid out below." **You decide—do you agree with us that policing is in a fourth era or do you believe that it is in phase two of the community era? Talk to your classmates and professor then send us an email to let us know your conclusion and how you arrived at your decision.**

THE INTELLIGENCE ERA, 2000s–PRESENT

The reform era focused on rooting out corruption and promoting policing to bona-fide professional status while the community era focused primarily on defining the role, methods, and practice of police. The textbook authors believe that policing has entered the next phase, as we are now seeing a refining and refocusing of the police function that is highly dependent on technology and research to further elevate policing from a primarily blue-collar occupation to a profession that requires a unique and highly developed skill set. As has been the case in each of the preceding eras, the changes that are occurring are most evident in large agencies and in specific parts of the country. To be sure, many US agencies continue to police the same way they have policed for the past 50 or more years.

Unlike earlier eras, which directly addressed problems that developed during the preceding eras, the intelligence era is better characterized as a response to society-changing external events, the shifting of focus toward the ideals of democratic policing, increased accountability, and the utilization of improved research and technology in the refinement and modification of strategies developed during the community era. Some may argue that we are still in the community era. That's okay. This is an ongoing discussion being had by academics and police executives around the United States, and even the world. Take a few minutes to read Box 3.3 to acquaint yourself with the issues. We think you will find this discussion of modern police history much easier to understand, and more interesting, once you do.

The terrorist attacks on the World Trade Center and the Pentagon on September 11, 2001, transformed both America and America's police. As a result of that infamous day the police mission unavoidably expanded to include homeland security and there has been a much greater emphasis on the value of intelligence (accurate and timely information) and on developing both an information-sharing culture within policing as well as avenues to share information between law enforcement agencies. In spite of the changes brought about by 9/11, the community era did not completely vanish; it was quietly overtaken by shifting priorities, including: (1) a focus on homeland security and intelligence gathering and sharing, (2) using evidence-based and intelligence-led practices to prevent and reduce crime and disorder, and (3) increasing industry accountability with a shift toward democratic policing and procedural justice principles. The importance of engaging community partners remains in the background, or in the case of some agencies, the foreground; as does problem solving.

The change in priorities after 9/11 away from community policing and toward other objectives, in particular fortifying homeland security, is revealed in past and current White House budgets. For example, federal funding for community policing remained steady at around $1.4 billion annually from 1995 to 2000 when funding was cut by more than half to $595 million. Some federal funding was restored for a few years (there was approximately $1 billion allocated annually FY2001–FY2003) but then funding was gutted again in FY2004 and has waned ever since (a mere $274 million was allocated to COPS in the FY2015 budget) (James, 2011; White House, 2014). While COPS has been virtually defunded, there have been large increases in allocations for anti-terrorism efforts (including technology, tools, and inter-agency collaboration activities) as well as small increases in funding for evidence-based policing strategies (White House, 2014).

FOCUS ON HOMELAND SECURITY AND INTELLIGENCE GATHERING AND SHARING

Federal law enforcement agencies were reorganized in 2002 as a result of the September 11 terrorist attacks. The Homeland Security Act of 2002 created the Department of Homeland Security and authorized the hiring of 180,000 new federal employees to fulfill the department's core

TABLE 3.4 Comparison of Four Eras of Modern Policing in U.S.

	Political Era 1845–920s	Reform (Professional) Era 1920s–1980s	Community Problem Solving Era 1980s–2000s	Intelligence Era 2000s–Present
Authorization for police…	Primarily political	Law and professionalism	Community support (political), law, professionalism	Public support (individuals, groups, & politicians), law, professionalism; terrorism
Police function	Crime control, order maintenance, broad social services	Crime control	Crime control, crime prevention, problem solving	Crime control, crime prevention, problem solving, order maintenance, terrorism
Police role	Political puppet	Professional crime fighter	Neighborhood cop. Warrior	Problem solver Guardian
Organizational design	Decentralized and geographical	Centralized, classical	Decentralization, task forces, matrices	Mix of centralized and decentralized generalists & specialists to facilitate information sharing & accountability; reorganization at federal level
Relationship to environment	Close and personal	Professionally remote	Consultative, police defend values of law & professionalism, but listen to community concerns	Professionally collaborative (community & other law enforcement agencies); democratic
Market & manage demand	Managed through links between politicians & precinct commanders, and face-to-face contacts between citizens & foot patrol officers	Channeled through central dispatching activities	Channeled through analysis of underlying problems	Civilianization; crime analysis, social media
Principal tactics employed	Foot patrol and rudimentary investigations	Preventative patrol and rapid response to calls for service	Foot patrol, problem solving, etc.	Intelligence-led, evidence-based, community policing & problem solving
Outcome measures	Political and citizen satisfaction with social order	Crime control	Quality of life, citizen satisfaction	Crime, quality of life, public satisfaction (individuals, politicians, media), procedural justice principles

mission to keep America safe from terrorist attacks as well as its secondary goals to enhance disaster preparedness and response, improve cyber-security, and increase security along the nation's borders. It was the largest reorganization of federal government since the National Security Act of 1947. As part of the reorganization efforts, this and similar Acts made it a priority for federal, state, and local law enforcement entities to share both intelligence and the responsibility for protecting critical infrastructure and information. These partnerships are most visible through Fusion Centers (discussed in Chapter 9) but are also evident in FBI-headed (and funded) Regional Computer Forensics Labs and INS cross-deputization programs. Not only has this emphasis on terrorism led to increased privatization of the police function, it has also meant that local police departments now need to provide more security at large events and critical venues than was typical pre-9/11 (at great expense to the general budget).

The types and quantities of information collected in the name of homeland security as well as the scope of data collection and length of retention have caused many Americans to question whether law enforcement and other government offices are violating citizens' civil rights. For example, the **USA PATRIOT Act** of 2001, in addition to providing substantial funding to bolster law enforcement's ability to gather and share intelligence, granted law enforcement agents much greater latitude in collecting intelligence, in particular allowing much greater use of surveillance (Gaines, 2014). There is much concern, particularly after Edward Snowden released secret government documents in 2013, that the federal government is collecting sensitive information on law-abiding individuals without proper legal authority. Although individual police departments have not been implicated, many Americans are alarmed at the possibility and fearful of illicit government monitoring by local, state, and federal law enforcement agencies. While technology has definitely improved policing and the focus on intelligence gathering has saved lives, there are significant unintended consequences that have arisen as a result of this effort, in particular distrust by a large segment of society. We'll return to this issue in a moment.

The new focus on homeland security also highlighted a need to equip police with additional resources, including military-grade equipment, to fight our "enemies." Interestingly, the **militarization** of law enforcement trend began prior to 9/11, at the same time as community policing and problem solving was taking hold. Except for a few academics and government watchers, no one really noticed the trend until the 2000s and 2010s; it was that unremarkable. Starting in the early 1990s, however, the military started quietly creeping into American law enforcement through technology, equipment, training, and personnel transfer (Kraska, 2001). The long-held tradition of separate military and civilian police organizations established by the *Posse Comitatus Act of 1878* cracked in the 1980s when President Reagan allowed the National Guard to be used in drug raids; a task not permitted by the spirit of the act but which was allowed under new laws which circumvented the 1878 law (Dunlap Jr., 2001). While the intent may have been benign—bringing all our resources to bear on a problem (drugs in the 1990s) and effectively equipping the police to respond to terrorism and other public safety incidents (2000s and beyond) —the result has been more heavily armed, quasi-military police forces that are prone to escalate, rather than deescalate, emotionally charged situations.

Police forces have adapted a number of military tactics for domestic law enforcement use. For example, SWAT-type tactical teams which are now commonly used for barricaded subjects, drug raids, proactive policing in hotspots, and a variety of other purposes have dramatically increased in number and deployments over the past 30 years. In the early 1980s, approximately 20% of small towns had a SWAT-type tactical team; by 2007, 80% of small towns had one, the numbers for large cities are even higher (Balko, 2013; Kraska, 2007). There were approximately 3,000 annual SWAT deployments throughout the United States in the early 1980s whereas by 2007, there were more than 45,000 annual deployments—a 15-fold increase (Kraska, 2007). This growth can be attributed to the government's surplus military equipment program, the fear of crime and terrorism, and the allure and desire to use "new toys" (often obtained at a steep discount).

Since the early 1990s, police departments have been allowed to obtain surplus military equipment such as armored personnel carriers, combat gear, assault rifles, night vision equipment, aircraft, and drones (Apuzzo, 2014) for free or at a highly reduced cost. This equipment, which is intended for war—not peace-keeping—is often seen by the public as a show of government force that sends the message that the police are to be feared, especially in minority-led communities that generally distrust police. Although police have legitimate reasons for wanting the equipment, the public is not always in favor of the acquisitions and as a result of this militarization many people have begun to see the police as an occupying force (an issue addressed by the **President's Task Force on 21st Century Policing**). As noted in Chapter 2, this is exactly what our ancestors feared and fought against, both in the United States and England. As a response to a general public perception that police have become too militarized, in May 2015 President Obama limited police department access to surplus military equipment and instituted a rule that departments must get jurisdictional (city council or board of supervisors) approval before accepting equipment (a reminder that police should consult with the public, *a la* community policing). Still, the militarization trend has caused some police executives and scholars to re-examine the role of police, re-consider how we want our police to be perceived, and discuss the negative effects that some of these policies have on specific segments of society, in particular in terms of legitimacy.

EVIDENCE-BASED AND INTELLIGENCE-LED POLICING STRATEGIES

Another defining feature of this era is an emphasis on evidence-based and intelligence-led approaches to crime prevention and crime reduction. **Evidence-based policing** strategies are those that have been deemed effective by rigorous scientific research; for example, hot spots policing, problem-oriented policing, and pulling levers strategies. As you recall, the Omnibus Crime Control and Safe Streets Act of 1968 instigated police research for the first time by providing federal research money for program evaluations. Since that time policing scholars and practitioners have learned a lot about "what works" but accumulated research has not guided policing until very recently. In fact, 1996 was the first year that Congress mandated that federally funded crime prevention programs be evaluated for effectiveness (Sherman et al., 1997). This mandate was part of a larger movement toward evidence-based practices that occurred in medicine, social services, education, and other industries around the same time. As part of this mandate, Lawrence Sherman and a team of University of Maryland researchers conducted the first-ever "state of the science report on what [was] known—and what [was] not—about the effectiveness of local crime prevention programs and practices" (Sherman et al., 1997, p. 1-1). It revealed that relatively little was known about effective policing practices at that time. Since then, however, much has been learned (see Chapters 9 and 10) and several organization, including the National Institute of Justice (NIJ), **International Association of Chiefs of Police** (IACP), **Police Foundation** (PF), **Police Executive Research Forum** (PERF), and the Center for Evidence-Based Crime Policy (CEBCP) at George Mason University, have taken a lead in disseminating these research findings to police executives and practitioners around the globe.

At the same time there has been an emphasis on gathering and using intelligence to reduce crime. This intelligence-led trend grew out of the availability and affordability of powerful computers and newer technologies that enabled police to easily collect, track, and disseminate information between agencies, agency personnel, and community partners; as well as the above-noted academic research that found the police were effective when they intentionally targeted crime hot spots. **Intelligence-led policing**, which will be discussed in great detail in chapter 9, has taken two forms, (1) identifying street level crime patterns in order to put "cops on the dots" and (2) identifying potential terrorists and any activities that support terrorism. Although intelligence-led policing was originally developed in England in the 1990s as a strategy to target career offenders (Ratcliffe, 2011), when the term was introduced in the United States after 9/11 it referred to the gathering of intelligence on potential terrorism activity and terrorists. Today it has been adopted by police departments across the country as a general commitment to use data to support crime reduction strategies and practices, though it still has a dual meaning in some departments. At its core, intelligence-led policing is about proactively managing and using information to effectively reduce crime. Intelligence-led approaches include crime analysis and Compstat, as well as strategies such as problem-oriented policing and hot spots policing that target specific problems based on collected data.

Importantly, the extent of well-educated police officers and executives in policing today has allowed evidence-based and intelligence-led strategies to take root and flourish. Having a highly educated workforce allows research to be understood, disseminated, adopted, and inculcated by officers within and between organizations. It is also required to interpret and use data to identify and target crime problems. The presence of college-educated officers has been almost as important as technology in moving policing forward in the 21st century. As you will learn in Chapter 6, the Omnibus Crime Control and Safe Streets Act of 1968 played a large role in increasing the proportion of college-educated officers by providing funding to colleges to create police science programs. Other social programs that made college more accessible for students from all socio-economic backgrounds also had a significant impact as can be seen by the fact that in 1960, only 3% of officers held a four-year degree but by 1988 about 23% did. Today, we suspect that about one-third of officers have a college degree. We don't have an official estimate because the percentage of officers with a college degree varies dramatically by department and there has not been a nationally-representative study in almost 30 years.

INCREASED POLICE ACCOUNTABILITY AND A SHIFT TOWARD DEMOCRATIC POLICING

Another relatively new feature in the intelligence era is increased police accountability and an overall shift toward democratic policing ideals. Police chiefs in the intelligence era are increasingly held accountable for "the three C's: crime, cost, and conduct" (Stone & Travis, 2011, p.12). They report feeling considerable political pressure to report low crime rates, contain costs, and hold officers liable for their conduct. Similar to the trend to be "evidence-based," increased accountability for measurable outcomes is part of a larger trend occurring in a variety of industries. While budget cuts and other recent events have required police chiefs to be much more cost-conscious than they had to be during most of the community era, tight budgets do not indicate a sea change. Accountability for crime and officer conduct, on the other hand, is indicative of a cultural change in policing.

It wasn't until the late 1990s/early 2000s that police executives (starting with Bill Bratton of NYPD) began claiming responsibility for lower crime rates (an easy thing to do when rates declined year after year). Prior to that point it was widely held that "police do not prevent crime" (Bayley, 1994, p.3). As crime rates continued to decline, police experimented with innovative programs, and evaluation research identified effective policing practices, politicians came to expect crime reduction from their chiefs. And chiefs began to expect it from their middle managers. This downward shift in accountability was a direct byproduct of Compstat, the management accountability system developed by NYPD in the mid-late 1990s to reduce crime.

In addition to being held accountable for crime, chiefs are also expected to hold officers accountable for their actions. Unlike in previous eras when officer misbehavior was likely to be ignored or under-punished, departments are now expected to use early warning systems to proactively monitor individual officers, conduct thorough, unbiased, and transparent investigations, and assign appropriate punishment for substantiated policy violations. Up until very recently, it was almost unheard of for a police officer to face criminal consequences for on-duty actions. This has changed in the past several years as citizens have captured many instances of questionable police behavior on their camera phones, and attorney generals have become increasingly likely to file charges against officers or empanel a grand jury to decide whether to file charges.

These videos showing problematic (and in some cases, criminal) behavior by police have caused many members of the public to question police authority and legitimacy in ways not seen since the 1960s. Some of these events, such as the deaths of Michael Brown (Ferguson, MO), Eric Garner (New York City), Tamir Rice (Cleveland, OH), Freddie Gray (Baltimore, MD), and Walter Scott (North Charleston, SC) (all black men) by police, triggered hundreds of public demonstrations and protests against police use-of-force practices across the nation. The early shootings spurred President Obama to establish the President's Taskforce on 21st Century Policing in November 2014. The task force, which was tasked with identifying best practices in policing, made building public trust and legitimacy one of the pillars of their recommendations (the others are contained in Figure 3.2 below).

The push for accountability along with deteriorating police–community relations in many communities have led police executives to embrace the ideals of democratic policing—legitimacy, accountability, and transparency. In particular, there has been a renewed focus on the importance of police *legitimacy* and the crucial role it plays in community cooperation and support. As explained in Chapter 1, legitimacy and public trust must be earned; they are not freely given. Toward this end, scholars and police executives recognized and began emphasizing the benefits of procedural justice for improving police legitimacy and community trust in the police. Leaders are also engaged in finding better ways (besides crime, arrest, and closure rates) to capture whether community members believe that police are doing a good job. One of the methods receiving much attention is surveying public satisfaction with police after encounters (both voluntary and involuntary). As traditionally measured crime rates have dropped to near 40–50 year lows, the profession is ready to consider new measures of effectiveness.

OVERARCHING RECOMMENDATIONS:

1. Create National Crime & Justice Task Force
2. Promote programs that address poverty, education, health, and safety

PILLAR 1: Building Trust & Legitimacy

1. Embrace guardian mindset & adopt procedural justice
2. Acknowledge role of policing in past & present injustice
3. Establish culture of transparency & accountability
4. Promote legitimacy internally within organization
5. Initiate positive nonenforcement activities to engage communities
6. Consider potential damage to public trust when implementing crime fighting strategies
7. Track the level of community trust in police
8. Employ a diverse workforce
9. Build trusting relationships with immigrant communities

PILLAR 2: Policy & Oversight

10. Collaborate with community members to develop policies
11. Create comprehensive use of force policies that are open for public inspection
12. Implement nonpunitive peer review of critical incidents
13. Adopt scientifically-supported identification practices
14. Make cencus data available to the public
15. Collect & analyze demographic data on all detentions
16. Create policies for policing mass demonstrations
17. Develop citizen oversight committee
18. Do not require officers to meet predetermined quotas
19. Require officers to seek consent prior to voluntary search
20. Require officers to fully identify themselves to members of the public & state the reason for the stop &/or search
21. Establish LGBTQ search and seizure procedures
22. Enforce policies prohibiting profiling and discrimination
23. DOJ to provide grants to help agencies
24. Expand register of decertified officers

PILLAR 3: Technology & Social Media

25. Establish national standards for research & development of new technology
26. Implement appropriate technology considering local needs aligned with national standards
27. Develop best practices to govern acquisition & use of auditory, visual, biometric data
28. Update public records laws
29. Adopt model policies & best practices for technology-based community engagement that increases community trust & access
30. Support development of "less than lethal" technology
31. Make development of segregated radio spectrum a top priority

PILLAR 4: Community Policing & Crime reduction

32. Develop policies & strategies that reinforce importance of community engagement
33. Infuse community policing throughout organizational culture & structure
34. Engage in multidisciplinary, community team approaches for responding to situations with complex causal factors
35. Support a culture & practice of policing that promotes dignity of all, especially the most vulnerable
36. Work with neighborhood residents to co-produce public safety
37. Adopt policies & programs that address the needs at-risk youth & reduce aggressive tactics that stigmatize & marginalize youth
38. Affirm & recognize youth voices in community decision-making

PILLAR 5: Training & Education

39. Promote consistent standards for high quality officer training across the country
40. Engage community members in training process
41. Provide leadership training to all personnel throughout their careers
42. Develop a national postgraduate institute of policing for senior executives with a standardized curriculum
43. Modify curriculum at FBI National Academy to align with this report
44. POSTs should make Crisis Intervention Training (CIT) a part of both basic recruit & in-service officer training
45. POSTs should include lessons to improve social interaction & tactical skills in basic recruit academy
46. POSTs should include information about addiction in basic recruit & in-service officer training
47. POSTs should include information about implicit bias & cultural responsiveness in basic recruit & in-service officer training
48. POSTs should include training on policing in a democratic society in basic recruit & in-service officer training
49. Federal government should encourage & incentivize higher education for law enforcement officers
50. Federal government should support efforts to develop technology that enhances police training
51. Federal government should support improved Field Training Officer programs.

PILLAR 6: Officer Wellness & Safety

52. U.S.D.O.J. should enhance & promote its multi-faceted officer safety & wellness initiative.
53. Promote safety & wellness at every level of the organization
54. U.S.D.O.J. should assist departments implement scientifically-supported shift lengths.
55. Provide anti-ballistic vests & tactical first aid kits & training to every officer
56. Expand efforts to collect & analyze data on officer deaths, injuries, & near-misses
57. Adopt policies that require officers to wear seat belts & bullet-proof vests
58. Congress should develop & enact peer review error management legislation
59. Explore the use of smart-car technology

Fifty years after the civil rights riots we might be reliving history, but this time police leaders are less inclined to blindly condone officers' bad behavior and officers who break the law are more likely to be fired and criminally charged than in previous eras. These recent public demonstrations and protests serve as stark reminders to police that public trust and support are fragile—they must be earned, cherished, and protected at all costs. Once again police must repair and rebuild relations with minority communities in order to regain legitimacy, which means re-emphasizing community policing, problem solving, and partnerships in conjunction with evidence-based and intelligence-led approaches. This is where we stand today—a push to be data-driven and community focused.

CONCLUSION

Policing in America has steadily evolved. It took modern police more than a century to become respected law enforcers. This vision of police and the distinct subculture is so entrenched that it has been difficult to break away. Still, agencies that have adopted a community policing orientation in preceding years continue to use this philosophy to guide operations. These agencies have used technological innovations to improve their response to crime and today, the modern police officer has tools at her disposal that officers 30 years ago considered science fiction. Time will tell how law enforcement agencies (approximately 18,000 of them in the United States) respond to the latest developments and whether they continue to engage the community or enrage the community.

REVIEW QUESTIONS

1. Name the four eras of policing and describe each.
2. Who were August Vollmer, O.W. Wilson, and William Parker? What were their contributions to modern policing?
3. What were the major technological innovations developed at the end of the 19th century and beginning of the 20th century? What impact did each have on policing?
4. What were the major technological innovations developed during the late 20th and early 21st centuries that changed policing? How did policing change with these innovations?
5. When someone says, "the police have become more militarized in the 21st century," what does the person mean?

GLOSSARY

Broken Windows theory a theory proposed by James Q. Wilson and George Kelling in 1982 that proposes that unkempt areas invite additional disorder and serious crime.

Community-Oriented Policing a policing philosophy that focuses on building community partnerships to reduce and prevent crime and improve police–community relations.

Compstat an intelligence-led approach developed by NYPD in the mid-1990s that entails holding middle managers accountable for crime and other performance indicators in their area.

Evidence-based policing policing strategies proven effective through social scientific research.

Intelligence-led policing a policing practice that uses crime intelligence and criminal intelligence to reduce and prevent crime.

International Association of Police Chiefs an association of police chiefs, formed in 1893, to advance the police profession.

Kerner Commission presidential commission formed to investigate the causes of the urban riots in the 1960s. The commission, which published its official report in 1968, was officially known as the National Advisory Commission on Civil Disorders.

Law Enforcement Assistance Administration a body created by the 1968 Omnibus Crime Control and Safe Streets Act to serve as a federal resource for local law enforcement agencies.

Lexow Committee a committee formed to investigate allegations of corruption within the New York Police Department in the late 1890s.

Militarization the increasing use of military equipment, technology, and personnel in policing since the 1980s.

Omnibus Safe Streets and Crime Control Act of 1968 a highly influential act passed by Congress that created the Law Enforcement Assistance Administration, provided grants for law enforcement personnel, education, training, equipment, and research.

Police Executive Research Foundation an independent research organization founded in 1976 devoted to critical issues in policing.

Police Foundation an organization established by a Ford Foundation grant in 1970 to advance policing through innovation and science.

President's Commission on Law Enforcement presidential commission formed to investigate law enforcement practices and the effects on citizens. The commission published its report, titled The Challenge of Crime in a Free Society, in 1967.

President's Task Force on 21st Century Policing presidential task force appointed to address police-community relations concerns in the wake of questionable police shootings of suspects in 2014–2015.

Problem-Oriented Policing a method of policing developed by Herman Goldstein in 1979 that broadens the role of police and involves identifying and addressing the root causes of problems.

Stop and frisk the police practice of stopping and detaining a "suspicious" person for further investigation. It may include a superficial pat down of the suspicious person's body and clothing for contraband, weapons, or other items if an officer can articulate reasonable suspicion that the person committed a crime or is a threat to public safety. The term has also been associated with New York City's aggressive style of policing that focuses on conducting these stops in high crime areas.

Team policing a method of policing developed in England during the 1970s that involved a team of officers assigned semi-permanently to a specific neighborhood; a pre-cursor of community-oriented policing.

USA Patriot Act a Congressional act passed shortly after the September 11, 2011, terrorist attacks in the United States, focusing primarily on providing law enforcement with legal authority to support efforts to fight terrorism. (KH)

Violent Crime Control and Law Enforcement Act of 1994

Volstead Act of 1919 an act that amended the constitution of the United States and prohibited the sale and manufacture of alcohol. Also known as Prohibition. It was repealed in 1933.

Wickersham Commission a presidential commission that published the first national comprehensive report on the state of the American criminal justice system in 1931. It focused much attention on law enforcement's concerns about Prohibition.

Zero tolerance policing an aggressive style of policing focused on eliminating low level disorder and disorderly behavior, based upon the broken windows theory. It was first instituted in New York City in the late 1980s to early 1990s.

REFERENCES

Ackerson, S. & Tully, D. (n.d.). *SFPD history: 150 years of history.* Retrieved from http://sf-police.org/index.aspx?page=1592

Akron (n.d.). *Akron police history.* Retrieved from http://www.akronhistory.org/police.htm

Apuzzo, M. (2014, June 8). War gear flows to police departments. *New York Times.* Retrieved from http://www.nytimes.com/2014/06/09/us/war-gear-flows-to-police-departments.html?_r=0

Balko, R. (2013). Rise of the Warrior Cop: The Militarization of America's Police Forces. New York: PublicAffairs.

Barker, T. (2010). Law enforcement assistance administration. In B.S. Fisher & S.P. Lab (Eds.) *Encyclopedia of victimology & crime prevention.* London: SAGE.

Bayley, D. (1994). *Police for the future.* New York, NY: Oxford University Press.

Bayley, D. & Nixon, C. (2010, September). *The changing environment for policing, 1985-2008.* National Institute of Justice Perspectives in Policing #NCJ 230576. Washington DC: Government Printing Office. Retrieved from https://www.ncjrs.gov/pdffiles1/nij/ncj230576.pdf

Boettcher, C. (1995). *Community policing: Is Santa Ana's acclaimed COP programme still a success?* Unpublished master's thesis. Cambridge University, Cambridge, England.

Braga, A. (2015, September). *Crime and policing revisited.* National Institute of Justice Perspectives in Policing #NCJ 248888. Washington DC: Government Printing Office. Retrieved from https://www.ncjrs.gov/pdffiles1/nij/248888.pdf

Bratton, W. & Knobler, P. (1998). *Turnaround: How America's top cop reversed the crime epidemic.* New York, NY: Random House.

Dulaney, W. M. (1996). *Black police in America.* Bloomington, IN: Indiana University Press.

Dunlap Jr., C. (2001). The thick green line: The growing involvement of military forces in domestic law enforcement. In P. Kraska (Ed). *Militarizing the American criminal justice system.* Boston, MA: Northeastern University Press.

Fagan, J., Geller, A., Davies, G. & West, V. (2010). Street stops and broken windows revisited: The demography and logic of proactive policing in a safe and changing city. In S.K. Rice & M.D. White (Eds.) *Race, Ethnicity, and Policing: New and essential readings.* New York, NY: New York University Press.

Gaines, L. (2014). Homeland security: A new criminal justice mandate. In S. L. Mallicoat and C. L. Gardiner (Eds.) *Criminal Justice Policy.* Newberry Park, CA: SAGE

Gaines, L. & Kappeler, V. (2008). *Policing in America, 6th edition.* Newark, NJ: LexisNexis Matthew Bender.

Gardiner, C. (2014). The influence of research and evidence-based practices on criminal justice policy. In S. L. Mallicoat and C. L. Gardiner (Eds.) *Criminal Justice Policy.* Newberry Park, CA: SAGE

Gardiner, C. (2015). *College cops: A report on education and policing in California.* Fullerton, CA: Center for Public Policy, California State University, Fullerton. Retrieved from http://cpp.fullerton.edu/

Gardiner, C. & Williams, S. (2014). Policing in California. In C. L. Gardiner & P. Fiber-Ostrow (Eds.) *California's criminal justice system.* Durham, NC: Carolina Academic Press.

Glensor, R. & Peak, K. (2012, September). New police management practices and predictive software: A new era they do not make. In D. Cohen McCullough & D. Spence. (Eds.). *American policing in 2022: Essays on the future of a profession.* Washington, DC: United States Department of Justice Community Oriented Policing Services. Retrieved from: http://www.cops.usdoj.gov/Default.asp?Item=2671

Goldstein, H. (1979). Improving policing: A problem-oriented approach. *Crime & Delinquency, 25*(2), 235–258.

Hartmann, F. (1988, November). *Debating the evolution of American policing: An edited transcript to accompany "The evolving strategy of policing."* National Institute of Justice Perspectives in Policing #NCJ 114214. Washington DC: Government Printing Office. https://www.ncjrs.gov/pdffiles1/nij/114214.pdf

James, N. (2011, January 4). *Community oriented policing services (COPS): Background, legislation, and funding.* Congressional Research Service report to Congress RL-33308. Retrieved from http://fas.org/sgp/crs/misc/RL33308.pdf

Kelling, G. & Moore, M. (1988, November). The evolving strategy of policing. National Institute of Justice Perspectives in Policing #NCJ 114213. Washington DC: Government Printing Office. Retrieved from https://www.ncjrs.gov/pdffiles1/nij/114213.pdf

Kraska, P. (2001). The military-criminal justice blur: An introduction. In P. Kraska (Ed). *Militarizing the American criminal justice system.* Boston, MA: Northeastern University Press.

Kraska, P. (2007). Militarization and policing Its relevance to the 21st century. *Policing.* New York, NY: Oxford University Press. Doi 0.1093/police/pam065. Retrieved from http://cjmasters.eku.edu/sites/cjmasters.eku.edu/files/21stmilitarization.pdf

Law Enforcement Assistance Agency (LEAA). (1978). *National Institute of Law Enforcement and Criminal Justice annual report, FY1978.* (NCJRS-59147)). Washington, DC: National Institute of Justice. Retrieved from http://www.ncjrs.gov/app/publications/abstract.aspx?ID=59147

Los Angeles Police Department (LAPD). (n.d.). *History of the LAPD.* Retrieved from http://www.lapdonline.org/history_of_the_lapd

Lyman, J. L. (1964). The Metropolitan Police Act of 1829. *Journal of Criminal Law and Criminology, 55*(1), 141-154.

Mastony, C. (2010, September 18). Tracking down the country's first female police officer. *Seattle Times.* Retrieved from http://seattletimes.com/html/nationworld/2012918942_1stpolicewoman19.html

Monkkonen, E.H. (1981). Police *in urban America 1860-1920.* New York, NY: Cambridge University Press.

Peak, K. (2009). *Policing America.* New York, NY: Pearson Publishing.

President's Commission on Law Enforcement and Administration of Justice (1967). *Task force report: The police.* Washington, DC: U.S. Government Printing Office.

President's Task Force on 21st Century Policing. (2015, May). *Final Report.* Washington DC: Office of Community Oriented Policing Services. Retrieved from http://www.cops.usdoj.gov/pdf/task-force/TaskForce_FinalReport.pdf

Ratcliffe, J. (2011). *Intelligence-led policing.* New York, NY: Routeledge.

Richardson, J. F. (1970). *The New York Police: Colonial times to 1901.* New York, NY: Oxford University Press.

Roberg, R. and Bonn, S. (2004). Higher education and policing: Where are we now? *Policing: An International Journal of Police Strategies & Management, 27*(4), 469–486.

Roosevelt, T. (1897). *American ideals and other essays social and political.* New York, NY: G.P. Putnam's Sons.

San Jose State University, Justice Studies Department (2005). 1930–2005: 75 *Years of educating and inspiring those who protect our property, our homes, our lives, and our rights.* http://www.sjsu.edu/justicestudies/docs/JS_75_Years_of_Excellence.pdf

Sherman, L.W. and The National Advisory Commission on Higher Education for Police Officers. (1978), *The quality of police education: A critical review with recommendations for improving programs in higher education*, Jossey-Bass, San Francisco, CA.

Sherman, L., Milton, C.H., & Kelly, T.V. (1973). *Team policing: Seven cities case studies*. Washington, DC: Police Foundation.

Starr, K. (1996). *Endangered dreams: The Great Depression in California*. New York, NY: Oxford University Press.

Stone, C. & Travis, J. (2011, March). *Toward a new professionalism in policing*. National Institute of Justice Perspectives in Policing #NCJ 232359. Washington DC: Government Printing Office. Retrieved from https://www.ncjrs.gov/pdffiles1/nij/232359.pdf

Uchida, C. (2004). The development of the American police: An historical overview. In Roger Dunham & Geoffrey P. Alpert (eds). *Critical Issues in Policing: Contemporary Readings*. Waveland Press, Inc. Retrieved from http://storage.globalcitizen.net/data/topic/knowledge/uploads/2009042815114290.pdf

Vila, B. & Morris, C. (1999). *The role of police in society: A documentary history*. Westport, CT: Greenwood Press.

Walker, S. (1980). *Popular justice: History of American criminal justice*. New York, NY: Oxford University Press.

White House. (2014). *Budget of the United States government, fiscal year 2015*. Office of Budget and Management. Retrieved from http://www.whitehouse.gov/sites/default/files/omb/budget/fy2015/assets/justice.pdf

Wilson, J.Q. & Kelling, G.L. (1982, March). Broken windows: The police and neighborhood safety. *The Atlantic Monthly, 249*, 29–38.

THE LAW ENFORCEMENT INDUSTRY

LEARNING OBJECTIVES

After reading this chapter, students should be able to:

1 Estimate the number of local law enforcement agencies in the United States.

2 Differentiate local, state, and federal law enforcement agencies.

3 Explain the differences between police departments and sheriffs' offices.

4 Name and describe different types of law enforcement agencies.

5 Describe the distribution of local agencies by size of agency.

6 Estimate the number of federal law enforcement agencies in the U.S.

7 Describe the extent of private police in the U.S.

KEY TERMS

Decentralized

Fragmented

Local police department

State police

Federal law enforcement

Department of Justice

Department of
    Homeland Security

Sheriff's office

Private police

OVERVIEW

In this chapter, we describe the nature and scope of the law enforcement industry in the United States. Students new or unaccustomed to the study of policing are often shocked to learn that there are roughly 18,000 state and local agencies in the United States as well as about 75

There are many different places for someone to work in law enforcement.

federal (nonmilitary) agencies. Agencies range from the very small (such as a part-time, one-officer police department) up to the massive (such as the New York City Police Department with about 36,000 officers). Collectively, across all federal, state, and local agencies, we are talking about roughly 900,000 full-time law enforcement officers. Functions and special jurisdictions range from the general (such as a general purpose local police department such as you might have in your home town) to the more esoteric (such as the U.S. Department of Energy's National Nuclear Security Administration, Office of Secure Transport). At least we know there are plenty of options out there for those who aspire to a career in law enforcement!

That being said, there is somewhat of an academic concern over what constitutes a law enforcement agency and/or a law enforcement officer, and we do not know with absolute precision how many officers and agencies there are in the United States (although we have a pretty good idea). You will encounter some oddities when you get down to the business of enumerating the many agencies and officers in the United States, with some agencies fading in or out of existence from time-to-time. By the end of the chapter, the reader should have a comprehensive understanding of the different types of law enforcement agencies in the United States, as well as differences in their basic functions, and legal jurisdictions.

WHEN IS A POLICE DEPARTMENT NOT A POLICE DEPARTMENT?

SORRENTO, LA.—This little Cajun town, surrounded by swamps and snake-bit with bad news of late, is about to hold one of the most divisive votes of this election season.

The contest over whether to eliminate the town's police department pits a mayor determined to close it against a 71-year-old great-grandmother with no police training who, nonetheless, was just sworn in as chief.

"If you lose the police department, what's next?" asked Fern Barnett, known here as "Miss Fern," as she sat in the chief's imitation-wood-paneled office.

Two rooms over in Sorrento's single-story town hall, Mayor Mike Lambert, 55, said the police department is a drain on the town's finances and has a history of costly lawsuits and other problems. He and the council laid off the department's six full-time employees. He wants the Ascension Parish Sheriff's Office to permanently take over patrolling Sorrento. "I had basically to treat the town like an intervention, like a family member having a drug problem," he said.

On November 4, Mr. Lambert wants voters to back a plan he says will save the town from years of mismanagement. Even if they don't, he won't fund the department, though the town will have to pay Ms. Barnett an as-yet-undetermined salary, he said.

The 3.1-square-mile town of squat homes, about 50 miles northwest of New Orleans, is surrounded by swampy forests of Cypress and Tupelo. While parts of Louisiana have flourished thanks to the booming energy sector, the town of 1400 has struggled. A community college left. Businesses closed. The 5-foot-tall Ms. Barnett, talkative and friendly, and Mr. Lambert, a burly 6-foot-4-inch former sheriff's deputy, are barely speaking. No one knows how the vote will go. Some lawn signs call to keep the department; others say "Stop The Embarrassment."

"It's making Sorrento more and more of a joke," said resident Bobby Brooks, a 39-year-old process operator at a chemical plant. He plans to vote to close the department.

"Sometimes it's bad to even say you're from Sorrento anymore," said Holly LeBlanc, 39, who supports Ms. Barnett.

After the old chief left, Ms. Barnett, who had been a part-time police clerk, decided to run for chief because she worried no one else would. After two possible candidates dropped out, she won by default. The great-grandmother of eight was sworn in October 21. She isn't allowed to do police work because she has no qualifications or training, so she directs inquiries to the sheriff.

She said she is prepared to sit at the desk, unpaid, for years to keep the department alive. "I'm not going anywhere."

[POSTSCRIPT: As of December, 2014, the citizens of the town of Sorrento had voted to close the police department and the town council approved the sale of police equipment as surplus property. However, Fern Barnett remains the default elected chief and is disputing her role (and salary) to run a department that apparently no longer exists.]

DECENTRALIZED, FRAGMENTED, AND LOCAL

Law enforcement in the United States is often described as **decentralized**, **fragmented**, and **local** in nature. Let's take these one at a time. Recall that a primary concern of the framers of the Constitution was the need to limit the power of those entrusted to public office by decentralizing authority both within and across levels of government, and explicitly reserving non-enumerated powers for the states and the people (i.e., the Tenth Amendment). The *police power* discussed in Chapter 1 (i.e., the power to regulate behavior through the enactment and enforcement of laws) is one such power. The United States has a tradition of *local control* over diverse matters not specifically reserved for the federal government in the Constitution. The general idea of local control is that the citizens living in a particular community are in the best position to know and determine the needs of that particular community. They are also the most invested (literally, in the form of taxation) in the specific services provided, the quality of those services, and the resulting quality of life within that community. Given their intimate knowledge of and personal investment in their community, they are perhaps the ideal decision-makers when it comes to the types and quality of services they desire for their community (as opposed to the oft-invoked and somewhat cynical image of decisions being made by "some bureaucrat in Washington, DC").

State laws and local ordinances vary greatly, and law enforcement must be somewhat flexible in order to accommodate these local variations. For example, recreational marijuana use is legal in Washington State, but not in neighboring Idaho. And even within Washington State, some local municipal governments have decided to pass local ordinances making recreational marijuana use illegal within their jurisdiction. Do the residents of a particular community want their own police department that understands and is responsive to the particular needs of their community? If they are incorporated and their tax base can support it, the answer is probably "yes" (law enforcement responsibility for unincorporated areas typically falls to the county sheriff). The alternative would be to contract for services with a nearby police department, county sheriff, or perhaps a primary state law enforcement agency. This is not to say that those contractual services will not result in quality services for the community, but it is perhaps less likely that officers will be as invested in the communities served as compared to a local police department. And both federal and state governments can still influence localities through policy and guidelines, and particularly by making any federal or state funding contingent on compliance with those policies and/or guidelines.

A centralized, national police force could address concerns related to the standardization of police training and to some degree standardization of police services, but a centralized police force is rather contrary to who we are as a people, and would probably not be desirable given the diversity of states and localities. A centralized national police force is something that we have historically feared, and perhaps for good reason in light of current debates about the increasing militarization of police. But maybe there are some things that could be standardized across agencies, such as policies concerning the use of force. Can there be any justification from the perspective of local control as to why every police department should have its own policies regarding the use of force? Couldn't we respect local control while requiring that agencies meet some minimum standard in areas such as this?

© arindambanerjee/Shutterstock.com

Do we have too many law enforcement agencies?

So, in a nutshell, our Constitution and our tradition of local control are why we today have a deliberately *decentralized* system of federal, state, and local law enforcement agencies. Is it efficient? Do we have too many law enforcement agencies? Are these agencies doing too many different things but also too many similar things (with duplication of effort)? Does it make coordinated action difficult when we are faced with national emergencies? Does it limit our ability to share information effectively (see Decentralized box)? These questions speak to the issue of fragmentation, a consequence of our decentralized system.

DECENTRALIZED, FRAGMENTED, AND LOCAL LAW ENFORCEMENT

Consider the following series of events:

- On April 1, 2001, police in Oklahoma stopped Nawaf al-Hazmi for speeding on Interstate 40 near the town of Clinton. A records check revealed no warrants, and the officer issued a ticket to Hazmi.

- On April 26, 2001, police at a random stop checkpoint near Fort Lauderdale, FL, stopped Mohamed Atta and issued him a citation for having no driver's license. He subsequently obtained a Florida driver's license on May 5, but then failed to show up for his required court hearing scheduled on May 26 (for the April 26 citation). An arrest warrant was issued for Atta on June 4, 2001. On July 5, 2001, police in Delray Beach, FL, stopped Atta for speeding. Unaware of the outstanding warrant (either due to a failure to check, or a failure to upload the warrant to databases in a timely fashion), police allowed Atta to proceed with a warning.

- On August 1, 2001, police in Arlington, VA, stopped Hani Hanjour for speeding and issued him a ticket, which he subsequently paid.

- On August 3, 2001, police in Broward County, FL, ran the plates on Mohamed Atta's rental car. The car was rented in his name but the arrest warrant did not return.

- Finally, on September 9, 2001, police in Maryland stopped and ticketed Ziad Jarrah for speeding.

Hazmi, Atta, Hanjour, and Jarrah were four of the hijackers (the latter three were the pilots) on the planes that were ultimately crashed into the World Trade Center, the Pentagon, and a field outside Shanksville, PA, on September 11, 2001. With the advantage of hindsight, it is perhaps unfair to ask whether these contacts between police and terrorists were "missed opportunities" to interrupt the September 11 terrorist attacks on the United States. But these contacts clearly highlight the new role that emerged for state and local law enforcement agencies in the aftermath of the attacks. The reality of terrorist "sleepers" within U.S. borders, combined with these specific local law enforcement contacts, made it clear that domestic terrorism was no longer a principally federal concern. Domestic terrorism is very much a local concern and state and local agencies play a much larger role as first responders to terrorist incidents as well as primary gatherers of intelligence. But can we realistically expect to be able to coordinate the activities of 18,000 state and local agencies? Is our decentralized, fragmented, and local system of law enforcement simply too unmanageable?

Law enforcement in the United States is often described as *fragmented*. Sometimes, the terms *decentralized* and *fragmented* are used synonymously, but fragmentation is really a consequence of our decentralized system of government, our tradition of local control, and the march of time—referring to our historical population growth and expansion. While we might agree that the framers of the Constitution clearly had respect for decentralized government and were genuinely fearful of the idea of a national police force, could the framers ever have envisioned a day when there would be 18,000 state and local law enforcement agencies? Would they have thought this a sensible thing, or would they have—with the benefit of foresight—supported a more centralized scheme? Figure 4.1 is a map with every federal, state, and local law enforcement facility (this figure includes such things as **State Police** barracks, not just headquarters facilities) in the United States plotted as a small dot. Examining the map, one is quickly taken by the fact that there's a whole lot of law enforcement out there—there are so many facilities that one really doesn't need the map outlines to see that these dots represent the shape of the United States.

When individuals say that law enforcement in the United States is fragmented, they are generally referring to the problems of overlapping physical and legal jurisdictions, duplication of effort, lack of standardized practice with regard to recruitment and selection, training, policy, and management, and inefficiency particularly with regard to the coordination of agencies. For example, in some parts of the country (particularly in large cities), there can be several different law enforcement agencies operating within their respective legal jurisdictions, but also in the same geographic jurisdiction as other agencies. This leads to the need for adequate systems to ensure *deconfliction*. For example, if the Drug Enforcement Administration (DEA) is going to conduct an operation in a city, the many other federal, state, and local agencies in the area need to know about it if only to ensure that they don't interfere with each other's ongoing operations. (In this example, local agencies may already be supporting federal agencies or participating on multi-agency task forces, which may alleviate or resolve some conflicts.) Computer software is often used by agencies to deconflict their operations with other agencies.

Finally, law enforcement in the United States is often described as *local* in nature. This stems from the simple fact that, due to our long tradition of local control, the vast decentralized and fragmented system of law enforcement agencies in the United States is comprised primarily of local agencies serving municipal governments. About 12,500 of the nearly 18,000 state and local agencies (or roughly 70%) are local police departments. We will return to these figures in detail later in the chapter.

WHO IS AN "OFFICER" AND WHAT IS AN "AGENCY"?

So, law enforcement in the United States is accurately described as decentralized, fragmented, and local. But before we get down to the "numbers" and examine in detail the scope of the law enforcement industry, we have to ask: what constitutes a law enforcement agency, and who constitutes a law enforcement officer? These might sound like silly questions, but re-read the box discussing the Sorrento, LA, police department and consider these questions again. It's not as simple as one might think.

There are three principal sources of national-level information about law enforcement employment in the United States: The Federal Bureau of Investigation's Uniform Crime Reporting (UCR) program (employee data are collected as part of the Law Enforcement Officers Killed and Assaulted—LEOKA—program within the UCR), the U.S. Census Bureau's Annual Survey of Public Employment and Payroll (ASPEP), and the Bureau of Justice Statistics Census of State and Local Law Enforcement Agencies (CSLLEA). These three government data collections are similar in some respects, but also differ in important ways. Predictably, the result is three different sets of numbers, but when they are combined they converge on what we understand to be an accurate picture of the nature and scope of the law enforcement industry.

Federal, State, and Local Law Enforcement Facilities in the U.S.

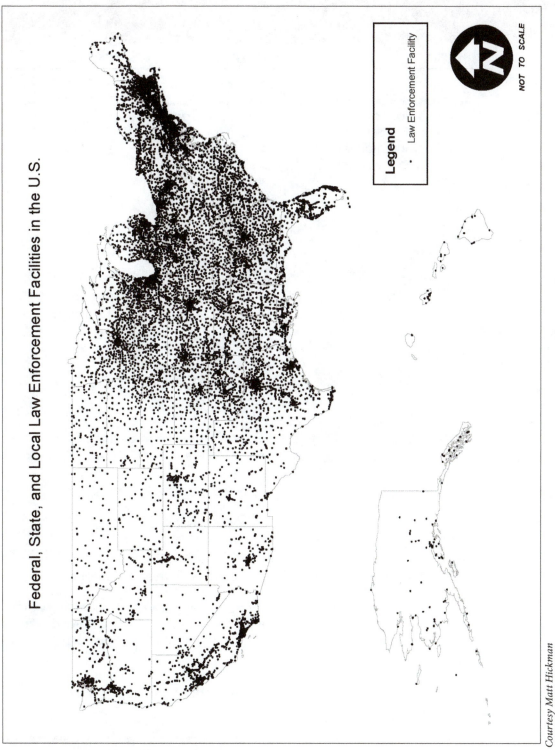

Law Enforcement Facilities in the United States

Courtesy Matt Hickman

TABLE 4.1. Comparing the Three National Sources of Law Enforcement Data

	LEOKA	ASPEP	CSLLEA
When conducted	Annually	Annually	Every 4 years
Agencies included	Government agencies having statutory power of arrest whose primary function is that of apprehension and detection	General police, sheriff, state police, and other governmental departments that preserve law and order, protect persons and property from illegal acts, and work to prevent, control, investigate, and reduce crime	State and local law enforcement and special jurisdiction agencies, such as campus police
Federal agencies	Excluded	Included	Excluded through 2008
Agencies that do not employ any sworn officers	Excluded	Included, provided they are classified as having a police protection function	Excluded
Campus police	Included	Excluded, categorized as having an education function	Included
Transit police	Included	Excluded, categorized as having a transit function	Included
Employees of agencies that perform primarily jail- or court-related functions	Excluded	Included, provided that they work for any agency defined as having a police protection function	Included
Definition of sworn employees	Individuals who carry a firearm and a badge, have full arrest powers, and are paid from government funds specifically set aside for sworn law enforcement representatives	Employees with the power of arrest in agencies designated as having a police protection function	Employees of eligible agencies with general arrest powers
Gender and race/ethnicity of employees	Available for officers killed or assaulted only	Not available	Available

Table adapted from: Banks, D., Hickman, M., Hendrix, J., & Kyckelhahn, T. (2016). *National Sources of Law Enforcement Employment Data.* Washington, DC: Bureau of Justice Statistics.

In addition to the problem of small agencies that may fade into or out of existence from time to time, there is also the problem of what constitutes a law enforcement agency. For example, the UCR LEOKA employment data are reported through Originating agency Identifiers (ORIs) that are issued to agencies by the Federal Bureau of Investigation (FBI) for purposes of NCIC access. But there are many agencies that have multiple ORI numbers. For example, a State police agency is often organized with multiple barracks across a state. Sometimes, an ORI is issued to each barracks for purposes of NCIC access, but crime data and employment data are reported through the main agency ORI. If you try to count agencies using the UCR file, you will find that all of these additional organizational entities are part of your count. Are the barracks of a State Patrol considered to be independent law enforcement agencies? No, they are part of the larger organization and should probably be excluded from an enumeration of law enforcement agencies. ORIs are also issued to investigative bureaus for purposes of NCIC access, but they are part of a larger organization.

One very important characteristic that is shared by all three data collections is that they are *voluntary*. While the rate of participation in these data collections is very high, and agencies may be incentivized to report to the UCR by the threat of becoming ineligible for certain types of federal funding if they do not report their data, some agencies still do not participate.

As can be seen in Table 4.1, the three government data collections use three distinct definitions of sworn employees, and some types of officers are excluded from counts. Agency counts can only be produced by the LEOKA and CSLLEA data collections, as the ASPEP collects government payroll data at the local jurisdiction level but does not allocate it across multiple agencies that may serve a given jurisdiction. Comparing LEOKA and CSLLEA, agency counts in CSLLEA are consistently higher than in LEOKA, although the gap (which has been as large as about 3700 agencies) is narrowing over time. Across the three government data collections, the number of full-time state and local sworn officers in 2008 ranged from about 693,000 in ASPEP to about 763,000 in LEOKA and to about 765,000 in CSLLEA. Because the CSLLEA provides the most comprehensive account of law enforcement agencies and employees, we present a detailed review of those data below.

STATE AND LOCAL AGENCIES

Table 4.2 presents a list of the different types of state and local agencies in the United States, along with the number of full-time sworn officers and other personnel employed in those agencies. Overall, at the last reported census there were 17,985 state and local agencies, employing about 1.1 million full-time personnel (including about 765,000 sworn personnel). These agencies also employ about 100,000 part-time personnel.

LOCAL POLICE DEPARTMENTS

As of 2008, there were 12,501 local departments including those operated by municipal or township governments (about 98% of all local departments), as well as those operated by county, city-county, and tribal governments, and regional or joint entities. These are generally the most visible law enforcement agencies and personnel, serving cities and towns and providing the primary response to calls for service in those communities. As mentioned earlier in the chapter, these agencies can range from the very small (a single officer) to the very large (the NYPD with its

Type of Agency	Agencies	Full-time Employees		Part-time Employees	
		Total	Sworn	Total	Sworn
All agencies	17,985	1,133,915	765,246	100,340	44,062
Local police	12,501	593,003	461,063	58,129	27,810
Sheriff's office	3063	353,461	182,979	26,052	11,334
Primary state	50	93,148	60,772	947	54
Special jurisdiction	1733	90,262	56,968	14,681	4451
Constable/marshal	638	4031	3464	531	413

Note: Excludes agencies employing less than one full-time officer or the equivalent in part-time officers. Adapted from: Reaves, B. (2011). *Census of State and Local Law Enforcement Agencies, 2008.* Washington, DC: Bureau of Justice Statistics.

36,023 full-time officers). We will discuss how these 12,501 agencies are distributed by size later in this section. There is also some state-level variation in the number of agencies; Pennsylvania, for example, has the greatest number of local police departments, nearly 1000 of them!

There are currently more than 150 tribal agencies in the United States, the largest of which is the Navajo Nation Department of Law Enforcement, with 365 sworn officers. Tribal agencies are interesting in that they provide a similar range of services as other local police departments, but the land area served can be quite different (e.g., the Navajo police cover tribal lands of more than 20,000 square miles across three states) and the legal jurisdiction over criminal offenses can belong to federal, state, or tribal agencies depending on the offense, the offender, the victim, and the offense location (see Hickman, 2003).

A Sheriff's Office often provides court-related and jail services in addition to law enforcement.

SHERIFF'S OFFICES

There are 3144 counties in the United States (including 137 county equivalents such as Alaska census areas, Louisiana parishes, independent cities in some states, and the District of Columbia), and almost all of the traditional counties and parishes have a **sheriff's office**. Sheriffs' offices typically provide traditional law enforcement functions, but also provide court-related services (such as process serving and court security), and about three-quarters of them also operate jails. As of 2008, there were 3063 sheriffs' offices in the United States with at least one full-time sworn officer. Some states do not have any sheriffs' offices, including Alaska, Connecticut, Hawaii, and Rhode Island. Like local police departments, sheriffs' offices range from the very small (a single sheriff) up to the very large (the largest is the Los Angeles County Sheriff's Department, with nearly 9500 full-time sworn personnel). For more information on sheriffs' offices, visit the Web site for the National Sheriffs' Association (www.sheriffs.org).

PRIMARY STATE AGENCIES

Each of the 50 states has a state law enforcement agency that provides general law enforcement services and is identified by the CSLLEA as the primary state agency. Some states may have other dominant state law enforcement agencies, such as the California Attorney General's Division of Law Enforcement which employs agents who conduct investigations in specialized areas; these types of agencies are considered "special jurisdiction" agencies in the CSLLEA, and are discussed below. The primary state agencies in CSLLEA are often identified as the "State Police," "State Patrol," "Highway Patrol," or "Department of Public Safety," and may have very different specific responsibilities, making comparisons difficult. The largest primary state agency is the California Highway Patrol, with 7,202 full-time sworn personnel, while the smallest is the North Dakota Highway Patrol, with 139. For more information on these primary state agencies, visit the Web site of the American Association of State Troopers (www.statetroopers.org).

SPECIAL JURISDICTION AGENCIES

In this category, we have those agencies serving both special geographic jurisdictions and/or special legal jurisdictions. There were 1733 of these special jurisdiction agencies in 2008, including:

- 1126 having jurisdiction in *public buildings or facilities* (such as colleges, public school districts, state government buildings, hospitals, and public housing);
- 246 *natural resources* agencies (such as fish and wildlife, parks and recreation, boating and water resources, environmental laws, and forests);
- 167 *transportation systems or facilities* agencies (airports, mass transit, commercial vehicle enforcement, harbors/ports, and bridges/tunnels);
- 140 *criminal investigations* agencies (state, county, or city investigations bureaus, fraud investigations, fire/arson investigation, and tax revenue agencies);
- 54 *special enforcement* agencies (dealing with such areas as alcohol, tobacco, agriculture, narcotics, gaming, and racing laws).

CONSTABLE AND MARSHAL OFFICES

There are 638 constable and marshal offices in the United States, primarily in the State of Texas, but they also exist in several other states. They are typically peace officers serving judicial precincts within counties. In some states, such as Connecticut, marshals have replaced sheriffs and perform their court-related duties. Texas constables are elected officials whose offices primarily serve the courts, either providing process serving duties and/or providing court security, but about half of them also respond to citizen calls for service, and about a third provide general patrol. Less than 10% of these offices handle criminal investigations. For more information on constable and marshal offices, visit the Web site for the National Constables and Marshals Association, which also offers links to state and local associations (www.nationalconstableandmarshalsassociation.com).

AGENCY SIZE DISTRIBUTION

While there are a large number of State and local law enforcement agencies in the United States, most of these (about 70%) are local police departments. And while there are a large number of local police departments, most of these agencies would be considered rather small: of the 12,501 local police departments, more than half of them (about 53%) have fewer than 10 officers (see Table 4.3). About three-quarters of them (76%) have fewer than 25 officers, and nearly 9 in 10 (88%) local police departments have fewer than 50 officers. In contrast, there are only 49 agencies in the United States with 1000 or more officers—less than half of 1% of all local police departments! When we think about police departments, we have a natural tendency to think of New York, Chicago, Los Angeles, Philadelphia, Houston—the largest local police departments in the country serving the largest populations—but the reality is that police departments in the United States would be more accurately characterized by very small town departments. Even the police department in Ferguson, MO, which most would probably regard as a "small town" police department, has 53 officers (at the time of writing) and would fall near the top 10% of departments in terms of size! Which is to say, roughly 90% of local police departments in the United States are smaller than the department in Ferguson, MO.

When looking at police employment, however, the story changes a little. While most agencies are small, most of the employment in law enforcement is among larger agencies. This makes sense: logically, a lot of very small agencies don't collectively employ as many officers as the less numerous but larger agencies. Thus, while nearly 9 in 10 (88%) local police departments have fewer than 50 full-time officers, these agencies only employ a little over one-quarter (27%) of all officers (see Table 4.4). Another way to think of it is that roughly three out of every four officers in the United States work for just 10% of all local police departments (those departments having 50 or more officers).

TABLE 4.3. Full-time Local Police Departments, by Size of Agency (number of full-time sworn), 2008

Size of Agency	Number of Agencies	Cumulative Percent of Agencies
All agencies	12,501	–
1000 or more	49	100.0
500–999	43	99.6
250–499	101	99.3
100–249	445	98.5
50–99	815	94.9
25–49	1543	88.4
10–24	2846	76.0
5–9	2493	53.3
2–4	2637	33.3
0–1	1529	12.2

Note: Excludes agencies employing less than one full-time officer or the equivalent in part-time officers. Adapted from: Reaves, B. (2011). *Census of State and Local Law Enforcement Agencies, 2008.* Washington, DC: Bureau of Justice Statistics.

TABLE 4.4. Full-time Local Police Employees, by Size of Agency, 2008

Size of Agency	Number of Full-time Sworn	Cumulative Percent of Full-time Sworn
All agencies	461,063	–
1000 or more	150,444	100.0
500–999	29,985	67.4
250–499	36,021	60.9
100–249	64,939	53.1
50–99	56,060	39.0
25–49	53,465	26.8
10–24	44,520	15.2
5–9	16,582	5.6
2–4	7694	2.0
0–1	1353	0.3

Note: Excludes agencies employing less than one full-time officer or the equivalent in part-time officers. Adapted from: Reaves, B. (2011). *Census of State and Local Law Enforcement Agencies, 2008.* Washington, DC: Bureau of Justice Statistics.

A common question is, how many officers *should* there be in a given jurisdiction? Is there an optimal ratio of officers to citizens? While there is no national standard or guidelines regarding the optimal number of officers-to-citizens, we can at least describe the current situation. On a population basis, there are approximately 2.5 sworn state and local law enforcement officers for every 1000 residents in the United States. However, this overall figure masks considerable state and local variation. In Washington State, the ratio is about 1.7 per 1000, while in Louisiana it is about 4.1 per 1000. At the city-level, Washington, DC tops the charts at about 7.2 per 1000.

INTERNATIONAL POLICE STRENGTH

How does the United States compare to other nations of the world? International comparative data are scarce and very difficult to collect and interpret. One such effort found wide variation, from about 1 per 1000 in Zambia up to more than 13 per 1000 in Saint Kitts and Nevis. Examine the table below listing different countries ranked by officer-to-population ratios. Does anything strike you as odd? Do you see any patterns or relationships? Does anything characterize countries with higher ratios vs. countries with lower ratios?

SWORN POLICE OFFICERS PER THOUSAND POPULATION

Nation	Year	#	Nation	Year	#
Saint Kitts and Nevis	1998	13.71	Ireland	1998	2.98
Antigua and Barbuda	1998	9.55	Hungary	1998	2.97
Singapore	1994	9.09	France	1994	2.95
Russia	1994	8.65	Scotland	1998	2.93
Northern Cyprus	1998	7.74	Kiribati	1994	2.91

Bermuda	1994	7.00	Czech Republic	1990	2.87
Niue	1990	6.71	Botswana	1990	2.68
Seychelles	1990	6.40	Marshall Islands	1994	2.54
Kuwait	1990	6.30	United States	1996	2.50
Mauritius	1994	6.30	Colombia	1994	2.48
Saint Vincent & the Grenadines	1994	6.03	Samoa	1994	2.47
Nauru	1998	5.90	England and Wales	1998	2.42
Tokelau	1991	5.71	Poland	1990	2.42
Italy	1998	5.68	Switzerland	1990	2.39
Hong Kong	1994	5.42	Fiji	1998	2.37
Kazakhstan	1994	5.21	Chile	1994	2.36
Lithuania	1998	5.01	Moldova	1994	2.35
Barbados	1990	4.57	Slovakia	1994	2.29
Malta	1998	4.55	Turkey	1998	2.26
Israel	1998	4.47	South Africa	1992	2.11
Tonga	1998	4.23	Solomon Islands	1998	2.05
Panama	1994	4.20	Liechtenstein	1998	2.03
Lebanon	1998	4.18	Swaziland	1990	2.02
Cook Islands	1991	3.96	Syria	1990	1.98
Ukraine	1994	3.95	New Zealand	1993	1.97
Latvia	1994	3.87	Greece	1990	1.96
Malaysia	1998	3.79	Romania	1994	1.95
Taiwan	1990	3.72	Australia	1994	1.92
Macedonia	1998	3.60	Denmark	1998	1.88
Austria	1998	3.57	Egypt	1994	1.88
Jamaica	1990	3.56	Korea, South	1990	1.87
Estonia	1994	3.55	Sweden	1998	1.85
Vanuatu	1998	3.44	Japan	1998	1.81
Slovenia	1994	3.43	Canada	1999	1.79
Croatia	1994	3.40	Finland	1998	1.53
Northern Ireland	1994	3.32	Norway	1990	1.37
Armenia	1986	3.24	Philippines	1994	1.36
Sri Lanka	1990	3.23	Nigeria	1998	1.09
Tuvalu	1991	3.21	Lesotho	1986	1.03
Peru	1994	3.16	Zambia	1994	1.01
Cyprus	1990	3.08			

Adapted from Table 3 in Maguire, E., & Schulte-Murray, R. (2001). Issues and patterns in the comparative international study of police strength. *International Journal of Comparative Sociology,* XLII (1–2): 75–100.

FEDERAL AGENCIES

As of 2008, there were 75 **federal law enforcement** agencies in the United States, including 33 offices of Inspector General that employed criminal investigators with arrest and firearm authority. These various federal agencies are responsible for enforcing particular categories of federal law and/or providing law enforcement services (such as custody and security functions) for particular federal jurisdictions. Law enforcement employment data for the Central Intelligence Agency and the Transportation Security Administration's Federal Air Marshals are classified, so the BJS census of federal law enforcement officers excludes these two agencies. Also excluded are law enforcement officers in the U.S. Armed Forces, and federal officers stationed in foreign countries. Table 4.5 lists each of the (non-IG) federal agencies by department or branch of government, along with the number of officers and their primary duties. Chances are there is at least one federal law enforcement agency appearing in that table of which you have not previously heard. Maybe it's the Federal Reserve Board Police? Or perhaps it's the Hoover Dam Police?

TABLE 4.5. Federal Law Enforcement Agencies and Employees, 2008			
Department or Branch of Government	**Federal Agency**	**Total Full-time Officers**	**Primary Duties of Law Enforcement Officers**
Agriculture	U.S. Forest Service, Law Enforcement and Investigations Organization	648	Uniformed law enforcement rangers enforce federal laws and regulations governing National Forest lands and resources. Special agents are criminal investigators who investigate crimes against property, visitors, and employees.
Commerce	Bureau of Industry and Security, Office of Export Enforcement	103	Special agents conduct investigations of alleged or suspected violations of dual-use export control laws.
	National Institute of Standards and Technology Police	28	Officers provide law enforcement and security services for NIST facilities.
	National Oceanic and Atmospheric Administration, Office of Law Enforcement	154	Special agents and enforcement officers enforce laws that conserve and protect living marine resources and their natural habitat in the U.S. Exclusive Economic Zone, which covers ocean waters between 3 and 200 miles off shore and adjacent to all U.S. states and territories.
Defense	Pentagon Force Protection Agency	725	Officers provide law enforcement and security services for the occupants, visitors, and infrastructure of the Pentagon, Navy Annex, and other assigned Pentagon facilities.

continued

Department or Branch of Government	Federal Agency	Total Full-time Officers	Primary Duties of Law Enforcement Officers
Energy	National Nuclear Security Administration, Office of Secure Transportation	363	Special agents, known as nuclear materials couriers, ensure the safe and secure transport of government-owned special nuclear materials during classified shipments in the contiguous United States.
Health and Human Services	National Institutes of Health, Division of Police	94	Officers provide law enforcement and security services for NIH facilities.
	U.S. Food and Drug Administration, Office of Criminal Investigations	187	Special agents investigate suspected criminal violations of the Federal Food, Drug, and Cosmetic Act and other related Acts; the Federal Anti-Tampering Act; and other statutes, including applicable Title 18 violations of the United States Code.
Homeland Security	Federal Emergency Management Agency, Security Branch	84	Officers are responsible for the protection of FEMA facilities, personnel, resources, and information.
	U.S. Customs and Border Protection	37,482	CBP officers protect U.S. borders at official ports of entry. Border patrol agents prevent illegal entry of people and contraband between the ports of entry. Air and marine officers patrol the nation's land and sea borders to stop terrorists and drug smugglers.
	U.S. Immigration and Customs Enforcement	12,679	Special agents conduct investigations involving national security threats, terrorism, drug smuggling, child exploitation, human trafficking, illegal arms export, financial crimes, and fraud. Uniformed immigration enforcement agents perform functions related to the investigation, identification, arrest, prosecution, detention, and deportation of aliens, as well as the apprehension of absconders.
	U.S. Secret Service	5226	Special agents have investigation and enforcement duties primarily related to counterfeiting, financial crimes, computer fraud, and threats against dignitaries. Uniformed Division officers protect the White House complex and other Presidential offices, the main Treasury building and annex, the President and Vice President and their families, and foreign diplomatic missions.

continued

Department or Branch of Government	Federal Agency	Total Full-time Officers	Primary Duties of Law Enforcement Officers
Independent	Amtrak Police	305	Officers provide law enforcement and security services for the passengers, employees, and patrons of the national railroad owned by the U.S. government and operated by the National Railroad Passenger Corporation.
	Federal Reserve Board Police	141	Officers provide law enforcement and security services for Federal Reserve facilities in Washington, D.C.
	National Aeronautics and Space Administration, Protective Services	62	Officers provide law enforcement and security services for NASA's 14 centers located throughout the U.S.
	Smithsonian National Zoological Park Police	26	Officers provide security and law enforcement services for the Smithsonian Institution's 163-acre National Zoological Park in Washington, D.C.
	Tennessee Valley Authority Police	145	Officers provide law enforcement and security services for TVA employees and properties, and users of TVA recreational facilities.
	U.S. Environmental Protection Agency, Criminal Enforcement	202	Special agents investigate suspected individual and corporate criminal violations of the nation's environmental laws.
	U.S. Postal Inspection Service	2324	Postal inspectors conduct criminal investigations covering more than 200 federal statutes related to the postal system. Postal police officers provide security for postal facilities, employees, and assets, as well as escort high-value mail shipments.
Interior	Bureau of Indian Affairs, Division of Law Enforcement	277	Officers provide law enforcement services in some tribal areas. In addition to providing direct oversight for these bureau-operated programs, the division also provides technical assistance and some oversight to tribally operated law enforcement programs.
	Bureau of Land Management, Law Enforcement	255	Law enforcement rangers conduct patrols, enforce federal laws and regulations, and provide for the safety of BLM employees and users of public lands. Special agents investigate illegal activity on public lands.

continued

Department or Branch of Government	Federal Agency	Total Full-time Officers	Primary Duties of Law Enforcement Officers
Interior *(continued)*	National Park Service, United States Park Police	547	Officers provide law enforcement services to designated National Park Service areas (primarily in the Washington, D.C., New York City, and San Francisco metropolitan areas). Officers are authorized to provide services for the entire National Park System.
	National Park Service, Visitor and Resource Protection Division	1416	Park rangers, commissioned as law enforcement officers, provide law enforcement services for the National Park System. Additional rangers serving seasonally are commissioned officers but are considered part-time and not included in the FLEO census.
	U.S. Bureau of Reclamation, Hoover Dam Police	21	Officers provide security and law enforcement services for the Hoover Dam and the surrounding 22-square-mile security zone.
	U.S. Fish and Wildlife Service, Office of Law Enforcement	603	Special agents enforce federal laws that protect wildlife resources, including endangered species, migratory birds, and marine mammals.
Judicial	Administrative Office of the U.S. Courts	4767	Federal probation officers supervise offenders on probation and supervised release. In seven federal judicial districts, probation officers are not authorized to carry a firearm while on duty and are excluded from FLEO officer counts.
	U.S. Supreme Court Police	139	Officers provide law enforcement and security services for Supreme Court facilities.
Justice	Bureau of Alcohol, Tobacco, Firearms and Explosives	2562	Special agents enforce federal laws related to the illegal use and trafficking of firearms, the illegal use and storage of explosives, acts of arson and bombings, acts of terrorism, and the illegal diversion of alcohol and tobacco products.
	Drug Enforcement Administration	4388	Special agents investigate major narcotics violators, enforce regulations governing the manufacture and dispensing of controlled substances, and perform other functions to prevent and control drug trafficking.

continued

Department or Branch of Government	Federal Agency	Total Full-time Officers	Primary Duties of Law Enforcement Officers
Justice *(continued)*	Federal Bureau of Investigation	12,925	Special agents are responsible for criminal investigation and enforcement related to more than 200 categories of federal law. Criminal priorities include public corruption, civil rights violations, organized crime, white-collar crime, violent crime, and major theft. FBI police officers provide law enforcement and security for FBI facilities.
	Federal Bureau of Prisons	16,993	Correctional officers enforce the regulations governing the operation of BOP correctional institutions, serving as both supervisors and counselors of inmates. They are normally not armed while on duty. Most other BOP employees have arrest and firearm authority to respond to emergencies.
	U.S. Marshals Service	3359	The agency receives all persons arrested by federal agencies and is responsible for their custody and transportation until sentencing. Deputy marshals provide security for federal judicial facilities and personnel.
Legislative	Library of Congress Police	85	Officers provided law enforcement and security services for Library of Congress facilities. On October 1, 2009, the agency ceased operations and its personnel, duties, responsibilities, and functions were transferred to the U.S. Capitol Police.
	U.S. Capitol Police	1637	Officers provide law enforcement and security services for the U.S. Capitol grounds and buildings, and in the zone immediately surrounding the Capitol complex. The U.S. Capitol Police assumed the duties of the Library of Congress Police on October 1, 2009.
	U.S. Government Printing Office, Uniformed Police Branch	41	Officers provide law enforcement and security services for facilities where information, products, and services for the federal government are produced and distributed.

continued

Department or Branch of Government	Federal Agency	Total Full-time Officers	Primary Duties of Law Enforcement Officers
State	Bureau of Diplomatic Security	1049	In the U.S., special agents protect the secretary of state, the U.S. ambassador to the United Nations, and visiting foreign dignitaries below the head-of-state level. They also investigate passport and visa fraud.
Treasury	Bureau of Engraving and Printing Police	207	Officers provide law enforcement and security services for facilities in Washington, D.C., and Fort Worth, Texas, where currency, securities, and other official U.S. documents are made.
	Internal Revenue Service, Criminal Investigation Division	2655	Special agents have investigative jurisdiction over tax, money laundering, and Bank Secrecy Act laws.
	United States Mint Police	316	Officers provide law enforcement and security services for employees, visitors, government assets stored at U.S. Mint facilities in Philadelphia, PA; San Francisco, CA; West Point, NY; Denver, CO; Fort Knox, KY; and Washington, D.C.
Veterans Affairs	Veterans Health Administration, Office of Security and Law Enforcement	3175	Officers provide law enforcement and security services for VA medical centers.

Note: Table excludes offices of inspectors general, U.S. Armed Forces (Army, Navy, Air Force, Marines, and Coast Guard), Central Intelligence Agency, and Transportation Security Administration's Federal Air Marshals.

Adapted from: Reaves, B. (2012). Census of Federal Law Enforcement Officers, 2008. Washington, DC: Bureau of Justice Statistics.

The major federal law enforcement agencies are located within the **Department of Justice** and the **Department of Homeland Security.** Within the Department of Justice are the FBI, the U.S. Marshal's Service (USMS), the DEA, and the Bureau of Alcohol, Tobacco, Firearms, and Explosives (ATF). Within the Department of Homeland Security are U.S. Customs and Border Protection (CBP), U.S. Immigration and Customs Enforcement (ICE), and the U.S. Secret Service (USSS). We briefly review here the major agencies of the Department of Justice, but encourage the reader to investigate all of these agencies and their respective histories on their Web sites.

- The FBI is perhaps the most widely known of the federal law enforcement agencies, due in some part to its long-running portrayal in popular media. Started as the Bureau of Investigation in 1908, and ultimately renamed the Federal Bureau of Investigation in 1935, the FBI has a long and storied history. The FBI has very broad criminal investigation and enforcement responsibilities in more than 200 categories of federal law. As of 2008, the FBI employed nearly 13,000 full-time law enforcement officers.

© Leonard Zhukovsky/Shutterstock.com

The FBI is perhaps the most widely known of the federal law enforcement agencies.

- The USMS is the oldest federal law enforcement agency (tracing its roots to 1789) and has also benefitted from long-running portrayals in popular media. The USMS handles individuals who are arrested by other federal law enforcement agencies, including custody and transportation through the sentencing phase. The USMS also provides security for the federal courts. And yes, they apprehend fugitives as well. As of 2008, the USMS employed nearly 3400 full-time law enforcement officers.

- The DEA was created in 1973 in response to the growing national problem of drug use and a desire to consolidate what was seen as a somewhat fragmented federal response to drugs. Prior to 1968, federal drug enforcement was carried out by multiple agencies focused on different aspects of drug policy and enforcement with roots going back to the Prohibition era. These early efforts were consolidated into the Bureau of Narcotic and Dangerous Drugs (BNDD), which existed from 1968 to 1973. The DEA was largely an outgrowth of BNDD, along with the consolidation of remaining federal drug intelligence, investigations, and policy functions in other agencies and offices. In addition to investigating drug trafficking, the DEA also enforces regulatory laws concerning the manufacture and dispensing of controlled substances. As of 2008, the DEA employed about 4400 full-time law enforcement officers.

- The ATF has a somewhat complicated history similar to that of the DEA, with different agencies (primarily the Internal Revenue Service) having addressed the regulation and taxation of alcohol since the Prohibition era, and later tobacco, firearms, and explosives. The ATF was established as a distinct bureau within the Department of Treasury in 1972, consolidating and removing alcohol, tobacco, and firearms responsibilities from the Internal Revenue Service. The ATF was moved into the Department of Justice after the September 11, 2001, terrorist attacks on the United States as part of a major reorganization (which included the creation of the Department of Homeland Security). The alcohol and tobacco taxation functions of ATF remained within the Department of Treasury. The ATF primarily enforces federal laws related to firearms trafficking, the use and storage of explosives, acts of arson and bombings, as well as diversion of alcohol and tobacco products. As of 2008, the ATF employed about 2600 full-time law enforcement officers.

Federal Offices of Inspector General are responsible for detecting, investigating, and preventing waste, fraud, and abuse related to federal programs, operations, and employees. While there are 69 IG offices in the United States, only 33 of them employ criminal investigators with firearms and arrest authority. Below is a list of the 33 offices of Inspector General, along with the number of full-time personnel. These IG offices employed a total of 3501 criminal investigators, ranging from the very small IG for the Library of Congress (with two full-time investigators) up to the IG for the U.S. Postal Service (with 508 investigators). As with the earlier list of federal agencies, chances are there is an agency on this list of which you were unaware. Perhaps is it the IG office for the U.S. Railroad Retirement Board?

TABLE 4.6. Offices of Inspectors General Employing Full-time Personnel with Arrest and Firearm Authority, September 2008

Office of Inspectors General	Number of Full-time Officers
Total	3501
U.S. Postal Service	508
Department of Health and Human Services	389
Department of Defense	345
Department of the Treasury, Tax Administration	302
Social Security Administration	272
Department of Housing and Urban Development	228
Department of Agriculture	164
Department of Labor	164
Department of Homeland Security	157
Department of Veterans Affairs	132
Department of Justice	122
Department of Transportation	94
Department of Education	85
General Services Administration	67
Department of the Interior	66
National Aeronautics and Space Administration	52
Department of Energy	48
Environmental Protection Agency	40
Federal Deposit Insurance Corporation	35
Small Business Administration	34
Department of State	32
Office of Personnel Management	28

continued

TABLE 4.6. Offices of Inspectors General Employing Full-time Personnel with Arrest and Firearm Authority, September 2008 *(continued)*

Office of Inspectors General	Number of Full-time Officers
Department of the Treasury	21
Tennessee Valley Authority	20
Department of Commerce	16
U.S. Railroad Retirement Board	16
Agency for International Development	13
Nuclear Regulatory Commission	13
Corporation for National and Community Service	9
National Science Foundation	6
National Archives and Records Administration	6
Government Printing Office	5
Library of Congress	2

Note: Excludes employees based in U.S. territories or foreign countries.

Adapted from: Reaves, B. (2012). *Census of Federal Law Enforcement Officers, 2008.* Washington, DC: Bureau of Justice Statistics.

OFFICES OF INSPECTOR GENERAL

If you are interested in a career with one of the many offices of Inspector General, visit the Web site for the Council of the Inspectors General on Integrity and Efficiency (CIGIE) at www.ignet.gov, where you will find information about IG offices as well as current job vacancies. Be creative about your career prospects and think about some of these less commonly known options within the realm of law enforcement.

PRIVATE POLICE

What? The U.S. has "private" police? The answer is yes, there are non-governmental **private police** in the U.S., and a chapter on the law enforcement industry would be incomplete without some discussion of this interesting area. Private police may be able to provide services that public police in some jurisdictions are otherwise unable to provide, such as spending additional time and attention on specific community concerns, addressing quality of life issues, and perhaps even helping to build the sense of community. On the other hand, there are important questions about the extent and quality of training for private police, as well as the scope of their authority.

The term *private police* is both subjective and contentious. As this is an introductory textbook, we will use Sparrow's broad definition and leave it to your professor to refine it to his or her liking. Sparrow defines *private policing* as the "provision of security or policing services other than by public servants in the normal course of their public duties" (2014, p. 2). Within this interpretation, *clients of private policing services* can be either public or private individuals or entities. For example, Santa Cruz Police Department (CA) contracts with private security firms to provide extra eyes in places it cannot afford to place a sworn officer in the same way that homeowners associations do (Lyons, n.d.). As part of his definition, Sparrow (2014) describes five categories of *providers of private police services:* volunteers, commercial security-related enterprises, specialist employees in private or not-for profit organizations, non-specialist employees in private or not-for profit organizations, and public police.

THINK ABOUT IT

Take some time to discuss each of these categories with your classmates and professor. Would you classify each of the individuals/groups described in these categories as private police? Which groups make the cut? Which do not? How would *you* define the term "private police?"

---

1. **Volunteers**—These are private individuals who are not paid for their services. Examples include individuals who join a neighborhood watch group or who patrol their neighborhood looking for suspicious activity or suspicious persons. It could also include volunteers who perform crossing guard duty to help children get to school safely or who sit in a park after school so children can play safely.

2. **Commercial security-related enterprises**—These are for-profit companies that provide some type of security and/or policing services. For example, private investigators, security guards, bounty hunters, and alarm and security companies all fit into this category. Many communities contract with private security companies for additional security patrol in their neighborhoods. These types of security personnel may serve as a visual deterrent, check on residences, report incidents to the police, and may even perform citizen's arrests of individuals. We bet you can name at least five companies in your area that provide such services. You might even know someone who works in this capacity.

3. **Specialist employees in private or not-for-profit organizations**—These are employees who perform security, investigative, or risk-management functions in a company or organization whose core mission is unrelated to security/policing. For example, store detectives, internal fraud investigators, computer network security specialists, etc. This is a particularly fast-growing category as national, multi-national, and small-medium sized companies alike are hiring former police detectives and executives with transferable specialty skills (such as computer forensics or intelligence gathering). On the not-for-profit side, Business Investment Districts and schools commonly employ their own security personnel. For example, the Business Improvement Districts in downtown Los Angeles employ their own private security guards (known by the shirt color they wear) to keep the streets clean and safe so that businesses can flourish; "purple shirts" even assisted LAPD officers during Occupy LA protests in late 2011 (Romero, 2011).

4. **Non-specialist employees in private or not-for-profit organizations**—These are employees with general duties who are asked to be observant for security issues. For example, retail store clerks looking for shoplifting activity, transportation personnel (airline, train, mass-transit) looking for passengers acting suspiciously, or event organizing staff who keep an eye out for suspicious activity (packages or people). If you work in retail, you probably fit into this category.

5. **Public police**—This category includes situations in which public police are paid by private clients to provide security or other police-related functions, either on-duty or off-duty. In all cases, they are hired because they are public police officers (or other employees such as dispatchers) with specific powers and/or training. Depending on how the contract is worded, officers might work for a private entity off-duty or as part of an overtime contract or be assigned to a special policing detail as part of their "normal" job duties but which was paid for by a private client. Examples of such events could include: sports matches, concerts, major political events, or V.I.P. security.

The growth of the private policing industry over the past 35 years is undeniable. Depending on how you measure, there are now 1.5 – 3 paid private police personnel for each public police officer in the United States (Bayley & Nixon, 2010). It has been argued that "nation-states are losing their monopoly on policing" and that the line between public and private policing is becoming increasingly blurred (Bayley & Nixon, 2010, p. 6). Despite this growth and the blurred lines, private police are not without controversy.

Beyond Sparrow's definition of private police is a special type of *private police officer* who by virtue of state authority can carry a firearm and possesses general police powers such as the authority to make arrests and issue citations for violations of law. We argue that these individuals, who are employed by non-governmental entities, represent an important sixth category of private police. Little is known about these private police officers on a systematic, nationwide basis, and there is great variation across the states. In some states, these individuals are referred to as "special police" or other titles, and the lines between private security and law enforcement may be very blurred and ill-defined at one extreme, or they may be treated as one and the same under some state laws and opinions.

PRIVATE POLICE CARRY GUNS AND MAKE ARRESTS, AND THEIR RANKS ARE SWELLING

Michael Youlen stopped a driver in a Manassas apartment complex on a recent night and wrote the man a ticket for driving on a suspended license. With a badge on his chest and a gun on his hip, Youlen gave the driver a stern warning to stay off the road.

The stop was routine police work, except for one fact: Youlen is not a Manassas officer. The citation came courtesy of the private force he created that, until recently, he called the "Manassas Junction Police Department."

He is its chief and sole officer.

He is a force of one.

And he is not alone. Like more and more Virginians, Youlen gained his police powers using a little-known provision of state law that allows private citizens to petition the courts for the authority to carry a gun, display a badge, and make arrests. The number of "special conservators of the peace"—or SCOPs, as they are known—has doubled in Virginia over the past decade to roughly 750, according to state records.

The growth is mirrored nationally in the ranks of private police, who increasingly patrol corporate campuses, neighborhoods, and museums as the demand for private security has increased and police services have been cut in some places.

The trend has raised concerns in Virginia and elsewhere because these armed officers often receive a small fraction of the training and oversight of their municipal counterparts. Arrests of private police officers and incidents involving SCOPs overstepping their authority have also raised concerns.

The Virginia legislature approved a bill on Friday increasing the training and regulation of SCOPs. The private officers would now be required to train for 130 hours, up from 40 hours—less than the state requires for nail technicians, auctioneers, and security guards.

In neighboring D.C., a similar designation called "special police" requires 40 hours of training. Maryland officials leave instruction to the discretion of employers but have no requirements. Other states have similar systems.

"There are a number of groups we regulate far more stringently than SCOPs carrying a gun," said Virginia Secretary of Public Safety Brian Moran, speaking prior to the passage of the bill.

INDEPENDENT AND INFORMAL

The conservator of the peace concept predates modern policing.

It has its origins in English common law, and the first Virginia statute was enacted in 1860 to allow proprietors of "watering places" to protect their establishments.

The designation still retains some of that informality. No authority regulates the conduct of SCOPs or addresses complaints against them, although a court can revoke their commissions. The state does not track the number of arrests they make or citations they issue.

Most SCOPs patrol corporate campuses, work for neighborhood associations, or perform code enforcement for counties or cities, but Youlen has pushed the model further by creating his own "department" and turning policing into an enterprise. He contracts his services to nine apartment and housing communities in the Manassas area. That's up from one in 2012.

SCOPs are free to call themselves "police" in Virginia, although the new bill would require court approval. Youlen recently dropped "police department" from the name of his operation, anticipating that lawmakers would restrict use of the term. It is now called Manassas Junction LLC.

Youlen, who is a former police officer, said he sees his work as a complement to the Manassas force, not a replacement for it. He said he provides the type of intensive policing, hands-on engagement with the community and attention to small problems that the city simply doesn't have the resources or manpower to provide.

"I'm a part-time police officer and a part-time advocate," Youlen said of his work. "And I would hope a part-time role model and steady security presence for these communities."

On the night Youlen wrote the suspended-license ticket, he pulled his black Ford Fusion with tinted windows out of the Colonial Village Apartments around 8 pm. Youlen, 30, spends his shifts circulating among the communities he covers until the early hours of the morning.

He deals mostly with loitering, traffic infractions, noise complaints, minor drug offenses, and nuisances that can impact quality of life. He said he has never pulled his gun.

At one point during another patrol, Youlen rolled up next to two mattresses that someone had propped against a tree in a townhome community. He said he would return later to investigate and possibly issue a citation to the violator.

At another point, he checked in with the mother of a teen who had gotten into trouble with neighbors to make sure the boy was still in school and playing football. Youlen wore a black flak vest with the word "police" emblazoned across it as he spoke to the woman.

Youlen said he turns any felony-type incidents, such as assaults, rapes or shootings, over to the Manassas police to handle, but if he does go to court, he testifies and provides evidence in cases just as a municipal police officer would.

Youlen said he was a police officer in upstate New York before spending several years on the Manassas force. He said he left to start a private investigator service and then became a SCOP after reading about a housing community in Stafford County called Aquia Harbour that had its own private police force.

In many ways, Youlen's operation functions much as any police department. Youlen has a dispatch number that residents can call and a daily blotter that he posts on the Manassas Junction Web site, along with fliers for suspects and notices about recent incidents. He gives reports about crime at homeowners' association meetings.

In 2014, Youlen recorded 77 arrests and ticket citations and handed out 162 parking violations, according to his statistics. He responded to 221 calls for service.

Manassas City Police Chief Douglas W. Keen said he has concerns about Youlen, saying his presence has created confusion among citizens, magistrates, and even judges. Keen said many who encounter him assume he represents the city.

"Any misunderstanding or confusion in this could greatly impact the relationships and trust within our community," Keen wrote in an e-mail.

Prince William County Commonwealth's Attorney Paul Ebert said SCOPs' lack of training and their backgrounds have sometimes undermined prosecutions, though he did not point to any specific cases. His office noted they had not had any issues with Youlen.

"The trouble of prosecuting cases from those folks is that we have to vouch for the credibility of the complainant," Ebert said. "A lot of them are not trained and don't have pasts that are conducive to law enforcement."

But Crystal Terrant, owner of Burke Community Management, which manages eight properties that Youlen patrols, said calls to police have dropped dramatically since she hired Youlen.

"He's cleaned up a lot of the petty crime and traffic stuff," Terrant said. "He offers a sense of security to residents. He's befriended the kids, so they respect the property more."

PROBLEMS BRING SCRUTINY

A handful of incidents involving SCOPs in Virginia and nationally have focused attention on the training and oversight of private police.

In 2009, a SCOP who owned a private security firm got into a heated argument with a woman over parking at a Newport News-area shopping center, according to court records.

Kevin Bukowski hemmed in the woman's vehicle, and then he and a partner pointed their guns directly at the woman and a friend as they sat in their car with two children, court records show. Bukowski was convicted of abduction, and the state revoked his SCOP registration in 2012.

"I was unjustly punished, but there are a lot of problems with the system," Bukowski said of SCOPs. "You got these guys running out there as security officers who couldn't make it as police officers."

In another incident in 2012, a SCOP on a motorcycle with flashing lights and various law enforcement-style stickers pulled over a Virginia State Police special agent driving on I-64 near the Hampton Roads Bridge-Tunnel, according to court records.

The SCOP asked the officer why he was going so fast. The officer replied, "Who are you?" and flashed his badge, according to court records. The SCOP then rode off.

The officer said the man on the motorcycle was likely a SCOP named Michael Tynan, who runs a security officer training academy in Virginia Beach.

Portsmouth police questioned Tynan after he was seen conducting another traffic stop in 2013, according to the court documents. He told officers his SCOP status allowed him to perform traffic stops. He also said he was a retired state trooper but later admitted he failed out of the academy.

The Virginia Attorney General's Office moved to strip Tynan of his SCOP commission in Portsmouth in 2013, and Tynan agreed to surrender it.

In an interview, Tynan said he was unaware of the allegations and would have challenged them if he had known about them. "I categorically deny these things," Tynan said.

The government's motion to vacate Tynan's SCOP commission in Portsmouth said he was "unfit for an appointment," but state records show Tynan is still registered as a SCOP in Virginia Beach.

Backers note that SCOPs can play a valuable role and that problems are rare.

John Hall, president of American Security Group in Richmond, said his company employs SCOPs. He said they provide an affordable way to boost security for many communities.

"There's a void in a lot of the [homeowner's associations], light rails and business parks," Hall said. "There has to be some type of role there between public and private."

Experts say Virginia's increase in SCOPs is part of a nationwide uptick in private security that began in the 1970s and accelerated after the September 11 attacks. The number of private security guards—nearly 1.1 million—dwarfs the 640,000 public police officers, according to the Bureau of Labor Statistics.

While the numbers have increased, training has not kept pace. A 2012 study from a University of Illinois College of Law assistant professor found that private police are "chronically undertrained" and nearly a third nationwide face almost no regulation.

States other than Virginia have faced issues as well. In 2012, more than 20 residents of the Cherry Hill neighborhood of Baltimore filed a $25 million lawsuit against a Cleveland security company, claiming its guards had abused residents and violated their civil rights by stopping them illegally and making false arrests. Two of the three guards named in the suit were "special police," a designation similar to SCOPs in Virginia.

In 2005, a special police officer tasked with guarding government buildings in D.C. was convicted of a felony after carrying out an armed robbery in Georgetown using the revolver issued by his security company.

To become a SCOP in Virginia, an individual must register with the Virginia Department of Criminal Justice Services. That requires the applicant to pass a criminal background check and an alcohol and drug test. The new bill ups the training requirement to 130 hours for armed SCOPs—still far less than the 580 to 1200 hours required of municipal police officers in the state.

The individual then petitions a circuit court to be commissioned with the sponsorship of an employer.

Virginia Gov. Terry McAuliffe is expected to sign the bill increasing training and regulation for SCOPs. Sen. Thomas K. Norment Jr., who sponsored it, said he would like to eventually bar SCOPs from calling themselves police and using flashing lights. The current bill allows them to do both, with the permission of the courts.

"I'm pleased with the progress, but there is still some work to do," Norment said.

CONCLUSION

In this chapter, we attempted to comprehensively describe the nature and scope of the law enforcement industry in the United States. If nothing else, you should be well prepared for a law enforcement version of the game *Trivial Pursuit*! Chances are that we covered at least one agency or type of agency that you were unaware of before reading the chapter. Owing to our long tradition and history of local control, we have a patchwork of law enforcement that is decentralized, fragmented, and local in nature. While we do not know with absolute precision how many agencies and officers there are in the United States, available data suggests that there are presently about 18,000 state and local law enforcement agencies in the United States, as well as about 75 federal (nonmilitary) law enforcement agencies, employing approximately 900,000 full-time law enforcement officers. We introduced you to agencies that are very small as well as to agencies that are quite large; agencies having very general jurisdictions and functions to those having very esoteric jurisdictions and functions. We also broached the subject of private police. The law enforcement industry in the United States is large and diverse, for better or for worse.

REVIEW QUESTIONS

1. Do you think there are simply too many local police departments in the United States? What are some of the pros and cons of our decentralized, fragmented, and local system of law enforcement? Would you suggest any changes, and how would we accomplish those changes?

2. To what extent are some of the current challenges and problems of modern law enforcement a reflection of our tradition of local control? Would you argue for the status quo, or for a greater federal role in some aspects of law enforcement?

GLOSSARY

Decentralized the idea that law enforcement authority is spread both within and across levels of government, as opposed to a single centralized law enforcement authority.

Department of Homeland Security an agency created by the Homeland Security Act of 2002 whose mission is to protect the homeland by preventing and reducing the country's vulnerability to terrorist attacks, as well as minimizing damage, assisting in recovery, and acting as a focal point for crises and emergency planning. (KH)

Department of Justice a department within the executive branch of the federal government designed to enforce the laws of the United States. (KH)

Federal law enforcement agencies responsible for enforcing particular categories of federal law and/or providing law enforcement services (such as custody and security functions) for particular federal jurisdictions.

Fragmented a consequence of our decentralized system of government, our tradition of local control, and our historical population growth and expansion; generally refers to the problems of overlapping physical and legal jurisdictions, duplication of effort, lack of standardized practice with regard to recruitment and selection, training, policy, and management, and inefficiency particularly with regard to the coordination of agencies.

Local Police Department operated by municipal or township governments (about 98% of all local departments), as well as those operated by county, city-county, and tribal governments, and regional or joint entities; these are generally the most visible law enforcement agencies and personnel, serving cities and towns and providing the primary response to calls for service in those communities.

Private Police non-governmental entities that may provide services that public police in some jurisdictions are otherwise unable to provide, such as spending additional time and attention on specific community concerns, addressing quality of life issues, and perhaps even helping to build the sense of community.

Sheriff's Office almost all traditional counties and parishes in the United States have a sheriff's office; typically provides traditional law enforcement functions, but also provides court-related services (such as process serving and court security), and about three-quarters of them also operate jails.

State police each state has a state law enforcement agency that provides general law enforcement services; often identified as the "State Police," "State Patrol," "Highway Patrol," or "Department of Public Safety," they may have very different specific responsibilities making comparisons difficult.

REFERENCES

Banks, D., Hickman, M., Hendrix, J., & Kyckelhahn, T. (2016). *National sources of law enforcement employment data.* Washington, DC: Bureau of Justice Statistics.

Bayley, D.H. & Nixon, C. (2010, September). The Changing environment for policing, 1985–2008. Washington DC: National Institute of Justice.

Hickman, M. (2003). *Tribal law enforcement, 2000.* Washington, DC: Bureau of Justice Statistics.

Lyons, J. (n.d.). *Privatization of police services.* Retrieved from http://www.fdle.state.fl.us/Content/getdoc/cbe81692-8662-46ed-a59b-b3861986f301/Lyons.aspx

Maguire, E., & Schulte-Murray, R. (2001). Issues and patterns in the comparative international study of police strength. *International Journal of Comparative Sociology,* XLII (1–2), 75–100.

Reaves, B. (2011). *Census of State and Local Law Enforcement Agencies, 2008.* Washington, DC: Bureau of Justice Statistics.

Reaves, B. (2012). *Census of Federal Law Enforcement Officers, 2008.* Washington, DC: Bureau of Justice Statistics.

Romero, D. (2011, December 8). Occupy L.A. demonstrators policed with help of private security known downtown as "The Shirts." LAPD says "that's not typical." LA Weekly. Retrieved from http://blogs.laweekly.com/informer/2011/12/occupy_la_lapd_assisted_private_security.php

Sparrow, M.K. (2014, September). Managing the boundary between public and private policing. Washington DC: National Institute of Justice.

5 LOCAL AGENCY STRUCTURE AND ORGANIZATION

LEARNING OBJECTIVES

After reading this chapter, students should be able to:

1 Define "mission statement" and explain its importance to an organization.

2 Explain how the size and structure of an organization is determined.

3 Describe Blau's four types of structural differentiation.

4 Explain the organizational transformation required for community oriented policing.

5 Name and describe three special function units.

6 Define multi-jurisdictional task force and give an example.

7 Describe a police paramilitary unit and explain their evolution.

KEY TERMS

Specialization

Division of labor

Mission statement

Hierarchy of authority

Spatial differentiation

Occupational differentiation

Functional differentiation

Hierarchical differentiation

Centralization

Span of control

Quasi-military organization

Multi-jurisdictional task force

Police paramilitary unit

Special Weapons and Tactics team (SWAT)

OVERVIEW

The previous chapter introduced you to the nature and scope of the law enforcement industry in the United States. If nothing else, you have hopefully come to appreciate the fact that there are a large number of law enforcement agencies in the United States, they come in all shapes and sizes, with varying jurisdictions, and operate at different levels of government. In this chapter, we will go deeper within local law enforcement organizations to gain a better understanding of variation in the goals and structures of these agencies. As we proceed, it is important to keep in mind that all organizations are created in order to achieve some goal or set of goals. In this regard, police departments are really no different than other organizations such as fire departments, colleges or universities, or the local widget factory. All of these organizations were created in order to achieve certain goals, and while an organization might articulate these goals in a fairly simple and straight-forward manner, when one digs down into the details one will generally find that there is actually a great deal of complexity involved in achieving those goals. While the underlying structure of these organizations may be just as diverse as the range of goals they seek to achieve, chances are that a given organization has sufficiently complex goals that they require certain structural characteristics associated with *bureaucracy*—a term that is often used derisively, but simply refers to a system of administration involving **division of labor**, hierarchy, and rules. Bureaucracies are often embodied by the ubiquitous "organization chart" consisting of boxes (showing individuals or collections of individuals) and lines (showing the relationships between the boxes). Police departments are no exception (see Figure 5.1).

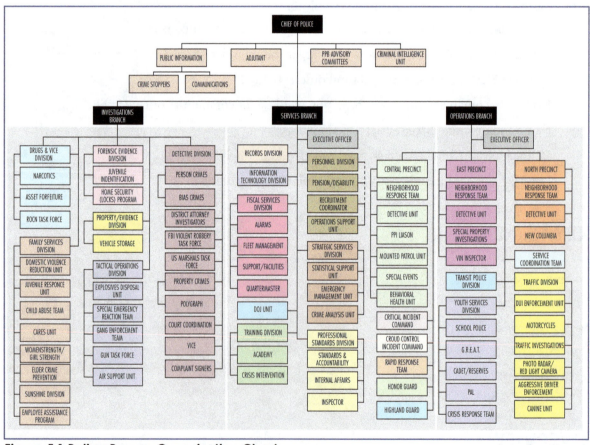

Figure 5.1 Police Bureau Organization Chart

This is not to say that the organization chart is chiseled in stone, nor that it is necessarily followed in practice or with absolute fidelity. The fact is that organizations change over time as personnel come and go, special units are banded and disbanded, political priorities arise and fall, not to mention the increasing automation of functions. Boxes on the organization chart may become unoccupied or irrelevant, and may lead to unnecessary duplication of effort, confusion and delay, and other inefficiency. (This is probably where the derisive use of the word "bureaucracy" comes in.) A police chief may, from time

A police chief may need to alter the organizational structure of his/her agency from time to time.

© Greg Browning/Shutterstock.com

to time, find it necessary to alter the organizational structure of his/her agency. It may have been a change a long time in the making, even before the chief arrived. Sometimes, change may be compelled by a particular event or string of events, or may be compelled by politicians or outside agencies. A recent example of such change in Portland, OR, is described in the box below.

INCOMING CHIEF O'DEA ANNOUNCES ORGANIZATIONAL AND COMMAND CHANGES

Thursday, December 11, 2014—Incoming Chief Larry O'Dea announced today organizational changes and personnel assignments for the Portland Police Bureau. Assistant Chief O'Dea will be appointed Chief of Police on January 2, 2015; these changes will be effective January 8, 2015.

The Bureau currently has three branches: Operations, Investigations, and Services. Under Chief O'Dea, the Bureau will add a fourth branch called Community Services. This branch will be responsible for the Traffic Division, Transit Police Division, Youth Services Division, and Tactical Operations Division. Emergency Management will also be in this branch, under the direction of the Traffic Division. These divisions were previously part of the Operations Branch.

"I fully support Larry O'Dea's changes and assignments," Mayor Charlie Hales said. "The incoming chief believes in engagement with the community; a personal passion of mine. He believes in the importance of diversity; another passion of mine."

Hales serves as Police Commissioner for the City of Portland.

The Operations Branch will contain the three precincts, Rapid Response Team, Critical Incident Command, and Crowd Control Incident Command.

"The most important reason for this change is to provide the senior leadership team the opportunity to oversee increased community engagement," said Chief O'Dea. "I discussed this priority when I was named Chief in October; it is vital that we increase our efforts in regard to community engagement. We must continue to build community relationships and trust. The value of these relationships is unmeasurable and critical as we move forward."

Adding a fourth branch will not cost any additional money and is fully supported by the staffing study that will be forthcoming in the first part of the year.

"Just as we moved ahead with Department of Justice (DOJ) recommendations prior to the settlement agreement being finalized, it's important that we adopt this reorganization that the staffing study will be recommending," said Chief O'Dea. "I can tell you from first-hand knowledge the workload in both the Operations Branch and the Services Branch is very heavy and doesn't allow for the necessary time to tackle additional initiatives such as community engagement."

Other changes include: The DOJ responsibilities and the new Equity/Diversity Manager will be direct reports to Chief O'Dea. The Information Technology Division will move from the Services Branch to the Investigations Branch.

Chief O'Dea also announced personnel assignments for the senior leadership team.

"I made these decisions after thoughtful consideration, and they were based on these individuals' ability to engage the community," Chief O'Dea said.

Source: http://www.portlandoregon.gov/mayor/article/435908

A revised organization chart appears in Figure 5.2. Compare and contrast Figure 5.1 (before) and Figure 5.2 (after). Does this appear to be a substantial change? Do you expect the department will operate very differently now? How so? What are your thoughts about placing the Tactical Operations Division under the Community Services branch? What about the other organizational changes made by the Chief?

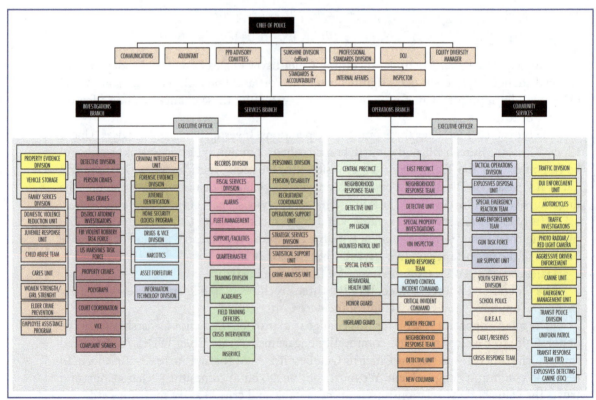

Figure 5.2 Police Bureau Organization Chart

ORGANIZATIONAL MISSION AND MISSION STATEMENT

Many police departments orient their operations around a **mission statement**: a clear statement of the organization's purpose, often including organizational goals and priorities and sometimes expressing organizational values, but ideally providing employees with a sense of direction about their work. The idea of a mission statement is that everything the employees of an organization are doing should in some way support the mission of the organization. If employees are doing something that doesn't support the mission, then one might rightly ask, "Why are you (we) doing that?" Consider the mission statement of the Seattle Police Department (SPD) as one example (Seattle Police Department Manual, 6/1/2015 revision): http://www.seattle.gov/police-manual/general-policy-information/mission-statement-and-priorities

Simple on the surface, but if you read the SPD mission statement a few more times and really think about it, this is actually a very complex mission. You can see below the Mission Statement that the SPD department manual helpfully elaborates with six bulleted explanations each point of the mission statement.

Departments may also use mission statements in order to articulate their overall approach to law enforcement. According to the latest available government data, more than two-thirds (68%) of local police departments in 2013, employing about 9 out of every 10 officers in the United States, had a mission statement that included a community policing component of some type (Reaves, 2015). We will discuss community policing in greater detail in Chapter 10, but this is an example of how a department can try to express the department's orientation toward public safety for both the public and their employees.

Here are a few other examples of police department mission statements; we have chosen some from the very largest police departments in the country, as well as from medium and smaller departments to give you a sense of variation. Read through these and see what kinds of themes you pick up:

Police departments often orient their operations around a mission statement.

© marekuliasz/Shutterstock.com

New York City Police Department
http://www.nyc.gov/html/nypd/html/administration/mission.shtml

Los Angeles Police Department
http://www.lapdonline.org/inside_the_lapd/content_basic_view/844

Chicago Police Department
http://www.cityofchicago.org/city/en/depts/cpd/auto_generated/cpd_mission.html

Mesquite [Texas] Police Department
https://www.cityofmesquite.com/442/Police

Beaver Police Department [Ohio]
http://beavertwp-oh.gov/police.htm

South Beaver [Pennsylvania] Police Department
http://www.southbeavertwp.com/#!police/c16v

When you consider some of the goals expressed in these mission statements, you can see goals that are broad and vague, goals that are narrow and well-defined, as well as ideas that might seem unrelated to your conception of what police "do." You might also be getting some sense of overall complexity in our understanding of the mission of a police department. Consider the goals of "enhancing" or "improving" the "quality of life" in a city, and contrast this with "enforcing the law" which is something that all police departments do regardless of whether they formally acknowledge it in a mission statement. Do you think we can tell something about a police department by reading their mission statement? What if they don't have one? Or, what if it's poorly written? Do you think that the mission statement really matters? Or does it depend on characteristics such as the size of the jurisdiction and organization? Are there any "essential" elements that you believe should be incorporated into a department's mission statement?

CHALLENGE YOURSELF: DRAFT A MISSION STATEMENT

Try drafting a mission statement for a hypothetical police department. You might use your local police department or sheriff's office as a model agency for your hypothetical police department, but don't research their mission statement before starting this challenge. Exchange drafts with a fellow student and cross-critique your mission statements. What similarities are there, and what major differences did you find?

BUREAUCRACY AND ORGANIZATIONAL STRUCTURE

An organizational chart and a mission statement are helpful, but are certainly not sufficient means to achieve organizational goals. If only it were that simple! In reality, the organizational chart is a rather superficial reflection of the underlying structure and functions of a police department. Sociologist Max Weber (1946) described the ideal features of bureaucracy in terms of economic rationality and efficiency, which enabled long-term and large-scale planning and subsequent economic growth and progress. But he also noted that while the goals of capitalism are well served by bureaucracy, with increasing bureaucratization comes increasing depersonalization—

© Joseph Sohm/Shutterstock.com

Enforcing the law in a city with a population of millions is a very different job than it is in a city with a few thousand residents.

less recognition of individual difference and tailoring to specific cases, more standardization of response and treatment of the average or typical case. Classic Weberian bureaucracies are characterized by **specialization** and *division of labor* meaning that employees train in and specialize in a particular type of work or area of focus, and are organized into work units based upon those specialized skills; a **hierarchy of authority**, meaning that the organization is characterized by the vertically higher-level supervision of lower-level employees; *explicit written rules* made at higher levels that govern decision-making at lower levels and ensure consistency throughout the organization; *impersonality*, meaning that the rules are followed and equally applied without exception for individual cases or circumstances; and *formal selection*, meaning that employment as well as advancement within the organization is based upon competence and technical qualifications.

The size and structure of an organization is generally related to the volume and diversity of tasks and services they must perform or provide. Enforcing the law in a city of 8 million residents is a very different task than enforcing the law in a township of several thousand residents. As organizations get larger in size, there is increasing specialization and division of labor, requiring a larger supervisory structure. Blau (1970) classically described organizational structures in terms of four types of structural differentiation, which describe how labor is subdivided as organizations grow in size: spatial, occupational, functional, and hierarchical. **Spatial differentiation** refers to the extent to which the organization's territorial coverage is divided up into localized units—think of a centralized headquarters facility, and localized branch or division offices, much like a local bank. Clients probably would not want to travel a great distance in order to do their banking at a single, unified headquarters building; this would present great inefficiency for both the client and the service provider (of course today, much banking is done online). Instead, labor is subdivided in order to facilitate banking services in particular local areas through a system of bank branches. In general, the larger the organization, the greater the degree of spatial differentiation one will find in the organization's structure. Consider the NYPD, the largest police department in the United States, with approximately 35,000 officers serving a population of about 8.4 million persons. The NYPD has its famous headquarters building, One Police Plaza, located in lower Manhattan, as well as 76 (yes, seventy-six!) police precincts spread out across the boroughs of New York City (with new additional precinct facilities underway at the time of writing). Would residents living in outlying boroughs want to travel to a hypothetical single headquarters building in lower Manhattan in order to report a crime? Would the police working there have extensive local knowledge of the issues being experienced in those outlying areas? Would it be an efficient means of organizing policing for the entire city? Of course not. Instead, the NYPD has a high degree (perhaps the highest degree) of spatial differentiation as compared with other police departments in the United States. Contrast this situation with a typical small-town police department which operates out of a single facility, likely shared with other city or governmental services, and may only have a single unified patrol area—a very low degree, or even the absence of, spatial differentiation.

Occupational differentiation describes the extent to which labor is subdivided among work tasks, some of which require very little specialized knowledge or skills, and those that require a higher degree of specialized knowledge or skills. In larger organizations, there tend to be more specialists (individuals who perform specific specialized tasks), as compared with generalists (individuals who perform a variety of tasks).

In larger police departments, there are more members who are specialists.

© a katz/Shutterstock.com

Many tasks within police departments are relatively nonspecialized and do not need to be performed by sworn officers (who have been extensively trained for law enforcement duties); these tasks can be performed more efficiently and effectively by civilian personnel. In addition, some highly specialized tasks can also be performed by civilian personnel having appropriate specialized knowledge and skills—crime analysis might be such an example.

In the largest police departments, one will find a very high degree of occupational differentiation with personnel situated in specific occupational positions; in smaller departments, personnel may wear many different "hats" as they fulfill a variety of tasks.

Functional differentiation describes the extent to which an organization has created subdivisions of specialized labor that are focused on a particular task. Here, labor is not only divided in terms of specialization, but it is also grouped by specialization in functional units. In larger organizations, there tends to be greater grouping of specialized labor. In the context of policing, some examples include the creation of such units as a homicide unit, crime scene investigation unit, or a crime analysis unit. Smaller agencies may still fulfill some of these tasks, but likely on a part-time or as needed basis by a designated officer or officers who have other duties. We review a variety of special functions and units later in this chapter.

Hierarchical differentiation refers to the levels of supervision in an organization. In general, the larger the organization, the greater the levels of supervision one will find in the organization's structure. In the context of police departments, this may be reflected in the rank structure of the department. As an example, a very rough sketch of the NYPD rank structure includes probationary police officer, police officer, detective (grades 3rd through 1st), sergeant, lieutenant, captain, deputy inspector, inspector, deputy chief, assistant chief, bureau chief, chief of department, deputy commissioner, first deputy commissioner, and police commissioner. The smallest police departments in the United States are one- or two-man shows, but more typical is a police chief with a few mid-level managers and several police officers working under them.

In addition to Blau's four forms of structural differentiation, Maguire (1997), writing in the specific context of police organizations, added the degree of **centralization**, formalization, and administration as core characteristics of police organizations. The degree of *centralization* in a police organization includes both spatial centralization (which is similar to Blau's concept of spatial differentiation) and centralization of authority, which is a bit more elusive in terms of observation and measurement. Centralization of authority refers to decision-making authority (and therefore, discretion) exercised at different units and supervisory levels of the organization. *Formalization* refers to the extent to which formal rules govern decision-making within the organization, and is thus also related in some respects to discretion. An agency with a greater number of formal, written rules might be said to be more formalized than an agency with fewer formal rules. The share of resources devoted to *administration* is reflected in both vertical (supervisory) and horizontal (functional) administrative resources, and these help describe organizations as more or less "top heavy." Vertical administration is related to supervisory **span of control**, or the number of subordinates for which supervisors are responsible. A lower span of control tends to be associated with a more vertical organization, while a higher span of control tend to be associated with a flatter organization.

Historically, police organizations have tended to be very vertical, perhaps reflecting the traditionally **quasi-military** nature of police organizations—a hierarchical rank structure with a unified chain of command—as emphasized in Vollmer's classic *Police Administration*, as well as Parker's re-organization of the LAPD (see Chapter 3). This quasi-military structure and its remnants are largely a reflection of the professional era, but what happens as we move toward community policing, or toward intelligence-led policing, or other models of policing? For example, do organizational structures need to change in order to accommodate core principles associated with community policing?

COMMUNITY POLICING AND ORGANIZATIONAL CHANGE

Consider as an example the idea of community policing, something that shows up in more than two-thirds of local police department mission statements (Reaves, 2015). That is to say, about two out of every three departments considers some aspect of community policing as part of their overall mission. *Organizational transformation* is necessary to achieve true community policing, and this is what distinguishes agencies that operate some community policing programs from those wholly committed to the community policing philosophy. Transformation involves changing the way the agency is structured and managed as well as changing the way officers think about their job and duties. It emphasizes organizational structures that support the elements of community policing and encourages departments to use modern management practices to improve effectiveness and efficiency. It takes place in four areas—agency management, organizational structure, personnel, and information systems/technology.

The key to infusing community policing throughout the department is by restructuring agency management, in particular making changes to the agency's climate and culture, leadership, decision-making methods, labor relations, strategic planning, policies and procedures, personnel evaluations, and transparency. Specifically, community policing works best within a climate and culture that encourages proactive decision-making and activities, values problem solving and partnerships, and allows the informal networks and communication methods used to support this orientation to thrive. One example might be encouraging officers to make time during their patrol shift to engage residents in positive interactions to gather opinions, input, and intelligence. Community-oriented Policing (COP) agencies select leaders who actively champion the ideals of community policing and role model positive risk-taking and building collaborative relationships with diverse individuals and interest groups to support and expand community policing. It calls for decentralization in command structure and decision-making to allow frontline officers to take responsibility and create solutions for problems in their area. This requires flattening the hierarchal organizational structure, increasing the agency's tolerance for risk-taking during problem solving, providing officers sufficient authority to coordinate resources to solve identified problems, and allowing officers increased discretion in handling calls, and establishing relationships and partnerships. It also emboldens agency command staff to work with labor union leaders in instituting organizational changes so that officers throughout the department are likely to adopt the values and practices associated with community policing.

A written statement expressing a department-wide commitment to the community policing philosophy as well as a strategy that fits operational goals to available resources and capabilities is highly recommended for all practicing agencies. Department policies and procedures are expected to match community policing principles and promote problem solving and partnerships. Additionally, agencies truly committed to COP expand the police performance measures they collect to include things such as community satisfaction, improvement in quality of life, fear of crime, and trust in police. Finally, community policing requires agencies to be transparent—to share information about crime and disorder problems as well as department policies, decisions, and operations with the public. This is often accomplished through public meetings, social media, or the agency Web site.

Community policing also requires an organizational structure that supports decision-making and accountability by frontline patrol officers. This is typically achieved through the geographic assignment of patrol officers and supervisors to specific areas on a long-term/semipermanent basis. Assigning officers to the same neighborhood for an extended period of time allows them to increase positive contact with the public, develop strong relationships with community members, get to know the culture of the neighborhood, and provide a high level of customer service. Geographic policing, a key component of COP, involves agencies restructuring their patrol divisions around place, rather than time. Meaning that patrol officers are organized into "platoons" based on the *area* they work, rather than the *shift* they work. A supervisor oversees each platoon, coordinates communication, and delegates tasks between members of the platoon who work different shifts, and is responsible for everything that happens in that geographic area. This is quite different from the traditional time-based patrol system whereby the shift supervisor coordinates activities and is responsible for what happens only during his/her shift. While there will always be a need for a shift supervisor to address daily issues (such as developing and coordinating a tactical response plan to an unfolding incident), geographic policing provides more accountability and allows for better coordination of officers and resources on a long-term basis. Some agencies align their beat and geographic boundaries with recognized neighborhood borders. This is a smart strategy because it makes coordinating public-service activities with other government departments easier and encourages a shared governance model.

To address the wide range of issues that often arise, officers work collaboratively, in a team environment with other officers, community members and groups, and other government departments. While patrol officers are expected to be generalists, able to handle anything that comes their way, agencies must have some specialist units (such as drugs, gangs, or vice units, a homeless taskforce, or school resource officers) that can handle particularly complex problems or partnerships. It is also important that the law enforcement agency, and the jurisdiction, allocate proper financial and human resources to support community policing and sustain partnerships and problem-solving efforts.

Employing the right personnel is of paramount importance to ensure community policing is inculcated and practiced throughout an agency permanently. Therefore, agencies must recruit, hire, select, and retain staff (both sworn and non-sworn) who are committed to the ideals of community policing, as well as train, supervise, and evaluate them on community policing values. In order to do this, some agencies describe community policing and problem-solving expectations in job announcements, ask interview questions to assess applicants' community policing values and skills, and recruit team players with a "spirit of service" rather than a "spirit of adventure" (COPS, 2014). Agencies also incorporate community policing principles and activities into performance evaluations. For example, personnel evaluations include measures such as engagement in problem solving, positive citizen contacts initiated, and active partnerships with community members and organizations; not just the traditional measures of citations issued, arrests made, cases cleared, or perpetrators prosecuted. Promotional procedures in COP agencies prefer individuals with solid problem-solving skills, experience with proactive policing and community collaboration, and high citizen satisfaction ratings. Moreover, training in COP agencies happens at all levels and includes identifying and practicing the skills that complement community policing and problem solving; skills such as creative, critical, and analytical thinking, interpersonal communication and networking, and problem and resource identification.

Finally, agency information systems (aka technology) in COP agencies must be able to support officers' need for time-sensitive and accurate crime information to address community concerns as well as have the ability to share pertinent information with the public in a timely and easily-accessible manner. Community policing encourages agencies to track, analyze, and utilize data to identify community concerns and solve problems and departments use many of the sophisticated intelligence-led policing resources and strategies introduced in Chapter 8 to do so. Technology also has the ability to improve communication between the police and the public as well as increase transparency and police accountability to the public. Many community policing departments communicate and share information with the public via Twitter, Facebook,

Instagram, and other applications as well as through e-mail and the department Web site. Some even take incident reports and citizen complaints, and provide almost real-time crime statistics on their Web site.

SPECIAL FUNCTIONS AND UNITS

While patrol and investigations are the common core functions of any law enforcement organization, we deal with these areas later in Chapters 8 and 12, respectively. Here, we take a look at some of the special functions and units that may be found in local agencies to varying degrees. As noted earlier in the chapter, occupational and functional differentiation tend to be correlated with agency size; as such, the Bureau of Justice Statistics reports data on special units grouped for agencies having 100 or more officers (larger agencies) versus those with fewer than 100 officers (smaller agencies). As can be seen in Table 5.1, there are a variety of crime-related issues that are addressed by agencies to varying degrees, but also varying in terms of specialized units versus designated personnel who perform that particular function on a part-time or as needed basis. For example, almost all large agencies (90%) address child abuse, and most (61%) do so through a special unit with full-time personnel devoted to that issue. A much lower proportion of smaller agencies (39%) address child abuse, and most (29%) do so with designated personnel rather than a full-time unit.

Among larger agencies, crime-related issues addressed by designated personnel or special units by a majority of the agencies included child abuse (90%), gangs (83%), juvenile crime (82%), domestic violence (81%), cybercrime (76%), impaired driving (75%), and victim assistance (62%). Less common were designated personnel or special units to address human trafficking (42%) and bias/hate crime (38%). Smaller agencies were much less likely to address these issues with either designated personnel or special units.

In 2007, BJS conducted a special survey of law enforcement gang units in order to better understand the different types of problems handled by these units, the nature of their operations and personnel, and characteristics of agencies having gang units (Langton, 2010). In that year, there were 365 large agencies that had a gang unit, employing a median of 5 officers per unit. A sizeable proportion of these gang units were created relatively recently; about half were formed between 2000 and 2007, with 43 units created in 2006 alone, although the oldest active unit reported being formed in 1975 (see Figure 5.3). Common functions of these units included monitoring gang graffiti (94%), tracking individual gang members (93%), monitoring internet sites for communication among gang members (93%), directed patrols (91%), and undercover surveillance operations (87%). Gang units also commonly reported distributing gang prevention literature to schools, parents, and other community groups and members (74%). A little over half (56%) participated in other prevention activities including mentoring programs, social skills and leadership training,

TABLE 5.1 Personnel Designated to Address Crime-related Issues in Local Police Departments, by Size of Department, 2013

Problem or Task	Departments Employing 100 Officers or More			Departments Employing 99 Officers or Fewer		
	Total (%)	Personnel Assigned Full time to Special Unit (%)	Other Designated Personnel (%)	Total (%)	Personnel Assigned Full Time to Special Unit (%)	Other Designated Personnel (%)
Bias/hate crime	38	10	28	15	5	10
Child abuse	90	61	29	39	11	29
Cybercrime	76	39	36	26	6	20
Domestic violence	81	54	28	28	8	20
Gangs	83	55	28	20	6	14
Human trafficking	42	15	27	11	3	8
Impaired driving	75	39	36	32	9	23
Juvenile crime	82	59	23	34	11	23
Victim assistance	62	37	26	21	6	14

Source: Bureau of Justice Statistics, Law Enforcement Management and Administrative Statistics (LEMAS) Survey, 2013.

drug prevention groups, and self-esteem building programs; nearly half took part in gang prevention activities with gang-involved youth or joined with faith-based organizations in gang prevention programs; and a third of the units had officers who taught prevention programs, such as the Gang Resistance Education And Training (G.R.E.A.T.) program. Interestingly, about 30% of these gang units examined a prospective officer's financial and credit history before allowing the officer to serve in the unit, suggesting that agencies recognize the large amounts of cash associated with gang activity (particularly those gangs involved in drug and/or weapons trafficking) and see officers with poorer financial backgrounds as potential risks.

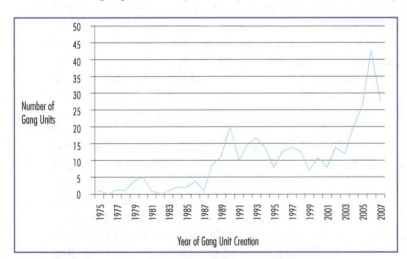

Figure 5.3. Number of specialized gang units established per year in large law enforcement agencies that had 100 or more sworn officers, 1975–2007 (Adapted from Langton, 2010)

TABLE 5.2 — Personnel Designated to Perform Special Operational Tasks in Local Police Departments, by Size of Department, 2013

Problem or Task	Departments Employing 100 Officers or More			Departments Employing 99 Officers or Fewer		
	Total (%)	Personnel Assigned Full time to Special Unit (%)	Other Designated Personnel (%)	Total (%)	Personnel Assigned Full Time to Special Unit (%)	Other Designated Personnel (%)
Bomb/explosive disposal	41	15	26	6	2	4
Fugitives/ warrants	68	41	27	24	7	17
Re-entry surveillance	21	7	14	8	2	6
Tactical operations (e.g., SWAT)	95	30	65	31	5	26
Terrorism/ homeland security	71	33	37	16	4	12

Source: Bureau of Justice Statistics, Law Enforcement Management and Administrative Statistics (LEMAS) Survey, 2013.

In addition to crime-related issues, police departments also have designated personnel and/or special units to handle a variety of special operational tasks. Even among larger departments, these operational tasks are more likely to be handled by designated personnel on a part-time or as needed basis rather than by full-time units. As can be seen in Table 5.2, almost all (95%) large police departments have a tactical operations function, but even among large departments only 30% have a full-time tactical operations unit. Also common among large departments are designated personnel and/or special units to handle terrorism/homeland security issues (71%) and fugitives/warrants service (68%). Less common are explosives disposal (41%) and re-entry surveillance (i.e., monitoring of individuals released from incarceration) (21%).

Aircraft are considered an important part of modern law enforcement services, though their presence in law enforcement actually dates back to the New York City Police Department's use of a fixed-wing aircraft as early as 1919. If for no other reason, aircraft are highly valued for their ability to provide an "eye in the sky"—a much better perspective on dynamic events such as foot and vehicle pursuits, crime scenes, and other situations where surveillance may be beneficial. These units may also assist with firefighting, search and rescue, and emergency medical response. They play an important role in

Police aircraft provide an "eye in the sky" during situations where surveillance is beneficial.

monitoring critical infrastructure such as power lines, pipelines, and reservoirs. A BJS study of police aviation units in large agencies (those having 100 or more officers) found about one in five large agencies in 2007 had such a unit. There were a total of 201 aviation units, operating almost 900 aircraft (about 600 helicopters and about 300 fixed-wing aircraft) in 46 states and the District of Columbia (Langton, 2009). Although many such aircraft are acquired through government surplus, cost is definitely a consideration with substantial annual costs related to maintenance, fuel, recurrent training, and so on. The majority of these units require pilots to be sworn law enforcement officers and/or have a minimum number of years of law enforcement experience.

MULTI-JURISDICTIONAL TASK FORCES (MJTFS)

Multi-jurisdictional task forces (MJTFs) are an efficient way to pool agency resources to both provide a service to several agencies that could not otherwise be provided by any single agency, as well as to address crime and public safety issues that are multi-jurisdictional in nature (such as gangs, drugs, human trafficking, and other regional issues). For example, a small agency likely cannot devote an officer full-time to address gang problems, but by contributing officer time to a MJTF that addresses gang issues, they leverage the resources of several agencies to address that problem. Regardless of agency size, MJTFs arguably enhance inter-agency communication and the sharing of intelligence among the participating agencies in order to more effectively address the problem with a unified, regional approach. In the absence of such coordination, agencies may inadvertently step on each other's toes with conflicted investigations and field operations. MJTFs may also, and often do, include agencies from different levels of government such as local, state, and federal law enforcement. As of 2013, about half (49%) of all local police departments in the United States participated in an MJTF focused on drugs, including almost a third of agencies serving the smallest jurisdictions (Table 5.3). Less common, except among agencies serving larger jurisdictions, was participation in MJTF's focused on gangs (13%) and human trafficking (4%).

TABLE 5.3 Task Force Participation by Local Police Departments, by Size of Population Served, 2013			
Population Served	**Drugs (%)**	**Gangs (%)**	**Human Trafficking (%)**
All sizes	49	13	4
1,000,000 or more	100	92	85
500,000–999,999	93	76	66
250,000–499,999	96	72	57
100,000–249,999	89	56	22
50,000–99,999	84	42	14
25,000–49,999	79	32	7
10,000–24,999	68	21	7
2,500–9,999	47	9	3
2,499 or fewer	31	3	—

—Less than 0.5%.

Source: Bureau of Justice Statistics, Law Enforcement Management and Administrative Statistics (LEMAS) Survey, 2013.

POLICE PARAMILITARY UNITS

Police paramilitary units (PPUs), such as **SWAT (Special Weapons and Tactics)** teams, are often featured in Hollywood movies. They make for great drama, but they are increasingly being used in real life by departments both large and small. Although the situations they are designed for (extremely serious or life-threatening events such as bank robberies, hostage situations, barricaded suspects, civil riots, and acts of terrorism) are very rare, departments are increasingly using these special units for more routine circumstances.

What, exactly, is a SWAT team? It is a heavily-armed unit within a police department, composed of specially-trained sworn officers, which responds to high-stakes incidents. These units have an array of military-grade equipment and are modeled after the special operations teams found in the branches of the military (for example, Navy Seals and Army Rangers). The officers wear battle dress uniforms (BDU's), Kevlar helmets, full body armor, and carry automatic weapons.

Philadelphia, PA created the first SWAT team in the country in 1964 in response to an increase in bank robberies (Dempsy & Forst, 2012). Since then the number of SWAT teams has grown tremendously. In the early 1970s, fewer than 10% of departments serving populations of 50,000 or greater had a PPU (see Figure 5.4). By 1995, that number had increased to 89% (Kraska & Kappeler, 1997). Additionally, 65% of departments serving 25,000-50,000 residents had a PPU by 1995 (Kraska, 2001). By 2013, 95% of departments with 100 or more officers had designated personnel serving on a PPU (Reaves, 2015).

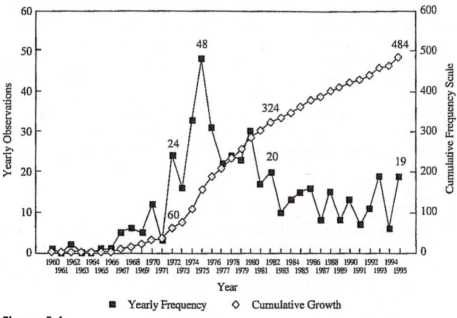

Figure 5.4

Just as the number of units grew during the 1980s and 1990s, so too did the average number of call-outs. In the early 1980s, the typical unit averaged just over one call-out per month (13–18 per year). By 1995, the typical PPU averaged about 7 call-outs per month; 75.9% of these were for "high risk warrant work" (often drug raids), not "barricaded suspects" (which accounted for 13.4% of call-outs), "hostage situations" (3.4% of call-outs), "civil disturbances" (1.3% of call-outs), or "terrorist activity" (0.09% of call-outs) (Kraska & Kappeler, 1997). In addition to call-outs, 20% of units also conducted pro-active patrol in urban neighborhoods in 1995 (Kraska & Kappeler, 1997). Keep in mind that 1995 was the height of the drug war in the United States and that PPU deployments may, or may not, look different today.

Still, the increase in paramilitary units and the activities they are used for indicate a militarization of policing in the United States. This militarization, which is juxtaposed against community policing, is supported by the Federal Government's 10-33 program, which shares surplus military equipment with American police forces. It is a double-edged sword: on the one hand, free equipment is good for taxpayers and the technology developed for military purposes has benefitted law enforcement (and the general public). On the other hand, military weapons and machinery put residents on edge and exacerbate emotional situations which strain the relationship between the police and the public. When deciding whether, when, and how to deploy a police paramilitary unit, law enforcement agencies should be cognizant of the negative effect that paramilitary units have on the citizenry and balance that with the need for power and force to protect the public and resolve a dangerous situation with minimal loss of life or property.

CONCLUSION

In this chapter, we explored variation in the goals and structures of local law enforcement agencies by looking at mission statements and organization charts, as well as the general characteristics of bureaucracies and organizational structure. We also looked at organizations through the lens of community policing and explored what types of organizational changes might be necessary in order to achieve true community policing. Finally, we looked at some of the special functions and units found in local law enforcement agencies to varying degrees, as well as multi-jurisdictional task forces. Just as there is extreme variation in the number, size, and types of agencies in the United States, when we look closely at local agencies we find just as much variation in the underlying organizational structures. Hopefully, the relationships between the size of an organization, the volume and diversity of tasks and services performed or provided, degree of specialization and division of labor, and resulting organizational structure have become clearer.

REVIEW QUESTIONS

1. Given the nature and scope of the law enforcement industry (as discussed in Chapter 4) and the basics of organizational structure from this chapter, do you think that true "economies of scale" could be achieved by consolidating smaller agencies? What types of organizational benefits do you see for consolidation, if any? What are some negative aspects of consolidation?

2. Research mission statements and organizational charts by looking at official agency Web sites. Can you find any examples of departments whose activities don't seem to align with their stated missions? How about the imagery on these Web sites? Does the imagery presented by these agencies match with their stated mission?

GLOSSARY

Centralization includes spatial centralization, but also refers to centralization of decision-making authority (and therefore, discretion) exercised at different units and supervisory levels of the organization.

Division of labor the idea that employees are organized into work units based upon specialized skills.

Functional differentiation describes the extent to which an organization has created subdivisions of specialized labor that are focused on a particular task.

Hierarchical differentiation refers to the levels of supervision in an organization.

Hierarchy of authority the idea that an organization is characterized by the vertically higher-level supervision of lower-level employees.

Multi-jurisdictional task force an efficient way to pool agency resources to both provide a service to several agencies that could not otherwise be provided by any single agency, as well as to address crime and public safety issues that are multi-jurisdictional in nature (such as gangs, drugs, human trafficking, and other regional issues).

Occupational differentiation describes the extent to which labor is subdivided among work tasks, some of which require very little specialized knowledge or skills, and those that require a higher degree of specialized knowledge or skills.

Police paramilitary unit a dedicated unit originally formed to deal with dangerous confrontations, but increasingly used in everyday policing. Also known as SWAT. (KH)

Quasi-military organization refers to a military-like structure; a hierarchical rank structure with a unified chain of command.

Span of control the number of subordinates a supervisor can effectively supervise.

Spatial differentiation refers to the extent to which the organization's territorial coverage is divided up into localized units.

Specialization the idea that employees train in and specialize in a particular type of work or area of focus.

Special Weapons and Tactics team (SWAT) a paramilitary policing unit originally formed to deal with dangerous confrontations, but increasingly used in everyday policing. (KH)

REFERENCES

Blau, P. (1970). A formal theory of differentiation in organizations. *American Sociological Review*, 35, 201–218.

Langton, L. (2009). *Aviation units in large law enforcement agencies*. Washington, DC: Bureau of Justice Statistics.

Langton, L. (2010). *Gang units in large local law enforcement agencies, 2007*. Washington, DC: Bureau of Justice Statistics.

Maguire, E. (1997). Structural change in large municipal police organizations during the community policing era. *Justice Quarterly*, 14, 547–576.

Reaves, B. (2015). *Local Police Departments, 2013: Personnel, policies, and practices.* Washington, DC: Bureau of Justice Statistics.

Seattle Police Department Manual, 6/1/2015 Revision. Retrieved from http://www.seattle.gov/police-manual.

Weber, M. (1946). *Essays in sociology.* New York, NY: Oxford University Press.

6 POLICE OFFICERS: HIRING AND TRAINING GUARDIANS

LEARNING OBJECTIVES

After reading this chapter, students should be able to:

1 Describe which personal qualities and characteristics make good officers.

2 Explain why hiring diverse officers is important for police-community relations.

3 Define police subculture and explain how it impacts officers and the profession.

4 Describe the state of education in policing.

5 List the sources of occupational stress in policing.

KEY TERMS

Police cynicism

Peace Officer Standards and Training

Police subculture

Symbolic assailants

Occupational stress

Successful democratic policing requires additional attention to the recruitment, selection, and training process. The need is for diverse men and women who can deal effectively with the realities of the job as a guardian of democracy rather than as a warrior in some kind of "war" on crime. This means recruiting individuals who are smart, reasoned, and service-oriented. The selection of the right individuals, combined with the proper training and enculturation process can be the difference between a department that garners a high degree of public trust and legitimacy, and one that lacks public confidence and spends a lot of time defending itself and its officers against allegations of impropriety and abuse of power.

In the review questions for the previous chapter, we asked you to take a look at official agency Web sites, in part to see whether the imagery presented by these agencies matched their stated missions. If you took up this challenge, your textbook authors are willing to bet that you saw some pretty interesting things as you surfed around—everything ranging from departments with elaborately produced recruitment videos that highlight SWAT team members being inserted by helicopters and "pie-ing" the entryway of a building with laser-sighted automatic weapons, to departments using the images of smiling actors in police uniforms posing on a city sidewalk with diverse and happy members of some fictitious community. Reality lies somewhere between these extremes. Do you think that this kind of imagery has any relationship to the pool of potential recruits that a department tends to attract, the subsequent quality of enforcement, and/or the legitimacy of the police in the eyes of the public?

In this chapter, we explore the recruitment, selection, and training process. We also look at the personal qualities and characteristics that make good officers, why the hiring of diverse and educated officers is important, and how diversity and education have impacted policing. In addition, we examine how officers change between recruitment and retirement and look at the impact that occupational stress has on officers and their families.

THE JOB OF POLICE OFFICER: FACT VERSUS FICTION

A time-persistent "problem" for the police has been dealing with the myth of the crime fighter—the idea that the police are first and foremost crime fighters who, were it not for their constant vigilance, prevent society from rapidly devolving into a chaotic world ruled by crafty, murderous criminals. The police are the "thin blue line" between order and chaos. These crime fighter police spend their entire shifts spotting crimes in progress, chasing and arresting criminals, as well as stopping crimes before they actually occur. All other activities are incidental. If they stop for lunch, they will drop their sandwich and coffee on the ground as soon as a call comes over the radio so they can get back into the fray. They do not have lives outside of their crime fighting role and their only off-duty activity is sleeping in preparation for another day of crime fighting. The lines between patrol officer and detective are blurred; forensic evidence of some type is utilized in every situation, but is still no match for physical crime fighting in the form of dramatic foot or car chases, gun play, and danger at every turn.

We put "problem" in quotes because at various times this crime fighter image has actually been quite useful for the police. For example, the crime fighter image serves the police quite well when they need to argue for additional resources. Recall also from the chapters on police history that there was a time that the police actively sought to portray themselves as crime fighters in order to help burnish their public image as detached, professional law enforcers. The police and popular media have occasionally managed to align their interests, with the police department seeing a public relations benefit and the media seeking increased viewership (and/or readership). The old television show, *Dragnet*, popular in the 1950s and again in the late 1960s, is a classic example of such cooperation.

Who doesn't like a good television police drama? The fact that there are so many police dramas being supplied by television producers tells you that there is a substantial public demand for them. *Hawaii Five-O, Hill Street Blues, NYPD Blue, COPS, Law and Order, CSI, The Wire*, just to name a few. Some of these shows are more realistic than others, but certainly all of them must emphasize the dramatic aspects of policing. Who would want to watch police officers fill out paperwork for an hour (or 2 hours, split into two exciting episodes)? Would it be any more interesting if in the second episode you got to see them standing around, talking to some people on the street? Maybe seeing them negotiate with and ultimately assist a mentally ill, homeless person to find a safer place to sleep and then connect them with available services? How about watching them clean the vomit out of the back of their patrol car after transporting an intoxicated person to the precinct?

The reality is that most of what the police do all day is not "crime fighting," but more of the order maintenance and service functions that will be discussed in detail in Chapter 8. As such, while it is certainly important that potential recruits be suited for, and trained and equipped to handle potentially violent situations, make arrests, and "catch bad guys," it is arguably more important that they be suited for, and trained and equipped for *service*. The more a potential recruit understands about the reality of policing, the more likely they are to successfully self-select into the profession. When there is a substantial disconnect between the image and the reality of policing, the potential exists for an unsuccessful recruitment and training process, as well as subsequent poor performance and negative behavior on the street. But the burden does not fall entirely on the potential recruit; much of the burden falls on the police themselves who bear some responsibility for "truth in advertising" in their recruitment process, as well as in the design of academy training.

In his classic study of **police cynicism**, Arthur Niederhoffer (1967) sought to explain why some officers "go wrong" during the course of their careers, especially in light of the increased standards for selection, better training, and high performance standards that came with the police professionalism movement. He proposed what is essentially a strain theory to explain the generation of cynical attitudes among police officers: police officers experience frustration and disillusionment when faced with this disconnect between the "ideal" expectations they pick up in the academy and the "reality" of police work on the street

While police officers perform a variety of duties, their ability to provide service is possibly most important.

(where they are told to forget the academy and rapidly learn how policing is really "done"), which generates cynicism and, without return to professional commitment, eventual apathy and alienation, or anomie. He argued that this process occurs over the course of officer careers, beginning with the contrast between academy training and initial field experience, and later as an effect of continued exposure to a police administration perceived as out of touch with street-level policing, the perceived failures of the criminal justice system, as well as contagion effects from other cynical officers (Neiderhoffer, 1967). In its worst form, an advanced stage of "aggressive cynicism" may develop; this is marked by overt hostility toward the sources of frustration and rejection of the goals or objectives that cannot be attained. Cynical attitudes will manifest in problem behavior as officers "act out" their frustrations in the course of their daily interactions with citizens and other officers (Niederhofffer, 1967). This cynicism, along with other ramifications of the selection process and the disjuncture between the myth and the reality of the job, help explain the existence and perpetuation of a distinctive police subculture—an issue that is discussed later in this chapter.

PATROL OFFICER JOB DESCRIPTION

Individuals are often drawn to police work because of the variability of the job. This variety makes the job of patrol officer very difficult to conceptualize and describe, more so than possibly any other occupation. Baehr and colleagues (1968) conducted comprehensive field observations and developed a behavioral analysis of a patrol officer's job and a list of the most important attributes required for success in the field. Although the behavioral analysis is more than 40 years old, it is still applicable today.

1. Endure long periods of monotony in routine patrol, yet react quickly and effectively to problem situations observed on the street or to instructions issued by the dispatcher.

2. Know the assigned patrol area, not only its physical characteristics but also of its normal routine events and behavior patterns of its residents.

3. Exhibit initiative, problem-solving capacity, effective judgment, and imagination in coping with the many complex situations he or she is called to face, such as a family disturbance, a potential suicide, a robbery in progress, an accident, or a disaster.

4. Make prompt and effective decisions, sometimes in life-and-death situations, and be able to size up a situation quickly and take appropriate action.

5. Demonstrate mature judgment, as in deciding whether an arrest is warranted by the circumstances or when facing a situation in which the use of force may be needed.

6. Demonstrate critical awareness in discerning signs of out-of-the-ordinary conditions or circumstances that indicate trouble or a crime in progress.

7. Exhibit a number of complex psychomotor skills, such as driving a vehicle in emergency situations, firing a weapon accurately under extremely varied conditions, maintaining agility, endurance, and strength; and showing competence in self-defense and apprehension.

8. Perform the communication and record-keeping functions of the job, including oral reports, formal case reports, and departmental and court forms.

9. Endure verbal and physical abuse from citizens and offenders while using only necessary force in the performance of his or her job.

10. Exhibit a self-assured professional presence and a self-confident manner when dealing with offenders, the public, and the courts.

11. Be capable of restoring equilibrium to social groups (e.g., when restoring order in a family fight, in a disagreement between neighbors, or in a clash between rival gangs).

12. Tolerate stress in a multitude of forms, such as meeting the violent behavior of a mob, coping with the pressure of a high speed chase or a weapon being fired, or assisting a woman bearing a child.

13. Maintain objectivity while dealing with a host of special-interest groups, ranging from relatives of offenders to members of the press.

14. Maintain a balanced perspective in the face of constant exposure to the worst side of human nature.

15. Exhibit a high level of personal integrity and ethical conduct.

Adapted from Baehr, M.E., Furcon, J.E., & Froemel, E.C. (1968). *Psychological assessment of patrolman qualifications in relation to field performance*. Department of Justice, pp. 11.3–11.5. Washington DC: U.S. Government Printing Office.

THE IMPORTANCE OF RECRUITMENT AND SELECTION

Law enforcement officers should have the wisdom of Solomon, the courage of David, the patience of Job, and the leadership of Moses, the kindness of the Good Samaritan, the diplomacy of Lincoln, the tolerance of the Carpenter of Nazareth, and finally, an intimate knowledge of every branch of the natural, biological, and social sciences.

—August Vollmer

In the opening chapter of this textbook, we introduced the idea of democratic policing and highlighted some innovative training going on at the centralized training academy in Washington State. This shift in their training model seeks to emphasize core democratic values and transition the police culture away from the warrior mentality (i.e., police as urban warriors equipped and trained for battle) and toward the idea of police officers as protectors and guardians of democracy (i.e., police as community guardians with a strong focus on procedural justice) (Rahr & Rice, 2015). As this guardian model of policing continues to accumulate national support, what kinds of characteristics are police leaders seeking in police recruits? Consistent with the broader emphasis on procedural justice, police leaders tend to emphasize critical thinking and independent decision-making skills, as well as the ability to socially engage with humans in a respectful manner, and to be effective at de-escalating conflict.

Critical thinking refers to the ability to objectively analyze a particular issue and independently form a conclusion or judgment about the issue. It is best thought of as a general way of thinking, not as a tool that can be applied to solve particular problems. Your professors are probably somewhat obsessed with critical thinking, since we are often evaluated on our ability to stimulate critical thinking in the classroom. We tend to approach critical thinking by encouraging students not to take things at face value; not to presume that something is so, simply because someone has said so or because it appears in a book; to dig deeper, try to free yourself from any preconceptions, do your own research, and come to an informed decision on your own. This is important in policing for a number of reasons. While police culture tends to emphasize adherence to policy and procedure, most would agree that memorizing the policies and procedures manual and attempting to follow it to the letter and apply it in every situation is a recipe for disaster. We need officers who can think on their feet and are comfortable with the exercise of discretion in unique and dynamic environments; if we wanted strict application of the policies and procedures manual, we could replace the officer with a robot—there would be no need for a reasoning human. In addition, officers who are good critical thinkers are open minded and empathetic, and as such they actively seek out different perspectives, different sources of information, and creative approaches to problems. When faced with a problem, good critical thinkers aren't looking for the "easy" answer, nor are they necessarily looking for the "right" answer—they seek the "best" decision given the information that is available to them.

Officers who are good critical thinkers are able to creatively approach problems.

Good critical thinking is essential to the guardian model of policing because of the increased importance placed on officer discretion, as well as the increased amount of discretion, necessary to fulfill the focus on procedural justice. Ultimately, the behavior of the police and the legitimacy of the police as an institution in the eyes of the public will be contingent on the perception of fundamental fairness in their use of coercive authority. As noted in Chapter 1, the intelligent use of coercion is the key; we need to ensure that the police are adequately trained to intelligently exercise discretion in their use of coercion, and seek to minimize unnecessary physical coercion. In addition to improved interactions with the public, as well as improvements in perceived legitimacy, there is also a benefit to officers in terms of increased safety. As Rahr and Rice (2015:5) note,

> … much recruit training focuses on physical control tactics and weapons, with less attention given to communication and de-escalation skills. The reasoning for this approach is the sacred mantra of officer safety. We train relentlessly—as we should—in physical tactics for the high-risk, low-frequency attacks. Less instructional attention is focused on human behavioral science. Yet seasoned cops and statistics tell us that the officer's intellect and social dexterity are often the most effective officer safety tools. For the sake of safety, voluntary compliance should be the primary goal in resolving conflict, with physical control reserved for those who present an immediate threat and cannot be managed any other way.

THE RECRUITMENT AND SELECTION PROCESS

Law enforcement agencies invest a considerable amount of time, money, and effort in selecting and hiring the highest quality candidates possible. The process to become a police officer is more extensive than almost every other job out there. There are stringent age, physical, and medical requirements as well as a battery of tests that reveal an applicant's suitability for the job and which may predict the applicant's likelihood of success.

ELIGIBILITY REQUIREMENTS

Because of the physically demanding nature of the job, police departments are generally looking for physically fit candidates between the ages of 21 and 38. Although there is not usually a stipulated maximum age, the minimum age is usually between 19 and 21 (depending on the state and the agency). Even though someone may meet the minimum age requirement, that is often not enough. Law enforcement agencies are looking for mature individuals with life experience, something than many candidates in their early twenties lack.

Beyond age, recruits must have good vision which is defined by each agency and is sometimes stipulated by the state Peace Officer Standards and Training office (POST). Departments also require candidates to meet minimum physical fitness standards which usually, though not always, involves meeting a specified height/weight ratio (or Body Mass Index), passing a medical test, and/or passing a physical agility test. Some departments require recruits to possess a 2-year or 4-year college degree but these are the exception rather than the rule. Most agencies only require candidates to have a high school diploma or equivalent (more on this). Finally, some departments have residency requirements which means that officers must reside in a specified geographical area for a defined period of time (possibly, the person's entire career); some departments extend this rule to recruits and only accept applications from individuals who live within the specified boundary.

TESTING AND SCREENING

The selection process also involves multiple stages of testing and screening, which serve as a weeding out process so that only the most mentally stable, morally upright, and qualified candidates become officers. In addition to a personal interview, criminal records check, drug test, and driving history check, which almost every recruit in America must pass, many recruits are also subjected to a psychological evaluation, a written aptitude test, and/or a drug test. Credit history checks and personality inventories are also common. Surprisingly, only about a quarter of agencies require candidates to pass a polygraph exam (Burch, 2012; Reaves, 2010). Each of these screening devices gives the agency unique information about the candidate. For example, the driving history check tells the department whether the applicant is a safe driver who can be trusted with agency equipment (multiple tickets

There are a variety of tests that an applicant must undergo to determine whether that person will be suitable for the job of police officer.

can indicate an unsafe and immature driver who places others' lives at risk unnecessarily and could be a liability for the department). The credit history check, on the other hand, tells the agency how well the applicant manages her money—whether she lives within her means and pays her debts. This not only provides information about the applicant's character but also indicates whether she might be tempted to steal evidence or take bribes on the job. The larger the agency, the more likely it utilizes most or all of these screening devices. Figure 6.1 shows which screening tools are most popular in the United States.

Other than the physical agility test and written aptitude test which are performed prior to any personal interview, the other tests are generally conducted as part of the background investigation process which happens after the agency has decided they are interested in hiring the applicant. These specialty tests are designed to predict whether a candidate will become a successful officer or whether they are likely to fail out of the grueling training program or become a liability for the department. Intelligence tests, in particular, are controversial because minority candidates tend to score more poorly than white candidates and there is much debate about whether or not they actually identify better qualified candidates. Even though many question the utility of personality tests and criticize their high false positive rate, the strongest predictor of job performance has been found to be the California Personality Inventory test.

Another important part of the process is the personal interview. These interviews are often panel interviews in which two to four officers of varying ranks question the job candidate. The point of the interview is to assess applicant qualities that are not easily evaluated through other means, such as an applicant's poise and demeanor, self-confidence, and interpersonal skills. Interviewers also assess a candidate's ability to communicate and think in a high-pressure environment, and whether he/she is easily provoked to anger. It is common for candidates to be given scenarios and asked how they would respond to the situation. Whether an interview is indicative of future job performance is up for discussion but interviews do help agencies determine which qualified candidates are good fits for the department.

The final stage of the process, the background investigation, happens after agency representatives have decided they want to hire a candidate. It involves an extremely thorough search into a

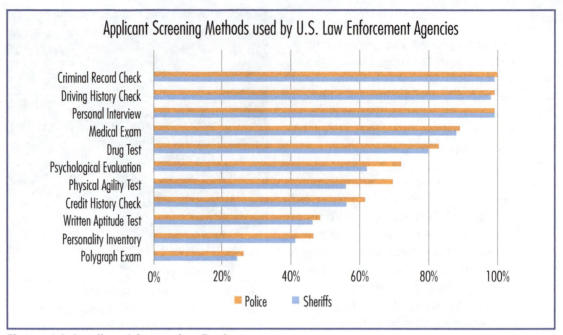

Figure 6.1 Applicant Screening Tools
Adapted from Reaves, B. (2010, December). *Local police departments, 2007.* Bureau of Justice Statistics, p. 35–36. Washington DC: U.S. Government Printing Office. And Burch, A.M. (2012, December). *Sheriffs' offices, 2007-Statistical tables.* Bureau of Justice Statistics, p. 8–9. Washington DC: U.S. Government Printing Office.

candidate's background to assess their character. Family members, past and present roommates and friends, current and previous employers, military colleagues and supervisors, and sometimes even instructors are contacted to verify the candidate's reputation, level of maturity, and integrity. This is the final check of trustworthiness and it takes months to complete.

TRAINING NEW RECRUITS

The Bureau of Justice Statistics conducted its first national study of law enforcement training academies in 2002, and updated the study in 2006 (Hickman, 2005; Reaves, 2009). The landscape of law enforcement training, much like the landscape of law enforcement in general, reflects the history and tradition of State's rights and local control. As such, law enforcement training across the states is done a little bit differently, depending on where you live. While there are no national standards for law enforcement training, there is a major professional association for those who are involved in establishing State-level training standards and administering law enforcement academies, the International Association of Directors of Law Enforcement Standards and Training, or IADLEST, www.iadlest.org. These individuals are generally associated with the many state POST agencies, boards, and/or commissions that determine the training standards for their states.

In the 2006 study, BJS identified 648 law enforcement training academies across the country providing basic training to entry-level recruits. In some states, all basic law enforcement training is conducted at a centralized state academy. Washington State is an example, where all basic law enforcement training is conducted at the Washington State Criminal Justice Training Commission facility, which is also the state POST agency (the exception is the Washington State Patrol, which operates their own basic academy). In other states, training is decentralized to the county-level, regional areas (including multiple counties), or to college, university, or technical school programs. Some larger municipal law enforcement agencies and sheriff's offices operate their own academies, and there are about 200 of these.

Excluding any field training component of academy curricula, the average length of basic recruits training programs was about 760 hours, or roughly 19 weeks. About a third of academies included a field training component, and this added about 450 hours on average to the total training time. Recruits typically had large instructional blocks related to learning firearms skills (the median instruction time is 60 hours) and self-defense skills (about 50 hours) (see Table 6.1). The next largest instructional block was health and fitness training (46 hours). Also common to all academies was training related to patrol procedures, investigations, and emergency vehicle operations (typically 40 hours each). You can see the wide variety of instructional areas and median instructional time listed in Table 6.1; consider these in light of Rahr and Rice's (2015) concerns regarding the lesser attention given to training in communication and de-escalation skills. It will be important to incorporate better measures of training in these areas in future iterations of the BJS training academy study.

More than 90% of academies also provided basic training on community policing topics in 2006. Very common topics included identifying community problems (provided in 85% of academies), and the history of community policing (83%) (Reaves, 2009). More than half of academies provided training on the environmental causes of crime (62%), prioritizing crime problems (62%), using problem-solving models (60%), and organizing/mobilizing the community (54%) (Reaves, 2009).

During 2006, an estimated 57,000 recruits started basic training in academies across the country. About 1 in 6 recruits that year were female, and in terms of race/ethnicity categories about 70% were white, 13% black, 13% Hispanic, and 4% in other categories. About 49,000 of the recruits who started basic training, or 86%, completed training and graduated from the academy (Reaves, 2009).

Completion rates varied by type of academy, with state police academies having lower completion rates on average as compared to other types of academies. Some of this may be explained by the academy training environment. Academy training environments can generally be characterized as falling along a continuum ranging from "stress-based," military boot-camp style academies, to "non-stress based" academies that may be more like academic campuses. According to the BJS study (Reaves, 2009:10),

A New York City Police Officer graduate takes his oath.

The more traditional stress-based model of training is based on the military model and typically includes paramilitary drills, intensive physical demands, public disciplinary measures, immediate reaction to infractions, daily inspections, value inculcation, and withholding of privileges. Proponents of this approach believe it promotes self-discipline in recruits resulting in a commitment to follow departmental policies, better time management, and completion of duties even when undesirable.

The non-stress model emphasizes academic achievement, physical training, administrative disciplinary procedures, and an instructor-trainee relationship that is more relaxed and supportive. Proponents of this approach believe it produces officers better able to interact in a cooperative manner with citizens and community organizations, and therefore more suited to the problem-solving approaches of community-oriented policing.

TABLE 6.1 Topics Included in Basic Training of State and Local Law Enforcement Training Academies (2006)

Topics	Percent of Academies with Training	Median Number of Hours of Instruction
Operations		
Report writing	100%	20
Patrol	99%	40
Investigations	99%	40
Emergency vehicle operations	99%	40
Basic first aid/CPR	97%	24
Computers/information systems	58%	8
Weapons/self-defense		
Self-defense	99%	51
Firearms skills	98%	60
Non-lethal weapons	98%	12
Legal		
Criminal law	100%	36
Constitutional law	98%	12
History of law enforcement	84%	4
Self-improvement		
Ethics and integrity	100%	8
Health and fitness	96%	46
Stress prevention/management	87%	5
Basic foreign language	36%	16
Community policing		
Cultural diversity/human relations	98%	11
Basic strategies	92%	8
Mediation skills/conflict management	88%	8
Special topics		
Domestic violence	99%	14
Juveniles	99%	8
Domestic preparedness	88%	8
Hate crimes/bias crimes	87%	4

Adapted from Reaves, B. (2009). *State and local law enforcement training academies, 2006*. Bureau of Justice Statistics. Washington DC: U.S. Government Printing Office.

The BJS data show that state police academies are more likely than other types of academies to fall into the stress-based end of the continuum, and this may contribute to the lower completion rates observed among recruits in those academies. Figure 6.2 below shows the distribution of training academies in terms of their training environment: 15% indicated a predominately stress-based environment, 38% more stress than non-stress based, 38% more non-stress than stress based, and 9% predominately non-stress based.

Academy completion rates in 2006 also varied by the race and gender of recruit. Males had higher completion rates (87%) than females (80%), and Whites had higher completion rates (87%) than Hispanics (82%) and Blacks (81%). In terms of race and gender interactions, white males had the highest average completion rate (about 95%), followed by white females and black males (about 88% each); Hispanic females had the lowest completion rates (see Figure 6.3). A related implication for stress-based training models is that there does appear to be a gender effect in completion rates. The BJS study found that in academies having a "predominantly non-stress" training environment, male and female recruits had an equivalent completion rate (89%). As the academy training environment moved toward an increasingly stress-based model, academy completion rates declined for both genders but at an accelerated rate for female recruits (see Figure 6.4). In academies having a "predominately stress" training environment, male recruits had a completion rate of 81% while female recruits had only a 68% completion rate.

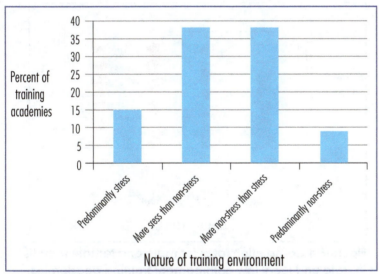

Figure 6.2 Training environment of state and local law enforcement training academies, 2006

Adapted from Reaves, B. (2009). *State and local law enforcement training academies, 2006*. Bureau of Justice Statistics. Washington DC: U.S. Government Printing Office.

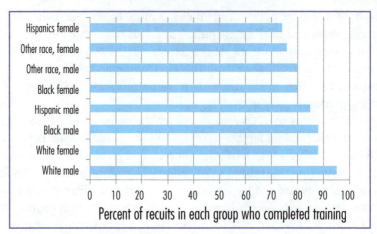

Figure 6.3 Completion rates for recruits in state and local law enforcement training academies, by race and gender, 2005–2006.

Adapted from Reaves, B. (2009). *State and local law enforcement training academies, 2006.* Bureau of Justice Statistics. Washington DC: U.S. Government Printing Office.

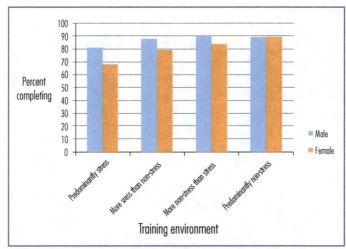

Figure 6.4 Completion rates for male and female recruits in state and local law enforcement training academies, by type of training environment, 2005–2006

Adapted from Reaves, B. (2009). *State and local law enforcement training academies, 2006.* Bureau of Justice Statistics. Washington DC: U.S. Government Printing Office.

THINK ABOUT IT

Recall from Chapter 1 that some of the innovative changes going on at the Washington State Criminal Justice Training Commission to support the Warriors to Guardians transition are aimed at reducing some of the militarization of the training environment, for example, eliminating "bracing," replacing the "tune-up" day with coaching, and generally moving away from the boot camp model. What do you think is the optimal training environment to support democratic policing?

THE EXTENT AND IMPACT OF DIVERSITY IN LAW ENFORCEMENT

As should be evident by now, becoming a police officer is a difficult process and not everyone makes the cut. It takes strength of character, integrity, sound judgment, and a variety of other traits to be selected for the job. Once selected, it takes commitment, tenacity, and about 12–24 months to make it through the background investigation, academy training, and field training before a new officer patrols the streets on her own. Who makes it through? Do the successful applicants and academy graduates who become law enforcement officers reflect the population at large? The answer is: it depends on where you live, but probably not.

Today, 1 in 8 officers (12.2%) are women. This represents an approximately 160% increase since 1987 when only 1 in 13 officers (7.6%) were women (Reaves, 2015). In fact, the proportion of female officers has grown every year since BJS began tracking this information (see Figure 6.5). As indicated in Table 6.2, the percentage of female officers is greatest in our largest police departments, where more than 16% of officers are female (that's 1 in every 6). While this is encouraging, women comprise almost 50% of the workforce, reminding us that women are still very much underrepresented as sworn officers. Females are also underrepresented as supervisors and chiefs. In 2013, only 9.5% of first-line supervisors and 3% of chiefs were women even though they comprised 12.2% of officers (Reaves, 2015).

© John Roman images/Shutterstock.com

The number of female officers continues to grow each year.

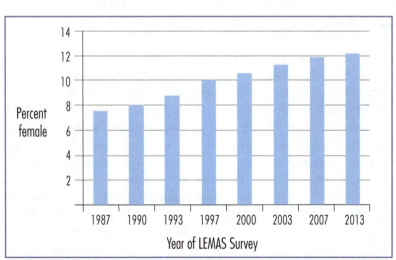

Figure 6.5 Female representation among full-time sworn personnel in local police departments, 1987–2013

Adapted from Reaves, B. (2015, May). *Local police departments, 2013: Personnel, Policies, & Practices.* Bureau of Justice Statistics, p. 4. Washington DC: U.S. Government Printing Office.

TABLE 6.2   Sex of Full-time Sworn Personnel in the United States

Population served	Male Police	Male Sheriffs	Female Police	Female Sheriffs
1,000,000 or more	82%	85%	18%	15%
500,000–999,999	84%	86%	16%	14%
250,000–499,999	85%	86%	15%	14%
100,000–249,999	88%	88%	12%	12%
50,000–99,999	90%	90%	10%	10%
25,000–49,999	91%	91%	9%	9%
10,000–24,999	92%	92%	8%	8%
2,500–9,999[a] Under 10,000[b]	93%	94%	8%	6%
Under 2,500	94%		6%	
ALL SIZES	88%	88%	12%	12%

[a]–police departments, [b]–sheriffs' departments   *may not equal 100% due to rounding

Adapted from Reaves, B. (2015, May). *Local police departments, 2013: Personnel, Policies, & Practices.* Bureau of Justice Statistics, p. 4. Washington DC: U.S. Government Printing Office. And Burch, A.M. (2012, December). *Sheriffs' offices, 2007-Statistical tables.* Bureau of Justice Statistics, p. 11. Washington DC: U.S. Government Printing Office.

As indicated in Table 6.3, the proportion of racial and ethnic minority officers has grown at a similar pace as female officers. In 1987, about one in seven officers (14.6%) identified as a racial/ethnic minority, today more than one in four officers (27.3%) identify as a racial/ethnic minority (Reaves, 2015). Black/African-American officers represent the largest minority-status group with 58,000 officers (12.2%). Hispanic/Latino officers are next with 55,000 (11.6% of all officers). The percentage of African-American officers has grown slowly from 9% to 12.2% over the past 26 years while the percentage of Hispanic/Latino officers has more than doubled (from 4.5% to 11.6%) in the same time frame. Members of other minority groups account for approximately 3% of all officers today, which is about a 400% increase since 1987 when they accounted for 0.8% of all officers (Reaves, 2015).

Does it matter that women and minorities are underrepresented in policing? Remember, police officers are not just people paid to enforce the law and keep the peace; they are visual symbols of the criminal justice system and of government. In poor, disadvantaged communities of color, that means that police officers are "the tangible target for grievances against shortcomings throughout [the criminal justice] system: Against assembly-line justice in teeming lower courts; against wide disparities in sentences; against antiquated correctional facilities; against the basic inequities imposed by the system on the poor—to whom, for example, the option of bail means only jail" (Kerner Commission Report, 1968 as cited in Vila, 1999, p. 190). For this reason, it is important that officers are able to relate to the community, not only to encourage law-abidingness but also so that community members will trust and support the police in their endeavors to protect the public's safety. Insofar as minorities are able to generate higher levels of trust among community members than white male officers, improving diversity is beneficial to departments.

As you learned in Chapter 3, there was deep-seated distrust and hostility between police and "ghetto communities" in the 1960s. This hostility resulted in numerous civil disturbances and riots during the decade. At this time, police officers were almost all white men. Both the President's Commission on Law Enforcement and the Administration of Justice and the Kerner Commission

TABLE 6.3 Race and Ethnicity of Full-time Sworn Personnel in the United States

Population served	White		Black/African American		Hispanic/Latino		Asian/Other Pacific Islander		American Indian/Alaskan Native		Two or more races	
	Police	Sheriffs	Police	Sheriffs	Police	Sheriffs	Police	Sheriffs	Police	Sheriffs	Police	Sheriffs
1,000,000 or more	56%	66%	17%	12%	25%	19%	4%	3%	<1%	<1%	<1%	<1%
500,000–999,999	60%	77%	23%	11%	10%	11%	5%	1%	<1%	1%	2%	<1%
250,000–499,999	67%	83%	19%	10%	11%	6%	2%	1%	<1%	<1%	<1%	<1%
100,000–249,999	74%	88%	12%	8%	11%	3%	3%	<1%	<1%	<1%	<1%	1%
50,000–99,999	80%	91%	8%	6%	9%	3%	2%	<1%	<1%	<1%	<1%	<1%
25,000–49,999	86%	88%	6%	8%	6%	4%	1%	<1%	<1%	1%	<1%	<1%
10,000–24,999	88%	88%	5%	9%	6%	2%	<1%	<1%	<1%	1%	<1%	<1%
2,500–9,999[a]	89%		4%		4%		<1%		1%		<1%	
Under 10,000[b]		91%		3%		5%		-%		1%		<1%
Under 2,500	85%		6%		5%		<1%		3%		<1%	
All Sizes	73%	81%	12%	9%	12%	8%	2%	1%	<1%	<1%	<1%	<1%

[a] –police departments, [b] –sheriffs' departments

* may not equal 100 % due to rounding

Adapted from Reaves, B(2015, May). *Local police departments, 2013: Personnel, Policies, & Practices.* Bureau of Justice Statistics, p. 4. Washington DC: U.S. Government Printing Office. And Burch, A.M. (2012, December). *Sheriffs' offices, 2007-Statistical tables.* Bureau of Justice Statistics, p. 10. Washington DC: U.S. Government Printing Office.

addressed the low number of minority law enforcement officers in their reports. The Kerner commission discovered that, in those cities that experienced significant civil unrest and disorder, the percentage of minority officers in the police department was dramatically lower than the percentage of minority community members. In spite of the importance of hiring minorities, The President's Commission recognized that "inducing qualified young men from minority groups to enter police work" was going to be a difficult task "in view of the distrust for the police felt by members of minority groups, especially by young men" (1967, p.102). Toward this end, the National Advisory Commission on Criminal Justice Standards and Goals (1973) set criteria to help agencies achieve increased minority and female recruitment to mirror the makeup of their surrounding community.

All else being equal, research consistently demonstrates that cities with a large minority population have more minority police officers than cities with a small minority population. Interestingly, research from public administration also shows that having a black or Latino mayor or city council members generally increases minority representation in the police force (Gustafson, 2013; Sharp, 2014; Zhao et al., 2005). Having a minority police chief and being the subject of a consent decree are also associated with greater police diversity (Gustafson, 2013). Agencies that want to increase department diversity must take affirmative steps to recruit women and minorities. This means developing recruitment materials that appeal to these groups as well as advertising in places that are likely to draw these groups.

THE EFFECTIVENESS OF FEMALE AND MINORITY OFFICERS

Are women effective officers? Yes. Two major studies, and several smaller studies, have shown women to be just as effective on patrol as men (Bloch & Anderson, 1974; David, 1984; Morash & Greene, 1986; Rabe-Hemp & Schuck, 2007; Schuck & Rabe-Hemp, 2005; Sichel et al., 1978; Stalans & Finn, 2000). For example, research has found no differences in arrest rates or conviction rates between male and female patrol officers, but has found that women receive fewer citizen complaints, are charged with improper conduct less often, and are seen by the community as more pleasant, respectful, and competent than men, which might explain why women are more likely than men to receive community support. A study of New York police officers found that men and women react very similarly to violent confrontations but that women are more emotionally stable and better able to deescalate potentially violent situations. Women are also less likely than their male counterparts to use a firearm, cause physical injury, or become physically injured on the job. In terms of improper behavior, women are significantly underrepresented in complaints, sustained use-of-force allegations, and agency civil litigation payouts. A review of LAPD civil litigation costs from 1990 to 1999 revealed that payouts for excessive force for male officers surpassed payouts for female officers by a ratio of 23:1 even though male officers outnumbered female officers by only 4:1 (National Center for Women & Policing, 2002).

Unlike the plethora of studies that have examined women as police officers, there is very little research on the performance of minorities as police officers. A recent study examined whether minority representation in government and in police agencies translates to police practice and found that black

Cities with a larger minority population tend to have more minority officers.

political representation reduces black order maintenance arrests but black representation on the police force does not (Sharp, 2014).

Additionally, a few studies have examined differences in attitudes between white and non-white officers and found some dissimilarities. For example, black officers are generally more supportive than white officers of community policing, citizen oversight, and police innovation in general. It has also been found that black officers take quality of life policing issues more seriously and place more importance on neighborhood conditions and fear of crime than their white counterparts (Boyd, 2010). One of the issues that affect black male officers more than any other demographic is the threat of being killed on the job by friendly fire. In particular, when African-American officers work plain clothes undercover assignments, they are at increased risk of being mistaken for a criminal and killed by a uniformed officer unfamiliar with the undercover officer.

THE PUSH FOR COLLEGE-EDUCATED OFFICERS

Although August Vollmer introduced the idea that education could improve policing in the 1920s, it was not really until the 1960s–1970s that the issue was debated in earnest in the United States. The increasing crime rate and urban riots of the 1960s pushed the issue to the forefront (Roberg & Bonn, 2004). The President's Commission on Law Enforcement and the Administration of Justice (1967) advocated for college-educated officers as a solution to the growing crisis of confidence in policing. In response, Congress passed the Omnibus Crime Control and Safe Streets Act (OCCSSA) of 1968.

> ### CHECK IT OUT!
> We discussed this bill in Chapter 2. Can you recall why it is important?

OCCSSA created the Law Enforcement Assistance Administration (LEAA) (and within it the Law Enforcement Education Program) and provided money for education, research, and equipment. As a result of newly available federal funding, the number of colleges offering police science or criminal justice degree programs increased exponentially. Unfortunately, the quality of the programs was not uniform and many programs were nonrigorous extensions of police academies (Roberg & Bonn, 2004; Sherman & the National Advisory Commission on Higher Education for Police Officers, 1978). This hurt attempts to increase education standards for entry-level officers. While poor quality instruction is no longer a pervasive issue, research on police education has yet to produce the clear, unequivocal results that many U.S. police leaders desire in order to change policy. Still, the value of a college-degree for officers holds much appeal; especially in light of the varied and complex tasks that today's police officers are expected to perform (tasks that were not expected of officers 30 years ago).

DOES A COLLEGE DEGREE MAKE A DIFFERENCE?

Research evidence on the value of a bachelor's degree for police officers is somewhat mixed; some studies find positive benefits but other studies find no correlation. On the whole, more research indicates positive effects than no correlation or negative consequences. Even though they typically receive higher salaries, research suggests that college-educated officers (those with a bachelor's degree or higher) save departments money. This is because research has found that college-educated officers take fewer sick days, have fewer on-the-job injuries and accidents, and have fewer individual liability cases filed against them (Carter & Sapp, 1989; Cascio, 1977; Cohen & Chaiken, 1972). They also may be better employees; college-educated officers are better report writers, more innovative, more reliable, more committed to the agency, more likely to take on leadership roles within the department, and more likely to be promoted than officers without a college degree (Carlan &Lewis, 2009; Cohen & Chaiken, 1972; Krimmel, 1996; Trojanowicz & Nicholson, 1976; Whetstone, 2000; Worden, 1990). If degree-holding officers are truly better report writers, that could translate into better investigations, higher court case filings, fewer evidentiary constitutional challenges, fewer false confessions or wrongful convictions, and/or more successful prosecutions.

It also has been found that college-educated officers are less resistant to change and more likely to embrace new methods of policing (Roberg & Bonn, 2004). They also have fewer citizen complaints filed against them, have fewer disciplinary actions taken against them, use force less often, and use less force than officers without a college degree (Chapman, 2012; Cohen & Chaiken, 1972; Fyfe, 1988; Kappeler et al., 1992; Lersch & Kunzman, 2001; Manis, Archbold, & Hassell, 2008; Roberg & Bonn, 2004; Rydberg & Terrill, 2010; Wilson, 1999). These last benefits may be particularly valuable for agencies which serve majority–minority communities where police-public relations are often strained. There are also benefits for agencies committed to community policing, problem solving, intelligence-led policing, as well as other newer policing strategies.

Balanced against these benefits are research findings that suggest that college-educated patrol officers may be less satisfied with their jobs, hold less favorable views toward management, and are less public service-oriented than their non-college educated peers (Paoline et al., 2015). Furthermore, college-educated officers are more likely to see police work as a "job," instead of a "calling" like their non-college-educated colleagues (Carlan & Lewis, 2009). Whether, or how, this impacts their service delivery is unknown.

MINIMUM EDUCATION REQUIREMENTS

Despite these known benefits, only the state of Minnesota and a handful of agencies in other states require applicants to possess more than a high school diploma. As Table 6.3 shows, only 1% of police departments and no sheriffs' departments in the United States require a 4-year college degree for employment as a police officer (Burch, 2012; Reaves, 2010). Fully 82% of police and 89% of sheriffs' agencies across the nation only require a high school diploma (or equivalent). Interestingly, higher education requirements are more popular among state police agencies than local agencies. In fact, 19 of the 50 primary state police agencies require at least some college (of those, four require a B.A. and five require an A.A.; the rest have a "units completed" requirement) (Burriesci & Melley, 2001). LEMAS (Law Enforcement Management and Administrative Statistics Survey) data tell us that larger agencies often have more stringent education qualification requirements than do smaller agencies. For example, 36% of police departments and 22% of sheriffs' departments that serve a population size of 1,000,000 or more require at least some college (Burch, 2012; Reaves, 2015). While a college degree is usually not required to become a police officer, it is required to promote through the ranks. A recent study of California law enforcement agencies found that merely one-third of agencies would promote an officer with only a high school diploma to sergeant and most agencies in the study required a 4-year degree to promote to lieutenant (Gardiner, 2015).

Why do so few agencies require a college degree to get hired? There are several reasons. One reason is because agencies generally have to pay a higher salary to attract college-educated officers and some agencies are unable to offer the competitive salaries necessary to recruit college graduates. Agencies with a small tax base (residential areas that serve predominately poor communities) have an especially difficult time offering competitive salaries. Another reason is because agencies do not think it is necessary to require a 4-year degree to recruit high quality candidates. Some think it would unnecessarily limit their ability to hire high quality candidates without degrees (e.g., individuals turning to policing as a second career or after military service).

Population served	High School Diploma		Some College		2-year College Degree		4-year College Degree	
	Police	Sheriffs	Police	Sheriffs	Police	Sheriffs	Police	Sheriffs
1,000,000 or more	64%	78%	7%	15%	29%	4%	0%	–%
500,000–999,999	70%	83%	19%	8%	7%	6%	4%	4%
250,000–499,999	70%	90%	15%	2%	9%	6%	7%	2%
100,000–249,999	78%	81%	8%	5%	10%	13%	3%	–%
50,000–99,999	75%	85%	8%	3%	12%	10%	4%	–%
25,000–49,999	75%	89%	4%	2%	18%	7%	2%	–%
10,000–24,999	81%	89%	6%	3%	12%	6%	–%	–%
2,500–9,999[a] Under 10,000[b]	86%	94%	2%	2%	9%	4%	1%	–%
Under 2,500	86%		3%		9%		–%	
All Sizes	84%	89%	4%	3%	10%	7%	1%	–%

[a] – police departments, [b] – sheriffs' departments

Adapted from Reaves, B. (2015, May). *Local police departments, 2013: Personnel, Policies, & Practices*. Bureau of Justice Statistics, p. 7. Washington DC: U.S. Government Printing Office. And Burch, A.M. (2012, December). *Sheriffs' offices, 2007-Statistical tables*. Bureau of Justice Statistics, p. 8. Washington DC: U.S. Government Printing Office.

Finally, some agencies are concerned about being able to recruit qualified minority or female candidates (Gardiner, 2015). The latter concern is unwarranted, as two recent studies have found that agencies with higher education requirements employ higher percentages of female officers than do agencies which only require a high school diploma (Gardiner, 2015; Schuck, 2014).

HOW MANY COPS HAVE A COLLEGE DEGREE?

Fifty years ago, in 1960, only 3% of officers held a 4-year degree (in comparison, 7.7% of U.S. residents 25 and older did) (Rydberg & Terrill, 2010; U.S. Census, 2006). By 1988, 22.6% of sworn officers in the nation were college graduates and for the first time, the percentage of officers with degrees was higher than the general population, which was at 20.3% (Carter & Sapp, 1990; U.S. Census, 1989). Unfortunately, we do not have a current, nationally-representative dataset that can tell us what percentage of officers nationwide have a college degree. We do, however, have several small studies that are informative and reveal two things about the state of education in policing: (1) the percentage of college-educated officers is increasing, and (2) there is great variability between departments. Of the departments which have been recently studied, the percentage of college-educated officers ranges

© Matt Benoit/Shutterstock.com

Less than half of officers across the nation have a college degree.

from 11.6% in three medium-sized, majority/minority communities in New Jersey to 65.2% in a medium-sized mid-west police department which requires at least some college to get hired and serves a 97% white population (Gardiner, 2015).

On average, it appears that between 25% and 45% of officers across the nation have a college degree. However, it is important to keep in mind that the percent of college-educated officers in a department is dependent on several factors, including:

1. The agency's minimum education requirements—agencies which require some college or an AA have a much higher percentage of officers with a BA;

2. Geography and demographics—in California, agencies located in urban areas with a high cost of living and an educated populous had more than twice as many officers with a college degree than did rural areas with a low cost of living and non-educated populous;

3. The size of the agency—larger agencies employ a higher percentage of college-educated officers than do smaller agencies;

4. Starting salary—though not a perfect relationship, the percentage of officers with a college diploma increases with starting salary (of course, starting salary is dependent on cost of living, type of county, surplus/deficit of qualified job candidates, and many other factors), and

5. Promotion requirements—departments that require a bachelor's degree to promote to lieutenant employ a higher percentage of college-educated officers than do agencies without this requirement (Gardiner, 2015).

POLICING: BLUE COLLAR OR WHITE COLLAR?

In the early days, policing was considered a blue-collar job. Depending on where you live in the country, this may no longer be true. Today there are many college-educated police officers earning high salaries and great benefits.

In California, many entry-level police officers make more money than college professors! What do you think—white collar or blue collar? Does knowing that you could make a good living change how you feel about possibly pursuing a career as a police officer? Should officers get paid more than professors? Why? Why not?

POLICE SUBCULTURE

Is there a distinct police "subculture?" Are police officers somehow different than people in the general population? Do they see the world differently than the average citizen? Do they behave or interact with other members of society differently than if they were teachers, engineers, or store clerks? Many scholars think so and research supports this view.

The term **police subculture** refers to the accepted norms, values, attitudes, and practices that are shared by officers. William Westley was the first scholar to propose a distinct police subculture in 1970. Based on his observations of police officers in Gary (IN), he suggested that the police subculture was defined by loyalty, secrecy, and a strong desire to help others in need. Since then, many scholars have studied and elaborated on the components that comprise the police subculture. As a result, we now consider a desire for adventure and excitement, a strong sense of mission, a macho attitude, political and ideological conservatism, authoritarianism, cynicism, and bravery to be among the traits shared by officers throughout the western world (Reiner, 1992; Waddington, 2008).

One of the most famous police scholars to write on this issue is Jerome Skolnick, who argued that the police subculture is shaped by three defining features of a police officer's job that are not found in the same combination in other jobs: *danger, authority,* and *efficiency.* According to Skolnick, these three occupational traits explain how officers develop a "working personality." First, recruits are taught the importance of being suspicious and developing a "sixth sense" to identify symbolic assailants—people who are unusual or look out of place, people who could cause harm to the officer—so that they (officers) may remain safe in a potentially dangerous job. The other defining aspect of the job, authority to enforce laws, puts officers at odds with many members of the society and exposes them to allegations of hypocrisy. According to Skolnick, officers become cynical and develop a "we vs. they" mentality because, by virtue of their job, they must be skeptical of all people, trusting no one except their fellow officers (*after* they have been vetted and passed the test). A situation made worse by a conceptualized "war on drugs" and "war on crime," which causes officers to see themselves as fighting against a specific enemy, further solidifies the cynical "us vs. them" mentality. This cynicism makes officers isolate themselves from others and increases group social solidarity, which is manifest in the police subculture. In addition to the cynicism and suspiciousness, officers feel a constant need to be efficient—to clear a call quickly so they can be available for the dispatcher and any other officer or member of the public who might need them at a moment's notice. Together, these three elements of the job push officers closer together and cause them to isolate themselves from the general public who, in their perception, "doesn't understand" the things they see and deal with every day.

While individuals who apply to become police officers are not much different than the rest of us, by the time they hit the streets in uniform they have begun to transform into the "thin blue line." Several studies have confirmed that a change in values takes place during academy training. Van Maanen (1973) and Harris (1973), for example, found that solidarity emerges during academy as recruits are taught the shared norms and values of the subculture, socialized into the depersonalized and defensive atmosphere of the job, and trained to take this interpersonal style to the streets (recall the discussion in Chapter 1 about changes made to Washington State's academy to transform the academy atmosphere from one that produced warriors to one that now produces guardians). The change in values happens through both enculturation (learning the system) and socialization (learning the rules of the game) not only during academy and field training especially, but also throughout one's career (Ruess-Ianni & Ianni, 2008). Researchers have documented that officers become more cynical after academy as the reality of the streets hits and they start to lose friends due to shift work and the nature of their chosen career. Their cynicism continues to grow during their first several years on the job but begins to decline in their mid-career years, possibly due to promotion or salary increase and as they begin to look toward retirement (Neiderhoffer, 1967). War stories are one of the main socialization tools used by veteran officers to teach recruits and newer officers about potential sources of danger, citizen complaints, and administrative difficulties (Waddington, 2008).

It used to be thought that police culture was homogeneous and stable but that view is no longer held, as research has affirmed that police culture has indeed changed as the workforce has become increasingly diverse and found that some agencies and specialty units develop their own unique subcultures (Waddington, 2008). While the "cop's code" that gives such pieces of advice as to not trust a new guy until you're sure about him, don't make waves, be aggressive but not too eager, and don't give up another cop (Ruess-Ianni & Ianni, 2008) still exists, it does so with more nuances and less conformity. For example, researchers have found distinct police cultures in rural and urban agencies, between routine patrol officers and community police officers, police paramilitary unit officers, and detectives. Research also indicates that subculture varies between officers of different races, different sexes, and different educational levels (Waddington, 2008).

Additionally, there are unique subcultures for middle managers and command staff, who arguably have different concerns than patrol officers (Ruess-Ianni & Ianni, 2008). It has been proposed that individual officers, rather than assume the entire police subculture as their own, now select the features they agree with from a pseudo-list of subculture characteristics and adopt only those elements that are congruent with their views and goals (Waddington, 2008).

The police subculture, which is sometimes viewed as negative, is functional and necessary in a job that is always unpredictable, often alienating, and sometimes dangerous (Chan, 2008). It gives meaning to officers' experiences and provides occupational self-esteem in a job that is largely invisible and autonomous (Waddington, 2008). It is also important because culture determines action and helps explain why officers support some policies and practices while ignoring or subverting other policies or innovations. How an officer sees herself (guardian or warrior; conflict negotiator or crime fighter) impacts how she approaches the job and interacts with her fellow officers and members of the community, both law-breaking and law-abiding. The warrior mentality is ingrained in the traditional police subculture and ethos which means that it may be quite difficult to shift officers who identify completely with this subculture toward a guardian, or community-oriented, philosophy. This suggests that in order to move away from a warrior/crime-fighter mentality toward a guardian mentality (or any other innovative practice that is not aligned with the traditional police subculture), police executives may need to first change the subculture. Besides orienting job performance, subculture can be a source of **occupational stress** for the growing number of officers who view themselves as "outside" of the subculture—an issue that will be discussed in the next section (Rose & Unnithan, 2015).

POLICE STRESS

There is little doubt that police officers experience occupational stress. The CareerCast.com annual jobs report usually ranks "police officer" among the top 10 stress-producing jobs in America. In addition to the typical personal stress that most individuals experience, as well as the standard organizational and administrative stressors that many working adults experience, officers are exposed to unique operational stressors by the nature of their job. But is this stress significantly greater than the level of stress experienced in most other jobs? And what effect does it have on officers and their families?

Oxford dictionary defines stress as "a state of mental or emotional strain or tension resulting from adverse or very demanding circumstances." There are five types of occupational (or workplace) stress—organizational structure/climate, interpersonal work relationships, career development, role in the organization, and factors unique to the job (Murphy, 1995).

- *Organizational structure/climate stress* results from the quasi-military, hierarchal structure of police agencies, and police work. In particular, the irregular working hours associated with shift work, having to work holidays, not having control over ones schedule (i.e., not being able to count on ending a shift on time) and inability of officers to participate in major decision-making or having influence over their general work activities contribute to officers' occupational stress.

- *Interpersonal work relationship stress* arises from problematic relationships and interactions with coworkers, administrators, or subordinates in the workplace. For example, antagonistic relationships between various work groups (such as command and line staff, separate specialty units, or officers on different shifts) but also work environments that include harassment, discrimination, bullying (from superiors or colleagues), threatened violence, rumoring, and intentional humiliation by others.

- *Career development stress* occurs when one feels "stuck" in their job. It can result from, among other things, job insecurity, being passed over for a promotion, being in a position with little potential for promotion, and lack of career development opportunities.

- *Role in the organization stress* occurs when one must perform multiple job duties due to short staffing or other issues and from role ambiguity. Employees feel particularly stressed when there are excessive work demands placed upon them or they are unclear about their job, their responsibilities, or how to satisfy their supervisor(s).

- *The factors unique to the job stress* category includes some of the job dimensions described above—unpredictability, the potential for danger, having to use force, perceived lack of support, the routinely negative interactions with the public, mediating other people's disputes, and needing to show courage in dangerous situations and to always be observant and attentive to evolving situations. It also includes the stress that results from the unique demands and constraints of the criminal justice system and its various actors.

Which factors cause officers the most stress? It turns out that it is a difficult question to answer. New York officers ranked killing someone in the line of duty, experiencing the death of a fellow officer, and being physically attacked at the top of their list of police stressors (Violanti & Aron, 1995) (see Table 6.5). Officers in Illinois, however, identified organizational factors (including interpersonal work relationships) as the most stress-inducing and concerns over occupational danger less stress-inducing (Crank & Caldero, 1991). Other studies have similarly found that officers report that organizational factors are more aggravating than job/task-related stressors (Buker & Wiecko, 2007; Gershon et al., 2009; Morash et al., 2006; Shane, 2010).

Many different circumstances in the job cause stress for police officers.

Why do these, and other, studies report divergent findings? One reason is different samples. The New York officers in Violanti and Aron's study worked for a large police department, and large departments are often located in urban cities with higher-than-average violent crime rates and higher perceived dangerousness. The Illinois officers, on the other hand, all worked for medium-sized departments which may have been perceived as less dangerous. Timing is another factor to consider—gang violence was near its height in the early 1990s when Violanti and Aron conducted their research and may have influenced their findings.

Another main reason the findings from multiple studies may differ is research methods—how a study is conducted. Most studies on police stress use a self-report survey approach that asks officers to rank order a variety of possible stressors according to the degree of stress the officer thinks each causes. There is very little direct measurement of stress in real-world settings (Hickman et al., 2011). This is important because stress induces psychological and physiological responses in the body. Acute stress, for example, activates the body's fight-or-flight response which triggers a complex set of physiological responses, including increased heart rate, elevated blood pressure,

TABLE 6.5 Highest Ranked Police Stressors

Stressor	Mean Score	Stressor	Mean Score
Killing someone in the line of duty	79.4	Insufficient personnel	58.5
Fellow officer killed	76.7	Aggressive crowds	56.7
Physical attack	71.0	Felony in progress	55.3
Battered child	69.2	Excessive discipline	53.3
High speed chases	63.7	Plea bargaining	52.8
Shift work	61.2	Death notifications	52.6
Use of force	61.0	Inadequate support (Supervisor)	52.4
Inadequate department support	61.0	Inadequate equipment	52.4
Incompatible partner	60.4	Family disputes	52.0
Accident in patrol car	59.9	Negative press coverage	51.9
		Overall mean score of 60 stressors	44.8

Adapted from Violanti, J. & Aron, F. (1995). Police stressors: Variations in percent among police personnel. *Journal of Criminal Justice, 23(3), 287-294.*

increased blood flow to the muscles, increased production of glucose, and elevated cortisol levels. Some of the physiological responses that indicate the body is under stress, especially those that continue for a prolonged period after the "danger" has subsided or those can be caused by other factors (such as headache, fatigue, inability to concentrate, muscle aches, etc.), go undetected by or are dismissed by the officer as not stress-related. Chronic stress can have some of the same effects on the body and is even more likely to go undetected or ignored. Thus, an officer's actual stress triggers may differ from her perceived stress triggers.

To date, it appears that only one study has used heart rate monitoring to directly and systematically measure police stress during a regular work shift. Anderson and colleagues (2002) studied 76 Canadian officers from 12 municipal police departments during their 12-hour shifts. They found that officers' heart rates were higher during their shift than before or after their shift. They further found that officers' average "above-resting" heart rates were highest at the beginning of their shift and lowest at the end of their shift (validating the idea that police work, in and of itself is stressful). Additionally, above-resting heart rates were highest when officers were wrestling with or handcuffing a suspect and elevated when an officer placed a hand on his gun, responded to a call to back up another officer, or drove "code 3" to an emergency call. Moreover, the researchers found that although officers' heart rates dropped after "critical incidents," their heart rates continued to be elevated for 30–60 minutes after the incident which indicates that officers remained in a hyper-vigilant mode long after the immediate threat subsided.

Hickman et al. (2011) expanded on this study by adding a GPS component to the real-time measurement of officer heart rates. One of the goals of the study was to be able to place the measurement of police stress in a space-time context so they could understand both when and where officers were likely to experience stress. Using monitoring units that simultaneously record heart rate as well as latitude and longitude enabled mapping of the stress data, and on a theoretical level, it would be possible to generate valid "hot-spot" style maps, although such maps would depict average officer heart rates (in density terms) instead of crimes. Figure 6.6 shows the heart rate trace of a test officer during his shift. The major "peak" in the chart corresponds to a particularly stressful incident. The initial call was for a "hit-and-run" by a pick-up truck that had hit several vehicles and stop signs. The test officer located the vehicle and pursued, but the driver did not respond to lights and siren. After some distance, the driver finally stopped his vehicle by means of hitting a curb. The test officer issued repeated commands over the PA system to the driver to turn off the ignition and throw his keys on to the pavement. The driver was nonresponsive. The test participant exited the cruiser and drew and pointed his service weapon at the suspect vehicle's driver compartment; at this point, his heart rate peaked at 165 bpm as depicted in the trace. The test officer advanced on the driver's vehicle, repeatedly issuing commands to the driver to put his hands out of the window. When the test officer arrived at the driver's window, he issued a command to unlock and open the door. The driver was again nonresponsive. Finally, the test officer opened the door and assisted the driver out of the vehicle, at which point the driver—obviously intoxicated—simply collapsed onto the ground. The test officer then rolled the driver onto his stomach and handcuffed him.

Figure 6.7 shows the mapped heart rate data from the officer's shift. As noted, the ellipse drawn within the map identifies the conclusion of this hit/run call that evolved into a DUI arrest at gunpoint. As the officer chased the vehicle through the city and began to realize that he was dealing with a non-compliant, potentially intoxicated and dangerous subject, his heart rate steadily increases. After the vehicle was stopped and several opportunities for compliance were offered, the officer's heart rate maximized at the exact moment that he decided it was necessary to draw his sidearm and began advancing on the vehicle. This is depicted in the map by the largest graduated point marker to the right side of the ellipse. Other notable incidents from the officer's shift included a call to assist a repo-man confronted by an angry car owner wielding a baseball bat (due East of the DUI incident described above), and a call reporting screaming and a possible knife within a Seattle Housing Authority apartment building (Northwest of the DUI incident).

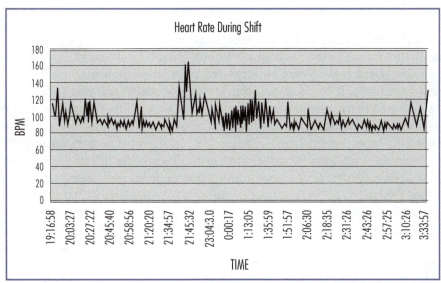

Figure 6.6 Heart rate recording of test officer

Adapted from Hickman, M., Fricas, J., Strom, K., & Pope, M. (2011). Mapping police stress. *Police Quarterly*, 14(3), 227–250.

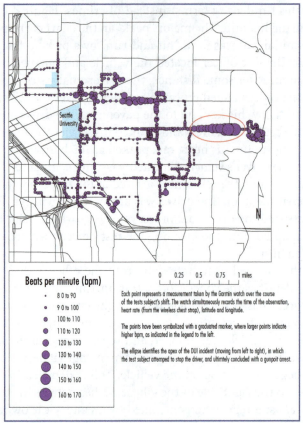

Beats per minute (bpm)

· 8 0 to 90
· 9 0 to 100
● 100 to 110
● 110 to 120
● 120 to 130
● 130 to 140
● 140 to 150
● 150 to 160
● 160 to 170

Each point represents a measurement taken by the Garmin watch over the course of the tests subject's shift. The watch simultaneously records the time of the observation, heart rate (from the wireless chest strap), latitude and longitude.

The points have been symbolized with a graduated marker, where larger points indicate higher bpm, as indicated in the legend to the left.

The ellipse identifies the apex of the DUI incident (moving from left to right), in which the test subject attemped to stop the driver, and ultimtely concluded with a gunpoit arrest.

Figure 6.7 Map of Point Data Collected via GPS-Enabled Heart Rate Monitor
Adapted from Hickman, M., Fricas, J., Strom, K., & Pope, M. (2011). Mapping police stress. *Police Quarterly*, 14(3), 227–250.

Stress mapping on a more systematic basis may enable hot-spot style analyses that could inform beat/district modification, with an eye toward balancing stress, and could assist departments in thinking about how officers are deployed in order to minimize repeated exposure to highly stressful situations. It could also inform stress inoculation training (SIT). Much like the inoculations delivered in the medical field to prevent the onset of more serious forms of disease, the idea here is that by exposing an individual to mild forms of stress you can improve their ability to cope with more severe forms of stress (e.g., Meichenbaum & Novaco, 1978; Novaco, 1977). Police training is designed to some extent with this process in mind; simulated stressful conditions are a common part of academy training that prepares recruits for real-world stressful condition (often referred to as "survival stress" training), particularly with regard to use of force (Hickman, 2005; Reaves, 2009). SIT models view stress as the product of the interaction between individual and environment; as such, knowledge of the micro-geography of police stress may assist with the design of survival stress training for individual police departments (as well as individual SIT treatments delivered by clinicians).

Do female officers experience stress differently than male officers? Yes and no. Whereas earlier studies showed distinct differences between male and female officers, recent studies show more similarities than differences. In general, the literature suggests that women and men have different views on what constitutes stress and different methods for coping with the stress (He et al., 2015). Women police officers encounter higher levels of harassment and overt hostility than male officers and this has led to higher levels of workplace stress (Kurtz, 2012). Research has also found that the higher stress levels reported by female officers are often caused, not by work-related experiences, but rather by family and marital issues; specifically the "second shift" of household chores and family responsibilities that await women (more so than men) after their official shift (Kurtz, 2012).

Are there any differences in how officers of different races experience stress? Research found that Latino and Black officers experience greater levels of polarization and discrimination by their fellow officers and fewer opportunities at work which can translate to higher stress levels (Stroshine & Brandl, 2011). There is also evidence that African American males report fewer symptoms of anxiety, stress, and depression than their white male counterparts and that African American male and female officers use more constructive coping strategies than their white counterparts (He, Zhao, & Ren, 2005).

This stress impacts both the officer and the officer's family. Some research has found that officers frequently employ negative coping mechanisms (such as drinking, smoking, and social isolation) and have higher rates of alcoholism, drug addiction, suicide, and health-related problems than the general public. But not all research studies concur, there is a lot of variation and some studies have found lower than average rates of these problems. One study of more than 4000 officers found that, although officers did not drink alcohol more often than the average adult, they did binge drink more frequently (Davey, Obst, & Sheehan, 2000). Further, 30% of the officers drinking behavior placed them in the "at-risk" for harmful alcohol consumption category and another 3% were classified as "alcohol dependent" based on their reported behavior. Surprisingly, 25% of these officers admitted to drinking alcohol while on-duty. Although research studies vary as to the amount, there is consensus that police officers commit suicide at elevated rates when compared to the general public and other government workers (Violanti, 2007); however, some of the precipitating factors (depression, alcoholism, divorce/separation, suffering a negative life event) are similar to the general public. Finally, current research on health-related issues suggests that it is officers' unhealthy lifestyles and diets that lead to health problems, not necessarily their occupational stress (Richmond et al., 1998). Despite the many occupational factors that place strain on officers' marriages and family life, research indicates that divorce rates among officers are similar to, and often lower than, the general population (McCoy & Aamodt, 2010).

CONCLUSION

In this chapter, we discussed the importance of hiring the right people to become police officers. Individuals who are service-oriented and compassionate guardians who recognize how their actions and responses affect not only citizens' willingness to follow established laws and provide assistance to law enforcement, but also affect the legitimacy of their department as well as their profession. We also examined how the academy format can impact which individuals graduate and how those graduates exercise discretion and perform their job in the field. While representation of women and minorities in policing is growing, neither of these groups is fully represented in policing as yet. There has also been major growth in the proportion of college-educated officers and this has had an effect on how we view policing as a profession and how officers see and experience the police subculture. Finally, we explored some of the realities of policing in the form of police occupational stress.

REVIEW QUESTIONS

1. What types of occupational stress do police officer experience and which categories do officers identify as most problematic?
2. What are some of the benefits of a college education for police officers?
3. How does the reality of policing differ from the myth of policing?

GLOSSARY

Occupational stress mental or emotional strain that results from circumstances that develop in or are related to a person's workplace or occupation.

Peace Officer Standards and Training organizations (usually state-level) that set eligibility and training standards for peace officers.

Police cynicism an attitude that develops among officers that they must be skeptical of all people and can trust no one.

Police subculture the accepted norms, values, attitudes, and practices shared by law enforcement offices.

Symbolic assailants an individual whose dress, behavior, and gestures indicate suspicion and possible danger to a police officer.

REFERENCES

Boyd, L. (2010). Light blue v. dark blue: Attitudinal differences in quality of life policing. *Journal of Ethnicity in Criminal Justice, 8*(1), 37–48.

Burch, A. (2012, December). *Sheriffs' Departments, 2007—Statistical Tables,* #NCJ 238558, Washington, DC: Bureau of Justice Statistics.

Burriesci, J. J., & Melley, M. (2001, January 19). *OLS research report: State Police educational qualifications and incentives.* Connecticut General Assembly, 2001-R-0092. Retrieved from http://www.cga.ct.gov/2001/rpt/2001-R-0092.htm

Carlan, P. E., & Lewis, J. A. (2009). Dissecting police professionalism: A comparison of predictors within five professionalism subsets. *Police Quarterly, 12*(4), 370–387. doi: 10.1177/1098611109348469

Carter, D. L., & Sapp, A. D. (1989). The effect of higher education on police liability: Implications for police personnel policy. *American Journal of Police, 8,* 153–166.

Carter, D. L., & Sapp, A. D. (1990). The evolution of higher education in law enforcement: Preliminary findings from a national study. *Journal of Criminal Justice Education, 1,* 59–85.

Cascio, W. F. (1977). Formal education and police officer performance. *Journal of Police Science and Administration, 5,* 89–96.

Chan, J. (2008). Changing police culture. In T. Newburn (Ed.), *Policing: Key readings*. Portland, OR: Willan.

Chapman, C. (2012). Use of force in minority communities is related to police education, age, experience, and ethnicity. *Police Practice and Research, 13*(5), 421–436. doi: 10.1080/15614263.2011.596711

Cohen, B., & Chaiken, J. M. (1972). *Police background characteristics and performance*. New York, NY: Rand Institute.

Davey, J., Obst, P., & Sheehan, M. (2000). Developing a profile of alcohol consumption patterns of police officers in a large scale sample of an Australian Police Service. *European Addiction Studies, 6*, 205–212.

Fyfe, J. (1988). Police use of deadly force: Research and reform. *Justice Quarterly, 5*(2), 15–205.

Gardiner, C. (2015). College Cops: A study of education and policing in California. *Policing: An International Journal of Policing Strategies and Management, 38*(4), 1–17.

Gustafson, J. (2013). Diversity in municipal police agencies: A national examination of minority hiring and promotion. *Policing: An International Journal of Policing Strategies and Management, 36*(4), 719–736.

Harris, R. (1973). *The police academy: An inside view*. New York, NY: Wiley.

He, N., Zhao, J., & Ren, L. (2005). Do race and gender matter in police stress? A preliminary assessment of the interactive effects. *Journal of Criminal Justice, 6*, 535–547.

Hilal, S., & Densley, J. (2013). Higher education and local law enforcement. *FBI Law Enforcement Bulletin, 82*(5), 1–3.

Kappeler, V. E., Sapp, A. D., & Carter, D. L. (1992). Police officer higher education, citizen complaints and departmental rule violations. *American Journal of Police, 11*(2), 37–54.

Krimmel, J. T. (1996). The performance of college-educated police: A study of self-rated police performance measures. *American Journal of Police, 15*(1), 85–96.

Kurtz, D. (2012). Roll call and the second shift: The influences of gender and family on police stress. *Police Practice and Research, 13*(1), 71–86.

Lersch, K. M. (1998). Exploring gender differences in citizen allegations of misconduct: An analysis of a municipal police department. *Women and Criminal Justice, 4*, 69–79.

Lersch, K. M., & Kunzman, L. L. (2001). Misconduct allegations and higher education in a southern sheriff's department. *American Journal of Criminal Justice, 25*(2), 161–172.

Manis, J., Archbold, C. A., & Hassell, K. D. (2008). Exploring the impact of police officer education level on allegations of police misconduct. *International Journal of Police Science and Management, 10*(4), 509–523. doi: 10.1350/ijps.2008.10.4.102

McCoy, S., & Aamodt, M. (2010). A comparison of law enforcement divorce rates with those of other occupations. *Journal of Police and Criminal Psychology, 25*, 1–16.

Morash, M., & Greene, J. (1986). Evaluating women on patrol: A critique of contemporary wisdom. *Evaluation Review, 10*, 230–255.

National Center for Women and Policing. (2002, April). *Men, women, and police excessive force: A tale of two genders, a content analysis of civil liability cases, sustained allegations and citizen complaints.* Retrieved from http://womenandpolicing.org/PDF/2002_Excessive_Force.pdf

Paoline, E. A., III, Terrill, W., & Rossier, M. T. (2015). Higher education, college degree major, and police occupational attitudes. *Journal of Criminal Justice Education, 26*(1), 49–73. doi: 10.1080/10511253.2014.923010

President's Commission on Law Enforcement and Administration of Justice. (1967). *The challenge of crime in a free society.* Washington, DC: Government Printing Office.

Rabe-Hemp, C., & Schuck, A. (2007). Violence against police officers: Are female officers at greater risk? *Police Quarterly, 4*, 411–428.

Reaves, B. (2015, May). *Local Police Departments, 2013: Personnel, policies, and practices.* Washington, DC: Bureau of Justice Statistics, Government Printing Office.

Reaves, B. (2010, December). *Local Police Departments, 2007.* Washington, DC: Bureau of Justice Statistics, Government Printing Office.

Reuss-Ianni, E., & Ianni, F. (2008). Street cops and management cops: The two cultures of policing. In T. Newburn (Ed.), *Policing: Key readings.* Portland, OR: Willan.

Richmond, R., Wodak, A., Kehoe, L., & Heather, N. (1998). How healthy are the police? A survey of life-style factors. *Addiction, 93*, 1729–1737.

Roberg, R., & Bonn, S. (2004). Higher education and policing: where are we now? *Policing: An International Journal of Police Strategies & Management, 27*(4), 469–486.

Rydberg, J., & Terrill, W. (2010). The effect of higher education on police behavior. *Police Quarterly, 13.* doi: 10.1177/1098611109357325

Schuck, A. M. (2014). Female representation in law enforcement: The influence of screening, unions, incentives, community policing, CALEA, and size. *Police Quarterly, 17*(1), 54–78. doi: 0.1177/1098611114522467

Schuck, A., & Rabe-Hemp, C. (2005). Women police: The use of force by and against female officers. *Women and Criminal Justice, 4*, 91–117.

Sharp, E. (2014). Minority representation and order maintenance policing: Toward a contingent view. *Social Science Quarterly, 95*(4), 1155–1171.

Sherman, L. W., and The National Advisory Commission on Higher Education for Police Officers. (1978). *The quality of police education: A critical review with recommendations for improving programs in higher education.* San Francisco, CA: Jossey-Bass.

Stalans, L., & Finn, M. (2000). Gender differences in officers' perceptions and decisions about domestic violence cases. *Women and Criminal Justice, 3*, 1–24

Trojanowicz, R. C., & Nicholson, T. (1976). A comparison of behavioral styles of college graduate police officers v. non-college-going police officers. *The Police Chief, 43*, 57–58.

U.S. Census Bureau. (1988). Years of school completed by persons 25 years old and over, by age and sex: Selected years 1940 to 1989. Retrieved from http://www.census.gov/

U.S. Census Bureau. (2006). A half-century of learning: Historical census statistics on educational attainment in the United States, 1940 to 2000: Detailed Tables. Retrieved from http://www.census.gov/

U.S. Census Bureau. (2012). Education attainment in the United States, 2012. Retrieved from http://www.census.gov/

Van Maanen, J. (1973). Observations on the making of policemen. *Human Organizations, 32*, 407–418.

Violanti, J. (2007). *Police Suicide: Epidemic in Blue 2nd edition*. Springfield, IL: Charles C. Thomas.

Waddington, P. A. J. (2008). Police (canteen) sub-culture: An appreciation. In T. Newburn (Ed.), *Policing: Key readings*. Portland, OR: Willan.

Westley, W. (1970). *Violence and the police*. Cambridge, MA: MIT Press (originally a Ph.D. dissertation: University of Chicago).

Whetstone, T. S. (2000). Getting stripes: Educational achievement and study strategy used by sergeant promotional candidates. *American Journal of Criminal Justice, 24*, 247–257.

Wilson, H. (1999). Post-secondary education of the police officer and its effect on the frequency of citizen complaints. *The Journal of California Law Enforcement, 33*, 3–10.

Worden, J. E. (1990). A badge and a baccalaureate: Policies, hypotheses, and further evidence. *Justice Quarterly, 7*, 565–592.

CHAPTER 7

POLICE DISCRETION

LEARNING OBJECTIVES

After reading this chapter, students should be able to:

1 Define and describe police discretion.

2 Explain the role of police officers as gate keepers.

3 Summarize the context specific correlates of police discretion.

4 Summarize the officer–level correlates of police discretion.

5 Describe the situation-specific correlates of police discretion.

6 Explain how organizational-level factors impact police discretion.

KEY TERMS

Police discretion

Watchman style

Rational Decision
Making Framework

Legalistic style

Service style

OVERVIEW

In 2003, voters in the City of Seattle approved Initiative 75 which set adult personal marijuana use as the lowest enforcement priority for the Seattle Police Department (SPD). In November 2012, voters in the State of Washington approved Initiative 502 (I-502), which legalized possession of small amounts of marijuana. Following the passage of I-502, some local jurisdictions within the state passed their own ordinances concerning marijuana: some allow it, others don't. In the City of Seattle, it is presently legal for persons aged 21 and over to *possess* small amounts of marijuana, but *consuming* marijuana in public still carries a civil fine. The City Council adopted legislation (Ordinance 124393), which sets the fines for smoking marijuana in public at the same level as public

© Stanimir G. Stoev/Shutterstock.com

In Seattle, smoking marijuana in public warrants a civil fine.

consumption of alcohol (presently a $27 fine). In addition, the ordinance notes that the Seattle Police Department (SPD) will issue a first warning to offenders, whenever practical, before issuing a citation. The ordinance also requires SPD to monitor marijuana enforcement actions by age, race, and sex of offender, as well as the geographic locations where citations are issued so that the City Council can evaluate whether the law is being equitably enforced. In order to assist the public with the transition to the new marijuana laws, the SPD issued a rather humorous citizen's guide which made national news headlines (see Box, "Marij what now?").

The data collection requirement imposed by the City Council is perhaps the most important part of this story. The first mandated analysis of marijuana enforcement data examined all enforcement actions from January 1 through June 30, 2014. SPD officers wrote a total of 82 tickets for public marijuana use during that period. The statistics were not pretty: Blacks comprised about 8% of the Seattle population, but 37% of the tickets issued; about half of the tickets were issued to homeless individuals. Even worse, however, it turns out that *a single officer* wrote 80% of the marijuana tickets. According to Police Chief Kathleen O'Toole, that officer also added some strange notes on the citations: "Some notes requested the attention of City Attorney Peter Holmes and were addressed to 'Petey Holmes'"; "In another instance, the officer indicated he flipped a coin when contemplating which subject to cite. In another note, the officer refers to Washington's voter-enacted changes to marijuana laws as 'silly'" (Miletich & Sullivan, 2014). In light of these findings, the City Attorney dropped all of the citations issued during this time period.[1]

In this chapter, we tackle the issue of **police discretion**. Most people are probably willing to recognize that we can't possibly enforce all of the laws all of the time, nor should we necessarily seek to do so. Instead, we must set enforcement priorities and allow criminal justice decision-makers to have some flexibility in their decision-making. For the police, this primarily refers to flexibility in the decision of whether to arrest as opposed to some informal outcome, but it also includes many other discretionary decisions that police officers must make on a daily basis. We also recognize that the law cannot possibly capture every contingency, nor is it designed to do so. If we can agree that not every infraction is identical, then we can probably agree that not every infraction will deserve the exact same response. Street-level circumstances may merit the exercise of discretion and we have to trust our police officers to use their professional judgment, grounded in their training and experience, and within the confines of departmental policy and rules. The problem lies in understanding what types of information influence the exercise of discretion, and with what kinds of consequences, with an eye toward ensuring due process and equal protection under the law. In the above example of Seattle's ongoing experiment with marijuana enforcement, it seems clear that extra-legal factors may have influenced the exercise of discretion in deciding whether to cite individuals for public marijuana consumption, and this likely played a role in the City Attorney's decision to drop all of the citations.

---

1   An analysis covering the second half of the year found that the disparities remained (Bush, 2015), and Chief O'Toole has since asked the City Council to clarify whether they want the SPD to continue issuing fines for public marijuana consumption (Young, 2015).

MARIJ WHAT NOW? A GUIDE TO LEGAL MARIJUANA USE IN SEATTLE

The people have spoken. Voters have passed Initiative 502 (I-502) and beginning December 6 (2012), it is not a violation of state law for adults over 21 years to possess up to an ounce of marijuana (or 16 ounces of solid marijuana-infused product, like cookies, or 72 ounces of infused liquid, like oil) for personal use. The initiative establishes a 1-year period for the state to develop rules and a licensing system for the marijuana production and sale.

Marijuana has existed in a gray area in Seattle for some time now. Despite a longstanding national prohibition on marijuana, minor marijuana possession has been the lowest enforcement priority for the SPD since Seattle voters passed Initiative 75 in 2003. Officers don't like gray areas in the law. I-502 now gives them more clarity.

Marijuana legalization creates some challenges for the SPD, but SPD is already working to respond to these issues head on, by doing things like reviewing SPD's hiring practices for police officers to address now-legal marijuana usage by prospective officers, as well as current employees.

While I-502 has decriminalized marijuana possession in Washington, the new state law does not change federal law, which classifies marijuana as a Schedule I narcotic. All Seattle Police officers have taken an oath to uphold not only state law but also federal law. However, SPD officers will follow state law, and will no longer make arrests for marijuana possession as defined under I-502.

The SPD and Mayor Mike McGinn have already begun working with state officials to navigate this conflict, and follow the direction of Washington voters to legalize marijuana.

In the meantime, the SPD will continue to enforce laws against unlicensed sale or production of marijuana, and regulations against driving under the influence of marijuana, which remain illegal.

Here's a practical guide for what the SPD believes I-502 means for you, beginning December 6, based on the department's current understanding of the initiative. Please keep in mind that this is all subject to ongoing state and local review, and that it describes the view of the SPD only. All marijuana possession and sale remains illegal under federal law, and Seattle Police cannot predict or control the enforcement activities of federal authorities.

CAN I LEGALLY CARRY AROUND AN OUNCE OF MARIJUANA?

According to the recently passed initiative, beginning December 6, adults over the age of 21 will be able to carry up to an ounce of marijuana for personal use. Please note that the initiative says it "is unlawful to open a package containing marijuana…in view of the general public," so there's that. Also, you probably shouldn't bring pot with you to the federal courthouse (or any other federal property).

WELL, WHERE CAN I LEGALLY BUY POT, THEN?

The Washington State Liquor Control Board is working to establish guidelines for the sale and distribution of marijuana. The WSLCB has until December 1, 2013 to finalize those rules. In the meantime, production and distribution of non-medical marijuana remains illegal.

DOES I-502 AFFECT CURRENT MEDICAL MARIJUANA LAWS?

No, medical marijuana laws in Washington remain the same as they were before I-502 passed.

CAN I GROW MARIJUANA IN MY HOME AND SELL IT TO MY FRIENDS, FAMILY, AND COWORKERS?

Not right now. In the future, under state law, you may be able to get a license to grow or sell marijuana.

CAN I SMOKE POT OUTSIDE MY HOME? LIKE AT A PARK, MAGIC SHOW, OR THE BITE OF SEATTLE?

Much like having an open container of alcohol in public, doing so could result in a civil infraction—like a ticket—but not arrest. You can certainly use marijuana in the privacy of your own home. Additionally, if smoking a cigarette isn't allowed where you are (say, inside an apartment building or flammable chemical factory), smoking marijuana isn't allowed there either.

WILL POLICE OFFICERS BE ABLE TO SMOKE MARIJUANA?

As of right now, no. This is still a very complicated issue.

IF I APPLY FOR A JOB AT THE SPD, WILL PAST (OR CURRENT) MARIJUANA USE BE HELD AGAINST ME?

The current standard for applicants is that they have not used marijuana in the previous 3 years. In light of I-502, the department will consult with the City Attorney and the State Attorney General to see if and how that standard may be revised.

WHAT HAPPENS IF I GET PULLED OVER AND AN OFFICER THINKS I'VE BEEN SMOKING POT?

If an officer believes you're driving under the influence of anything, they will conduct a field sobriety test and may consult with a drug recognition expert. If officers establish probable cause, they will bring you to a precinct and ask your permission to draw your blood for testing. If officers have reason to believe you're under the influence of something, they can get a warrant for a blood draw from a judge. If you're in a serious accident, then a blood draw will be mandatory.

WHAT HAPPENS IF I GET PULLED OVER AND I'M SOBER, BUT AN OFFICER OR HIS K9 BUDDY SMELLS THE OUNCE OF SUPER SKUNK I'VE GOT IN MY TRUNK?

Under state law, officers have to develop probable cause to search a closed or locked container. Each case stands on its own, but the smell of pot alone will not be reason to search a vehicle. If officers have information that you're trafficking, producing or delivering marijuana in violation of state law, they can get a warrant to search your vehicle.

SPD SEIZED A BUNCH OF MY MARIJUANA BEFORE I-502 PASSED. CAN I HAVE IT BACK?

No.

WILL SPD ASSIST FEDERAL LAW ENFORCEMENT IN INVESTIGATIONS OF MARIJUANA USERS OR MARIJUANA-RELATED BUSINESSES THAT ARE ALLOWED UNDER I-502?

No. Officers and detectives will not participate in an investigation of anything that's not prohibited by state law.

DECEMBER 6 SEEMS LIKE A REALLY LONG WAYS AWAY. WHAT HAPPENS IF I GET CAUGHT WITH MARIJUANA BEFORE THEN?

Hold your breath. Your case will be processed under current state law. However, there is already a city ordinance making marijuana enforcement the lowest law enforcement priority.

I'M UNDER 21. WHAT HAPPENS IF I GET CAUGHT SMOKING POT?

It's a violation of state law. It may refer to prosecutors, just like if you were a minor in possession of alcohol.

Source: Seattle Crime News - SPD Blotter by Jonah Spangenthal-Lee.

WHAT IS DISCRETION?

Discretion exists anytime an individual is faced with a decision to make, and they are free to select from among two or more alternative courses of action. This is a fairly broad definition of discretion; under this definition you exercise discretion all the time, such as deciding whether to attend class (please don't tell your instructor that we view that as a discretionary decision—you should always attend class!). To more precisely define discretion within the criminal justice system, we can refine the definition to add that the criminal justice decision-maker is acting upon the authority vested in their official position and/or office, and they are using their professional judgment to select from among decision alternatives within the structure of the law as well as agency policies and rules. Both types of discretion (the discretion you exercise in your daily life, and the discretion exercised by criminal justice officials) are important to consider, however, and citizen discretion—in the form of the victim's decision whether to report a crime to the police—is perhaps the most important as it has a substantial impact on what types of cases come to the attention of the criminal justice system as well as the sequence of events and official decisions that follow.

Police discretion is not a modern phenomenon; discretion in the criminal justice system has been acknowledged for quite some time (Pound, 1913, 1930). It is probably safe to say that discretion has existed as long as the police have existed, and it has certainly been acknowledged by police chiefs, other criminal justice actors, the news media, and the public for a very long time. But the formalized recognition of discretionary decision-making as central to the administration of justice, and the academic study of police discretion, *are* both relatively modern phenomena. Scholars generally point to the field research and surveys conducted by the American Bar Foundation in three states, starting in 1956, as the impetus for subsequent social science research on the nature of discretion (Walker, 1992; see also Walker, 1993). The American Bar Foundation study observed widespread informal resolutions to the tension between the public demand for order maintenance and the constraints of procedural law, and that these resolutions were largely hidden from public view or record. They also observed widespread discretionary decision-making in the absence of formal rules, and came to the view of criminal justice as an integrated system of decision stages rather than as a collection of relatively independent entities. The findings made their way into the scholarly literature, notably for police discretion in the works by Joseph Goldstein (1960) and Wayne LaFave (1965), and in a broader sense by the subsequent shift in academic view of the criminal justice system. The empirical study of police discretion rapidly followed with important studies focused on police interactions with juveniles (Piliavin and Briar, 1964) and a long line of inquiry into the role of suspect demeanor in police officer decision-making by several authors, as well as individual, situational, neighborhood, and organizational factors (discussed below).

We adopt here the **rational decision-making framework** articulated by Gottfredson and Gottfredson (1988). Following from the literature of the 1960s and 70s, they approach the criminal justice system as a series of decision points, with criminal justice actors making discretionary decisions about how particular cases should be handled. Thus, we have police officers deciding whether to arrest, prosecutors deciding whether and how to charge, juries making determinations of guilt, judges making sentencing decisions, correctional officials determining conditions of confinement, parole boards making decision about parole, and so on. In making these varied decisions, criminal justice actors have *goals* that they are seeking to achieve, *alternative* courses of action from which to choose, and *information* about the alternatives (such as the likelihood of a particular outcome, given the choice of a particular alternative) which may guide their selection (Gottfredson & Gottfredson, 1988).

These decision points are perhaps best visualized in terms of the classic "flowchart" of criminal justice, which first appeared in the 1967 report of the President's Commission on Law Enforcement and Administration of Justice and was last revised in 1997 by the Bureau of Justice Statistics on the 30th anniversary of the Commission (Figure 7.1). The flowchart depicts the major decision arenas as "entry into the system" (encompassing both victims and police), "prosecution and

What is the sequence of events in the criminal justice system?

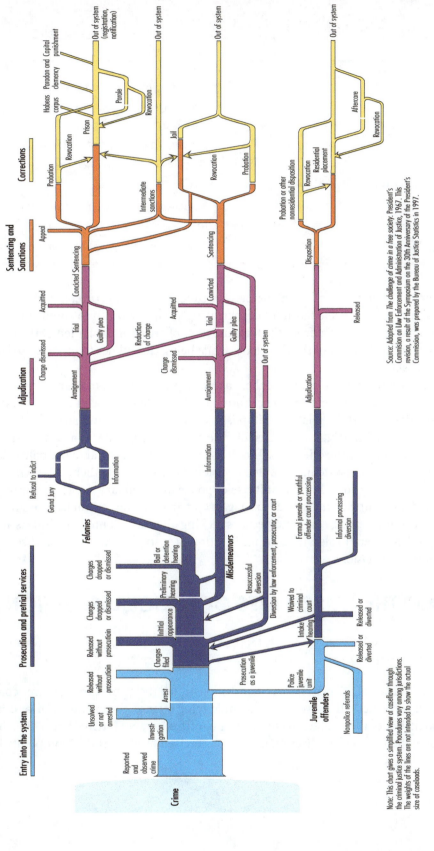

Note: This chart gives a simplified view of caseflow through the criminal justice system. Procedures vary among jurisdictions. The weights of the lines are not intended to show the actual size of caseloads.

Source: Adapted from *The challenge of crime in a free society*. President's Commission on Law Enforcement and Administration of Justice, 1967. This revision, a result of the Symposium on the 30th Anniversary of the President's Commission, was prepared by the Bureau of Justice Statistics in 1997.

Figure 7.1 The Classic "Flowchart" of the Criminal Justice System

TABLE 7.1 Examples of Police Discretionary Decisions

Decision	Alternatives
Dispatch an officer	Do not dispatch, deprioritize follow-up, inform citizen how to report crime
Take the call	Radio unavailable to take call, respond as back-up
On-view action	Ignore the incident, refer to other officer
Issue citation	Give verbal warning, ignore
Investigate reported crime	Do not investigate
Arrest	Separate, mediate, counsel, warn, ignore
Engage in pursuit	Break off
Use physical force	Don't use force, level of force used

pretrial services," "adjudication," "sentencing and sanctions," and "corrections." The major decision points and pathways are depicted as lines of increasingly narrow width to simply indicate that there is overall attrition as cases proceed from the total universe of crime at the far left of the flowchart, to capital punishment at the far right of the flowchart (while being careful not to imply actual caseloads in the width of the lines).

Police play an early and important role here as, perhaps, the second most important decision-makers (next to victims), as "gatekeepers" of the criminal justice system. We can certainly expand the police decision categories beyond the relatively simplistic depiction in the flowchart, which only includes the decisions of whether to investigate a reported or observed crime, whether to arrest a suspect, and includes a separate pathway for juvenile offenders. The decision to arrest is central to the police decision-making role in the criminal justice system, since that decision determines whether a case will proceed to prosecutors for charging decisions. But the universe of police discretionary decision-making is much larger than arrest, and it is a little disingenuous to suggest that arrest is the central feature since the police play an important role in diverting cases and perhaps seeking alternative outcomes. This is arguably of equal importance to their overall role in the administration of justice. Below is a list of several examples of police discretionary decisions.

WHAT ARE THE CORRELATES OF POLICE DISCRETION?

STARTING WITH THE BIG PICTURE: COMMON CRIMINAL JUSTICE DECISION CORRELATES

A large body of social science research has demonstrated the significance of three common criminal justice decision correlates—the severity of the underlying offense, the offender's prior criminal conduct, and the relationship of the offender to the victim (Gottfredson & Gottfredson, 1988).The more serious the underlying offense, the less discretion will be exercised at various decision points in the criminal justice system; rather, full system processing is the most likely outcome. The less serious the offense, the greater discretion will be exercised at different decision points, and case attrition or exit from formal processing (and toward less formal alternatives) is likely. Homicides are likely to receive full system processing with very little discretion exercised at any given decision point. Simple drug possession is likely not to receive formal processing, and great discretion will be exercised in, for example, the police decision to arrest, issue a citation, warn the individual, or ignore it altogether.

Police officers exercise discretion when issuing traffic citations and warnings.

When offenders have extensive criminal histories, less discretion will be exercised at various criminal justice system decision points and full system processing is more likely. On some level, this probably appeals to one's sense of justice—that an offender with an extensive criminal history might be treated more strictly by the criminal justice system, and afforded fewer opportunities for alternative resolutions. In contrast, first-time offenders are more likely to benefit from less formal or less serious alternatives.

Less discretion tends to be exercised for "stranger" offenses (i.e., when the victim and offender do not know each other) as compared to intimate offenses, where the victim and offender do know each other or have a relationship of some type. Criminal justice actors tend to seek alternatives when the participants are relatives or friends, whereas stranger offenses are more likely to receive full system processing.

The prominence of these three decision correlates in criminal justice decision-making—the severity of the underlying offense, the offender's criminal history, and the victim/offender relationship—led to what Gottfredson and Gottfredson (1988) conceptualized as "two systems" of criminal justice. One of these conceptual systems is characterized by serious violent offenses committed by strangers, and less serious offenses committed by individuals with extensive criminal histories. Very little discretion is exercised and full system processing is likely in this first system. The other conceptual system is characterized by less serious offenses, offenses committed by first-time or low-level offenders, and offenses involving intimates or no victim at all. Great discretion is exercised and very limited and/or alternative processing is likely in this second system.

In the first system, because very little discretion is being exercised, extra-legal factors such as an individual's race or demeanor are unlikely to play a significant role in criminal justice decision-making. But in the second system, where great discretion is exercised, these extra-legal factors are much more likely to rear their ugly heads. As demonstrated by Seattle's early experience with Marijuana enforcement in light of recent legislation to legalize possession but to restrict public consumption (described at the beginning of the chapter), this wide discretion provides officers with the flexibility necessary to handle otherwise vague ordinances, but can also have significant consequences in terms of any disparate impact on persons of particular races and/or statuses, such as minorities and the homeless.

POLICE DISCRETION CORRELATES: CONTEXT, INDIVIDUAL, SITUATION, AND ORGANIZATIONAL FACTORS

CONTEXT

Neighborhood characteristics that describe police officer work environments are an important place to start. Smith (1986) situated this area of research in the historical context of early delinquency studies where disproportionate arrest of poor juveniles was attributed to police disproportionate attention to juveniles from poorer neighborhoods, and in later work arguing that variation in police activity across neighborhoods is a kind of adaptation implicit in the police role (e.g., Whyte, 1943; Banton, 1964; Reiss and Bordua, 1967). Classic observational studies of the 1960s and 70s (Black and Reiss, 1967; Skolnick, 1966; Wilson, 1968; Rubinstein, 1973) provided confirmation of differential behavior across neighborhoods, and sparked the development of formal theory of the law and social control (e.g., Black, 1976).

The research literature demonstrates that neighborhood characteristics are in fact strongly correlated with officer behavior and decision-making. In particular, the racial/ethnic composition of neighborhoods, taken with indicators of

© 1000 Words/Shutterstock.com

Poor neighborhoods often have a higher rate of arrests.

structural disadvantage (e.g., neighborhoods with high rates of unemployment, high rates of poverty, low rates of owner-occupied housing), have been shown to be empirically related to arrest as well as the use of force. This growing body of research suggests that "context matters" and that these neighborhood characteristics are essential to understanding police behavior. Smith's (1986) oft-cited analysis of data collected as part of the 1977 Police Services Study identified several variables related to neighborhood context that account for differences in police behavior between neighborhoods. In particular, neighborhood socioeconomic status, racial heterogeneity, percent non-white, crime, and instability were found to be important contextual measures.

Socioeconomic status was the strongest predictor of the police decision to arrest, net of the effects of individual- and encounter-level characteristics. Specifically, as neighborhood socioeconomic status increased, the probability of arrest decreased. In addition, neighborhood-level racial heterogeneity was found to interact with complainant preference for arrest such that the effect of preference on arrest was stronger in more racially homogeneous neighborhoods.

With regard to police coercion (physical force, verbal threats of arrest, force, or surveillance), percent non-white and racial heterogeneity were significant predictors of coercion net of individual- and encounter-level characteristics. As percent non-white and racial heterogeneity increased, the probability of police coercion increased. That is, police are more likely to use force in non-white and mixed neighborhoods. In addition, percent non-white was found to interact with suspect race such that police coercion was more likely to be used against black suspects in largely non-white neighborhoods.

Neighborhood crime and instability predicted the filing of official incident (victimization) reports. As the level of crime increased, the probability of official reporting decreased, and as the level of instability increased, the probability of official reporting increased. Victim race was found to interact with neighborhood racial heterogeneity such that police reporting was less likely for black victims in both predominately white and non-white neighborhoods, but approximately equal (with whites) in mixed neighborhoods.

Collectively, Smith's findings suggest that the study of police behavior must include consideration for the context in which such behavior occurs. Research findings are likely to be misleading (and perhaps even incorrect) when context is not controlled. Although Smith offered a number of potential explanations for his findings, he did not go so far as to articulate a theory of police behavior that explained behavior in context. David Klinger (1997) was probably the first to do so.

Klinger's ecological theory is largely based on the notion that police district-level characteristics structure the reality of policing for the officers who work there. Klinger argues that police behavior is an outgrowth of officers' shared understanding of district-level deviance. In large part, district-level deviance is defined by the types of calls for service that are actually dispatched (i.e., subsequent to dispatcher filtration processes), and the shared experience of officers as they respond to the district workload. But the perception of district-level deviance is also influenced by other characteristics that officers associate with deviance:

> Police officers know from experience what social scientists have "discovered" through research: Deviance is correlated with numerous territorial properties, such as population density, standard of living, and the physical condition of areas. By paying attention to the sights, sounds, and smells of patrol, officers gain an impression of levels of crowding, deterioration, and living standard in their districts. While handling details, they gain impressions of household crowding, residents' standard of living, and the state of (dis)repair of commercial and residential structures. The more crowded the general area and individual domiciles seem to be, the more poverty stricken the area and

its inhabitants appear, the more dilapidated the property, and the more that
garbage litters the landscape and graffiti cover the walls, the greater the level
of perceived deviance. (Klinger, 1997:289)

Klinger argues that the level of deviance in a police district in turn structures the way in which officers understand and regulate deviance within that district. Holding constant the seriousness of behavior in police–citizen encounters, the degree of police "vigor" (the degree to which officers exercise their authority via arrests, taking reports, etc.) is expected to be *lower* in districts where the level of deviance is understood by officers to be higher. Crimes that might be regarded as "extreme" in police districts with generally low levels of deviance may be regarded as "normal" by police in other districts with higher levels of deviance. Victimization, too, may be regarded as a somewhat "normal" event, with less attention consequently being devoted to victims in these areas. This bears out in Smith's (1986) study, where he found that as the level of neighborhood crime increased, the probability of police reporting (i.e., filing of official incident reports) decreased. At the least, it suggests that police may set thresholds for what constitutes "serious" crime (i.e., deserving of official reaction) based on the level of crime in the neighborhood. In addition, Klinger (1997) points out that workload pressures tend to be greater in districts with high levels of deviance; thus, less attention can be devoted to the full range of behavior that occurs there.

More recent work by Mastrofski and his colleagues, based on the 1996–97 Project on Policing Neighborhoods (POPN), has tended to reinforce the importance of context. In their study of police disrespect toward the public,[2] Mastrofski et al. (2002) found that while several encounter-level variables were predictive of police disrespect, a measure of neighborhood concentrated disadvantage, while problematic (due to the confounding of a variety of ecological measures), also predicted disrespect: the greater the level of neighborhood disadvantage, the more likely police are to behave disrespectfully of citizens. Importantly, citizen race was only significant when neighborhood context was controlled (such that white citizens are more likely to experience police disrespect), although this appears to be driven primarily by data from one of the three cities studied (St. Petersburg, Florida).

Terrill and Reisig (2003) explored the role of concentrated disadvantage and homicide rate on the level of force employed by police. While controlling for 26 encounter-level variables, they found that both concentrated disadvantage and homicide rate were predictive of the level of force used by police. That is, police were found to use higher levels of force in areas characterized by greater levels of concentrated disadvantage and higher crime (as indicated by homicide rate). Similar to Smith (1986), they also found that the encounter-level effect of minority status on level of force used by police was mediated by concentrated disadvantage.

INDIVIDUAL

When considering decisions made by individual actors, it is perhaps somewhat natural to focus on any individual characteristics that may or may not influence decision-making and the exercise of discretion. Examples include officer demographics such as education, age and/or experience, gender, and race.

As you learned in Chapter 6, the role of higher education in police performance has a long history, and there has been several decades' long push to increase the education standards for entry to policing. In general, it is hypothesized that college-educated officers will perform better than

---

2   "Disrespect" was operationalized as any instances of "name calling, derogatory remarks about the citizen or the citizen's family, belittling remarks, slurs, cursing, ignoring the citizen's questions (except in an emergency), using a loud voice or interrupting the citizen (except in an emergency), obscene gestures, or spitting" (Mastrofski et al., 2002:529–530).

less educated officers. Rydberg and Terrill (2010) recently examined the effect of officer education on arrest, search, and use of force, using observational data from Indianapolis and St. Petersburg collected as part of the POPN study. In a subsample of more than 3300 police–citizen encounters in those two cities, they found no effect of higher education (officer having either some college, or a 4-year degree, as compared to non-college-educated officers) on arrest or search decisions, but reported that higher education reduced the likelihood of using force, a finding consistent with previous research on these outcomes.

Officer age and years of experience tend to be highly correlated because policing is a physically demanding job that is most attractive to young adults and police departments often have higher age limits for entry-level hire. Also, assignment practices tend to be correlated with years of experience, with newer officers typically receiving more "active" and less desirable assignments than more experienced officers (who, by virtue of their seniority, typically have preference and are more likely to attain choice assignments). These combine to make it very difficult to disentangle whether one is seeing an age effect or an experience effect in the data. Typically, research hypotheses in policing specify an effect of years of service rather than age and try to control for confounders such as assignment. There is some evidence that the volume of work may decline but the quality of work (such as the quality of arrests) improves with years of experience.

Officer gender is a bit of a mixed bag, with some studies suggesting differences and others suggesting no differences in the exercise of discretion. One problem is that, historically, females have only comprised a small percentage of total employment in law enforcement. It is only in recent years that substantial growth in the percentage of female officers has been realized (and even so, as of 2013 females still comprised only about 1 out of every 8 officers, and 1 out of every 10 supervisors, although these figures are higher among the largest agencies; see Reaves, 2015). Much research has been focused on such issues as sexual harassment and tokenism, and less so on gender differences in performance, and officer gender is typically treated as a control variable rather than an explanatory variable. Researchers have typically hypothesized that female officers will exhibit less aggression with attendant benefits to police-community relations, but recent research has not supported that claim; for example, Paoline and Terrill (2004) found no substantive gender differences in the use of verbal or physical coercion in the POPN data.

Similarly, research on officer race offers little guidance on stable effects. In some cases, observed race effects may be masking other substantive considerations. For example, Fyfe (1978) found that the apparent relationship between officer race and use of deadly force in New York City (such that black officers used deadly force to a greater extent than white officers) was spurious in that black officers were disproportionately assigned to high-crime neighborhoods where the likelihood of having to use deadly force was higher. Some research shows black officers tending to be more coercive than white officers (Sherman, 1980); and less likely to arrest than white officers (Brown & Frank, 2006); while other research shows no relationship or that the relationship between officer race and various outcomes is contingent on neighborhood

Many factors go into a decision by an officer to use force in a given situation.

© bikeriderlondon/Shutterstock.com

context, suspect characteristics, and other situational factors (e.g., Sun & Payne, 2004; Brown & Frank, 2006).The role of officer race and ethnicity in understanding officer behavior is a complex and evolving area.

On balance the evidence on individual officer characteristics is mixed, and the effects of individual characteristics are typically weaker than contextual and situational variables.

SITUATION

The scholarly literature also points to the influence of situational characteristics, such as suspect demographic characteristics (e.g., age, gender, and race), suspect demeanor (e.g., cooperativeness, rudeness, aggressiveness), complainant preference (e.g., the complainant's preference for police to arrest a suspect), and the way in which police encounter the situation (responding to a call for service, or coming across the situation in the course of proactive patrol). Suspect demeanor in particular has been shown to be a relatively strong correlate of police behavior. As one might expect, when suspects are noncompliant, disrespectful, uncooperative, and/or behave antagonistically toward the police, they are more likely to be arrested, as well as to have force used upon them, and higher levels of force, than a compliant suspect in equivalent circumstances. There is some debate about the conceptual differences between suspect noncompliance with commands and statements indicating disrespect for authority, but on balance the available research shows a relatively robust effect of suspect demeanor.

The role of suspect demographic characteristics, such as suspect age, race, and gender in police decision-making is less clear. While suspect race is a highly contentious issue that rapidly moves toward concerns about racial profiling, or racially-biased policing, the research on balance tends to demonstrate that suspect demeanor outweighs the effect of suspect race in predicting things like police use of force. We will explore racially-biased policing in greater detail in Chapter 13.

Finally, the two principle means by which police encounter suspects are (1) responding to citizen-initiated calls for service, and (2) police-initiated activity, also called proactive or "on-view" encounters. As you might hypothesize, the dynamic is somewhat different when the police have been called to a scene as compared to when they come across something that may or may not (in the eyes of the participants) require their intervention. In the former, their presence has been specifically requested by someone either involved or witnessing the incident; in the latter, the police are much more likely to be seen as illegitimate, antagonistic, intrusive, "over-stepping," discriminatory, and/or oppressive. There is some evidence that the police are more likely to arrest, use force, and receive citizen complaints in on-view incidents as compared to citizen-initiated contacts.

ORGANIZATION

Finally, it is important to consider organizational factors. James Q. Wilson's (1968) classic, *Varieties of Police Behavior,* described variation in police organizational styles based upon the frequency and the formality of police–citizen interaction, and he theorized that the style of policing was largely a reflection of local political culture as well as community characteristics. These styles of policing include the **watchman, service,** and **legalistic** organizational styles. In watchman style police departments, there is relatively less frequent interaction with citizens, very little emphasis on arrests, and the primary focus is on the order maintenance function of policing. Officers in watchman style departments exercise great discretion in determining what should be done, if anything, and although Wilson did not describe the formality of interaction for these departments it might be considered less formal on balance. In service oriented departments, which tend to be relatively low-crime suburban cities, police interact with citizens regularly and seek to provide a response to all citizen requests (thus the service orientation), but these interactions tend to be less formal and officers tend to avoid arrest. Finally, in legalistic departments, the primary focus is on the law enforcement function of policing. Police in legalistic departments interact with citizens regularly and in a formal manner. The law is the primary determinant of whether and how officers respond to situations in these departments, and there is emphasis on issuing citations and making arrests. In general, research has demonstrated variability in the frequency and formality of police–citizen interactions and resulting policing styles across large samples of agencies, but has not demonstrated a relationship between local political culture and policing style, although this may be due to limited ability to fully measure the key theoretical mechanisms (Liederbach & Travis, 2008).

CONTROLLED DISCRETION

No two cases are identical in every possible regard, and a "one-size-fits-all" approach to law enforcement is as unrealistic as a "one-size-fits-all" approach to clothing. While on the whole the Constitutional requirements of due process and equal protection push us toward a preference for ensuring equity in the administration of justice, the police also need the flexibility to tailor their responses to specific situations. Police need the freedom to select among alternative courses of action, but the police should not be completely unrestrained in doing so. In order to provide some structure and guidance to officers, administrative rulemaking (in the form of formal, written policies) seeks to specify what officers are not allowed to do, and where officers can use discretion. The goal is not to eliminate discretion but to structure and guide the exercise of discretion. Almost all police departments in the U.S. have formal written policies concerning the use of deadly force (97%), and departments typically have a number of formal policies for such matters as handling domestic disputes; in fact, about 9 out of 10 departments in the U.S. in 2007 had such a policy, including all of the very largest departments (Reaves, 2010). Other examples include handling juveniles (90%), the mentally ill (69%), homeless (34%), persons with limited English proficiency (32%), and checking immigration status (20%) (Reaves, 2010). One important correlate is the size of the agency: larger agencies serving larger jurisdictions are much more likely to have formal written policies on a diverse range of issues, as compared to smaller agencies serving smaller jurisdictions.

THE LACK OF FEEDBACK LOOPS IN POLICING

Returning for the moment to the issue of common decision correlates and the consequent impact on the exercise of discretion, another major theme identified by Gottfredson and Gottfredson (1988) is the absence of feedback in criminal justice, which is to say, the absence of adequate *information* to enable rational, goal-oriented decision-making about alternatives. This includes information about the decisions of colleagues faced with similar situations (i.e., "how consistent is my decision-making in relation to other decision-makers?"), as well as information about the specific outcomes of decisions and whether they matched the goals of the decision (i.e., "I arrested this individual because … with the goal to … and did that actually happen? Was this the correct decision, given the goal?"). *The textbook authors are unaware of any police department that systematically collects, maintains, and/or utilizes a database concerning the goals and outcomes of police decision-making, along with feedback loops to the individual officers. How delighted we would be to learn that a department was doing so.* In practice, this may occur on a "gut" level, or may be less formally communicated among individual criminal justice actors (e.g., prosecutors may communicate to police officers about the quality of the cases being presented for possible prosecution by denying to file charges or communicating with an officer or a department's command staff). However, if the goal is to inform the exercise of discretion and improve the quality of police decision-making, systematic data collection, analysis, and reporting would seem to be a critical step.

CONCLUSION

Discretion—the ability to select among alternative courses of action—is a necessary and even desirable feature of policing, but uncontrolled discretion and arbitrary decision-making are not. Our system of law enforcement requires that we trust police officers to exercise discretion intelligently, using professional judgment based upon their training and experience, and within the structures of the law as well as agency policy and rules. Much criminal justice decision-making is explained by common correlates, including the severity of the underlying offense, the offender's prior criminal history, and the relationship between the offender and any victim. In addition, police decision-making can also be explained by a multitude of contextual, individual, situational, and organizational factors. The challenge comes in recognizing that police officers are humans who are tasked with dealing with extremely complex and rapidly evolving situations, no two of which are exactly alike. They must make decisions about "what to do" using the information that is available, and this requires the exercise of discretion. Officers need adequate guidance in their exercise of discretion, which is often provided in the form of written policies, but they also need information and feedback about the outcomes of their decisions such that the quality of police decision-making can be assessed over time. It is in this latter area where there is arguably much room for improvement.

REVIEW QUESTIONS

1. Do police officers have too much discretion? If yes, what are the areas in which you believe police discretion to be excessive, and how would you further limit the amount of discretion that officers can exercise in those areas? If no, are there any changes you would recommend to further structure discretionary decision-making?

2. Do you think that police officers could ever be replaced with robots? What kinds of programming would be necessary to ensure equal protection and due process, while balancing the idiosyncrasies of particular situations as well as the needs/desires of the community served? Could they outperform a human?

GLOSSARY

Police discretion decision-making authority of officers to choose a course of action based on suspect, situational, and contextual factors.

Watchman style a police style, proposed by James Q. Wilson, in which police have relatively less frequent interaction with citizens, there is very little emphasis on arrests, and the primary focus is on the order maintenance function of policing; officers exercise great discretion in determining what should be done, if anything.

Service style a police style, proposed by James Q. Wilson, in which police interact with citizens regularly and seek to provide a response to all citizen requests, but these interactions tend to be less formal and officers tend to avoid arrest.

Legalistic style a police style, proposed by James Q. Wilson, in which the primary focus is on the law enforcement function of policing; interactions with citizens are regular and formal; the law is the primary determinant of whether and how officers respond to situations, and there is emphasis on issuing citations and making arrests.

REFERENCES

Banton, M. (1964).*The Police in the Community.* New York, NY: Basic Books.

Black, D. (1976). *The Behavior of Law.* New York, NY: Academic Press.

Black, D., and Reiss, A. J. (1967). Patterns of behavior in police and citizen transactions. In *Studies of crime and law enforcement in major metropolitan areas.* Washington, DC: Government Printing Office.

Bush, E. (2015). Tickets for pot use in Seattle still skew toward blacks, men. *The Seattle Times,* July 17. Retrieved from http://www.seattletimes.com/seattle-news/marijuana/tickets-issued-for-pot-use-in-seattle-continue-to-skew-toward-blacks-men/

Fyfe, J. (1978). *Shots fired: An examination of New York City Police firearms discharges.* Ph.D. Dissertation, State University of New York at Albany.

Goldstein, J. (1960). Police discretion not to invoke the criminal process; low-visibility decisions in the administration of justice. *Yale Law Journal, 69*(4), 543–588.

Gottfredson, M., & Gottfredson, D. (1988). *Decision making in criminal justice: Toward the rational exercise of discretion.* New York, NY: Plenum.

Klinger, D. (1997). Negotiating order in police work: An ecological theory of police response to deviance. *Criminology, 35,* 277–306.

LaFave, W. (1965). *Arrest.* Boston, MA: Little, Brown & Co.

Liederbach, J., & Travis, L. (2008). Wilson redux: Another look at varieties of police behavior. *Police Quarterly, 11*(4), 447–467.

Mastrofski, S. D., Reisig, M., & McClusky, J. (2002). Police disrespect toward the public: An encounter-based analysis. *Criminology, 40,* 519–551.

Miletich, S., & Sullivan, J. (2014). SPD investigates cop who wrote 80 percent of pot tickets. *The Seattle Times*, July 31. Retrieved from http://www.seattletimes.com/seattle-news/spd-investigates-cop-who-wrote-80-percent-of-pot-tickets/

Paoline, E., & Terrill, W. (2004). Women police officers and the use of coercion. *Women and Criminal Justice, 15,* 97–119.

Piliavin, I., & Briar, S. (1964). Police encounters with juveniles. *American Journal of Sociology, 70*, 206–214.

Pound, R. (1913). The administration of justice in the modern city. *Harvard Law Review, 26*, 302–328.

Pound, R. (1930). *Criminal justice in America.* New York, NY: Henry Holt and Co.

Reaves, B. (2015). *Local Police Departments, 2013: Personnel, policies, and practices.* Washington, DC: Bureau of Justice Statistics.

Reaves, B. (2010). *Local Police Departments, 2007.* Washington, DC: Bureau of Justice Statistics.

Reiss, A. J., & Bordua, D. (1967). Environment and organization: A perspective on the police. In D. Bordua (Ed.), *The police: Six sociological essays.* New York, NY: Wiley.

Rubenstein, J. (1973). *City Police.* New York, NY: Noonday Press.

Rydberg, J., & Terrill, W. (2010). The effect of higher education on police behavior. *Police Quarterly, 13*(1), 92–120.

Skolnick, J. H. (1966). *Justice without trial: Law enforcement in democratic society.* New York, NY: Wiley.

Smith, D. (1986). The neighborhood context of police behavior. In A. Reiss & M. Tonry (Eds.), *Communities and crime* (pp. 313–341). Chicago, IL: University of Chicago Press.

Terrill, W., & Reisig, M. (2003). Neighborhood context and police use of force. *Journal of Research in Crime and Delinquency, 40*, 291–321.

Walker, S. (1992). Origins of the contemporary criminal justice paradigm: The American Bar Foundation survey, 1953-1969. *Justice Quarterly, 9*, 201–230.

Walker, S. (1993). *Taming the system: The control of discretion in criminal justice, 1950-1990.* New York, NY: Oxford University Press.

Wilson, J. Q. (1968). *Varieties of police behavior.* Cambridge: Harvard University Press.

Whyte, W. (1943). *Street Corner Society.* Chicago, IL: University of Chicago Press.

Young, B. (2015). SPD chief asks council: Stop writing $27 pot tickets or not? *The Seattle Times,* July 20. Retrieved from http://www.seattletimes.com/seattle-news/spd-chief-asks-council-stop-writing-27-pot-tickets-or-not/

8

THE BASIC FUNCTIONS OF POLICE WORK

LEARNING OBJECTIVES

After reading this chapter, students should be able to:

1. Name and describe the three basic functions of policing

2. Explain why dispatchers are considered gate keepers.

3. Describe the difference between reactive policing and proactive policing.

4. Explain how an officer's job might vary by the beat and/or shift she works.

5. Name four methods used to patrol and explain the benefit of each.

6. Describe the research on police response time and when rapid response might make a difference in suspect apprehension.

7. Explain the research on the ideal number of patrol officers (one or two).

8. Summarize the research on preventative patrol.

9. Name and describe three types of targets patrol practices.

KEY TERMS

Law enforcement

Service

Order maintenance

Dispatcher

Differential response

Computer aided dispatch

Random routine patrol

Discovery crime

Involvement crime

Newark Foot Patrol Experiment

Preventative patrol

Minneapolis Hot Spot Study

Kansas City Preventative Patrol Experiment

Directed patrol

Saturation patrol

Crackdowns

Crime control

What, exactly, do police officers do during a shift? Television shows and movies would have us believe that a police officer's shift is packed full of one exciting call after another. In truth, such a portrayal is more myth than reality. While it is true that officers respond to a variety of calls and perform a multitude of tasks, both law enforcement and non-law enforcement related, many of the calls that police officers respond to are routine and might even be considered boring. Of course, an individual officer's experience depends tremendously on his or her jurisdiction and assigned beat.

This chapter explores the basic functions of police work and the various methods officers use to achieve their objectives. It starts with an explanation of the basic functions (objectives) of policing and how these objectives have changed over time. It then moves to a discussion about how agencies manage calls for service from the citizenry. From there, we investigate the patrol function and what research has taught us about the effectiveness of various strategies. Finally, the chapter introduces students to special teams and the functions they perform.

BASIC FUNCTIONS

In general, police work can be classified into three main categories: law enforcement (some say crime control), order maintenance, and service. **Law enforcement** is the function that people are most familiar with and encompasses those tasks that are directly related to enforcing the law and controlling crime. Briefly, it involves things like making arrests, taking crime reports, investigating crimes, and writing traffic citations. Meanwhile, *order maintenance* entails those activities that promote an orderly and peaceful society, for example, providing public safety during events that draw large crowds (such as sporting matches, parades, and civil protests), ensuring safe traveling conditions for vehicles and pedestrians, and regulating the use of public space. Finally, police officers provide a variety of **services** to the general public, including emergency medical services, supporting community events and schools, crime prevention training, and aiding individuals in need. These basic functions overlap and some tasks can be classified under two or more categories (more on this in a moment).

LAW ENFORCEMENT (AKA CRIME CONTROL)

Crime control is the function that we most equate with a police officer's job. Ironically, it is the function that officers spend the least amount of time doing (Green & Klockars, 1991; Johnson & Rhodes, 2009; Scott, 1981; Wilson, 1968). The law enforcement function includes tasks such as taking crime reports, investigating crimes, interviewing witnesses and suspects, collecting evidence, making arrests, patrolling hotspots, running DUI checkpoints, and performing undercover operations. It is primarily *reactive*, meaning police respond and perform these tasks after a crime has been reported, not before. We will discuss this in more detail later in this chapter, but suffice to say that few victims interact with the perpetrator during the commission of the crime; most discover that they were victimized after the crime took place and the perpetrator is long gone. Law enforcement can be *proactive* as well, meaning that police officers observe a law violation and make contact with the suspect on their own, without being alerted to the law violation by a member of the community. Sometimes this happens when an officer is randomly patrolling, but it can also happen when an officer is participating in an undercover sting operation or sitting inconspicuously in an area known for criminal activity (such as an open air drug market or a street known for prostitution, illegal gambling, or street racing). The line between the law enforcement function and the **order maintenance function** (discussed below) can be particularly blurred in blighted areas known for high levels of criminal activity.

ORDER MAINTENANCE

Order maintenance is essentially the peace keeping part of a police officer's job. It includes things such as helping resolve disputes between neighbors (loud music, for example); limiting the amount of disorder caused by homeless persons and their belongings; quelling public disturbances; removing prostitutes from busy avenues; and addressing issues caused by teens, street racers, and drug addicts. As can be seen, there are a wide array of activities that are involved in order maintenance. Almost all police activities that attempt to reduce disorder and decay or provide for a more peaceful environment could be considered order maintenance.

This is the part of the job that Egon Bittner was referring to when he said that police are the people we call when "something-ought-not-to-be-happening-about-which-something-should-be-done-NOW!" (Bittner, 1974, p. 30 reprinted in Klockars, 1985, p.16). For example, your neighbor is playing his music very loudly at 1:00 am. You don't appreciate his taste in music, and besides, you have an early class and need to get some sleep. Do you walk to your neighbor's door and

The law enforcement function includes such tasks as collecting evidence.

ask him to turn the music down? Maybe you know your neighbor to be a reasonable and considerate person so you "do the neighborly thing" and talk to him about the issue and resolve the situation peacefully. Perhaps, instead, you've asked him to turn down his radio in the past and he, in a rather passive-aggressive manner, turned up his radio in response to your request. Do you call the cops now? Many people do. The police respond to your call that your neighbor is "disturbing the peace" and officers help you resolve the problem with your inconsiderate neighbor. If necessary, they will help you perform a citizen's arrest of your neighbor (since police officers cannot be victims of "disturbing the peace," they are there as mediators only—unless there is a noise ordinance that your neighbor is breaking or until the neighbor does something else that is against the law). Ideally, your neighbor recognizes the officer's authority and power and turns down his music.

Natural disasters are another good, though thankfully not routine, example of the order maintenance function. Occasionally when there is pre-warning of potential danger, such as spreading wildfires or ash from volcanic eruptions, police alert residents of evacuation orders as well as establish and maintain safety perimeters. After the disaster, police are the ones dealing with the chaotic aftermath. Sometimes, like in New Orleans after Hurricane Katrina in 2005 and in New York and New Jersey after Hurricane Sandy in 2012, neighborhoods which experienced an unprecedented natural disaster find themselves in chaos and disarray. Power outages cause traffic problems as well as potential health problems, and people get scared and frustrated. There is sometimes widespread looting and violence. The police are stretched thin in these circumstances because they are inundated with calls for help and must prioritize the many essential tasks that are (or become) their responsibility (traffic safety, protecting downed power lines, search and rescue, evacuating people out of the danger zone, etc.). In such situations, guarding businesses (crime control) is less important than saving and protecting lives (order maintenance, service).

One of the most important order maintenance functions is keeping the peace during civil disturbances—whether acts of civil disobedience, political protests, sports celebrations, or riots. During the 1960s and early 1970s, officers were frequently called upon to quell disturbances related to the civil rights movement and the Vietnam War. Since that time, and prior to the Ferguson, MO, grand jury decision, there had been relatively few such orchestrated events. Most recently, police throughout America have responded to protests over the economy and social inequality (Occupy Movement; One-Percenters), the wars in Iraq and Afghanistan, and police use of force incidents (Ferguson, MO; New York City, NY; Baltimore, MD). Unfortunately, protests in reaction to police's use of force incidents are becoming much more regular and officers fully outfitted in riot gear responding in armored vehicles will tend to exacerbate the already highly emotional nature of these situations.

More commonly, order maintenance is associated with blighted neighborhoods, open air drug markets, and red light districts. Officers in these areas may remove abandoned or nonfunctioning vehicles, repair or demolish buildings that are uninhabitable, remove trash, fix street lights, and enforce code violations in an effort to reclaim the area. Some cities have special teams (e.g., vice or problem-oriented policing) that focus specifically on these areas. It is worth mentioning here that concerted and sustained efforts to reduce disorder and decay in blighted neighborhoods in an attempt to reduce serious crime has evolved into its own policing strategy based on the idea of broken windows. This will be discussed in detail in Chapter 9 but should not be confused with order maintenance as a basic function of policing (which is the target of the policing strategy).

As you can see, order maintenance tasks can be large-scale or small-scale and proactive or reactive. Sometimes tasks that begin as order maintenance can become law enforcement and/or service. The 2013 Boston Marathon is a good example of how one function of policing can quickly morph into other functions, sometimes without warning. On April 15, 2013, almost 27,000 runners took part in the 117th running of the Boston Marathon (BAA, 2014). Boston Police Department (BPD) officers were on duty and stationed throughout the 26 miles course for basic crowd control and general safety purposes, something they do every year, and what we would consider to be order maintenance. As you are probably aware, at 2:49 pm, 4 hours into the race (2 hours after the elite runners crossed the finish line) two pressure-cooker bombs exploded near the finish line killing three spectators and injuring 264 others (Levs & Plott, 2013). At that moment, some police officers became service providers, aiding injured victims, and other officers became law enforcers, investigating the initial cause of the explosions as accidental or intentional and sealing off a perimeter around each blast site. Still other officers, not in the immediate vicinity of the explosions, continued in their order maintenance role by diverting remaining runners and spectators away from the finish line, as per the emergency plans. In the days and weeks ahead, BPD continued in a law enforcement role, working with national agencies such as the FBI, BATF, CIA, DEA, and other agencies to identify and apprehend the suspects. BPD also continued in a service role by setting up and running a helpline for worried relatives and friends of runners and spectators.

SERVICE

The last, but not least, basic function of police is the provision of services to members of the community. This category includes activities that do not (or only minimally) involve maintaining order, controlling crime, or enforcing laws; activities such as looking for missing children, seniors, and runaways; performing emergency medical services; responding to burglar alarms; assisting stranded motorists; teaching crime prevention, bike safety, and citizen academy classes; engaging with local youth through outreach programs like the Police Explorers and Police Athletic League; and doing K-9 demonstrations, child fingerprinting, and show-and-tell at elementary schools.

For at least 40 years (and probably much longer), police departments have been educating the public about crime prevention. This can take the form of presentations to community groups, pamphlets handed out during community events, and information about target hardening provided to victims by responding officers. Today, such information is often shared via Twitter feeds, Facebook pages, Instagram, and department Web sites. While you are probably too young to remember this, in the 1970s and 1980s, police departments loaned out electric engravers so that residents

K-9 demonstrations are an example of a police service function.

could engrave their valuables (televisions, VCRs, tools, ATARI game consoles) with a personal identifier (usually a driver's license number or name and phone number) so that the item could be returned in the event that it was stolen. Ask your parents; perhaps, they still have an engraved item or two. Many departments have a designated crime prevention officer, often a non-sworn civilian or trained volunteer, to assist in this capacity.

Service, like law enforcement and order maintenance, can be reactive, as in the case of the Boston marathon, a drowning child, or even a request to participate in a community carnival. It can also be proactive, such as when a department initiates a citizen academy or other program not specifically requested by the community, when an officer stops his car to play catch with a young boy who has no one to play with, when an officer delivers a meal to a homebound senior in her beat, or when an officer helps an abused woman move herself and her children out of their home before the abuser returns.

The amount of time officers spend in service depends on the level of crime in an area—officers assigned to higher crime areas generally have less time to devote to community service. It also depends on the type of neighborhood—residents in more affluent areas often expect, and tend to receive, a higher level of service than residents in impoverished communities. This is a luxury afforded to these communities because officers in these neighborhoods spend less time responding to crimes and performing order maintenance tasks. There are other socio-demographic reasons as well, such as affluent communities often generating a tax base that supports higher staffing levels. Officer characteristics also play into how much attention a particular officer devotes to service. Some officers are naturally more comfortable with service-related activities than other officers.

There was a renewed focus on service activities in the 1990s when community policing gained popularity. While police have always, and will always, provide some basic services to the general public, community policing emboldened departments, especially large departments, to step out of their comfort zone to develop deeper and more collaborative partnerships with community groups in their jurisdiction. A benefit of this is that officers trained in the community policing philosophy have learned the importance of providing information and service to crime victims after taking a report. Today, unlike during the political and professional eras, it is common for patrol officers to spend extra time with a victim talking them through "what happens next," the steps they need to take (if any) to comply with the law, providing contact information for valuable resources (such as a victims' compensation fund, shelters, drug and alcohol resources), and sometimes, basic counseling. One of the authors worked with a patrol officer who, for many months, attended group grief counseling sessions with a mother who lost her daughter to suicide. She was afraid to attend alone and he felt it was important that she go to counseling so he volunteered his personal time to take her (now that is going above and beyond!).

MANAGING CALLS FOR SERVICE

Although police officers are generally considered the main gatekeepers of the criminal justice system, **dispatchers** are typically the *first* gatekeepers that residents encounter when requesting police services. In 2011, approximately 31 million U.S. residents age 16 and older requested police assistance—about 15% of the population. Most of these individuals reported a crime, disturbance, or suspicious activity (Durose & Langton, 2013). The vast majority of these requests for service, about three-quarters, were phoned in to police as opposed to stopping a police officer on the street or driving to a police station (Durose & Langton, 2013).

It has been found that, nationwide, dispatchers answer about 23 million calls annually. Call volume is not evenly divided, with residents living in impoverished communities more likely than those living in affluent communities to call the police (Schaible & Hughes, 2012) and large cities receive a disproportionate number of calls in comparison to small towns. Baltimore police dispatchers, for example, answer approximately 1,000,000 calls per year (Mazerolle, et al., 2002). Smaller departments answer considerably fewer. In order to manage high call volumes, police departments have created special procedures and phone numbers to triage requests and manage responses (see 211 and 311 Systems box).

211 AND 311 SYSTEMS FOR GENERAL PUBLIC SERVICES

The general public calls the police for help with a variety of concerns, regardless of whether they are law related. To report a clogged sewer that is causing water to pool in the street, an inoperable traffic light, graffiti, a stampede of horses running down a suburban street, a woman walking unevenly in the roadway and talking to herself; to find out the time for high tide, sunset, or whether he just experienced an earthquake, or to get advice on whether to get out of a bad relationship, and where to go for help. Believe it or not, one of the authors has fielded all of these citizen requests for assistance (some of which are legitimate police issues). Why do we call the police when we need help with something not technically crime related? The answer is simple; it is generally the one public agency that is always open (24 hours per day, 7 days per week, 365 days a year) and we have the number memorized. It is also because most of us have been taught that police are there to help us even when we don't know where else to turn.

In response to these realities, and the burden such as high call volume places on police departments, some cities and counties (e.g., Chicago, Houston, Los Angeles, San Francisco, New York, and Washington D.C.) have instituted 211 and 311 systems alongside the 911 emergency system (some jurisdictions use 511, the traffic system, for non-police services). The 311 hotline is intended to be a one-stop call center for all city service (and in some cities such as Chicago, nonemergency police service) requests—clogged sewers, graffiti removal, snow removal, pothole and street light repair, malfunctioning train crossing barriers, weather-related emergency shelters, health code violations, and even senior citizen welfare checks.

Since the number was approved by the Federal Communications Committee 2000, 211 has been the one-stop shop for community health and human service resources. It contains information for those needing assistance with:

- *basic human needs*—food and clothing, banks, shelters
- *physical and mental health support*—medical and insurance information, crisis intervention, support groups, and counseling
- *work support*—job training, education programs, transportation, and financial assistance
- *services for seniors and residents with disabilities*—adult day care, home health care, community meals, transportation
- *resources for children, youth, and families*—parenting, after-school programs, summer camps, mentoring, tutoring, protective services
- *suicide prevention* (FCC, 2013).

Some regions, such as Orange County, CA, also include reentry resources for previously incarcerated individuals as well as legal resources on their 211 Web sites.

Both systems, in particular 311, are intended to divert non-emergency calls for service away from police dispatch centers to allow more resources to be devoted to emergency calls for service. Research has found that 311 systems can dramatically reduce non-emergency calls for service to 911 and that cost and police personnel workload savings are greatest when calls are routed to a non-police dispatch center (Mazerolle, Rogan, Frank, Famega, & Eck, 2002).

Dispatchers are the first gatekeepers that residents encounter when requesting police services and are often the public's first impression of the police. Like police officers, dispatchers are street-level bureaucrats who exercise tremendous discretion in determining who gets service, when, and the level of service received. Dispatchers use discretion as they screen calls, categorize callers' problems, and determine and assign the most appropriate response given department resources. They field a wide variety of calls, many of which do not require police assistance. Some requests for service require the skills, expertise, and powers of a sworn officer but many others are easily handled by non-sworn (civilian) staff. Similarly, some requests require an immediate response (due to a life-threatening situation) but most do not. It is up to the discretion of the dispatcher to determine the urgency and validity of each call and assign appropriate resources.

As you might imagine, it can get very hectic in the dispatch center, especially if there are multiple urgent calls for assistance at the same time (see Dispatching box for a description of

Dispatchers use discretion as they screen and prioritize calls.

© hhltdave5/Shutterstock.com

the dispatch process). In order to manage all the calls for service and make sure officers respond to the most critical calls first, dispatchers triage (prioritize) calls based on urgency and seriousness. Just like when you go to a hospital emergency room and a person having a heart attack gets seen by doctors before a person with a broken arm (even if the patient with the broken arm was waiting for a longer time), the most urgent calls for service get dispatched first (even if someone else called first). For instance, officers will respond to a silent robbery alarm call (where an alarm button is pushed by a bank or store employee indicating they are being robbed) more quickly and before responding to a burglary alarm call (where an alarm company indicates that a building's security system was triggered), which they will respond to before responding to a non-combatant shoplifter call, which they will respond to before taking a report of a fraud that occurred earlier in the day. Sometimes dispatchers must ask officers to "break" from a non-emergency call to respond to a more serious and urgent call. The practice of prioritizing calls for service, or triaging, is also known as **differentiated response**.

DISPATCHING A CALL FOR SERVICE

Depending on the size of the population served, a standard police dispatch center will have dispatchers assigned to three different roles—call taker, primary dispatcher, and secondary dispatcher. Larger agencies, sheriff's departments, and those which also dispatch fire or emergency medical services may have dispatchers assigned to additional roles. The *call taker* answers both non-emergency and emergency calls for service and passes the information to the primary dispatcher. The *primary dispatcher* is responsible for the movement of all the patrol officers in the field. She or he assigns officers to calls, decides the priority of the call, tracks officers' movements, and importantly, keeps the Code 7 (lunch) list, among a host of other duties. The *secondary dispatcher* assists the primary dispatcher with officer requests, such as calling for a tow truck, the power company, the emergency contact for a school or business (after a false alarm), another law enforcement agency, or running a warrant check on a suspect. In very small departments, one person may do all three jobs at the same time! In very large departments, there may be multiple people assigned to each role, based on geography. For example, a large metropolitan area or a sheriff's department may have a primary and one or more secondary dispatchers for each region or station in their jurisdiction. In most small to medium agencies, a dispatcher is hired and trained to do all three jobs and the roles are rotated each shift.

What happens when a caller dials 911 or the non-emergency police number to request service? If there is more than one dispatcher, a caller will likely speak with a call taker. The police call taker will ask questions to determine the nature and urgency of the request for assistance. As the call taker is gathering this information from the caller (victim, witness, or bystander), she is typing it into a computer and sending it to the primary dispatcher so that an officer can be assigned to the call. If it is a very urgent call, the call taker will send little bits of information at a time so that the primary dispatcher can assign the call and get an officer headed toward the emergency as soon as possible. For example, the first page may only contain a code for the nature of the incident (such as 901 for traffic accident with injuries), the address of the incident, and a brief note (multiple vehicles, possible serious injuries). This small amount of information allows the primary dispatcher to assign the closest available officer with the appropriate call priority (code three—lights and sirens in this scenario). While the primary dispatcher is dispatching an officer, the call taker continues to gather information from the caller and provides updates to the primary dispatcher as quickly as her fingers can type (sometimes the call taker and primary dispatcher will talk, rather than type, if they are seated close to each other and events are unfolding rapidly).

Sometimes, call takers ask what might sound like silly questions. For example, if a caller states she was "robbed," the call taker will likely ask the caller "how do you know?" Callers will often say "because I came home and my TV was gone." The call taker would then ask follow-up questions to verify that the caller was a victim of a burglary (not a robbery) and that the suspect (if known) is no longer in the vicinity. Alternatively, a caller might respond, as your author's first robbery caller did, "because I was tied up!" This response indicates that we need to get the police there as quick as possible (unlike a past burglary report, which does not require an urgent response).

If a call for assistance is non-urgent (for instance, in the case of a past burglary with no suspect information), the call taker will gather all the information before passing the service request to the primary dispatcher. In some cases, the call taker may transfer the call to another dispatch center (e.g., if the incident happened in another city or the caller needs services the department does not provide—such as EMS or fire). The primary dispatcher assigns an officer based on several factors—geographic location of the call, urgency, and availability of officers, the type of call (some go to special teams or to civilian report writers), and occasionally officer characteristics (sometimes female rape victims request a female officer, if available).

RESOURCES

How much information a dispatcher has about a caller and his location depends on which number (911 or non-emergency) the person called, whether the agency is equipped with enhanced 911 services, and the extent to which the dispatch center is computerized. If the caller dials 911, his phone number and location will display on a computer screen at the call taker's station in the dispatch center, if the agency has the capability to do this. Agencies that have Enhanced 911 have the ability to display the caller's location. As Table 8.1 indicates, one-third of sheriffs' departments and one-fifth of police departments that serve very small populations (less than 10,000) do not have the capability to display caller location. Even among the agencies that have Enhanced 911 systems, relatively few agencies are able to display a wireless caller's exact location (latitude and longitude); most can only get a general location (nearest cell tower). For more information about 911, including the history of emergency numbers and how the number 911 was selected, see Box 8.3.

Population Served	Total 911		Enhanced 911		Basic 911	
	Police	Sheriffs	Police	Sheriffs	Police	Sheriffs
1,000,000 or more	100%	93%	100%	81%	0%	11%
500,000–999,999	100%	84%	100%	82%	0%	2%
250,000–499,999	100%	88%	91%	82%	9%	6%
100,000–249,999	99%	92%	94%	87%	5%	5%
50,000–99,999	99%	97%	91%	85%	8%	12%
25,000–49,999	97%	96%	90%	87%	6%	9%
10,000–24,999	96%	94%	84%	77%	12%	17%
2,500–9,999[a] Under 10,000[b]	91%	95%	75%	62%	17%	33%
Under 2,500	86%		65%		21%	
All Sizes	91%	95%	74%	78%	16%	16%

[a]–police departments, [b]–sheriffs' departments

Adapted from Reaves, B. (2010, December). *Local police departments, 2007.* Bureau of Justice Statistics, p. 15. Washington DC: U.S. Government Printing Office. And Burch, A.M. (2012, December). *Sheriffs' offices, 2007-Statistical tables.* Bureau of Justice Statistics, p. 11. Washington DC: U.S. Government Printing Office.

THE 911 SYSTEM

HISTORY

The very first three-digit emergency telephone number system, 999, was established in London, England on July 8, 1937 (Allen, 2014). It took another 20 years before a similar system was implemented in Sydney, Australia in September 1957 and 30 years before the United States was close to adopting such a system. As late as 1966, such a universal emergency telephone number was discounted in the United States because it was thought to be cost-prohibitive and impractical (Allen, 2014). However, in 1967 the President's Commission on Law Enforcement and the Administration of Justice issued a recommendation that "wherever practical, a single police telephone number should be established, at least within a metropolitan area and eventually over the entire United States" (PCLEAJ, 1967, as cited in Allen, 2014). This was essentially the beginning of 911 in the United States.

From there, things moved quickly and the first 911 call was placed in Haleyville, Alabama from Alabama Speaker of the House, Rankin Fite, at the Haleyville City Hall to U.S. Representative Tom Bevill at the Haleyville Police Department on Friday, February 16, 1968 (Allen, 2011; NENA, n.d.). Although AT&T (the major carrier at the time) was heavily involved in setting up the national system, the competitive head of Alabama Telephone Company, Bob Gallagher, wanted to be the first one to implement the number and beat AT&T to the punch by 13 days (Allen, 2014). Just in case you're curious, the phone used to answer the first 911 call was a bright red, rotary dial phone (it is now in a museum in Haleyville but you can find pictures of it floating around the internet).

By the end of 1976, approximately 16% of the U.S. population had access to 911 (NENA, n.d.). That percentage grew to about 26% by 1979 and 50% by 1987. Today, about 95% of the U.S. population is covered by 911—most (about 75%) with enhanced 911 features (Burch,

2012; NENA, n.d.; Reaves, 2010). Interestingly, 911 did not become the "official" universal emergency number in the United States until 1999, when congress passed the Wireless Communications and Public Safety Act, which directed the Federal Communications Commission to facilitate "the prompt deployment of a nationwide, seamless communications infrastructure for emergency services" (FCC, 2014, para. 1).

HOW WAS THE NUMBER 9-1-1 CHOSEN?

Actually, there was much more debate about the number than one might expect. The committee that developed the system at AT&T wanted dialing to be as easy as possible from rotary dial phones (touch tone phones were not commonplace until the late 1970s). The committee knew that the first number could not be "0" (which was used to summon the operator) or "1" (which was used for international calling), so it had to be a number from 2-9. The second and third digits had to be "1" (there were technical and logistical reasons for this). So the only real question was what would the first number be? The committee decided that "9" was the best number because if someone needed to call in the dark, they could easily find the "0" (the last hole on the phone dialer) and go up one space to the 9. This logic also worked for touch tone phones—callers could find the lowest right button (the # key) and go up one to find the 9.

911 TODAY

Today, many callers call 911 from their cell phone, or by using a VoIP or satellite service. These "new" technologies were not immediately compatible with most 911 systems. In fact, some carriers could not connect to 911 in the early days of cellular technology. Today, all wireless callers can connect to a local law enforcement agency by dialing 911. However, depending on the area of the country you are in, your phone number may or may not appear on the dispatcher's console and your location may or may not be available to the dispatcher. Getting these technologies to talk to each other is an involved, and in some cases costly, multistep and multi-partner process. To see where your jurisdiction is at in the process, check out this Web site: http://nena.ddti.net/Default.aspx. Zoom in to find out whether and how much location information your local law enforcement agency will receive if you dial 911 from your cell phone (nearest cell tower or latitude and longitude coordinates). You can see from the map that some parts of the country only have basic 911 service (no ability to transmit caller's location) while other pockets only have wireless 911 (no 911 access from a landline—meaning the phone in your house or school building).

Sources:

Allen, G. (2014). History of 911. *DISPATCH Monthly Magazine. Retrieved from: http://www.911dispatch.com/911/history/*

Burch, A.M. (2012, December). *Sheriffs' offices, 2007-Statistical tables.* Bureau of Justice Statistics. Washington DC: U.S. Government Printing Office.

Retrieved from http://www.bjs.govFederal Communications Commission (FCC) (2014). 9-1-1 and E9-1-1 services. *FCC Encyclopedia.* Washington DC: U.S. Government Printing Office. Retrieved from http://www.fcc.gov/encyclopedia/9-1-1-and-e9-1-1-services

National Emergency Number Association (NENA). 9-1-1 origin and history. Retrieved from https://www.nena.org/?page=911overviewfacts

President's Commission on Law Enforcement and Administration of Justice (PCLEAJ) (1967). *Task force report: The police.* Washington, DC: U.S. Government Printing Office.

Reaves, B. (2010, December). *Local police departments, 2007.* Bureau of Justice Statistics. Washington DC: U.S. Government Printing Office. Retrieved from http://www.bjs.gov

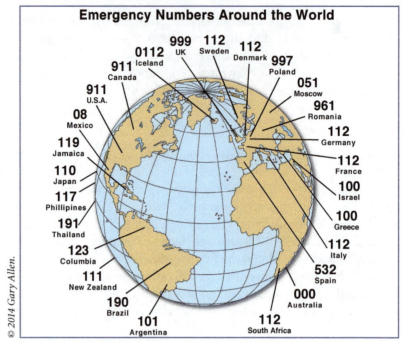

Figure 8.1 EMERGENCY NUMBERS AROUND THE WORLD

TABLE 8.2 Existence of Computer Aided Dispatch and in-field computers throughout the United States

Population Served	Computer Aided Dispatch (CAD)		In-field Computers & Terminals		Use in-field Computers for Field Reports		Use in-field Computers for Communication	
	Police	Sheriffs	Police	Sheriffs	Police	Sheriffs	Police	Sheriffs
1,000,000 or more	100%	96%	100%	96%	46%	93%	100%	89%
500,000–999,999	94%	89%	100%	96%	74%	73%	84%	79%
250,000–499,999	93%	86%	98%	86%	85%	66%	89%	55%
100,000–249,999	97%	83%	97%	85%	73%	73%	80%	67%
50,000–99,999	95%	77%	97%	66%	77%	62%	76%	45%
25,000–49,999	90%	74%	92%	49%	72%	40%	69%	23%
10,000–24,999	79%	70%	77%	43%	57%	44%	52%	26%
2,500–9,999[a]	51%	43%	59%	30%	50%	43%	35%	13%
Under 10,000[b]								
Under 2,500	23%		43%		46%		18%	
All Sizes	49%	69%	59%	53%	52%	51%	35%	32%

[a]–police departments, [b]–sheriffs' departments

Adapted from Reaves, B. (2010, December). *Local police departments, 2007.* Bureau of Justice Statistics, p. 22-23. Washington DC: U Government Printing Office. And Burch, A.M. (2012, December). *Sheriffs' offices, 2007-Statistical tables.* Bureau of Justice Statistics, 15-16. Washington DC: U.S. Government Printing Office.

Population Served	Vehicle Records		Driving Records		Warrants		Protection Orders		Interagency Information Sharing		Calls-for-service History		Criminal History Records	
	Police	Sheriffs	Police	Sheriffs	Police	Sheriffs	Police	Sheriffs	Police	Sheriffs	Police	Sheriffs	Police	Sheriffs
1,000,000 or more	100%	96%	100%	96%	100%	93%	92%	85%	69%	70%	85%	78%	77%	78%
500,000–999,999	100%	94%	87%	92%	94%	94%	71%	77%	61%	66%	61%	68%	58%	77%
250,000–499,999	98%	80%	93%	78%	98%	80%	89%	66%	65%	49%	83%	56%	63%	62%
100,000–249,999	93%	73%	86%	71%	88%	68%	68%	58%	59%	59%	71%	54%	52%	51%
50,000–99,999	93%	55%	85%	54%	86%	52%	71%	44%	58%	38%	76%	32%	53%	37%
25,000–49,999	88%	30%	81%	28%	81%	24%	66%	21%	60%	25%	66%	17%	50%	14%
10,000–24,999	70%	24%	65%	20%	68%	20%	58%	18%	47%	18%	47%	11%	45%	14%
2,500–9,999ᵃ	54%		49%		48%		44%		38%		30%		34%	
Under 10,000ᵇ		16%		15%		16%		12%		12%		5%		10%
Under 2,500	33%		31%		31%		28%		25%		22%		21%	
All Sizes	52%	37%	48%	36%	48%	35%	42%	29%	37%	28%	34%	22%	32%	24%

ᵃ–police departments, ᵇ–sheriffs' departments

Adapted from Reaves, B. (2010, December). *Local police departments, 2007.* Bureau of Justice Statistics, p. 23. Washington DC: U.S. Government Printing Office. And Burch, A.M. (2012, December). *Sheriffs' offices, 2007-Statistical tables.* Bureau of Justice Statistics, p. 17. Washington DC: U.S. Government Printing Office.

Computer aided dispatch *(CAD)* systems, which are used by most agencies in the United States, have automated and improved the dispatching process greatly. These systems help dispatchers and officers manage loads of information seamlessly and instantaneously, which is important because the dispatch center is a very fluid environment where things can change in, literally, an instant. For example, these systems will immediately transfer call information from the call taker's screen to the primary dispatcher's screen, verify the validity of the address, prioritize the calls on the primary dispatcher's screen in order of urgency and seriousness (show the most serious calls above the least serious calls), suggest the most proximate available officer, and once assigned, will transfer call information directly to the laptop or mobile data terminal (MDT) in the responding officer's patrol vehicle (if the vehicle is so equipped). Some systems also pull previous call histories and notes on the location, suspect, and/or victim. While not all systems have the same capabilities and small departments are less likely than larger agencies to have complete functionality, this is a huge improvement over the pre-CAD days (pre-1980s/1990s) when call takers handwrote call information on index cards, passed the cards to the primary dispatcher who looked up the address in a map book to ascertain which beat it was in, and read the information over the radio to an officer who wrote the address and call details on a notepad in his patrol car. Table 8.2 depicts the latest information about U.S. agencies which utilize CAD and Table 8.3 indicates what information is available to officers in the patrol car. Notice how agency capabilities differ by size and agency type. As you can see, there is much divergence between police departments and sheriffs' departments of different sizes.

PATROL PRACTICES

Patrol, which is the backbone of policing, has three main objectives—deter crime, maintain order, and provide services for 24 hours per day, 7 days per week. It is a vital function of all police departments and a cornerstone of policing. In general, 60%–70% of an agency's officers are assigned to patrol (Burch, 2012; Reaves, 2010). Almost all local law enforcement officers begin their careers in patrol (sheriffs' deputies generally start in the jails prior to moving to patrol). This is seen as an important first step for officers because much of an officer's experience is developed in the field. Patrol exposes officers to a wide variety of unusual activity and hones their observation, communication, and officer safety skills. It also serves as a bonding experience between officers enhancing the police culture and allows field training officers to inculcate the department's philosophy and expectations in new officers.

Uniformed patrol officers are not only the most visible part of the criminal justice system, they are also the main gatekeepers of the system and can be a citizen's first, and sometimes only, encounter with the criminal justice system. For these reasons, the way patrol officers exercise discretion and interact with citizens is immensely important. They are a department's best opportunity for encouraging cooperation, developing camaraderie, and establishing legitimacy in the community. Conversely, poorly trained, biased, or "trigger happy" patrol officers can be a department's worst democratic policing nightmare.

Patrol officers spend much of their shift responding to calls for service, what we would call, *reactive* policing. In order to respond to calls quickly, officers are assigned to a designated *beat*, or small geographic area, to patrol. When patrol officers are not on a call for service, they usually drive around their beat looking for suspicious activity and waiting to be assigned a call for service. This random driving around, hoping to discourage criminal activity through visibility, is often referred to as **random routine patrol**. These two activities, responding to calls for service and random routine patrol, have defined a patrol officer's job since the 1960s.

It might surprise you to learn that approximately 70% of an officer's shift is uncommitted time—when she is not on a call and is available to dispatchers in case something happens (Famega, 2005). It is during uncommitted time that officers involve themselves in proactive activities such as patrol or administrative tasks. While the mix of activities varies by agency, beat, and shift, studies of patrol have revealed that officers spend approximately 29% of their time on crime-related incidents, 24% on traffic regulation and enforcement, 23% on order maintenance activities, and 24% on service and other activities (Mastrofski, 1983; see also Green & Klockars, 1991) and this hasn't changed much since the professional era. Interestingly, one study found that officers in urban and rural agencies received the same proportion of law enforcement calls (about 35%) but opposite levels of order maintenance and service calls—officers in urban agencies received approximately 40% order maintenance calls and 25% service calls while officers in rural agencies received approximately 40% service-oriented calls and 25% order maintenance calls (Johnson & Rhodes, 2009).

PATROL PERSONNEL DEPLOYMENT: BEATS

The patrol function, which goes back to Peel's London Metropolitan Police, is organized around beats (sometimes called geographic areas). Beats are essentially small service areas within a jurisdiction that indicate an officer's area of responsibility (territory). Drawing appropriate boundaries and assigning an appropriate number of officers to each beat serves to improve coverage and response time. During the political era, beats were very small and officers walked around their beat, checking in periodically on call boxes to verify that they were indeed "making their rounds." When police cars became commonplace in the professional/reform era, beats became larger and, for the first time, providing rapid response to calls for service became a main policing objective and measure of success.

The process of subdividing a jurisdiction can be (and has historically been) an arduous, and sometimes political, endeavor. Beat boundaries are based on several factors, most importantly the volume and types of calls for service in an area, the number of Part I and Part II crimes, the daytime and nighttime populations of an area (and population density), and natural geographic or sociocultural borders. Some departments also factor in the number of traffic accidents and the number of bars, clubs, high schools, colleges, half-way houses, sober living homes, and other establishments that require a disproportionate amount of police resources.

It used to be that beats were static and rarely changed; that is no longer the case in some departments. Today's technology allows police administrators the ability to routinely monitor the amount of activity in each beat by running a report of officers' *downtime* by beat area, shift, day of the week, month, etc. Downtime is anytime an officer is NOT assigned to a call or police activity (e.g., report writing, eating lunch, driving around randomly on routine patrol). Police managers then analyze the work load patterns and can alter beat boundaries when the workload per officer is not balanced across beats. Some departments rarely change beat boundaries while other departments alter boundaries by season, day of the week, or even by shift.

The factors that influence beat boundaries also affect the number of officers assigned to particular beats at different times of the day and night. Residential areas typically receive more calls for service during the evening hours than during the day because many people leave home to work during the standard work week (although this is certainly changing). Thus, most departments will schedule more officers in the evening hours than in the daytime in these areas. While these beats may need more officers in the evening shifts, other beats—those occupied primarily by corporate businesses open 8am–5pm, may require more officers during the daytime. Departments using their resources wisely allocate personnel according to these dimensions and schedule more officers in the evening hours and fewer during the early morning hours (when there is little activity). Additionally, as previously mentioned, crime is not evenly distributed within the community; so, high crime beats generally require more officers than other beats, even during the same shift.

PATROL PERSONNEL DEPLOYMENT: SHIFTS

In years past, officers (like most other employees in the United States) worked five 8-hour shifts per week. More recently, police departments have experimented with alternate work schedules; some of the most popular are four 10-hour shifts per week (called 4–10s), three 12-hour shifts every week plus one 8-hour shift every other week (called 3–12s), and nine 8–9-hour shifts every 2 weeks (called 9–80s). Using alternative shift schedules allow departments to manage their personnel and budget in a way that provides adequate coverage at all times of the day. A recent study by the Police Foundation compared the traditional (5–8s) schedule to a 4–10s schedule and a 3–12s schedule and found that although there were no differences in health or performance outcomes, officers on the 4–10s schedule indicated much greater satisfaction with their schedule, increased sleep, and significant reductions in overtime hours (Amendola et al., 2011).

Just as beats have unique characteristics that affect patrol officers, work shifts also affect the duties that officers perform. Regardless of the length of shifts employed, most departments have a "day shift," roughly 6 am–4 pm, a "swing shift," roughly 2 pm–12 am, and a "graveyard shift," roughly 10 pm–8am. Some departments have a fourth shift (from evening to bar closing) to provide additional personnel during the most demanding times, while some very small departments close down at night and contract with a larger agency to provide essential emergency services. In general, the busiest shift is swing shift; officers who work this shift run from call to call while officers on graveyard fight off boredom during the early morning hours.

Officers working the *day shift*, typically the officers with the most seniority, provide traffic control; take reports; perform official errands; attend meetings with other government departments, schools, and citizen groups on behalf of the police department; respond to crimes involving businesses (such as fraud, shoplifting, and bank robbery); and answer a lot of citizen questions. Some officers do not like this shift because police administrators (chief, captains, and lieutenants) are on duty and citizens are prone to complaining. Day shift officers usually have more citizen encounters than officers working the graveyard shift.

Swing shift officers typically respond to the most domestic disputes and burglary alarm calls. They also take a lot of reports and assist with traffic accidents. Officers on this shift tend to remain busy and for this reason it is preferred over day shift by some senior officers. If the jurisdiction has a sports or concert arena, swing shift officers may be called to work traffic snarls or peace keeping assignments during or after the event. Recently, it has become customary for departments to charge the venue for extra police staffing (which is then offered to officers as an overtime shift)—this is good public policy, as it shifts the cost burden for public safety at these special events from taxpayers to the event promoters and attendees—the users of the service.

The overnight shift, known as the *graveyard shift* since the 1800s, typically starts off busy and tapers off after about 2 am. This shift is worked mainly by young officers with low seniority because of the toll it takes on a person's body and social life. After the bars close and activity dies down, graveyard officers spend the remainder of their shift on random routine patrol, driving around looking for suspicious persons (which is almost anyone on the street at 3 am) in areas known for drug or prostitution activity, commercial districts, and residential areas. They also spend time talking with other officers and shift workers (such as at gas stations and restaurants) and running license plates (looking for stolen vehicles) to pass the time and alleviate the boredom.

TYPES OF PATROL

Historically, officers patrolled on foot and on horseback. Today, officers still patrol this way but they also patrol in cars and boats, on motorcycles, bicycles, ATVs, snowmobiles, and Segways, and even in helicopters and planes (see Table 8.4); someday we may even see Unmanned Aerial Vehicles (aka drones) used in patrol. How an area is patrolled is very much dependent upon the terrain and traffic in the area. For example, foot patrol as the primary method of patrol is limited to small beats in large urban cities, town centers of small and medium sized towns, and other unique areas not easily accessible by vehicle. It would be impossible to patrol a sprawling rural area or even a small suburban city only on foot. Similarly, it can be very difficult to patrol a very congested, pedestrian-dominated, metropolitan city center (such as New York City's Times Square) primarily in a vehicle. For these reasons, police departments use a variety of deployment methods for patrol.

Foot Patrol

Prior to the 1950s, foot patrol was the primary method of patrol. Officers walked a beat and were expected to get to know the members of the community—both the law-abiding citizens and the troublemakers. Only about 4% of all patrol today is on foot (Burch, 2012; Reaves, 2010). Most foot patrols are in areas that are not easily accessible to vehicles, such as beaches and downtown city centers and pedestrian malls or areas with a high concentration of tourists. Many departments encourage, or require, officers in cars to park and walk around portions of their beat (such as parks and shopping centers) periodically so they can get the best of both worlds—the efficiency of the automobile combined with the personal touch of foot patrol.

Even though foot patrol is not very efficient, it is beneficial to the department because it is a good way to build and maintain community trust and support through positive interactions. Foot patrol officers become part of the community and the people living and working in the beat become familiar with, and begin to trust them. Officers on foot, more so than officers in vehicles, are seen as resources by community members, someone they can turn to for help when they do not know who to call or are reluctant to call the dispatch center or another agency. In addition to being good for building relationships, research has found that foot patrol can also decrease citizens' fear of crime and provide other benefits (more on this shortly).

Vehicle Patrol

Motorized patrol is much more efficient than foot patrol, but as we discovered in the 1970s, it is also more alienating. The patrol vehicle, more than any other police innovation, profoundly changed policing for the better and the worse. At the same time, it improved coverage area and response time, it also caused the police to grow more distant from the general public. As discussed in Chapter 3, citizens can summon the police and they arrive quickly but the trade-off is that officers are isolated and have fewer positive interactions with law-abiding members of the public, which breeds distrust on both sides of the patrol vehicle. Today, most patrol is conducted in a motorized police car. While generally safe, vehicle patrol can be dangerous, especially when officers are responding to an emergency with lights and sirens, involved in a car chase, or even just reading information on their MDT or laptop screen while driving. As can be seen in Table 8.5,

TABLE 8.4 Types of regularly scheduled patrols, other than automobile, in Agencies throughout the United States

Population Served	Foot Police	Foot Sheriffs	Bicycle Police	Bicycle Sheriffs	Motorcycle Police	Motorcycle Sheriffs	Marine Police	Marine Sheriffs	Transporter Police	Transporter Sheriffs	Horse Police	Horse Sheriffs	Air Police	Air Sheriffs
1,000,000 or more	92%	44%	100%	67%	100%	81%	69%	63%	31%	22%	77%	41%	100%	59%
500,000–999,999	81%	44%	100%	42%	94%	61%	52%	42%	29%	8%	61%	17%	71%	31%
250,000–499,999	78%	28%	89%	42%	91%	34%	26%	50%	24%	5%	50%	17%	57%	30%
100,000–249,999	59%	23%	71%	22%	90%	25%	12%	41%	15%	1%	17%	4%	14%	12%
50,000–99,999	56%	25%	69%	10%	74%	11%	12%	37%	6%	3%	5%	4%	5%	3%
25,000–49,999	52%	25%	58%	5%	55%	3%	6%	23%	4%	1%	2%	2%	1%	4%
10,000–24,999	50%	19%	44%	4%	25%	1%	5%	14%	2%	2%	1%	3%	1%	4%
2,500–9,999[a]	58%		36%		8%		4%		1%		<0.5%		0%	
Under 10,000[b]		29%		1%		<0.5%		9%		<0.5%		2%		4%
Under 2,500	54%		15%		4%		1%		<0.5%		0%		<0.5%	
All Sizes	55%	25%	32%	9%	16%	9%	4%	23%	2%	2%	1%	4%	1%	7%

[a]–police departments, [b]–sheriffs' departments

Adapted from Reaves, B. (2010, December). *Local police departments, 2007.* Bureau of Justice Statistics, p. 15. Washington DC: U.S. Government Printing Office. And Burch, A.M. (2012, December). *Sheriffs' offices, 2007–Statistical tables.* Bureau of Justice Statistics, p. 12. Washington DC: U.S. Government Printing Office.

TABLE 8.5 — Officer deaths in the United States, 2004–2013

Population Served	2004	2005	2006	2007	2008	2009	2010	2011	2012	2013	Total
Aircraft accidents	3	2	3	3	3	4	2	1	3	1	25
Automobile accident	51	43	46	61	44	39	51	44	27	28	434
Bicycle accident	0	0	2	0	0	0	1	0	0	0	3
Boating accident	0	0	0	1	0	0	1	0	0	0	3
Drowned	3	4	0	4	1	0	3	4	0	2	21
Fall	1	4	0	3	0	0	1	4	4	6	23
Horse-related Accident	0	0	0	0	0	0	0	0	1	0	1
Job-related illness	19	24	21	19	23	18	21	20	8	13	186
Motorcycle accident	10	5	11	10	9	3	6	5	7	4	70
Shot	59	60	54	70	41	50	60	73	50	31	548
Stabbed	1	1	1	0	2	0	0	2	5	2	14
Struck by vehicle	13	16	16	14	18	11	13	10	14	11	136
Terrorist attack	1	1	1	5	0	0	0	1	0	0	9
Other[1]	4	3	1	1	5	1	2	7	2	2	28
Total	165	163	156	191	147	125	161	171	122	100	1501

[1] "Other" category includes beaten, bomb-related incident, electrocuted, poisoned, strangled, struck by falling object, struck by train.

Adapted from National Law Enforcement Officers Memorial Fund (NLEOMF). (2014, April 14). *Causes of law enforcement officer deaths over the last decade (2004-2013)*. Retrieved from http://www.nleomf.org/facts/officer-fatalities-data/causes.html

vehicle accidents are the second leading cause of line-of-duty deaths among law enforcement officers in the United States each year, they are second only to shooting deaths (NLEOMF, 2014).

Other methods of patrol

In addition to foot patrol and the standard patrol car, many agencies also use motorcycles and bicycles to patrol. Motorcycles, in particular, are often associated with and used for traffic control and enforcement because of their maneuverability, acceleration, and ability to

Horse patrols are still used in some cities.

hide in plain sight. Overall, more than 90% of police departments serving 100,000 or more residents use them. Unfortunately, their small profile can also make them dangerous for officers. Each year approximately six officers are killed in motorcycle crashes in the line of duty, making them the fifth leading cause of police officer deaths each year in the United States (NLEOMF, 2014). Bicycles are another popular method of patrol. They are more efficient than foot patrol, and great

Bicycles are a popular method of patrol.

Air patrol is used in larger police agencies.

for areas that are not easily accessible to vehicles, such as public housing developments, college campuses, tourist areas, and business complexes. As Table 8.4 indicates, 32% of all police departments and 100% of those serving populations over 500,000 maintain bicycle patrols. They are also very safe—only three officers have been killed in bicycle accidents in the past decade (NLEOMF, 2014).

Beyond these typical patrol vehicles, jurisdictions also utilize a variety of other special vehicles depending on the terrain and geography of their particular jurisdiction. For example, departments that patrol beach cities often use ATVs on the sand and Segways on pedestrian pathways adjacent to the sand. Segways are also popular in tourist areas and shopping malls. ATVs are also used in mountain and desert communities. Snowmobiles are used in mountain areas, rural areas, and for search and rescue. Some agencies also have boats and other types of watercraft to patrol harbors, lakes, bayous, rivers, and other bodies of water that criminals use to transport illegal products or that residents use for entertainment. Horse patrols are still used in many large cities across America, as well as a few small ones. They are particularly good for parks and mountains, as well as crowd control situations. Although expensive to purchase and maintain, many departments see horses as a public relations tool and worth the investment.

Finally, helicopters and airplanes can be found in a majority of police departments that serve more than 250,000 residents (Reaves, 2010). Because of the enormous cost to purchase, operate, and maintain aircraft, only large agencies can afford to own them (although many small- and medium-sized agencies have acquired aircraft through the federal government's 10–33 surplus military equipment program). Smaller agencies generally "contract" with larger agencies to patrol on a routine basis, or more generally, on an "as-needed" basis for an agreed upon cost. Contracting services (paying for them on an as-needed basis) from another law enforcement agency is a popular method used by smaller departments which cannot afford the array of law enforcement tools that are useful, but not often needed (such as bomb-detecting robots).

RESEARCH ON PATROL PRACTICES

The Omnibus Crime Control and Safe Streets Act of 1968 provided money for law enforcement agencies to purchase equipment and for researchers to conduct studies to ascertain which strategies employed by police officers were most successful, and under which conditions. The research conducted during the 1970s as a result of this act taught us many things about policing, in particular that the strategies developed during the professional era were not nearly as effective at reducing crime and apprehending suspects as police and the public thought they were. In this section, we examine the research (old and new) that challenges some of these fundamental assumptions about policing.

RAPID RESPONSE TO INCIDENTS

Conventional wisdom tells us that if the police arrive to a call really fast, they will catch the criminal. Unfortunately, research does not support this conventional wisdom. The problem with this assumption is that it does not take into account the entire process of events leading up to an officer arriving on scene, which includes:

1. *Citizen discovery and reporting time*: The time it takes for a person (victim or witness) to discover that a crime was committed and then call the police department to request an officer (this can happen during or after the crime occurred).

2. *Police dispatch time*: The time it takes for the dispatcher/s to process the call—to determine what happened and where it happened, and assign an available officer.

3. *Officer travel time*: The time taken for a responding officer to acknowledge the call, finish what he is doing, and then travel to the scene of the crime.

All of the above, in particular discovery and reporting time, increase the actual time it takes for an officer to arrive on a scene. According to research on the topic, dispatch time averages 2–3 minutes, travel time averages 5–6 minutes, and reporting time averages 10 minutes or more, depending on the type of the crime (Cordner, Greene, & Bynum, 1983; KCPD, 1978; Spelman & Brown, 1984). Although most law enforcement agencies strive for rapid response times, the fact is that it usually does not matter.

One of the main reasons that response time is not particularly important is because most crimes are noticed after the crime has been committed. In fact, 75% of all crimes are **discovery crimes**, meaning they were discovered after the crime had been committed and the perpetrator had fled (e.g., burglary, larceny, and motor vehicle theft are commonly discovered long after the criminal committed the crime). Only 25% of crimes are considered to be **involvement crimes**, those in which the victim was confronted by the suspect (such as a robbery, assault, or rape). Research tells us that response time has little to no impact on solving the crime or apprehending a suspect in discovery crimes (Spelman & Brown, 1984). However, rapid response can increase the likelihood of apprehending a suspect in an involvement crime if the crime was reported by the citizen immediately. In Spelman and Brown's study (1984), there was a 35% chance of making a response-related arrest if the involvement crime was reported *while* the crime was in progress; however, this dropped to 18% if the victim/witness waited just 1 minute after the crime was over to report it. Unfortunately, most residents delay reporting crimes by several minutes while they verify a crime occurred, call a friend, regain their composure, and/or decide if they want to call the police. This means that any police response time would be too slow to make a response-related arrest.

More recent research, however, has found some support for the assertion that rapid response can improve the likelihood of catching a burglar in the act (Chican et al., 2012; Coupe & Blake, 2005). Although other variables also played a role in whether a suspect was arrested, rapid response was a contributing factor. Additionally, research found that response time varies considerably across neighborhoods. Contrary to expectations, it is shortest in neighborhoods with concentrated disadvantage, high immigrant concentration, and high call rates; this means that residents who live in impoverished areas enjoy the lowest response times to in-progress calls (Chican et al., 2012).

What about public satisfaction? Certainly, citizens are happier with the police when they arrive quickly. Well, yes and no. Victims and other members of the public are definitely more satisfied when they experience a rapid response time from police (Brandl & Horvath, 1991; McEwan et al., 1984). However, satisfaction is not directly tied to the amount of time it takes an officer to arrive on scene; what is most important is how long the citizen thinks it will take the officer to arrive. Regardless of how long it actually takes the officer to arrive, citizens are more satisfied when the officer arrived sooner than the citizen expected them to arrive (Pate et al., 1976). Thus, if I expected the officer to arrive in 3 minutes and she arrived in 5 minutes, I'm unhappy; but if I expected her to arrive in 15 minutes and she arrived in 5 minutes, then I'm happy. It's all about managing expectations. This knowledge has inspired police agencies to train dispatchers to provide realistic estimates of officer arrival time whenever possible, develop telephone reporting units for non-serious crimes, and institute *differentiated response times* for all calls for service. Differentiated response time is the triage system described earlier whereby dispatchers prioritize calls according to their seriousness and urgency. These findings also encouraged officers to spend more time with victims, providing crime prevention tips and developing rapport (which also improves public satisfaction with police).

TWO OFFICERS VERSUS ONE

Two person patrol cars were the standard when the automobile replaced foot patrol. Although many foot patrol officers patrolled on their own, two-officer patrol cars were thought to be safer and more effective than single-officer units due to the complexity of the job and the required multitasking—driving, listening to the police radio, talking on the police radio, and observing suspicious behavior. Police chiefs at the time debated whether officers were physically and intellectually up to the task (Brannon, 1956). Also, conventional wisdom suggested that two-officer units would be more proactive in their investigations of suspicious activity than one-officer units.

In December 1953, the Kansas City (MO) Police Department became the largest police department in the nation to experiment with a patrol division composed completely of single-officer units (Brannon, 1956). A department study revealed that patrol activity (calls answered, reports taken, pedestrians and vehicles checked, etc.) increased by a whopping 438% while the number of suspects resisting arrest increased only marginally and on-the-job injuries declined slightly (Brannon, 1956). There was also some indication that patrol officers experienced fewer personality clashes and arguments with other officers as a result of working solo. The experiment also proved very cost-effective: $50,000 to purchase 16 new vehicles and accessories and $37,000 to maintain the additional automobiles (much of which was recouped through increased parking and traffic tickets issued by one-officer units). This is compared to $583,000, which is what it would have cost to hire 16 additional officers to maintain two-officer patrol units.

What little research there is on the topic suggests that, although single-officer units are generally more cost-effective, both types of units are useful and necessary for public safety and service. Single-officer units increase police visibility, respond more quickly to calls, and can cover about 71% more area than dual-officer units (Kaplan, 1979; Larson & Rich, 1985; Tarr, 1978); however, they routinely require backup support which decreases their cost-effectiveness and can impact public perception of safety and police response when numerous cars respond to a single call. Dual-officer units clear calls more quickly, are more cost-effective than single-officer units which require backup support, and may be more proactive (Boydstun et al., 1977; Wilson, 1990). Research is mixed on which units write more tickets, make more arrests, and write more reports—some studies show that single-officer units do these things more (Boydstun et al., 1977; Brannon, 1956) while others show that two-officer units do (Wilson, 1990; Wilson & Brewer, 1991). The research is also mixed on which units are safer. Boydstun and colleagues (1977) found that single-officer units were less likely to be involved in resisting arrest incidents while Wilson and Brewer (1992) found that single-officer units were more likely to be injured if assaulted. There is also a perception that dual-officer units are more likely to take a hardline approach toward offenders while one-officer units more typically take a conciliatory approach (Demers et al., 2007; Wilson & Brewer, 1991).

FOOT PATROL

As automobiles gained popularity, foot patrols went on the endangered list and, in many communities, became extinct. The reason, of course, was efficiency—driving is almost always more efficient than walking. However, research has found that foot patrols have positive benefits that cannot be achieved when officers remain in their cars.

The **Newark Foot Patrol Experiment**, conducted during 1978–1979, tested the effects of different levels of foot patrol on crime, arrest rates, citizen attitudes, and officer attitudes. The study varied the amount of foot patrol each beat in the city received and then compared the results. Researchers found that foot patrol had no impact on crime or victimization, but it did impact citizens' perception of crime. In areas with additional foot patrol, residents felt safer and believed serious crime was down in their neighborhood (even though it was not) (Police Foundation, 1981). Citizens in areas with standard (or reduced) levels of foot patrol did not express the same feelings. Interestingly, business respondents felt the opposite—they believed crime was going up when they saw additional foot patrol officers in the area. This is likely because business owners were accustomed to seeing officers only when a crime report needed to be taken or a criminal arrested; so when they saw additional officers, they assumed there was more crime in the surrounding businesses. (Note: this false perception can be addressed when officers stop and talk to business owners in casual conversation.) One of the most important, and surprising, findings of this study was that officers assigned to foot patrol reported more job satisfaction than officers assigned to motor vehicles. This is a result of foot patrol officers having more positive encounters with supportive community members than officers in vehicles who spent more of their time with crime victims and perpetrators. A simultaneous study of foot patrol in Flint, Michigan confirmed the above findings.

Although earlier research failed to find any crime reduction effects of foot patrol, two recent studies have found that foot patrol can reduce violent crime when implemented in high crime places. In Philadelphia (PA), for example, violent crime was reduced by 23% and in Newark (NJ), it was reduced by 30% (Piza & O'Hara, 2012; Ratcliffe et al., 2011). Research suggests that targeted and concentrated foot patrols in violent crime hotspots can reduce crime when it increases the certainty of perpetrators' getting caught and arrested; however, the activities undertaken by foot patrol officers can undermine crime reduction efforts if police legitimacy is decreased (which happens when prolonged Terry stops are conducted) (Song et al., 2013). Interestingly, researchers found that Philadelphia foot patrol officers performed different activities than vehicle patrol officers; specifically, foot patrol officers spent most of their time initiating pedestrian stops and dealing with disorder incidents while vehicle officers responded to most of the reported crimes in the area (and thus wrote most of the crime reports) (Groff et al., 2015).

PREVENTATIVE PATROL

Probably, the most well-known study to come out of this period was the **Kansas City Preventative Patrol Experiment**. This study, more than any of the ones mentioned above, rocked the policing world by challenging the effectiveness of random preventative patrol. Researchers from the Police Foundation, led by George Kelling, divided the city into 15 beats—five groups of three matched beats. The beats were matched on population demographics (race/ethnicity and median income), crime types and rates, and calls for service. One of the beats in the group (the proactive beat) received extra **preventative patrol** which amounted to two–three times the amount of visible patrol cars. Another one (deemed the reactive beat) received no preventative patrol; officers were to stay out of the beat unless responding to a call and were instructed to patrol only the perimeter or in an adjacent proactive beat. The third beat (called the control beat) operated as they did in the past and there was no change to patrol procedures or staffing levels.

Researchers measured crime rates and surveyed residents and found that random preventative patrol had no effect on crime rates, public perception of police services, citizens' fear of crime, officer response time or the public's satisfaction with officer response time, or the number of traffic accidents (Kelling, Pate, Dieckman, & Brown, 1974). Essentially, the researchers discovered that randomly driving around in a patrol car does not deter crime. So what does? What should police officers do instead?

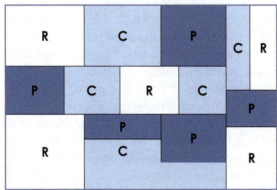

Figure 8.2 Schematic representation of the 15-beat experimental area.

P = Proactive C = Control R = Reactive
Adapted from Kellng, G., Pate, T., Dieckman, D., & Brown, C.E. (1974). *The Kansas City preventative patrol experiment: A summary report.* Washington DC: Police Foundation. Retrieved from http://www.policefoundation.org/content/kansas-city-preventive-patrol-experiment-0

One of the reasons that random preventative patrol is not effective is because crime is not randomly distributed throughout a city. Another important study, the **Minneapolis Hot Spot Study**, was the first to find that a very small percentage of a city's addresses produce a large portion of its calls for service, these are known as "hot spots" of criminal activity (Sherman, Gartin, & Buerger, 1989). In the case of Minneapolis (MN), 64% of calls for service came from just 5% of the city's addresses (Sherman, Gartin, & Buerger, 1989). Sherman and Weisburd (1995) randomly assigned 110 of these hot spots to an experimental group or a control group. The experimental group received 3 hours of targeted patrol daily (in 10-minute segments) for 8 months while the control group received the normal amount of patrol during the study. There were fewer calls for service and less disorder in the experimental hot spots which led the researchers to conclude that preventative patrol implemented in the right areas can reduce crime and disorder. Further research has revealed that the optimum time to spend in a hotspot is 12–15 minutes; up until this time, there is an additional deterrent effect for each minute spent at the hot spot; after this point, there are diminishing returns (Koper, 1995). This is known as the *Koper Curve.*

TARGETED PATROL PRACTICES

These studies have led police to develop and implement a variety of targeted patrol practices that are focused on specific problem areas. Given that crime disproportionately happens in small clusters of places at specific times of the day and specific days of the week, effective officers concentrate their efforts on specific places at specific times to decrease crime. This section serves as a brief introduction to these strategies, as we will discuss targeted patrol practices and supporting research in much greater detail in later chapters.

Directed patrol involves increasing patrol in a specified area to address a specific issue or as a general attempt to reduce crime or disorder in a high crime area. It could be as simple as an officer sitting in the parking lot of the nearest convenience store after school lets out for the day to deter juveniles from causing trouble (you might find this hard to believe, but crime increases near high schools immediately after school); or driving around an apartment complex that has been the site of numerous vehicle burglaries at night. It could also involve traffic officers writing tickets for unsafe driving on a specific stretch of road that has had a lot of accidents. The key is that officers are focused on the places in their beat that are generating a disproportionate amount of calls for service, either in the short-term or over the long-term.

Saturation patrol uses a dramatic and sudden increase in patrol officers in a specific area to increase police visibility and deter potential criminal behavior. For example, after a gang shooting, a city might deploy additional patrol officers in an attempt to avert retaliatory violence by a rival gang. Beach cities (and other touristy destinations) routinely schedule additional officers on holiday weekends and during the summer to discourage drinking in public and other unruly behaviors in places where they expect, based on previous experience, to have trouble. Usually, these supplementary officers come from the jurisdiction's own forces but sometimes additional officers come from neighboring jurisdictions or even the National Guard. You may recall that in November 2014, more than 2,000 Missouri National Guard arrived in Ferguson, MO the week before the grand jury decision whether to indict Officer Wilson in the shooting death of Michael Brown was announced, as a show of police presence to deter violent protests and to encourage peaceful demonstrations (some argue that it had the opposite effect).

Crackdowns are short-term, intensive operations that target an unwanted behavior and usually include a lot of arrests and/or citations. Often crackdowns require additional officers to achieve the crime reduction goal, but not always. For example, officers might hide near the entrance of an elementary school and issue tickets to every speeding motorist between 7:30 and 8:00 am on weekdays for a week. Or, a city may ticket and tow every vehicle illegally parked on a main thoroughfare during commuting hours. A college town might crackdown on drinking in public by issuing citations to everyone with an open alcoholic beverage on game days. Although crackdowns can be aimed at any crime or illegal behavior, often they are aimed at prostitution, drugs, and impaired, distracted, or otherwise unsafe drivers. State highway patrol departments routinely schedule crackdowns on texting (or talking) while driving, driving without a seatbelt, and intoxicated driving. Some agencies crackdown on gang violence by instigating intensive enforcement of truancy laws, curfew laws, gun laws, traffic laws, and/or extensive use of field interviews and searches. Studies show that crackdowns and saturation patrol are generally effective at deterring crime for a short period of time (Scott, 2003; Sherman, 1990)

Targeted patrol practices also include *suspect-oriented techniques*, such as stakeouts, bait cars, and decoys. These particular techniques target known offenders or classes of individuals who violate, or are thought to violate, a particular law or set of laws. They are used by detectives and officers assigned to special teams as well as by patrol officers. Stakeouts involve officers watching either (a) a specific person or group of people, such as a gang, or (b) a specific place with known or suspected criminal activity, such as a drug house or secret gambling establishment. Stakeouts are labor-intensive, but can be highly effective if they target repeat offenders (more on this strategy in Chapter 10).

Bait cars, which are unoccupied vehicles that have been outfitted with a camera and a kill switch on the ignition, are another useful suspect-oriented strategy designed to catch car thieves. They are not patrol vehicles; rather, they are common passenger vehicles that are popular with car thieves. Once a thief gets into the car and starts driving, the officers lock the doors, stop the car remotely, and then arrest the car thief. The entire event is usually caught on video. Maybe you've seen one of these videos circulating around the Internet—some thieves can be rather funny.

Although decoys are often thought of as people, such as when a female officer dresses as a prostitute to attract potential johns, police vehicles are also effective decoys. Have you ever seen an empty patrol car parked near an intersection with a four-way stop or along a straight stretch of open road that invites fast driving? If so, the police department may have been running a decoy operation to reduce traffic violations along that street. The city that one of the authors grew up in regularly used this strategy and often placed an inflatable officer in the decoy car to make it look occupied. It was quite realistic, until you were right next to the car (by which point you were following all traffic laws and the decoy car accomplished its purpose). Decoy vehicles are cost-effective and versatile. They can be used to reduce many types of unwanted behavior in downtown areas, parks, business complexes, shopping centers, schools, and public housing projects by giving the perception of police presence in the area. An often overlooked benefit is that they are "community friendly"—meaning that they can deter problem behaviors in the short term without issuing citations or making arrests (which can alienate community members).

SPECIAL PATROLS

Some problems are pervasive enough that a law enforcement agency will develop a special patrol or a special team to address this issue. Some of the most common special teams were introduced in Chapter 5 and will be discussed in depth in Chapter 10. Whereas special teams are typically a permanent unit with its own chain of command, special patrols are usually implemented on a short-term or seasonal basis within the patrol division. For example, many college towns have designated "party cars" on Thursday, Friday, and/or Saturday nights when school is in session. These units, which are usually composed of two officers, respond to all the noise complaints (suspected parties) in a specified portion of the city (or the entire city, depending on size). Cities with a lively night life routinely employ "bar cars" that serve a similar purpose; these may be in service every weekend or only the first one or two weekends of the month

© bikeriderlondon/Shutterstock.com

Traffic stops are how most people encounter police officers each year.

(when people have money to spend on alcohol). Some departments designate a roaming "felony car" to respond to serious crimes throughout the city (or a subsection of the city) on specific nights. Once again, this is usually a two-person unit and allows the dispatcher to send a single two-officer unit rather than having to wait for two one-officer units to be available. Many larger departments also employ "DUI cars," whose main purpose is to identify intoxicated drivers. These units (also composed of two officers) can respond to high-level calls for service when needed.

TRAFFIC FUNCTION

Traffic is considered a special patrol function even though it is routinely performed by regular patrol officers in most cities. It is also the police function that brings most people into contact with the police each year. In 2011, just about 63 million people aged 16 and older reported having contact with police, 42% of whom (26 million people) had been stopped for a traffic violation (Langton & Durose, 2013). This means that a little more than 10% of all registered drivers in the United States were stopped by police in 2011 for a traffic infraction (Langton & Durose, 2013). To put this in a little more perspective, three million more people were stopped for a traffic violation than reported being a crime victim in 2011 (Langton & Durose, 2013; Truman & Plantry, 2012).

This highlights the importance of traffic stops for democratic policing and perceptions of police legitimacy. As can be seen in Table 8.6, overall 88.2% of drivers stopped for a traffic violation believed the police officer behaved properly and this differed only slightly by driver sex, age, and race (Langton & Durose, 2013). Even 88.6% of drivers issued a ticket felt the officer behaved properly (93.3% of drivers

TABLE 8.6 Demographic Characteristics of Those Stopped for Traffic Violations in 2011			
		Percent of stopped drivers	
Demographic Characteristics	**Percent of all drivers in United States**	**Total**	**Reported Police Behaved Properly**
Total	10.2%	100%	88.2%
Sex			
Male	11.9%	58.8%	86.9%
Female	8.4%	41.2%	89.9%
Race			
White	9.8%	69.3%	89.4%
Black	12.8%	12.6%	82.7%
Hispanic/ Latino	10.4%	12.2%	86.5%
American Indian	15.0%	0.6%	74.2%
Asian/Pacific Islander	9.4%	4.0%	89.5%
Two + races	13.4%	1.3%	94.8%
Age			
16–17	9.0%	1.8%	92.3%
18–24	17.8%	19.5%	85.1%
25–34	12.7%	22.4%	88.1%
35–44	11.3%	19.8%	87.9%
45–54	9.4%	17.9%	88.7%
55–64	7.1%	11.4%	89.7%
65 and older	4.8%	7.2%	92.3%

Adapted from Langton, L. & Durose, M.. (2013, September). *Police behavior during traffic and street stops, 2011.* Bureau of Justice Statistics, p. 15. Washington DC: U.S. Government Printing Office.

given a warning felt the same way). However, the percentage of drivers believing the officer behaved properly dropped significantly when the driver believed the reason for the stop was not legitimate (it was unfair) (see Table 8.7). The perception of whether the stop was legitimate varied by the reason given for the traffic stop as well as driver race. As Table 8.8 illustrates, some violations were less likely to be seen as legitimate as others (e.g., stop sign/light violations and illegal turn/lane changes), and when the officer gave no reason for the stop, drivers were much more likely to believe the stop was not legitimate. The take-away for officers is that providing a reason for a traffic stop can dramatically improve a driver's perception of the legitimacy of the stop and the officer's behavior during the encounter, even if the driver is ticketed. This is a great illustration of procedural justice.

TABLE 8.7 Perception that Reason for Traffic stop was Legitimate and that Police Behaved Properly, 2011

Race & Ethnicity of Driver & Officer	Total	Reason for Stop Was Legitimate[c]	Police Behaved Properly[d] — Reason for Stop Was Legitimate	Police Behaved Properly[d] — Reason for Stop Was Not Legitimate
Total	100%	80.0%	93.9%	65.0%
White driver[a]	100%	83.6%	93.9%	64.5%
White officer	81%	84.0%	93.8%	67.2%
Black officer	4.3%	82.3%	96.6%	60.3%
Hispanic/Latino officer	3.3%	76.5%	98.0%	63.5%
Black driver[a]	100%	67.5%	94.2%	58.7%
White officer	65.3%	70.2%	93.6%	58.3%
Black officer	13.8%	70.7%	91.6%	87.1%
Hispanic/Latino officer	5.7%	46.8%	100%	55.4%[!]
Hispanic/Latino driver	100%	73.6%	94.7%	60.1%
White officer	64.9%	74.3%	94.2%	64.1%
Black officer	3.2%	74.1%	94.2%[!]	64.3%[!]
Hispanic/Latino officer	16.7%	77.4%	93.8%	54.4%[!]
Other[a,b] driver	100%	78.4%	91.9%	78.7%
White officer	72.3%	80.3%	93.1%	75.0%
Black officer	3.1%[!]	52.7%[!]	51.2%[!]	79.4%[!]
Hispanic/Latino officer	5.8%[!]	76.9%[!]	100%[!]	100%[!]

! Interpret with caution. Estimate based on 10 or fewer cases or the coefficient of variation is greater than 50%.

[a] Excludes persons of Hispanic or Latino orgin.

[b] Includes persons identifying as American Indian, Alaska Native, Asian, Native Hawaiian, or other Pacific Islander, and persons of two or more races.

[c] Denominator includes approximately 3% of respondents who did not know or did not report whether the reason for the stop was legitimate.

[d] Denominator includes approximately 1% of drivers who thought the stop was legitimate and 6% of drivers who did not think it was legitimate who did not know or did not report whether the police behaved properly.

Adapted from Langton, L. & Durose, M.. (2013, September). *Police behavior during traffic and street stops, 2011.* Bureau of Justice Statistics, p. 15. Washington DC: U.S. Government Printing Office.

Reason for Traffic Stop	Percent of All Drivers Stopped for This Offense	Percent of Stopped Drivers Reporting Reason Was Legitimate				
		All	White[a]	Black	Hispanic/ Latino	Other[b]
Any reasons	100%	80%	83.6%	67.5%	73.6%	78.4%
Police gave reason as:						
Speeding	46.5%	87.1%	89.6%	72.8%	83.1%	87.3%
Vehicle defect	14.1%	81.2%	86.4%	69.0%	74.4%	79.3%
Record check	9.7%	80.0%	80.9%	83.0%	70.7%	81.2%
Roadside sobriety check	1.3%	79.4%	86.0%	–	56.6%!	68.1%!
Seatbelt or cell phone violation	6.6%	79.7%	84.0%	63.8%	77.3%	69.0%!
Illegal turn or lane change	7.0%	73.0%	75.4%	65.0%	72.6%	67.1%
Stop sign/light violation	6.7%	68.4%	68.8%	69.2%	63.6%	74.6%
Other reason	5.1%	59.1%	65.2%	21.6%!	61.9%	67.8%!
Police did not give reason	3.1%	44.6%	51.0%	36.6%!	18.3%!	59.8%!

! Interpret with caution. Estimate based on 10 or fewer cases or the coefficient of variation is greater than 50%.

[a] Excludes persons of Hispanic or Latino orgin.

[b] Includes persons identifying as American Indian, Alaska Native, Asian, Native Hawaiian, or other Pacific Islander, and persons of two or more races.

Adapted from Langton, L. & Durose, M.. (2013, September). *Police behavior during traffic and street stops, 2011.* Bureau of Justice Statistics, p. 15. Washington DC: U.S. Government Printing Office.

Tasks Specialized traffic units perform a variety of tasks meant to facilitate traffic flow and reduce the frequency and severity of auto accidents. Enforcing traffic laws is the most obvious, but officers also investigate traffic accidents, educate the public about traffic safety, monitor traffic flow, and ensure safe traveling conditions by closing roads when it is unsafe to pass, regulating traffic at intersections when necessary, or recommending changes to roads or intersections to improve vehicle, bicyclist, or pedestrian safety. For agencies that are not large enough to have a specialized traffic division (most agencies), these tasks fall on patrol officers.

Traffic enforcement varies broadly by department—some departments write a lot of tickets, others write very few. Priorities and enforcement practices are determined by formal and informal department policy, individual officer discretion, community pressure and the number, severity, and determined causes of traffic accidents in the area. Research on whether aggressive enforcement of traffic law violations results in fewer accidents, fewer crimes, or more arrests is highly mixed but generally supportive when conducted in/near hot spots (more on this in Chapter 10).

CONCLUSION

This chapter examined the basic functions of police in American society and how those basic functions are carried out on a daily basis. It explores the distinctions between proactive and reactive policing as well as between the law enforcement, order maintenance, and service functions of policing. Patrol officers are tasked with a multitude of assignments and this has not changed much since the 1960s. We have, however, learned much about effective patrol strategies since the 1960s. Today, there is a much greater emphasis on directed patrol strategies aimed at specific problem areas and techniques, such as saturation patrol and crackdowns that can reduce crime.

REVIEW QUESTIONS

1. What are the three main functions of policing? Provide an example of each.
2. What are the various methods used by officers to patrol specific areas? What are the strengths of each?
3. What did the Kansas City Preventative Patrol Experiment teach us about routine patrol?
4. What did we learn from the Newark Foot Patrol Experiment?
5. What did the Minnesota Hot Spots Study teach us about the distribution of crime? What were the implications of the study?

GLOSSARY

Computer-aided dispatch an automated computer system that assists police dispatchers receive calls for service, then assign and manage responding officers and information.

Crackdowns short-term, intensive operations that target an unwanted behavior and usually include a lot of arrests and/or citations.

Differential response a method of triaging calls for service in which the most urgent calls are dispatched first.

Directed patrol spending an allotted amount of time patrolling a specific area of the community that is considered to be a high-crime area.

Discovery crime crimes that are discovered by the victim after the suspect fled the scene.

Dispatcher a person who answers emergency and non-emergency calls for police services from the public and coordinates the movements of officers in the field.

Involvement crime crimes in which the victim is confronted by the suspect.

Kansas City Preventative Patrol Experiment the first study conducted on the effectiveness of random patrol in the early 1970s.

Law enforcement activities performed by peace officers that are directly related to enforcing the law and controlling crime.

Minneapolis Hot Spot Study a study conducted during the mid-1980s which found that crime is not evenly distributed and that focusing patrol resources on the specific places that produce the most calls for service effectively reduces crime.

Newark Foot Patrol Experiment a study conducted during the late 1970s that tested the effects of different levels of foot patrol on crime, arrest rates, citizen attitudes, and officer attitudes.

Order maintenance activities performed by peace officers that promote and orderly and peaceful society.

Preventative patrol patrolling the community on an unpredictable and routine or random basis.

Random routine patrol the practice of police officers randomly driving around their beat, hoping to discourage criminal activity through visibility.

Saturation patrol a dramatic and sudden increase in patrol officers in a specific area to increase police visibility and deter potential criminal behavior.

Service activities performed by peace officers that are considered a public or community service.

REFERENCES

Amendola, K. L., Weisburd, D., Hamilton, E.E., Jones, G., & Slipka, M. (2011). *What we know about 8-, 10-, and 12- hour shifts in policing.* Washington, DC: Police Foundation. Retrieved from http://www.policefoundation.org/

Boston Athletic Association (BAA). (2014). *Boston Marathon participation.* Retrieved from http://www.baa.org/races/boston-marathon/boston-marathon-history.aspx

Boydstun, J., Sherry, M., & Moelter, N. (1977). *Officer patrol staffing in San Diego: One or two-officer units?* Washington, DC: Police Foundation.

Brannon, B. C. (1956). Report on one-man police patrol cars in Kansas City, Missouri. *Journal of Criminal Law and Criminology, 47*(2), 238. Retrieved from http://scholarlycommons.law.northwestern.edu/cgi/viewcontent.cgi?article=4489&context=jclc

Burch, A. M. (2012, December). *Sheriffs' offices, 2007 – Statistical tables.* Bureau of Justice Statistics (p. 12). Washington, DC: U.S. Government Printing Office.

Chian, A., Zhang, Y., & Hoover, L. (2012). Police response time to in-progress burglary: A multilevel analysis. *Police Quarterly, 15*(3), 308–327. doi: 10.1177/1098611112447753

Cordner, G., Greene, J., & Bynum, T. (1983). The sooner the better: Some effects of police response time. In Richard R. Bennett (Ed.), *Police at work.* Beverly Hills, CA: Sage.

Coupe, R., & Blake, L. (2005). The effects of patrol workloads and response strength on arrests at burglary emergencies. *Journal of Criminal Justice, 33*, 239–255.

Demers, S., Palmer, A., & Griffiths, C. (2007). *Vancouver police department patrol deployment study.* Vancouver, BC: City of Vancouver.

Durose, M., & Langton, L. (2013). *Request for police assistance, 2011.* Washington, DC: Bureau of Justice Statistics. Retrieved from http://www.bjs.gov/index.cfm?ty=pbdetail&iid=4780

Famega, C. (2005). Variation in officer downtime: A review of the research. *Policing: An International Journal of Police Strategies & Management, 28*(3), 388–414.

Federal Communication Commission (FCC). (2013, March 31). Dial 211 for essential community services guide. Washington, DC. Retrieved from http://www.fcc.gov/guides/dial-211-essential-community-services

Greene, J. R., & Klockars, C. (1991). What police do. In C. Klockars & S. D. Mastrofski (Eds.), *Thinking about police* (pp. 281–291). New York, NY: McGraw-Hill.

Groff, E., Johnson, L., Ratcliffe, J., & Wood, J. (2015). Exploring the relationship between foot and car patrol in violent crime areas. *Policing: An International Journal of Police Strategies & Management, 36*(1), 119–139.

Hickman, M., & Reaves, B. (2006). *Local police departments, 2003.* Washington, DC: Bureau of Justice Statistics.

Johnson, R. R., & Rhodes, T. N. (2009). Urban and small town comparison of citizen demand for services. *International Journal of Police Science & Management, 11*(1), 27–38.

Kansas City Police Department (KCPD). (1978). *Response time analysis: Executive summary.* Washington, DC: U.S. Government Printing Office.

Kaplan, E. (1979). Evaluating the effectiveness of one-officer versus two-officer patrol units. *Journal of Criminal Justice, 7,* 325–355.

Kelling, G., Pate, T., Dieckman, D., & Brown, C. E. (1974). *The Kansas City preventative patrol experiment: A summary report.* Washington, DC: Police Foundation. Retrieved from http://www.policefoundation.org/content/kansas-city-preventive-patrol-experiment-0

Koper, C. (1995). Just enough police presence: Reducing crime & disorderly behavior by optimizing patrol time in crime hotspots. *Justice Quarterly, 12*(4), 649–672. doi: 10.1080/07418829500096231

Langton, L., & Durose, M. (2013, October). *Police behavior during traffic and street stops, 2011.* Washington, DC: Bureau of Justice Statistics. Retrieved from http://www.bjs.gov/content/pub/pdf/pbtss11.pdf

Larson, R., & Rich, T. (1985). *Use of operational models in considering implementation strategies for combined use of two- and one-officer cars.* National Institute of Justice Report 103174. Washington, DC: National Institute of Justice.

Levs, J., & Plott, M. (2013, April 18). Boy, 8, one of 3 killed in bombings at Boston Marathon; scores wounded. CNN.com. Retrieved from http://www.cnn.com/2013/04/15/us/boston-marathon-explosions/index.html

National Law Enforcement Officers Memorial Fund (NLEOMF). (2014, April 14). *Causes of law enforcement officer deaths over the last decade (2004-2013).* Retrieved from http://www.nleomf.org/facts/officer-fatalities-data/causes.html

Piza, E., & O'Hara, B. (2012). Saturation foot-patrol in a high-violence area: A quasi-experimental evaluation. *Justice Quarterly.* E-pub ahead of print.

Police Foundation. (1981). *The Newark foot patrol experiment.* Washington, DC: Police Foundation. Retrieved from http://www.policefoundation.org/content/newark-foot-patrol-experiment-report

Ratcliffe, J., Tanaiguchi, T., Groff, E., & Wood, J. (2011). The Philadelphia foot patrol experiment: A randomized controlled trial of police patrol effectiveness in violent crime hotspots. *Criminology, 49*(3), 795–831. doi: 10.1111/j.1745-9125.2011.00240.x

Reaves, B. (2010, December). *Local police departments, 2007.* Bureau of Justice Statistics (p. 15). Washington, DC: U.S. Government Printing Office.

Schaible, L. M., & Hughes, L. A. (2012). Neighborhood disadvantage and reliance on the police. *Crime & Delinquency, 58,* 245. Originally published online 8 September 2008. doi: 10.1177/0011128708322531

Scott, E. (1981). *Calls for service: Citizen demand and initial police response.* Washington, DC: U.S. Government Printing Office.

Scott, M. (2003). *The benefits and consequences of police crackdowns.* Washington, DC: Office of Community Oriented Policing Services.

Sherman, L. W. (1990). Crackdowns: Initial and residential deterrence. In M. Tonry & N. Morris (Eds.), *Crime and justice: A review of research* (Vol. 12). Chicago, IL: University of Chicago Press.

Sherman, L. W., Gartin, P. R., & Buerger, M. E. (1989). Hot spots of predatory crime: Routine activities and the criminology of place. *Criminology, 27*(1), 27–56. doi: 10.1111/j.1745-9125.1989.tb00862.x

Sherman, L. W., & Weisburd, D. (1995). General deterrent effects of police patrol in crime "hot spots": A randomized, controlled trial. *Justice Quarterly, 12*(4), 625–648. doi: 10.1080/07418829500096221

Song, E., Haberman, C., Ratcliffe, J., & Groff, E. (2013). Foot patrol in violent crime hot spots: The longitudinal impact of deterrence and post treatment effect of displacement. *Criminology, 51*(1), 65–102. doi: 10.1111/j.1745-9125.2012.00290.x

Spelman, W., & Brown, D. K. (1984). *Calling the police: Citizen reporting of serious crime.* Washington, DC: US Government Printing Office. Retrieved from https://www.ncjrs.gov/pdffiles1/Digitization/82276NCJRS.pdf

Wikipedia. (n.d.). *2013 Boston marathon.* Retrieved from http://en.wikipedia.org/wiki/Boston_Marathon_bombings

Wilson, C. (1990). Research on one- and two-person patrols: Distinguishing fact from fiction. *National Police Research Unit,* Report Series No. 104.

Wilson, C., & Brewer, N. (1991). One- and two-person patrols: Summary report. *National Police Research Unit,* Report Series No. 108.

Wilson, C., & Brewer, N. (1992). One- and two person patrols. *Journal of Criminal Justice, 20,* 443–454.

Wilson, C. (1991). How police forces protect the single-officer patrol. *National Police Research Unit,* Report Series No. 94.

Wilson, J. Q. (1968). *Varieties of police behavior.* Cambridge, MA: Harvard University Press.

9 IDENTIFYING PROBLEMS

LEARNING OBJECTIVES

After reading this chapter, students should be able to:

1   Name and describe the two main computer systems agencies use to store information.

2   Explain intelligence-led policing.

3   Describe the three levels of crime analysis and when each would be used.

4   Summarize the analytic process of crime analysis.

5   Describe the four main types of analysis.

6   Summarize predictive policing.

7   Describe Compstat, including the components and the process

8   Explain the benefits and problems associated with Compstat

9   Differentiate real time crime centers from regional intelligence centers

KEY TERMS

Computer aided dispatch (CAD)

Records management system (RMS)

Uniform Crime Report (UCR)

National Incident Based Reporting System (NIBRS)

Intelligence-led policing (ILP)

Crime analysis

COMPSTAT

Predictive policing

Real time crime center

Regional intelligence center

Fusion center

Crime mapping

Tactical analysis

Operational analysis

Strategic analysis

Crime trend analysis

Intelligence analysis

Investigative analysis

Operational analysis

217

In the previous chapter, we learned that patrol is the backbone of policing but that randomly driving around a beat does not reduce crime and rapidly responding to most calls does not catch criminals. We also learned that devoting extra attention to crime hotspots can do both—reduce crime and catch criminals. In this chapter, we examine how officers know where these crime hotspots, or problem areas, are in their beat. As you might recall from Chapter 3, the current state of policing could be best described as the intelligence era. This chapter explains why. It describes the vast information available to personnel in law enforcement agencies across the country and illuminates how these personnel decipher and contextualize that information to develop appropriate strategic responses to police issues. The chapter depicts intelligence-led policing (ILP) as a commitment to use data to reduce crime. Also, it describes some of the common approaches used by police departments that are congruent with the ILP paradigm and which support efforts to improve police competence through data analysis and data sharing, including crime analysis, COMPSTAT, real-time crime centers, and fusion centers.

ILP uses data to reduce crime and police departments have many resources now at their disposal.

© VLADGRIN/Shutterstock.com

GATHERING INFORMATION

Consider for a moment that you are a patrol officer. You are enthusiastic and want to be as effective as you can be at your job. Specifically, you want to reduce crime and make people in your beat feel safe. What should you do to accomplish your goals? You now know that you should focus on the places that cause the most trouble. But how do you know which places those are and whether there are trouble makers there all the time or just sometimes? To start, you have your own personal observations and experiences. While on patrol you notice things—things such as how many people are typically in a particular place (such as a park or street corner) at a particular time; you notice who they are (children, teenagers, adults, senior citizens, college students, "gang bangers," and so on) and what they are doing (playing a friendly game of basketball, chess, or jump rope rather than drug dealing, gambling, or prostituting); whether they are getting along peacefully or whether there seems to be tension. You also notice the places in your beat that you are frequently called to keep the peace or take crime reports. Beyond these personal observations and experiences, what other information might be available to help you determine the places with the most or biggest problems?

SOURCE OF INFORMATION

Officers and agencies collect a lot of data (information). It is collected from a variety of sources, including calls for service, crime reports, field interview cards, traffic citations, offenders who are required to register with the police (e.g., sex offenders, drug offenders, and arsonists), intelligence from special teams and investigations (such as the names and addresses of drug dealers, gang members, prostitutes, and other one-time and serial offenders), and other criminal justice agencies (such as probation and parole).

Computer Aided Dispatch (CAD) Remember, in Chapter 8 we said that most departments use **computer aided dispatch (CAD)**. This means that you could print a report of calls-for-service. Depending on the computer system, you might be able to get a list of addresses with the highest number of calls for service—though it isn't usually this easy and often requires some work on your part, like counting the number of times an address appears on the list (thankfully the calls can usually be sorted by address so it isn't difficult—just tedious). Some CAD systems allow an officer to build a report that includes days and times of calls and call summary information (the call type and disposition), but not all systems are this flexible or useful for this purpose. Agencies that use NIBRS (more on this in a moment) may have an advantage here since that system requires the collection and tracking of more information than the traditional UCR reporting system.

Information collected from calls from the public might include suspect information—physical description, possibly a name or address, and maybe vehicle information such as make and model of car, color, or license plate. It also generally includes caller information (unless the caller requests to remain anonymous), location of the incident, and the nature of the incident (what is happening or what happened). Call information is stored in the agency's CAD system for a specific period of time, which varies by agency and network capabilities and may be based on state law. The information retained in the CAD system is sometimes only accessible to dispatchers and responding officers, and others by specific request. Important call information (names of confirmed involved parties and locations) is transferred to the records management system (RMS).

Records Management System (RMS) Most law enforcement agencies that use computers have a **records management system (RMS)** that stores and secures their most important data. In the case of a police department, that would be information from crime reports, accident reports, arrests, restraining orders, warrants, criminal registrants (narcotics, arson, and sex), and sometimes field interview cards. For example, information contained in crime reports is entered into the agency's RMS by records clerks. Here, it is stored for future retrieval for an indefinite period of time (or until the computer system is severely strained and inactive records must be purged or archived in order to avoid a system crash). This is the system that is typically used to report crime activity to the FBI's **Uniform Crime Report (UCR)** program each year. Often, the information in the RMS database is integrated with the CAD system so that dispatchers and officers in the field have access to the information contained in it, along with station personnel.

How much and which information from the crime report gets entered into the RMS depends on the agency. Some agencies enter very little information, perhaps only contact information for the parties involved (victim, witness, suspect, guardian), address of occurrence, call type, disposition, and basic descriptions of property stolen (and identifying marks). Other agencies record a lot more information specific to the crime and perpetrators, including details of the crime. How much information is entered depends on the agency's computer system capabilities as well as the degree to which the agency's administrators value and encourage the use of information by department personnel.

As you may have learned in a "research methods" or "introduction to criminal justice" class, almost every local law enforcement agency in the United States voluntarily reports criminal activity known to them to the FBI to be included in the *UCR*. This annual report summarizes information on crimes reported to police, number of arrests made by police, and other agency-level information (such as counts of police personnel). Because it only provides counts of Part I and Part II crimes, it does not require significantly detailed crime information from police agencies. So, police agencies are not obligated to capture, track, or report detailed characteristics of crimes (which generally means less data entered into the

> **TEST YOURSELF!**
>
> Can you name the Part I crimes?

© Levente Gyori/Shutterstock.com

The NIBRS uses information such as the time of day of the crime, point of entry, and weapon used to show patterns of criminal activity.

RMS). The **National Incident Based Reporting System (NIBRS)**, on the other hand, requires quite a bit of detailed information about criminal events. Thus, agencies participating in this reporting process record a lot more information specific to the crime (as well as lesser and included offenses) and perpetrators, including characteristics of the offenders and victims as well as relationship of victim to suspect, types and values of property stolen, and details of the crime such as time of day, point of entry (e.g., front door of building, garage, rear entry door, pet door,…), and weapon used (e.g., knife, handgun, rifle,…). This information can be valuable when looking for patterns of criminal activity and suspects with a unique *modus operandi*. If you are unfamiliar with the UCR and NIBRS programs, visit the crime statistics section of the FBI's Web site at: https://www.fbi.gov/stats-services/crimestats.

Other systems Beyond the RMS, officers and analysts rely on other specialized databases such as field interview cards, pawn slips, traffic citations, gang members, and community policing projects to provide useful information. Often, these databases are integrated into the RMS as separate modules. However, some agencies are working with an antiquated RMS that was not built with these modules and cannot be expanded to include these modules. These agencies typically build separate databases (usually in MS ACCESS or EXCEL) to track and store the information they want to retrieve. It should be noted that most custom-built RMS systems are extremely expensive (in the hundreds of thousands to millions of dollars range) and take years to develop (and even more time to debug once personnel start using the new system). For small agencies that cannot afford such a substantial expenditure, there are companies (for example, CrimeStar) that sell complete, customizable, "off the shelf" CAD and RMS systems for a few thousand dollars, which allows even very small departments to be intelligence-driven.

Some agencies also have access to information from other criminal justice agencies; the most common examples are probation and parole agencies. Often, these community corrections agencies provide the names (including aliases), contact information, and parole/probation conditions for each individual currently under supervision along with the supervising agent's contact information. Some systems, such as Parole LEADS (operated by the California Department of Corrections and Rehabilitation), also include photos of the offender and his/her scars, marks, and tattoos, as well as his/her vehicle information, aliases, and a Google map of his/her addresses (home, work) (CDCR, n.d.). California law enforcement officers can search the Parole LEADS database using a variety of criteria (such as suspect physical descriptors, commitment offense, city of residence, registration requirements, etc.). This database and others like it are valuable investigative and crime control tools for officers.

Some states have created secure mobile apps that allow officers to access confidential information (including suspect photos and GPS coordinates) on their mobile phones and tablet computers. For example, California's JusticeMobile app allows officers to query state and federal databases such as vehicle registration and driver's license systems, criminal history, wanted persons, firearms systems, mental health, and stolen property, as well as department and regional databases. Other states have created apps that contain legal code books and other pertinent information for officers. Some even allow officers to scan suspect fingerprints, use facial recognition software to identify a suspect, or create a photo lineup in the field. The Federal Bureau of Alcohol, Tobacco, and Firearms (BATF) produced an app to assist local law enforcement officers identify recovered firearms. Additionally, many cities have developed apps that connect the police department to their constituency and allow citizens to file police reports, compliment an officer, get crime and community resource information, and receive alerts from the police department. There are also other private label apps designed to assist officers organize their field interview cards and help field supervisors establish perimeters, set schedules, and perform a variety of other tasks. Interestingly, officers who started their careers prior to the mid-1980s (a mere 30 years ago) used a pen to write down call information from the dispatcher on a notepad when they were rookies; now those same officers are receiving suspect photos and warrant information on their cell phones.

Police officers in some jurisdictions can get suspect photos and warrant information on their cell phones.

© Chad Zuber/Shutterstock.com

Why is all this information important? Because these computer systems store the information that officers and analysts retrieve and use to identify hotspots and problem people. How much information is easily available and how long it takes to decipher determines how much of the information stored in the computer gets used, how often, and by whom (administrators, analysts, or patrol officers). The technological (information) revolution that began in the mid-1980s with the accessibility of personal computers and soon after, the Internet and World Wide Web, changed policing and incrementally moved the profession toward what we now call ILP. Yet, the notion of ILP has roots that go back to the crime prevention purpose emphasized by Sir Robert Peel and his commissioners in 1829 and the forward-thinking officers' around the world who began creating pin maps to track crimes as far back as the early 1900s.

INTELLIGENCE-LED POLICING

At its core, **ILP** is about proactively managing and using information to effectively reduce crime. The paradigm was proposed in the 1990s in Britain, but did not gain momentum in the United States until after the terrorist attacks of 9/11. It was developed at the same time that crime analysis and **COMPSTAT** were gaining popularity in American police departments. All of these were the direct result of the third technological revolution (the digital information revolution, which made powerful computers affordable and extensive networking possible). Each of these concepts will be discussed separately; however, it is important to understand that they are not completely distinct from one another but rather, interrelated. A department can have a well-resourced crime analysis unit without using COMPSTAT or being committed to an overall intelligence-led approach; while an agency that uses COMPSTAT may or may not have a separate crime analysis unit, it is most likely committed to an ILP approach. Conversely, an agency that ascribes to an ILP model almost certainly has a crime analysis unit, a COMPSTAT unit, or both.

ILP is based on two essential truths: (1) a small number of prolific offenders commit a large portion of crime and (2) crime is clustered in a small number of problem places. These two facts suggest that if police focus their attention on these crime-prone places and people, they can achieve a large crime reduction effect. Hence, ILP is a proactive policing philosophy that focuses on *crime intelligence*, which is defined as the combination of *crime analysis* (which focuses on crime events) and *criminal intelligence* (which focuses on the behavior and relationships of offenders), to direct police resources (Ratcliffe, 2011).

The idea of ILP is still in its infancy and thus police administrators, officers, and scholars are discussing what it actually means from their unique vantage points and for day-to-day police operations. In an effort to establish a universal definition of the paradigm, Ratcliffe has proposed the following:

> *intelligence-led policing is a business model and managerial philosophy where data analysis and crime intelligence are pivotal to an objective, decision-making framework that facilitates crime and problem reduction, disruption and prevention through both strategic management and effective enforcement strategies that target prolific and serious offenders. (2011, p.89)*

Although the definition presents ILP as a formal management philosophy and business model, we portray it here as a general policing paradigm in which the key component is using "crime intelligence to objectively direct police resource decisions" (Ratcliffe, 2011, p.87). We have chosen to do this because there is not a consensus on how U.S. law enforcement agencies are implementing ILP. For example, although ILP calls for a data-driven, top-down hierarchal management style, some agencies successfully practice ILP using the bottom-up community-centered managerial approach advocated by community policing (more on this in Chapter 10) or include it within traditional or modified management structures (see Chapter 4). Although ILP is operationally different from community policing, many departments across the United States are successfully integrating the two.

Police executives and scholars who advocate the ideals of democratic policing like ILP because data-driven focus on crime-prone individuals and addresses (identified using crime data), not of it's racial or cultural stereotypes or preconceptions. For this reason, it is able to stand up to scrutiny and provide answers when residents ask police why they are "targeting" a particular neighborhood, business, or group of individuals. At the same time, police scholars and the general public question the constitutionality of some of the extensive information-gathering tactics that can be involved in ILP, particularly nontargeted "fishing expeditions" that ensnare law-abiding citizens (such as cell phone record downloads, surveillance cameras, license plate readers that feed into a computerized database, etc.). How individuals feel about ILP really depends on how it is practiced, and how much trust the public has in its police department.

It should be noted that ILP encourages police departments to focus intelligence-gathering efforts on prolific criminals, not random community members, and for that reason does not promote "fishing expeditions"; however, anytime there is an effort to gather intelligence, there will always be information collected on law-abiding individuals as part of the process. For example, an officer may conduct research on a known gang member. As part of her research, the officer will likely learn about the gang member's known associates, both criminal and law abiding. If anything "criminally interesting" turns up, then the officer may follow this new lead in an attempt to discover how this person or business may be involved in the known gang member's criminal enterprise. This is the process of research and crime intelligence and is to be expected, just not exploited.

How does an agency practice ILP? The cornerstone of ILP is **crime analysis**, but there are other practices that also promote the process, such as COMPSTAT, real-time crime centers, and fusion centers. The size and scope of ILP practices will depend on the type, size, and location of an agency. Some police departments have a single crime analyst (depending on the size of the agency, this person may be part-time), some departments have several analysts that work in a crime analysis unit, others include crime analysis within another bureau (e.g., detectives, research and training, or problem-oriented policing). Some agencies have formalized, routinized, and integrated crime analysis into a management accountability system known as COMPSTAT while other agencies have developed elaborate computer systems that integrate public surveillance cameras and other tools into "real-time" crime centers. Other departments participate in a fusion center, which is a joint effort among local, state, and federal law enforcement agencies to provide intelligence on organized crime with the purpose of preventing terrorism and other crimes. COMPSTAT, real-time crime centers, and fusion centers are enhanced iterations of crime analysis.

CRIME ANALYSIS

Crime analysis is the "systematic study of crime and disorder problems as well as other police-related issues—including socio-demographic, spatial, and temporal factors—to assist the police in criminal apprehension, crime and disorder reduction, crime prevention, and evaluation"(Santos, 2012, p.2). Although the elements of crime analysis have arguably been part of policing for a very long time, crime analysis as defined above is a relatively new development in policing. Crime analysis has firm roots in the 1960s when O.W. Wilson referenced it by name in his 1963 book, *Police Administration*, and federal money allowed some large departments to place sworn officers in a crime analysis capacity. However, the field did not really expand or become commonplace until the 1990s when modern technology allowed departments to store enormous amounts of data and agencies needed qualified personnel who could easily retrieve and analyze the data in order to inform police practices. As can be seen in Table 9.1, almost every municipal police department that serves 100,000 or more residents performs crime analysis but only about two-thirds to four-fifths of large sheriff's departments do.

Crime analysis is extremely valuable because repeat offenders, and in fact most people, tend to be creatures of habit and they tend to be lazy. They frequently commit crimes in and around the same places, during the same times, days of week, or by the same method. Crime analysts, among other things, monitor these crime patterns and report their existence to the patrol and investigative units so that tactical and/or strategic action plans can be developed. Due to the large amount of data that are collected over time, crime analysts can provide patrol officers and investigators with suspect leads, MO patterns, and other information to assist in identifying criminals as well as the possible location of future criminal activity. They also perform other types of analysis which will be discussed shortly.

LEVELS OF ANALYSIS

Analysis happens at three different levels—tactical, operational, and strategic—in accordance with the way police departments operate (Ratcliffe, 2011). Tactical analysis supports officers working in front-line assignments such as patrol, investigations, and special enforcement teams (drugs, prostitution, and gangs for example). In typical police departments, analysts spend most of their time engaged in tactical analysis (crime trend analysis, investigative analysis, intelligence analysis, suspect identification, etc.) (O'Shea & Nicholls, 2003).

Operational analysis is one step up and includes analysis which supports deploying department resources to most effectively reduce crime or achieve other operational goals—for example, examining the number of calls for service by day, time, type, and geographic location for the station commander so that patrol beats and shifts can be restructured to balance workload across officers. It could also involve analysis of underlying community problems and support for

TABLE 9.1 Analytic Functions of Computers in Agencies throughout the United States

Population Served	Intelligence Gathering		Crime Analysis		Analysis of Community problems		Crime Mapping		Hotspot Identification	
	Police	Sheriffs	Police	Sheriffs	Police	Sheriffs	Police	Sheriffs	Police	Sheriffs
1,000,000 or more	85%	81%	100%	81%	77%	59%	100%	78%	92%	52%
500,000–999,999	90%	65%	100%	71%	81%	52%	100%	63%	100%	44%
250,000–499,999	93%	64%	100%	66%	80%	43%	100%	55%	80%	30%
100,000–249,999	82%	66%	96%	66%	75%	38%	94%	58%	66%	33%
50,000–99,999	72%	51%	88%	47%	70%	30%	82%	41%	56%	18%
25,000–49,999	63%	46%	69%	34%	52%	19%	60%	27%	31%	8%
10,000–24,999	49%	40%	53%	25%	43%	13%	41%	19%	19%	7%
2,500–9,999[a]	42%	40%	37%	20%	27%	9%	23%	9%	9%	4%
Under 10,000[b]	26%		21%		14%		11%		5%	
Under 2,500										
All Sizes	40%	47%	38%	36%	28%	21%	27%	29%	13%	13%

[a] – police departments, [b] – sheriffs' departments

Adapted from Reaves, B. (2010, December). *Local police departments, 2007.* Bureau of Justice Statistics, p. 22. Washington DC: U.S. Government Printing Office. And Burch, A.M. (2012, December). *Sheriffs' offices, 2007-Statistical tables.* Bureau of Justice Statistics, p. 16. Washington DC: U.S. Government Printing Office.

short-term operations. For instance, determining where, how, and when to deploy a roaming task force of officers to eradicate a persistent crime problem. This is the level at which COMPSTAT operates.

Strategic analysis is the top level, and as the name indicates, it is concerned with informing broader department policies, strategies, and ways of doing business. For example, examining when and under what circumstances juvenile crime is occurring to help the chief decide whether to ask the city council to pass a juvenile curfew ordinance, or looking at the effects of arrest practices for specific crimes (such as domestic violence) to decide whether there are any clear best practices that should be incorporated into department policy.

The type and scope of analysis that happens at each level depends on the size, type, and location of an agency. As Figure 9.1 shows, the analysis that happens in a rural agency is much more localized than analysis that is conducted in a state or federal agency. Large metropolitan cities like Chicago, Dallas, Los Angeles, and New York will have analysts focused on broader public safety issues than smaller municipal departments that are not major tourist destinations and that do not host major banking centers. Although there are crime analysts in state and federal law enforcement agencies, this chapter focuses on crime analysis in local law enforcement agencies.

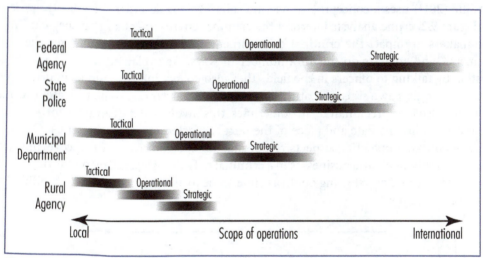

Figure 9.1 Scope of crime intelligence within different types of agency (adapted from Ratcliffe 2007)

INFORMATION DISSEMINATION

Analysts are master disseminators and for that reason, a law enforcement agency that values intelligence and collaboration will position analysts as the main information hub of the agency, both physically within the station and operationally. This structure facilitates the flow of information because analysts work closely with personnel throughout the department.

The relationship between analysts and officers is reciprocal, meaning that information flows in both directions—from officers to analysts and from analysts to officers. Analysts also facilitate the dissemination of information between units (such as between officers who work opposite shifts or at different sites, like undercover drug officers who work primarily at night and patrol officers who work day shift). For example, when one of your textbook authors was an analyst, the southern business park on the west side of the freeway was rarely the site of crimes other than fraud (and there were not many of those). All of a sudden one week, there were a couple vehicle burglaries reported in the area. Odd, but not a pattern nor a concern quite yet. The following week there were several more vehicle burglaries and a few other crimes. No pattern emerged (the crimes occurred on different days and at different times), but it was still noteworthy; so, your author spoke to patrol officers at day shift briefing and asked if they had any ideas. Several officers spoke up and said, "Yes, a parole office just opened in that complex." Well, that explained it. From that point on, officers spent more time patrolling that business park. This information was shared with graveyard officers who were unaware of the new tenant or crime wave.

THE ANALYTIC PROCESS

The standard intelligence cycle includes five steps: direction, collation, analysis, dissemination, and feedback and review. Analysts take direction (someone asks them to analyze something or they notice something on their own to investigate), collate pertinent information, and then analyze it. After analyzing the data, they disseminate the findings to the person who made the initial request (and/or other pertinent personnel who could benefit from the information) and receive feedback and review (the receiver of the analysis may have additional questions or be satisfied that the question was answered appropriately). At that point, the cycle ends or begins again.

Ratcliffe (2011) uses a conceptual model he calls "3-i" to describe the analytic process. As seen in Figure 9.2, crime analysts interpret the criminal environment so that they can influence decision-makers to impact the criminal environment. The first step is "interpret the criminal environment," and analysts do this in a number of ways. As explained above, analysts collect information by talking to officers in the field. They also collect information from crime reports, field interview cards, pawn slips, and other data sources. Analysts do not just collate information; however, they also interpret (analyze) it. Sometimes, this involves identifying potential crime patterns and calculating the date and place of the next suspected crime in the series. Other times, it involves identifying potential suspects responsible for specific crimes or uncovering relationships between individuals and businesses in a criminal network. Depending on the department, it might even involve an analyst going out to a crime scene to assess a target's vulnerability (though this is not very common).

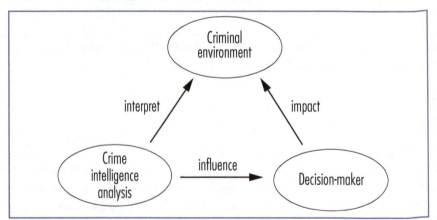

Figure 9.2 The 3-i model (interpret, influence, impact) (adapted from Ratcliffe 2003).

Once an analyst has interpreted the criminal environment (analyzed the data), she will provide her findings to the appropriate decision-makers (patrol officers, detectives, special teams, or police leaders, for example). Depending on the situation and the department, this often involves

COMPSTAT

Compstat (which stands for compare statistics) is a strategic management tool that was introduced by Commissioner William Bratton and Deputy Commissioner Jack Maple of the NYPD as a way to track crime and hold managers accountable for achieving agency goals (crime reduction). It was Bratton's attempt to fix a highly dysfunctional and moribund department (Weisburd et al., 2003). Although it revolves around a computer system that provides decision-makers' immediate access to information about crime trends and disorder problems, it is much more than that. It is a change in management structure that holds middle managers accountable for setting and achieving mission goals (crime reduction, for example).

It was developed around the same time, and for the same reasons, that crime analysis was becoming popular in police departments across the county. In particular, rising crime and the failure of traditional policing methods to control crime left many police leaders searching for inventive ways to reduce it. New policing philosophies, such as problem-oriented policing and community policing, that stressed problem solving also contributed to the creation of Compstat and the rise of crime analysis. Of course, as we've previously discussed, the availability of powerful computers and software was the essential prerequisite that made these analytic innovations possible. Probably, the most notable distinction in the development of Compstat that was not echoed in the diffusion of crime analysis was NYPD Commissioner Bill Bratton's "reacceptance of responsibility for controlling crime" (Moore, 1997, p. 67) and his resolute desire to disprove academics and other skeptics who thought that police could not impact crime.

Compstat became very popular very fast. Within the first 5 years, one-third of U.S. law enforcement agencies with 100+ sworn officers claimed to have implemented a "Compstat-like program" and another one-fourth were planning on implementing the program (Weisburd et al., 2003). Numerous law enforcement agencies in the United Kingdom and Australia have also adopted it, as have corrections agencies, park departments, health departments, and other public service agencies (Eterno & Silverman, 2010; Silverman, 2006; Weisburd, et al., 2003). Although it was developed for use in a police department, it can be used in any public service agency wanting to improve performance.

Weisburd and colleagues (2003) argue that one of the reasons that Compstat resonated so well with police executives, and why it diffused so quickly, is its strong reliance on the traditional bureaucratic and hierarchical police structure that has defined policing since Peel's original force. They suggest that Compstat was offered as an alternative to community policing, a major policing innovation which emerged in the 1980s (more on this in Chapter 10). Whereas community policing advocates a bottom-up organizational style that emphasizes command decentralization and public partnerships, Compstat requires a top-down management style that emphasizes accountability and control. Compstat is embraced because many police executives and officers are more comfortable with paramilitary procedures than community collaboration; however, today it is common to find departments that utilize Compstat as a managerial approach and practice community policing.

THE COMPONENTS

Compstat is based on the premise, "what gets measured, gets done." Weisburd and colleagues (2003) identified six key elements:
1. mission clarification
2. internal accountability
3. geographic organization of command

4. organizational flexibility

5. data-driven problem identification and assessment, and

6. innovative problem solving.

Mission clarification means that the organization has clearly identified a mission/objective that is measurable and that leaders can be held responsible for achieving (e.g., reduce crime by 10%). Internal accountability means that "people in the organization are held directly responsible for carrying out organizational goals … and can expect consequences if they are not knowledgeable about or have not responded to problems that fit within the mission of the department" (Weisburd et al., 2003, p. 428). In this case, it is the middle managers who are accountable for crime problems. Additionally, geographic organization of command dictates that accountability rests with managers of geographic units and decision-making is shifted to supervisors with territorial responsibility (beat or precinct commanders, for example). This means that precinct commanders are typically able to make decisions about staffing and deployment of extra patrols without getting permission from headquarters.

Organizational flexibility requires that middle managers are provided the resources necessary to accomplish their mission and the flexibility to deploy those resources; however, she or he feels is best. That might include, for example, allowing patrol officers to perform tasks normally delegated to special teams (such as drug enforcement). Likewise, timely and accurate data must be available to relevant personnel for problem identification and assessment. Without it, Compstat would fall apart. Finally, commanders are expected to employ innovative problem-solving tactics. Experimentation is encouraged and commanders are expected to develop strategies based on knowledge of what works, not based on what was done yesterday.

THE PROCESS

As part of the process, agency goals are identified, data are collected on a wide variety of performance measures, and reports are produced—for example, the number of crimes committed, arrests made, citations issued, Terry stops conducted, crimes cleared, sick days taken, overtime shifts, car accidents, and citizen complaints, are commonly tracked. This information is compiled regularly (usually daily) so district commanders can be aware of all developing issues and take appropriate action quickly. Although the process differs slightly in each agency that uses Compstat, it is possible to describe a typical process.

On a routine basis (every week usually), there is a Compstat meeting between the command staff (police chief or deputy police chief and other administrators) and some of the district commanders. Each meeting focuses on one (or two) districts, so only the commanders of that (those) districts are "on the hot seat" that week. During the Compstat meeting (sometimes called accountability meeting), the district commanders are presented with analyses of current and past statistics, and then grilled about the issues that command staff view as problems. These analyses are contained in three types of reports: (1) a Compstat report that compares and ranks each district on crime, arrests, and other factors; (2) a commander profile report that depicts personnel issues (such as citizen complaints, officer car accidents, on-duty injuries, sick days used, overtime shifts) within the context of the individual district (taking into account population demographics and size, etc.) and compares commanders throughout the department; and (3) crime maps detailing crimes and calls for service in the district (Henry, 2002). These are highly stressful meetings, and district commanders are expected to show knowledge of the problems and discuss how they are responding to them. Sometimes, commanders bring lieutenants, sergeants, or special team officers with them to present information on operations or tactics being used to address specific crime problems, but accountability always rests with the commander. Commanders are expected to experiment with innovative tactics. These meetings facilitate communication between the ranks and can help reduce bureaucratic "red tape" when trying to implement solutions.

IS IT EFFECTIVE?

Compstat has been called "arguably one of the most significant strategic innovations in policing in the last couple of decades" (Editorial Introduction: Compstat, 2003) and "perhaps the single most important organizational/administrative innovation in policing during the latter half of the 20th century" (Kelling & Sousa, 2001, p. 6). It received the Innovations in American Government Award from the Ford Foundation and Harvard University as well as Vice President Gore's Hammer Award for government innovation (Barry, 1998; Silverman, 2006). It definitely makes departments smarter and more efficient. However, the verdict is still out on whether or not it actually reduces crime.

One of the problems with the research is that it is very difficult to disentangle the crime reduction benefits of Compstat from the policing strategies it instigates. For example, Compstat is associated with the major crime decline in New York City (NYC). From the early 1990s through 2009, crime in NYC declined by about 75%, and while this decline was larger and longer than any other decline in the nation, many things changed in NYC at the same time and it is clear that Compstat was only part of the reason for the decline (expansion of the police force, hot spot policing, and targeted violence-prevention programs share much of the credit) (Zimring, 2012). Compstat has been associated with a rise in some "broken windows"-type arrests and decreases in property and total index crime in Texas (Jang, Hoover, & Joo, 2010) as well as a decline in unlawful entry offenses and the total number of reported offenses in Queensland, Australia (Mazerolle et al., 2007). What we can say with confidence is that Compstat is almost certainly part of the solution because it helps commanders use current crime information (intelligence) to tailor crime control responses to specific problems.

PROBLEMS WITH COMPSTAT

The main criticism of Compstat is that its emphasis on statistics and crime reduction unintentionally encourages managers to use unethical practices to achieve set goals. For middle managers who are accountable for crime trends, having statistics that go in the right direction is highly important; not just so they look good during the Compstat meeting, but also so they are promotable (Eterno & Silverman, 2012, 2010). This intense pressure is transferred to subordinates who are encouraged to change procedures to support goal achievement. Some of the unethical reporting practices that have been documented by researchers include down grading felonies (serious crimes) to misdemeanors (minor crimes) or non-crimes (such as lost property or embezzlement), under-valuing property stolen so that the crime is not a felony, reporting a series of crimes as a single event, and making it so difficult to report a crime that victims give up, rather than file a report (Eterno & Silverman, 2012, 2010; Zink, 2004).

A group of retired NYPD commanders reported that the pressure to reduce index crime increased significantly and manager's demand for integrity in crime statistics decreased significantly after Compstat was implemented (Eterno & Silverman, 2010). One of the most important findings was that, before Compstat was instituted, the demand for integrity in crime statistics was greater than the pressure to reduce index crime and after Compstat was introduced, the pressure to reduce index crime was greater than the demand for integrity in crime statistics! Compstat-induced crime misclassification has also been reported in Atlanta, Philadelphia, Los Angeles, New Orleans, and Broward County, Florida, as well as departments in the United Kingdom and

Australia (Gardiner, 2017). The extent of the "numbers fixing" is unknown. It is possible that the problem is limited to a small number of people in a very small number of departments (bad apples), all of which have been reported in the media. It is also possible that the media has investigated only the "tip of the iceberg" and that the problem is more pervasive than reported.

REAL-TIME CRIME CENTERS

More and more agencies across the United States are developing real-time crime centers. These are centralized technology and analysis centers that use advanced data mining, analytic, and forecasting software and high-tech tools to provide near-real-time information to patrol officers, detectives, and police managers. These centers, which are extremely expensive to develop, can be found in New York (NY), Houston (TX), Memphis (TN), Ogden (UT), Albuquerque (NM), Charlotte-Meckleberg (NC), Philadelphia (PA), Seattle (WA), and a host of other cities. It is believed that New York City was the first to establish a real-time crime center in 2005 (D'Amico, 2006). Usually they are single agency efforts, but occasionally they can be multi-jurisdictional endeavors. South Sound 911 is an example of a multi-jurisdictional center that serves the entire Pierce County, Washington region (southsound911.org, n.d.).

Centers operate 24/7, and the difference between a real-time crime center and a dispatch center is that real-time crime centers are staffed by analysts around the clock, not dispatchers. The analysts provide up-to-the-minute access to technology, analysis, and investigative support. What makes these centers unique from standard crime analysis units is the following:

- the staffing structure (24/7, not 8-5)
- constant monitoring of calls for service allows analysts to provide valuable information to officers and detectives while they are on scene (or en route to calls)
- a highly sophisticated, integrated network of technology provides access to billions of bits of information almost instantaneously as well as the ability to merge queries from a variety of databases
- state-of-the-art data analysis software that easily combines information from multiple databases and other technologies (videos, license plate readers, etc.) to identify and locate suspects quickly
- superb data-viewing capabilities—centers are outfitted with numerous large screen monitors and televisions to display multiple crime scenes, traffic cameras, and news programs simultaneously.

Analysts at the centers expertly and seamlessly glean information from public records databases (including Facebook, Twitter, Instagram, and other social media) as well as databases with information on crimes, calls for service (both 911 and 311), criminal records, probation and parole files, traffic and parking tickets, pawn systems, gang membership, and court records—all at the push of a button. They also have access to traffic and other surveillance cameras, license plate readers, gunshot detection sensors, radiation sensors, satellite imaging, mapping, link analysis, and a variety of other resources to solve crimes. The "domain awareness system" (DAS) software, specifically developed for NYPD (but sure to be adopted by others), collects and analyzes this information, maps it, and even compares it to potential threat lists (i.e., terrorist watch lists, known gang members, drug dealers, etc.) (Joh, 2014). Even with all of these tools and resources, real-time crime center analysts do not have access to all the information that is available to fictional characters such as FBI analyst Penelope Garcia from Criminal Minds or her colleagues on CSI, NCIS, and similar shows.

Still, real-time crime centers are pretty amazing. For example, in Houston, a witness who saw a man kill his wife called police and the analyst from the real-time crime center "cross-referenced the murder scene's address with information on the suspect... [then] used that to get the OnStar in his car activated... [Officers arrested the suspect] within two hours of the shooting" (Oberg, 2010; para.9-10). In New York, a man who posed as an electrician burglarized elderly couples and on one occasion left a business card with a first name and phone number on it. Real-time crime center analysts discovered that the phone number was associated with a previous 911 call from a night club. Detectives contacted the caller, who then identified the suspect, who was then arrested (D'Amico, 2006).

ST. LOUIS OPENS 'REAL TIME CRIME CENTER'; CRITIC CALLS IT 'SPY HUB'?

ST. LOUIS • When a 911 call comes in, St. Louis police now may be able to see the scene before responding officers have time to arrive.

It's part of the Real Time Crime Center, opened Thursday to bring together an array of electronic resources—including a network of public and private surveillance cameras that could put eyes on a location within seconds.

Eight officers and a sergeant will run the around-the-clock operation inside police headquarters, at 1915 Olive Street. They will have access to data from cameras, license plate readers, red light cameras, hot-spot crime mapping and the ShotSpotter microphone system that can track the source of gunfire.

"Today is a great day for law enforcement and a bad day for criminals in the city of St. Louis," Chief Sam Dotson declared.

But the concept is not without controversy.

John Chasnoff, long-time member of the activist organization Coalition Against Police Crimes and Repression, called it "a spy hub for the whole city of St. Louis." He was among about 20 protesters gathered outside headquarters as officials toured the center.

"This is a big step toward mass surveillance of the city's population," Chasnoff complained. "People going about their business who have given no indication they have committed an offense are still being watched by their government and police."

Dotson sees the center as the linchpin of a safer community, helping police both fight and prevent crime. It puts his department in line with dozens of police agencies with similar capabilities, including Chicago, Houston, and Kansas City.

REGIONAL INTELLIGENCE CENTERS

Regional intelligence centers (also called **fusion centers**) were initiated after the 9/11 terrorist attacks to address the major gaps in information sharing that existed between federal, state, and local law enforcement agencies in the United States at that time. Fusion centers bring together federal, state, and local law enforcement agencies within a region for the purpose of gathering, receiving, analyzing, and disseminating intelligence on criminal enterprises (Department of Homeland Security, n.d.). There are currently 78 regional intelligence centers spread across the United States (see Figure 9.3). Each of the fusion centers are owned and operated by state or local agencies with federal support through the U.S. Department of Homeland Security. Each center functions as a terrorism early warning group and coordinates all counter-terrorism efforts in the defined jurisdiction, including protecting critical infrastructures, assessing

Figure 9.3 Map of Fusion Centers in US.

threats, monitoring infectious disease outbreaks, and working with both public and private entities to identify suspicious activity.

Unlike real-time crime centers, which are more concerned with local crime and criminals, fusion centers were created to prevent terrorism and coordinate emergency responses. However, this does not mean they are limited to terrorism and emergency responses, and most fusion centers assist authorities investigate local crimes and address complex problems such as gangs, narcotics, violence, and human trafficking. The goal is for each center to function as a multi-jurisdictional analysis unit that supports crime prevention and investigation as part of a larger focus on criminal enterprises, terrorism, and emergency response within the region. As many law enforcement agencies have discovered, sometimes local criminals committing standard crimes (such as shoplifting) have international ties to terrorism. See the Field Perspectives box for an example from the Orange County, CA fusion center.

FIELD PERSPECTIVES: TECHNOLOGY, INTELLIGENCE, AND COLLABORATION

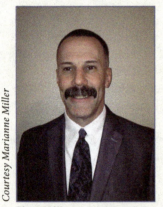

Courtesy Marianne Miller

Tim Miller

By: Lt. Tim Miller, Fusion Center Director

Like all aspects of society, modern law enforcement has been changed forever by technology. For many years, law enforcement methods changed little in how crimes were solved. Witnesses were interviewed, crime scenes were checked for the suspect's fingerprints which were classified, then checked by hand for a match against known records; suspects were identified through old booking photos, detectives checked the prior booking documents for the latest address and knocked on the door in hopes of finding the suspect at home to make an arrest. In more serious cases, detectives conducted surveillance, waiting for the suspect to show themselves before attempting contact.

In the last several decades, computer automation has made the process more efficient by making tremendous amounts of data available to utilize in solving crimes and identifying problem locations and people. The human element continues to perform as the critical component in law enforcement investigations; however, the data comes in a variety of forms and still requires the need for deeper analysis. The same witness interviews occur, but are now enhanced by audio and video recordings at or near a crime scene which may capture images of the suspect and/or his vehicle and occasionally the license plate on the car. Automated License Plate Reader software technology now helps officers identify where suspect vehicles have recently been seen, giving law enforcement additional options for locating suspects. Fingerprints are still sought at crimes scenes, but are now enhanced by DNA collection and other forms of trace evidence left behind by suspects. While the human element has not been completely replaced in the world of fingerprint classification and identification, the process has been enhanced by automation and technology.

Information available through system checks regarding suspects has grown exponentially with data being linked together by complex networks which check for data across a variety of systems simultaneously. More detailed suspect profiles are available through law enforcement data bases, open source, and social media analysis. A variety of images related to a suspect are now available and may aid in providing the most accurate depiction of a suspect's current appearance. High-tech surveillance methods now supplement traditional "eyes on" surveillance.

Fusion Centers are a relatively new resource available to assist law enforcement. Created after the terrorist attacks on "9-11," Fusion Centers assess threats and help to collect, analyze and disseminate information in a multi-agency, multi-disciplined task force environment effort to help improve communication among various public safety agencies and the public, while respecting the public's privacy, civil rights and civil liberties. Fusion Centers receive tips and leads on suspicious activity from members of public safety and the public and analyze data from a variety of sources in order to identify and prevent terrorist activity. Suspicious activity is frequently identified as common criminal behavior and communicated to the appropriate agency for investigation.

Recently, a police vehicle was stolen from a law enforcement facility. Data was analyzed from a variety of sources in solving the crime. Shortly after the vehicle was stolen, a witness observed a police vehicle being driven erratically some distance from the scene of the theft. The witness reported her observations to local law enforcement that investigated the tip, but were at that time unaware of the theft. Once the theft was reported to the local agency providing service to the area where the theft occurred, assistance was requested of the local Fusion Center. A comprehensive search of data by personnel at the Fusion Center revealed the information regarding the police vehicle being driven erratically some distance from the location of the theft, but shortly after the theft probably occurred. A re-interview of the original witness revealed additional information regarding a possible second suspect and vehicle involved.

Through leveraging a variety of data bases, including Automated License Plate Reader software, the investigation revealed identifying information on a possible second suspect vehicle. An analysis of real-time open-source information revealed a group of individuals openly buying and selling vehicle parts on the internet from typical police vehicles as members of this group sought to recreate realistic looking police vehicles as a hobby. Investigators from the local agency investigating the vehicle theft were able to obtain specific information related to the suspects' identity and location through the courts. Detectives then traveled approximately 100 miles to a neighboring county and contacted the suspects. Detectives conducted thorough interviews obtaining additional information from parties involved and received enough information to obtain a search warrant on suspects' residences and ultimately recovered vehicle parts removed from the stolen police vehicle as well as the vehicle itself. This led to the successful prosecution of the parties involved.

This is a typical example of traditional law enforcement methods being enhanced by the interpretation and analysis of data, interjection of modern technology, and collaboration between partners. In this exponentially advancing age of technology, law enforcement must constantly look for new ways to piece together data from a variety of sources in its many forms to help identify problem people and locations. It is this leveraging of information that will propel law enforcement ahead in its fight against a criminal element that is ever-increasing in sophistication.

Tim Miller is a Lieutenant for a local law enforcement agency in Southern California. He currently serves as the Director of a Department of Homeland Security recognized Fusion Center. Tim has been an officer for over 29 years and served in and led a variety of assignments including Patrol, Narcotics, Career Criminal Apprehension, Gang Enforcement, Community Policing, Training, Emergency Management and SWAT.

The centers are staffed by personnel from federal, state, and local government agencies and often include members from fire departments, hospitals, public health agencies, and probation and parole departments in addition to local and state law enforcement agencies. Staff gather crime and intelligence information from member agencies, members of the public, and private companies within the jurisdiction, as well as the federal government, and anyone else who has pertinent information to share (usually via an anonymous tip line). Additionally, as part of a public-private partnership, fusion centers work with Information Sharing and Analysis Centers (ISACs)—trusted private entities that provide detailed analyses of specific sectors (such as aviation, maritime, financial, IT, health, energy, real estate, nuclear, public transit, oil and coal, water, defense, etc.). Fusion center analysts have access to local, state, and federal databases of suspicious incidents, crimes, investigations, criminal networks, terrorist tactics and suspects, as well as a variety of other types of information. They then analyze the information from all the different sources and disseminate the analysis to the appropriate constituents. Fusion centers were created to facilitate communication and information sharing between member agencies to improve public safety and coordinated emergency responses.

CONCLUSION

In this chapter, we learned how departments store information and how officers use information to identify problem locations and solve crimes. Officers today have a variety of high-tech tools at their disposal that were unimaginable 30 years ago. There is little doubt that the most recent technological revolution has pushed us into a new policing era that is driven by intelligence—analysts gather, track, and analyze data, link it together, and disseminate it to officers as quickly as possible. Crime analysis, Compstat, real-time crime centers, and fusion centers are integral parts of this intelligence-led policing effort.

REVIEW QUESTIONS

1. How might an officer use CAD and RMS to identify problems in his jurisdiction?
2. What is the general premise of intelligence-led policing? How does it differ from standard policing?
3. What is crime analysis? Why is it useful?
4. How does Compstat compare to standard crime analysis?

GLOSSARY

Compstat an intelligence-led approach developed by NYPD in the mid-1990s that entails holding middle managers accountable for crime and other performance indicators in their area.

Computer-Aided Dispatch an automated computer system that assists police dispatchers receive calls for service, then assign and manage responding officers and information.

Crime analysis The analysis of crime data and other sources of information by police personnel for the purpose of targeting responses to reduce crime, catch a perpetrator, or otherwise improve the efficiency or effectiveness of police.

Crime mapping a process of using a geographic information system to conduct spatial analysis and investigation of crime.

Crime trend analysis A type of analysis that involves analyzing specific types of crime looking for patterns. it is often called crime pattern analysis.

Fusion Center an information sharing center that allows federal, state, and local law enforcement personnel to collaborate to assess potential terrorist threats and implement corrective action.

Intelligence-led policing a policing practice that uses crime intelligence and criminal intelligence to reduce and prevent crime.

Intelligence analysis A type of analysis that focuses on the relationships between persons and organizations involved in illegal activity. It is often referred to as network analysis or link analysis.

Investigative analysis A type of analysis that provides insight in the type of criminal and his/her motivation for committing a crime. It is also known as criminal profiling.

National Incident-Based Reporting System (NIBRS) a national crime data collection program created and implemented during the 1980s in an effort to enhance the methodology for collecting, analyzing, and publishing crime data.

Operational analysis The analysis of department data for the purpose of deploying department resources most effectively to reduce crime or achieve other operational goals

Operations analysis A type of analysis that examines how department resources are deployed. It is sometimes called administrative analysis.

Predictive policing an emerging strategy that uses computer software to model historical crime data in order to predict future crime events.

Real-time crime center centralized technology and analysis centers that use advanced data mining, analytic, and forecasting software and high-tech tools to provide near-real-time information to police personnel.

Records Management System a computer system that stores pertinent information on crimes, suspects, victims, and other incidents and can be searched and queried.

Regional intelligence center an information sharing center that allows federal, state, and local law enforcement personnel to collaborate to assess potential terrorist threats and implement corrective action. Also called Fusion Center.

Strategic analysis The analysis of department data to inform department policies and strategies.

Tactical analysis The analysis of crime and other data to support officers working front-line assignments.

Uniform Crime Report (UCR) an official data-reporting tool created in 1930 to provide uniform definitions of crimes and annual summaries of crime and arrest data for the vast majority of local and state law enforcement agencies in the United States.

REFERENCES

California Department of Corrections and Rehabilitation (CDCR). (n.d.). *Parole LEADS2.0.* Retrieved from http://www.cdcr.ca.gov/Parole/docs/LEADS2_facts.pdf

D'Amico, J. (2006, September). Stopping crime in real time. *The Police Chief, 73*(9). Retrieved from http://www.policechiefmagazine.org/

Department of Homeland Security. (n.d.). *National network of fusion centers fact sheet.* Retrieved from http://www.dhs.gov/files/programs/gc_1296484657738.shtm

Editorial Introduction: Compstat. (2003). *Criminology & Public Policy, 2*(3), 419.

Eterno, J. A., & Silverman, E. B. (2006). The New York City police department's Compstat: Dream or nightmare? *International Journal of Police Science and Management, 8*(3), 218–231.

Eterno, J. A., & Silverman, E. B. (2010). The NYPD's Compstat: Compare statistics or compose statistics? *International Journal of Police Science & Management, 12*(3), 426–449. doi: 10.1350/ijps.2010.12.3.195

Federal Bureau of Investigation. (n.d.). *NIBRS general FAQs.* Retrieved from http://www.fbi.gov/about-us/cjis/ucr/frequently-asked-questions/nibrs_faqs

Gardiner, C. (forthcoming, 2016). Is Compstat a good policing strategy? In S. Mallicoat. *Crime and Criminal Justice: Concepts and Controversies.* Thousand Oaks, CA: Sage.

Henry, V. E. (2002). *The COMPSTAT paradigm.* Flushing, NY: Looseleaf Law.

Jang, H. J., Hoover, L. T., & Joo, H. J. (2010). An evaluation of Compstat's effect on crime: The Fort Worth experiment. *Police Quarterly, 13*(4), 387–412. doi: 10.1177/1098611110384085

Joh, E. (2014). Policing by numbers: Big data and the fourth amendment. *Washington Law Review, 89*(1), 35–68.

Mazerolle, L., Rombouts, S., & McBroom, J. (2007). The impact of Compstat on reported crime in Queensland. *Policing: An International Journal of Police Strategies and Management, 30*, 237–256.

Oberg, T. (2010, September 2). HPD's high-tech center helping solve crimes. *ABC13 Eyewitness News.* Retrieved from http://abc13.com/archive/7642890/

O'Shea, T. C., & Nicholls, K. (2003). Police crime analysis: A survey of U.S. police departments with 100 or more sworn personnel. *Police Practice & Research, 4*, 233–250.

Ratcliffe, J. (2011). *Intelligence-led policing.* New York, NY: Routledge.

Santos, R. B. (2012). *Crime analysis with crime mapping.* Thousand Oaks, CA: Sage.

Silverman, E.B. (2006). Advocate: Compstat's innovation. In D. Weisburd & A.A. Braga (Eds.), *Police Innovation: Contrasting perspectives.* Cambridge, England: Cambridge University Press.

Weisburd, D., Mastrofski, S. D., McNally, A., Greenspan, R., & Willis, J. J. (2003). Reforming to preserve: Compstat and strategic problem solving in American policing. *Criminology & Public Policy, 2*(3), 421–456.

Zimring, F. (2012). *The city that became safe: New York's lessons for urban crime and its control.* New York, NY: Oxford University Press.

Zink, R. (2004, Summer). The trouble with Compstat. *PBA Magazine.*

10 RESPONDING TO PROBLEMS

LEARNING OBJECTIVES

After reading this chapter, students should be able to:

1. Differentiate between organizational and operational approaches to crime control.

2. List and describe the main components of community policing.

3. Discuss the extent of community policing in America.

4. Explain the research on community policing.

5. Describe the problem-oriented policing process, including the SARA model and problem analysis triangle.

6. Explain the research on problem-oriented policing.

7. Distinguish community policing from problem-oriented policing.

8. Describe BWP and the relevant research.

9. Contrast zero tolerance and stop-and-frisk tactics with the broken windows theory.

10. Explain hot spot policing and the relevant research.

11. Describe banishment orders.

12. Explain and provide examples of Situational Crime Prevention.

13. Describe focused-deterrence and the relevant research.

14. Summarize evidence-based policing practices.

15. Explain the importance of both effectiveness and equity in policing strategies.

KEY TERMS

Community policing

Problem-oriented policing

SARA

Broken windows policing

Broken windows theory

Zero tolerance policing

Stop and frisk

Quality of life policing

Terry stop

Terry v. Ohio

Hot spots policing

Banishment orders

Civil orders

Exclusion orders

Off-limits orders

Trespass laws

Trespass affidavit programs

Situational crime prevention

Crime Prevention Through Environmental Design (CPTED)

Focused deterrence

Pulling levers

Evidence-based policing

In the 1970s, most officers went "10–8" (on duty) in their patrol car and, when not assigned a call, randomly drove around their beat without a plan. As we now know, randomly driving around is not a successful strategy. Officers need to be intentional in their efforts to control crime. This chapter describes some of the most popular philosophies and strategies used by police agencies to reduce crime and promote order, and presents the research evidence on which policing practices are most effective. It builds on the last chapter by showing how officers *use* the crime intelligence they gather from all those sources we discussed.

To help us differentiate the approaches, we have grouped them into two categories: organizational methods and operational methods. Although not a perfect delineation, organizational methods tend to require more commitment and coordination from the entire agency than do operational methods. They also tend to be long-term, defining philosophies that require significant organizational change. Operational methods, on the other hand, require fewer resources than do organizational methods and they can operate within an already existing organizational philosophy. Also, operational strategies can come and go more easily than ingrained organizational approaches. As we define them here, organizational methods are those that expect a commitment to the approach/philosophy by the entire organization (nearly all personnel in a police agency), while operational methods are those that expect a commitment from only a small segment of the agency (e.g., patrol or a drug enforcement team).

Before we dive into the different types of methods, it might be useful to agree on the terminology. The terms strategy, approach, and philosophy are often used interchangeably; however, there are nuanced

Figure 10.1 A Comparison of Organizational and Operational Methods

differences that separate them from one another (at least as we use them here). Of the three, philosophy is the broadest. The Merriam-Webster dictionary defines philosophy as "the most basic beliefs, concepts, and attitudes of an individual or group." An agency's guiding philosophy is what orients all of its approaches, strategies, and operations. It is often expressed in an agency's mission and goals. As you will see in a moment, the community policing philosophy promotes a specific set of principles, includ-

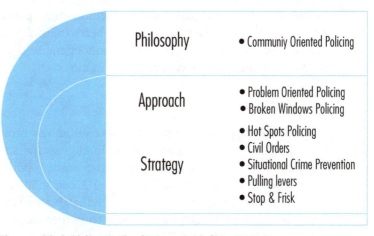

Philosophy	• Communiy Oriented Policing
Approach	• Problem Oriented Policing • Broken Windows Policing
Strategy	• Hot Spots Policing • Civil Orders • Situational Crime Prevention • Pulling levers • Stop & Frisk

Figure 10.2 Philosophy/Approach/Strategy

ing community engagement, personal service, and problem solving; agencies that ascribe to the community policing philosophy use these principles to mold the organization and guide its operations.

Meanwhile, approach means "a way of doing or thinking about something; a particular manner of taking steps … toward a particular purpose" (Merriam-Webster.com). It is the middle level between philosophy and strategy. It is broader than a specific strategy but not quite as all-encompassing as a philosophy. For example, problem-oriented policing is an approach that encourages departments to investigate discrete pieces of information in order to develop better solutions for dealing with specific issues. It promotes thoughtful analysis of recurring problems. Agencies that utilize this approach incorporate strategies and design operations that employ this method (problem identification and analysis).

Finally, the term strategy refers to "a plan, method, or series of maneuvers or stratagems for obtaining a specific goal or result" (dictionary.com). It is the closest to ground-level operations (in comparison to philosophy which guides the organization and is determined at the top administration level). A strategy is essentially an "action plan" for achieving a specific outcome (e.g., fewer crimes, fewer accidents, or less disorder in a specifically defined area). The strategy indicates the resources to be devoted to a particular issue as well as how, when, and where those resources will be deployed.

ORGANIZATIONAL METHODS

Organizational methods are those that expect a commitment to the strategy, approach, or philosophy by the entire organization (nearly all personnel in a police agency), all the time. Organizational methods include community-oriented policing, problem-oriented policing, and sometimes, order maintenance policing. Community policing, in particular, requires a wholesale commitment to change the way policing is done in an agency. It refocuses the department on working *with* the public, rather than *for* the public, and is antithetical to traditional policing. While both

© lev radin/Shutterstock.com

Community policing focuses on working *with* the public.

community-oriented policing and problem-oriented policing require strong organizational commitment to the approach/philosophy, **broken windows policing** (BWP) can be adopted as a department-wide organizational approach or as an operational strategy intended to address one or more hot spots (problem places) on a temporary basis.

COMMUNITY-ORIENTED POLICING

Community policing (also known as community-oriented policing, or COP) is a policing philosophy that calls for police agencies to develop partnerships and engage in problem solving with community stakeholders in order to foster positive police–public relationships, promote order, and reduce crime. As discussed in Chapter 3, community policing was a response to the tumultuous 1960s—the rising crime rates, the civil rights movement, the poor police-community relations, and other consequences that arose from the professional policing era, as well as the policing research conducted in the 1970s that called into question the effectiveness of traditional police strategies. Its roots can be traced to Robert Trojanowicz's Flint foot patrol experiment, which found the public and officers were more satisfied when they had positive interactions with each other, Wilson and Kelling's broken windows hypothesis (which we'll cover in detail shortly), and Goldstein's problem-oriented policing approach. The scholars and practitioners who developed community policing sought to improve police-community relations and police effectiveness.

Components of Community Policing So, what is community policing? It is "an overall philosophy that redefines the overall mission of policing as well as its operational methods and administrative form" (Moore, 1994, p. 290). It incorporates crime prevention, problem solving, community engagement, and partnerships to reduce crime and improve an area's quality of life (QOL). It balances the need to reactively respond to calls for services with the practice of proactive problem solving. It places a premium on community partnerships because police officers need community support to solve crimes, maintain order, and enforce law. Unlike traditional policing, which views the police function very narrowly (anything outside of "law enforcement" is not "real" police work), community policing views policing

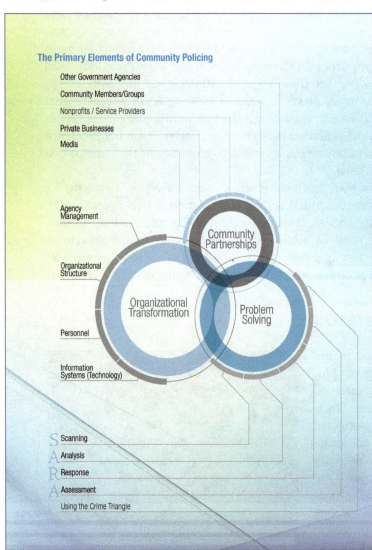

Figure 10.3 Primary elements of community policing.

very broadly and gives legitimacy to the many order maintenance and service functions that officers routinely provide. It encourages officers and agencies to address the community concerns that impact QOL, not just the incidence of crime. As articulated by the USDOJ Office of Community Oriented Policing Services (COPS), there are three core elements at the center of community policing: community partnerships, problem solving, and organizational transformation (COPS, 2014).

Community partnerships are the hallmark of community policing and involve working with the public, formally and informally, to increase public trust in police, reduce crime, and address other problems. These collaborative partnerships are between the law enforcement agency and any community organizations and individuals who have a stake in the community. Agencies which ascribe to and practice community policing establish multidisciplinary partnerships with other city/county departments, community members and groups, non-profit organizations, businesses, academic institutions, and the media, as each contributes a unique perspective and distinctive resources. The most successful partnerships happen when the law enforcement agency and each of the community partners bring a sincere commitment to work together on community policing activities as well as adequate resources.

Developing robust partnerships begins with a dedication to agency transparency and seeking citizen input. Some departments accomplish this by holding regularly-scheduled community meetings or open forums, conducting periodic resident surveys, establishing citizen advisory boards, or offering citizen academies. Department Web sites, blogs, social networking, and social media are also very popular methods to relay information to the public as well as gather public opinion and concerns. The important part is that departments are not only asking for citizen input but that they are also incorporating what they learn into their daily operations. Knowing what is important to community members allows an agency to tailor its service to the needs of the community. Agencies which provide personal service and adapt their practices to local norms and values are not only responsive to citizen concerns but they may also enjoy greater community support than agencies which do not engage the community in these ways.

CHECK IT OUT!

Check out your local law enforcement agency—What information is available on your department's Web site? Can you see crime statistics? Are the crime statistics reported in real time or are they delayed? Can you send an e-mail directly to the Chief/Sheriff from the Web site? Does the Web site provide the agency's street address? Can you report a crime online? Can you compliment an officer? Does the Web site contain any of the agency's policies or its latest annual report? Does your agency have Facebook, Instagram, or Twitter accounts? Does your agency have a smartphone "app" to stay connected to residents?

Another key to achieving healthy and productive partnerships with the community is to have officers maximize the number of positive interactions they have with individual community members. In general, citizen encounters with police officers tend to be negative because they often involve unpleasant experiences such as a victimization, arrest, or citation. Without intentional efforts to create positive encounters, both officers and citizens can feel alienated from one another. Officers can increase positive encounters with community members simply by rolling down the window of their patrol vehicle, driving slowly through a neighborhood, and greeting residents. Even better, officers can (and are highly encouraged to) park their vehicles, get out,

USING SOCIAL MEDIA TO IMPROVE POLICING

Hassan Aden is the current Director of Research and Programs at the International Association of Chiefs of Police (IACP). He was formerly the Chief of Police for the Greenville (NC) Police Department. The following is a partial except of his testimony before the Task Force on 21st Century Policing on January 31, 2015. You can find the original document here: http://www.iacp.org/Portals/0/documents/pdfs/TaskForceTestimonyHassan-AdenSocialMedia.pdf

Law enforcement agencies of all sizes across the United States are using many forms of social media in innovative and effective ways. According to the fifth annual Center for Social Media Survey completed in late 2014, 95% of law enforcement agencies surveyed stated they were using some form of social media. Of those using social media, 78.8% indicated social media had helped to solve a crime in their jurisdiction and 77.5% stated that social media had improved police-community relations in their jurisdiction (IACP Center for Social Media Annual Survey, 2014).

Social media allows law enforcement agencies to reach a broad, diverse audience, quickly, and in an unfiltered manner. These platforms also allow police to reach out in conversational ways to open lines of communication and show examples that break down stereotypes. By using these tools thoughtfully, agencies develop new levels of transparency and provide exceptional customer service, thereby enhancing relationships with individuals, businesses, and organizations throughout their community, not just online, but offline as well.

When I went to Greenville Police Department (GPD), I found a place where morale was low, the crime rate was unacceptable, and relationships with some elected officials, the news media, and community members were in need of repair. On day one, I met with the local news outlets and established an expectation of inclusion and transparency. I later created a deliberate media plan that included a new media relations position, filled by a local news anchor that came to the department and provided a new, positive perspective.

In my first year at GPD we enhanced our Facebook presence, adding 4,000 new followers, and also established new Instagram and Twitter accounts to connect with the public. We used informative messaging, listening to what the community wanted from us and building transparency. We established Twitter Town Halls, where officers from various units shared pictures and answered questions about their role in the department and community. We also did Tweet-alongs where we shared updates, photos, and videos throughout an officer's shift, providing a virtual ride-along experience. Using social media, we were able to create opportunities for people to interact with us in a way the public almost never gets to.

One example of how GPD utilized their social presence was during an unseasonably cold winter. We sent messages across social media platforms telling people that if they see a homeless person out in the bad weather to please call GPD as we had a block of rooms at a local hotel (paid for by Angel Corps, a local nonprofit). If individuals chose not to go, officers carry wool blankets that they can provide. This message of community caretaking spoke volumes to the residents of Greenville.

We consistently received great responses to our social media efforts. When I left two years later, there was a 13% reduction in violent crime and a 5% reduction in property crime. Department morale was at an all-time high. And, we had repaired, improved, and built new relationships with all local stakeholders. Much of this can be attributed to the open lines of communication we created and the transparency we facilitated, often using social media tools. By working together, police and media outlets are able to benefit the community with comprehensive, timely reporting. This type of relationship shows that the agencies have nothing to hide and are a true partner, tightly integrated with those they serve.

Social media has brought a new perspective to many agencies, and that is that both the law enforcement profession as well as their department are a brand. When an individual comes across an agency patch, badge, or logo, they will get certain feelings and have certain expectations. If those images are paired with consistent messaging that portrays honesty, integrity, and trustworthiness, then those values will become part of that law enforcement agency brand. This should also be paired with exceptional customer service. Social media has changed expectations, and many people now turn to these channels to voice a complaint or ask a question. [Responding in those instances] shows the community we care.

Austin (TX) Police Department (APD) engages in conversations and shares information about the things they have identified as important or concerning to citizens. For example, through thoughtful listening, they found out that when the APD helicopter was seen, many residents grew apprehensive and wanted to know what was going on in their city. So, APD now takes a proactive approach by tweeting information each time the helicopter goes up and their citizens thank them for it.

Palo Alto (CA) Police Department (PAPD) has been using social media for years, and has established their brand identity and built relationships throughout their community using social media tools. In November 2014, a group of activists gathered in Palo Alto to protest the police actions that had occurred in New York City and Ferguson. The protestors took over the downtown area, and PAPD set up their Emergency Operations Center and began implementing their communication plan, which included a strong social media component. PAPD started the day with a tweet to all their followers that included the hashtag being used by the demonstrators. They indicated that the protest was happening and that they looked forward to working with the protestors for a peaceful demonstration. PAPD continued to send out information throughout the day, providing information to those that were impacted by the demonstration as well as to the protestors themselves. As the events stayed nonviolent, PAPD repeatedly used the word "peaceful" throughout the day to describe the event and participants.

As the day went on, groups involved in the protests, including Stanford University's Black Student Union engaged with the police department, retweeting some of the department's messaging and including PAPD in their own tweets. Protestors thanked PAPD for their professional response and noted their appreciation for the terminology used throughout the day. This strategy of using strong, positive messaging; communicating early and often; and engaging participants has been successfully replicated in subsequent events.

Social media allows agencies to reach beyond geographic, cultural, demographic, and other boundaries that exist throughout the country. Social channels can be a vital tool in starting the conversation on many topics and can help foster and build new relationships with community members and groups. Social media is just one more way that agencies can keep their presence known and constantly share information and the status of any situation of compelling public interest.

There are many opportunities for officers to increase positive encounters with community members.

and engage citizens—on the basketball court, in and around stores/shopping centers, on the street, at senior centers and schools, and at other popular hang outs. Remember those viral videos of officers playing ball with kids that we mentioned back in Chapter 7; those are great examples of officers creating meaningful, positive contacts in accordance with the principles of community policing.

Unlike traditional departments which are predominately reactive, community policing departments emphasize prevention and manufacture ways to be proactive. Problem solving is one example of this proactive, prevention orientation. *Problem solving* involves identifying and addressing the root causes of recurring problems, usually using the SARA model (see the next section on problem-oriented policing). Instead of treating each call-for-service as its own unique situation, unrelated to other calls or common occurrences, community policing agencies engage in proactive problem solving to prevent crime and reduce disorder and other issues. This means that officers throughout the organization are encouraged, and expected, to proactively develop solutions to the underlying issues that cause, or contribute to, crime and other public safety problems. *Organizational transformation* is necessary to achieve true community policing, and this distinguishes agencies that operate some community policing programs from those committed to a community policing philosophy—these types of organizational structures and changes in culture were discussed in great detail in Chapter 5.

Community Policing in Practice Approximately two-thirds of law enforcement agencies across the United States could be said to practice community policing—they include it in their mission statement, utilize geographic policing, and train their recruits in its principles. This is an increase from a decade ago when only 47% of agencies had a mission statement that included community policing (Reaves, 2015). Almost 9 out of every 10 locally employed sworn police officers in the United States now work for an agency committed to community policing. The percent of agencies that use geographic assignment for patrol officers increased from 31% in 2003 to 44% in 2013. In fact, almost every agency that serves a population of 100,000 or more now uses geographic assignment for patrol officers. We've also seen improvements in the percent of agencies that actively encourage patrol officer involvement in problem-solving projects (from 24% in 2003 to 33% in 2013), in the percent of agencies that include problem solving in patrol officers' performance evaluations (from 14% in 2003 to 30% in 2013), and in the percent that train their recruits for at least 8 hours in community policing and problem-solving principles (from 39% in 2003 to 60% in 2013).

The percentages listed above represent the average for all police departments in the United States, big and small. As you know from Chapter 4, most agencies in the United States are very small (fewer than 10 sworn officers or serve a population of less than 10,000), but most officers are employed by (and residents served by) medium and large departments (100 or more sworn officers or serve a population of more than 100,000). As you can see in Tables 10.1 and 10.2,[1]

---

1   The in-text data are from the 2013 LEMAS report on police departments. Tables 10.1 and 10.2 contain data from the 2009 LEMAS report because the 2013 LEMAS report for sheriffs' departments had not been released when this book went to press.

TABLE 10.1 Community Policing Policies Throughout the United States

Percentage of Departments with

Population Served	Mission Statement with Community Policing Component		Formal Written Community Policing Plan		Full-time Community Police Officers		Separate Full-time Community Policing Unit	
	Police	Sheriffs	Police	Sheriffs	Police	Sheriffs	Police	Sheriffs
1,000,000 or more	100%	81%	69%	37%	100%	89%	85%	52%
500,000–999,999	84%	61%	71%	29%	97%	78%	61%	50%
250,000–499,999	93%	57%	65%	29%	98%	68%	61%	34%
100,000–249,999	86%	54%	49%	12%	94%	65%	61%	23%
50,000–99,999	89%	43%	43%	13%	87%	45%	58%	9%
25,000–49,999	76%	37%	27%	8%	69%	33%	33%	9%
10,000–24,999	70%	31%	19%	8%	50%	35%	17%	6%
2,500–9,999[a] Under 10,000[b]	56%	27%	12%	5%	42%	39%	7%	8%
Under 2,500	35%	—	11%	—	39%	—	9%	—
All Sizes	53%	38%	16%	10%	47%	43%	14%	12%

[a]–police departments, [b]–sheriffs' departments

Adapted from Reaves, B. (2010, December). *Local police departments, 2007.* Bureau of Justice Statistics, p. 26–27. Washington DC: U.S. Government Printing Office. And Burch, A.M. (2012, December). *Sheriffs' offices, 2007-Statistical tables.* Bureau of Justice Statistics, p. 18–19. Washington DC: U.S. Government Printing Office.

participation in community policing is much higher in larger agencies which means that most residents are served by a police department that says it is practicing community policing. For example, whereas 44% of all agencies (36% of very small agencies) use geographic policing, 93% of medium and large agencies do. Likewise, 73% of medium and large agencies actively encourage officers to problem solve (in comparison to 33% of all agencies and 26% of very small agencies). Additionally, 57% of large agencies include problem solving in officer performance evaluations (compared to 30% of all agencies and 25% of very small agencies) (Reaves, 2015). The same pattern holds true for training recruits in community policing principles, 86% of medium and large agencies do this while only 51% of very small agencies do. Importantly, the numbers above reveal how policing differs by community size, type, and region.

The elements noted above comprise some of the ideal characteristics of agencies committed to community policing and the numbers are encouraging. In practice, however, few agencies employ all of the obligatory components. Organizational transformation is the most difficult aspect of community

| Population Served | Geographic Assignments for Patrol Officers | | Trained Some or all Recruits for 8+ Hours | | Patrol Officer Involvement in Problem-solving Projects | | | |
| | | | | | Activity Encouraged | | Included in Performance Evaluation | |
	Police	Sheriffs	Police	Sheriffs	Police	Sheriffs	Police	Sheriffs
1,000,000 or more	92%	70%	100%	70%	62%	37%	62%	30%
500,000–999,999	97%	65%	94%	73%	61%	31%	39%	21%
250,000–499,999	83%	65%	93%	60%	61%	27%	52%	21%
100,000–249,999	89%	55%	80%	51%	57%	28%	46%	15%
50,000–99,999	81%	56%	82%	51%	57%	11%	39%	10%
25,000–49,999	65%	36%	75%	41%	33%	16%	29%	5%
10,000–24,999	52%	33%	65%	34%	29%	8%	17%	12%
2,500–9,999[a] / Under 10,000[b]	26%	14%	62%	25%	21%	7%	15%	3%
Under 2,500	14%	—	37%	—	11%	—	7%	—
All Sizes	31%	38%	56%	40%	21%	13%	15%	10%

[a]–police departments, [b]–sheriffs' departments

Adapted from Reaves, B. (2010, December). *Local police departments, 2007.* Bureau of Justice Statistics, p. 26. Washington DC: U.S. Government Printing Office. And Burch, A.M. (2012, December). *Sheriffs' offices, 2007-Statistical tables.* Bureau of Justice Statistics, p. 18. Washington DC: U.S. Government Printing Office.

policing to accomplish, and many agencies that are community oriented never achieve complete agency transformation. A recent study found that 92% of police and sheriffs' departments in California said they ascribe to a community policing philosophy; yet only 60% said they had an organizational structure that matched (Gardiner, 2015). The most popular community policing activities, implemented by more than 75% of California agencies, were problem solving with other organizations, expecting all officers to routinely problem solve, organizing a neighborhood watch program, and recognizing employees for good community policing work (see Figure 10.4).

It is important to understand that community policing varies by jurisdiction. What it looks like in a large, metropolitan city is probably not what it looks like in a small, rural area. As a practical matter, community policing adapts to the environment and community. A police department in a community with a highly engaged and mobilized citizenry will be able to access more resources than a department with no active citizen groups. Likewise, the problems that a small township routinely deals with are almost certainly different from those of a large city, and the resources they have to work with are considerably more limited.

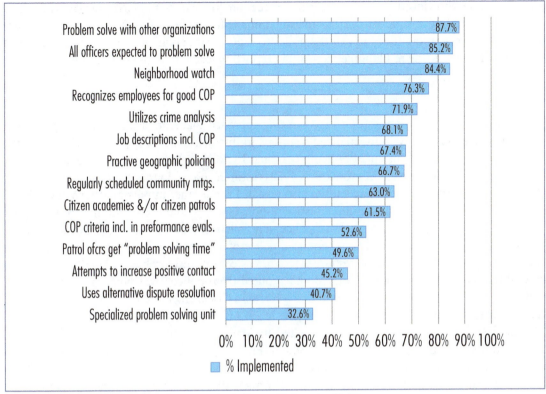

Figure 10.4 The most popular community policing activities.

Used by permission. Copyright Gardiner, C. (2015). The state of education and policing in California. Center for Public Policy. Fullerton, CA: California State University, Fullerton.

Research on Community Policing Researching community policing is very difficult for two main reasons. First, the community policing philosophy is ambiguous; there are several components but no clear, concise, agreed-upon definition. Because the concept is vague, it is difficult to define and even more difficult to measure "success." The ambiguity of community policing also makes it hard to implement. A recent survey of police leaders from across the country found that most agencies have a very difficult time securing the financial resources required to fully implement community policing and many also have difficulty gaining the

Community policing improves police-community relations.

support of line-level officers (Mastrofski, 2006). As previously mentioned, most agencies do not fully implement community policing, but rather adopt the "language of community oriented policing" (Gill, 2014; Trojanowicz et al., 1998).

Despite these limitations, a recent review of research found that community policing increases citizen satisfaction of the police, improves perceptions of disorder, and increases police legitimacy (Gill et al., 2014). This is interesting, and important—the main benefit of community policing appears to be improving police-community relations, not reducing crime. Why is this important?

Because people who view the police as legitimate are more likely to comply with the law and police officers and offer more support during investigations (Mazerolle et al., 2013; Kirk & Matsuda, 2011). They are also more likely to call the police to report crime (which may be why researchers often do not find a crime reduction effect—more reporting leads to higher crime, not lower).

PROBLEM-ORIENTED POLICING

Problem-oriented policing (POP) is a policing approach that emphasizes identifying, analyzing, and developing highly individualized solutions to intrinsic community problems. Like community policing, problem-oriented policing is rooted in police scholars' and professionals' desire to improve police effectiveness. As you know, 1970s research studies found that traditional policing methods were ineffective; but these studies also revealed some other important information. First, they discovered that traditional criminal justice responses (arrest and prosecution) were not highly effective. The studies further observed that police were called to handle a wide variety of community problems (not just crime); and that experienced police officers had tremendous discretion as well as access to a variety of tools and resources to address community problems. Finally, the studies showed that community members valued and profited from police involvement in non-criminal problems (POP Center, 2015). These findings led Herman Goldstein, a professor at the University of Wisconsin, to develop problem-oriented policing in 1979 (Goldstein, 1979 and 1990).

The first POP experiments were conducted in Madison (Wisconsin), Newport News (Virginia), Baltimore County (Maryland), and London (England) in the early 1980s. Police used POP to address the problems of theft, burglary, and domestic violence in Newport News (Eck & Spelman, 1987) and fear of crime in Baltimore County (Cordner, 1988). After these successful evaluations were published (and discussed at annual police leadership meetings), POP spread to police departments across the nation. Since 1993, agencies from across the globe have competed annually for the coveted Herman Goldstein Award for the most innovative POP project. As popular as POP is in the United States, applications for this award indicate that it is just as popular in England.

You might have recognized that community policing and problem-oriented policing developed concurrently. In the early days, scholars debated (1) whether problem-oriented policing was its own distinct approach or was an aspect of the community policing philosophy and (2) whether the ideas were complementary or competing (Capowich & Roehl, 1994; Eck, 2006). Although POP and COP intersect in both philosophy and practice and share some of the same features and goals, they are two distinct models of policing. Table 10.3 shows a comparison of the two philosophies/approaches. Probably, the most important defining difference between the two is that community policing emphasizes building positive police–community relations through public partnerships while problem-oriented policing emphasizes solving substantive community problems within the police purview. Problem-oriented policing, although theoretically separate and unique from community policing, has become an integral part of community policing as evidenced by community policing's dual focus on partnerships and problem solving (many scholars and practitioners refer to community policing as community-oriented policing and problem solving (COPPS).

Principles of Problem-Oriented Policing At the heart of problem-oriented policing is identifying recurring community problems and fixing them so that they no longer require significant public resources. It is proactive and prevention oriented. POP advocates an organizational problem-solving approach. This means that problem solving is "standard operating procedure," not a special occasion strategy. It also means that everyone in the agency is expected to engage in problem solving on a routine basis and that organizational and operational decisions are based on systematically gathered information. Collaborating with outside agencies, especially those with unique resources to address specific problems, is part of the problem-solving process, as is

TABLE 10.3 Community Policing and Problem-Oriented Policing: Some Comparisons

Principle	Problem-Oriented Policing	Community Policing
Primary emphasis	Substantive social problems within police mandate	Community engagement in policing process
Police and community collaboration	Determined on a problem by problem basis	Always or almost always
Priority given to problem analysis	Highest priority given to thorough analysis of problems	Encouraged, but less important than community collaboration
Police role in organizing & mobilizing community	Advocated only if warranted by specific problem response	Strong emphasis for officers in some assignments
Importance of geographic decentralization & continuity of officer beat assignment	Preferred, but not essential – aids in problem identification and resource commitment	Essential – primarily to improve police-community relations and partnerships, secondarily for problem identification
Decision making authority	Ultimate decision-making authority rests with police, but strongly encourages input from public	Emphasizes sharing decision-making authority with community
Officer skills	Emphasizes intellectual and analytical skills	Emphasizes interpersonal skills

Adapted from: POP Center (2015). Model Academic Curriculum, Module 2, Community Policing, Selected Comparisons between problem-oriented policing and community policing principles table on page 21. Retrieved from http://www.popcenter.org/

incorporating community input and participation. Including other public agencies in the problem-solving process establishes a "team work" approach and acknowledges the multidimensional nature of intrinsic social problems while including the community in the process provides an important opportunity for community stakeholders to share in the responsibility for public safety and welfare.

The key features of problem-oriented policing, as articulated by Scott and Goldstein (1988), are:

- The basic unit of police work is a problem (not a crime, case, call, or incident).
- A problem is something that causes harm to or concerns citizens, not just the police.
- Addressing problems means tackling conditions that create problems, not just concocting quick fixes.
- Police officers must systematically analyze problems before trying to solve them and departments must create procedures and systems to facilitate problem analysis.

- An analysis of a problem must be thorough, but not necessarily complicated.
- Problems must be accurately and precisely defined and dissected.
- Problems must be analyzed from the multiple perspectives of affected stakeholders.
- Current responses to the problem must be understood and the effectiveness honestly evaluated so that new, and better, responses may be developed.
- All potential responses to a problem should be considered initially; nothing should be "dismissed out of hand" or "off the table."
- Police must be proactive to solve problems rather than reactive.
- Police agencies must increase officers' discretion and ability to make important decisions and officers must be responsible for their decision-making.
- The effectiveness of new responses must be evaluated so that results can be shared with others in the department, the community, and throughout law enforcement to add to the knowledge of what does and does not work.

Officers may use the SARA model to determine why a rash of car burglaries is happening in an area.

The trademark of POP is SARA, a four-step model used to guide the problem-solving process. SARA stands for Scanning, Analysis, Response, and Assessment. Box 10.1 (below) presents the entire model, as articulated by Eck and Spelman (1987). During the first stage, officers **scan** the problem. At the most basic level, this involves identifying the four w's (who, what, where, and when) of the problem. Who is involved (victim and offenders)? What is happening (robberies, traffic accidents, commercial burglaries, assaults…)? Where is it happening (in a four-block area bordered by W, X, Y, Z streets; all bars or just specific bars…)? When is it happening (every Friday night, weekdays during the morning coffee rush, at sunset during the summer months, only during a full moon …)? At this stage, officers or analysts recognize that a pattern may exist and try to learn more about it so they can isolate the specific issue, then diagnose it, and eventually treat it; much like doctors do when we go into the office complaining about a mysterious illness/injury. Say, for example, we find that most of the vehicle burglaries in our jurisdiction are occurring in the afternoon and evening hours at one specific shopping center. The cars that are broken into are a variety of makes and models and the thieves are stealing miscellaneous items.

During the second stage, officers **analyze** the problem. They try to determine "why" the problem is occurring and attempt to understand the distinctive elements that contribute to the specific situation. They ask questions such as why is it happening in this place, at this time, between these people? For example, is there something about the design of this shopping center that encourages thefts from vehicles? Are the vehicle burglaries occurring randomly throughout all parking lots of the shopping center or is one section particularly problematic? The answers to these questions inform the department's intervention.

Next is stage three, when officers **respond** to the problem. At this point, officers research potential solutions, as well as design and implement a unique action plan fitted for the specific problem. Here, officers ask questions that help them narrow the specific cause and effect sequence. In our example, what can we do to make vehicle burglary less attractive in this center? Should we improve lighting or make egress out of the center more cumbersome? Would strategically placed cameras, or additional security guards, discourage potential thieves? In our example, we found that most of the vehicles that were burglarized were parked in the employee lot, far from store entrances. Neither lighting nor egress was a contributing factor. Using all the gathered information, we developed a three-pronged response. First, the private security guards were alerted and agreed to provide extra patrols in the area. Second, the shopping center owners agreed to add a parking lot surveillance system for added security so that any future criminals can be caught and prosecuted. Third, employees were alerted to the problem and provided crime prevention tips through flyers on their windshields and an e-mail to all store managers. What are some other possible responses that we didn't mention?

POP emphasizes responses that are "preventative in nature, that are not dependent on the use of the criminal justice system, and that engage other public agencies, the community, and the private sector when their involvement has the potential for significantly contributing to the reduction of the problem" (Goldstein, 2001).

Finally, in stage four, officers **assess** the response. Was it successful? Did it reduce, displace, or eliminate the problem? Were there any unintended consequences (or benefits)? A variety of measures are used to ascertain operational success. For example, police reported measures such as fewer reported crimes, fewer complaints, fewer accidents, or fewer calls for service. Alternatively, observational measures such as more kids playing in the park, more business patrons, fewer empty store fronts, or the establishment of new neighborhood watch and community groups can demonstrate success. Additionally, community survey responses indicating positive public perceptions and satisfaction with the police are also used as indicators of success. In our example, we looked to see whether the number of vehicle burglaries at the shopping center decreased. We also examined the number of vehicle burglaries throughout the jurisdiction to make sure we didn't displace crime. What else should we measure?

THE SARA MODEL

Scanning:

- Identifying recurring problems of concern to the public and the police.
- Identifying the consequences of the problem for the community and the police.
- Prioritizing those problems.
- Developing broad goals.
- Confirming that the problems exist.
- Determining how frequently the problem occurs and how long it has been taking place.
- Selecting problems for closer examination.

Analysis:

- Identifying and understanding the events and conditions that precede and accompany the problem.
- Identifying relevant data to be collected.
- Researching what is known about the problem type.
- Taking inventory of how the problem is currently addressed and the strengths and limitations of the current response.
- Narrowing the scope of the problem as specifically as possible.
- Identifying a variety of resources that may be of assistance in developing a deeper understanding of the problem.
- Developing a working hypothesis about why the problem is occurring.

Response:

- Brainstorming for new interventions.
- Searching for what other communities with similar problems have done.
- Choosing among the alternative interventions.
- Outlining a response plan and identifying responsible parties.
- Stating the specific objectives for the response plan.
- Carrying out the planned activities.

Assessment:

- Determining whether the plan was implemented (a process evaluation).
- Collecting pre- and post-response qualitative and quantitative data.
- Determining whether broad goals and specific objectives were attained.
- Identifying any new strategies needed to augment the original plan.
- Conducting ongoing assessment to ensure continued effectiveness.

Source: www.popcenter.org

THE PROBLEM ANALYSIS TRIANGLE

The Problem Analysis Triangle

While the *SARA model* is useful as a way of organizing the approach to recurring problems, it is often very difficult to figure out just exactly what the real problem is. The problem analysis triangle (sometimes referred to as the crime triangle) provides a way of thinking about recurring problems of crime and disorder. This idea assumes that a crime or disorder results when (1) likely offenders and (2) suitable targets come together in (3) time and space, in the absence of capable guardians for that target. A simple version of a problem analysis triangle looks like this.

Offenders can sometimes be controlled by other people: those people are known as handlers. Targets and victims can sometimes be protected by other people as well: those people are known as guardians. And places are usually controlled by someone: those people are known as managers. Thus, effective problem solving requires understanding how offenders and their targets/victims come together in places, and understanding how those offenders, targets/victims, and places are or are not effectively controlled. Understanding the weaknesses in the problem analysis triangle in the context of a particular problem will point the way to new interventions. A complete problem analysis triangle looks like this.

Problems can be understood and described in a variety of ways. No one way is definitive. They should be described in whichever way is most likely to lead to an improved understanding of the problem and effective interventions. Generally, incidents that the police handle cluster in four ways:

1. *Behavior.* Certain behavior(s) is (are) common to the incidents. For example, making excessive noise, robbing people or businesses, driving under the influence, crashing vehicles, dealing drugs, and stealing cars. There are many different behaviors that might constitute problems.

2. *Place.* Certain places can be common to incidents. Incidents involving one or more problem behaviors may occur at, for example, a street corner, a house, a business, a park, a neighborhood, or a school. Some incidents occur in abstract places such as cyberspace, on the telephone, or through other information networks.

3. *Persons.* Certain individuals or groups of people can be common to incidents. These people could be either offenders or victims. Incidents involving one or more behaviors occurring in one or more places may be attributed to, for example, a youth gang, a lone person, a group of prostitutes, a group of chronic inebriates, or a property owner. Or incidents may be causing harm to, for example, residents of a neighborhood, senior citizens, young children, or a lone individual.

4. *Time.* Certain times can be common to incidents. Incidents involving one or more behaviors, in one or more places, caused by or affecting one or more people may happen at, for example, traffic rush hour, bar closing time, the holiday shopping season, or during an annual festival.

There is growing evidence that, in fact, crime and disorder does cluster in these ways. It is not evenly distributed across time, place, or people. Increasingly, police and researchers are recognizing some of these clusters as:

- Repeat offenders attacking different targets at different places.

- Repeat victims repeatedly attacked by different offenders at different places.

- Repeat places (or hot spots) involving different offenders and different targets interacting at the same place.

The problem analysis triangle was derived from the routine activity approach to explain how and why crime occurs. This theory argues that when a crime occurs, three things happen at the same time and in the same space:

- a suitable target is available.

- there is the lack of a suitable guardian to prevent the crime from happening.

- a motivated offender is present.

Source: www.popcenter.org/

Research on Problem-Oriented Policing Research suggests that POP can be used effectively to address a wide variety of problems, such as convenience store robberies, construction thefts, common bar/nightclub problems, prostitution, and more (Braga & Weisburd, 2006). Problem-oriented policing strategies have been shown to moderately reduce crime and disorder and are more effective than traditional responses on all three types of problems: repeat places, repeat criminals, and repeat victims (Eck, 2006; Weisburd et al., 2010). Property and drug crimes appear to be particularly well suited to POP techniques (Mazerolle et al., 2013). Furthermore, when alternatives to enforcement (such as landlord interventions, education, or street improvements) are incorporated alongside focused enforcement (such as crackdowns), results are more positive than when additional methods are not included (Eck, 2006). POPCenter.org maintains a full library of research articles and reports, successful POP projects shared by practitioners, as well as MOOC modules developed for practitioners.

A recent case study of Colorado Springs Police Department (CO) (CSPD), an internationally recognized POP leader, is very instructive. The most common types of problems tackled by CSPD included places/people with numerous calls for services, noise disturbances/parties, drug activity/intoxication, traffic issues, parking congestion, and graffiti/vandalism (notice, these are not what most people would consider to be major crimes) (Maguire et al., 2015). Of the 753 POP projects undertaken by CSPD officers in the 6-year study period, most were focused on a single business or a single neighborhood; the next most popular "target" was a whole district, followed by a single house, then a single apartment complex/mobile home park. Most of the problems were identified using police data, about a quarter were identified by police personnel, slightly less than 10% by residents, and a handful by business owners/managers/customers or school employees. Some cases took only one day to solve while others took as much as 3 years. On average, it took CSPD officers 130 days (slightly more than 4 months) to complete a project. Some of the most popular case resolution strategies used by CSPD were providing education to businesses/citizens, making environmental changes, routine patrol/spot checks, and a stricter enforcement/zero tolerance approach.

FIELD PERSPECTIVES

HERMAN GOLDSTEIN AWARDS FOR EXCELLENCE IN PROBLEM-ORIENTED POLICING

By Michael S. Scott, Director—Center for Problem-Oriented Policing, Inc.

Photo courtesy of Arizona State University

Michael Scott

The Herman Goldstein Award for Excellence in Problem-Oriented Policing was established in 1993 to complement the annual Problem-Oriented Policing Conference. Its principal purpose is to recognize exemplary problem-oriented policing practice and to inspire further such good work. Over the years, approximately 1100 "POP projects" have been submitted to this award program from police agencies across the United States, Canada, the United Kingdom, Australia, and New Zealand. There have also been a few submissions from Bermuda, Chile, Colombia, Japan, the Netherlands, Norway, and Spain. The United Kingdom sponsored its own POP awards program—the Tilley Awards—for several years and, recently, New Zealand launched its own. Expert judges recognize each year's best submissions. As a long-time judge and current chair of the Goldstein Award program, several projects exemplify for me the quality of this type of police work and the range of public-safety problems which it is employed to address.

Problem-oriented approaches have been used to address community problems ranging from those involving threats to people's physical safety, property, and peace of mind, as well as misuse of police resources.

In 1998, the Boston Police Department was recognized for its now widely renowned *Operation Ceasefire*, a POP initiative that brought new insights about the nature of youth-gang gun violence to bear on the problem. A collaboration among Boston police, prosecutors and probation officials; Harvard researchers; African-American clergy; and social-service providers applied a so-called "focused deterrence" approach to the most prolific and danger-ous gangs and, as a result, reduced gun violence among this population by over 60% and, at least for 1 year, reduced gun homicides among this population to zero. In 2006, the focused-deterrence approach was successfully applied to violent drug markets in High Point, North Carolina. These two POP projects have inspired many other communities across the United States to adapt focused-deterrence approaches to their particular violent-crime problems. [Note: This problem-oriented policing project was so successful that it instigated a new oper-ational strategy (see pulling levers in the next section).]

Threats to people's physical safety also come in the form of deaths and injuries from traf-fic crashes. In 2002, the California Highway Patrol was recognized for its Safety and Farm Vehicle Education Program. Motivated by the deaths of thirteen farm workers in one crash, CHP analyzed the problem to identify the riskiest times and locations for such crashes and to pinpoint the most significant contributing factors to serious injuries and deaths. As a direct result of this analysis, state laws were changed to mandate that seat belts be worn in all vehi-cles transporting farm workers and create a stricter inspection regime to ensure compliance. Through non-punitive inspections and a public-education campaign targeted at the farming-community, a 73% reduction in farm-vehicle crashes and zero fatalities were realized in the period following implementation of these new measures.

Other exemplary projects that reduced risks to people's personal safety include the Charlotte-Mecklenburg (NC) police's Baker One Domestic Violence Intervention Project, the Lancashire Constabulary's (UK) Smashing Time—Or Not? initiative to reduce injuries from bar fights, and the Safer Travel at Night campaign in London (UK) to reduce assaults on passengers in unlicensed taxis.

Among the projects that best typify how POP can reduce and prevent threats to people's property are the Port St. Lucie (FL) "Bulldozing" Construction Site Burglary project and the Chula Vista (CA) Residential Burglary Reduction Project. In both projects, police analysis of the problems demonstrated how improved security practices by house developers and build-ers could prevent the burglaries from occurring in the first instance.

Police efforts to control public nuisances can be tremendously beneficial to entire com-munities affected by them and thereby help keep communities viable and stable. Among my favorite efforts of this sort are San Diego police's "Glitter Track" project to control a street-prostitution market operating in a business district without resorting to extensive and inef-fective criminal law enforcement and Glendale (CA) police's Day Laborer Project that not only reduced the disorder of an unregulated day-laborer market but also improved working wages and conditions for both the day laborers and those who hired them.

One of my favorite projects that reduced the inefficient, ineffective use of police resources was Salt Lake City (UT) police's False Alarm Solution: Verified Response. Not only did it reduce demand on police resources by over 90%, but also it did so without compromising public safety and by shifting greater responsibility for the problem to the entity most responsible for creating it. This project has encouraged other communities across the United States to similarly shift responsibility for reducing false alarms from the police and taxpayers to the alarm companies and owners.

Michael Scott is a clinical professor at Arizona State University's School of Criminology & Criminal Justice and the director of the Center for Problem-Oriented Policing. He chairs the judging committee for the Herman Goldstein Award for Excellence in Problem-Oriented Policing. Scott was formerly a clinical professor at the University of Wisconsin Law School; chief of police in Lauderhill, Florida; special assistant to the chief of the St. Louis, Missouri, Metropolitan Police Department; director of administration of the Fort Pierce, Florida, Police Department; legal assistant to the police commissioner of the New York City Police Department; and a police officer in the Madison, Wisconsin, Police Department. He was a senior researcher at the Police Executive Research Forum (PERF) in Washington, D.C. In 1996, he received PERF's Gary P. Hayes Award for innovation and leadership in policing. Scott holds a law degree from Harvard Law School and a bachelor's degree from the University of Wisconsin–Madison.

BROKEN WINDOWS POLICING

Broken windows policing (a.k.a. disorder policing, order maintenance policing) is based on Wilson and Kelling's (1982) proposition that physical deterioration of an area leads to fear of crime and more serious crime. Their hypothesis, often referred to as "**broken windows theory**," is that physically (and socially) disordered areas send a message to neighborhood residents that the area is unsafe, which causes law-abiding residents to stay out of the area for fear of victimization. At the same time, it sends a message to potential criminals that no one cares about the area and that they are able to operate without fear of getting caught breaking the law. The idea is that if small offenses (graffiti, vandalism, public intoxication, panhandling, drug use, prostitution, etc.) are left unchecked, more serious crimes will appear and flourish, driving out the law-abiding element completely.

Consider for a moment, a vacant warehouse building. If it is in good condition (paint is somewhat fresh, windows are intact, there is no graffiti, etc.), it will likely stay that way—people will leave it alone. However, if no one is around the building, one day someone (maybe a group of juveniles messing around for no reason other than they are bored) comes by and throws rocks at the windows and breaks one. If the owner of the building discovers the damage and repairs it quickly, the message to the misbehaving juveniles is that someone cares about the building and they are unlikely to break more windows (especially if the building owner takes other preventative measures, such as adding new cameras, lights, or signs promising prosecution). On the other hand, if the owner does nothing about the damage, the message to the juveniles is "no one

© Roy Pedersen/Shutterstock.com

If a building is left in disrepair, it invites an increase in crime in the area.

cares about this property" and they interpret that to mean that they can hang out, cause trouble, and break as many windows as they want without getting into trouble. The additional damage is seen by others in the area who see an opportunity to make their mark (maybe they spray paint a message on a wall or urinate on it). Eventually, a group of miscreants seize the building for their own use (force their way into the building and use it as a drug den, homeless camp, etc.). Meanwhile, law-abiding citizens notice the changes in the building's appearance and the congregating misfits and are now afraid to walk near the building (because the broken windows and graffiti signal that criminals are in the area). Soon, there are fewer law-abiding citizens and more criminals in the area and crime increases.

CORE IDEAS OF BROKEN WINDOWS

1. Disorder and fear of crime are strongly linked;
2. Police negotiate rules of the street. "Street people" are involved in the negotiation of those rules;
3. Different neighborhoods have different rules;
4. Untended disorder leads to breakdown of community controls;
5. Areas where community controls break down are vulnerable to criminal invasion;
6. The essence of the police role in maintaining order is to reinforce the informal control mechanisms of the community itself;
7. Problems arise not so much from individual disorderly persons as from the congregation of large numbers of disorderly persons;
8. Different neighborhoods have different capacities to manage disorder.

Source: Sousa, W.H. & Kelling, G.L. (2006). Advocate: Of "broken windows," criminology, and criminal justice. In D. Weisburd & A. Braga, *Police Innovation: Contrasting Perspectives*. New York, NY: Cambridge University Press.

As you can see from the above core ideas, broken windows is more complex than its name (and the previous warehouse example) would suggest. In particular, many practitioners (and academics) ignore the important role that the theory says police play in helping neighborhoods reinforce their own informal social control mechanisms. Although the theorists place it within the community-policing framework, there has been quite a bit of debate about BWP and whether it promotes aggressive police tactics and is inherently biased against residents living in poor, minority neighborhoods (Kelling & Coles, 1997). Our stance is that broken windows is neither inherently aggressive nor community oriented. It can be implemented in either manner, but how it is implemented determines whether the police-public relationship is weakened or strengthened. Heavy-handed, or aggressive, police tactics reduce citizens' perception of police legitimacy while community-oriented policing tactics increase citizens' perception of police legitimacy (Gill et al., 2014; Fagan et al., 2010).

BWP in practice Agencies that adopt BWP as an organizational approach use these core concepts to guide general crime prevention efforts throughout the department on an ongoing basis. In contrast, agencies that utilize BWP as an operational strategy tend to use it on an "as needed" basis to address specific problem areas. Regardless of how entrenched the practice of BWP is within an agency, any approach that attempts to reduce unwanted behavior or physical blight while reinforcing the social controls in the neighborhood could be considered BWP.

Proposed around the same time as problem-oriented policing and community-oriented policing, BWP is popular with police officers and administrators because it makes sense to them, it tells them what to do (but not necessarily *how* to do it), and it fits within law enforcement's traditional organizational culture. Like community-oriented policing and problem-oriented policing, BWP has had some difficulty gaining traction among line-level officers, especially when implemented as a top-down strategy. Unlike COP and POP, which both require a significant shift in organizational thinking and practice away from traditional methods, BWP allows officers to use traditional tactics (such as arrests) on traditionally defined problem places (and people).

BROKEN WINDOWS IN THE NEW YORK SUBWAY SYSTEM: THE CLEAN CAR PROGRAM

The New York City Transit Authority (NYCTA) was one of the first to test broken windows theory. Although it might be hard to believe now, the New York City subway in the 1980s was extremely disorderly—robberies were common, graffiti riddled every train in the fleet (inside and out), aggressive panhandlers littered every station (and train), people urinated and defecated in the stations (and trains), and fare evasion was the norm. As an initial response, NYCTA started the "Clean Car Program" in 1984. This project entailed each of the transit authority's 10,000 trains being enrolled in program, a few cars at a time. Once a train was enrolled in the program and cleaned, it was not allowed to run with graffiti on it again. If it was vandalized, the train was removed from service until the graffiti was removed. All clean cars had a transit police officer assigned to protect the train from further graffiti. Within 5 years, all 10,000 trains had been cleaned and graffiti was all but gone from subway trains (they are now some of the cleanest in the world).

In theory, BWP is congruent with community policing and problem-oriented policing. In practice, even though broken windows is routinely implemented in community police agencies and as problem-oriented policing projects, it is most often associated with heavy-handed police tactics (such as zero tolerance). While broken windows started as a coproduction model of crime control (whereby residents play an active role in crime prevention and social control), it has become associated with an aggressive set of police tactics aimed at reducing easily targeted incivilities (Taylor, 2006).

This is partly because significant attention has been paid to New York Police Department's (NYPD) version of broken windows. William Bratton, who is currently on his second term as police commissioner of NYPD, is a strong and vocal proponent of BWP. Bratton, who was with the Transit Police during the clean car program, took over leadership of the agency in 1990 just after the start of Operation Enforcement (in October 1989). Operation Enforcement was a multifaceted program aimed at reducing disorder in the subway system. It had all the components of a problem-oriented policing project including months of scanning, analyzing, and planning. When Bratton took over the transit police, his mission was to "take back the subway" by focusing on a trilogy of crimes: farebeating, disorder, and robbery (Kelling & Coles, 1997). Officers were instructed to inform misbehaving citizens of their improper behavior, warn them to stop, and if they refused, to eject them from the subway. Ejections and misdemeanor arrests in the subway skyrocketed immediately after Bratton took office (Kelling & Coles, 1997).

TABLE 10.4 Comparison of Major Policing Approaches

	Community Policing	Problem-Oriented Policing	Broken Windows Theory	Zero Tolerance/ Stop and Frisk
To reduce crime...	Engage the community (through positive interactions, partnerships, and problem solving)	Identify, analyze, and respond to substantive social problems	Reduce disorder	Deter criminals by using Terry stops and/or heavily enforcing laws against minor crimes and infractions
Police and community collaboration	Always or almost always	Determined on a problem by problem basis	Police reinforce rules and informal social control mechanisms & help residents improve collective efficacy	None
Main Priority	Positive police-community relations & police legitimacy	Problem analysis and response	Maintain physical environments that discourage criminal activity	Discourage unwanted behavior through general & specific deterrence
How accomplish	Geographic policing, positive interactions, problem solving, partnerships, organization transformation	SARA problem-solving process; intelligence-led policing (crime analysis and mapping)	Clean up disorder; increase collective efficacy; enforcement of disorderly behaviors	A high level of citizen stops, cites, and arrests for low level criminal activity
Service, Order Maintenance, or Law enforcement focused	Service	Order maintenance, Service	Order maintenance	Law enforcement
Officer skills	Emphasizes interpersonal skills	Emphasizes intellectual and analytical skills	Depends on whether implementation follows COP, POP or ZT model	Emphasizes traditional police tactics
Impact on crime/ disorder	Limited effects on crime; can improve perceptions of disorder	Moderate reductions in crime and disorder; best results when non-enforcement strategies combined with enforcement	Depends on implementation; best when implemented as POP	May reduce crime if implemented as hotspots policing or focused deterrence
Impact on police legitimacy	Improves legitimacy, trust in police, and citizen satisfaction of the police	Unknown—probably project dependent; potential for positive	Depends on implementation (see COP, POP, ZT)	Reduces legitimacy and trust in police Strains police–community relations

© littleny/Shutterstock.com

New York subway trains are clean and free of graffiti.

NYPD took a particularly strong stance against farebeating, establishing roving teams to target law violations and setting up "booking buses" onsite to aid in the booking process. Early on, they discovered that many of the individuals booked for farebeating either were carrying illegal weapons or had an outstanding warrant for their arrest. Even though there were other components to the program (such as the newly created position of station manager to coordinate services and act as a form of social control) that were equally important to the sustained success of the initiative, those were overshadowed by the officers' realization that serious criminals also commit minor crimes and that arresting individuals for violating small infractions often led to felony arrests. This important, but unexpected, finding had the effect of reorienting the practice of broken windows toward aggressive enforcement strategies that rely on searching and arresting minor law violators.

Zero tolerance It was this lesson that Bratton brought with him when he became police commissioner of the NYPD for the first time in 1994 and implemented his QOL policing initiative. Based on the logic of broken windows and the experience gained through Operation Enforcement, this was a concerted attempt to reduce the incidence of 25 specific Quality of Life offenses in NYC using an aggressive arrest approach. Soon, **quality of life policing** became known as **zero tolerance policing** (and the general understanding of broken windows began to morph into something other than what it had been up to this point).

Thanks to New York City's major crime decline, Commissioner Bratton's marketing prowess, and the strategy's perfect alignment with the very popular "tough on crime" philosophy in the 1990s, the "zero tolerance" ideology quickly spread to other cities across the nation as well as to other institutions concerned with controlling disorderly behavior (most notably, schools!). Today, the term "zero tolerance policing" refers to very strict enforcement of unwanted behavior that uses misdemeanor arrests (or other penalties/consequences) as the key component of the strategy.

Stop and Frisk The next iteration of NYPD's BWP strategy, **stop and frisk** or *stop-question-and-frisk (SQF),* developed during Commissioner Raymond Kelly's leadership from 2002 to 2013. Like the other iterations, it too has become a tactic used by police departments across the country. The approach is similar to zero tolerance but uses pedestrian stops (instead of misdemeanor arrests) as the primary method of reducing crime. Pedestrian stops, which are also called **Terry stops** (named for the court case which made them legal, and described more extensively in Chapter 12), are police-initiated stops of suspicious individuals for investigative purposes. **Terry v. Ohio** (1968) granted officers the right to stop and question a person they reasonably suspected of being involved in criminal activity and also conduct a limited pat down (frisk) of the detained person if the officer reasonably suspected the person was in possession of a weapon. Anything more extensive than a limited pat down for weapons is considered a search, and requires probable cause, a search warrant, or the individual's consent.

Pedestrian stops have been a part of policing for many decades; what is new is their use as a systematic crime prevention strategy. Historically, these stops have involved individual officers stopping specific persons upon observing suspicious behavior in order to interrupt a potential crime in progress. Officers did not go 10–8 (on duty) with a directive to stop, question, and frisk everyone they could articulate to be suspicious in a particular area in the name of crime prevention. The rationale for using pedestrian stops as a crime prevention tool is that increasing the number of pedestrian stops by police increases the risk of a person being stopped and searched, which discourages would-be offenders from carrying contraband or weapons. Although it is associated with NYPD's zero tolerance policing practice, as a criminal justice student you may have noticed that the tactic is actually more rooted in deterrence theory than broken windows. As we'll discuss in the next section, this strategy is generally implemented as an operational tactic, not an organizational approach.

NYPD'S CONTROVERSIAL STOP AND FRISK POLICY: THE EFFECT ON POLICE-COMMUNITY RELATIONS

Between 2002 and 2011, NYPD saw a dramatic rise in the annual number of SQF conducted by officers from 97,000 to 685,000 (Ward, 2014). The constitutionality and racially biased nature of these stops was questioned in a lawsuit, *Floyd et al. v. City of New York*, filed in 2008. In making her decision, Judge Scheindlin relied on SQF data collected by NYPD and others for the time period January 2004–June 2012. Some of the more profound uncontested facts of the case are:

- NYPD conducted more than 4.4 million SQFs (a.k.a. Terry stops) during this time.
  - 84% (about 3.7 million) of these were performed on Black or Hispanic persons.
- 52% of all stops included a frisk for weapons.
  - Only 1.5% of these resulted in a weapon being found on the person. Thus, no weapon was found in 98.5% of the 2.3 million frisks.
- 8% of all stops led to a search of the person's clothing (based on the officer feeling what s/he thought was a weapon or recognized to be contraband).
  - In 9% of the cases, the felt object was, indeed, a weapon (91% of the time it was not).
  - In 14% of the cases, the felt object was, indeed, contraband (86% of the time it was not).
- 6% of all stops resulted in an arrest and another 6% resulted in summons.
  - 88% of the stops resulted in no further law enforcement action.
- 52% of stops were of Blacks (in comparison, Blacks represent 23% of NYC's population); 31% of stops were of Hispanics (who comprise 29% of NYC's population); 10% of stops were of Whites (who constitute 33% of NYC's population.
- Use of force was recorded in 17% of White stops, 23% of Black stops, and 24% of Hispanic stops.
- Weapons were seized in 1.0% of Black stops, 1.1% of Hispanic stops, and 1.4% of White stops.
- Contraband (other than weapons) was seized in 1.7% of Hispanic stops, 1.8% of Black stops, and 2.3% of White stops.

In her analysis of the data, Judge Scheindlin further determined that

- at least 200,000 (of the 4.4 million) were made without reasonable suspicion (the legal standard required for conducting a *Terry stop*).
- Blacks and Hispanics were more likely than Whites to be stopped, even after controlling for other factors.
- Between 2004 to 2009, Blacks were 30% more likely to be arrested (rather than receive summons) than Whites for the same suspected crime.

The judge found that NYPD acted with "deliberate indifference" and that NYPD's policies and practices emphasized productivity and put pressure on officers to make a particular number of stops, or risk consequences. The impact of this policy was particularly impactful on young, minority males who were unfairly targeted.

NYPD's use of SQF's declined by 60% from 2012 to 2013 and Commissioner Bratton states the number has declined even more since he resumed leadership of the agency in 2013, but many in the community question whether the NYPD culture has sincerely changed because they see the same tactics being used (Ward, 2014). The question is, can NYPD regain the legitimacy they lost in prior years?

Judge Scheindlin was adamant that the court's role is to assess the "constitutionality of police behavior, not its effectiveness as a law enforcement tool" and that "the enshrinement of constitutional rights necessarily takes certain policy choices off the table" (p.5). What do you think? Should effectiveness as a law enforcement tool be considered? Why or why not?

Research on BWP Research on BWP has been highly mixed, with some studies indicating a large impact on crime and many others showing little or no reduction in serious crime (Braga et al., 2015; Weisburd & Eck, 2004; Weisburd et al., 2013). The key research finding on order maintenance policing is that the types of strategies deployed matters immensely. In general, aggressive strategies that focus on individual disorderly behaviors (such as QOL policing or zero tolerance policing) do not reduce crime (Braga et al., 2015). Furthermore, aggressive strategies that increase misdemeanor arrests have the unintended effect of reducing police legitimacy and trust in police in low-income, minority communities—the specific communities where relationship building is most needed (Skogan & Frydl, 2004; Stroudt et al., 2011). On the other hand, strategies that use community problem-solving approaches to reduce physical and social disorder at particular places reduce crime by a substantial amount (Braga et al., 2015). Community problem-solving approaches often have an added benefit of improving public perception of and trust in the police (Gill et al., 2014)

Officers frisk a man on the street.

© ChameleonsEye/Shutterstock.com

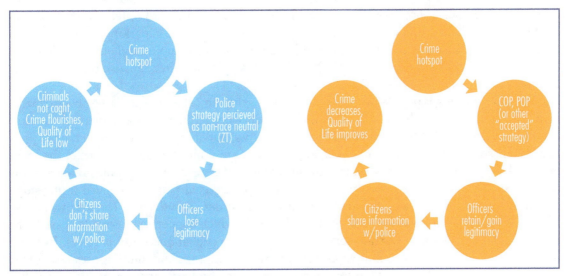

Figure 10.5 Effect of police practice on citizens and crime.

OPERATIONAL METHODS

Operational strategies are those that require a commitment from a small segment of agency personnel, not the entire department. For example, an operational strategy could involve all patrol officers or just those working a specific area; or only officers assigned to a drug, vice, or gang enforcement team. These strategies can be place-based, offender-based, offense-based, or victim-based, and can be utilized in both traditional departments and community policing departments, as a problem-oriented policing approach, or within a broken windows framework. The individual strategies can be quite varied but are typically focused on a particular area or set of potential offenders.

Place-based strategies, such as **hot spots policing**, attempt to reduce crime by focusing on the places that generate the most crimes or calls for service. Meanwhile, *offender-based strategies* attempt to reduce crime by focusing on the people that generate the most crime or calls for service. Criminal sweeps and pulling levers are two examples of offender-based strategies. Some strategies, such as gang injunctions and banishment orders, could be considered both offender-based and place-based. Additionally, these strategies can target crime in general or a specific crime problem (such as gun violence, robberies, or underage drinking). They can be proactive, reactive, or a combination of both. Finally, operational strategies generally exist for a finite (temporary) period of time, but this is not always the case. In some instances, short-term operational strategies evolve into formalized, long-term approaches, especially when an operation produces positive results. As we identify effective strategies through research, more agencies adopt the strategies on a temporary, semipermanent, or permanent basis.

PLACE-BASED STRATEGIES

Hot Spot Policing This is one example of a place-based operational strategy to reduce crime. It is defined as "the application of police interventions at very small geographic units of analysis" (Braga & Weisburd, 2010, p.9). It is based on the fact that crime is not normally distributed but rather concentrated in a few "hot spots." Some of the most common examples of small geographic units of analysis (a.k.a. hot spots) are a specific address, street segment, intersection, block, or cluster of blocks. A hot spot could also be an apartment complex, park, parking lot, business, or shopping center. Hot spots are typically identified through crime mapping and other intelligence-led procedures (crime analysis and COMPSTAT, for example), but they can also be identified by community members (Koper, 2014).

Hot spots policing is popular among practitioners, with almost every very large police department, and most small/medium, medium, and large police departments in the United States using the strategy (Reaves, 2010). It can take a variety of forms, but always involves some type of pro-active focused activity intended to reduce a specific issue at a micro-location. Some of the most popular hot spot policing strategies used by law enforcement agencies are problem analysis and problem solving, community policing and partnerships, directed patrol, enhanced traffic stops and field interviews, buy and bust/reverse stings, and order maintenance (broken windows) (Koper, 2014). Other popular hot spot-policing strategies (which happen to be offender-based) are targeting known offenders, warrant service, and checks on probationers and parolees. In addition, numerous agencies use mobile suppression or saturation units and multi-agency task forces to combat crime at hot spots. Note that hot spot policing can work under a problem-oriented policing approach, a community policing philosophy, or as part of a broken windows strategy.

A substantial body of research has shown hot spot policing to be effective at reducing crime and disorder (Braga & Weisburd, 2010; Koper, 2014; National Research Council, 2004). Although displacement is always a concern in place-based strategies, research shows that hot spot policing tactics more often diffuse benefits (reduce crime/disorder in areas that did not receive the intervention) than displace crime (move crime from targeted area to another area not targeted for intervention) (Koper, 2014).

Banishment Orders Using broken windows for theoretical support, **banishment orders** (also sometimes called **civil orders**) combine criminal and civil processes and penalties to reduce social disorder in defined places. Because these orders most often impact individuals experiencing homelessness, mental illness, and substance abuse, some scholars contend that the purpose of these orders is to exclude "socially marginal" people from public space (Beckett & Herbert, 2009; Herbert & Beckett, 2010). Beckett and Herbert (2009) identified three common types of banishment orders in use by police departments in America—parks exclusion laws, off-limits orders, and trespass laws.

Exclusion orders ban a person from a specific park (certain parks, or all parks) within a jurisdiction for up to 1 year. They are issued by police, without a hearing, to individuals who are caught committing an infraction (such as possessing alcohol, littering, urinating in public, being present after hours, etc.). The order is considered a civil law, but violating the order is a crime (usually a misdemeanor).

Off-limits orders are typically a condition of probation or parole for individuals convicted of (and sometimes just arrested and given diversion for) specific crimes. They require individuals to stay out of a specified geographic area. For example, Seattle (WA) residents convicted of (or diverted for) prostitution-related crimes may receive a SOAP (Stay Out of Areas of Prostitution) order while those convicted of drug crimes might receive a SODA (Stay Out of Drug Areas) order. This means that those individuals may not go into the area defined by the court for any reason, even to visit family or receive public services. Sometimes the defined exclusion area is very large. Violation of one of these orders is treated as a criminal offense or as a violation of probation/parole.

Trespass laws allow private property owners to limit access to their property. As a new innovation, cities are conveying (transferring) ownership rights to private property owners (such as businesses, libraries, recreation centers, public housing complexes, public transportation stations, etc.) so the owners can place restrictions on who can access the property (cities can't limit access). Police departments are facilitating this practice by implementing formal **trespass affidavit programs**. For example, private property owners can prohibit people from sleeping in the doorstops (and doing other things) by signing trespass papers that allow the police to arrest persons who do not have a "legitimate purpose" for being on the property. Property that was once public is now private for the purposes of exclusion (and order maintenance). Interestingly, because these are civil procedures, individuals do not have due process rights. Those who are trespassed cannot contest the admonishment. For example, in Seattle, public housing authorities ban nearly all non-residents/non-invited from the properties (NYC has a similar provision). Likewise, a person banned from one parking lot in Seattle is banned from all 320 parking lots (which makes parking in the city extremely difficult).

CHECK IT OUT!:

Google the search terms "police trespass affidavit" or "trespass affidavit program" and see how many cities across the country have implemented a similar program.

POLICE NOTICE

All City Police Department Officers are authorized representatives to advise any person to leave these premises, includeing parking lots. Failure to vacate the premises after being so instructed may result in an arrest for trespass after warning.

State Statute Section 810.09

Trespass affidavit program

CHICAGO PD'S CRIMINAL TRESPASS AFFIDAVIT PROGRAM

This is an example of a Trespass Affidavit Program policy. It is directly from Chicago PD's Web site.

Policy—The Trespass Affidavit Program is a valuable tool to prevent, detect, and take necessary enforcement action regarding narcotics, prostitution, and other illegal activity occurring in lobbies, stairwells, basements, and other common areas of privately owned buildings. The Trespass Affidavit Program will not be used to mitigate landlord–tenant disputes or other civil matters where ownership is in dispute.

Criminal Trespass Affidavit—A document signed and sworn to by a private property owner that (1) authorizes department members to enter a privately owned building to patrol common areas for trespassers and other criminal activity, (2) eliminates the need for the property owner to sign a criminal complaint at the time of an arrest, and (3) enhances crime intelligence and problem solving by facilitating communication between police and property owners.

TWENTY FIVE TECHNIQUES OF SITUATIONAL PREVENTION				
Increase the Effort	**Increase the Risks**	**Reduce the Rewards**	**Reduce Provocations**	**Remove Excuses**
1. **Target harden** • Steering column locks and immobilisers • Anti-robbery screens • Tamper-proof packaging	6. Extend guardianship • *Take routine precautions: go out in group at night, leave signs of occupancy, carry phone* • "Cocoon" neighborhood watch	11. Conceal targets • Off-street parking • Gender-neutral phone directories • Unmarked bullion trucks	16. Reduce frustrations and stress • Efficient queues and polite service • Expanded seating • Soothing music/muted lights	21. Set rules • Rental agreements • Harassment codes • Hotel registration
2. Control access to facilities • Entry phones • Electronic card access • Baggage screening	7. Assist natural surveillance • Improved street lighting • Defensible space design • Support whistleblowers	12. Remove targets • Removable car radio • Women's refuges • Pre-paid cards for pay phones	17. Avoid disputes • Separate enclosures for rival soccer fans • Reduce crowding in pubs • Fixed cab fares	22. Post instructions • "No Parking" • "Private Property" • "Extinguish camp fires"
3. Screen exits • Ticket needed for exit • Export documents • Electronic merchandise tags	8. Reduce anonymity • Taxi driver IDs • "How's my driving?" decals • School uniforms	13. Identify property • Property marking • Vehicle licensing and parts marking • Cattle branding	18. Reduce emotional arousal • Controls on violent pornography • Enforce good behavior on soccer field • Prohibit racial slurs	23. Alert conscience • Roadside speed display boards • Signatures for customs declarations • "Shoplifting is stealing"
4. Deflect offenders • Street closures • Separate bathrooms for women • Disperse pubs	9. Utilize place managers • CCTV for double-deck buses • Two clerks for convenience stores • Reward vigilance	14. Disrupt markets • Monitor pawn shops • Controls on classified ads. • License street vendors	19. Neutralize peer pressure • "Idiots drink and drive" • "It's OK to say No" • Disperse troublemakers at school	24. Assist compliance • Easy library checkout • Public lavatories • Litter bins
5. Control tools/ weapons • "Smart" guns • Disabling stolen cell phones • Restrict spray paint sales to juveniles	10. Strengthen formal surveillance • Red light cameras • Burglar alarms • Security guards	15. Deny benefits • Ink merchandise tags • Graffiti cleaning • Speed humps	20. Discourage imitation • Rapid repair of vandalism • V-chips in TVs • Censor details of modus operandi	25. Control drugs and alcohol • Breathalyzers in pubs • Server intervention • Alcohol-free events

Figure 10.6 Techniques of situational prevention.

Source: www.popcenter.org/25techniques

Although the use of banishment orders and their effect on society's most marginalized populations is well documented, there are no studies that directly assess the effectiveness of these orders on reducing crime or disorder.

Situational Crime Prevention (SCP) Based on the routine activities theory (Cohen & Felson, 1979), which stipulates that a crime occurs when three things converge in space and time (a motivated offender, a suitable target, and the absence of capable guardians), situational crime prevention tackles the situational context of criminal events. It typically focuses on specific problems in specific places; however, it is extremely versatile in the fact that it can be a place-based strategy, an offense-based strategy, an offender-based strategy, or a victim-based strategy. Situational crime prevention calls on police (in partnership with property owners, store managers, event organizers, and others) to (1) increase the effort required to commit a crime, (2) increase the risks associated with committing a crime, (3) reduce the rewards derived from committing a crime, (4) reduce provocations that lead a crime, and (5) remove the excuses for committing crime (Clarke, 1983; Cornish & Clarke, 2003).

For example, consumers used to buy cough medicine with pseudoephedrine in the medicine aisle. You didn't have to ask, nor provide your name to the pharmacist, and you could buy as much as you wanted to buy. However, as methamphetamine use and manufacturing became a serious problem in the late 1990s, laws were created to restrict access to pseudoephedrine (which is one of the main ingredients needed to cook methamphetamine). The situational crime prevention tactic worked by increasing the effort needed to commit the crime (manufacture the methamphetamine) but it also instigated a new crime wave of pharmacy robberies in some places for a short time, which led to more target hardening and eventually a reduction in the original and subsequent crimes. Other examples of situational crime prevention you might be familiar with include speed bumps on long straight streets (prevents speeding and drag racing), electronic sensors on clothing and other often stolen merchandise,

CCTV, height charts affixed to entry/exit doors at convenience stores and other retail establishments, educational signs (such as those on little league fields reminding parents "it's just a game and they're just kids"; or those on the freeway reminding drivers how expensive it is to get caught texting and driving or drinking and driving), extremely large packaging for small ink cartridges for your printer, knobs on rails and benches to prevent skateboarding, and the "greeter" at your favorite store in the mall, etc. Can you name some others? See Figure 10.6 above for additional examples.

Speed bumps are an example of situational crime prevention.

© nulimukas/Shutterstock.com

Similar to situational crime prevention, **crime prevention through environmental design (CPTED)** attempts to reduce crime by altering the environmental conditions that present criminal opportunities (Jeffrey, 1971). Based on the premise that the built environment can facilitate or hinder criminal offending and also impact how safe we feel in a particular space, it urges architects to

FIELD TRIP!

Go to your nearest mall to see SCP and CPTED in action. If you can afford it (or live nearby), visit any of the Disney theme parks (and parking lots) for LOTS of examples of SCP and CPTED. How many different examples can you find?

design buildings and public spaces that discourage criminal offending and increase feelings of safety. It can also be used to alter already-built environments to reduce crime. For example, using motion-sensor lights in front of your home, keeping the lights on in a store or bank over-night, making egress out of a shopping center time-consuming enough that potential robbers decide that none of the stores in the center are a suitable target; placing bollards in front of the large entry doors to a store (to prevent cars from driving directly into the store after closing and stealing the merchandise), roping off aisles in an outdoor public amphitheater or beach concert venue so that concert-goers don't get their fingers stepped on or their personal items stolen by passers-by trying to get to the bathroom or the snack bar.

SCP and CPTED are often included as part of a comprehensive strategy to alleviate crime in a specific hot spot. Studies have shown that these strategies can be used successfully to reduce crime. Although SCP and CPTED responses are highly unique to the individual crime location/problem, research indicates that targeted approaches can reduce crime. *Displacement*, an issue that occurs when crime moves from the targeted site to a nontargeted site, has been shown to occur; however, it is usually less than the accompanying *diffusion* benefits (when non-targeted sites also experience a drop in crime) (Guerette & Bowers, 2009; Johnson et al. 2012). This is similar to research findings on other hot spot policing strategies that find more diffusion benefits than displacement effects (Bowers et al., 2011; Telep et al., 2014).

Other place-based strategies discussed under BWP include zero tolerance policing and stop and frisk. Also, directed patrol, saturation patrol, and crackdowns are considered place-based strategies and have some research support. For example, directed patrol in high gun crime areas can reduce gun carrying and gun-related violence (Telep & Weisburd, 2012). Depending on how these are deployed (in a small, micro-place identified as a hot spot versus on a larger, more general area such as a beat or jurisdiction), these strategies could be considered hot spot policing. In fact, Weisburd and colleagues (2013) found that NYPD's SQF practice (in particular, "Operation Impact" which placed new recruits in high crime areas to conduct SQFs) was strategically implemented in concentrated high crime areas and could be considered hot spots policing.

OFFENDER-BASED STRATEGIES

Focused Deterrence Focused deterrence (a.k.a. pulling levers) is a prime example of an offender-based operational strategy used to reduce crime. This tactic, developed in Boston as part of Operation Ceasefire, uses the legal system and available social services to encourage identified individuals (violent gang members in Boston) to refrain from committing crime. Specifically, Boston gang members were notified that gang violence would not be tolerated and anyone who engaged in violence would be subjected to every possible legal consequence that could be directed at them. At the same time, social services were provided to individuals who requested the services and committed to be violence-free. Unlike some of the other strategies, pulling levers is generally implemented on a city-wide basis (to a specific audience) and involves partners from other agencies (such as the district attorney's office, probation department, community leaders, etc.) (Telep & Weisburd, 2012). Research conducted thus far suggests this is a strategy that "works." Interestingly, this approach got its start as a POP project—not surprisingly, it won the Herman Goldstein Award for excellence the year it was nominated (1998).

Other Other offender-based strategies can include warrant service, checks on probationers and parolees, sweeps of probation and parole violators, bait cars, decoys, banishment orders, and gang injunctions. Offender-based strategies are often employed as part of hot spots, or place-based, approach and are regularly included in problem-oriented policing strategies.

It is important to recognize that some of these strategies, even if they are effective, may be viewed unfavorably by the public and reduce police legitimacy. In particular, aggressive policing approaches have been shown to erode public trust and confidence in the police (Kochel, 2011; Telep & Weisburd, 2012). To reduce this possibility and increase the likelihood that citizens approve of the department's crime prevention tactics, comply with officers' directives, and view the police as legitimate, police should incorporate aspects of procedural justice (include citizens in the decision-making process, use neutral strategies, treat citizens with dignity and respect, and be fair) (Taylor, 1990; Telep & Weisburd, 2012). Although many of these operational tactics have been shown to effectively reduce crime, a strategy that causes a department to lose legitimacy could erase short-term crime prevention gains and increase crime in the long run.

EVIDENCE-BASED POLICING

Evidence-based policing takes all the information we have on police methods and uses it to identify the practices and strategies that accomplish police missions most cost-effectively (Sherman, 2013). Some of the earliest studies showed that traditional policing methods (random patrol, rapid response to incidents, and reactive investigations) do not effectively reduce crime. Since those early studies, other studies have identified police strategies that do effectively reduce crime. It is not enough, however, for academics to know which strategies "work" if police professionals do not use the research and implement the strategies deemed effective. Toward this end, renowned police scholar Lawrence Sherman proposed the "Triple-T" strategy of policing—targeting, testing, and tracking—to increase implementation of best practices in policing (Sherman, 2013).

1. *Targeting*: "Police should conduct and apply good research to target scarce resources on predictable concentrations of harm from crime and disorder" (p.383).

2. *Testing*: "Once police choose their high-priority targets, they should review or conduct tests of police methods to help choose what works best to reduce harm" (p.383).

3. *Tracking*: "Once police agencies use research to target their tested practices, they should generate and use internal evidence to track the daily delivery and effect of those practices, including public perceptions of police legitimacy" (p.383).

A SUMMARY OF THE EVIDENCE ON POLICING PRACTICES

So, what do we know about which police strategies are most effective? There are three main sources of information that are easily accessible to students and practitioners. The first, crimesolutions.gov, is a U.S. Department of Justice operated Web site that provides evidence-based practices for the entire criminal and juvenile justice systems (you may have heard about it in one of your other criminal justice classes). It provides information on "effective," "promising," and "no effects" programs and practices, as judged by the available scholarly research. As of August 2015, there were 51 policing programs listed on the Web site—12 considered effective, 34 considered promising, and 5 considered to have no effect. The 12 effective programs are, by and large, small and highly focused programs designed to address a specific issue in a specific place. There were also 7 policing practices listed—1 deemed effective (hot spots policing), 5 deemed promising, and 3 stated to have no effects. Why a particular policing strategy was categorized as a practice or a program is not completely clear, but it appears that "practices" were more generally focused than "programs." Check out the Web site for yourself!

The second source of information on policing practices is the Campbell Collaboration, an international organization of researchers that conducts, maintains, and disseminates systematic reviews on many socially relevant topic areas, including criminal justice. A systematic review is a review of all the research on a specific topic using a special analytic technique called meta-analysis. There are at least 14 systematic reviews on policing which can be found at campbellcollaboration.org. Unlike crimesolutions.gov, which classifies programs as effective/could be effective/not effective, Campbell systematic reviews provide a much more comprehensive review of a particular strategy. Sometimes, these reviews provide the research used by crimesolutions.gov to categorize a strategy.

Finally, the most extensive list of police studies can be found on a Web site maintained by scholars at George Mason University's Center for Evidence-Based Crime Policy (http://cebcp.org/evidence-based-policing/the-matrix/). They developed the "Evidence-Based Policing Matrix" to help scholars and practitioners identify the most effective policing strategies. As part of the project, they examined the research evidence on more than 100 different police practices and then plotted the results in a three-dimensional figure, as shown in Figure 10.7:

(X) is the type or scope of target (individuals, groups, micro places, neighborhood, jurisdiction, nation)

(Y) is the specificity of prevention mechanism (general or focused)

(Z) is the level of proactivity (reactive, proactive, highly proactive)

As you can see from the matrix in Figure 10.7, each dot represents a separate research study on a particular strategy—the different colored shapes tell us whether the strategy was effective (black dot), not effective (clear dot), had mixed effects (grey dot), or was harmful (red triangle). Plotting research findings in this three-dimensional figure allow scholars to identify clusters of effective police strategies. These "realms of effectiveness" show that, in general, police strategies that are (1) focused, place-based, and highly proactive; (2) general, micro-place or neighborhood-based, and proactive, or (3) focused, jurisdiction-wide, and proactive are effective. Furthermore, it reveals that individually focused police strategies are typically not effective or have mixed effects.

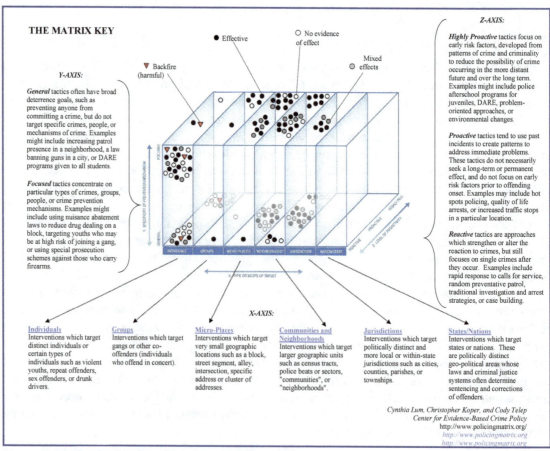

Figure 10.7 The evidence-based policing matrix.

To summarize the general research knowledge, the scholars at GMU categorized policing strategies into four categories, based on the research evidence of effectiveness (Lum, 2009; Lum, Koper, & Telep, 2011). Here is what they found:

What Works

Hot Spots Policing
Problem-oriented policing
Focused deterrence strategies
Directed patrol for gun violence
DNA for police investigations

What's Promising

Information-gathering interrogation approach
Community policing & procedural justice
CCTV

What Doesn't Work

"Traditional" policing tactics
(random patrol, rapid response...)
Second responder programs
DARE (Drug Abuse Resistance Education)

What we need to know more about

Broken windows policing
Increasing department size
Investigations by detectives
Counterterrorism strategies
Police technology (shot spotter, drones, license plate readers, body worn cameras)

EFFECTIVENESS AND EQUITY

Throughout this chapter, we have presented some of the most popular policing practices in the United States and attempted to highlight their effectiveness as well as their impact on the community being policed. Police scholar Robin Engel recently reviewed policing strategies on two dimensions, effectiveness and equity, to ascertain whether specific strategies could achieve both effectiveness and equity or whether the two concepts represent opposing goals (Engel, 2014). Before diving into her findings, we need to define our concepts. Equity, as it is used here, means perceived fairness in both process and outcome (a.k.a. procedural justice and a just outcome) while effectiveness refers to how well a strategy reduces crime or disorder (or achieves other stipulated police objectives). Engel examined four different policing models—traditional/standard policing, community policing, problem-oriented policing, and (what she calls) focused policing. She arranged each model along two dimensions, the range of interventions (narrow to wide) and level of attention on specific problems (unfocused to highly focused), then summarized the research literature on equity and effectiveness for each general model (see Figure 10.8).

While not a perfect dichotomy, her findings suggest that highly focused strategies (those on the right side of the figure) are the most effective but have either unknown equity or low equity ratings. She reiterates our earlier point that how policing is done matters immensely for citizen perception of police (perceived equity). Engel makes a strong case that "equity" should be part of all evaluations of police strategies and that only strategies that are both effective and equitable should be endorsed as evidence-based.

	Community		Problem-Oriented	
Wide Range	*Focus:* community partnerships *Examples:* Foot patrols, neighborhood stations, community meetings and involvement		*Focus:* systematic analysis of problems with individually designed responses *Examples:* problem analysis, SARA process, multi-agency partnerships, risky facility interventions, repeat victimization	
	Effectiveness: LOW	*Equity:* HIGH	*Effectiveness:* HIGH	*Equity:* UNKNOWN (potential for high)
	Standard		**Focused**	
Narrow Range	*Focus:* all crimes across jurisdiction *Examples:* random patrol, intensive and broad enforcement, rapid response, traditional investigative methods		*Focus:* repeat places, offenders, crimes *Examples:* Hotspots patrol, repeat offenders, temporal/spatial crackdowns	
	Effectiveness: LOW	*Equity:* LOW	*Effectiveness:* HIGH	*Equity:* LOW (potential for change)

Interventions (vertical axis label)

| *Unfocused* | **Attention** | *Highly Focused* |

Figure 10.8 Equity vs effectiveness in policing strategies.

Adapted from Engel, R. (2014, June 25). *Effectiveness vs. equity in policing: Is a tradeoff inevitable?* Police Foundation, Ideas in Policing Lecture. Washington, DC.

CONCLUSION

In this chapter, we explained some of the most prominent policing methods used in the United States (and other predominately Anglo-Celtic countries around the world—e.g., Canada, Australia, New Zealand, and the United Kingdom). As you already know, policing differs by community size, type, and region. A practice that is right and works for one community may be all wrong for another community. We also summarized the knowledge base on police strategies and underscored the importance of strategies that are both effective at reducing crime and/or disorder and supported by the public who live in the area being policed. By and large, practices that are highly focused and target specific problems (locations, offenders, or victims) are effective at reducing crime, but practices that incorporate the community as partners improve police legitimacy and perceptions of equity.

REVIEW QUESTIONS

1. What are the three organizational policing strategies introduced in this chapter? Can you describe each one?

2. Which approaches have strong research support? Support your answer with the relevant research.

3. How do community policing, problem-oriented policing, and broken windows differ? How are they similar?

4. Why is implementation so important in BWP?

5. Explain each of the place-based operational strategies introduced in this chapter. Which of these are supported by research?

6. Describe evidence-based policing. Which strategies are most consistently supported by research?

GLOSSARY

Banishment orders orders that combine civil and criminal processes and penalties to reduce social disorder in defined places. Also known as civil orders.

Broken windows policing a method of policing based on the broken windows theory that focuses on reducing low level disorder and disorderly behavior in order to reduce serious crime.

Broken windows theory a theory proposed by James Q. Wilson and George Kelling in 1982 that proposes that unkempt areas invite additional disorder and serious crime.

Civil orders orders that combine civil and criminal processes and penalties to reduce social disorder in defined places. Also known as banishment orders.

Community Policing a policing philosophy that focuses on building community partnerships to reduce and prevent crime and improve police—community relations.

Crime Prevention Through Environmental Design (CPTED) crime prevention strategy that attempts to reduce crime by altering the environmental conditions that present criminal opportunities.

Evidence-based policing policing strategies proven effective through social scientific research.

Exclusion orders orders that ban a named person from a specific place within a jurisdiction for a defined period of time.

Focused deterrence a proactive policing strategy that uses the legal system and available social services to encourage identified individuals to refrain from committing crime. Also known as pulling levers.

Hot spots policing a proactive approach that devotes police resources to reduce crime or other problems at small geographic places based on crime, calls for service, or other data.

Off-limits orders orders requiring an individual to stay away from a specified geographic area as a condition of probation or parole.

Problem-oriented Policing a method of policing developed by Herman Goldstein in 1979 that broadens the role of police and involves identifying and addressing the root causes of problems.

Pulling levers a proactive policing strategy that uses the legal system and available social services to encourage identified individuals to refrain from committing crime. Also known as focused deterrence.

Quality of life policing NYPD Chief Bratton's version of broken windows policing, first instituted in 1994. It later became known as zero tolerance policing.

SARA acronym for scan, analyze, respond, and assess—the four stages of the problem-oriented policing strategy.

Situational crime prevention crime prevention strategy based on routine activities theory that focuses on making it harder to commit a crime or reducing the rewards for committing a crime.

Stop and frisk The police practice of stopping and detaining a "suspicious" person for further investigation. It may include a superficial pat down of the suspicious person's body and clothing for contraband, weapons, or other items if an officer can articulate reasonable suspicion that the person committed a crime or is a threat to public safety. The term has also been associated with New York City's aggressive style of policing that focuses on conducting these stops in high crime areas.

Terry stop The standard for allowing police officers to stop and search suspicious persons as defined in *Terry v. Ohio*.

Terry v. Ohio 1968 US Supreme Court case that granted police officers the right to stop and question a person they reasonably suspected of being involved in criminal activity and also conduct a limited pat down of the detained person if the officer reasonably suspected the person to be in possession of a weapon.

Trespass affidavit programs a program whereby private property owners sign a document authorizing a law enforcement agency to enforce trespass laws in the property owner's absence.

Trespass laws allow private property owners to limit access to their property.

Zero tolerance policing an aggressive style of policing focused on eliminating disorderly behavior through a high number of arrests and citations. Based upon the broken windows theory, it was first instituted in New York City in the late 1980s to early 1990s.

REFERENCES

Approach. (n.d.) *Merriam-Webster Dictionary*. Retrieved from http://www.merriam-webster.com/dictionary

Beckett, K., & Herbert, S. (2009). *Banished: The new social control in urban America*. New York, NY: Oxford University Press.

Bowers, K., Johnson, S., Guerette, R. T., Summers, L., & Poynton, S. (2011a). Spatial displacement and diffusion of benefits among geographically focused policing interventions. *Campbell Systematic Reviews, 7*(3).

Braga, A. A., & Weisburd, D. L. (2010). *Policing problem places: Crime hotspots and effective prevention*. New York City, NY: Oxford University Press.

Braga, A. A., & Weisburd, D. L. (2006). Critic: Problem-oriented policing: The disconnect between principles and practice. In D. Weisburd & A. Braga (Eds.), *Police innovation: Contrasting perspectives*. New York, NY: Cambridge University Press

Braga, A. A., Welsh, B. C., & Schnell, C. (2015). Can policing disorder reduce crime? A systematic review and meta-analysis. *Journal of Research in Crime and Delinquency, 52*(4), 567–588. doi 10.1177/0022427815576576

Capowich, G. E., & Roehl, J. A. (1994). Problem oriented policing: Actions and effectiveness in San Diego. In D. P. Rosenbaum (Ed.), *The challenge of community policing: Testing the promises*. Thousand Oaks, CA: Sage.

Clarke, R. V. (1983). Situational crime prevention: Its theoretical basis and practical scope. *Crime and Justice, 4,* 225–256.

Cohen, L., & Felson, M. (1979). Social change and crime rate trends: A routine activity approach. *American Sociological Review, 44*(4), 588–608.

COPS. (2014). *Community policing defined*. Washington, DC: US Department of Justice. Retrieved from http://www.cops.usdoj.gov

Cordner, G. W. (1988). A problem-oriented approach to community-oriented policing. In J. R. Greene & S. D. Mastrofski (Eds.), *Community policing: Rhetoric or reality*. New York, NY: Praeger.

Cornish, D. B., & Clarke, R. V. (2003). Opportunities, precipitators and criminal decisions: A reply to Wortley's critique of situational crime prevention. *Crime Prevention Studies, 16,* 41–96.

Eck, J. E. (2006). Advocate: Science, values, and problem-oriented policing: Why problem-oriented policing? In D. Weisburd & A. Braga (Eds.), *Police innovation: Contrasting perspectives*. New York, NY: Cambridge University Press.

Eck, J. E., & Spellman, W. (1987). *Problem-solving: Problem-oriented policing in Newport News*. Washington, DC: Police Executive Research Forum.

Engel, R. (2014, June 25). *Effectiveness vs. equity in policing: Is a tradeoff inevitable?* Police Foundation, Ideas in Policing Lecture. Washington, DC.

Fagan, J. A., Geller, A., Davies, G., & West, V. (2010). Street stops and Broken Windows revisited: The demography and logic of proactive policing in a safe and changing city. In S. K. Rice & M. D. White (Eds.), *Race, ethnicity, and policing: New and essential readings*. New York: New York University Press.

Gardiner, C. (2015). *The state of education and policing in California*. Fullerton: Center for Public Policy at California State University, Fullerton.

Gill, C., Weisburd, D., Telep, C. W., Vitter, Z., & Bennett, T. (2014). Community-oriented policing to reduce crime, disorder and fear and increase satisfaction and legitimacy among citizens: A systematic review. *Journal of Experimental Criminology, 10,* 399–428. doi: 10.1007/s11292-014-9210-y

Goldstein, H. (1979). Improving policing: A problem-oriented approach. *Crime & Delinquency, 25*(2), 235–258.

Goldstein, H. (1990). *Problem-oriented policing*. New York, NY: McGraw-Hill.

Goldstein, H. (2001). *What is POP?* Retrieved from http://www.popcenter.org/about/?p=whatiscpop

Guerette, R. T., & Bowers, K. J. (2009). Assessing the extent of crime displacement and diffusion of benefits: A review of situational crime prevention evaluations. *Criminology, 47*(4), 1331–1368.

Herbert, S., & Beckett, K. (2010). 'This is home for us': Questioning banishment from the ground up. *Social & Cultural Geography, 11*(3), 231–245. doi: 10.1080/14649361003637661

Johnson, S. D., Guerette, R. T., & Bowers, K. J. (2012). Crime displacement and diffusion of benefits. In B. C. Welsh & D. P. Farrington (Eds.), *The Oxford handbook of crime prevention* (pp. 337–353). New York, NY: Oxford University Press.

Kelling, G. L., & Coles, C. M. (1997). *Fixing broken windows: Restoring order and reducing crime in our communities.* New York, NY: Touchstone.

Kirk, D., & Matsuda, M. (2011). Legal cynicism, collective efficacy, and the ecology of arrest. *Criminology, 49,* 443–472.

Kochel, T. R. (2011). Constructing hot spots policing: Unexamined consequences for disadvantaged populations and for police legitimacy. *Criminal Justice Policy Review, 22,* 350–374.

Koper, C. S. (2014). Assessing the practice of hot spots policing: Survey results from a national convenience sample of local police agencies. *Journal of Contemporary Criminal Justice, 30*(2), 123–146. doi: 10.1177/1043986214525079

Lum, C. (2009). Translating police research into practice. *Ideas in American Policing, 11.* Washington, DC: Police Foundation.

Lum, C., Koper, C., & Telep, C. W. (2011). The evidence-based policing matrix. *Journal of Experimental Criminology, 7,* 3–26.

Maguire, E., Uchida, C., & Hassell, K. (2015). Problem-oriented policing in Colorado Springs: A content analysis of 753 cases. *Crime & Delinquency, 61*(1), 71–95. doi: 10.1177/0011128710386201

Mastrofski, S.(2006). Critic: Community policing: A skeptical view. In D. Weisburd & A. Braga (Eds.), *Police innovation: Contrasting perspectives.* New York, NY: Cambridge University Press.

Mazerolle, L., Darroch, S., & White, G. (2013). Leadership in problem-oriented policing. *Policing: An International Journal of Police Strategies & Management, 36*(3), 543–560. doi: 10.1108/pupsm-06-2012-0055

Moore, M. H. (1994). Research synthesis and policy implications. In D. P. Rosenbaum (Ed.), *The challenge of community policing.* Thousand Oaks, CA: Sage.

National Research Council. (2004). In W. Skogan & K. Frydl (Eds.), *Fairness and effectiveness in policing: The evidence.* Washington, DC: National Academies Press.

Philosophy. (n.d.) *Merriam-Webster Dictionary.* Retrieved from http://www.merriam-webster.com/dictionary

POP Center. (2015). *History of policing.* Retrieved from http://www.popcenter.org/about/?p=history

Reaves, B. (2010, December). *Local police departments, 2007.* Bureau of Justice Statistics. Washington, DC: U.S. Government Printing Office.

Reaves, B. (2015, May). *Local police departments, 2013.* Bureau of Justice Statistics. Washington, DC: U.S. Government Printing Office.

Scott, & Goldstein, H. (1988). *The key elements of problem-oriented policing.* Retrieved from http://www.popcenter.org/about/?p=elements

Sherman, L. W. (2013). The rise of evidence-based policing: Targeting, testing, and tracking. *Crime and Justice, 42*(1), 377–451.

Skogan, W., & Frydl, K. (Eds.). (2004). *Fairness and effectiveness in policing: The evidence.* Washington, DC: National Academies Press.

Sousa, W. H., & Kelling, G. L. (2006). Advocate: Of "broken windows," criminology, and criminal justice. In D. Weisburd & A. Braga (Eds.), *Police innovation: Contrasting perspectives.* New York, NY: Cambridge University Press.

Strategy. (n.d.). *Dictionary.com Unabridged.* Retrieved from http://dictionary.reference.com/browse/strategy

Stroudt, B., Fine, M., & Fox, M. (2011). Juvenile justice reform in New York: Growing up policed in the age of aggressive policing tactics. *New York Law School Law Review.*

Taylor, T. R. (1990). *Why people obey the law: Procedural justice, legitimacy, and compliance.* New Haven, CT: Yale University Press.

Taylor, T. R. (2006). Critic: Incivilities reduction policing, zero tolerance, and the retreat from coproduction: Weak foundations and strong pressures. In D. Weisburd & A. Braga (Eds.), *Police innovation: Contrasting perspectives.* New York, NY: Cambridge University Press.

Telep, C. W., & Weisburd, D. (2012). What is known about the effectiveness of police practices in reducing crime and disorder? *Police Quarterly, 15*(4), 331–357. doi: 10.1177/1098611112447611

Telep, C. W., Weisburd, D., Gill, C. E., Vitter, Z., & Teichman, D. (2014). Displacement of crime and diffusion of crime control benefits in large-scale geographic areas: A systematic review. *Journal of Experimental Criminology, 10*(4), 515–548. doi: 10.1007/s11292-014-9208-5

Trojanowicz, R. C., Kappeler, V. E., Gaines, L. K., & Bucqueroux, B. (1998). *Community policing: A contemporary perspective.* Cincinnati, OH: Anderson.

Ward, S. F. (2014). Stopping stop and frisk. *ABA Journal, 100*(3), 38–45.

Weisburd, D., & Eck, J. E. (2004). What can police do to reduce crime, disorder, and fear? *The Annals, 593,* 42–65.

Weisburd, D., Telep, C., & Lawton, B. (2013). Could innovation in policing have contributed to the New York City crime drop even in a period of declining police strength? The case of stop, question, and frisk as a hot spots policing strategy. *Justice Quarterly, 31*(1), 129–153. doi: 10.1080/07418825.2012.754920

Weisburd, D. L., Telep, C. W., Hinkle, J. C., & Eck, J. E. (2010). Is problem-oriented policing effective in reducing crime and disorder? *Criminology & Public Policy, 9*(1), 139–172.

Wilson, J. Q., & Kelling, G. L. (1982, March). Broken windows: The police and neighborhood safety. *The Atlantic Monthly,* 29–38.

COURT CASES

Terry v. Ohio, 392 U.S. 1 (1968).

Floyd, et al. v. City of New York, et al., 08 Civ. 1034 (2013).

11

POLICING SPECIAL POPULATIONS

LEARNING OBJECTIVES

After reading this chapter, students should be able to:

1 Discuss how policing individuals experiencing homelessness is different than policing other populations.

2 Describe three ethical trade-offs that police face when dealing with homeless individuals.

3 Explain the "criminalization of homelessness."

4 Explain how policing individuals with mental illness is different than policing other populations.

5 Describe CIT, how they work, and why they are beneficial.

6 Describe the extent of juvenile delinquency in America.

7 Explain how police treat juveniles differently than adults.

8 Recall the top youth issues for law enforcement.

9 Discuss the school to prison pipeline and the role that zero-tolerance policies and school resource officers play.

10 Define a gang and describe the prevalence of gangs in America.

11 Describe the risk factors for gang joining.

12 Explain typical crimes committed by gang members and the extent of gang crime in the United States.

13 Outline possible and popular police responses to gang crime.

KEY TERMS

Mercy booking

Crisis intervention team (CIT)

Reasonable suspicion

School-to-prison pipeline

School resources officer (SRO)

Risk factor

Protective factor

Gang graffiti

Tagging

Primary prevention

Secondary prevention

Tertiary prevention

Suppression

Civil gang injunctions

Pulling levers

This chapter describes some of the special populations police encounter on a regular basis. Due to the nature of the job, police officers are often called to deal with people who are not necessarily criminals but whose behavior brings them into contact with law enforcement. For example, individuals who are homeless, have a diagnosed mental illness, or suffer drug or alcohol addiction tend to have more contact with police than individuals who do not have any of these characteristics. Likewise, juveniles and gang members also have increased contact with police, which has motivated many departments to establish special policies and teams for these populations.

The extent to which an officer encounters the populations described in this chapter depends on several agency factors: (1) the level of government—federal, state, county, municipal; (2) the size of the agency—very small to very large; (3) jurisdiction characteristics—urban, suburban, rural; and (4) the location of the agency—West coast, East coast, South, Mid-west, proximity to major tourist or political centers. How individual agencies respond to these special populations is also dependent on these factors. As you can see in Table 11.1, most law enforcement agencies have special policies in place for encounters with juveniles and mentally ill persons, but only about a third of agencies have a policy in place for persons experiencing homelessness or those with limited English proficiency. Larger agencies are much more likely than smaller agencies to have articulated specific policies.

POLICING PERSONS EXPERIENCING HOMELESSNESS

For many reasons, individuals experiencing homelessness disproportionately come from America's most disadvantaged neighborhoods—those with high levels of crime, family violence, unemployment, and low educational attainment. A significant portion become homeless as a result of a financially devastating medical diagnosis but a large portion also end up homeless due to job loss, addiction (usually alcohol, drugs, or gambling), and/or difficult transitions from foster care, incarceration, psychiatric hospitals, and the military. The lack of affordable housing plays a major role in homelessness in most cities (USCM, 2014). While the number of people experiencing homelessness grew from the 1980s until 2007, it has since declined slightly (mostly due to a higher number of temporary shelter beds and efforts to house veterans) (NAEH, 2015). Recent estimates place the number of individuals experiencing homelessness in the United States at approximately 578,424 (NAEH, 2015). Of which, 216,197 are people in families and 362,163 are individuals. Somewhere between 9% and 13% of people experiencing homelessness are veterans, 15% are victims of domestic violence, and approximately 8% are unaccompanied youth and children (NAEH, 2015; USCM, 2014).

TABLE 11.1   Special Population Policies throughout the United States

Population Served	Juveniles		Mentally Ill Persons		Homeless Persons		Persons with Limited English Proficiency	
	Police	Sheriffs	Police	Sheriffs	Police	Sheriffs	Police	Sheriffs
1,000,000 or more	100%	100%	100%	85%	69%	44%	85%	59%
500,000–999,999	100%	98%	97%	84%	57%	21%	73%	36%
250,000–499,999	98%	92%	96%	81%	50%	20%	67%	36%
100,000–249,999	98%	92%	93%	85%	38%	24%	47%	46%
50,000–99,999	99%	89%	88%	83%	40%	25%	45%	33%
25,000–49,999	98%	92%	85%	75%	39%	30%	43%	35%
10,000–24,999	96%	85%	82%	68%	40%	29%	40%	37%
2,500–9,999[a] / Under 10,000[b]	93%	83%	72%	66%	34%	32%	31%	34%
Under 2,500	84%		57%		29%		25%	
ALL SIZES	90%	88%	69%	74%	34%	28%	32%	36%

[a]–police departments, [b]–sheriffs' departments

Adapted from Reaves, B. (2010, December). Local police departments, 2007. Bureau of Justice Statistics, p. 16. Washington DC: U.S. Government Printing Office. And Burch, A.M. (2012, December). Sheriffs' offices, 2007-Statistical tables. Bureau of Justice Statistics, p. 12. Washington DC: U.S. Government Printing Office.

It is important to understand that distinctions exist between the general "homeless" population and the "chronic homeless" population. The homeless count includes those who have nowhere to live and live with family, friends, in shelters, or on the streets. Many of these individuals remain homeless on a temporary basis after a financial difficulty or family breakdown. These temporary homeless populations attract little police attention. At the same time, chronic homeless (people living on the streets) may have a home, but chose not to live in it for reasons including, but not limited to, alcoholism, drug addiction, or mental illness. Approximately 15% of homeless individuals (and 3% of families) are considered chronically homeless and approximately 28%–39% have been diagnosed with severe mental illness (NAEH, 2015; USCM, 2014).

In addition to mental illness, drug and alcohol addiction further complicate the homelessness crisis for police. Studies estimate that between 25% and 45% of individuals living on the streets struggle with alcohol or drug addiction; exposing the homeless to frequent infractions for public intoxication, drug possession, and nuisance (Lane, 2014; NLCHP, 2014). Mental illness and public intoxication prompt many residents and business owners to fear homeless individuals or treat them as a drain on commerce, leading many to call the police for assistance. This further strains police resources, and pushes public officials to advocate the containment of homeless populations in areas away from public centers.

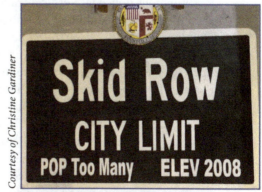

Courtesy of Christine Gardiner

Skid Row has been a center of homelessness for many years.

Los Angeles' Skid Row presents perhaps the most vivid example of this point. Located in downtown Los Angeles, blocks from the financial, jewelry, fashion, and entertainment districts, Skid Row has been a center of homelessness and poverty since the 1960s. Characterized by crimes such as prostitution, open air drug markets, dumping, and public intoxication, Skid Row has become the public face of policy failure in the media while compounding problems for police struggling to contain the area's numerous problems (Berk & MacDonald, 2010). To be sure, New York, Chicago, and many other cities (both big and small) face similar problems. How a city chooses to address its homeless population, in particular the number of shelter and transitional beds and other services it provides (and where), are important factors in the existence and size of its "skid row" and the extent of problems which require police action. As you learned in Chapter 10, New York City had a considerable crime problem in the 1980s and 1990s, much of it concentrated in the downtown area. As you are also aware, the city was able to reduce its level of crime significantly. But what you may not realize is that New York City's major crime decline was the result of many factors, including police action, real estate development, gentrification, and, important for present purposes, addressing the city's homelessness problem. One of the things that NYC did, besides making lots of arrests for minor law violations, was dramatically increase the number of shelter beds available and expand social services in the city. In short, it was a concerted and multifaceted approach undertaken by many different entities—public, private, and nonprofit—not just the police.

POLICE CONCERNS

How police interact with individuals experiencing homelessness in their jurisdiction depends on how extensive the homeless population is and whether it is deemed a "problem" by decision-makers. Residents and politicians of many cities see homelessness as blight and a catalyst for crime. As such, numerous jurisdictions have established laws (codes and ordinances) prohibiting behaviors that are associated with homelessness in an effort to change behavior or to change where the behavior is performed; in other words to "hide," "regulate," or "contain" homelessness within the jurisdiction. According to the most recent report by the National Law Center on Homelessness & Poverty, most cities prohibit sitting or lying down, camping, loitering, and begging in public (see Figure 11.1) (NLCHP, 2014). Police are necessarily tasked with enforcing these codes. A recent national survey of homeless individuals found that 50% had been cited (30% arrested) for sleeping in public, 43% had been cited (26% arrested) for loitering, and 41% had been cited (25% arrested) for sitting or lying down in public (see Figure 11.2) (NLHCP, 2014).

Ultimately, police face ethical trade-offs in three principal arenas when dealing with homeless individuals: (1) conflicts over public spaces, (2) public demand for enforcement, and (3) providing services to disenfranchised people. From public restrooms and subway/transit stations to sidewalks and public streets, police are frequently forced to intervene when homeless individuals impede the use of public space. Keep in mind that there are many legitimate users of public space in areas with large homeless populations. In a typical skid row, for example, there are business owners, employees, and patrons, real estate owners and developers, service providers and clients, school teachers and students, as well as homeless residents and advocates. The main issue arises when one party wants to use a public space differently than another party. For example, a homeless person wants to sit or lay on the sidewalk in the shade while a shopper wants to walk safely between stores without being harassed or feel like they are invading someone's personal space when they step on or over an individual's person or belongings.

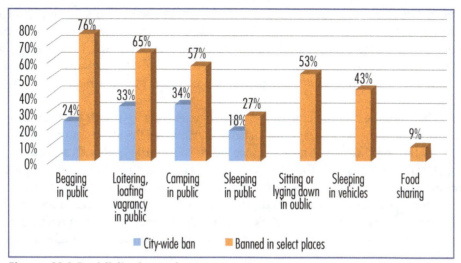

Figure 11.1 Prohibited conduct

Adapted from National Law Center on Homeless & Poverty (NLCHP). (2014, December). *No safe place: The criminalization of homelessness in U.S. cities.* Retrieved from: http://www.nlchp.org/documents/No_Safe_Place

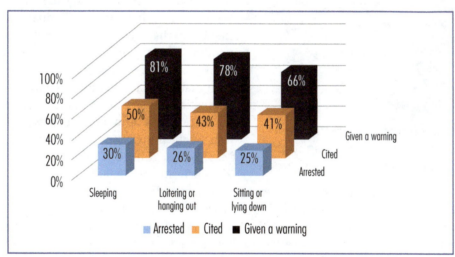

Figure 11.2 Police Contact

Adapted from National Law Center on Homeless & Poverty (NLCHP). (2014, December). *No safe place: The criminalization of homelessness in U.S. cities.* Retrieved from: http://www.nlchp.org/documents/No_Safe_Place

Ultimately, police are neutral arbiters of the law with tremendous discretion—present to help disagreeing parties interpret the law and to take a proper course of action according to the law. As such, police must consider the laws (codes and ordinances) passed by their jurisdiction when deciding an outcome and course of action when encountering a situation involving homeless individuals. However, police are also agents of the state and jurisdiction beholden to supervisors, the chief, and other decision-makers.

Second, police must manage public demands for enforcement. Calls involving mentally ill persons experiencing homelessness create the greatest challenge as police attempt to balance a compassionate response while treating the needs of the individual and considering the needs of the community. As we discuss in the next section, calls involving mentally ill individuals not only consume more of an officer's time than a standard call but also require special training and patience.

Third, police face the challenge of providing police services to disenfranchised people. With significant portions of the homeless being victims of crimes, police must find a balance between enforcement of the law and providing assistance. With substantial trade-offs associated with any response, police interactions with the homeless are wide and varying. As previously stated, police most commonly interact with homeless individuals when they are involved either as victims or perpetrators in a crime. Over 38% of the homeless have reported lost or stolen property; however, since much of the interactions the homeless have with police are order maintenance based, few trust the police enough to report crimes committed against them. Homeless males are most likely to exhibit this pattern.

Though many homeless report stolen property, few trust the police enough to report crimes committed against them.

Negative public image has done little to stop police from using order maintenance techniques to drive away homeless persons from city centers and boundaries. Despite disapproval from the courts, police frequently use minor infractions to drive homeless individuals away with the hope that crime will follow (*ala* broken windows theory). Bratton's "Main Street Pilot" (MSP) project (which later became the Safer Cities Initiative [SCI]) attempted to reduce homeless population density by increasing the number of nuisance-based infractions such as public urination, public intoxication, and jaywalking (Berk & MacDonald, 2010). The campaign produced over 9000 arrests and 12,000 infractions in the first year (Stuart, 2013). The aggressive enforcement was later followed with services in an attempt to use the citations and arrests to cajole individuals into treatment and housing (by dismissing the citation/arrest upon program completion). However, there was no money allocated to the program piece which meant that very few individuals actually received services. While crime decreased and order improved after the MSP and SCI, improvements were difficult to sustain and LAPD's actions spurred the ACLU and other organizations to file civil rights lawsuits against the city. Subsequent studies of Bratton's approach have shown limited effect on crime reduction as a result of the project (Berk & MacDonald, 2010).

It has become increasingly popular for business investment districts (BIDs) across America to hire private security to provide extra enforcement. In Los Angeles' Central City East Business Investment District, which includes the area known as Skid Row, security guards carry batons, chemical spray, handcuffs, and sometimes handguns (if the guard has a valid CCW—concealed weapons permit). Known as "Red Shirts" (due to the color shirt they wear), guards make citizen arrests and alert the police to illegal activity. By law they only have the authority to move someone off *private* property, yet that does not usually stop them from asking homeless individuals to identify themselves and consent to a search of their person or property in public spaces

(Harcourt, 2005). Excessive use of this practice has resulted in LAPD officers sometimes coming to the defense of homeless residents (Harcourt, 2005). Although LAPD has a large number of officers assigned to patrol skid row (sometimes as high as 50 for a 50 square block area), Red Shirts provide even more surveillance and enforcement potential.

These approaches have led many to note a so-called criminalization of homelessness especially with the rise of city ordinances banning panhandling, loitering, and even feeding the homeless in public places. As Figure 11.1 showed, a 2014 study from the National Law Center on Homelessness and Poverty found that of 187 major cities surveyed, 53% prohibited sitting or lying in some public place, 34% prohibited camping in public throughout the city, and 24% prohibited panhandling citywide, policies which have been increasing in prevalence since 2009 (NLCHP, 2014). The laws, some of which were discussed in Chapter 10, are also referred to as banishment orders or civility laws. On the flip side, these laws can also help officers "shepherd" homeless individuals into shelters that provide housing and programs that teach life skills, job skills, general education courses, and addiction management. This is the strategy that LAPD has been using since about 2007; collaborating with the mega-missions in skid row, officers act as "recovery managers" by using these laws to make residents sleeping on the streets so uncomfortable that they may prefer to enter a shelter's treatment program to get them back on their feet (Stuart, 2014). Of course, not everyone is happy with this controversial approach.

Some police departments have community service officers who help the homeless find shelter.

These approaches follow a general pattern of reactive strategies toward dealing with homelessness and are found to be much more costly and less effective than other, noncriminal justice alternatives such as providing housing and case managers (Lane, 2014). Recently, leaders have encouraged the use of proactive strategies in dealing with homelessness. Some departments have increased the use of community service officers with specialized training by social service agencies to respond to incidents with homeless individuals by encouraging them to find shelter, treatment, or both. Other departments have established teams of sworn Homeless Liaison Officers which attempt to reach out and connect with residents experiencing homelessness. These officers get to know as many homeless residents as possible and serve as a department's homeless and social service experts (*ala* community policing).

These types of strategies have produced more constructive relationships between homeless persons and police, reducing the ingrained suspicions that have characterized relationships between the two groups. Some have even advocated turning areas of dense homelessness like Skid Row into so-called recovery zones in which social services, nonprofit charities, and religious institutions are encouraged to increase their presence as a means of reducing the need for order maintenance (Stuart, 2013). This is a strategy that LAPD, LA's Mega Missions, and others have partnered together to advance.

POLICING PERSONS WITH MENTAL ILLNESS

As first responders, police are given an "impossible mandate" (Manning, 1977) to enforce law, maintain order, and provide services. Manning calls this the "impossible mandate" because enforcing the law is inherently political even though police officers themselves are required, in theory, to be apolitical. As explained in the previous section, police officers must negotiate competing interests and the tensions between order maintenance, the political machine, individuals' civil rights, and what is "best" for the person/s involved. This is especially true for officers called to help a person having a mental health crisis, especially when that person is also experiencing homelessness.

With access to health services limited for the mentally ill poor, mental illness has shifted from an issue between families and doctors to a significant police problem. The deinstitutionalization process of the 1960/70s, which had so substantially contributed to the homelessness crisis, systematically limited access to mental health services particularly for those severely impaired or financially unable to maintain expensive treatments. While the goal was to treat individuals with mental illness in the community, rather than psychiatric hospitals, the necessary funding for community mental healthcare providers and treatment never materialized. The result was a steady increase of calls to police to assist with persons having mental health crises and the criminalization of mental illness.

The increasing number of calls for assistance, coupled with criminalization laws and ordinances, improper dosing of medication and addiction, and privatization of mental health services at price ranges above the reach of the poor have all contributed to the problem. While studies disagree as to how high arrest rates are among the mentally ill, it is estimated that 7–10% of all police encounters involve "Persons with Mental Illness" (PMI) and that 56% of state prison inmates, 45% of federal inmates, and 64% of U.S. jail inmates have a diagnosed mental illness (Frazier et al., 2015; Lord & Bjerregaard, 2014). Contact between PMI and police is primarily initiated from four types of citizen encounters:

1. Family members of an individual who cannot handle a mental health crisis situation alone.

2. Persons with mental illness (PMI) who are victims of crimes.

3. Business owners and landlords who fear an encounter with a PMI will reduce business or cause property damage.

4. Citizens who feel a PMI is threatening the safety of others in a public space.

Despite the consistent increase in the number of encounters between police and PMI, few law enforcement professionals are adequately trained to handle the gamut of situations that arise during these encounters. Some studies have found that as many as 50% of officers feel inadequately trained or even threatened by PMI in crisis. As a result, inadequate training can lead to a chaotic interaction—more than 50% of encounters between police and PMI result in an arrest in some jurisdictions (Kesic & Thomas, 2014). Psychologists are quick to note that PMI respond differently to environmental and interpersonal cues, ignoring standards of authority making force more likely. Kesic and Thomas (2014) however emphasize that the most common triggers for police using force to resolve a conflict with a PMI are alcohol impairment and the perception of irrationality.

Use of violence and force has been met with considerable public outcry and has prompted policy changes in departments across the United States. Although often inconsistent and inadequate, police training in mental illness can improve officers' self-confidence in dealing with mentally ill persons as well as outcomes for the PMI (Bonfine, Ritter, & Munetz, 2014). For this reason, some states now require police recruits to complete a training module on handling incidents involving people with mental illness during the basic academy. California, for example, requires recruits to receive a minimum of 6 hours of training in this area. Beyond that, 54% of departments in California voluntarily provide additional training on handling mental health crisis situations as part of officers' continuing education (Gardiner, 2015). While this is laudable, the extra training provided to officers by most agencies is a mere 1–4 hours every couple of years. It is, however, an improvement over previous years when patrol officers received no training whatsoever.

POLICE RESPONSE

Several traditional options exist to deal with PMI causing disturbances; however, many of these techniques have proved ineffective. With constitutional constraints on treating PMI without consent, police often find their hands tied especially when inadequate training is provided.

1. Hospitalization is frequently used when a PMI exhibits suicidal tendencies.

2. Arrest sometimes takes the form of a **mercy booking** in which an individual is arrested because better treatments exist while in custody than while living free. As with hospitalizations, arrested PMI often present a danger either to themselves or others.

3. Informal disposition or psychiatric first aid involves police attempting to diffuse a crisis situation without resorting to arrest. Often, these techniques require more advanced training.

Subsequent reforms have emphasized the creation of specialized procedures and protocols in dealing with calls involving a PMI. These protocols seek to provide officers with options—options that most often include guiding a PMI to seek mental health services as opposed to arrest. Specialized police-based responses involve advanced training for a subset of police officers responsible for responding to calls for service. These responses also require departments to hire (or collaborate with) mental health professionals to respond to calls involving a PMI with a duty officer. Finally, these responses generally dictate that the mental health professionals take the lead in dealing with PMI in crisis. Research has found that these specialized police-based responses are beneficial. Specifically, they have been found to increase linkages between PMIs and mental health treatment, reduce arrests of people with mental illness, reduce the stigmatization of individuals with mental illness, and increase time in the community for individuals with mental illness (Simpson, 2015).

Most innovative are so-called collaborative **Crisis Intervention Teams** (CIT) which incorporate emergency medical, police, and social service units trained to respond to calls involving PMI. Beginning in Memphis, Tennessee in 1988, the approach has proved both effective and popular. There are currently 2,956 CIT programs across the United States in every state but three (Alabama, Arkansas, and West Virginia) (CIT, n.d.). The goal of these crisis teams remains focused on keeping PMI out of prison and jail while allowing the resources accrued through cross-agency collaboration to triage PMI before taking them to a hospital, conducting an arrest, or using force. The result has been a reduction in the number of incidents involving deadly force and arrest with some studies even attributing an increase in officer confidence after receiving CIT training (Bonfine, Ritter, & Munetz, 2014). Unfortunately, the departments which have formed specialized units (CITs) to handle PMI calls are the exception, not the rule. As you can see in Figure 11.3, only 14% of law enforcement agencies in California have a designated team of trained officers that respond to mental health crisis calls. Most agencies in the state rely on patrol officers with standard (or no) training to handle these incidents. We expect that this situation is similar throughout the country, an assumption supported by the fact that there are approximately 3,000 CITs but 18,000 local police and sheriffs' departments in the United States.

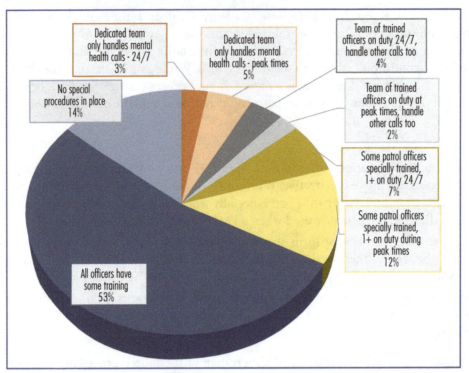

Figure 11.3 Mental health crisis response.

Source: Gardiner, C. (2015). The State of Education and Policing in California. Fullerton, CA: Center for Public Policy at California State University.

POLICING JUVENILES

Juveniles account for a disproportionate amount of crime perpetrators and victims relative to their size of the U.S. population. This is because offending peaks during the teenage years and drops in the early 20s. Although it is impossible to know the exact number of crimes committed by juveniles in the United States, we do know that police "arrested" 1.3 million youth under the age of 18 in 2012 (Puzzanchera, 2014). The vast majority of these were for minor crimes, including larceny/theft (224,000), misdemeanor assault (173,100), drug violations (140,000), disorderly conduct (120,100), liquor law violations (77,800), and curfew and loitering (70,200). In comparison, police arrested more than 7 million adults (FBI, 2014). As Figure 11.4 indicates, 71% of the juveniles taken into custody (arrested) were male, 72% were between 15 and 17 years old, and 65% were white (Puzzanchera, 2014). Between 2002 and 2012, the juvenile arrest rate declined by 37% while the adult arrest rate declined by a mere 4% (FBI, 2014). In fact, the 2012 juvenile arrest rate was the lowest it has been in at least 30 years. Self-report studies suggest that this represents a real crime decline (Males, 2015).

© Fotosenmeer/Shutterstock.com

A majority of juvenile arrests are for minor crimes.

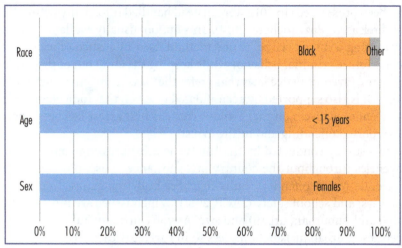

Figure 11.4 Juvenile Arrest Demographics, 2012

Even though juveniles are developmentally different than adults, police officers (for the most part) treat juveniles the same as adults. There are a few age-related legal distinctions between the two groups. For example, police must notify a parent/guardian when they take a juvenile into custody, but they generally do not need to tell them where or why the juvenile is being held. Furthermore, although the U.S. Supreme Court (U.S.S.C.) ruled in *J.D.B. v. North Carolina (2011)* that police must take a child's age and maturity into account when deciding whether a child is "in custody" and entitled to a Miranda warning, few states actually require juveniles to consult with a lawyer or parent before waiving their Miranda rights (Feld, 2013; IACP, 2012). This is problematic because, as you will learn in Chapter 12, juveniles are much more likely than adults to falsely confess to committing a crime under certain circumstances. The International Association of Chiefs of Police (IACP) recommended several best practices for interviewing juveniles, including encouraging the presence of a "friendly adult" and providing a simplified Miranda warning to juveniles that only requires a third-grade comprehension level (the typical warning requires a tenth-grade comprehension level) (IACP, 2012). Some police departments have implemented policies and procedures that provide juveniles extra protections, but in most states it is not required.

Additionally, the rules of search and seizure of juveniles on school grounds generally differ from the standard rules of search and seizure that apply to adults (and juveniles not on school grounds). On school grounds, school officials (and usually law enforcement officers) only need **reasonable suspicion,** not probable cause, to search a student's person, backpack, locker, and/or vehicle (*New Jersey v. TLO, 1985*). Note, many schools require students to sign agreements at the beginning of the school year that they will *consent* to a search of their locker at any time, for any reason; in this case, reasonable suspicion is not required because students consented to the search.

Another distinction is that, whereas an officer must witness an adult committing a misdemeanor in order to arrest him, an officer usually can take a juvenile into custody for committing a misdemeanor without personally witnessing the act. In fact, in most jurisdictions, a police officer can "arrest" a juvenile for a misdemeanor or felony without a warrant as long as the officer reasonably believes that the juvenile committed the crime. A law enforcement agency can pursue consequences against a juvenile even if she is not charged with a crime (this option does not exist for adults). This can include informal probation or other diversion programs (such as Teen Court) and means that a juvenile can be ordered to attend educational classes by a law enforcement agency without ever being petitioned in court. Approximately 22% of youth who were arrested (and could have been prosecuted) in 2012 were instead handled informally within the law enforcement agency and released (Puzzanchera, 2014). This option, usually available to first-time offenders caught committing a minor crime, is one method used by justice officials to admonish the offender and deter future criminal behavior while keeping the child out of the court. It is in keeping with many states' juvenile justice laws that prefer the "least restrictive alternative" when dealing with juveniles. It is also supported by accumulated research that indicates that the best course of action with juveniles is diversion that avoids arrest, as first arrest has been shown to increase subsequent self-reported offending and future arrest.

According to a survey conducted by the IACP, the most pressing youth issues affecting law enforcement agencies throughout the country are: substance abuse; physical, sexual, and emotional abuse; juvenile repeat offenders; bullying/cyber-bullying; gangs; Internet crimes involving youth; runaways; and school safety (IACP, 2011). Which issues are most concerning vary by agency location (rural, suburban, urban) and size. As you can see in Table 11.2, gangs are a major concern for agencies in urban jurisdictions, less so in rural jurisdictions.

Many, though not all, law enforcement agencies have personnel assigned specifically to juvenile operations. The larger the agency, the more likely it will have at least one dedicated juvenile unit. Eighty-two percent of police departments which employ at least 100 sworn officers have selected personnel who work with juveniles (59% of the agencies have full-time personnel assigned

TABLE 11.2   Top Youth Issues for Law Enforcement, by Jurisdiction

Youth Issue	Rural	Urban	Suburban
Abuse	71%	57%	56%
Substance abuse	70%	51%	75%
Juvenile repeat offenders	52%	53%	46%
Bullying/Cyberbullying	49%	43%	56%
Internet crimes involving youth	42%	29%	40%
School safety	40%	26%	42%
Runaways	33%	38%	40%
Juveniles with mental illness or other disabilities	30%	16%	19%
Truancy and drop outs	28%	30%	22%
Gangs	27%	62%	39%
Lack of positive police/youth interactions	19%	15%	18%
Crimes committed by or incidents involving adolescent girls	9%	13%	10%
Gun violence	7%	23%	8%
Increase in violence by children 11 and under	6%	5%	5%
Disproportionate minority contact	4%	8%	7%
Child trafficking	3%	7%	6%
Other	2%	6%	6%

Adapted from IACP. (2011, July). *Juvenile justice training needs assessment: A survey of law enforcement.* Tables 7–9. Alexandria, VA: IACP. Retrieved from http://www.iacpyouth.org/Portals/0/Content_Files/2011_Needs_Assessment_Report.pdf

to a special juvenile unit and another 23% have designated personnel who handle juveniles as part of their duties) (Reaves, 2015). On the other hand, only one-third of agencies with fewer than 100 sworn officers have personnel dedicated to juvenile crime (and most of these address it as part of their other duties, not as their sole duty). The most common specialized assignments are school resource officers (sworn officers assigned to work full-time in schools) and detectives assigned to investigate crimes committed against children or by children. Many agencies also have officers assigned to a gang unit, which deals with a mixture of juveniles and adults. Large school districts sometimes have their own police department, separate from the city police department.

The IACP has spearheaded a recent movement toward youth-focused policing (YFP), a proactive strategy that encourages police to intervene with youth to reduce and prevent delinquency, victimization, and prolonged involvement with the juvenile and criminal justice systems (see Figure 11.5 below). As part of their effort, they provide an online resource center that includes a clearinghouse of information related to youthful offenders and victims, sample documents and policies, training, and a searchable program directory of YFP programs and activities in use by departments across America.

> ## CHECK IT OUT!:
>
> You can find IACP's resource center and program directory here: http://www.iacpyouth.org/. What programs does your community offer?

The Effects of Adolescent Development on Policing 4

10 Strategies to Improve Law Enforcement Interactions with Youth

1. Approach youth with a calm demeanor, conveying that you are there to help them. Aggression may cause the youth to shut down and make the situation worse. Refrain from pushing back (arguing). If necessary, de-escalate using a calm, focused, and non-confrontational verbal approach. Use a nonjudgmental tone. Youth are particularly attune to both verbal and non-verbal judgment from adults.	**6. Repeat or paraphrase their statements. Affirm their emotions.** Seek clarity and understanding through the use of these three methods. *Repeating* what they say gives you a chance to confirm you heard what they said. *Paraphrasing* shows them you are listening. *Affirming* their emotions (e.g. You're frustrated with your parents) shows them genuine interest.
2. Establish rapport. Developing rapport is fundamental to successful youth interactions. They are not likely to open up if they feel unsupported or uncomfortable. Give them your undivided attention. Convey that you want to listen and can be trusted. Listen openly and non-judgmentally.	**7. Take caution with nonverbal communication.** Avoid challenging gestures. Approach youth in a natural manner, not actively seeking or avoiding eye contact. Don't demand eye contact. Convey your warmth over your authority. Get on their level (e.g. sit if they are sitting), lean in when listening, and hold your arms and body in a relaxed manner.
3. Be patient. Don't act hurried, like you don't have time to talk with the youth. Give the youth a chance to ask questions and be honest with your responses. Convey that you want to hear what they have to say. Give them a chance to explain what happened. Build in extra time to assess their emotions and to work around blocked thinking due to emotion.	**8. Model and praise calm confidence.** Adolescents seek validation and praise while acting indifferent towards it. They act confident, even when feeling self-doubt. They tend to be most calm and cooperative when provided with adult modeling and sincere praise for their ability to make good decisions.
4. Model the respect you expect in return. Avoid criticism and lecture. Refer to them by name as much as possible. Avoid correcting them or making statements that may communicate disrespect. You may lessen their aggression and defiance by demonstrating respect and support for their autonomy, views, and choices.	**9. Empower them through choices.** Adolescents need to feel they have choice and control over their thoughts and actions. They are sensitive to external influence and likely to feel coerced, even when there is no explicit effort to coerce them. Yet, they rely on others to validate their decisions. Provide them a range of options and explain their choices in simple terms. Give them a chance to ask questions.
5. Use age-appropriate language. Adolescents do not have adult capacity to organize thoughts. They may not fully understand what you tell them and may need time to process information. Keep it simple. Use open-ended questions and be prepared to help them sort out information. Don't expect a long attention span.	**10. Serve as a positive adult role model.** Positive relationships with adults are a vital component of healthy youth development. Develop programs in your agency that focus on positive youth development, such as mentoring, job skills training, and recreational programs.

Figure 11.5 IACP Recommended strategies to improve law enforcement interactions with youth

Reprinted from *The Affects of Adolescent Development on Policing*, page 4, 2015. Copyright held by the International Association of Chiefs of Police, Inc., 44 Canal Center Plaza, Ste 200, Alexandria, VA 22314. Further reproduction without express permission from IACP is strictly prohibited.

ZERO TOLERANCE, SRO'S, AND THE SCHOOL-TO-PRISON PIPELINE

Somewhere between four and five million 16–19-year-olds have contact with police each year (IACP, n.d.). Many of these contacts take place at school; and some involve suspension, expulsion, or formal criminal charges. This is referred to as the "school-to-prison pipeline" and describes the situation that has evolved over the past 30 years whereby school officials increasingly refer students' school misbehavior to law enforcement officials for formal criminal prosecution and processing, thereby introducing and exposing students to the criminal justice system early in their lives. A key component of the school-to-prison pipeline is the presence of police officers on school campuses across America. This path from classroom misbehavior to prison is particularly pronounced for minority children from disadvantaged backgrounds (Amurao, 2013; Fader et al., 2015). By and large, this pipeline was created by zero-tolerance policies and exacerbated by the increase of school resource officers (Fader et al., 2015; Price, 2009).

Zero-tolerance policies became very popular in the 1990s in response to rising crime (in general) and a prediction that juveniles would develop into "super-predators" (DiIlulio, 1995; Fadar et al., 2015). By 2000, 90% of schools had at least one zero-tolerance policy that required suspension, expulsion, or criminal charges for violation of a school policy (Fadar et al., 2015). If you graduated high school recently, you are probably familiar with these policies and the serious repercussions that can result from a violation.

Combined with these zero-tolerance policies was a dramatic increase in police officers on school campuses, in particular after the 1999 Columbine High School shooting. In 2004, more than 70% of students between the ages of 12 and 18 reported having police at their school; this represented a 30% increase from only 5 years earlier (Price, 2009). Together, these two factors led to an increase in the number of students arrested (rather than sent to the principal's office) for school misbehavior (Fader et al., 2015). For instance, the number of student arrests in Clayton County, GA increased 600% in the 3 years after they hired SRO's (Fader et al., 2015). This is not atypical and other research (Dohrn, 2001; Johnson, 1999; Theriot, 2009) has documented similar patterns across the country. Not unexpectedly, the impact is disproportionately felt by Black and Latino students who are suspended, expelled, referred to law enforcement, and arrested at much higher rates than their white peers (USDOE-OCR, 2014).

Unfortunately, there are severe consequences for juveniles referred to the criminal justice system for school misbehavior, including falling behind academically, lower attachment to school and friends, a greater likelihood of dropping out of school, not graduating, and ending up in prison. Furthermore, students who live in communities which rely heavily on SRO's demonstrate less respect for police and are less likely to be "scared straight" by officers outside of school (Price, 2009). Although juvenile arrests have been decreasing for many years now, it appears that a fair percentage of juvenile arrests are due to students' misbehavior at school. Thus, how schools and law enforcement choose to deal with adolescent misbehavior in school is very important. The more student misbehavior that is handled by the school (rather than law enforcement), the better it is for the students and their future.

POLICING GANGS

What is a gang? The public conceptualization of a gang is perhaps more informed by popular portrayals in Hollywood movies than in the reality behind them. In truth, there is no single, generally accepted definition of a "gang," and each jurisdiction is left to create its own definition. Still, practitioners commonly use the following criteria to classify groups as a gang.

1. Three or more members

2. A common sign, symbol, or name

3. Ongoing group or organization (the group has some permanence)

4. Members engage in a pattern of criminal activity, either individually or collectively

Media portrayals, police statements, and popular imagery give the illusion that gangs are highly organized networks of crime and disorder, yet these groups are far less centralized than these reports suggest. Unlike prison gangs, terrorist gangs, motorcycle gangs, and criminal gangs (a.k.a. organized crime), which tend to have much greater levels of organization and a sophisticated and strong leadership structure, street gangs (sometimes called youth or neighborhood gangs) generally are loosely structured with transitory leaders and members. Though many street gangs operate drug sales and prostitution rings, few meet the criteria to be classified as "organized crime."

Gangs in the United States are organized and draw members largely along ethnic lines. Black and Hispanic gangs are both territorial; they are relatively similar in structure but have some unique differences, for instance, Hispanic gangs are typically multigenerational. Most Asian/Pacific Islander gangs are nonterritorial (Filipino gangs are a common exception) and well organized. White gangs (sometimes called "skinheads") are not territorial and are often categorized as "hate groups" rather than gangs in recognition of the fact that they are generally organized around racial issues and commit crimes in furtherance of their racist beliefs. Of course, you may know of gangs in your area that do not fit the above descriptions; this is because gangs vary regionally.

Gang scholars and police investigators define four levels of gang members with stratified involvement in the gang's organization. "Hardcores" are the most involved and violent actors in a gang and seek to use whatever means possible to defend the honor of the gang. "Associates" never achieve full membership and may have misgivings about the actions of the group, but see membership as a means of gaining social prestige in the community. "Peripherals" are the least integrated in the gang hierarchy, joining simply for protection. The final group comprises the "wannabes" who never kill for the sake of the gang and as such are viewed as inferior by the "hardcores." These groupings can vary with gang type—for example, in Hispanic gangs, the more relevant categories are "veteranos"—the long-time gang members and shot callers, "soldiers"—who do much of the work, and "youngsters"—the new kids who want to prove themselves to the gang.

GANG PREVALENCE

Modern gang violence began in southern California in the early-twentieth century, which might help explain why California, in particular southern California, is considered the gang capital of the United States, if not the world (Brown, 2014). From there gangs moved east and migrated to other large cities like Chicago and New York first and then to suburban counties and eventually to rural counties (Klein, 1995). According to the latest National Youth Gang Survey (NYGS), which collects data from law enforcement agencies across the country, there were approximately 30,700 street gangs and 850,000 gang members in the United States in 2012 (NGC, 2014). While

TABLE 11.3 Distribution of Gang Members

Gang Member Distribution	Larger Cities	Suburban Counties	Smaller Cities	Rural Counties
% of all gang members reside in	57.3%	24.4%	15.6%	2.7%
# of gang members in Jurisdiction				
No data reported	6.0%	23.0%	19.5%	26.1%
Fewer than 25	6.7%	15.8%	28.2%	27.5%
25–50	7.2%	11.5%	26.3%	23.2%
51–100	12.1%	9.8%	11.5%	9.4%
101–250	19.5%	11.1%	9.5%	10.1%
251–500	16.5%	11.7%	4.2%	3.6%
501–1000	13.0%	6.8%	0.8%	0.0%
1001–2500	10.4%	5.7%	0.0%	0.0%
More than 2500	8.6%	4.7%	0.0%	0.0%

Adapted from National Gang Center. (2014). *2012 National Youth Gang Survey Analysis.* Retrieved [date] from http://www.nationalgangcenter.gov/Survey-Analysis.

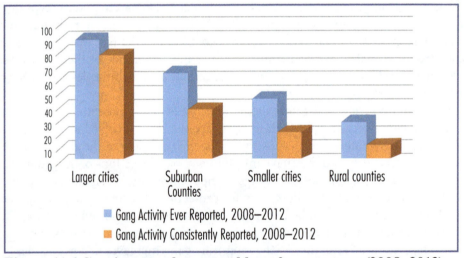

Figure 11.6 Consistency of gang problems by area type (2008–2012).

Adapted from National Gang Center. (2014). 2012National Youth Gang Survey Analysis. Retrieved [date] from http://www.nationalgangcenter.gov/Survey-Analysis.

there has been much fluctuation in the past 20 years, these numbers are almost identical to those from 1996 (when there were 846,500 reported gang members in 30,800 gangs). As you might imagine, a large proportion of gang members (57%) live in larger cities (see Table 11.3). One-third of larger cities (and 17% of suburban counties) reported more than 500 gang members in their jurisdiction. In comparison, less than 1% of smaller cities and no rural counties reported more than 500 gang members. On the contrary, 28% of smaller cities and rural counties reported fewer than 25 gang members. This indicates that gangs, and the associated problems, are concentrated in specific places and differ accordingly.

TABLE 11.4 Demographics of Gang Members

Gang Member Characteristics	Larger Cities	Suburban Counties	Smaller Cities	Rural Counties
Race				
Black/African American	39.0%	32.7%	20.3%	56.8%
Hispanic/Latino	45.5%	51.0%	53.8%	24.8%
White	9.7%	9.1%	14.6%	14.9%
Other	5.8%	7.2%	11.3%	3.4%
Age				
Juvenile (less than 18)	32.6%	36.7%	48.0%	58.9%
Adult (18 or older)	67.4%	63.3%	52.0%	41.1%
Sex				
% Gangs with female members	22.8%	45.3%	43.0%	49.5%

Adapted from National Gang Center. (2014). *2012 National Youth Gang Survey Analysis.* Retrieved from http://www.nationalgangcenter.gov/Survey-Analysis.

In 2012, over 3,100 jurisdictions reported gang problems, representing 30% of all jurisdictions in the nation (NGC, 2014). This is a decrease from 1996 when 40% of jurisdictions reported gang problems. Interestingly, having a gang problem one year does not mean that the jurisdiction will "forever more" have a gang problem. As indicated in Figure 11.6, a good percentage of jurisdictions do not have durable (long-lasting) gang problems. This provides optimism that law enforcement can have an impact on gang issues.

DEMOGRAPHICS OF GANG MEMBERS

The NYGS reports that 46% of gang members in the United States are Hispanic/Latino, 35% are Black/African American, 11.5% are white, and 7% are another race/ethnicity (NGC, 2014). These percentages are virtually unchanged since 1996. As you might expect, ethnic breakdowns vary by jurisdiction (see Table 11.4). According to law enforcement, females account for roughly 7% of all gang members; academics say it's somewhere between 20% and 46% (Hagedorn & Chesney-Lind, 2014; NGC, 2014). Approximately 45% of gangs have female members (in all jurisdiction types except larger cities where only 23% of gangs have female members). Contrary to popular beliefs, law enforcement reports that most gang members (65%) are over the age of 18 (NGC, 2014). In every type of jurisdiction except rural counties, adult gang members outnumber juveniles. Once again, academic research finds that gang members are younger than police records indicate. These discrepancies are due to several factors, including the fact that the average age (and sex) reported is a function of the samples—youth surveyed by academic researchers vs. youth who come into contact with law enforcement.

Although only a small number of youth join a gang (8% nationally, as much as 15% in some urban cities), those that do commit a lot of crime—especially violent crime. Research shows that juveniles commit more crime while they are in a gang than either before they join a gang or after they leave a gang. For example, one meta-analysis found that gang members (who comprised 15–30% of the sample) self-reported committing 65–85% of all violent offenses reported.

Fortunately, most youth do not remain in a gang for very long (1–2 years on average). Surprisingly, less than 1% of gang members remain in a gang for 4 or more years, and the vast majority of kids who live in disadvantaged areas do not join a gang (NGC, 2014).

RISK FACTORS FOR GANG MEMBERSHIP

Given the tremendous amount of crime that gang members commit while they are in the gang, understanding what drives youth to join gangs allows law enforcement and others to fashion programs to prevent or interrupt gang membership. Based on many studies with gang members, researchers have found that youth are "pulled" and/or "pushed" into a gang. *Pulls* are internal characteristics of the gang that are attractive to youth, such as friendship; increased reputation; cultural, family, or neighborhood pride; the promise of power, money, drugs, or excitement; or belonging to a "family." *Pushes* are the opposite; they are external factors that make the gang look attractive. For example, a youth joins a gang for protection from neighborhood crime or bullies, because he fears the consequences of not joining, or because he has a highly stressful home life or feels ignored. Although a youth can be simultaneously pulled and pushed into a gang, most youth report being "pulled" into a gang. Thus, programs and strategies that make gangs look less attractive by (1) disrupting the gang pulls (suppressing gang activities and breaking the bonds between members), (2) pulling the youth into an alternative, prosocial activity (youth–adult mentoring, sports), or (3) eliminating the pushes (provide more supervision and adult leadership to provide more protection; change the environment, reduce victimization) could be successful. It is important to remember that the decision to join a gang is generally a gradual process—it does not happen "overnight," it happens "over time."

There are many **risk factors** that increase the likelihood that a youth will join a gang. The six most consistently supported risk factors for joining a gang are (Maxson, 2011):

1. Critical life events (a serious injury or illness, disruption in intimate social relationship—divorce or death, for example)
2. Nondelinquent problem behaviors (risk taking, impulsivity, antisocial tendencies)
3. Delinquent beliefs (acceptance of antisocial behavior)
4. Weak parental monitoring
5. Peer delinquency
6. Negative peer influence

See Figure 11.7 for a list of some of the other risk factors. Keep in mind that having a single risk factor is not important. What is important is the *accumulation* of risk factors. There is no single risk factor that will cause a youth to join a gang. However, youth who have many risk factors are *more likely* to join a gang. On the flip side, **protective factors** can actually decrease the likelihood that a youth will join a gang.

GANG CRIME

There is some debate regarding what should be counted as gang crime—is it any crime committed by a member of the gang or does the crime need to be committed on behalf of, or in furtherance of, the gang to count. The answer to this question depends on the jurisdiction and sometimes the actual crime. This is one of the reasons that gang crime is impossible to count accurately. Most agencies record homicide and graffiti as "gang related" but there is much less consensus on all the other crimes (NGC, 2014). In many jurisdictions, sentencing laws (specifically gang enhancements) dictate which crimes get counted as "gang crime." Less than one-third

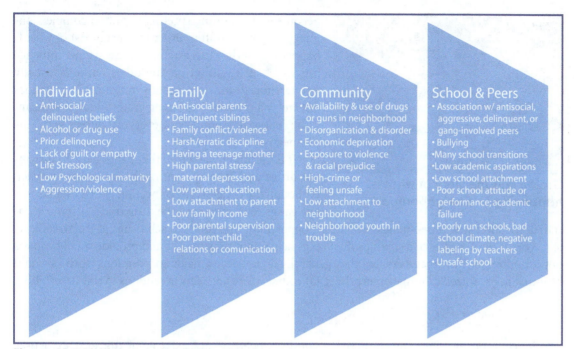

Figure 11.7 Risk Factors for Gang Membership

Source: Office of Juvenile Justice and Delinquency Prevention (OJJDP). (n.d.). *Strategic Planning Tool, Risk Factors*. Retrieved from https://www.nationalgangcenter.gov/SPT/Risk-Factors

of agencies record robbery, aggravated assault, firearms use, burglary, motor vehicle theft, larceny/theft, or drug sales as gang-related. Thus, we know very little about how much gang crime really exists and whether it has increased or decreased in recent years.

It might be useful to note that gang crime entails both instrumental crimes and expressive crimes. *Instrumental crimes* are crimes that are committed for an economic purpose (robbery, drug sales, fraud, prostitution, etc.). *Expressive crimes*, on the other hand, are crimes that are committed in response to someone else's action, generally in response to an ongoing conflict or rivalry between gangs (shooting in response to perceived disrespect). Research confirms that the motive for gang violence is most often expressive, not instrumental (NGC, 2014).

Law enforcement agencies reported 2,363 gang-related homicides in 2012 to the NYGS; most of these were in larger cities (NGC, 2014). Combined with UCR data (which shows 14,827 murders for the same time period), this suggests that approximately 15% of homicides in America were likely gang-related. In some areas, the percentage is much higher. For example, in Chicago and Los Angeles, the two major "gang capitals," 50% of all homicides were gang-related in 2012. Moreover, these two cities together accounted for 25% of all gang-related homicides reported to NYGS in 2011 and 2012. This demonstrates that gang violence is significantly concentrated in the largest cities in the United States. Further, law enforcement agencies have reported steady or increasing numbers of gang-related homicides in the past several years, a trend that is opposite to the national homicide trend. This provides further evidence that the "urban homicide problem" is really a "gang homicide problem" (NGC, 2014).

Graffiti, which should not be confused with tagging, is a visual reminder of gang activity and is relatively easy to attribute to gang members. Different strokes provide information on the gang claiming a given territory and their relationship with other gangs. **Gang graffiti** is often described as the "newspaper of the streets." It tells the story of what is happening in a neighborhood—it announces peace deals as well as threats, challenges, and declarations of war. For this reason, officers

Graffiti tells the story of what is happening in a neighborhood.

become experts in interpreting the often complex language of gang graffiti in order to stay abreast of what is happening so they can attempt to thwart any impending violence. **Tagging**, on the other hand, is usually not territorial and is generally more artistic; it does not "relay a message" like gang graffiti does. It is meant to be "enjoyed," though not everyone agrees with this perspective.

It is commonly asserted that gangs exist to distribute drugs and thereby control the local drug market. Although the drug–gang connection is well established, few gangs revolve around the drug trade. A more accurate description would be—gangs provide an opportunity for youth to sell drugs at the street level (e.g., corner boys) and earn a small profit. Gangs help establish networks and provide small business opportunities for their members, but they generally do not act as major corporations (such as would be found in organized criminal enterprises). Of course, there are a few exceptions to this description.

POLICE RESPONSE TO GANG CRIME

Police responses center on the activities of the *gang unit*—at least a single officer who focuses on gang control and violence prevention. Cities have increased the number of specialized gang units in the past decades. Eighty percent of police department with 100 or more sworn officers and 20% of agencies with fewer than 100 sworn officers have dedicated gang officers (Reaves, 2015). Some agencies also have officers assigned to a multi-agency gang taskforce. Approaches for dealing with gang members and gang crime fall into three categories—prevention, intervention, and suppression, each of which is described below.

Prevention and Intervention There are three levels of prevention programs. **Primary gang prevention** programs are aimed at youth in general with a goal of keeping youth from joining a gang. These programs are given to an entire "population" without determining which youth are at elevated risk for gang joining. For example, an SRO (School Resource Officer) talks to all elementary children in a school district about the dangers of gangs, or the police department films anti-gang public service announcements which are played in schools or on television. Most Police Athletic League and Explorer programs would also fit here. Due to the nature of these programs, they are generally not very effective at reducing gang involvement (or delinquency); however, they are inexpensive and can reach a large number of youth with minimal to moderate effort and may have other benefits (such as improved public perception of and cooperation with police). It should be noted that there are some primary prevention strategies, such as Communities That Care (CTC), that are very comprehensive and highly effective.

Secondary gang prevention programs target youth at an elevated risk of gang joining—for example, a gang prevention program such as Gang Resistance Education and Training (GREAT) for youth in a gang neighborhood or an adult–youth mentorship program like Big Brothers/Big Sisters (BB/BS) if targeted appropriately. The GREAT program is the most prominent example of this category. It is considered a "promising program" on crimesolutions.gov and a large study (with a very strong research design) showed that it can moderately reduce gang membership as well as improve pro-social attitudes (Esbensen et al., 2012). Programs at this level are more involved than primary prevention strategies and the most effective programs are usually focused on specific outcomes related to the identified risk and protective factors for gang membership. BB/BS is another promising/effective program that has been shown to reduce some of the risk factors for gang joining and increase the presence/strength of some of the protective factors.

Tertiary **prevention programs** are intervention programs for youth already involved in gangs. These programs aim to reduce the time youth are in a gang and/or the crime they commit while in a gang. Chicago's Ceasefire program is one such example which reduced the number of gang shootings and retaliatory gang homicides (it should not be confused with Boston's Operation Ceasefire which was a pulling levers approach). The program in Chicago used community mobilization and public education campaigns, outreach workers, community partners who provided a variety of educational, job, and other services, and "violence interrupters" who mediated conflicts between gangs (Skogan, et al., 2009).

Suppression Gang **suppression** programs, which exist to reactively challenge the dominance of gangs within the community, are based on deterrence and rational choice theories which assert that individuals choose to join a gang and commit crime because the benefits outweigh the costs. The programs are focused on the arrest, prosecution, and incarceration of gang members, and police agencies play a major role. Some examples of gang suppression strategies include specialized gang units, vertical prosecution programs, truancy and curfew enforcement, metal detectors in schools, increased surveillance, and targeted crackdowns. Vertical prosecution is a program whereby police, prosecutors, and probation officers work together as a single team to improve criminal justice system efficiency and effectiveness during investigation, prosecution, and sentencing. Other examples, described below, include **civil gang injunctions** (CGI) and **pulling levers** programs. With few exceptions, gang suppression strategies are not highly effective at reducing gang crime or membership beyond the initial implementation period.

CGI have become the most prominent technique in this category. CGIs target territorial gangs. They take the form of "safety zones," which are court-ordered restrictions on where and when an individual or group can hang out with the hopes of squashing group identity (Papachristos, 2013). Injunctions, which are based on the premise that gangs constitute a "public nuisance," prohibit named gang members from being in particular places, at particular times, with any other individuals named in the injunction and from engaging in prohibited activities (including some normally legal activities such as wearing gang clothing or carrying markers) (Brown, 2014).

While increasingly popular, CGIs have faced considerable legal challenges particularly from civil rights groups who argue that such restrictions constrain constitutional freedom of association and travel (Hennigan & Sloane, 2013; Melde, 2013). As the name implies, CGIs are civil orders (like the banishment orders we discussed in Chapter 10), which means that violations can be prosecuted in civil or criminal court. If prosecuted in civil court, the defendant is not entitled to an attorney (unless they are already on probation) and the burden of proof is "a preponderance of the evidence;" however, the maximum penalty is usually a fine or a few days in jail. Alternatively, if prosecuted in criminal court, a defendant is entitled to an attorney, the burden of proof is "beyond a reasonable doubt," and penalties can include a fine and up to 6 months in jail. The main deterrent benefit of CGIs comes from the gang members knowing they are being watched and are subject to court action for violation.

The research on CGIs is limited and ambiguous (Esbensen, 2013). A few studies have found short-term violence reduction results in the 12 months after the injunction while others have found an increase in gang presence, disorder, and victimization (Brown, 2014). The difference between the effects may be in implementation—when the group feels threatened, the CGI serves to *increase* group cohesion (and crime) rather than decrease it (Hennigan & Sloane, 2013; Papachristos, 2013). To avoid increasing cohesion, researchers stress the importance of intervention over suppression in enforcing CGIs and focusing efforts on targeted individuals within the gang rather than the gang as a whole (these approaches have the most positive benefits).

Pulling Levers This comprehensive suppression/intervention strategy was introduced in Chapter 10, but is covered in greater depth here. This strategy is based on the belief that conflict between gangs over mutual disrespect is the predominant reason for violence. It threatens gang members with heavy legal consequences if violence continues and simultaneously offers substantial social services for gang members (and their families) who refrain from violence. The Boston Operation Ceasefire experiment presents the most cited example of such a program. Beginning in the mid-1990s, the Boston program emphasized zero tolerance for gang activity and threatened to increase enforcement of minor offenses within a gang community if violence continued. Partnering organizations such as churches and social service agencies continued to offer services, but were instructed to stress that ceasing violent activity would bring an end to heightened enforcement. Initial estimates of effectiveness were staggering—63% decrease in youth homicides. Subsequent studies have lowered these estimates while still attributing significant success (31% reduction in total shootings) to the program (Braga, Hureau & Papachristos, 2013). It is considered an "effective" program and some have argued that similar programs should be emphasized over the more popular CGIs due to the limited opportunity for litigation (Melde, 2013).

As you can see, there are a wide variety of programs and strategies that can be employed by law enforcement and others to respond to and reduce gang crime. Crimesolutions.gov provides information on several research-tested and approved strategies. The IACP youth-focused policing Web site provides a plethora of innovative, but mostly untested, programs implemented by law enforcement agencies. The National Gang Center, in conjunction with the Office of Juvenile Justice and Delinquency Prevention, also publishes information about research-validated programs to reduce the risk factors associated with gang joining and the incidence of crime by gang members. It can be found at: https://www.nationalgangcenter.gov/SPT/Program-Matrix. The key to reducing gang violence is to focus on disrupting the specific mechanisms that lead youth to join gangs and/or commit crime while in the gang.

CONCLUSION

In this chapter, we covered some of the special populations that police encounter on a regular basis and why they each pose a unique challenge to law enforcement. Police officers acting according to democratic policing principles must be respectful and exercise discretion in ways that enhance procedural justice for all members of the public. This sometimes requires special procedures and training and usually requires extra patience (and empathy) when dealing with individuals experiencing homelessness and/or mental illness and juveniles. As discussed in the chapter, the most successful strategies for handling these populations are responses that avoid arrest or further criminal justice involvement and link individuals to appropriate programs (such as education, life skills, or treatment) while the best responses to gang members are those that decrease gang involvement and/or reduce the time that an individual is in a gang.

REVIEW QUESTIONS

1. How does policing individuals experiencing homelessness differ from policing individuals with shelter?
2. How is policing individuals with severe mental illness unique to the general population?
3. What is the school-to-prison pipeline and what roles do school resource officers and zero-tolerance policies play in it?

4. How do police respond differently to juveniles than adults?

5. What are the top youth issues identified by law enforcement officers?

6. Approximately how many gangs and gang members are there in the United States? Where are they located?

7. How do police respond to gangs? Are there any established best practices?

GLOSSARY

Civil gang injunctions a police suppression program that involves getting a court order to prohibit gang members from being in particular places, with specifically named people, and/or engaging in specified prohibited activities.

Crisis intervention team (CIT) specially trained officers who responded to mental-health related calls.

Gang graffiti words, numbers, and symbols that provide information on the gang claiming a given territory and their relationship with other gangs; considered to be the "newspaper of the streets."

Mercy booking arresting an individual for the purpose of accessing services (for example, food, shelter, medical care, treatment).

Primary prevention prevention programs that target an entire population without discerning which individuals are at elevated risk of committing criminal activity.

Protective factor biological, psychological, family, social, and environment factors that decrease the risk that an individual will commit delinquent/criminal acts.

Pulling levers A suppression/intervention strategy that threatens gang members with heavy legal consequences if they engage in violence and simultaneously offers social services to gang members who refrain from violence.

Reasonable suspicion a reasonable belief, based on objective factors and officer experience, that a crime has been or is about to be committed; it is the standard of proof that is necessary for officers to stop a suspect and/or conduct a search.

Risk factor biological, psychological, family, social, and environmental factors that put an individual at increased risk of committing delinquent/criminal acts.

School-to-prison pipeline the term used to describe the trend of school officials referring student misbehavior to law enforcement officers for formal criminal justice system processing, rather than traditional school discipline.

School resources officer (SRO) a sworn police officer assigned to a school or set of schools as part of his/her normal duties to act as a liaison and address student misbehavior and criminal behavior.

Secondary prevention Prevention programs that target individuals deemed to be at an elevated risk of committing criminal activity.

Suppression programs aimed at reducing the influence of gangs in a community.

Tagging artistically painted pictures, words, and symbols generally considered to be vandalism but which are usually intended to be enjoyed as art by the "artist"; it is often confused with gang graffiti.

Tertiary prevention intervention programs that target individuals already engaged in repeated or serious delinquency.

REFERENCES

Amurao, C. (2013). Fact sheet: How bad is the school-to-prison pipeline? Prepared for Travis Smiley Reports, Episode 6: Education under arrest. PBS. Retrieved from http://www.pbs.org/wnet/tavissmiley/tsr/education-under-arrest/school-to-prison-pipeline-fact-sheet/

Berk, R., & MacDonald, J. (2010).Policing the homeless: An evaluation of efforts to reduce homelessness-related crime. *Criminology & Public Policy, 9*(4).

Bonfine, N., Ritter, C., & Munetz, M. (2014). Police officer perceptions of the impact of crisis intervention team (CIT) programs. *International Journal of Law and Psychiatry, 37,* 341–350. doi: 10.1016/j.ijlp.2014.02.004

Braga, A., Hureau, D., & Papachristos, A. (2013). Deterring gang-involved gun violence: measuring the impact of Boston's operation ceasefire on street gang behavior. *Journal of Quantitative Criminology, 30,* 113–139. doi: 10.1007/s10940-013-9198-x.

Brown, G. (2014). Gangs and the California Criminal Justice System. In C. Gardiner & P. Fiber-Ostrow (Eds.), *California's criminal justice system* (2nd ed.). Durham, NC: Carolina Academic Press.

Crisis Intervention Team (CIT). (n.d.). Homepage. Retrieved from http://cit.memphis.edu/

DiLulio, J. (1995, November 27). The coming of the super-predators. *The Weekly Standard.* Retrieved from http://www.weeklystandard.com/Content/Protected/Articles/000/000/007/011vsbrv.asp

Dohrn, B. (2002). The school, the child, the court. In M. K. Rosenheim, F. E. Zimring, D. S. Tanenhaus, & B. Dohrn (Eds.), *A century of juvenile justice* (pp. 267–309). Chicago, IL: Chicago University Press.

Esbensen, F. (2013). Civil gang injunctions. *Criminology & Public Policy, 12*(1), doi: 10.1111/1745-9133.12007

Esbensen, F., Peterson, D., Taylor, T. J., & Osgood, D. W. (2012). Results from a multisite evaluation of the G.R.E.A.T. program. *Justice Quarterly, 29*(1), 125–151. doi: 10.1080/07418825.2011.585995

Fader, J. J., Lockwood, B., Schall, V. L., & Stokes, B. (2015). A promising new approach to narrowing the school-to-prison pipeline: The WISE arrest diversion program. *Youth Violence and Juvenile Justice, 13*(2), 123–142. doi: 10.1177/1541204014521249

Federal Bureau of Investigations (FBI). (2014). *Uniform Crime Reports Ten Year Arrest Trends 2003-2012*. Retrieved from https://www.fbi.gov/about-us/cjis/ucr/crime-in-the-u.s/2012/crime-in-the-u.s.-2012/tables/32tabledatadecoverviewpdf

Feld, B. (2013). Kids, cops, and confessions: Inside the interrogation room. New York: New York University Press.

Frazier, B., Sung, H., Gideon, L., & Alfaro, K. (2015). The impact of prison deinstitutionalization on community treatment services. *Health and Justice, 3*(9). doi 10.1186/s40352-015-0021-7

Gardiner, C. (2015). *The state of education and policing in California*. Fullerton: Center for Public Policy at California State University.

Hagedorn, J., & Chesney-Lind, M. (2014). America's "war on gang:" Response to a real threat or a moral panic? In S. Mallicoat & C. Gardiner (Eds.), *Criminal Justice Policy*. Thousand Oaks, CA: Sage.

Harcourt, B. (2005). Policing L.A.'s Skid Row: Crime and real estate redevelopment in Downtown Los Angeles [An experiment in real time]. *The University of Chicago Legal Forum*, 325–403.

Hennigan, K., & Sloane, D. (2013). Improving civil gang injunctions: how implementation can affect gang dynamics, crime, and violence. *Criminology & Public Policy, 12*(1), doi: 10.1111/1745-9133.12000

International Association of Chiefs of Police (IACP). (2011, July). *Juvenile justice training needs assessment: A survey of law enforcement*. Tables 7-9. Alexandria, VA: IACP. Retrieved from http://www.iacpyouth.org/Portals/0/Content_Files/2011_Needs_Assessment_Report.pdf

International Association of Chiefs of Police (IACP). (2012, September). *Reducing risks: An executive's guide to effective juvenile interview and interrogation*. Alexandria, VA: IACP. Retrieved from http://www.theiacp.org/Portals/0/pdfs/ReducingRisksAnExecutive-GuidetoEffectiveJuvenileInterviewandInterrogation.pdf

International Association of Chiefs of Police (IACP). (2014). *Effects of adolescent development on policing*. Promising Practice Briefs Alexandria, VA: IACP. Retrieved from http://www.theiacp.org/Portals/0/documents/pdfs/IACPBriefEffectsofAdolescentDevelopmentonPolicing.pdf

Johnson, M. (1999). School violence: The effectiveness of a school resource officer program in a southern city. *Journal of Criminal Justice, 27*, 173–192.

Kesic, D., & Thomas, S. (2014). Do prior histories of violence and mental disorders impact on violent behavior during encounters with police? *International Journal of Law and Psychiatry, 37*, 409–414. doi: 10.1016/j.ijlp.2014.02.012

Klein, M. (1995). *The American street gang*. New York, NY: Oxford University Press.

Lane, M. (2014). *Social welfare: Fighting poverty and homelessness*. Detroit, MI: Gale Cengage Learning.

Lord, V., & Bjerregaard, B. (2014). Helping persons with mental illness: Partnerships between police and mobile crisis units. *Victims & Offenders: An International Journal of Evidence-based Research, Policy, & Practice, 9*(4), 455–474. doi 10.1080/15564886.2013.878263

Males, M. (2015, May). The plummeting arrest rates of California's children. CJCJ Research Report. Retrieved from http://www.cjcj.org/

Manning, P. (1977). *Police work: The social organization of policing* (2nd ed.). Prospect Heights, IL: Waveland Press.

Maxson, C. (2011). Street gangs. In J.Q. Wilson and J. Petersilia (Eds.), *Crime and public policy.* New York, NY: Oxford University Press.

Melde, C. (2013). The practicalities of targeted gang interventions. *Criminology & Public Policy, 12*(1). doi: 10.1111/1745-9133.12004

National Alliance to End Homelessness (NAEH). (2015, April). *The state of homelessness in America 2015.* Retrieved from http://www.endhomelessness.org/

National Gang Center (NGC). (2014). *2012 National Youth Gang Survey Analysis.* Retrieved from http://www.nationalgangcenter.gov/Survey-Analysis.

National Law Center on Homeless & Poverty (NLCHP). (2014, December). *No safe place: The criminalization of homelessness in U.S. cities.* Retrieved from http://www.nlchp.org

Office of Juvenile Justice and Delinquency Prevention (OJJDP). (n.d.). *Strategic planning tool, risk factors.* Retrieved from https://www.nationalgangcenter.gov/SPT/Risk-Factors

Office of Juvenile Justice and Delinquency Prevention (OJJDP). (2014, December 16). *OJJDP statistical briefing book.* Online. Retrieved from http://www.ojjdp.gov/ojstatbb/crime/qa05101.asp?qaDate=2012.

Papachristos, A. (2013). The importance of cohesion for gang research, policy, and practice. *Criminology & Public Policy, 12*(1). doi: 10.1111/1745-9133.12006

Price, P. (2009). When is a police officer an officer of the law? The status of police officers in schools. *The Journal of Criminal Law and Criminology, 99*(2), 541–570. doi: 0091-4169/09/9902-0541

Puzzanchera, C. (2014, December). *Juvenile Arrests 2012.* Juvenile Offenders and Victims National Report Series. Washington, DC: Office of Juvenile Justice and Delinquency Prevention (OJJDP). Retrieved from http://www.ojjdp.gov/pubs/248513.pdf

Reaves, B. (2015, May). *Local police departments, 2013.* Bureau of Justice Statistics. Washington, DC: U.S. Government Printing Office.

Simpson, J. (2015). Police and homeless outreach worker partnerships: Policing of homeless individuals with mental illness in Washington, D.C. *Human Organization, 74*(2), 125–134. doi: 0018-7259/15/020125-10$1.50/1

Skogan, W., Hernett, S., Bump, N., & Dubois, J. (2009). *Evaluation of CeaseFire Chicago.* Retrieved from http://skogan.org/files/Evaluation_of_CeaseFire-Chicago_Main_Report.03-2009.pdf

Stuart, F. (2013). From 'rabble management' to 'recovery management': Policing homelessness in marginal urban space. *Urban Studies, 51*(9), 1909–1925. doi: 10.1177/0042098013499798

Theriot, M. T. (2009). School resource officers and the criminalization of student behavior. *Journal of Criminal Justice, 37*(3), 280–287. doi: 10.1016/j.jcrimjus.2009.04.008

United States Department of Education Office for Civil Rights (USDOE-OCR). (2014, March). *Civil Rights Data Collection data snapshot: School discipline.* Issue Brief No. 1. Retrieved from http://ocrdata.ed.gov/Downloads/CRDC-School-Discipline-Snapshot.pdf

United States Conference of Mayors (USCM). (2014, December). *Hunger and homelessness survey: A status report on hunger and homelessness in America's cities.* Retrieved from http://usmayors.org/pressreleases/uploads/2013/1210-report-HH.pdf

COURT CASES

J.D.B. v. North Carolina, 131 S. Ct. 2394 (2011).

New Jersey v. TLO, 1985.

12 INVESTIGATIONS AND INTERROGATIONS

LEARNING OBJECTIVES

After reading this chapter, students should be able to:

1 Recount the history of investigations.

2 Describe the basic structure of the typical detective unit.

3 Explain the investigative process, including the preliminary investigation and secondary investigation.

4 Explain the main types of evidence.

5 Name three cases that govern police searches and the importance of each.

6 Describe how forensic scientists evaluate the evidence and the available federal databases that assist in suspect identification.

7 Differentiate a police interview from an interrogation.

8 Describe typical suspect interrogations.

9 Explain the legal rules governing police questioning.

10 Discuss the problem of false confessions and name the practices that lead to false confessions.

11 Identify four ways that detectives can prevent false confessions.

12 Name at least five recommendations offered by IACP to reduce wrongful convictions.

KEY TERMS

Preliminary investigation

Secondary investigation

Clearance rate

Physical evidence

Digital evidence

Documentary evidence

Testimonial evidence

Biometrics

Ballistics

US v. Davis

Weeks v. US

Mapp v. Ohio

Fruit of the poisonous tree doctrine

Exclusionary rule

Public safety exception

Inevitability of discovery exception

Good faith exception

Criminalistics

Next Generation Identification (NGI)

DNA Profiling

Interview

Interrogation

Reid technique

Gideon v. Wainwright

Miranda v. Arizona

Voluntary false confession

Coerced-compliant false confession

Miranda rights

In Chapter 9, we discussed ways in which officers within the agency use proactive investigative tactics to reduce and prevent repeated crimes (both reported and unreported). In this chapter, we focus on the investigative function and how detectives go about solving crimes that have been reported to police. We begin with a brief history of the investigative function and describe a typical detective bureau. Then we explain the investigative process from the first officer on scene through case closure, including an introduction to the science behind evidence processing and the rules that govern evidence collection. Finally, we examine the interview process, the rules that govern police questioning, commonly used interrogation strategies, and explain how interrogations can produce false confessions.

HISTORY OF INVESTIGATIONS

The first time the word "detective" was used was probably in 1842, when the London Metropolitan Police created the first "detective unit." Kuykendall, a police historian, breaks the history of American investigations into three semi-distinct, but overlapping, periods.

1850S–1920S: THE SECRETIVE ROGUE

Investigators during this period were generally plain clothed, poorly trained, and corrupt. They focused their efforts on criminals (not crimes) because criminals were easy targets and reward money provided a strong incentive. Due to the systemic corruption that existed at all levels at this point in history, detectives were sometimes instructed by politicians to focus their investigative efforts on specific individuals (namely, the enemies of those in power) or lose their job. They performed their job in secret much of the time and fraternized with criminals in order to infiltrate criminal organizations.

1890S–1960S: THE INQUISITOR

By the turn of the century, police became associated with brutal practices and a rash of abuse. The "third degree" was widely and systematically practiced and came to define investigations during this period. Detectives inflicted physical and psychological pain and suffering on individuals to obtain information about crimes and coerce suspects to confess. (See the Common Interrogation Practices box for some examples of methods used during this time.) This torture occurred almost "without restraint" and many police executives publicly supported the practice up through the 1930s (Leo, 2008). The Wickersham Commission, which published its report in 1931, heavily criticized the abusive practices and called for an immediate stop.

When policing moved into the reform (professional) era, there were increased expectations on detectives to solve crimes and make arrests. As crime detection methods became more "scientific" and police training and education improved, the need for abusive interrogation practices waned. Police began to collect evidence and rely more on "modern" (psychological) interrogation practices that were persuasive but not abusive. Use of the third degree declined substantially in the 1930s, 1940s, and 1950s (first in large, urban departments and then in small, rural agencies). By the mid-1940s, the practice had ceased in most places and by the time the President's Commission was assembled in 1967, the practice had all but disappeared (except for a few rare and isolated cases—Chicago, Il. for example).

COMMON INTERROGATION PRACTICES 1890S–1930S

In the heyday of the third degree, journalist Ernest Jones Hopkins wrote that "there are a thousand forms of compulsion; our police show great ingenuity in the variety employed" (Hopkins, 1931, p. 194; in Leo, 2008, p.48). There were purely physical techniques, purely psychological ones, and many that incorporated both physical and psychological elements. Some were simple and straightforwardly brutal while others were more sophisticated" (Leo, 2008, p46). Many police stations had specially designed interrogation cells known as "third-degree rooms" or "incommunicado" (Chicago PD was infamous for the torture detectives inflicted on suspects in the "fishbowl" or "Goldfish room"). These practices were able to exist because unlike today when we have numerous mechanisms in place to keep police power "in check" (e.g., the exclusionary rule and Miranda), no such mechanisms existed at this time in history. All of the examples and quoted materials below were taken from Leo, 2008, pp. 46–54.

- **Blatant physical abuse:** suspects were kicked or beaten with nightsticks, baseball bats, blackjacks, loaded leather saps, pistol butts, brass knuckles, and many other items. "Variations included holding up or hanging a handcuffed suspect over the top of an open door and pretending that he was a human punching bag…" (p. 47). Blatant physical abuse also included acts such as putting lighted matches, cigarettes, cigars, or pokers against a suspect's body; tying a suspect to a hot water pipe and forcing his body against

Brass knuckles

© tarapong srichaiyos/Shutterstock.com

the hot furnace; having a dentist drill into the nerves of the suspect's teeth; and adding a blindfold to the torture.

- **Deniable physical abuse:** Although some suspects came into court "with their faces so bandaged that only their eyes showed" (p.47), much of the physical abuse meted out by detectives was meant to be deniable in court. For instance,

  - Rubber hoses (and similar devices) which did not break the skin but did cause tremendous pain.

  - "An interesting Chicago discovery was that the local telephone book, weighing several pounds, would knock a man down if swung hard enough against his ear, yet would leave no marks" (Hopkins, 1931, p. 219 in Leo, 2008, p. 49).

  - "… administering tear gas, sometimes into a large box that had been placed over the suspect's head" (p. 49).

  - Making a suspect stand for hours on end, bending and twisting his fingers, wrists, and arms backward, choking him with a necktie, dragging or lifting the suspect by his hair, "pulling his hair out and stuffing it in his mouth" (p. 49), "hanging him out a window or suspending him in a room by steel handcuffs around his ankles" (p. 49), stripping him naked and making him sit in an ice bath.

- **Orchestrated physical abuse:** Some of the more common torture techniques used by police were:

  - **Sweat box**—suspect is placed in a small, dark cell next to a stove for hours or days; the stove was stoked with miscellaneous items to create extremely hot temperatures and horrible smells.

  - **Water cure** (a.k.a. water boarding)—suspect's head is placed underwater and held down until he almost drowned, then forcing the suspect to lie on his back while water is poured over his nostrils or a water hose is shoved into his mouth or throat until he nearly drowns.

  - **Electric mat**—a barefooted suspect is forced to walk across an electrically-charged mat or carpet; sparks fly and cause the suspect to dance in agony, faint, or confess.

  - **Cannonball**—a heavy cannonball was placed several feet above the floor, in a box fastened to the wall. The trap door on the box was controlled by a cord which, when sprung, released the cannonball. The suspect was sat, bound, directly underneath the cannonball—with the cord attached to one of his legs, which had to stay at a 90 degree angle in order to not deploy the cannonball above his head while the detectives taunted him.

- **Isolation, deprivation, and duress:** Some of the more common (and outrageous) psychological techniques used by police in the early part of the 20th century. Some of these are still in use today, though not to the extremes used 100 years ago.

  - "Losing" a suspect by transferring him between stations for 2–3 days at a time (for up to 6 weeks!) so that an attorney, friends, or family could not find him to intervene and detectives could have more time to gain a confession (in Philadelphia they called this practice "cold storage," in Detroit it was known as "sending a man around the loop" (p. 54); detectives would sometimes avoid filing charges against the suspect for days for the same purpose.

- Shining a bright strobe light in the suspect's face.
- Depriving suspects of food, water, sleep, medical care, etc.
- Detectives staged mock executions—complete with blood-curdling screams, the sounds of falling bodies, and other disturbing noises—to encourage suspects to confess.

1940S–PRESENT: THE HIGHLY SKILLED PROFESSIONAL

The professionalization era put pressure on detectives to be more accountable for their behavior and more professional (less brutal). Detectives began to focus on specific crimes and respond to individual victims (rather than focusing solely on criminals). The due process revolution of the 1960s placed new constraints on officers which (they thought) would make it more difficult to obtain confessions (as you'll see, it didn't work out that way). The new legal constraints did, however, force detectives to place a greater emphasis on investigative procedures and the accompanying paperwork to demonstrate that evidence and confessions were obtained lawfully. Investigators must now rely on developing solid cases which means collecting better evidence and working more closely with victims and witnesses. At this point, detectives are highly trained and skilled in the art and science of investigations and interrogations.

THE DETECTIVE UNIT

The size of the detective unit depends on the size of the agency. In general, about 10–15% of a department's sworn staff are assigned to the detective bureau (also called investigations). In small departments, one or two detectives (investigators) work on every type of crime whereas in larger departments detectives are assigned to work on specific types of crimes. For organizational purposes, it is common for medium-sized (and larger) departments to subdivide the detective bureau into some of the following divisions: property crimes, sex crimes, computer crimes, and violent crimes. In large agencies, these are often further subdivided into homicide, robbery, domestic violence, fraud, and juvenile crime. While these are common divisions, agencies are free to divide cases into any categorization scheme that works for the agency. In general, the larger the agency (and the more reported crime), the larger the number of subdivisions in the investigations bureau.

THE INVESTIGATIVE PROCESS

The criminal investigator's primary goal is to identify the perpetrator of a crime and aid in the prosecution of the perpetrator. Another key objective is to recover stolen property and return it to the victims. The Investigative Objections box lists the main objectives of an investigation. The investigative process is generally broken down into two separate stages: the preliminary investigation and the secondary investigation.

PRELIMINARY INVESTIGATION

The **preliminary investigation** is conducted by the initial responding patrol officer. It is the initial inquiry into a reported crime. Typically, officers spend approximately an hour on the preliminary investigation—slightly less for property crime, slightly more for violent crimes. There are six main objectives at this stage:

1. *Gather initial facts*—On the way to the crime scene and upon arriving on the scene, the responding officer gathers the initial facts to determine whether a crime was committed and whether the crime was committed within the officer's jurisdiction. Some initial facts might include the type of crime that occurred as well as when and how it occurred, suspect description and location (which direction they fled or if they are still on scene), suspect vehicle description (if any), suspect weapon, and victim injuries.

2. *Locate and apprehend fleeing suspects (and collect any discarded evidence)*—Based on the description given to the dispatchers, the responding officer is on the lookout for the suspect while she is driving to the call. She also retrieves (or more commonly, radios to dispatch the location of) any evidence discarded by the suspect/s in their attempt to flee from the crime scene (such as weapons, disguise used to commit the crime, money bags, or other identifying property taken during the crime).

3. *Assess scene and request additional help*—It is the responding officer's responsibility to determine what additional resources are needed at the crime scene. For example, it is common for Emergency Medical Services (EMS) to respond to provide medical care to injured parties. (Note: in some consolidated public safety departments, police officers are cross-trained

Any evidence left behind at the crime scene needs to be documented by responding officers.

as firefighters and/or paramedics.) If the suspect is thought to be in the area but his exact whereabouts are unknown, a K9 unit or a helicopter might be requested to help locate the suspect. Alternatively, if a suspect is barricaded in a building, the SWAT team might be called. Many agencies have a team of specially trained evidence technicians (a.k.a. CSI—Crime Scene Investigators) which respond to collect evidence. In some cases (such as a bank robbery, homicide, or other major crime), it may be customary to call out the detective/s who will be assigned the case to the initial crime scene. In the event of a death, the coroner is generally called. Some of these resources (e.g., SWAT, K9, helicopter) usually require the approval of a patrol supervisor while others (such as EMS, tow trucks, CSI, and detectives) do not.

4. *Secure crime scene*—This involves taking control of the crime scene and directing personnel and onlookers. Sometimes this requires taping off the crime scene and keeping people out of the area. In a major incident, an officer will keep a log of everyone who enters a crime scene as well as how long they are there. Many departments now require officers to carry specially designed booties in their gear bag—these are to wear over their shoes at a crime scene to prevent contamination and preserve the integrity of the evidence.

5. *Identify and interview individuals with information about the crime*—The responding officer takes statements from the reporting party, as well as any victims, witnesses, potential suspects, and others with information. These individuals (and their contact information) are listed on the initial report so that the detective assigned to the case can conduct follow-up interviews, if necessary.

6. *Write report*—Finally, the assigned officer writes an initial report summarizing what occurred and who was involved. It contains suspect and victim information as well as a description of any stolen property and individual statements made by involved parties. Sometimes, photos of injuries, damage, or stolen property are included. This is the report that the investigator uses to start his **secondary investigation**. In some cases, when there were many victims and witnesses, other responding officers may interview some of the involved parties and write a "supplemental" report containing the individuals' statements.

SECONDARY INVESTIGATION

This is the stage when the detective assumes responsibility for the case and starts to "fill in the blanks." The first thing that a detective does is confirm that a crime was committed within her jurisdiction and that there are clues that could lead to the perpetrator of the crime and/or recovery of stolen property. The detective maintains a case file that includes the initial report (written by the responding patrol officer) as well as all supplemental reports (written by others who responded to the initial call and the detective). As part of the investigation, the detective conducts follow-up interviews, reviews reports and crime scene photos, runs criminal history checks on named suspects, checks suspect descriptions in the department's RMS and other databases (see Chapter 9), interprets evidence analysis, and performs other investigatory tasks to solve the case.

The detective is the main point of contact for others working the case. For example, if a death occurred, the county coroner usually autopsies the body and provides a report to the investigator. Likewise, many agencies employ specially trained evidence technicians (sometimes called crime scene investigators) who collect and/or analyze **physical evidence**. Some large agencies have their own crime lab, but most agencies rely on their county or state crime lab to process DNA and perform other analyses (such as toxicology, serology, ballistics, etc.). Additionally, a specially trained computer forensic examiner might be used to collect and preserve any **digital evidence**. These highly skilled experts are necessary because there are strict rules that apply to handling evidence and documenting the chain of custody of evidence so that pertinent evidence can be admitted into court.

Interestingly, most of a detective's time is spent on reviewing files and reports. One seminal study found that investigators spent 93% of their time on non-productive activities (tasks that did not lead to solving previously reported crimes) (Greenwood, Chaiken, & Petersilia, 1977). A more recent study found that detectives spent 65.6% of their time on six activities: contacts with victims and witnesses (19.9%), supplemental report preparation (17.0%), login and review of case (9.2%), computer searches for suspect information (6.7%), suspect interviews/interrogations (6.4%), and case preparation (6.4%) (Womack, 2007).

Case Screening

Because detectives work multiple cases at once, it is necessary to use a triage system to identify the cases that are most likely to be solved and allocate time accordingly; this means screening cases for solvability potential. Not all reported crimes are assigned to a detective for follow-up. If there are no leads and no evidence, the case probably will not be assigned to a detective. Instead, the case will be suspended and only reopened if new leads or evidence are discovered or if stolen property is recovered. The seriousness of the crime and the number of workable leads are the prime determinants of how hard a detective works a case. Some cases may take precedence over other cases—in particular serious crimes, serial crimes, and crimes that are considered high profile for another reason (such as area crime was committed, victim status, suspect status, or media attention). Other factors may also influence how much attention gets devoted to a case.

A study by Eck (1983) determined that there are essentially three types of cases:

1. *Already solved*—The suspect has been identified by a victim or witnesses and needs to be apprehended. These cases have strong evidence and generally require little effort from the detective. They are relatively common. For example, a bar fight between two known acquaintances where injuries were sustained by one party (the victim) but the other party (suspect) left before police arrived. The victim gave the police the suspect's name and address. Domestic violence cases are another example of "already solved" cases that are assigned to detectives for follow-up.

2. *Solvable*—These cases contain a moderate amount of clues that can be used to solve the crime with some effort. For example, a witness observed a subject tag a wall (which happened to be monitored by a surveillance camera) and provided a detailed suspect description. The detective can try to use the surveillance camera image, as well as other techniques, to identify the suspect. It will probably take some effort but the case can be solved.

3. *Unsolvable*—It is very common for victims to report crimes that have no or insufficient clues to follow. In these cases, where there is little or no information, the case cannot be solved without additional information, regardless of the effort put forth by the detective. For example, you parked your car at the grocery store and returned to find that your laptop had been stolen from the front seat. There were no tool marks or other physical evidence, no eyewitnesses, and no security cameras. Without some additional information, the detective cannot solve this crime.

HOW SUCCESSFUL ARE INVESTIGATORS?

The "clearance rate" is the measure that is typically used to determine the effectiveness of police investigators. It compares the number of cases closed by arrest or "exception" (exceptional cases where the case is considered solved but no one was arrested) to the number of crimes reported. Although this is the traditional measure of police effectiveness (the percent of cases solved), it is not highly reliable because (1) there is no universal method to calculate the clearance rate (each police department decides for itself what it considers "solved"), (2) it uses reported crimes as the denominator (meaning it does not account for unreported crimes), and (3) it is subject to manipulation (attributing multiple crimes to one suspect already in custody inflates the rate, as does reclassifying thefts as "lost property" and "unfounding" other crimes that are unlikely to be solved—see Chapter 8 and the discussion on Compstat).

There are many factors that are important to whether a case is solved. The key factor is how much information is obtained by the initial officer—specifically, whether victims or witnesses provide a suspect name or description. A study by RAND (Greenwood, Chaiken, & Petersilia, 1977) found that 80% of all cases cleared are the result of arrests made by patrol officers or because a victim provided the suspect's name. Most cases are solved because victims

Opportunistic Burglar
- Unlawful entry—Entry left open
- No preparation or tools
- Unoccupied residence
- Low value items stolen
- Little evidence left behind
- Young offenders
- Adolescent onset
- Short criminal career
- Low offending frequency
- Do not know victim
- Mostly male, but some female offenders
- Versatility, prior petty theft/shoplifting arrests
- Do not have car

Organized Burglar
- Clean but forced entry
- Tools brought to scene
- No evidence left behind
- High value items stolen that often require fence or network
- Older offenders
- Adolescent onset
- High offending frequency
- Limited versatility—prior arrests for theft/burglary
- Often have a car
- Cohabitating or have partner
- May have met victim

Disorganized Burglar
- Forced entry
- Scene left in dissary
- Tools &/or evidence left
- Low value or no items stolen
- Young offenders
- Early onset
- Long criminal career
- High offending frequency
- Do no know victim
- Versatility, past arrests for drug offenses
- Do not know victim

Interpersonal Burglar
- Occupied residence
- Target is victim—not objects
- Attempted, threatened, or committed violence at scene
- Personal items stolen
- Adult aged
- Late criminal onset
- Solo offender
- Have a car
- Single/not cohabitating
- No record—but if arressted usually for violence
- Know of victim

Source: Adapted from Fox & Farrington (2015)

Figure 12.1 Burglary offense styles and features of offenders who commit them.

and witnesses provide straight-forward, consistent, and correct information. For instance, a suspect's description, name, photo, clothing description, or address, and a vehicle description or license plate number are all useful to detectives. In fact, the RAND researchers found that only 3% of cases were solved through "extraordinary detective work."

Much of what we know about investigations is based on research conducted decades ago, when computers did not play much, if any, role in solving crimes. Although we know that technology has had a profound effect on some aspects of policing, we do not know what impact it has had on investigations—the process or the clearance rate. Certainly, computers have changed the way investigators do their job (reread Chapter 9 if you have any doubts), but it is unknown whether technology has actually improved clearance rates. Research does confirm, however, that "trust in police" is important to solving crimes because residents are more likely (than officers) to notice suspicious behavior in the neighborhood and residents that trust the police are more likely to alert the police to the observed suspicious behavior and/or provide the information to officers (either voluntarily or when asked).

New studies have focused on how detectives can work smarter. For at least the last two decades, some detectives have incorporated the use of behavioral profiles in difficult rape and homicide investigations and have reported, anecdotally, that they help solve these unique cases. A first-of-its-kind study recently found detectives can significantly improve arrest rates for burglary by using behavioral profiles of burglars (Fox & Farrington, 2015). Using a matrix of burglary offense styles and the features of offenders who commit those types of burglaries (see Figure 12.1), detectives were able to limit the pool of potential suspects and concentrate their efforts on the potential suspects (who were already known to police) who, statistically speaking, were most likely to have committed the type of burglary they were investigating. The burglary arrest rate rose from 11.29% before the matrix was employed to 30.06% after it was employed (Fox & Farrington, 2015). Because this is only the first study to examine this issue, we need to be cautiously optimistic about this strategy.

EVIDENCE—THE KEY TO SOLVING CRIMES

As mentioned, police solve crimes when victims and witnesses provide straightforward, consistent, and correct suspect information. The suspect's name and whereabouts are particularly helpful. Beyond that, and even when a suspect has been named, the detective uses evidence to tie a suspect to the crime. There are several common (and not so common) types of evidence that investigators rely upon to solve cases.

TYPES OF EVIDENCE

Physical evidence

This is the widest category of evidence and includes any physical item related to the case that can be seen and felt, such as a note, weapon, dye pack contained in stolen bank money, an item of clothing, a shoe, a phone, a duffle bag, a carpet, a plane, train, or bus ticket, bank statements, receipts, anything you can imagine. It could also include a shoe print impression or a finger print.

Biometrics Considered a subcategory of physical evidence, biometrics is the term used to refer to biological evidence. It includes things such as blood, DNA, hair or fiber samples that can be used to learn something about the persons involved in the crime (victim or suspect), and finger prints.

Ballistics Ballistics is the identification of firearms and bullets. This category, which is also a subcategory of physical evidence, includes bullet shell casings and guns found at the crime scene.

Digital evidence

Anything and everything that can be found in a computer, cell phone, or tablet. This category includes the computer itself, along with any files on the computer as well as the search history of the web browser. It includes all the personal information we've entered into our favorite apps and programs—our personal contacts, calendar, music, phone numbers we've dialed (or received calls/texts from), GPS coordinates of places we've been (or just searched), and posts on social media. It can also include images from traffic and other surveillance cameras and license plate readers. Digital evidence is extremely valuable because it is often date- and time-stamped, which is difficult for the standard user to fabricate or erase.

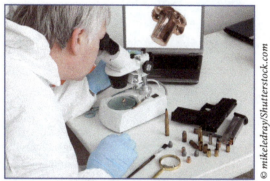

A forensics lab technician examines a bullet for evidence to be used in a court case.

Documentary evidence

This category includes documents that are part of a crime; in particular crimes that are considered "white collar" or that were committed for financial gain. For example, a log of crematorium clients listing tracking numbers and body parts which were illegally disarticulated from the client's body prior to cremation; or a bank account or other financial records indicating fraud, money-laundering, or criminal personal gain. The documents can be in hardcopy or digital format (thus this category overlaps with the physical evidence and digital evidence categories).

Testimonial evidence

This category includes knowledge and memories provided by individuals—victims, witnesses, suspects, and key others (conspirators, agents, etc.). While definitely important in an investigation, research reveals that human memory is not reliable. Not only do our minds alter and embellish things that did happen; they sometimes manufacture incidents that did not happen (former NBC Nightly News Anchor, Brian Williams, is a prime example of this phenomenon—see Parker-Pope, 2015).

Eyewitness testimony Information provided by someone who witnessed the commission of the crime firsthand. It is often seen as being the most important evidence in a case but it is not always reliable. This is because most people have very weak observational skills and poor memories. Witnesses also often misinterpret what they see, hear, and experience. Eyewitness identifications are particularly suspect when the witness and perpetrator are of different races and/or when the identification is of a violent crime, an accident, or a catastrophic event (Kozinski, 2015). Eyewitness accounts must be carefully vetted for accuracy, as eyewitness misidentification is THE leading cause of wrongful convictions in the United States, playing a role in 72% of the 330 DNA exonerations since the late 1980s (Innocence Project, 2015). Addressing the role that mistaken eyewitness accounts play in wrongful convictions, the National Academy of Sciences recently issued a report on memory and eyewitness identification and identified four best practices for police interviews (see Figure 12.2).

Victim testimony Unless something about the victim's recounting of the incident "doesn't add up," detectives generally believe a victim's account of the crime. Victims are typically considered to be truth-tellers, having little incentive usually to make up a story or falsely accuse another person of committing a crime. Still, false accusations occur regularly and it is up to the detective

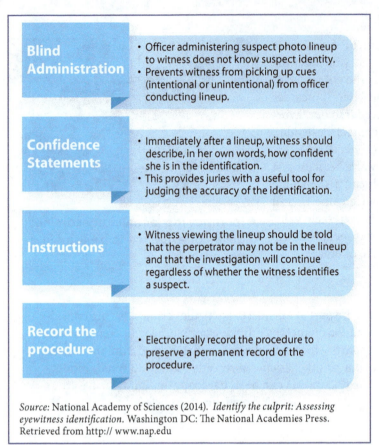

Blind Administration	• Officer administering suspect photo lineup to witness does not know suspect identity. • Prevents witness from picking up cues (intentional or unintentional) from officer conducting lineup.
Confidence Statements	• Immediately after a lineup, witness should describe, in her own words, how confident she is in the identification. • This provides juries with a useful tool for judging the accuracy of the identification.
Instructions	• Witness viewing the lineup should be told that the perpetrator may not be in the lineup and that the investigation will continue regardless of whether the witness identifies a suspect.
Record the procedure	• Electronically record the procedure to preserve a permanent record of the procedure.

Source: National Academy of Sciences (2014). *Identify the culprit: Assessing eyewitness identification.* Washington DC: The National Academies Press. Retrieved from http:// www.nap.edu

Figure 12.2 Best practices for police eyewitness identification procedures.

to detect when this has happened. Of the 1625 documented exonerations that occurred between 1989 and 2014, 56% of them involved a false accusation or perjured testimony, including the very first DNA exoneration in 1989 (National Registry of Exonerations, 2015a). False accusations are most likely to occur in child sex abuse cases (80% of these exonerations involved a false accusation) and homicide cases (67%) (National Registry of Exonerations, 2015b).

Conspirator testimony Information provided by someone who is considered a crime partner—someone who helped, aided, or abetted the suspect in the commission of the crime. As depicted on our favorite crime shows, coconspirators can be helpful for obtaining the details of the crime.

Informant testimony Information provided in exchange for leniency by someone who has information about the crime. The informant is either in jail or has potential legal action pending against him. The court accepts the testimony of informants but often looks at the information with some skepticism. Typically informant testimony requires corroboration from a person or piece of evidence.

Undercover agent testimony Information provided by a law enforcement agent working undercover. The agent may work for the arresting agency or another agency.

LEGAL RULES GOVERNING EVIDENCE

There are many legislated laws and Supreme Court rulings that pertain to evidence gathering and its admissibility in court. These cases are primarily focused on our Fourth Amendment protection against unreasonable search and seizure. The primary concerns are what constitutes an unreasonable search and what happens if a detective collects evidence from an unreasonable search.

In order for a search to be considered *un*reasonable, (1) an individual must have an *expressed expectation of privacy* and (2) that expectation must be reasonable (*Katz v United States, 1967*). Since Katz was first decided, the court's interpretation of "reasonable" has changed multiple times; and

FOURTH AMENDMENT OF THE CONSTITUTION OF THE UNITED STATES

The right of the people to be secure in their persons, houses, papers, and effects, against unreasonable searches and seizures, shall not be violated, and no warrants shall issue, but upon probable cause, supported by oath or affirmation, and particularly describing the place to be searched, and the persons or things to be seized.

it will continue to change as technology advances and societal expectations of privacy change. For example, closed-circuit cameras are now part of our daily lives and we expect that we are on camera when we shop at retailers, walk through airports, and drive through some intersections (in other words, we no longer have an expectation of privacy in most public spaces). Individuals have the strongest protections against unreasonable searches inside their homes. Fourth Amendment protections diminish the farther one goes away from one's actual house. Curtilage (the area immediately surrounding the home—back yard, front yard, short driveway) provides some privacy protections but open fields on one's property provide virtually no privacy protections over public space.

New technologies can aid investigations in many ways, but the rules that police must abide by are constantly changing and evolving. For instance, investigators can conduct surveillance on suspects

WHAT DO YOU THINK?

Question: *If you are arrested for a crime, can an officer search your smartphone without a warrant?* **Answer:** The courts are still addressing this issue, but in general, no—as of June 25, 2014, cell phones *cannot* be searched without a warrant incident to arrest, except under specific circumstances (*Riley v. California, 2014*). Cell phones may be searched once a warrant has been obtained.

Question: *Can an investigator look at your social media account without a warrant?*

Answer: It depends on several factors. In deciding this question, justices are considering the suspect's privacy settings along with the size of her circle of "friends" to determine the individual's expectation of privacy (the larger the circle of "friends" or "followers," the less expectation of privacy). In general, however, police need a search warrant for anything that is not "public" information. Although the Riley decision did not address this issue specifically, it governs it—at least to the extent that a warrant is required.

by following the suspect's car or by attaching a GPS monitoring device to a suspect's vehicle. In *Jones v. U.S. (2010)*, the U.S. Supreme Court enumerated rules for when police needed a search warrant for using a GPS device based on where the car was located when the GPS device was attached and how long the device could remain without violating a person's right to privacy. Since then, the Third Circuit Court of Appeals ruled in *U.S. v. Katzin (2013)* that police always need a search warrant to affix a GPS tracking device to a suspect's vehicle, regardless of where the car is parked when police affix the device, or how long the device remains on the car.

Likewise, whereas detectives used to be able to retroactively track suspects via their cell phones without a warrant, as of 2014 that is no longer the case. The Eleventh Circuit Court of Appeals ruled in **U.S. v. Davis** *(2014)* that investigators need a search warrant to obtain cell site location data for a suspect. Investigators who gain access to a suspect's cell phone, tablet, or computer have a wealth of potentially incriminating evidence at their fingertips.

It is important for an investigator to know when a search requires a warrant and to follow the rules to avoid collecting evidence illegally. What happens if a detective performs an unreasonable search? One of the first cases on the matter, *Weeks v. U.S.* (1914), established the **exclusionary rule** and prohibited illegally obtained evidence from being used in Federal trials. *Mapp v. Ohio* (1961), perhaps the most important of these cases, extended the federal exclusionary rule to the states and articulated the **"fruit of the poisonous tree" doctrine** which specifies that *any* evidence obtained illegally is inadmissible in court, including testimony obtained by the suspect prior to being read his (Miranda) rights. The exclusionary rule and fruit of the poison tree doctrine are based on the premise that police will willfully violate a suspect's due process rights (in the name of justice) unless there are severe consequences that act as a deterrent. Making illegally obtained evidence inadmissible in court provides the necessary incentive for officers to "play by the rules" or risk the criminal "going free." Over the past 50 years, the U.S. Supreme Court (U.S.S.C.) has delineated

PUBLIC SAFETY EXCEPTION: BOSTON MARATHON BOMBING SUSPECT • DZHOKHAR TSARNAEV

The most famous recent application of the public safety exception was in the case of the 2013 Boston Marathon Bombing. Dzhokhar Tsarnaev, the only surviving suspect, was taken to the hospital immediately upon being apprehended by the FBI in April 2013. He had been shot and was in and out of consciousness for the first couple of days. This postponed the interrogation for 5 days. When he awoke, the FBI questioned Tsarnaev for 16 hours without Mirandizing him, choosing instead to invoke the public safety exception (Wright, 2013). The main question for the court will be whether the statements made by Tsarnaev during those 16 hours of questioning are admissible. If the judge rules that the public safety exception applies in this case, Tsarnaev's statements will be able to be used against him during his trial. If, on the other hand, the judge rules that the public safety exception does not apply, then his statements will not be allowed because the officers would have violated Tsarnaev's due process rights. Side note: some media outlets hypothesized that the police would not need his testimony because of the amount of evidence they had amassed against the suspect. If this was true, investigators may not have been concerned about the admissibility of his testimony.

Tsarnaev's lawyers requested that the court exclude the statements he made in the hospital, arguing that (1) Tsarnaev repeatedly asked for a lawyer but was denied one (even though he had been assigned a public defender), and (2) questioning covered topics not associated with a public safety threat (such as sports, school history, future career goals, and religious beliefs) and continued after it was clear that the public was not in danger (Gerstein, 2014). In their opposition filling, the Federal Government argued that, because they did not intend to use Tsarnaev's statements in their "case-in-chief," the issue was moot. For this reason the judge never officially ruled on the issue.

YOU DECIDE: What do you think? Should the FBI be allowed to question a suspect under the public safety exception 5 days after the crime occurred? Should his statements be admissible in court?

several exceptions to the exclusionary rule in an attempt to balance law enforcement's efforts to control crime and provide public safety with suspects' due process rights.

One of these, the **public safety exception** (which is actually an exception to the 5th Amendment protection against self-incrimination), allows officers to use information and evidence gathered as a result of questioning a suspect prior to his **Miranda rights** being read to him *if* the concern for public safety is so great as to outweigh adherence to the rules. The public safety exception is intended to permit law enforcement officers to question suspects immediately after a crime was committed in order to locate the weapons used by the suspect that could (and likely would) cause great public harm if not located quickly.

The second exception, **inevitability of discovery exception**, allows evidence that eventually would have been discovered through the normal investigative process to be used in court, even if the evidence was initially found as the result of an illegal search. Essentially, if the prosecutor can convince the judge that detectives would have located the same evidence on their own, without benefit of the illegal search, the evidence can be used against the suspect in court.

Finally, the **good faith exception** allows evidence from an invalid search warrant to be presented in court. If it turns out that the search warrant was not valid (there was not sufficient probable cause to issue it), the evidence obtained can still be used in court as long as the officer acted in good faith (did not lie on the affidavit or defraud the court in some way). In this case, the mistake was made by the judge, not the officer, which is why the evidence is admissible.

Together, these cases establish a set of narrow and specific rules that law enforcement officers must adhere to if they want the evidence they gathered to be admissible in court. It is important to know that these rules are not static and they can (and do) change when new appeals are taken up by the U.S. Supreme Court in regard to new technology, new threats, and new social norms. In particular, exceptions to the rules have expanded, especially as they apply to suspected terrorists after 9/11.

SCIENCE—EVALUATING THE EVIDENCE

Criminalistics is the "application of scientific techniques in collecting and analyzing physical evidence in criminal cases" (Merriam-Webster dictionary, n.d.). The discipline has evolved greatly since its birth in the 19th century when it primarily involved crime scene photography, fingerprint analysis, handwriting analysis, and ballistics. Today, it has expanded into what we call *forensic science*, "the application of scientific methods and techniques to matters under investigation by a court of law" (Oxford Dictionary, n.d.). The field is expansive and includes numerous specialties from the physiological sciences, social sciences, digital forensics, and criminalistics.

There are 411 publicly funded crime labs in the United States (Durose et al., 2012). Some labs are small (employing fewer than 10 employees) and specialized (performing only three functions on average) while others are large (employing more than 100 employees) and versatile (performing seven tasks on average). See Table 12.1 for a list of the functions performed by labs in the United States. Together these labs received approximately 4.1 million requests for forensic services in 2009. The most popular

TABLE 12.1 Functions Performed by Publicly Funded Forensic Crime Labs, by Type of Jurisdiction (2009)					
Forensic Function	**All Labs**	**State**	**County**	**Municipal**	**Federal**
Controlled Substances Identification of drugs and other illegal controlled substances	82%	86%	85%	75%	59%
Latent Prints Comparison of finger or palm prints lifted from crime scenes	60%	54%	63%	78%	65%
Forensic Biology Examines evidence for the presence of stains from blood, saliva, and other physiological fluids. Includes DNA analysis.	59%	64%	66%	49%	26%
Firearms/Tool marks Comparison of evidence resulting from the discharge of firearms; the comparison of marks made by various tools.	55%	55%	63%	62%	21%
Crime Scene Identification, documentation, collection, and interpretation of physical evidence at a location where crime occurred	52%	44%	62%	71%	44%

continued

TABLE 12.1 Functions Performed by Publicly Funded Forensic Crime Labs, by Type of Jurisdiction (2009) *(continued)*

Forensic Function	All Labs	State	County	Municipal	Federal
Trace Evidence Any analytical procedure using microscopy or chemical and instrumental techniques. Includes the examination of gunshot residue, explosives, hair, fibers, and fire debris.	50%	50%	55%	44%	50%
Impressions Identification, documentation, collection, and interpretation of 2D and 3D impressions and imprints found at crime scenes (incl. footwear and tire tread)	44%	44%	53%	43%	24%
Toxicology Analysis of biological samples for the presence of drugs and other potentially toxic materials.	42%	50%	43%	35%	9%
Digital Evidence Investigation of various types of analog or multi-media evidence, such as the recovery, extraction, and analysis of computer files, film, tape, magnetic and optical media.	19%	10%	21%	32%	44%
Questioned Documents Examination of printed, typed, or written material for the purpose of identifying the source, determining alterations, or gaining information about the item or the circumstances surrounding its production.	16%	13%	13%	24%	29%
Other Functions Includes tasks such as polygraph, bloodstain pattern analysis, environmental forensics, and forensic pathology.	13%	10%	14%	12%	24%

Source: Durose, M.R., Walsh, K.A., & Burch, A. M. (2012, August). Census of publicly funded forensic crime laboratories, 2009. #NCJ238252. Washington DC: U.S. Department of Justice, Bureau of Justice Statistics.

requests were for screening or DNA analysis of biological evidence (34% of all requests), controlled substance analysis (33%), and toxicology analysis (15%).

Using fingerprints to identify suspects was one of the first "scientific" developments in policing in the 19th century. By the early 20th century, detectives lifted latent fingerprints at crime scenes to compare to the collection of finger print cards they had amassed at the station. Of course, at this time they had to hand search each and every card for comparison (which took a very long time and was limited to the cards in the station house). Now, most fingerprints collected by law enforcement officers are digitized and stored in a national database managed by the FBI called *NGI* (**Next Generation Identification**), which makes comparisons much easier than in the past years. Prior to NGI, the national fingerprint database was called IAFIS (Integrated Automated Fingerprint Identification System). IAFIS was launched in 1999 and replaced by NGI in September 2014. NGI is the largest criminal fingerprint database in the world—housing more than 70 million sets of prints in the criminal master file and another 34 million in the civil print file. Of the 60% of crime labs that processed latent prints in 2009, 78% used IAFIS (Durose et al., 2012). In addition to housing fingerprints, NGI contains (1) a Repository for Individuals of Special Concern (RISC)—a small file of wanted individuals, known or suspected terrorists, and sex offender registry subjects that is designed to help law enforcement officers make rapid identifications in the field; (2) Interstate Photo System (IPS)—a searchable compilation of photos (such as front and side facing suspect views and tattoos) received with fingerprint cards from law enforcement agencies; (3) Latents and National Palm Print System (NPPS)—a database of palm prints

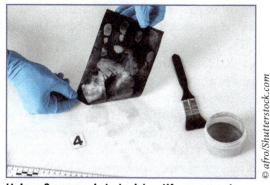

Using fingerprints to identify suspects was an early scientific development in policing.

and latent fingerprints collected from crime scenes and submitted for queries; and (4) Iris Recognition (IR)—a pilot program to identify subjects using a person's iris (FBI, n.d.).

Important research note: Historically, fingerprints have been thought to be completely unique to a single person and that no two people could share the same markers; however, recent research has begun to question this infallibility assumption, especially as it pertains to latent fingerprints. Latent fingerprints are invisible prints that are "lifted" from a crime scene surface using powder or a chemical developing agent. The prints are rarely complete; they are usually incomplete, blurred, overlapping, and distorted in other ways. This makes them particularly difficult to match to prints inked or scanned by police under ideal conditions. Probably, the best known example of a match error happened when a latent print taken from the 2004 Madrid terrorist train bombing was matched to Brandon Mayfield, an innocent Oregon attorney, by the FBI. Eventually, Spanish investigators matched the latent print to another suspect (from Spain), but not before Mr. Mayfield's life was turned upside down.

Discovered in the 1980s, **DNA profiling** has had a profound effect on the way civilians view law enforcement and the criminal justice system. It uses variations in the genetic code to identify individuals, similar to the way that fingerprint analysis uses the variations of ridges, whirls, and loops to identify individuals. Specifically, it uses highly variable sequences of DNA that are unique to individuals, but similar in close family relatives (which means that suspects sometimes can be identified from familial samples). The vast majority (75%) of all forensic biology requests to publicly funded labs in 2009 were to process DNA samples from convicted offenders and arrestees (Durose et al., 2012). This makes sense because every state in the nation, the District of Colombia, and the Federal government require the submission of DNA from convicted offenders (and some extend the requirement to offenders arrested for certain crimes) (Durose et al., 2012). These samples are stored in a set of nationally shared databases called CODIS (Combined DNA Index System), which like NGI is administered by the FBI. CODIS contains more than 11 million DNA samples from offenders and arrestees as well as missing persons, relatives of missing persons, and unidentified human remains. Of the crime labs that performed forensic biology services in 2009, 81% used CODIS. In order to be useful, DNA evidence must meet both a scientific standard as well as a legal standard. Seen as incontrovertible proof of a suspect's guilt or innocence, it has,

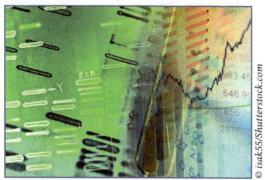

DNA profiling uses variations in the genetic code to identify individuals.

almost singlehandedly, illuminated the issue of wrongful convictions. Unfortunately, due to backlogs and other issues, it has not transformed investigations the way that our favorite crime dramas suggest it has.

Ballistics is the analysis of bullets, bullet impacts, and firearms to identify a firearm that was used in a crime. The first identification of a criminal from a bullet occurred in 1835 when an English detective found a bullet mold in the murder's house that matched the bullet taken from the victim. *Ballistic fingerprinting* refers to the set of procedures that are used to match a bullet to the gun that it was fired from. It is based on the premise that all firearms have internal variations from the machining process that are unique to the specific firearm and which leave microscopic marks on the bullets as they are ejected. The Bureau of Alcohol, Tobacco, Firearms, and Explosives' (BATF) maintains the National Integrated Ballistics Information Network (NIBIN). This database includes digital images of cartridge casings from crime scenes or crime gun test fires. Of the 55% of crime labs that process firearms evidence, 78% use NIBIN (Durose, 2012). BATF recorded 68,000 hits (potential matches) between 1999 and 2015; exactly how many turned out to be actual matches is unknown but BATF listed 18 success stories on its Web site (BATF, 2015a and 2015b). In addition, some states (Maryland and New York for example) have built their own databases but have generally found them to be very costly and not at all effective. This is because, unlike human fingerprints and DNA, a gun's ballistic fingerprinting can change over time with use (or by replacing the gun's barrel) (Lott, 2002). Studies on the topic have found that computer matching is not very effective but that manual matching can be effective when detectives have actual guns to match to bullets found at a crime scene.

FIELD PERSPECTIVES: AN INVESTIGATOR'S JOB

By: Det. Brian Meux

Courtesy Vitaly Prokopchuk

Brian Meux

Criminal cases are, for the most part, solved and prosecuted through the interviews and interrogations that law enforcement investigators conduct. Of course, we hear a lot about the importance of physical evidence such as DNA, fingerprints, and video surveillance footage, but that evidence is only as good as the statements that put it in context. "How did it get there? Who put the evidence there? What other reasonable explanation is there for the presence of that evidence?" The answers to these and many more questions are obtained from the wide variety of people interviewed by investigators.

The goal of every law enforcement interviewer should be to obtain the most complete, accurate, and truthful information he or she can from every interview. Every statement must be compared and contrasted to everything else known to the investigative team. How does this statement compare to what other witnesses have said? Does the story match the physical evidence? What motivations might this person have to minimize, embellish, or lie about the facts? If the answers given don't make sense to the investigator, ask the questions again.

Pulling information out of humans is not like accessing a computer; it never hurts to spend a little more time to go over the statement again; and maybe again. A committed investigator is never satisfied with taking a statement at face value. He or she should always be looking beyond the interview to help make the case better. "Who else should I talk to in order to validate or debunk the information I just obtained?" "What other evidence should I seek to bolster my case?" Corroboration is the glue that holds a case together, making prosecutors willing to file a case and juries willing to convict. Every interrogator strives for getting "the confession," hearing a person admit to the crimes they are being accused of. Even confessions should be looked at with a degree of skepticism because it is not unheard of for people to admit to acts they did not commit. What might their motive be to "falsely confess?" Are they protecting a loved one? Did they feel unduly pressured by the tactics used by the interrogator? A person's confession should be subjected to the same vetting process as any other statement, comparing and contrasting it to the other evidence and statements known to the investigator.

All told, being tasked with gathering information through interviews and interrogations is a privilege, and a great responsibility, bestowed upon the law enforcement investigator. With patience, diligence, and a commitment to always seeking the truth, the interviewer can rest assured that his or her efforts will be used to further the cause of justice.

Brian Meux has been in law enforcement for over 19 years, serving in both the military and in several California law enforcement agencies. Meux has worked as a police detective in the fields of child abuse, sexual assault, and homicide. Meux teaches interview and interrogations courses to law enforcement officers from throughout California.

INTERVIEWS AND INTERROGATIONS

Depending on the types of crimes an investigator is assigned to, she may spend a considerable amount of time questioning witnesses, victims, and suspects. When a detective questions a victim or witness, it is called an interview. When a detective questions a suspect, it may be considered an interview or an interrogation. As Figure 12.3 illustrates, there are some not-so-subtle distinctions between interviews and interrogations. **Interviews** are intended to be information-gathering sessions. They are generally inquisitive and conciliatory, not accusatory. The format of an interview may resemble a dialogue between interviewer (detective) and interviewee or a friendly "Q and A" session. **Interrogations**, on the other hand, are different from interviews in that they are only conducted with suspects (not witnesses or

	Interview	Interrogation
Tone	Inquisitive (non-accusatory)	Accusatory
Format	Dialogue (Q and A format)	Monologue (detective talking)
Goals	1. Gather information about the crime and the subject's involvement 2. Assess the subject's truthfulness	1. Ellicit the truth about subject's involvement in crime 2. Obtain a court-admissible confession (if suspect is thought to be guilty)

Adapted from Jayne, B. & Buckley, J. (2014). *A field guide to the Reid Technique.* Chicago, IL: John E. Reid & Associates, Inc.

Figure 12.3 Interview vs. Interrogation—Some Distinctions

victims), and they are aimed at learning the truth about the suspect's involvement and ultimately, eliciting a confession. Unlike interviews, which are generally inquisitive in nature, interrogations in America are usually accusatory (though it is not this way in other parts of the world). The detective generally has some solid information about the suspect's involvement in the crime prior to commencing an interrogation.

The most common interview method used in the United States is the **Reid Technique** (Kassin et al., 2010). Since 1974, more than 500,000 investigators and security personnel have been trained in the Reid Technique which is composed of three stages: factual analysis, behavior analysis interview, and interrogation (Jayne & Buckley, 2014). The first stage involves a factual analysis of the crime facts to determine whether a potential suspect could possibly be the person who committed the crime (based on factors such as suspect demographics and physical description, opportunity and access to commit the crime, knowledge needed to commit the crime, motivations and propensity to commit the crime). During the second stage, a behavioral analysis interview is conducted to assess the suspect's truthfulness using a structured set of "behavior provoking" questions that elicit specific behavioral responses that are supposed to differ based on a suspect's guilt or innocence. Finally, the interrogation is a nine-step process that is primarily confrontational and intended to be used on suspects whose guilt is reasonably certain (see the Reid Interrogation Technique box).

THE REID INTERROGATION TECHNIQUE

The suggested interrogation method has nine distinct steps:

1. **Positive confrontation**—confronting the suspect with evidence of guilt.

2. **Theme development**—using minimization techniques, the detective provides the suspect with possible moral justification for the crime.

3. **Handling denials**—according to the model, innocent and guilty suspects deny involvement in different ways; innocent suspects do not go past this stage, they reject any suggestion of guilt.

4. **Overcoming objections**—suspects provide emotional, factual, and moral objections (arguments why they couldn't have committed the crime).

5. **Procurement and retention of the suspect's attention**—the detective closes the physical distance between suspect and investigator.

6. **Handling the suspect's passive mood**—empathize and sympathize with the suspect and help him relieve his embarrassment.

7. **Presenting an alternative question**—ask contradictory questions based on the selected theme (justification) where the suspect must choose one option or the other (e.g., did you plan this out or did it happen on the spur of the moment?).

8. **Having the suspect orally relate details of the crime**—obtain a statement of reinforcement that corroborates the suspect's admission of guilt.

9. **Convert an oral confession to a written confession**—ideally using an electronic recording of the confession.

Source: Inbau, F.E., Reid, J.E., Buckley III, J.P., & Jayne, B.C. (2013). Criminal interrogation and confessions, 5th edition. Chicago, IL: John E. Reid and Associates, Inc.

Research indicates that there are some best practices for conducting effective information-gathering interviews that investigators should practice. As shown in Figure 12.4, these include asking open-ended questions, using active listening, remaining nonjudgmental, and employing the 80:20

rule whereby the investigator listens 80% of the time and speaks 20% of the time. Unfortunately, research finds that few investigators adhere to these best practices; in particular, violating the 80:20 rule and asking the wrong types of questions (Snook at al., 2012). In addition to following these best practices, investigators should follow legal guidelines and avoid practices that have been shown to unintentionally elicit false confessions from innocent suspects (more on these in a minute).

TYPICAL SUSPECT INTERROGATIONS

There are four basic types of interrogation strategies that are contained within the nine steps of the Reid Interrogation Technique and which are practiced by investigators using other interrogation methods. The first, *isolation, rapport, and minimization*, involves the detective isolating the suspect away from family and friends, developing a rapport with the suspect, and minimizing the moral seriousness of the crime. The second, *confrontation*, involves confronting the suspect with a statement of guilt (and a case file to appear there is evidence against him); essentially the detective accuses the suspect of the crime and suggests that the paperwork in the file establishes his guilt.

The third technique, *threatening the suspect*, has the detective threaten the suspect with consequences if she doesn't tell the truth. The fourth technique, *presentation of evidence*, involves showing the suspect some of the actual evidence against her.

Almost all suspect interrogations include the following elements: (1) isolating the suspect away from family and friends; (2) placing the suspect in a small, private room; (3) identifying contradictions in the suspect's account; and (4) trying to establish a rapport with the suspect to gain trust (Kassin et al., 2007). Many interrogations also involve the detective confronting the suspect with evidence of guilt and appealing to the suspect's self-interests.

Typically, a suspect interview/interrogation lasts for 1.6 hours and is conducted during normal waking hours (Kassin et al., 2007). Most suspects are questioned three times, on average, during an investigation (the first couple are certainly interviews while the later (or last) one is customarily an interrogation).

Interestingly, very few suspects (19%) invoke their Miranda rights and most suspects (81%) choose to talk to investigators.

1. Ask as many open-ended questions as possible

2. Avoid yes-no, forced-choice, multiple-choice, and leading questions.

3. Use active listening; do not interrupt.

4. 80:20 rule: Interviewer should listen 80% of the time and talk 20% of the time.

5. Remain non-judgemental; do not share own opinions.

Source: Snook, B., Luther, K., Quinlan, H., & Milne, R. (2012). Let 'em talk! A field study of police questioning practices of suspects and accused persons. *Criminal Justice and Behavior, 39*(10), 1328–1339. doi: 10.1177/0093854812449216

Figure 12.4 Best Practice for information-gathering interviews

© iQoncept/Shutterstock.com

Presenting a file of evidence to a suspect is one popular interrogation strategy.

Of those who agree to answer police questions, two-thirds make self-incriminating statements (38% of suspects make a partial admission and 30% of suspects make a full confession); about one-third (32%) make no admission or confession during questioning.

Why do so many suspects make self-incriminating statements? It is probably because they think they can talk their way out of trouble, that they are somehow "smarter" than the investigator conducting the interview. Unfortunately, that is rarely the case. Today, most detectives are highly trained interviewers, masters in the law, and skilled in the art of psychological persuasion. This is due to advanced education and the training that the vast majority of detectives receive upon being promoted into the position.

LEGAL RULES GOVERNING POLICE QUESTIONING

As is the case with evidence collection and processing, there are many court cases that have enumerated citizens' due process rights when it comes to questioning by police and criminal prosecution. By and large, the cases governing police interrogations focus on our Fifth Amendment right to due process and against self-incrimination and our Sixth Amendment right to be informed of all formal charges and to the assistance of counsel.

FIFTH AMENDMENT OF THE CONSTITUTION OF THE UNITED STATES

No person shall be held to answer for a capital, or otherwise infamous crime, unless on a presentment or indictment of a grand jury, except in cases arising in the land or naval forces, or in the militia, when in actual service in time of war or public danger; nor shall any person be subject for the same offense to be twice put in jeopardy of life or limb; nor shall be compelled in any criminal case to be a witness against himself; nor be deprived of life, liberty, or property, without due process of law; nor shall private property be taken for public use, without just compensation.

SIXTH AMENDMENT OF THE CONSTITUTION OF THE UNITED STATES

In all criminal prosecutions, the accused shall enjoy the right to a speedy and public trial, by an impartial jury of the state and district wherein the crime shall have been committed, which district shall have been previously ascertained by law, and to be informed of the nature and cause of the accusation; to be confronted with the witnesses against him; to have compulsory process for obtaining witnesses in his favor; and to have the assistance of counsel for his defense.

The first major U.S.S.C. case pertaining to police interrogation was *Escobedo v. Illinois* (1964). This case provided that a person's right to counsel begins as soon as the person is a primary suspect (when questioning becomes accusatory), not upon appearing in court on a felony charge (as was the previous decision). It came one year after **Gideon v. Wainwright** (1963), which established that indigent defendants accused of felonies in state courts have a right to counsel provided for them. A mere two years later, the U.S.S.C. supplanted the Escobedo decision with **Miranda v. Arizona** (1966), which stipulated that officer's must advise suspects of their rights to free legal representation and against self-incrimination.

Owing to the plethora of crime drama shows on television and the many court-enacted exceptions to the requirement, Miranda is often misunderstood. However, it is actually quite simple. The Miranda notification requirement kicks in when two conditions are simultaneously met: custody and interrogation (police questioning). When a person is "in custody" (not free to leave) *and* is being questioned about a crime, police need to provide the Miranda notification.

If a person is being questioned, but is not in custody (is free to leave), no warning is required. Similarly, a person who is in custody but is not being questioned does not need to receive the Miranda warning (an officer might choose to provide the warning, but he is not required to at that point). A suspect must be unequivocal in his request for counsel.

At first, police were afraid Miranda would destroy their ability to solve crimes and gain confessions, but studies have found that Miranda has had very little effect on law enforcement's ability to apprehend suspects, elicit admissions of guilt, solve crimes, or gain convictions. There are two reasons Miranda has had such a minimal effect. First, most suspects routinely waive their Miranda rights. As mentioned above, only 19% of suspects invoke their Miranda rights immediately upon being informed of them (Kassin et al., 2007). Most suspects (81%) waive their Miranda rights and talk with officers. A small portion of suspects (13%) waive their rights initially and then invoke them at some time during police questioning. A full two-thirds (68%) never invoke their rights during police questioning. Second, police comply with the letter of the law, but not always the spirit of the law. For example, after giving warning, an officer might put a suspect (or two) in the back of a patrol vehicle or an interview room (with cameras rolling) to capture incriminating statements, or an officer may make statements about the crime in the suspect's presence that are very tempting for the suspect to respond to, or an officer may continue asking the suspect questions until the suspect says the exact words "I want a lawyer."

As it turned out, Miranda (along with other professional developments) transformed interrogations without undermining detectives' crime-solving capacity. Contrary to original feelings when the decision became law, police have come to embrace Miranda as a legitimating symbol of their professionalism. Some scholars argue that Miranda motivated police to develop more sophisticated interrogation techniques (Leo, 2008).

THE PROBLEM OF FALSE CONFESSIONS

Richard Leo, a police scholar who has studied interrogations extensively, has noted that there is a significant power imbalance in the interrogation room that puts suspects at a major disadvantage and can cause some suspects to falsely confess. This imbalance is caused by multiple factors: (1) detectives are highly trained interviewers and experts in the law; (2) suspects are generally not knowledgeable about the law or interview rules and are unaware that police can legally use deception during questioning (career criminals and streetwise offenders, especially those who are part of a criminal network, may be exceptions to this assumption); (3) detectives have the ability to frame the suspect's actions to other criminal justice practitioners (put in a good word with the prosecutor, for example); (4) suspects' movements are controlled by detectives (suspect must ask detective to use the bathroom, eat, drink, take a break); (5) suspects have a lot more at stake than the detective (namely, their freedom); and (6) interrogations take place in the police station, a place that is very comfortable for detectives but not suspects.

© Photographee.eu/Shutterstock.com

A suspect may give a false confession in an effort to stop the interrogation.

False confessions are not a new problem. The issue has existed for many years. The cause of the problem, however, has changed as interrogation techniques have evolved. Unlike 80 years ago, when false confessions typically resulted from physical coercion (the "third degree"), today they result from the highly persuasive psychological interrogation practices used by detectives (Leo, 2008). Although a minority of suspects make false confessions, it is an important issue and one that has drawn increased scrutiny in recent years because false confessions are one of the leading causes of false convictions (the others are eyewitness misidentification and unvalidated/improper forensics) (Innocence Project, 2015). Of more than 300 innocent defendants exonerated by DNA evidence in the past 25 years, 27% made incriminating statements, confessed, or pled guilty (Innocence Project, 2015).

Despite the fact that it is hard for most of us to understand why a sane person would admit to committing a crime they did not commit, it happens. There are three main reasons why suspects offer false confessions (Kassin & Wrightsman, 1985). Some individuals provide a **voluntary false confession** to gain fame or notoriety, to protect another person, or because they (due to a mental or psychological condition) are unable to discern reality from fantasy. Others provide a **coerced-compliant false confession** in response to "extreme methods of interrogation" because they want to stop the interrogation and believe that confessing to the crime will result in a more positive outcome than continuing to tell the truth (to the detective's dismay and the suspect's discomfort). Finally, some suspects provide a **coerced-internalized false confession** because they have been convinced (incorrectly) of their guilt.

More than 250 interrogation-induced false confessions have been documented in the past 50 years. Detectives are more skeptical of (and more likely to recognize as untruthful) voluntary false confessions than police-induced false confessions (Leo, 2008). Thus, false confessions that lead to false convictions are typically coerced (police-induced). Also, because the pressure to solve a case is greatest for serious crimes, false confessions happen most frequently in very serious cases. Of the 873 exonerations that occurred in the United States between 1989 and 2012, 135 (15%) involved false confessions; most (80%) of these were coerced and 75% happened in homicide cases (Cutler, Findley, & Loney, 2014).

PRACTICES THAT LEAD TO FALSE CONFESSIONS

Scholars have noted several police interrogation practices that are likely to lead to false confessions. These are *minimization and promises of leniency, presentation of false evidence*, and *lengthy interrogations*. In addition, suspects from specific *sensitive populations* have been found to be unusually susceptible to making false confessions.

Minimization and Promises of Leniency

The two interrogation techniques that have been consistently linked to false confessions are minimization and the presentation of false evidence. Detectives use *minimization techniques* to provide the suspect with moral justification for having committed the crime using a variety of "themes." For example, the detective might empathize with the suspect, normalize the crime, and then offer excuses (justifications) of why the suspect might have committed the crime (for instance, he was provoked, he succumbed to peer pressure, he was under the influence of drugs, or it was accidental). Such tactics encourage the suspect to make a confession and implicitly insinuate that a confession will be rewarded with leniency in the court and other privileges (like going home, having a meal, leaving the interrogation room).

Presentation of False Evidence Though very popular on television shows, *presenting false evidence* to a suspect in an interrogation is controversial in real life. It is allowed by U.S. law, but is not condoned by some law enforcement agencies because it has been implicated in the majority of documented police-induced false confessions (Kassin et al., 2010). Here, detectives pretend to have incriminating evidence against the suspect. Detectives may make false assertions (say they have evidence that they don't actually have), but they may not fabricate evidence (create an actual report/piece of evidence with the suspect's name on it to back up their fictional story). They may, however, use "props" as long as the props cannot be mistaken for actual evidence against the suspect (e.g., a bag containing clothing fibers from another case is acceptable). Deceptive practices cause suspects to question their memory and make incriminating statements based on their false belief that they were somehow involved.

Lengthy Interrogations

As previously mentioned, the standard interrogation is short; it lasts between 30 minutes and 2 hours (Kassin et al., 2010). Interrogations that lead to false confessions, however, are much longer—16.3 hours on average! In a study of proven false confessions, researchers found that 73% of false confession interrogations lasted 6 or more hours (34% lasted 6–12 hours and another 39% lasted 12–24 hours). Prolonged isolation from significant others and other deprivations can exaggerate a suspect's distress and provide the motivation to "do whatever it takes" to get out of the situation. Similarly, sleep deprivation (which is an aspect of extremely long interviews) impairs human functioning, including decision-making ability.

Sensitive Populations

Police must be particularly careful when conducting interrogations of individuals from sensitive populations who are more suggestible or who may not understand the long-term consequences of their statements. In particular, juveniles and individuals with mental impairment are overrepresented in the "proven false confessions" population. Children and adolescents are less mature (both psychosocially and cognitively) than adults and are prone to impulsive decision-making and risk taking, more susceptible to negative influences, and less able to predict long-term consequences (Kassin et al., 2010). These facts put them at much greater risk of providing a false confession. Likewise, individuals with diminished mental capacity are overrepresented in false confessions for many of the same reasons, especially a heightened susceptibility to influence, desire to please, and inability to understand the interrogation process and consequences (Kassin et al., 2010). Detectives should avoid presenting false evidence to suspects who have no recollection of the event due to alcohol or drug intoxication, injury, or other issue.

COULD YOU BE CONVINCED TO CONFESS TO A CRIME YOU DID NOT COMMIT?

It is easy to believe that we could never be convinced to admit to something we didn't do. However, new research questions that assumption.

According to an NPR (National Public Radio) article, after a 28-year-old jogger in New York City's Central Park had been beaten and raped in 1989, five teen boys were accused of the high profile crime. The boys quickly confessed to the crime and were convicted of it.

They, however, maintained their innocence and stated they only confessed because of intense pressure by police during questioning. The boys served more than 10 years in prison before new evidence came to light that showed they didn't do it. They were eventually released but their case highlights the role police interview tactics can play in convincing suspects to falsely confess to crimes they did not commit.

A recent study of undergraduate students shows that you can be convinced you did something you didn't do (even committed a crime) if the person telling you about the event has some true background information about you. After some time spent discussing the true information, along with the invented material, a person blends it together and can believe that it really happened. Not only does a subject believe the false memory, but their belief allows their imagination to run with the story, adding in details about the "crime" that make it seem even more real and filling in any holes in the narrative of what transpired. All together, the researchers "convinced" 70% of research participants that they had committed a minor crime during their adolescence (Researchers "debriefed all research subjects to ensure they understood that they did not, in fact, commit the crimes they were convinced they committed.).

What do you think? What would it take to convince YOU that you committed a crime?

Source: Siegel, N. (2015, January 29). You can be convinced to confess to an invented crime, study finds. NPR.

PRACTICES THAT REDUCE FALSE CONFESSIONS

What can police detectives do to prevent false confessions? Scholars offer four suggestions (some of which are starting to become standard practice in some agencies and states across America): (1) electronically record interrogations, (2) reform interrogation practices that disproportionately lead to false confessions, (3) require all confessions to have corroborating evidence, and (4) improve police training (Leo, 2008; Kassin, et al., 2010).

Electronically record interrogations Not only does an electronic recording create an accurate, objective, comprehensive, and reviewable record of an interrogation, but it also lessens the likelihood that investigators will use questionable tactics during the interrogation and protects the suspect's due process rights. Furthermore, like body-worn cameras on patrol officers, a recording of the interrogation is a valuable investigative tool and compelling court evidence. A recording preserves the suspect's initial statement (which can be played back for the suspect or others later). It also allows the detective to review the interrogation as the case develops and new evidence is uncovered. Additionally, without the burden of note taking, the investigator can focus more intently on the interview and the suspect's statements and nonverbal behaviors. Although many detectives and law enforcement officers were vehemently opposed to recording interrogations a few years ago, many who have experimented with the practice now endorse it and find that the many advantages outweigh the few concerns. As Table 12.2 shows, currently 19 states require the recording of some interrogations and another 2 strongly suggest it (Innocence Project, 2015).

TABLE 12.2 Practices to Prevent False Conviction

State	Eyewitness Identification Reform	Recording of Interrogations	Post-conviction DNA Testing
Alabama	None	None	Capital offenses
Alaska	None	Must record custodial interrogations, if feasible	Any serious felony
Arizona	None	None	Any felony
Arkansas	None	None	Any crime
California	None	None	Any felony
Colorado	Blind administration, proper instructions, proper fillers, confidence statements	None	Any prisoner
Connecticut	Blind administration, proper instructions, proper fillers, confidence statements	Must record all felony interrogations	Any crime
Delaware	None	None	Any crime
District of Columbia	Blind administration	Must record all violent crime interrogations conducted in MPD interview rooms	Any violent crime
Florida	None	None	Any felony
Georgia	Blind administration, proper instructions, proper fillers, confidence statements	None	Any serious violent felony
Hawaii	None	No state law; Honolulu PD (covers 80% population) req. recording custodial interrogations	Any crime
Idaho	None	None	Any crime
Illinois	Witness instructions, proper filler selection, blind or blinded administration	Must record custodial interrogation of homicide and sexual assault	Any crime
Indiana	None	Unrecorded statements are inadmissible in felony prosecutions, unless exception proved	Murder or Class A, B, or C felony
Iowa	None	Recordings of custodial interrogations encouraged but not required	Any felony
Kansas	None	None	Murder or rape only
Kentucky	None	None	Capital offense, violent or other certain felonies
Louisiana	None	None	Any felony
Maine	None	Must abide by standards set by Maine Criminal Justice Academy	Any crime punishable by 1+ years imprisonment
Maryland	Blind administration, proper instructions, proper fillers, confidence statements	Must make reasonable efforts to record custodial interrogations of murder, rape, sexual assault	Murder, manslaughter, rape, and sexual offense

continued

TABLE 12.2   Practices to Prevent False Conviction *(continued)*

State	Eyewitness Identification Reform	Recording of Interrogations	Post-conviction DNA Testing
Massachusetts	None	Jury instructions if unrecorded statements used in court; most depts. record custodial interviews	Any crime
Michigan	None	Time stamped, audiovisual recording required of any custodial interrogation of major felony suspect	Any felony for which prison time being served
Minnesota	None	Custodial interview must be recorded when feasible/ occurs at a place of detention	Any crime
Mississippi	None	None	Any crime
Missouri	None	Must record interrogations of certain serious crimes	Any crime
Montana	None	Must record interrogations of all felony crimes	Any felony
Nebraska	None	Must record interrogations at a place of detention in crimes	Any crime
Nevada	Agencies must adopt lineup policy.	None	Any felony punishable by 1+ years in prison
New Hampshire	None	Recorded final statements offered into evidence only admissible if entire post-Miranda interrogation session was recorded.	Any crime
New Jersey	Blind administration, sequential presentation, proper instructions, proper filler, confidence statement	Must record all custodial interrogations of certain felony suspects conducted in place of detention	Any prisoner while they are serving time
New Mexico	None	All police departments must record custodial interrogations	Any felony
New York	None	None	Any crime
North Carolina	Blind administration, sequential presentation, proper filler, proper instructions, confidence statement, record if possible	Must record homicide interrogations	Any crime
North Dakota	None	None	Any crime
Ohio	Blind administration, proper instructions, proper fillers, confidence statements	Presumes statements made during recorded interrogation are voluntary.	Any serious felony
Oklahoma	None	None	Allowed, no details
Oregon	OACP developed model policy is used to train officers according to *Lawson* decision	Must record entirety of custodial interrogations of class A and B felonies and homicides in law enforcement facilities	Murder, sex crime, or person felony

continued

TABLE 12.2   Practices to Prevent False Conviction *(continued)*

State	Eyewitness Identification Reform	Recording of Interrogations	Post-conviction DNA Testing
Pennsylvania	None	None	Any crime
Rhode Island	Task force recommended policies and procedures	None	Any crime
South Carolina	None	None	Any offense listed in §17-28
South Dakota	None	None	Any felony
Tennessee	None	None	Any crime listed in T.C.A. §40-30-303
Texas	Blind administration, proper instructions, proper fillers, confidence statements	None	Any crime
Utah	None	None	Any felony
Vermont	Blind administration, proper instructions, proper fillers, confidence statements	Must record custodial interrogation of homicide or sexual assault suspects	Certain offenses
Virginia	State board created model policy and training standards: Blind administration, proper instructions, proper fillers, confidence statements	None	Any felony
Washington	None	None	Any felony
West Virginia	Agencies must adopt written policy; 2/3 of policies require blind administration, proper instructions, proper fillers, sequential presentation, confidence statements, recording procedure	None	Any felony
Wisconsin	Agencies must adopt written policy; WI Attorney General suggested best practices	Must record felony interrogations	Any crime
Wyoming	None	None	Any felony

Source: Innocence Project. (2015). How is your state doing? Retrieved from http://www.innocenceproject.org/how-is-your-state-doing

Reform interrogation practices that disproportionately lead to false confessions

Scholars recommend changing the interrogation practices that have been shown to produce false confessions. In particular,

- Regulate or *ban the use of minimization techniques that include (explicit or implicit) promises of leniency* because they lead innocents to confess by suggesting that complying with the detective's request will lessen punishment or lead to other benefits, especially when the minimization techniques are coupled with threats that pleas of innocence will not be entertained and prosecution is inevitable (maximization techniques).

- *Forbid threats of physical harm or certain consequences* for the same reason as above.

- *Prohibit or further regulate the use of deceptive, false, and misleading interrogation techniques* because police lying about evidence is almost always necessary for eliciting false confessions. Except in rare circumstances, false confessions do not occur without police deception.

- *Restrict the length of interrogations* because long interrogations increase the risk of false confessions by fatiguing suspects and impairing their ability and motivation to resist police pressures.

- *Disallow depriving suspects' of physical essentials* such as food, water, sleep, medicine, bathroom, and supportive human contact because doing so drains suspect's resolve and increases the likelihood of an involuntary and false confession that is later recanted.

- *Provide additional safeguards for vulnerable populations* (juveniles, mentally handicapped, mentally ill) that are more easily led into giving involuntary and unreliable statements and are disproportionately documented in false confession cases.

- *Transform interrogations from the current antagonistic* (confrontational) *approach to an investigative approach* (such as the PEACE model used in England).

Require all confessions to have corroborating evidence

Detectives should make a practice of comparing the fit of the suspect's confession to the crime facts to ensure that the suspect's statement is corroborated by independent evidence. A false confessor's narrative (accounting of events) will have guesses and errors and will be either inconsistent with or contradicted by available evidence. Three indicators of reliability that have been offered by Leo and Ofshe (1998) are:

Does the statement:

1. Lead to the discovery of new evidence (specifically evidence unknown to the police)?
2. Include identification of highly unusual elements of the crime that have not been made public (e.g., an unlikely method or tool for killing, or entry method)? and
3. Include an accurate description of the mundane details of the crime which are not easily guessed and have not been reported publicly (for instance, how the victim was clothed or positioned, how the room was decorated, what was taken, etc.)?

Improve police training

Studies show that investigators are no better than laypeople at discerning a person's guilt or innocence based on their perception of demeanor, body language, and other nonverbal behavior (though they are much more confident in their truth-detecting abilities than the average lay person). Detectives should also be trained on the variety and causes of police-induced false confessions so that they can be aware of and identify potential unreliable confessions and distinguish them from reliable and truthful confessions.

LAW ENFORCEMENT'S COMMITMENT TO REDUCE WRONGFUL CONVICTIONS

In 2012, the International Association of Chiefs of Police, in conjunction with the U.S. Department of Justice, convened a summit on wrongful convictions specifically aimed at discussing how law enforcement can help reduce the incidence of wrongful convictions (and wrongful arrests). It is difficult to convey just how much policing has changed throughout history and since the first DNA exoneration occurred in 1989 for this to happen. Law enforcement professionals now not only acknowledge that there is a problem (which means accepting responsibility that law enforcement officers have made mistakes) but they also want to be a part of the solution (reduce the likelihood of future wrongful arrests and convictions and help true innocents gain freedom). This is because they recognize the damage that these cases cause for the criminal justice system, the public's trust in police, and public safety (since the true perpetrator is still at large). Noting the importance of the front end of the process, much of the committee's work during the summit focused on improving the investigations process and culture so that detectives are receptive to new information, use proper protocols and best practices, leverage available technology, and share collective ownership of investigations (investigators and prosecution teams). The committee made a total of 30 recommendations, some of which are listed below:

- Use established best practices for eyewitness identification (warnings, double-blind administration, sequential lineups, avoid confirmatory feedback, gather certainty statement, document the process).

- Gather corroborating evidence in cases of jailhouse testimony of informants.

- Conduct supervisory review to assess whether investigative bias adversely affected a case; develop protocols to acknowledge, address, and limit investigative bias; train investigators in risk-based decision-making.

- Improve timeline of DNA testing and delivery of results and ensure dissemination of results to all parties in a timely manner.

- Create a wrongful arrest risk-assessment tool, incorporating an investigative checklist or point system to guide pre-arrest decisions and post-arrest reevaluation.

- Establish accountability at every level in law enforcement agency for major case investigations; create a culture of critical thinking and openness to new information and incentivize using promising investigative practices (rather than focusing on speedy actions and outcomes).

- Create critical case review opportunities to increase transparency and decrease agency vulnerability to lawsuits.

- Improve training and protocols for evidence collection, preservation, and retention; invest in emerging technology that can enhance investigative quality and accuracy.

- "Law enforcement should take a leadership role in developing greater openness to re-examination [of closed cases when credible evidence calls into question prior decision-making]—both on a national level with the IACP and a local level with each executive leading that charge in every investigation" (IACP, 2013, p.20).

CONCLUSION

In this chapter, we introduced the investigative function. Starting with a history lesson, we explained how investigations have evolved from the early days of corruption and politics through the years marked by extreme physical punishment inflicted upon suspects to the current point where investigators are highly skilled professionals. We described the typical detective unit as well as the investigative process. Next, we explained the types of evidence investigators rely on to solve cases, the reliability of specific types of evidence (particularly as it pertains to wrongful convictions), and the science behind the evidence. We also discussed the various laws pertaining to the collection of evidence and questioning of suspects. Finally, we took up an important conversation about interrogations, the problem of false confession, and the practices that lead to false confessions as well as wrongful convictions. To be sure, police are just as concerned as the public about the possibility of wrongful convictions and have begun to take steps to address this serious issue.

REVIEW QUESTIONS

1. How did the Secretive Rogue period of history differ from the Inquisitor period and the Highly Skilled Detective period?
2. What were some common interrogation practices between the 1890s and 1930s?
3. What are the eight investigative objectives?
4. What happens during the preliminary investigation? Who conducts this investigation?
5. What happens during the secondary investigation? Who conducts this investigation?
6. What are the three types of cases described by Eck?
7. What does the research indicate about the effectiveness of investigators?
8. What are the different types of evidence mentioned?
9. What federal databases exist to assist in the identification of suspects through evidence evaluation?
10. What is the difference between an interview and an interrogation?
11. What are the four basic types of interrogation strategies used by detectives?
12. What practices have been shown to increase the likelihood of a false confession?
13. What can police do to prevent false confessions?
14. What are some of the recommendations made by IACP to reduce wrongful conviction?

GLOSSARY

Ballistics the scientific identification of firearms and bullets.

Biometrics a method of authenticating a person's identity through behavioral or physiological characteristics such as iris scanners and fingerprinting.

Clearance rate the measure that is often used to assess the effectiveness of the police; it compares the number of cases closed by arrest or exception to the number of crimes reported.

Coerced-compliant false confession a suspect who confesses to a crime in response to extreme interrogation methods; the suspect believes that confessing to the crime will result in a more positive outcome than continuing to tell the truth.

Coerced-internalized false confession a suspect who confesses to a crime because he/she has been convinced (incorrectly) of their guilt.

Criminalistics using scientific methods to collect and analyze physical evidence in criminal cases.

Digital evidence items related to a criminal case that can be found in a computer, cell phone, tablet, or other electronic device such as a camera.

DNA Profiling a forensic science procedure that uses variations in the genetic code to identify individuals.

Documentary evidence items related to a criminal case that provide information about or document activities or transactions affiliated with a crime.

Exclusionary rule US Supreme Court ruling that any evidence seized by police in violation of the Constitution cannot be used in court against a defendant.

Fruit of the poisonous tree doctrine US Supreme Court ruling that any evidence obtained by law enforcement as a result of an illegal search or seizure is inadmissible in court, as is any additional evidence obtained after the illegal search; it is an extension of the exclusionary rule.

Gideon v. Wainwright 1963 US Supreme Court case which established that indigent defendants accused of felonies in state courts have a right to counsel provided for them.

Good faith exception an exception to the exclusionary rule that allows evidence from an invalid search warrant to be presented in court, provided the police acted in good faith.

Inevitability of discovery exception an exception to the exclusionary rule that allows illegally obtained evidence to be used if police can prove that it would have been discovered eventually as the result of legal investigative procedures.

Interrogation a formal conversation between a police investigator and a crime suspect in which the purpose is to determine the suspect's involvement in the crime and elicit a confession; often takes an accusatory tone in the United States.

Interview a formal dialogue between a police officer or investigator and an individual who has knowledge of or is potentially associated with a crime (for example suspect, victim, or witness); the goal is to gather information about the individual's knowledge of and/or potential involvement in a crime under investigation.

Mapp v. Ohio 1961 US Supreme Court case that extended the exclusionary rule to the states and articulated the "fruit of the poisonous tree" doctrine.

Miranda rights the obligation of police officers to inform suspects of their right to remain silent and their right to an attorney.

Miranda v. Arizona 1966 US Supreme Court case that established the Miranda rule which requires police officers to advise suspects of their constitutional rights.

Next Generation Identification (NGI) a database of digitized fingerprints, palm prints, and photos held by the FBI; it is the largest fingerprint database in the world.

Physical evidence any physical item that can be seen or felt and is related to a criminal case.

Preliminary investigation evidence-gathering activities performed at the scene of a crime immediately after the crime was reported to or discovered by the police.

Public safety exception an exception to the exclusionary rule and the 5th Amendment protection against self-incrimination that allows officers to use information and evidence obtained by questioning a suspect prior to advisement of his/her Miranda rights if the concern for public safety is so great as to outweigh adherence to the rules.

Reid technique the most common interview and interrogation method in the United States.

Secondary investigation investigation conducted by detective to identify suspects and prepare a case file for prosecution.

Testimonial evidence knowledge and memories provided by victims, witnesses, suspects, and key others about a crime or suspect.

U.S. v. Davis 2014 11th Circuit Court of Appeals case that ruled that investigators need a search warrant to obtain cell phone location data for a suspect.

Voluntary false confession a suspect who voluntarily confesses to a crime to gain fame or notoriety, protect another person, or because they (due to a mental or psychological condition) are unable to discern reality from fantasy.

Weeks v. U.S. 1914 US Supreme Court case that established the exclusionary rule and prohibited illegally obtained evidence from being used in Federal trials.

REFERENCES

Bureau of Alcohol, Tobacco, Firearms, and Explosives (BATF). (2015a, February 1). *Fact sheet: National Integrated Ballistics Information Network (NIBIN).* Retrieved from https://www.atf.gov/resource-center/pr/atf-fact-sheet-national-integrated-ballistic-information-network-nibin

Bureau of Alcohol, Tobacco, Firearms, and Explosives (BATF). (2015b, June 16). *National Integrated Ballistics Information Network (NIBIN) success stories.* Retrieved from https://www.atf.gov/firearms/success-stories

Criminalistics (n.d.). *Merriam-Webster Dictionary.* Retrieved from http://www.merriam-webster.com/dictionary

Cutler, B., Findley, K.A., & Loney, D. (2014). Expert testimony on interrogation and false confession. *UMKC Law Review, 82,* 589–622.

Durose, M. R., Walsh, K. A., & Burch, A. M. (2012, August). *Census of publicly funded forensic crime laboratories, 2009.* #NCJ238252. Washington, DC: U.S. Department of Justice, Bureau of Justice Statistics.

Federal Bureau of Investigation (FBI). (n.d.). *Next Generation Identification (NGI).* Retrieved from https://www.fbi.gov/about-us/cjis/fingerprints_biometrics/ngi

Forensic Science. (n.d.) *Oxford Dictionary.* Retrieved from http://www.oxforddictionaries.com/

Fox, B., & Farrington, D. (2015). An experimental evaluation of the utility of burglary profiles applied in active police investigations. *Criminal justice and behavior, 42*(2), 156–175. doi: 10.177/0093854814548446

Gernstein, J. (2014, May 7). Tsarnaev defense: Suppress hospital statements. *Politico.* Retrieved from http://www.politico.com/blogs/under-the-radar/2014/05/tsarnaev-defense-suppress-hospital-statements-188142.html

Greenwood, P., & Petersilia, J. (1975). *The criminal investigation process: Summary and policy implications.* Washington, DC: U.S. Government Printing Office.

Hopkins, E. J. (1931). *Our lawless police: A study of the unlawful enforcement of the law.* New York, NY: Viking Press.

International Association of Chiefs of Police (IACP). (2013, August). National summit on wrongful convictions: Building a systemic approach to prevent wrongful convictions. Alexandria, VA: IACP. Retrieved from http://www.theiacp.org/portals/0/documents/pdfs/Wrongful_Convictions_Summit_Report_WEB.pdf

Inbau, F. E., Reid, J. E., Buckley, J. P., & Jayne, B. C. (2013). *Criminal Interrogation and confession* (5th ed.). Chicago, IL: John E. Reid and Associates, Inc.

Innocence Project. (2015). The causes of wrongful conviction. Retrieved from http://www.innocenceproject.org/causes-wrongful-conviction

Innocence Project. (2015). How is your state doing? Retrieved from http://www.innocenceproject.org/how-is-your-state-doing

Jayne, B., & Buckley, J. (2014). *A field guide to the Reid Technique.* Chicago, IL: John E. Reid.

Kassin, S. M., Drizin, S. A., Grisso, T., Gudjonsson, G. H., Leo, R. A., & Redlich, A. D. (2010). Police-induced confessions: Risk factors and recommendations. *Law and Human Behavior, 34,* 3–38. doi: 10.10979-009-9188-6

Kassin, S. M., Leo, R. A., Meissner, C. A., Richman, K. D., Colwell, L. H., Leach, A. M., et al. (2007). Police interviewing and interrogation: A self-report survey of police practices and beliefs. *Law and Human Behavior, 31,* 381–400.

Kassin, S., & Wrightsman, L. (1985). Confession evidence. In S. Kassin & L. Wrightsman (Eds.), *The psychology of evidence and trial procedure* (pp. 67–94). Beverly Hills, CA: Sage.

Kozinski, A. (2015). Criminal law 2.0. *Georgetown Law Journal Annual Review of Criminal Procedure, 44,* iii–xliv.

Leo, R. (2008). *Police interrogation and American justice.* Cambridge, MA: Harvard University Press.

Leo, R. A., & Ofshe, R. J. (1998). The consequences of false confessions: Deprivations of liberty and miscarriages of justice in the age of psychological interrogation. *Journal of Criminal Law and Criminology, 88,* 429–496.

Lott, J. R., Jr. (2002). Bullets and bunkum: The futility of 'ballistic fingerprinting' *National Review, 54*(21), 28–30.

National Academy of Sciences. (2014). *Identify the culprit: Assessing eyewitness identification.* Washington DC: Author. Retrieved from http:// www.nap.edu

National Registry of Exonerations. (2015a). *% exonerations by contributing factors.* Retrieved from http://www.law.umich.edu/special/exoneration/Pages/ExonerationsContribFactors-ByCrime.aspx#

National Registry of Exonerations. (2015b). *Basic patterns.* Retrieved from http://www.law.umich.edu/special/exoneration/Pages/Basic-Patterns.aspx

Northwestern University School of Law. (n.d.). *First DNA Exoneration: Gary Dotson—The rape that wasn't the nation's first DNA exoneration.* Retrieved from http://www.law.northwestern.edu/legalclinic/wrongfulconvictions/exonerations/il/gary-dotson.html

Ofshe, R., & Leo, R. A. (1997). The social psychology of police interrogation: The theory and classification of true and false confessions. *Studies in Law, Politics, and Society, 16,* 189–251.

Parker-Pope, T. (2015, February 8). Was Brian Williams a victim of false memory? *The New York Times.* Retrieved from http://well.blogs.nytimes.com/2015/02/09/was-brian-williams-a-victim-of-false-memory/?_r=0

Siegel, N. (2015, January 29). You can be convinced to confess to an invented crime, study finds. *NPR.* Retrieved from http://www.npr.org/2015/01/29/382483367/you-can-be-convinced-to-confess-to-an-invented-crime-study-finds

Snook, B., Luther, K., Quinlan, H., & Milne, R. (2012). Let 'em talk! A field study of police questioning practices of suspects and accused persons. *Criminal Justice and Behavior, 39*(10), 1328–1339. doi: 10.1177/0093854812449216

Womack, C. L. (2007). *Criminal investigations: The impact of patrol officers on solving crimes.* Master's thesis. University of North Texas, Denton.

Wright, J. (2013, September). Applying the public safety exception to Dzhokhar Tsarnaev: Restricting criminal procedural rights by expanding judicial exceptions. *Columbia Law Review Sidebar.* Retrieved from http://columbialawreview.org/

CASES

Riley v. California, No. 13-132 (U.S.S.C., 2014).
U.S. v. Katzin, No. 12-2548 (3d. Cir., 2013).
U.S. v. Davis, No. 12-12928 (11h. Cir., 2014).

13 POLICE BEHAVIOR

LEARNING OBJECTIVES

After reading this chapter, students should be able to:

1 Describe the relationship between actual and perceived police behavior, and explain why it is important for police departments to be aware of this relationship.

2 Describe and discuss the four pillars of procedural justice.

3 Discuss the history of racial profiling as a topic of scientific inquiry in policing.

4 Describe the difference between police deviance and police integrity, and describe different varieties of police deviance.

5 Explain the Supreme Court's approach to understanding the reasonableness of police use of force.

6 Discuss what we presently "know" about the nature and extent of police use of force in the United States, and how we know it.

KEY TERMS

Police legitimacy	Rotten apple	Meat eaters
Procedural justice	Rotten pockets	Police integrity
Biased policing	Rotten orchard	Force factor
Racial profiling	Knapp Commission	Reasonable force
Occupational deviance	Grass eaters	Excessive force
Abuse of authority		

OVERVIEW

We begin this chapter with a dilemma for you to consider. We often talk about holding officers to a higher standard than we hold ourselves, and that officers must also hold themselves to this higher standard. We spend an awful lot of resources on screening, selection, and training processes designed to ensure that we are employing high-quality personnel in law enforcement. Police chiefs may diligently follow the research evidence and employ "best practices" in all aspects of departmental management and administration. And maybe, as a result, your local police department consists of officers who could be appropriately characterized as a bunch of "boy scouts"—they consistently provide high-quality police services, follow the rules to a tee, and generally do a fine job. Here's the dilemma: Does any of the above matter, if the public just doesn't see it that way? The reality is that it doesn't matter if your officers are "boy scouts," for if the public doesn't see it that way, you have a problem.

In this chapter we tackle police behavior and in particular try to understand this relationship between actual and perceived police behavior. This is not a new concept; police administrators, reformers, and others have long recognized a perceptual component of policing. That is, police behavior has direct consequences for public perceptions of the police and subsequent trust and confidence in the police, but there can also be a disconnect between the perception and the reality of police behavior, which can be highly problematic. As Figure 13.1 below depicts, there can be two kinds of disconnect: that which occurs when actual police behavior is not necessarily poor, but the public perceives it to be poor (Disconnect I); and that which occurs when police behavior is poor but the public is unaware or does not view the behavior as problematic (Disconnect II). In the other two cells both actual and perceived behavior are in alignment, one in a positive direction (No Problem) and the other in a negative direction (Serious Problem).

		Actual police behavior	
		Exemplary	Less than exemplary
Public perception of police behavior	**Exemplary**	**No problem**—Police behavior is optimal and your department likely has strong public confidence	**Disconnect II**—Your department may not have a problem now, but is likely to have a serious problem in the future that will undermine public confidence
	Less than exemplary	**Disconnect I**—Police behavior is not necessarily problematic, but the public does not agree and your department may lose public confidence	**Serious problem**—Your department has either already lost or will soon lose public confidence

Figure 13.1 Contrasting actual and perceived police behavior.

The grid above can play out over the long-term, as well as the short-term; a police department may find itself generally in the "No Problem" category but can move to other cells in the wake of high-profile incidents. In response to several such incidents over the past couple of years, the police have in some cases struggled with "Disconnect I." In these instances, the police maintain that what their officer(s) did was legal and proper, but the public simply does not agree. In some cases, such as incidents involving the use of force, the public perception may not align with departmental policy, or with the law. And, while it can be easy to lose confidence, most would agree it can be very difficult to regain it once it is lost. The public is expected to presume that officers have been subjected to a rigorous screening, selection, and training process, and that police agencies are vigilant in monitoring and responding to officer behavior. However, because policing is such a visible occupation, involving direct personal contacts with citizens, this presumption can be eroded by incidents involving poor officer behavior or what may be perceived as poor officer behavior. The public experiences officer behavior through direct police–citizen contact, and indirectly through exposure to the experiences of family, friends, and acquaintances, as well as media reports of police misbehavior and portrayals in the entertainment industry. The proliferation of mobile electronic devices, such as smart phones with high-definition video cameras (and the coming wave of police body cameras), has each produced countless hours of video footage of police–citizen interactions. It is not difficult to find videos of police doing apparently bad things uploaded on the Internet.

One of the ways the public experiences officer behavior is through direct police-citizen contact.

As we suggested in Chapter 1, one way to think about democratic policing is that the principal concern of democratic policing is not the behavior of citizens; it is the behavior of the police. And, as we have been arguing above, it is not just the behavior of the police, but also the public perception of police behavior. A critical piece of this is the need for the police to first acknowledge the behaviors that the public views as a violation of their trust (regardless of whether the police agree), and then the police must seek to either explain or correct the identified problems in a timely manner. In the next chapter we will argue that this is an essential component of police accountability, but for now let's consider it in the broader context of understanding police behavior.

As we continue through this chapter, we will be examining the effect of police behavior on legitimacy and citizen cooperation, we will look at the issue of racially biased policing, explore different forms of police deviance, and we will take up the issue of police use of force. As you progress through the chapter, we want you to consider the framework above for understanding the relationship between actual police behavior and the public's perception of that behavior.

EFFECT OF POLICE BEHAVIOR ON CITIZEN COOPERATION

KEY CONCEPTS: LEGITIMACY AND PROCEDURAL JUSTICE

Legitimacy is formally defined by Tyler (1990: 375) as "a psychological property of an authority, institution, or social arrangement that leads those connected to it to believe that it is appropriate, proper, and just." When individuals believe that an institution is appropriate, proper, and just, they are more likely to comply with rules and defer to the institution's authority (Sunshine and Tyler, 2003). So that "psychological property" of the institution is very important, and it is highly dependent on police behavior—both actual and perceived. **Police legitimacy**, then, can be thought of as the extent to which we recognize and are willing to defer to the authority of the police to regulate our behavior. Further, we can conceptualize police legitimacy as falling along a continuum ranging from strong to weak, with the position along the continuum being determined by police behavior and, importantly, the public's perception of that behavior.

Researchers have explored many different factors that might improve police legitimacy, and have generally focused their efforts on the idea of **procedural justice**. The idea here is that the process by which decisions are made is very important to the formation of citizen's attitudes, not only with regard to the specific interaction but also generally toward the police. There are four key aspects (or "pillars") of procedural justice: *citizen participation* (i.e., citizens feel that they've had "voice" in the matter and have been able to explain their side of things prior to the police making a decision); perceived *neutrality* on the part of the police in making the decision; police treating all parties with *dignity and respect* during the interaction; and whether the police convey *trustworthy motives*. Mazerolle et al. (2013), in their systematic review of the legitimacy in policing literature, specify four other pathways to police legitimacy, including high performance, distributive justice, legality, and tradition (see Figure 13.2), although they focus on the procedural justice linkage. The anticipated outcomes include improved citizen satisfaction with the police, willingness to cooperate with the police, trust in the police, and confidence in the police. Some have also pointed out that there is an additional benefit to officers in the form of improved safety, insofar as compliance and cooperation are increased and violent interactions may be less likely.

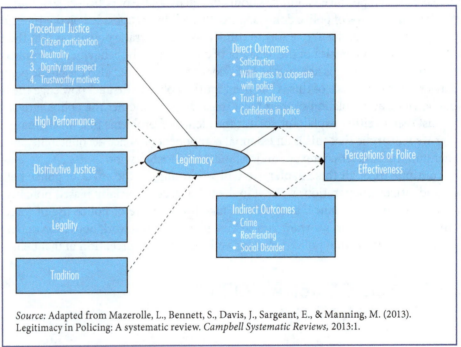

Source: Adapted from Mazerolle, L., Bennett, S., Davis, J., Sargeant, E., & Manning, M. (2013). Legitimacy in Policing: A systematic review. *Campbell Systematic Reviews*, 2013:1.

Figure 13.2 Theoretical Model of Police Legitimacy Process.

Mazerolle et al.'s (2013) review of the literature focused on police-led interventions (such as community policing) that were designed to improve police legitimacy or used one of the four principles of procedural justice. They identified more than 900 studies on police legitimacy and/ or procedural justice in policing, 163 of which reported on police-led interventions. They pared down the list to a final set of 30 studies (including 41 different assessments) that employed certain experimental or quasi-experimental methods, with which they performed a meta-analysis. Seven of the studies assessed legitimacy as an outcome, 14 assessed procedural justice, 8 assessed compliance or cooperation, 29 assessed satisfaction or confidence, and 26 assessed reoffending. In sum, they reported that the largest effects were found for improved satisfaction or confidence in the police, followed by compliance or cooperation, and procedural justice. They concluded that "... police interventions that comprised dialogue with a procedural justice component (or stated specifically that the intervention sought to increase legitimacy) did indeed enhance citizens' views on the legitimacy of the police, with all direct outcomes apart from legitimacy itself being statistically significant. Our review shows that by police adopting procedurally just dialogue, they can use a variety of interventions to enhance legitimacy, reduce reoffending, and promote citizen satisfaction, confidence, compliance and cooperation with the police" (Mazzerole et al., 2013:11).

BIASED POLICING

Biased policing, whether actual or perceived, is one area in which legitimacy can break down rapidly, as biased policing undermines fundamental fairness in the administration of justice. As discussed in Chapter 7 with regard to police discretion and decision-making, there have been concerns about racial discrimination, and indeed discrimination of all forms, in policing for a very long time. Researchers have long studied the effects of an individual's race on criminal justice decisions and outcomes generally, and police behavior in particular. However, starting in the 1990s, there was renewed attention to the role of race within the particular context of traffic stops. The Drug Enforcement Administration in the mid-1980s had developed a drug courier profile to help stop the flow of drugs along Interstate-95 from Miami, Florida, to the Northeastern states (called "Operation Pipeline"), and the profile was comprised of several characteristics including driver race/ethnicity. This information was disseminated and taught to State and local agencies along the I-95 corridor as a means of increasing the efficiency of enforcement. Although the historical roots of "**racial profiling**" and "driving while black" are arguably very deep, the term racial profiling came to popular usage in the wake of legal actions against the New Jersey State Police and the Maryland State Police in the early 1990s, as well as intense political attention to the issue and subsequent legislation.

Engel et al. (2002) argued that much of the early research on racial profiling was weak because the knowledge base on police decision-making, particularly theoretical explanations other than the individual biases of officers, was generally ignored. Data collection became the mantra for agencies (whether legislatively proscribed or not), but left to the side were important considerations about what types of data were necessary to answer particular questions, and once agencies had collected the data, what should be done with them analytically. There were lots of questions about the appropriate

Racial profiling by police continues to be an issue as shown in this 2014 protest.

population base against which to compare traffic stop demographics (the so-called denominator problem or the benchmark problem—i.e., in order to calculate the rate of traffic stops, what is the appropriate "at-risk" population?). As this line of inquiry expanded beyond traffic stops into other areas of police intervention, such as stop-and-frisks, even more methodological development occurred. Yet, a recent assessment (Ridgeway and MacDonald, 2010) concluded that a "best" benchmark approach for identifying the at-risk population for police interventions has not yet been determined, although some methods are more promising than others.

Racial profiling has been expanded to the broader "bias-based policing" in recognition of biases beyond race (such as gender, age, and sexual orientation), and, in the post-September 11, 2001, era, religious bias is also increasingly a concern. The profiling of Muslims has been a very controversial topic, and only limited academic attention has been directed at interactions with the justice system. Rice and Parkin (2010: 457), for example, cited public opinion data showing that "... Muslim Americans identified discrimination, racism, and prejudice as the number one problem facing their communities, while the number two problem was being viewed as a terrorist.

Seventy-three percent of native-born Muslims believe that anti-terrorism policies single out Muslims, compared to 47% of foreign-born Muslims."

Much of the current research focus on biased policing has shifted away from benchmarking research and empirical analyses of police administrative data, and toward helping officers to gain self-awareness of *implicit bias* (i.e., unconscious bias) and the potential impacts, as well as strategies for managing and minimizing these potential impacts in their work. Take a look at the box on the Implicit Association Test (IAT) for more on this.

TAKE AN IMPLICIT ASSOCIATION TEST (IAT)

Researchers associated with *Project Implicit* have developed several tests for assessing both conscious and unconscious preferences for many different things, such as skin tone, race, religion, gender, and weight. Their goals are to collect data through their Internet-based IATs for research purposes and to provide information to the public about hidden biases. For example, you can go to their website (https://implicit.harvard.edu/implicit/) and take the Race IAT, which assesses your ability to distinguish faces of European and African origin. After answering several survey questions, you will begin a series of word and image sorting tasks. One task will ask you to sort images of faces into the categories of European or African; another task will ask you to sort words into the categories of Good or Bad; a third task will combine the first two sets of categories so that you sort into "Good or African" and "Bad or European" categories; then, you will sort into the categories of European or African, but the categories will be reversed; finally, you will sort images of faces into the categories "Bad or African" and "Good or European." Your score on the IAT is based on the average time it takes you to sort the words in the third task as compared to the fifth task. If you are faster to sort when European faces and Good words were classified together than when African faces and Good words were classified together, your results would be described as an automatic preference for European American, with further qualifiers of "slight," "moderate," "strong," or "little to no preference" depending on the magnitude of the difference in the sorting times. Try it out!

POLICE DEVIANCE

For some reason, there is a strong marketplace for movies about police officers who have gone bad either by themselves, as part of a small but tightly knit group of officers, or as part of an entire police department. Perhaps there is something broadly appealing about these tales of abused authority and systemic corruption? *Bad Lieutenant, Cop Land, The Departed, L.A. Confidential, Night Falls on Manhattan, Prince of the City, Serpico, Training Day*, just to name a few. Some of these movies are based on true events while others are simply elaborate fictions. How can we organize and understand the broad nature of police misbehavior, as well as the "reality" or extent of misbehavior?

Scholars have developed a number of different classification schemes for describing the varieties of police misbehavior, typically referred to as *police deviance,* including both criminal and norm-violative behavior (e.g., Barker and Carter, 1994; Kappeler et al., 1994; Palmiotto, 2001). In order to understand police deviance, we must begin by recognizing that the key factor differentiating police deviance from general deviance is the fact that police deviance occurs in the specific context of an individual's role as a police officer. Barker and Carter (1994) synthesized existing classification schemes and proposed a general typology that distinguishes between police **occupational deviance** and police **abuse of authority**:

> *Police occupational deviance*—Criminal and non-criminal behavior committed under the guise of police authority or in the course of normal police activity, including *corruption* and *misconduct*.

> *Police abuse of authority*—Actions committed "without regard to motive, intent, or malice that tends to injure, insult, trespass upon human dignity, manifest feelings of inferiority, and/or

Citizens gather for the Stop Murder by Police protest.

violate an inherent legal right of a member of the police constituency in the course of performing 'police work'" (Barker and Carter, 1994:7), including *physical, psychological,* and *legal abuse.*

While both types of deviance are inherently occupational in nature, the distinction is made based on the locus of the behavior. Physical, legal, and psychological abuses are conceptualized as acts with an external locus—namely, citizens. These abuses are motivated by the intent to accomplish some police goal, and emerge out of the "practice of policing" (Barker and Carter, 1994:6, 9). These acts are also likely to have greater levels of peer acceptance or tolerance. Examples would include brutality (physical abuse), improper searches (legal abuse), and verbal harassment (psychological abuse).

On the other hand, corruption and misconduct are conceptualized as acts with an internal locus—that is, these acts are related to how officers perform as members of the organization, although they may have indirect effects on citizens. These acts are motivated by personal profit or gain, and they emerge out of the individual's role as an employee. These acts are likely to have lower levels of peer tolerance. Examples would include using confidential information for personal use (misconduct) and soliciting bribes to ignore violations (corruption).

Scholars, practitioners, and others have also proposed various classification schemes to describe the officers involved in corrupt activities, as well as the degree of involvement within agencies. For example, the idea that an officer who engages in corrupt activity on their own is a **rotten apple** or that small groups of officers who engage in such behavior together are **rotten pockets**, and a larger group of corrupt officers (such as a unit or station) is a **rotten orchard**. The terms *pervasive unorganized* and *pervasive organized* corruption refer to the spread of corrupt behavior within a police department (Sherman, 1974). Pervasive unorganized corruption refers to a large proportion of officers engaged in corrupt behavior, but independently of one another, while pervasive organized corruption describes a large proportion of officers working together in corrupt activities. The **Knapp Commission**, formed in 1970 to investigate corruption in the NYPD in the wake of the allegations of officer Frank Serpico, rejected the idea of "rotten apples" as simplistic and a hindrance to police reform. Instead, they identified two categories of corrupt officers, fairly widespread "**Grass Eaters**" and less-widespread "**Meat Eaters.**" Grass eaters were engaged in relatively low-level corruption in that they accepted gratuities and low dollar bribes but did not actively seek out such opportunities, and mainly accepted such money in order to demonstrate their loyalty to fellow officers—indeed taking the money to keep quiet. Meat eaters, on the other hand, actively sought out opportunities for financial gain (primarily from drug dealers and those engaged in other vice crimes) and rationalized it by diffusing responsibility to their criminal victims.

VARIETIES OF POLICE DEVIANCE

How do we know about the nature and extent of these behaviors? Our knowledge of the varieties of police deviance comes from a broad range of data sources. Just as in our approach to understanding crime in general, there is a sizeable "dark figure" of police deviance and we try to get at a good estimate through the same types of data sources. Official data on police deviance may be found in the form of police department records (such as records of citizen complaints, internal investigations, and disciplinary action) as well as court records. As an example, researchers and practitioners alike have examined cases where officers were officially disciplined in order to explore the distribution of underlying behaviors. Plitt (1983) noted that the underlying behaviors were quite diverse, including: abuse of sick leave, perjury, off-duty drunkenness, sexual improprieties, off-duty firearms incidents, disobedience of orders, acceptance of gratuities, and excessive use of force. While this is certainly part of the puzzle, this kind of data is very similar to official data on offenses known to the police (i.e., the UCR). That is, disciplinary data and all other official, departmental data of this nature are just that: behavior known to and officially recognized by the police administration. While the official disciplinary data are useful, it only represents a subset of all such deviant behavior within a police department—that which was officially detected.

© Bogdan Vija/Shutterstock.com

Profit-motivated crimes such as bribery account for 16% of career-ending misconduct.

Nevertheless, when researchers can gain deep access to records we can learn quite a bit from these studies. Kane and White (2009; 2013), for example, had deep access to NYPD records as part of their involvement with the NIJ-funded "Bad Cops" study of the late James Fyfe (a former NYPD officer turned policing scholar). This was a study of career-ending misconduct in the NYPD during the period 1975–1996. They collected extensive information on 1,543 officers who separated from the NYPD for misconduct, along with a matched sample of 1,543 officers, each of whom were randomly selected from the same academy class as their respective study officer. This study design enabled them not only to describe the nature and prevalence of career-ending misconduct in the NYPD, but also the characteristics of officer's personal background histories and their police careers that tended to predict whether an officer would get "jammed up" (Kane and White, 2013). With regard to the prevalence of career-ending misconduct, the 1,543 officers represented about 2% of all officers during the 22-year period, leading the authors to conclude that it is relatively rare. With regard to the nature of career-ending misconduct, they noted that about 30% of the charges involved administrative offenses, such as attendance, performance, obedience, and reporting; about 19% involved drug sales, possession, or failure of a drug test; and 16% involved profit-motivated crimes (such as bribe-taking, larceny, fraud, burglary, and gratuities).

In terms of what predicts career-ending misconduct, their multivariate analyses showed that the following were the strongest risk factors: officer was black or Hispanic; citizen complaints; working in inspector precincts; having a criminal history; and having prior employment problems. They also identified some protective factors (i.e., factors that lead to lower likelihoods of career-ending misconduct): more years on the job; having a college degree at the time of appointment;

older at the time of appointment; officers whose fathers had served in the NYPD; and achieving a supervisory rank.

Another example of official data would be court records concerning civil or criminal actions against officers. Bickel's (2001) case studies of misconduct cases brought for prosecution, and Chiabi's (1996) analysis of Section 1983 cases in the Eastern and Southern Districts of New York are good examples. Bickel (2001), for example, highlights cases involving sexual assault, murder, domestic violence, and robbery. These cases, however, clearly represent only the smallest portion of the iceberg in terms of the full scope of behavior.

Researchers may not have access to data of the detail described above, nor may some departments keep such records. Thus, in addition to accepting the fallibility of official measures, it may also be necessary to rely on proxy measures for underlying problem behaviors. For example, absent extremely detailed information on the circumstances and content of police-citizen interactions, researchers may have to rely on less-detailed indicators of problem behavior, such as counts tallying the generation of citizen complaints, the launching of investigations, and the filing of disciplinary charges. These events are driven by officer behaviors of varying degrees of severity, and a collection of such events may then be taken as indicative of more serious underlying behaviors for a given officer. At the least, these events individually and collectively raise concern over officer performance.

Although this is starting to change in the wake of recent public attention to police and the lack of data about police-citizen interactions, for a variety of legal, administrative, and political reasons, police agencies have been either unable or unwilling to provide even basic descriptive data about police misbehavior. And even when an agency is able or willing to produce data, the quality of the data varies greatly across agencies. This is not to say that attempts haven't been made to collect national-level data (e.g., Pate and Fridell, 1993; Hickman, 2006), but there are a number of methodological hurdles that must be overcome if these kinds of questions are to be addressed. For example, in order to conduct meaningful aggregate or comparative analyses, police agencies would have to adopt standardized definitions. As this is being written, this is not the case and the prospect for such standardization remains rather dim. So, researchers have little choice but to explore alternative and complementary methods.

Observational data have been a useful source of information about police deviance. A classic example is Black and Reiss' study of more than 5,000 police–citizen interactions in Washington, DC, Chicago, and Boston, during the Summer of 1966. Thirty-six observers rode or walked with officers on patrol in these three cities and recorded mobilization "incidents" (an event beginning when the officer becomes aware of a situation that requires police action, by radio, by a citizen, or by the officer's own detection, and concludes when the officer leaves the scene). The study necessarily involved a little bit of deception, in that officers under observation were informed that the study was of citizen behavior toward the police and not police behavior; in fact, the primary purpose of the research was to study both officer and citizen behavior.

Key findings reported from this study relevant to police deviance (Reiss, 1971) included officers being verbally and physically abusive toward citizens, and some officers violated the law including acceptance of bribes, the use of "drop guns," and receipt of stolen property, among other offenses. The incidence of police criminal violations included: officer accepts money to alter testimony report (4 cases); officer carries weapon to leave on citizen (2 cases); officer receives money/merchandise on return of stolen property (2 cases); officer takes money/property from deviants (10 cases; 6 directly observed); officer gives no citation for traffic violation and gets money (9 cases; 4 directly observed); officer takes merchandise from burglarized establishment (6 cases; 3 directly observed); and officer receives money or merchandise from a business (excluding

© bikeriderlondon/Shutterstock.com

Most people stopped for traffic violations say that the police behaved properly and respectfully during the encounter.

free meals and small favors, 19 cases; 17 directly observed). Other directly observed infractions included: drinking on duty, sleeping on duty, neglect of duty, and falsification of reports. The rate of all such criminal violations was reported as an astonishing 23.7 per 100 in "City X," 21.9 in "City Y," and 16.5 in "City Z" (Reiss, 1971:156).

Victimization surveys are another potentially useful source of information on police deviance, wherein citizens report on their experiences with the police. One example is the Police-Public Contact Survey (PPCS), conducted as part of the National Crime Victimization Survey (NCVS), which we have already discussed in this text. A recent analysis of PPCS data (Langton & Durose, 2013) for 2011 shows that of the nearly 63 million residents age 16 or older who had a contact with the police during that year, about half (49%) said their most recent contact was police-initiated (such as a traffic stop, street stop, or other involuntary contact including arrest) as opposed to citizen-initiated or voluntary contacts. Among respondents reporting traffic stops, 86% said that the police behaved properly and respectfully during the encounter compared to 66% among those reporting street stops (see Figure 13.3).

Likewise, during traffic stops about 10% reported that the police did not behave properly, compared to 25% among those reporting street stops. Belief that the reason for the stop was legitimate, as well as searches of vehicles and/or persons, and the use of force (including shouting or cursing, verbal threats, and physical force) were related to beliefs that the police behaved properly during the encounter. In both cases, less than 5% of those who said the police behaved improperly filed a citizen complaint. While the PPCS does not ask questions about the types of police misbehavior we have been discussing thus far (and would likely be unable to do so given sample size issues), it is not inconceivable that victimization surveys could be useful for studying some forms of police deviance.

Recently, there have been several attempts to collect data via media-aggregation. For example, the Cato Institute's *National Police Misconduct Statistics and Reporting Project* (www.policemisconduct.net) is based upon media reports of police misconduct incidents. In their latest annual statistical report (2010), they reported tracking 4,861 incidents involving 6,613 officers. The misconduct data were recently used as the dependent variable in an agency-level analysis reported by Eitle et al. (2014). A related endeavor has been undertaken by policing scholar Phillip Stinson, who developed a system for harvesting news reports of police officers who have been arrested. These data have enabled him to study such diverse topics as police sexual misconduct (Stinson, Liederbach, Brewer, & Mathna, 2014), drunk driving (Stinson, Liederbach, Brewer, & Todak, 2013), drug-related corruption (Stinson, Liederbach, Brewer, Schmalzried, Mathna, & Long, 2013), and most recently, violence (Stinson, Brewer, & Bridges, 2015).

There have also been some recent attempts at the "crowd-sourcing" of police misconduct. The law surrounding videotaping of the police remains quite controversial in some jurisdictions, but smartphone applications for recording video and audio of police–citizen interactions are becoming increasingly available. The Civil Liberties Unions of New York, New Jersey, and California all have phone applications that are freely distributed. The New York version is called

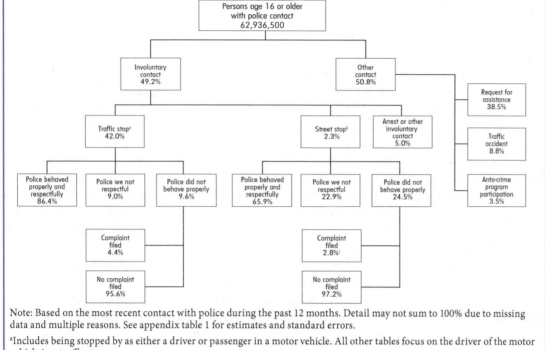

Note: Based on the most recent contact with police during the past 12 months. Detail may not sum to 100% due to missing data and multiple reasons. See appendix table 1 for estimates and standard errors.

[a]Includes being stopped by as either a driver or passenger in a motor vehicle. All other tables focus on the driver of the motor vehicle in a traffic stop.

bIncludes being stopped by police in a public place, not a moving vehicle.

! Interpret with caution. Estimate based on 10 or fewer sample cases or the coefficient of variation is greater than 50%.

Source: Bureau of Justice statistics, National Crime Victimization Survey, Police-Public Contact Survey, 2011.

Source: Langton, L., & Durose, M. (2013). *Police Behavior during Traffic and Street Stops, 2011.* Washington, DC: Bureau of Justice Statistics.

Figure 13.3 Perceptions that police behaved properly and respectfully during most recent contact with persons age 16 or older, by type of contact, 2011.

"Stop and Frisk Watch" and allows the user to record interactions, as well as to monitor the use of the application by others nearby, and to submit the video with survey data to the NYCLU. Another application that has received quite a bit of media attention, if only because it was created by three teenagers in Georgia, is "Five-O," which in addition to video and audio allows users to rate specific officers, and has community boards for different counties in order to support data collection by community activists.

A largely unexplored option is officer self-reports. Some scholars have argued that traditional social science methods, such as the use of self-report survey methodology, are inappropriate for this type of research (e.g., Klockars et al., 1997; Goldstein, 1977). On the surface, self-report surveys probably don't sound like a reasonable approach. Can we expect to obtain meaningful data by asking police officers to report the number of times they, for example, physically abused citizens in the past year? Would police officers be willing to provide this kind of information about themselves? One study made some preliminary investigations in this area by comparing officer self-reported citizen complaints to official departmental records of citizen complaints (Hickman, 2007) and found a relatively high degree of correspondence between the two (in a sample of 440 officers, self-reports of citizen complaints corresponded with official records for 77% of respondents), although, much additional study is necessary in determining the viability of self-reports. However, a related but alternative strategy focuses on the measurement of police integrity.

POLICE INTEGRITY

Rather than study police misbehavior directly, which is methodologically challenging at best, some scholars have instead turned their attention toward the study of **police integrity**. Police integrity is defined as "the normative inclination among police to resist temptations to abuse the rights and privileges of their occupation" (Klockars, et al., 2006, p. 251) and thus assesses attitudes toward misconduct and corruption rather than studying behaviors directly. Klockars and colleagues asked officers about their attitudes and intentions within the context of morally ambiguous, potentially deviant situations. Their method presents officers with scenarios depicting such behaviors, and they ask officers to indicate how serious they consider the behavior to be, what level of punishment should and likely would follow, and how likely they would be to report a fellow officer who engaged in such behavior. They do not collect any identifying information (not even any basic officer demographics) in order to enhance the anonymous nature of the survey. Their approach decreases the likelihood that officers will perceive a question as threatening, yielding a more truthful response. Through an exploration of police integrity, one can more readily assess how prevalent and persistent corruption is in a law enforcement organization by measuring the strength of organizational integrity (Kutnjak Ivkovich, 2009; Kutnjak Ivković and Kang, 2012). By aggregating the responses for an agency, the approach allows one to characterize the agency's "culture of integrity" and also compare (and rank) the agency with other agencies. Their 30-department study (Klockars et al., 2000) found wide variability in integrity measures across departments, that the seriousness of the behavior was strongly related to the willingness to report (as well as the level of discipline), and that these data can be used to characterize an agency's occupational culture of integrity relative to other agencies, both nationally and internationally. Several subsequent studies have reported similar findings.

MEASUREMENT OF POLICE INTEGRITY

Consider the following scenarios from Klockars et al. (2000), and answer the questions below them (from your perspective). Then compare your responses with the averages from more than 3,200 police officers in 30 police departments across the country (provided at the bottom). How do your answers compare with the average officer responses?

1. A police officer routinely accepts free meals, cigarettes, and other items of small value from merchants on his beat. He does not solicit these gifts and is careful not to abuse the generosity of those who give gifts to him.

2. At 2 A.M. a police officer, who is on duty, is driving his patrol car on a deserted road. The officer sees a vehicle that has been driven off the road and is stuck in a ditch. The officer approaches the vehicle and observes that the driver is not hurt but is obviously intoxicated. The officer also finds that the driver is a police officer. Instead of reporting this accident and offense, the officer transports the driver to his home.

3. A police officer stops a motorist for speeding. The officer agrees to accept a personal gift of half the amount of the fine in exchange for not issuing a citation.

For each of the scenarios above, answer the following questions:

a. How serious do YOU consider this behavior to be?

Not at all serious				Very Serious
1	2	3	4	5

b. How serious do MOST POLICE OFFICERS IN YOUR AGENCY consider this behavior to be?

Not at all serious				Very Serious
1	2	3	4	5

c. If an officer in your agency engaged in this behavior and was discovered doing so, what, if any, discipline do YOU think SHOULD follow?

1 None   4 Period of suspension w/o pay

2 Verbal reprimand   5 Demotion in rank

3 Written reprimand   6 Dismissal

d. If an officer in your agency engaged in this behavior and was discovered doing so, what, if any, discipline do YOU think WOULD follow?

1 None   4 Period of suspension w/o pay

2 Verbal reprimand   5 Demotion in rank

3 Written reprimand   6 Dismissal

e. Do you think YOU would report a fellow police officer who engaged in this behavior?

Definitely not				Definitely yes
1	2	3	4	5

f. Do you think MOST POLICE OFFICERS IN YOUR AGENCY would report a fellow police officer who engaged in this behavior?

Definitely not				Definitely yes
1	2	3	4	5

Below are the average responses from the officer sample. Did you find any of the scenarios to be more serious than the officers? How about less serious? Compare the levels of discipline you thought warranted, as well as willingness to report a fellow officer. If you noted a substantial difference between your responses and those of the officers, what might explain that, and do you see any problems or concerns with those differences? Do you think that these types of data are useful for understanding an agency's culture of integrity?

Scenario 1: a – 2.6; b – 2.3; c – 2.1; d – 2.4; e – 1.9; f – 1.8
Scenario 2: a – 3.0; b – 2.9; c – 2.8; d – 3.2; e – 2.3; f – 2.3
Scenario 3: a – 4.9; b – 4.8; c – 4.9; d – 4.9; e – 4.2; f – 3.9

EXPLAINING POLICE DEVIANCE

There have been many attempts to explain police deviance through either inductive or deductive approaches, the latter drawing heavily from existing theories of deviance. The perspectives are quite varied, including psychological explanations (generally individual-level explanations, such as the idea of the "rotten apple" described earlier, and the search for individual-level risk factors that predict poor behavior), sociological (focused primarily on the nature of police work), anthropological (viewing policing as an occupational subculture with structural characteristics that facilitate deviance), and organizational perspectives (focused on leadership and organizational tolerance) (Kappeler et al., 1994; Worden, 1995). Applications of criminological and/or deviance theory have been rather diverse, including neutralization theory (Hunt and Manning, 1993), control balance theory (Hickman et al., 2001), deterrence theory (Pogarsky & Piquero, 2004), and social learning theory (Chappell & Piquero, 2004).

Recently, Harris (2009) demonstrated the potential utility of the life-course perspective in criminology for understanding police deviance. He examined complaints generated by a cohort of 1,138 officers in an anonymous Northeastern police department. These officers entered the department in the late 1980s (1987–1990), and Harris collected data up through 2001 (thus representing about 11 to 15 years of service). Harris reported that the average *onset* of problem behaviors was about 3 years into officer careers, the behavior *duration* was about 6 to 7 years on average, and *desistance* occurred around the ninth year of service.

While much of this work is promising (particularly the life-course perspective), to date no satisfactory theory of police deviance has emerged from the accumulated research with broad application, support, and consensus.

POLICE COERCION AND THE USE OF FORCE

UNDERSTANDING WHY THE POLICE USE FORCE

As we noted in Chapter 1, a major purpose of government is to protect the core natural rights of life, liberty, and property that we so deeply cherish, and we accomplish this by granting government the power to regulate behavior through the enactment and enforcement of laws (i.e., the so-called *police power*). And, as you have learned over the previous 12 chapters, the police do many things in everyday life that go well beyond our typical conceptions of what the police "are" and what they "do." Yet, as we strip-away these many complex layers of activity in search of the core function of the police, we return to the idea that no matter what the police are doing ("… caring for those who cannot care for themselves, attempting to solve a crime, helping to save a life, abating a nuisance, or settling an explosive dispute …") what makes the police different from all others who might try to do those things is the capacity of the police to both verbally and physically coerce individuals to do things that they are not otherwise inclined to do, particularly those individuals who are not obeying the rules.

Unfortunately, the reality is that not everybody plays by the rules and they may threaten the life, liberty, and/or property of others. These individuals who are not obeying the rules may also reject the authority of the police, who we have entrusted with the job of enforcement. If the police intervene and are not able to achieve compliance through lesser means, they may need to use verbal or physical force in order to gain control of an individual and/or situation, make the situation safe, and/or obtain compliance from the parties involved.

Sometimes coercion can take the form of simple physical presence. Think to the last time you were out driving and saw a police car by the side of the road—did you take your foot off the gas, straighten up in your seat, and make certain that you used your turn signal properly at the next corner? Why did you do that? Perhaps in your mind it was in order to avoid the possibility of getting a ticket, but didn't the officer succeed in changing your behavior merely through his/her presence? How about the last time you were walking down a street and saw a police officer on foot—did you avoid direct eye contact, or change what you were doing in any way? We are being a little bit facetious here; these are very benign examples. In fact, many conflicts between people can be avoided or resolved by an officer simply being present. Their presence and body language is a means of asserting control over the situation, and their continued presence indicates a commitment to maintaining control until the matter is satisfactorily resolved. Highly skilled officers may avoid the need for any greater level of coercion by verbally *deescalating* the situation and seeking (and achieving) voluntary compliance from the parties; this may cross over into the next category of coercion.

A step higher than coercion in the form of physical presence would be verbal coercion. Direct orders issued by an officer to a citizen, such as orders to sit or stand at a particular location, keep one's hands visible, and so on,

Often just the presence of an officer helps to avoid conflict situations.

are examples. Moving higher is some form of physical control; at the low end this would include simple directional contact such as steering an individual toward a police cruiser, but also includes "escorts" to the ground, various takedowns, use of pressure points, and temporary restraints. Still higher would be the use of a weapon, and this may include impact weapons such as batons, chemical spray, an electronic control device (ECD) or conducted energy weapon (CEW) such as a Taser, and use of police canines. Focused physical blows with fists or arms may also be included

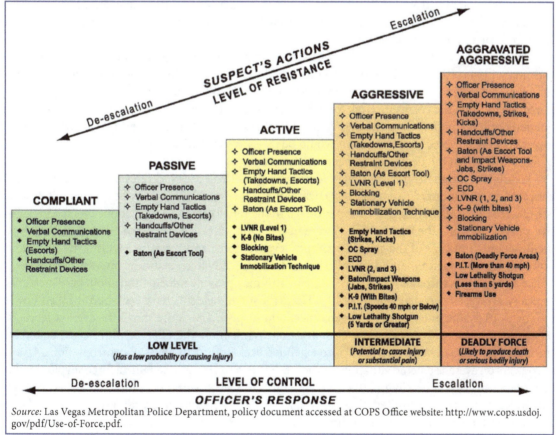

Figure 13.4 An example of a force continuum.

Source: Las Vegas Metropolitan Police Department, policy document accessed at COPS Office website: http://www.cops.usdoj.gov/pdf/Use-of-Force.pdf.

at this level. The highest level would be the use of deadly force. Firearms are obviously lethal, but this may also include carotid artery holds, strikes to the head, and other potentially lethal physical control techniques.

What we have described above is essentially a force *continuum*, ranging from physical presence at the lowest end of the continuum, up to deadly force at the highest end of the continuum. The idea is that the police response to noncompliance ought to be relatively proportional to the degree of suspect resistance. A force continuum provides a visual guide for officers showing the level of force parallel to the level of suspect resistance. That is, police in exercising their coercive authority should seek to use force not only as a last resort but use the lowest level of force necessary to achieve control of the suspect. However, as their goal is to obtain control of the situation, a level of force higher than the level of suspect resistance may be expected. Ultimately, they will be judged by whether the level of force was reasonable, as discussed below. Figure 13.4 presents one example of a force continuum; please keep in mind that there are many variants of force continuums and little standardization across agencies. They come in all shapes and sizes, and some agencies choose not to adopt a continuum model.

Policing scholar Geoffrey Alpert (Alpert & Dunham, 1997; see also Alpert & Dunham, 2004) proposed quantifying the levels of force and resistance in the form of a *force factor*, a summary score which relates the degree to which police use of force is proportional to suspect resistance. By scoring the level of force and the level of resistance on parallel ordinal scales, one then subtracts the level of officer force from the level of suspect resistance. For example, in Figure 13.5 below, we present an example of two parallel scales used in a recent study of police use of force in Seattle, WA (Hickman & Atherley, 2012). This compares the maximum force applied by the officer to the maximum level of suspect resistance on scales ranging from 1 to 7. By taking the difference between the two values for a given scenario (i.e., officer force level minus suspect resistance level), the result is a numeric value ranging from -7 to 7, the force factor for a given incident.

For example, if the maximum level of suspect resistance was "Resistance level 4," and that was met with a comparable level of officer force ("Force level 4"), this would result in a force factor equal to zero, indicating a proportional response. If the officer used a higher level of force, say Force level 5, then the corresponding force factor would be (5 – 4 = +1), indicating the officer used one level of force higher than the degree of suspect resistance. If the officer used a lower level of force, say Force level 3, the force factor would be (3 – 4 = –1), indicating the officer used one level of force lower than the degree of suspect resistance.

Figure 13.6 shows the distribution of force factors for 1,240 use of force events in Seattle during a recent two-and-a-quarter year period (Hickman & Atherley, 2012). As can be seen, about 80% of use of force incidents during this time period fell in the range of 0 to +2, and about 14% fell in negative categories, while the remaining 6% were in the +3 to +5 range. This shows the distribution of incidents only in terms of the static maximum levels of force and resistance within the incidents; however, the force factor method can also be used dynamically to code dyadic interactions between police and suspects throughout a given incident. This may provide information about how incidents typically evolve, as depicted in Figure 13.7. Here, the force incidents have each been broken down into up to 10 dyadic interactions between officer and suspect. The figure shows the average levels of officer force and suspect resistance at each iteration. While more than half of all the cases ended by the fourth iteration, several continued into extended back-and-forth physical confrontations. Overall, officers on average entered situations at a force deficit, and transitioned into a force surplus by the third iteration. This generally reflects initial attempts to reason with noncompliant suspects either with voice commands or limited physical contact, with officers ultimately taking control by about the third exchange and most cases ending at the fourth iteration.

The distribution of force factors for use of force events can be instructive for a department, not only for purposes of monitoring, understanding, and responding to force events, but for engaging with the public in conversations about the use of force. For example, police departments might use

Level	Description	Level	Description
Resistance 1	No resistance. The Subject is offering no resistance or threat.	Force 1	Officer presence in uniform or marked police vehicle.
Resistance 2	Verbal resistance to complying with lawful orders. Subject may challenge authority or standing and may present as "dead weight."	Force 2	Issuance of lawful orders and light physical contact to include guiding, leading and/or handcuffing. No intentional infliction of pain for the purpose of compliance.
Resistance 3	Use of posture and verbal threats of physical violence. Subject may attempt to intimidate or otherwise pose a physical threat to officers.	Force 3	Chemical agents for the purpose of crowd dispersal or distraction. Tactic is often reserved for large gatherings, civil disobedience and fight disturbances.
Resistance 4	Physical non-compliance including refusal to give up hands for cuffing andattempts to flee.	Force 4	Physical control tactics such as pain compliance holds,joint manipulation and open handed strikes.
Resistance 5	Active physical resistance to compliance. Subject may attempt to strike officers, kick and struggle free from holds and compliance positions.	Force 5	Advanced physical control tactics including closed fisted strikes, knee and elbowstrikes to the body and the extremities.
Resistance 6	Use of non-lethal weapons to injure or otherwise actively assault officers. Drug paraphernalia, beverage containers and rocks may be employed as cutting and impact weapons.	Force 6	Intermediate weapon use, deployment of electronic control weapons and impact weapons for pain compliance and strikes to the body andextremities.
Resistance 7	Use of lethal force as presented by whatever means are available:firearms, knives, and motor vehicles.	Force 7	Use of lethal force includingcarotid artery holds, headstrikes, and intentional discharge of firearms.

Source: Hickman, M., & Atherley, L. (2012). *Police Use of Force in Seattle, January 2009–March 2011*. Seattle, WA: Northwest Justice Solutions.

Figure 13.5 Suspect Resistance and Officer Force Levels.

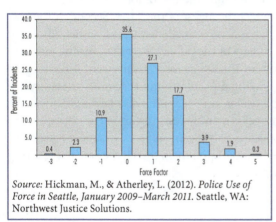

Source: Hickman, M., & Atherley, L. (2012). *Police Use of Force in Seattle, January 2009–March 2011*. Seattle, WA: Northwest Justice Solutions.

Figure 13.6 Force factors in Seattle (WA), 2009–2011.

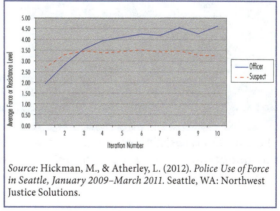

Source: Hickman, M., & Atherley, L. (2012). *Police Use of Force in Seattle, January 2009–March 2011*. Seattle, WA: Northwest Justice Solutions.

Figure 13.7 Dynamic force and resistance levels.

force factors for descriptive reporting purposes, such as in external reports to the public. Internally, force factors may enhance the supervisory review of force incidents; such a method was suggested by Atherley & Hickman (2014), who demonstrated that by recording force factors as well as relevant *Graham* factors (see below) a simple pointer system for identifying incidents where the use of force is potentially excessive is possible. Stewart (2013) suggested a similar approach, termed constitutional force analysis (CFA), using force factors, variables pertaining to information available to the officer prior to arrival on-scene, information available on-scene and up to the use of force, and other administrative variables. The potential benefits of the approach included improved analysis of use of force, improved quality control, and an improved debriefing process (Stewart, 2013).

THE REASONABLENESS OF FORCE

What we have described thus far mostly relates to the *proportionality* of force, but it does not describe whether the use of force was *reasonable* as opposed to *excessive*. Legal guidance comes from the Supreme Court case *Graham v. Connor* (1989), in which the justices acknowledged that while we must balance the government's interest in apprehending a criminal suspect against the suspect's Fourth Amendment rights, there is no precise mechanism or definitions for accomplishing this. The Court articulated a three-prong test (sometimes summarized as a four-prong test with the third-prong split into two) for balancing the government's interest vs. the suspect's Fourth Amendment rights, and these are often referred to as the *Graham factors*: (1) the severity of the underlying offense; (2) the immediate threat posed by the individual to officers and the public; and (3) active resistance to arrest or flight. The justices also determined that use of force should be judged by an *objective reasonableness* standard: In deference to the dynamic situations officers face and the split-second decisions that they must make, whether a particular use of force is reasonable "… must be judged from the perspective of a reasonable officer on the scene, rather than with the 20/20 vision of hindsight" and that "… the 'reasonableness' inquiry in an excessive force case is an objective one: the question is whether the officers' actions are 'objectively reasonable' in light of the facts and circumstances confronting them, without regard to their underlying intent or motivation."

Thinking about the Graham factors a little bit will demonstrate their practicality. First, consider the severity of the underlying offense. All things being equal, we would probably prefer that force not be used upon a jaywalker as compared to a homicide suspect. What we really mean here is that the government has less interest in intervening with the jaywalker as compared to the homicide suspect, and thus the use of force is more reasonable to affect the arrest of the latter. Second, if the suspect poses no immediate threat to either officers or members of the public, there can be little justification for the use of force. Conversely, if the suspect is waving a pistol around the threat is immediate and use of force is more reasonable. Finally, if the suspect is actively resisting arrest, or attempting to evade arrest by fleeing officers, it is more reasonable to use force upon them than if they are not resisting or fleeing.

© Photographee.eu/Shutterstock.com

If a suspect is resisting arrest, it is more reasonable to use force upon them.

Over time, the courts have considered several other factors relevant to the determination of reasonableness, including such considerations as the suspect's impaired rational ability (for example, as evidenced by poor balance, incoherent or slurred speech, alcohol or drug use, mental illness, indications of suicidal tendencies, and so on). There are also additional constraints on the use of deadly force—in the earlier case of *Tennessee v. Garner* (1985) the Supreme Court held that a police officer pursuing an unarmed fleeing suspect may not use deadly force to prevent escape unless "… the officer has probable cause to believe that the suspect poses a significant threat of death or serious physical injury to the officer or others." This was an important decision in that it ended the so-called fleeing felon rule that permitted officers to use deadly force to prevent the escape of an individual suspected of committing a felony.

Thus, while information about the proportionality of force (for example, the force factors discussed earlier) is important, it does not necessarily follow that proportional force is **reasonable force**. The determination of the reasonableness of a particular use of force is very complex under the law, and it is difficult for citizens to understand or appreciate this whereas proportionality is rather intuitive. This may account for some of the disconnects between the police use of force under department policy and the law, compared with public perceptions of the use of force.

NATURE AND EXTENT OF USE OF FORCE

What do we know about the nature and extent of police use of force in the United States, and how do we know it? Similar to our discussion of police deviance, we have a variety of different data sources, some of which capture different aspects of the phenomenon, and a substantial remaining "gray figure." At present, we simply do not know how often or to what extent the police in the United States use force upon its citizens in any given year. We are getting closer to knowing how often the police use lethal force. We have absolutely no idea how often police use **excessive force**.

To return briefly to Chapter 4, part of the problem (or challenge) is that we have roughly 18,000 state and local law enforcement agencies, and about 75 federal (non-military) agencies, to try to track. There is no law requiring these agencies to collect and report data on the use of force, and there is no commonly accepted or standard method for doing so. Absent any action by Congress to pass such a law, the only mechanism for "encouraging" these agencies to collect and report use of force data would be to make it a condition of receiving federal funding. And, to be fair, there are no resources being provided to assist agencies with the standardization and/or collection of use of force data, so there is very little incentive to do so voluntarily.

There is a federal law requiring the collection of data about the use of excessive force by law enforcement officers. This law has as its roots in the 1994 Violent Crime Control and Law Enforcement Act of 1994, also referred to as the "Clinton Crime Bill" or the "1994 Crime Act." In the wake of the Rodney King incident in Los Angeles, the 1994 Crime Act included a provision expanding the authority of the US Justice Department's Civil Rights Division to investigate police departments that they believe are engaging in unconstitutional "patterns or practices" of conduct and seek corrective action (this was codified as 42 USC 14141). These investigations typically center on the use of force, racially discriminatory policing, and procedural violations, and we discuss this important accountability mechanism in detail in the next chapter. Important for present purposes, however, is another provision that came along with the pattern or practice authority, often referred to as the "data collection requirement" (codified as 42 USC 14142), and which we briefly mentioned in Chapter 1. Below is the full text of the data collection requirement. It is rather brief and includes three subsections:

TITLE 42 UNITED STATES CODE, SECTION 14142: DATA ON USE OF EXCESSIVE FORCE

(a) Attorney General to collect

The Attorney General shall, through appropriate means, acquire data about the use of excessive force by law enforcement officers.

(b) Limitation on use of data

Data acquired under this section shall be used only for research or statistical purposes and may not contain any information that may reveal the identity of the victim or any law enforcement officer.

(c) Annual summary

The Attorney General shall publish an annual summary of the data acquired under this section.

Given that this data collection requirement has been on the books since 1994, one might reasonably ask, "So where are these annual summaries of the data?" The answer is that there are none; a long string of Attorneys General have failed to make any meaningful progress on this requirement. The current Attorney General as of this writing, Loretta Lynch, might be the first to do so, spurred on by the many high-profile incidents over the past couple of years as well as the President's Task Force on 21st-Century Policing.

To be fair, satisfying the requirement to "acquire data about the use of excessive force by law enforcement officers" is not an easy task. Shortly after the data collection requirement was enacted, the Bureau of Justice Statistics (BJS) and the National Institute of Justice (NIJ) jointly held a workshop on police use of force, bringing together the expertise of criminal justice researchers and practitioners to bear on the data collection requirement. There were two key products that emerged from this meeting: One was a summary of prior research and data collection on police use of force, which highlighted some of the challenges and pitfalls of data on police use of force (McEwen, 1996); the other was the Police Public Contact Survey (PPCS), which we discussed briefly earlier in this chapter. The PPCS has been conducted every three years since 1999, and generally asks citizens about their interactions with police officers during the previous 12-month period, including incidents involving the use of force by officers. The PPCS was and is, as of this writing, the principal federal response to the data collection requirement, and it is the only systematic, national-level data collection on police–citizen interactions.

The goals of the PPCS are to provide national estimates of the incidence and prevalence of citizen contacts with the police, describe the nature of those contacts, including whether the police used or threatened the use of force, the specific actions the police took, as well as any potentially provoking citizen behaviors. A recent analysis (Hyland et al., 2015) of the four administrations

More than half of those experiencing use of force by the police reported that they themselves had been disrespectful, resisted, or had been under the influence at the time.

of the PPCS during the period 2002–2011 demonstrated that the PPCS results have been very consistent over that time frame. In any given administration, about 19% of the public aged 16 or older (about 44 million persons, on average) experienced at least one direct contact with a police officer during the previous year. Of those who reported having a contact with police, 1.6% (about 715,500 persons, on average) reported that officers used or threatened the use of force during the encounter. Males, blacks, and youth are more likely to experience the use of force. About three-quarters of those who experienced the threat or use of force (about 535,300 persons, on average) reported that they thought it was "excessive" and 87% believed police acted improperly. Although the study notes that the perception that force was excessive varies by the different types of force that police used, the study did not address citizen behavior during this time period. However, in earlier administrations of the PPCS, it was found that the types of force used by officers primarily involved being pushed or grabbed by the officer, with less than 1 in 5 individuals reporting an actual injury as a result. Further, more than half of those experiencing threat or use of force reported that they themselves had been disrespectful, resisted, or had been using drugs or alcohol at the time. On balance, while victimization surveys are useful for estimating the prevalence of citizen contacts with the police, their utility for estimating the prevalence of the use of excessive force by police is probably quite limited.

Another source of data was the 2002 BJS Survey of Inmates in Local Jails (SILJ), which provided some information about police use of force, although BJS has never analyzed or reported on these data. The SILJ is a computer-assisted personal interview conducted with a nationally representative sample of jail inmates that covers a broad range of topics. Importantly, the 2002 SILJ contained questionnaire items that paralleled those included in the PPCS at the time; thus, jail inmates were asked about the use or threat of force experienced at the time of their arrest. This addresses a long-standing criticism of the PPCS that it underestimates force due to the exclusion of a "high-risk" population for the use of force by police: recent arrestees. Analysis of the inmate data demonstrates that the PPCS does in fact underestimate force due to the exclusion of the recently incarcerated from the NCVS-based sample; the inmate sample is more likely to experience force, a much higher level of force, and is more likely to report injury from force (Hickman et al., 2008). However, demographic characteristics are substantively similar across the two data sources: Males, blacks, and youth are more likely to experience force.

The FBI's Supplemental Homicide Reports (SHR), part of the UCR program, is designed to collect additional detail on victim and offender demographic characteristics, type of weapon used, victim/offender relationship, and the circumstances of the homicide (e.g., "Victim shot by robber"). The SHR captures justifiable homicides by police; however, the SHR is widely criticized for substantially undercounting (by as much as half) when compared with other sources, and as Klinger et al. (2015) recently points out, is severely lacking as a national indicator of police use of deadly force since the police frequently shoot but miss suspects, and/or suspects are shot by police but survive (neither of which would be captured in data pertaining to homicides).

The BJS Arrest Related Deaths (ARD) program, formerly known as the Deaths in Custody Reporting Program (DCRP), had been conducted annually from 2003 to 2009 and again in 2011. The ARD program is a national census of individuals who died during the process of arrest or while in the custody of local, county, or state law enforcement personnel. The ARD program captures deaths related to police use of force, as well as other deaths in custody (such as suicide, accidental, or natural causes). Over the entire data collection period, the annual average estimate of persons experiencing deadly force by police during arrest was 1,242 (this is the upper-bound of the range around the estimate) (Hyland et al., 2015). In 2014, the ARD program was suspended due to coverage concerns; specifically it was estimated that the program only captured between 50–70% of all arrest-related deaths (Hyland et al., 2015).

The ARD data on law enforcement homicides (both justifiable and unjustifiable) are substantively similar to those obtained by the FBI's SHR although concerns regarding under-counting plague both data collections due to the voluntary nature of reporting, problems with classification of homicides as justifiable or non-justifiable, and other data quality issues. In a 2007 analysis, it was reported that 97% of law enforcement homicides involved a male subject, the average age was 33 years, more than 80% were killed by a handgun, and about 30% involved a black subject (Mumola, 2007), very similar to the SHR statistics. About 56% of all arrest-related deaths involved a minority subject (suicide is the only category of arrest-related deaths in which whites are the majority) (Mumola, 2007).

Finally, the BJS LEMAS survey (you will recall from earlier chapters, particularly Chapter 4), which is presently the most systematic and comprehensive source of national data on law enforcement personnel, expenditures and pay, operations, equipment, and policies and procedures, also has collected data on use of force. The LEMAS surveys have been conducted roughly every three years since 1987, and provide national estimates for all state and local law enforcement agencies based on a representative sample of about 3,000 agencies. In the 2003 and 2007 iterations of LEMAS, data were collected on formal citizen complaints about police use of force (these complaints data are discussed in detail in the next chapter). The LEMAS data provide information on the volume and rate of complaints as well as complaint dispositions. Hickman (2006) suggested that sustained citizen complaints about police use of force might serve as an indicator of the incidence of use of excessive force. The International Association of Chiefs of Police (IACP) defined sustained force complaints as incidents of excessive force (IACP, 2001), and the underlying logic is that a sustained complaint indicates there was sufficient evidence of the allegation for the agency to justify disciplinary action against the officer (Hickman, 2006). Hickman reported about 2,000 sustained force complaints among large agencies (those with 100 or more officers), which results in an overall rate of one incident of excessive force for every 200 full-time sworn officers during the year studied. However, there are many problems with citizen complaints data that we discuss in the next chapter.

The above resources, to the best of the authors' knowledge at the time of writing, comprise the full extent of national-level, systematic data collections on police use of force in the United States. To be clear, none of these data collections satisfactorily addresses the 1994 requirement to "acquire data about the use of excessive force by law enforcement officers" and "publish an annual summary of the data acquired." However, to be fair, if you read the text of the statute very literally, there is no requirement that the Federal government take the lead role—or ANY role—in primary data collection on the use of excessive force. While it seems implied that the burden falls on the US Attorney General to "acquire data," in theory, the reporting requirement could be satisfied by simply compiling and reporting on state-level and non-government initiated efforts.

Otherwise, much of what we know about the nature and extent of police use of force is subnational, and consists primarily of single-agency studies. In a recent review of the literature conducted as part of an effort to construct an improved national estimate of police use of nonlethal force by combining the PPCS and SILJ data, Hickman et al. (2008) found that the majority of studies producing an incident-based rate of police use of force were based on data from a single jurisdiction, and the methods were quite diverse (including analyses of arrest reports, independent observations, surveys of police, surveys of suspects, and use of force forms), as were the definitions of force and the units of analysis. As a result of this diversity, it is perhaps not surprising that across 36 studies reporting on the amount of nonlethal force used by the police, they found that incident-based rates of force varied from about a tenth of 1% up to almost 32%. They concluded their review by stating that "… the existing research literature—although extensive and informative for other purposes—does not provide a reasonable basis for estimating either the amount of force used by police in the United States or the correlates of force" (Hickman et al., 2008:572). While recognizing the inherent value of the diversity of methodological approaches, Engel (2008) noted that the literature reflects a failure to adequately conceptualize and measure police use of force, and that current approaches to understanding force on a national level are not achieving those goals.

CONCLUSION

In this chapter, we discussed the importance of both actual police behavior and the public perception of police behavior, as well as potential disconnects between the two, and how these can affect police legitimacy. We also explored the problem of biased policing (and hope that you took that Implicit Association Test!) and addressed a broad range of police deviance, including both police occupational deviance (corruption and misconduct) and police abuse of authority (including physical, psychological, and legal abuses), as well as the idea of police integrity. Finally, we examined police coercion and the use of force.

While we have invested a great deal of resources in understanding crime and criminal behavior, we know relatively little about police behavior. Most importantly, we know very little about the use of force by police. As this book goes to print, *we have no idea how often the police in the United States use force upon its citizens, and we know even less about the use of excessive force. We are slowly beginning to improve our understanding of police shootings, but much work remains to be done.* This situation is fundamentally at odds with the idea of democratic policing and must be corrected if we are to truly engage in the process of democratic policing in the United States. It remains to be seen whether the President's Commission on 21st Century Policing or the related President's Data Initiative will deliver on spurring data transparency in this area, but we can hope for the best.

REVIEW QUESTIONS

1. To what extent do you believe that police misconduct is any more/less prevalent than misconduct in other professions, such as might be found among physicians, lawyers, accountants, and so on? Is it different for police? Why or why not?

2. What do you think is the most significant problem to be overcome in the quest for valid and reliable national-level data on police use of force? How would you go about setting up a national database on police use of force? What specific steps would need to be taken in order to achieve this goal?

GLOSSARY

Abuse of authority misuse of power by an officer in the course of duty.

Biased policing making a choice to stop, cite, or arrest a person based on the person's race, ethnicity, gender, sexual orientation, economic status, or other personal trait.

Excessive force level of force used by an officer on an individual that is considered to be more than was appropriate or necessary.

Force factor a single value describing the proportionality of officer force relative to suspect resistance.

Grass eaters those police officers who engage in relatively passive forms of inappropriate behavior by accepting small favors or money for looking the other way when illegal activities are taking place.

Knapp Commission commission created to investigate allegations of widespread corruption in the NYPD in the early 1970s.

Meat eaters police officers who are more aggressive in their illegal behavior and actively search for ways to make money illegally while on duty.

Occupational deviance criminal and non-criminal behavior committed under the guise of police authority or in the course of normal police activity, including corruption and misconduct.

Police integrity defined by Carl B. Klockars as the normative inclination among police to resist temptations to abuse the rights and privileges of their occupation.

Police legitimacy the extent to which we recognize and are willing to defer to the authority of the police to regulate our behavior; can be conceptualized as falling along a continuum ranging from strong to weak, with the position along the continuum being determined by both police behavior and the public's perception of that behavior.

Procedural justice the idea that the process by which decisions are made should be fundamentally fair, which is very important to the formation of citizen's attitudes about both specific interactions and generally toward the police; four key aspects of procedural justice include: citizen participation (or "voice"); perceived neutrality on the part of the police; police treating all parties with dignity and respect during the interaction; and whether the police convey trustworthy motives.

Racial profiling selection of individuals based solely on the race or ethnicity of the person or group.

Reasonable force the acceptable amount of force that officers can use when subduing a suspect or making an arrest.

Rotten apple corruption theory that states that individual officers within an organization are corrupt, not the entire organization. Corrupt officers are referred to as "rotten apples."

Rotten orchard a large group of corrupt officers (such as a unit or station)

Rotten pockets small groups of corrupt officers within an organization.

REFERENCES

Alpert, G., & Dunham, R. (1997). *The force factor: Measuring police use of force relative to suspect resistance.* Washington, DC: Police Executive Research Forum.

Alpert, G. & R. Dunham. (2004). *Understanding police use of force: Officers, suspects, and reciprocity.* Cambridge: Cambridge University Press.

Atherley, L., & Hickman, M. (2014). Controlling use of force: Identifying police use of excessive force through analysis of administrative records. *Policing: A Journal of Policy and Practice, 8*(2), 123–134.

Barker, T. (1978). "An empirical study of police deviance other than corruption." In T. Barker and D.L. Carter (eds.), *Police deviance* (3ʳᵈ ed.), Cincinnati: Anderson Publishing (pp. 123–128).

———, and D.L. Carter. (1994). "A typology of police deviance." In T. Barker and D.L. Carter (eds.), *Police deviance* (3ʳᵈ ed.), Cincinnati: Anderson Publishing (pp. 3–11).

Bickel, W. (2001). "An analysis of section 1983 litigation dealing with police misconduct." In M.J. Palmiotto (ed.), *Police misconduct*, New Jersey: Prentice Hall (pp. 415–427).

Chappell, A., & Piquero, A. (2004). Applying social learning theory to police misconduct. *Deviant Behavior, 25*, 89–108.

Chiabi, D.K. (1996). "Police Civil Liability: An Analysis of Section 1983 Actions in the Eastern and Southern Districts of New York." *American Journal of Criminal Justice, 21*(1), 85–104.

Eitle, D., D'Alessio, S., & Stolzenberg, L. (2014). The effect of organizational and environmental factors on police misconduct. *Police Quarterly, 17*, 103–126.

Engel, R. S., Calnon, J. M., & Bernard, T. J. (2002). Theory and racial profiling: Shortcomings and future directions in research. *Justice Quarterly, 19*(2), 249–273.

Engel, R. (2008). Revisiting critical issues in police use-of-force research. *Criminology & Public Policy, 7*, 557–561.

Graham v. Connor 490 U.S. 386 (1989).

Harris, C. (2009). Exploring the relationship between experience and problem behaviors: A longitudinal analysis of officers from a large cohort. *Police Quarterly, 12*(2), 192–213.

Hickman, M. (2007). Validity of officer self-reported citizen complaints: A research note. *Police Quarterly, 10*(3), 332–341.

Hickman, M. (2006). *Citizen complaints about police use of force*. Washington, DC: Bureau of Justice Statistics.

Hickman, M., & Atherley, L. (2012). *Police Use of Force in Seattle, January 2009–March 2011*. Seattle, WA: Northwest Justice Solutions.

Hickman, M., Piquero, A., & Garner, J. (2008). Toward a national estimate of police use of nonlethal force. *Criminology & Public Policy, 7*(4), 563–604.

Hickman, M., Piquero, A., Lawton, B., & Greene, J. (2001). Applying Tittle's control balance theory to police deviance. *Policing: An International Journal of Police Strategies & Management, 24*(4), 497–519.

Hunt, J. & Manning, P. (1993). The social context of police lying. *Symbolic Interaction, 14*, 51–70.

Hyland, S., Langton, L., & Davis, E. (2015). *Police use of nonfatal force, 2002–11*. Washington, DC: Bureau of Justice Statistics.

International Association of Chiefs of Police. (2001). *Police use of force in America, 2001*. Alexandria, VA: IACP.

Kane, R., & White, M. (2013). *Jammed up: Bad cops, police misconduct, and the New York City police department.* New York: NYU Press.

———. (2009). Bad cops: a study of career-ending misconduct among New York City police officers. *Criminology & Public Policy, 8*(4), 737–769.

Kappeler, V.E., R.D. Sluder, and G.P. Alpert. (1994). *Forces of deviance: Understanding the dark side of policing.* Illinois: Prospect Heights.

Klinger, D., Rosenfeld, R., Isom, D., & Deckard, M. (2015). Race, crime, and the micro-ecology of deadly force. *Criminology & Public Policy*, forthcoming.

Klockars, C.B., Kutnjak Ivković, S., Harver, W.E., and Haberfeld, M.R. (2000). *The measurement of police integrity.* Washington, DC: National Institute of Justice.

Langton, L., & M. Durose. (2013). *Police behavior during traffic and street stops, 2011.* Washington, DC: Bureau of Justice Statistics.

McEwen, T. (1996). *National data collection on police use of force.* Washington, DC: National Institute of Justice.

Mazerolle, L., Bennett, S., Davis, J., Sargeant, E., & Manning, M. (2013). Legitimacy in Policing: A systematic review. *Campbell Systematic Reviews*, 2013:1.

Mumola, C. (2007). *Arrest-related deaths in the United States, 2003–2005.* Washington, DC: Bureau of Justice Statistics.

Palmiotto, M.J. (2001). "Police misconduct: What is it?" In M.J. Palmiotto (ed.), *Police misconduct.* New Jersey: Prentice Hall (pp. 32–41).

Pate, A., & Fridell, L. (1993). *Police use of force: official reports, citizen complaints, and legal consequences* (Vol. 1). Washington, DC: Police Foundation.

Plitt, E. (1983). "Police Discipline Decisions." *Police Chief* (March), pp. 95–98.

Pogarsky, G., & Piquero, A. (2004). Studying the reach of deterrence: Can deterrence theory help explain police misconduct? *Journal of Criminal Justice, 32*, 371–386.

Rice, S., & Parkin, W. (2010). "New avenues for profiling research: The question of Muslim Americans." In S. Rice & M. White (eds.) *Race, ethnicity and policing: New and essential readings*, New York: NYU Press (pp. 450–467).

Ridgeway, G., & MacDonald, J. (2010). "Methods for Assessing Racially Biased Policing." In S. Rice & M. White (eds.) *Race, ethnicity and policing: New and essential readings*, New York: NYU Press (pp. 180–204).

Sherman, L. (1974). The sociology and social reform of the American police: 1950-1973. *Journal of Police Science and Administration, 2*(3), 255–262.

Stewart, G. (2013). *A quantitative method for the analysis of constitutional factors in police use of force* (Unpublished master's thesis). Portland State University, Portland, OR.

Stinson, P., Liederbach, J., Brewer, S., & Mathna, B. (2014). Police sexual misconduct: A national scale study of arrested officers. *Criminal Justice Policy Review*, forthcoming.

Stinson, P., Liederbach, J., Brewer, S., & Todak, N. (2013). Drink, drive, go to jail? A study of police officers arrested for drunk driving. *Journal of Crime and Justice, 37,* 356–376.

Stinson, P., Liederbach, J., Brewer, S., Schmalzried, H., Mathna, B., & Long, K. (2013). A study of drug-related police corruption arrests. *Policing: An International Journal of Police Strategies & Management, 36,* 491–511.

Stinson, P., Brewer, S., & Bridges, J. (2015). Violence-related police crime arrests in the United States, 2005–2011. Presented at the annual meeting of the Academy of Criminal Justice Sciences, Orlando, FL.

Sunshine, J., & Tyler, T. (2003). The role of procedural justice and legitimacy in shaping public support for policing. *Law & Society Review, 37*(3), 513–548.

Tennessee v. Garner 471 U.S. 1 (1985).

Tyler, T. R. (1990). *Why people obey the law.* New Haven, CT: Yale University Press.

Worden, R. (1995). The "causes" of police brutality: Theory and evidence on police use of force. In Geller, W., & Toch, H. (eds.) *And justice for all: Understanding and controlling police abuse of force.* Washington, DC: PERF.

14

LEGITIMACY AND ACCOUNTABILITY IN A DEMOCRATIC SOCIETY

LEARNING OBJECTIVES

After reading this chapter, students should be able to:

1   Explain police accountability using the general framework introduced in the chapter.

2   Explain, in general terms, citizen complaints and disciplinary processes as well as some of the general conclusions that can be drawn from the research literature in these areas.

3   Describe the nature and work of Internal Affairs units.

4   Compare and contrast different citizen oversight models.

5   Discuss police officer decertification, the nature and extent of decertification practices, and the purpose of the National Decertification Index.

6   Describe and discuss the role of the U.S. Department of Justice Civil Rights Division in police accountability

KEY TERMS

Accountability

Early warning systems

Citizen oversight

Officer decertification

Federal pattern or
    practice investigation

Consent decree

OVERVIEW

In the previous chapter, we discussed some negative police behaviors as well as their impact on the perceived integrity of the police and the potential consequences, such as reduced citizen deference to police authority and reduced cooperation. In this chapter, we discuss the variety of mechanisms for holding the police accountable for these negative behaviors. We present a general framework for understanding police accountability, and describe in detail some of the internal and external mechanisms for identifying problematic police behavior and, perhaps most importantly, responding to it. By the end of the chapter you should be able to describe the importance of citizen complaints about police behavior in general, as well as some of the challenges and pitfalls in interpreting the throughputs of citizen complaint processes. You should also be able to describe internal affairs functions, disciplinary systems, civilian oversight structures, decertification processes, and the role of federal intervention. All of these accountability mechanisms—perhaps best conceptualized as "layers" of accountability—are designed to help ensure public confidence in the police. However, as a recent newspaper story described in the box below demonstrates, simply having an accountability structure in place is no guarantee that it will actually function as intended. This reinforces the need for multiple layers of accountability.

CHICAGO RARELY PENALIZES OFFICERS FOR COMPLAINTS, DATA SHOWS

In 2014, Chicago police officer Jason Van Dyke fatally shot 17-year-old Laquan McDonald, who was armed with a knife. A dash-cam video of the shooting was released in late 2015, and showed the officer emptying his 16-round magazine into the teenager in just a few seconds, with little apparent justification and seeming contradictions to the official police account of the incident. There are many unanswered questions about this event as this textbook goes to press, but the officer has been charged with murder; the Police Chief has been asked by the Mayor to resign; and, the US Department of Justice Civil Rights Division has announced its intent to investigate. In the wake of this tragic event, much media attention has been focused on the Chicago Police Department; excerpts from an article that appeared in the *New York Times* discussing citizen complaints and discipline in the Chicago Police Department are presented below.

"In 18 years with the Chicago Police Department . . . Jerome Finnigan had never been disciplined—although 68 citizen complaints had been lodged against him, including accusations that he used excessive force and regularly conducted illegal searches. Then, in 2011, he admitted to robbing criminal suspects . . . and ordering a hit on a fellow police officer he thought intended to turn him in. He was sentenced to 12 years in prison."

The article uses Mr. Finnigan as an example, albeit an extreme case of Chicago officers who have been the subject of formal citizen complaints but not been disciplined over an approximately four-and-a-half year period (2011–2015). The data were obtained and released by two groups, the Mandel Legal Aid Clinic of the University of Chicago Law School, and the Invisible Institute, a Chicago-based journalism group focused on transparency issues. The article reported that there were more than 28,500 citizen complaints against Chicago police officers during this time period, and that the vast majority—97%—resulted in no discipline of officers. Their analysis also showed that when officers were punished, the punishment rate for black officers was twice that of white officers for similar offenses. In addition, they found that while the majority of complaints were filed by black citizens, complaints filed by white citizens had higher sustain rates.

For purposes of this chapter, it is important to note that Chicago has both internal and external systems of complaint review. In addition to the CPD's Internal Affairs Division (IAD), there is the Chicago Independent Police Review Authority (IPRA). The IPRA handles some types of complaints while the IAD handles others. According to the IPRA website, the IPRA:

... intakes all allegations of misconduct, whether generated externally by the public, or internally by Police Department personnel. When an allegation involves excessive force, domestic violence, coercion though violence, or verbal bias-based abuse, IPRA conducts the investigation into the allegation and recommends the result. All other allegations are referred to the Internal Affairs Division for appropriate resolution. In addition to investigating allegations of misconduct, IPRA investigates or reviews all officer involved shootings, extraordinary occurrences in lock-up, and uses of Tasers.

The CPD's IAD website notes that the allegations handled by IAD may include criminal misconduct, improper searches, arrest/lockup procedures, operations/personnel violations, substance abuse, and off-duty incidents that require departmental oversight. Regardless of whether a matter is investigated by IAD or IPRA, ultimate disciplinary action is at the discretion of the Superintendent.

The *New York Times* article reported that the CPD disputes the discipline figures reported by the University of Chicago / Invisible Institute, stating that the percentage not disciplined is actually lower. The reason for this is not particularly encouraging from an accountability point-of-view: Illinois law requires a signed, sworn affidavit before an investigation can be initiated, so the CPD does not count those citizen complaints where the citizen had not sworn-out their complaint; they also did not include complaints where the citizen did not know the identity of the subject officer.

Source: Williams, Timothy. Chicago Rarely Penalizes Officers for Complaints, Data Shows. New York Times, November 18, 2015, accessed at: http://mobile.nytimes.com/2015/11/19/us/few-complaints-against-chicago-police-result-in-discipline-data-shows.html?referer=&_r=0

A FRAMEWORK FOR UNDERSTANDING ACCOUNTABILITY

In Chapter 1, we discussed accountability to the public as a key component of democratic policing. Specifically, law enforcement agencies in a democratic society should be accountable to the public for police behavior. As we framed it, being accountable requires a few different elements: First, there must be some means of receiving feedback from the constituency. The chief executive of a law enforcement agency typically reports to an elected official (such as a Mayor) and/or an elected body (such as a City Council), and may themselves be an elected official (common among county Sheriffs). In this sense, they are in theory—if not practice—politically responsive to the electorate. But the feedback requirement that we discuss here is more direct and institutional in nature. There must be a formal mechanism for the police department to receive feedback directly from the public, and it is important that it be tracked through ultimate resolution.

Second, when apprised of a problem, the police must clearly acknowledge the behaviors that are being viewed as a violation of the public trust. The police don't need to necessarily agree that the behaviors are trust violative at this point, but they need to acknowledge that the public has alleged something to have happened. It may be a perceptual issue about the use of force or a misunderstanding concerning police procedure, or whatever the case may be. It doesn't matter; what is required is some formal acknowledgment that the public has identified a particular police behavior as problematic.

Third, the police must then investigate, explain, and correct, if necessary, the identified problem in a timely fashion. These three components are the necessary requirements to conclude that an accountability structure exists and that the police might be minimally held "accountable" to the public for police behavior. Extending this a bit, accountability structures can be internal to the organization as well as external to the organization. Internal accountability structures are commonly found in the form of a citizen complaint process, an internal affairs function (or equivalent), and a disciplinary process. With regard to external accountability structures, we are primarily referring to **citizen oversight** of the police. Walker (2001: 5) defines citizen oversight as "a procedure for providing input into the complaint process by individuals who are not sworn officers." Thus, citizen complaint processes may also be external to the agency.

When problems arise, the police need to acknowledge the issue.

It is important to note that police accountability occurs at both the agency and the individual levels. Thus far, we have discussed police accountability as it relates to individual officers, but police departments can also be held accountable for systemic behavioral problems; we discuss this intriguing aspect of police accountability toward the end of the chapter. In the next section, we discuss the primary mechanism for citizens who wish to address the behavior of individual officers—filing a complaint.

COMPLAINING ABOUT THE POLICE

We are typically taught at a very young age that a core component of our democratic society is the absolute right (some would also say 'duty') of citizens to complain about the quality of governance and seek resolution. This derives from the First Amendment to the Constitution, including the rights of free speech, assembly, and "to petition the Government for a redress of grievances"— that is, the right to complain, without fear of punishment, and seek resolution to the identified problems. This applies to the branches of government at both the federal and state levels, but is generally interpreted to mean that an individual can complain and seek relief in the courts (and as such it is important to note that external accountability also takes the form of criminal and/ or civil liability for officer actions). But we also see this in the form of peaceful protest, which we have seen historically with regard to police behavior (and there has certainly been much of this activity in the past couple of years). We are a people who explicitly reject tyrannical governance and require that our institutions of government are responsive to the people. When these institutions of government and their agents do wrong, they are to be held to account for their behavior. This is not a trivial matter in that the police are fundamentally exercising coercive authority and restricting liberty—it is absolutely essential that there be a mechanism by which improper behavior be brought to light, and if wrongdoing is determined to have occurred, those actors punished. But before we get too carried away, keep in mind that we are

Recently police behavior has been the reason for many protests.

not just talking about egregious behaviors to which criminal and/or civil liability may attach—we are also talking about the *quality* of enforcement.

A typical police complaint process involves four general steps: (1) intake; (2) classification; (3) fact finding; and (4) disposition. With regard to intake, citizen complaints can be received a number of different ways, and there is great variation across departments in terms of their intake procedures. Excluding departments that have no formal complaints process, this variation in intake procedures can be described in terms of a continuum. At one end of the continuum, some departments require citizens to physically present themselves at a police facility and swear-out their complaint (i.e., they must sign the complaint attesting to its truthfulness, and may even be apprised of state law that makes it a crime to file a false complaint). At the other end of the continuum, some departments may allow citizens to file a complaint through a variety of means (telephone, website, e-mail, written letter, in person, etc.) at a variety of locations (police department, City Hall, local prosecutors office, etc.), and may allow third-party complaints (witnesses, friends and relatives, attorneys, etc.) as well as anonymous complaints to be filed. A police department's position on this continuum speaks to the accessibility of the complaint process. Consider the former example, wherein a citizen is required to physically present themselves at a police facility, request a complaint form, complete it, sign it, and submit it to police personnel. This can be a very intimidating process, and it may even be so by design. There have been media accounts of precinct desk personnel in several cities trying to convince citizens not to file a complaint, blatantly lying about the availability of complaint forms, and even threatening arrest (for example, the hidden-camera investigations by the now defunct www.policeabuse.org, which received many broadcasting awards and have been used by more mainstream media outlets such as NBC's Dateline program). If nothing else it may also lead to more informal resolutions of complaints, for better or for worse. When comparing complaint volumes across departments, the accessibility of the complaint process is an important consideration.

When a complaint is received, it should be logged no matter the circumstances. This is a key part of the accountability process—a record of *all* incoming complaints regardless of their veracity. Some departments will maintain a call-log that keeps a record of all contacts, including those contacts for which no complaint is made or taken—informational requests would be logged, for example. This is an oft-overlooked but important part of documenting the work of the oversight personnel/unit. At this point, if a complaint is being made, intake personnel will generally try to assemble as many details about the nature of the complaint and the complainant as they possibly can.

The next general step is *classification*. This includes initial determination of the appropriate allegations under the policy manual. A complainant may allege that an officer used excessive force during an incident, but based upon review of the initial details intake personnel may determine that other actions warrant additional allegations about discourtesy, or search and seizure issues, for example. Or, review may determine that different allegations are appropriate. These initial allegations may change as the case proceeds.

Not all complaints will receive the same workflow. Some complaints may be considered *de minimus* in nature (i.e., if the alleged behavior was sustained it would not constitute serious misconduct) and can be addressed by an officer's supervisor. For example, minor issues related to demeanor or courtesy, or standards violations such as not wearing one's hat during a traffic stop,

All complaints should be logged, regardless of the circumstances.

can be investigated and addressed by a supervisor. Some complaints may be amenable to a mediation process, wherein the complainant and the officer are (voluntarily) brought together in front of a private mediator to try and arrive at an understanding about the incident. Typically, if both the citizen and the officer agree to mediation, then the case will not be subject to possible disciplinary action. If the alleged behavior would constitute serious misconduct if sustained, then the complaint will typically be routed for internal investigation. One exception is that if an officer has been charged with a crime, the internal investigations process will generally be limited to administrative review until the criminal process is resolved. It is important to note that these classifications are not fixed in stone, and they can change if new information comes to light.

The next general step is *fact finding*. If the underlying alleged behavior is *de minimus* in nature and routed for investigation and resolution by a supervisor, the supervisor may address the behavior with the officer by simply having a conversation with them about it, correcting behavior perhaps through additional instruction/training, and in some departments may even be empowered to administer low-level or informal disciplinary action (we address the discipline process later in the chapter). Typically, any supervisory action taken is then reported back through the complaints process to indicate how the complaint was addressed, and then a determination of whether to close the case and report the resolution can be made.

If the underlying behavior would constitute serious misconduct, then internal investigators will then try to determine the facts of the case through review of administrative records about the incident, interviews with officers, complainants, and witnesses, and other common investigative procedures.

Typically, an internal investigation concludes with a recommended finding or *disposition* for each allegation. In some cases, this finding may be determined by supervisory internal investigations personnel as they review the complete investigative file. Although there is some variation in the actual categories of complaint disposition, they generally conform to the following five categories:

Sustained:	When a complaint allegation is sustained, it means that there was sufficient evidence to justify disciplinary action against the officer or officers involved.
Not Sustained:	When a complaint allegation is not sustained, it means that there was insufficient evidence to prove the allegation.
Exonerated:	A disposition of exonerated means that the alleged incident occurred, but the officer's action was determined to be lawful and proper.
Unfounded:	An unfounded allegation means that the allegation was not based on facts, or the reported incident did not occur.
Other:	Other dispositions for complaints can include administrative closures, withdrawn complaints, training referrals, mediations, and so on.

If a complaint allegation is sustained, then disciplinary action may result. The disposition of complaints and appropriate level of discipline are generally recommendations to the Chief, who is typically responsible for imposing disciplinary action (we discuss disciplinary action later in the chapter). Finally, it is important to communicate with the complainant and the subject officer(s) about the ultimate disposition of the complaint. This "closes the loop" in the process and strengthens confidence in the responsiveness of the department to citizen concerns as well as the procedural fairness of the process. The general complaint process we have outlined above may be performed completely internal to the organization, completely external to the organization, or in some cases, both. There are also hybrid internal/external models. We discuss external models later in the chapter.

RESEARCH ON COMPLAINT CASE PROCESSING

It is important to understand the history and nature of citizen complaint processes, so we review here studies about the receipt and processing of complaints, the characteristics of officers who are the subjects of complaints, and the characteristics of complainants. There is also literature focused on the correlates of complaint volumes and dispositions, such as agency organizational characteristics, the presence of external review entities, agency policies and procedures, and community demographics. We review this literature chronologically below, highlighting some of the most important and interesting findings, and then offer some synthesis.

Probably the first significant empirical study of police complaints from a social science perspective was Hudson's (1970) analysis of the Philadelphia Police Advisory Board (PAB). From a historical perspective, the PAB is considered to be the "first significant oversight agency" in the United States (Walker, 2001: 23). Hudson's analysis looked at nearly 700 complaints filed with the PAB during its first 10 years of operation, and for which an investigation was conducted. A large proportion of the complaints (46%) resulted from on-view incidents, which is a very meaningful and important finding when compared with the classic Black & Reiss (1967) three-city observational field study of the same era, which found that on-view actions were relatively rare (16%) as a proportion of all officer mobilizations. This provided some of the first evidence that on-view incidents are more likely to result in complaint as compared to incidents where officers are responding to a call for service. As noted in Chapter 7 with regard to police discretion, this makes sense because the dynamic is rather different when the police have been called to a scene (i.e., their presence has been specifically requested by someone) as compared to when they come across something that may or may not require their intervention and they are more likely to be seen as antagonistic or intrusive.

Hudson (1970) found that complainants were mostly male (76%) and minority (70%). The latter statistic is particularly striking when taken in contrast to the population of Philadelphia at the time (about 25% minority). This provided some of the first empirical evidence that complainants are disproportionately minority. In nearly two-thirds (62%) of the incidents giving rise to complaint, the principal complainant had been arrested, with a slightly higher proportion for minorities (65%) than whites (56%). This difference was more substantial when location (public vs. residence) was controlled; when the incident took place at the complainant's residence, 62% of minorities were arrested compared with 46% of whites. Resisting charges were more likely in arrests of minorities (38%) compared to whites (26%). As one of the earlier studies of citizen complaints, Hudson's data and analysis helped researchers to appreciate the importance of situation, status, and context in explaining negative police–citizen interactions that give rise to complaint.

In a pair of articles, Wagner (1980a; 1980b) explored complainant and officer characteristics in a sample of nearly 600 complaint cases during 1971 and 1973 in the pseudonymous "Metro City" police department. Included were all complaints of physical and verbal abuse, and a random sample of other allegations. Wagner (1980a) found that blacks comprised 41% of the population served, but 67% of complaints filed against police. Complainants were also disproportionately male (46% of the population, and 77.5% of complainants) and young (16% of the population was aged 15–24 years, but this age group filed 43% of complaints). A quarter of complainants were unemployed and another 17% were students at the time of the incident. About a quarter of complainants had been arrested for resisting or interfering with officers. When allegation types were separated, blacks were found to complain about physical and verbal abuse proportionately more so than individuals in other complaint categories. Females were found to complain more about verbal abuse than males, and unmarried individuals complained more about physical abuse.

Across the two years studied by Wagner (1980a), just 5% of complaints were sustained. Sustain rates varied by allegation type, with physical force having the lowest rate (2%) compared to verbal abuse (9%) and other allegations (11.5%). Upon further investigation, half of the sustained physical abuse complaints were against off-duty officers involved in disputes with family or friends.

In terms of officer characteristics, Wagner (1980b) examined rank, assignment, race, sex, age, years of service, training, education, height, as well as radio status at time of incident (patrol, foot, detective, and single or two-officer), and mobilization type. Wagner reported that the characteristics of officers who were the subject of complaints were not distinctive. In terms of race, whites comprised 80% of all officers and 85% of all complaints. Officers in two-officer cars were more likely to have complaints than those in one-officer cars, and on-view incidents comprised 71% of all complaints.

A study found that officers in two-officer cars were more likely to have complaints than those in one-officer cars.

Littlejohn (1981) reported on 2,323 citizen complaints (representing more than 4,000 allegations) received by the Detroit Police Department during 1975. This represented a substantial increase in complaint volume over prior years, following the introduction of a new civilian complaints investigations structure in that city during 1974. About one-quarter (24%) of allegations were related to officer demeanor, followed by force complaints (21%) and complaints related to procedure (16%). Fifteen percent of the 2,251 complaint investigations closed in 1975 had at least one sustained finding.

Dugan and Breda (1991) reported on a 1988 survey of all 259 law enforcement agencies then operating in Washington State. They asked for the number and types of complaints received during a 12-month period spanning 1987 and 1988, as well as the number of sustained complaints. Forty-seven percent of the responding agencies reported one or more investigated complaints; the total during the one year period was 691 complaints (an average of 4.2 per agency), involving 437 officers. Most officers received just one (64.5%) or two (22.4%) complaints. The largest complaint category was verbal conduct (41.5% of all complaints), followed by physical force (17.5%). The overall complaint sustain rate was 25%, varying from 12% for physical force complaints to 30% for failure to act complaints. An "other" complaint category comprised 18% of all complaints and had a sustain rate of 37%; this category included a wide variety of behaviors that could be characterized as serious misconduct.

In the wake of the Rodney King incident, as part of a broad review of the Los Angeles Police Department, the Christopher Commission (Independent Commission on the Los Angeles Police Department, 1991) examined complaints and discipline in that agency. They found that a small number of officers had very high rates of complaints and could have been identified from internal records. Of the 1,800 officers who had a use-of-force allegation during the four-year study period, 44 had six or more such allegations. These 44 officers averaged 7.6 force-related complaints in comparison to .6 complaints for all other officers. The study further revealed that a mere half of 1% of officers accounted for 15% of all allegations of excessive force. The Commission expressed the public's frustration with the department, noting that just 3% of the 3,149 allegations of excessive force or improper tactics during the period 1986–1990 were sustained. The Commission noted that sustain rates for these complaints were much higher for investigations conducted by the Internal Affairs Division (15%) as compared to division level investigations (5%), the former generally handling more serious cases than the latter.

Probably the first national-level study of complaints was conducted by Pate & Fridell (1993) for the Police Foundation. Their study focused on police use of force broadly (including agency policies and procedures, training, official reports, citizen complaints, and so forth), and collected data via an establishment survey of 1,111 agencies. 840 agencies provided data on citizen complaints about police use of force. Collectively, they reported 15,608 complaints during 1991, with rates of complaint varying by size and type of agency. Pate & Fridell (1993, p. 95) reported that minorities composed 48.4% of the population served and 58.6% of those filing complaints of excessive force among 215 city police departments. Blacks, in particular, were overrepresented, composing 21.4% of the population served but 42.3% of those filing complaints. Sustained complaints also varied by race of complainant, with black complainants accounting for 27.3% of sustained complaints. In terms of officer characteristics, black officers comprised 13.3% of sworn officers in city police departments, and 12.5% of those with citizen complaints of excessive force (in contrast, Hispanic and "other" officers were overrepresented in complaints). However, black officers were disproportionately represented in sustained complaints (17.3%) compared to other race/ethnicity categories.

Griswold (1994) studied the influence of the seriousness of complaints, the frequency with which an officer is the subject of complaints, and the complaint origin (internal or external) on complaint dispositions during a two-year period in a large suburban sheriffs' department (860 officers) in south Florida. A total of 573 complaints were filed during this period, and about half (49%) were sustained. Most officers (73%) had no complaints filed against them. About 40% of the complaints were filed by citizens, while the remainder was either initiated by internal affairs (38%), or other individual officers (22%). Violations of standard operating procedures accounted for 42% of complaints, and another 22% related to unnecessary force. Multivariate analysis found that complaints filed by other officers were significantly more likely to be sustained, and complaints alleging excessive force were less likely to be sustained. The null effect for frequency of complaints should be considered in light of the fact that prior complaints were limited to those within the two-year study period. In addition, it should be noted that no other variables (such as officer characteristics) were controlled.

Lersch and Mieczkowski (1996) examined 527 complaints over a three-year period in the "Sunnyville" police department. These complaints involved 274 officers, or a little over half of all officers in the department, and a total of 682 allegations. Half of the complaints were classified as harassment, and another 22% were force related. A small group of 37 "repeat" officers who accumulated five or more complaints during the study period (about 7% of all officers) accounted for 35% of all complaints. Overall, 11% of complaints were sustained. They found that minority citizens in the city of Sunnyville composed 22% of the population but about 50% of those filing complaints against Sunnyville police officers. Minority officers comprised 18% of the department, and were the subject of 22% of complaints.

In a second study of a "large police department in the Southeast," Lersch and Mieczkowski (2000) examined whether external (citizen-initiated) complaints were a valid indicator of problem officers, when using internal (officer-initiated) complaints as a criterion measure. Out of 854 misconduct allegations over a three-year period, 174 (or 20.4%) were internal. These internal allegations involved 121 officers, or about 24% of all officers in the department. External allegations involved 259 officers. There were 87 officers who received both internal and external complaints, representing 17% of all officers; these officers were responsible for nearly half (46.6%) of all internal and external complaints during the study period. Minority officers were overrepresented in internal complaints, but not external complaints. Minority officers comprised about 18% of the officers, and 20% of external complaints, but 39% of internal complaints (31% combined external and internal). Gender (male), age (younger), and years of service (fewer) were also related to complaint generation. About a third of the external complaints were related to officer performance (32%) or demeanor (29%), and about a fifth alleged unnecessary force (22%). Internal complaints were similar only in that officer performance was the most frequent category (31%); however, there were no internal allegations of unnecessary force, and just 6% related to demeanor.

At the census tract level, Lersch (1998) found that tracts with higher-than-average numbers of complaints had higher percentages of non-White residents as well as lower median income levels, lower educational levels, a greater percentage living in poverty, and greater unemployment. Similar to Lersch (1998), Lawton et al. (2001) found that complaint locations clustered geographically within the City of Philadelphia (i.e., citizen complaint "hot spots"), and were also correlated with measures of community disadvantage at the precinct-level. Complainant residences were also strongly correlated with precinct-level measures (Lawton et al., 2001). Interestingly, some police precincts had very high proportions of complaints that originated from residents within the precinct, while those in the center city area had very low percentages of complaints originating from persons residing within those areas.

A reanalysis of Pate and Fridell's (1993) data reported by Cao (1999) and Cao et al. (2000) found that the presence of a civilian complaint review board (CCRB), larger percentages of African American officers, higher numbers of arrests, and larger jurisdiction sizes were associated with a higher rate of citizen complaints about excessive physical force. Longer average officer tenure, the presence of a Field Training Officer (FTO) program, and greater levels of in-service training were associated with a lower rate of complaints.

As part of organizational shifts toward community policing in the Philadelphia Police Department, Hickman et al. (2000a) studied a cohort of officers assigned to community policing roles with funding from the Office of Community Oriented Policing Services (COPS), in comparison to officers fulfilling more traditional police roles. They reported no difference in the volume or types of complaints received by officers fulfilling either role, while controlling for several individual background characteristics and demographic characteristics that were related to complaint generation.

Brandl et al. (2001) examined the effects of officer gender, race, education, age, length of service, assignment, patrol area, and arrest activity on citizen complaints about use of force in a random sample of 800 officers from a "large mid-western municipal police department" during 1993. Bivariate models indicated that high-complaint officers (3 or more complaints) were more likely to be younger, with fewer years of experience, assigned to higher crime areas within the city, and with higher arrest activity. Multivariate models indicated that officer gender (male), age (younger), and arrest activity (greater activity), were significantly related to receipt of more complaints about use of force.

Worrall (2002) studied whether agencies with an internal affairs function, CCRB, personnel monitoring system, and automated complaint databases received more complaints than other agencies while controlling for percentage minority, unemployment, crime rate, agency training and education requirements, department size, and ratio of officers to citizens. Multivariate models indicated that agencies having automated complaint databases receive more complaints than agencies not having such databases. Agency size was also related to greater complaints, and crime rate was related specifically to greater force complaints. Worrall suggested that automated systems may indicate a greater level of professionalism and agency concern about citizen complaints, and citizens may be more comfortable complaining. Another explanation offered was that agencies with automated databases have a higher incidence of complaints because the records are perhaps more accurate or at least more accessible.

Hickman (2006) integrated questions regarding the number of citizen complaints about police use of force, as well as complaint dispositions, into the Law Enforcement Management and Administrative Statistics (LEMAS) program administered by the Justice Department's Bureau of Justice Statistics (BJS). These data provided a cross-sectional view of complaints processed by nearly 800 large law enforcement agencies during 2002, including municipal and county police, county sheriffs' offices, and the primary state agencies. Collectively, municipal police departments received more than 22,200 complaints during the year, or 9.5 force complaints per 100 full-time sworn officers, with an overall sustain rate of 8%. There was variation in complaint and sustain rates by agency size as well as organizational characteristics (such as CCRBs, formal internal affairs units, personnel monitoring systems, collective bargaining, and agency policies).

Hickman and Piquero (2009) merged the BJS agency data with Census demographics in order to explore macro-level correlates of police use of force complaints, including organizational, administrative, and environmental factors. They reported that: rates of force complaints were higher among agencies having greater spatial differentiation (see Chapter 5), internal affairs units, and higher violent crime rates; the percentage of complaints sustained was higher among agencies characterized by greater formalization and lower where collective bargaining was authorized for officers; and minority representation among sworn officers relative to the communities served was unrelated to complaint rates nor to the percentage of complaints sustained.

Liederbach et al. (2007) studied all complaints against officers assigned to one patrol district of the "Midwest" city police department during the period March, 2000, through December, 2003. A total of 206 complaints were filed during this time period. 12.6% were internal (police-initiated) complaints, of which 69% were sustained. In contrast, citizen-initiated complaints were sustained against only three officers (a roughly 2% sustain rate), with large proportions of complaints "not sustained" (as compared to unfounded or exonerated). The patrol district was overall 82% non-white (with neighborhood level variation from 47% to 98%), and most complainants were also non-white (78%). Subject officers were mostly white (78%), although comparison departmental demographics were not reported. Complaint allegation types were fairly evenly distributed among verbal misconduct, physical misconduct, failure to serve, and unlawful behavior, with fewer property complaints. Just over half (52%) of complaints involved white officers and non-white citizens, and physical misconduct complaints in these incidents were more likely (20%) than in incidents involving white officers and white citizens (10%). Liederbach et al. focused on the underlying reasons for not sustained findings, and found that the most commonly cited reason (31% of not sustained complaints) was the presence of conflicting "he said/she said" accounts and the lack of independent witnesses. Lack of cooperation from the complainant was also commonly cited (23% of not sustained complaints).

Hassell and Archbold (2010) examined complaints against patrol officers in a "Midwestern" municipal police department during 2002–2005. Both formal and informal (citizen contacts with internal affairs for which no formal complaint was filed) complaints about police action/practice, work performance, and policy violations were included. Officer productivity measures (including arrests, reports, and citations) were collected in addition to demographics (gender, years of experience, and education). Only the productivity variables (arrests and citations) were related to the frequency of both formal and informal complaints against officers. Work performance and departmental policy complaints were more likely to be sustained than police action/practice complaints, and when there was more than one officer at the scene complaints were less likely to be sustained.

It should be noted that BJS collected one additional wave of data on citizen complaints about police use of force in the 2007 LEMAS, but never reported on those data. Hickman and Poore (2015) merged the two waves of data at the agency-level for the purposes of both reporting on the second wave of data, as well as exploring validity and reliability. Reliability was assessed by looking at the distribution of within-agency changes in complaints across the two waves; validity was assessed by drawing a subsample of agencies for external validation of their reported data using publically available reports, records, and/or data, as well as direct contacts with agency personnel via telephone, mail, or electronic inquiry.

For example, they found that the largest raw decrease in complaints about use of force was reported by the Detroit Police Department: 1,172 were reported in the 2002 LEMAS, and 160 were reported in 2006, yielding a decrease of 1,012 complaints, or 86%. In communicating with the Detroit Board of Police Commissioners, it was confirmed that the 1,172 figure for 2002 was approximately the total number of citizen complaints or allegations in that year (their records showed 1,113 total complaints comprising 1,154 total allegations in 2002, 160 of which were force allegations), while the 160 figure for 2006 was determined to be the accurate total use of force allegations in that year; thus, there were 160 force-related allegations in both years–no change at all.

In sum, Hickman and Poore (2015) found that the item wording in the LEMAS data collection was not sufficiently precise, or was not being interpreted and used by respondents as intended, to yield valid and reliable measurement, resulting in net inflation of complaints data. They identified the following list of problems encountered, with some agencies having one or more of these problems in one or both years of reported data:

- Reporting total citizen complaints rather than the subset involving use of force;
- Combining citizen complaints with internal complaints;
- Combining or replacing citizen complaints with officer-reported uses of force;
- Reporting total force allegations within complaint cases, rather than cases involving any force allegation;
- Reporting total complaints investigated, rather than complaints received; and
- Undetected data entry errors (either on the part of the agency or the data collection agent).

Hickman and Poore (2015) concluded that these citizen complaints data do not provide a valid and reliable basis for comparative statistical reporting and research purposes, and should not be used for these purposes, nor for purposes of litigation involving the conduct of law enforcement agencies. This is not to say that the data cannot be collected in a valid and reliable manner, just that additional research and development is necessary.

Most recently, Terrill and Ingram (2015) studied more than 5,500 citizen complaint allegations in eight cities over a two year period. Many of their findings were consistent with the literature: A small percentage of officers accounted for a large percentage of complaints; excessive force and discourtesy allegations were most frequent; younger officers and those with less experience received more complaints; male and non-white complainants were more likely to allege use of force violations; and black complainants were less likely to have their complaints sustained. Importantly, they found that in cities where the internal affairs unit served as the investigatory entity, but complaint dispositions were by an external civilian oversight agency, sustain rates were higher.

One of the challenges in synthesizing this literature is that police complaint processes are somewhat idiosyncratic, owing to different intake processes, unique codes of conduct, varying types and layers of decision-making processes, different degrees of internal and external review, as well as differing policies and procedures, some of which are negotiated with collective bargaining units. Much of the idiosyncrasy is tied to the individual department histories and traditions. This is why large-scale data collection is so problematic and why synthesis is difficult at best. Nevertheless, the available literature on complaint processing indicates that in general:

- A relatively small proportion of officers are responsible for a large proportion of complaints, but this has generally been linked to arrest activity and other measures of productivity;
- On-view incidents and more "proactive" policing assignments may be more likely to lead to complaints than dispatched calls;

- Minority citizens complain in numbers disproportionately greater than their representation in the population served, and this is particularly true for black citizens;
- Minority officers are disproportionately the subject of citizen complaints, as well as internal (police-initiated) complaints;
- There is wide variation in sustain rates across agencies, some of which is attributable to structural differences, but also to idiosyncrasies in the processing of complaints;
- In general, sustain rates are lower for physical force complaints as compared to other types of complaints;
- Internal (police-initiated) complaints tend to have higher sustain rates than citizen complaints;
- Minority representation among officers, relative to the communities served, does not appear to be related to agency complaint volumes or dispositions;
- There are serious measurement concerns that require serious attention when collecting and using multi-agency data.

INTERNAL MECHANISMS

INTERNAL INVESTIGATIONS

Internal affairs units (also referred to as internal investigations, professional standards, professional accountability, and many other names) are typically—though not always—staffed by police investigators whose focus is the organization itself. These units typically have responsibility for investigating citizen complaints as well as internal complaints (complaints by departmental personnel), conducting proactive internal investigations, monitoring legal actions involving officers, and they may also be tasked with reviewing police shootings and/or officer use of force reports. Proactive investigations may take the form of monitoring an officer when allegations of improper behavior arise, as well as conducting *integrity tests*, wherein evidence or cash may be marked and/or left for a subject officer to discover in order to determine whether correct procedures are subsequently followed.

These units may also have responsibility for the maintenance and operation of so-called **Early Warning Systems** (or Early Intervention Systems), computer-based applications that attempt to apprise supervisors of potential problem behaviors. The early versions of these systems tended to be fairly crude, "3-strikes" style systems based on the occurrence of a specified number of events within a specified period of time. For example, an officer who generates three citizen complaints in a month might be flagged for intervention by supervisors. More sophisticated systems may take into consideration the officer's particular assignment. Some types of assignments or parts of a city may give an officer greater exposure to the likelihood of complaint, and it might be the case that the generation of three complaints in a month is "normal" for that particular assignment or location. This is highly controversial, but without such considerations these systems are likely to produce many "false positives." The goal is to identify officers who are having trouble and are in need of assistance in the form of training, counseling, or other remedies, and salvage a career rather than end it.

Recall that in chapter 5, we explored structural differentiation in law enforcement organizations. One form of structural differentiation is functional differentiation, or the extent to which an organization has created subdivisions of specialized labor that are focused on a particular task. In larger organizations there tends to be greater grouping of specialized labor; we gave the examples of special units such as a homicide unit, crime scene investigation unit, or a crime analysis unit. Smaller organizations may still fulfill these tasks, but they likely do so on a part-time or as-needed basis with designated officers who have other regular duties. Internal affairs units staffed with full-time personnel, integrity testing programs, and early warning systems are more likely to be found in larger agencies. Smaller agencies may have a designated investigator who conducts internal investigations on an as-needed basis. The very smallest agencies may request a larger outside agency to handle an internal investigation.

Hickman (2006) reported that, among large police departments (those with 100 or more officers), 82% had an internal affairs or equivalent special unit staffed with full-time personnel. In addition, 33% of large police departments had a currently operational, computer-based personnel performance monitoring and/or assessment system (such as an early warning or early intervention system) for monitoring or responding to officer behavior patterns before they become problematic.

DISCIPLINARY ACTION

Given that a complaint allegation has been sustained, an appropriate punishment may be administered. The primary purpose of a disciplinary process is to hold individual officers directly accountable for their behavior and hopefully to change behavior–not only in the individual but in a broader sense by communicating to the department that poor behavior will not be tolerated and that real consequences follow. However, a disciplinary process that focuses entirely on punishment and not constructive alternatives that could be appropriate (such as training) may tend to undermine the effectiveness of the disciplinary process. In addition, it must be seen by officers as procedurally fair in order to be effective. As you will see shortly, disparity in police disciplinary proceedings has been a long-running topic in the field, and the scant empirical literature on police disciplinary processes has been largely focused on disparity. In general, a disciplinary process will involve several stages and/or levels of review, and may involve legal counsel in determining the appropriate level of punishment based upon the strength of the case as well as precedent set by previous disciplinary decisions, and considerations of what would be defensible in an administrative hearing or legal action. Among the commonly used options are *reprimands* (both oral and written), *suspensions* from duty, *demotion*, and *termination*. Where substantial punishments are involved, such as suspension, demotion, or termination, a *Loudermill* hearing may be convened. Here, the officer has an opportunity to plead their case before the Chief prior to a final decision being made. The officer may be accompanied by legal counsel and/or union representation. The decision to impose discipline is typically at the discretion of the Chief, and can be modified as a result of this hearing—for example, if an officer takes responsibility for their actions and is appropriately remorseful, ultimate discipline could be more lenient. In some cases, severe punishments may require approval by a municipal entity or external board, and there may be extensive appeal processes in some jurisdictions.

Reprimands are commonly used as discipline measures.

The academic literature reflects relatively little attention to case processing in police disciplinary systems. There is ample material on the purpose and goals of discipline systems, as well as suggested disciplinary procedures (e.g., Stephens, 2011; Bender et al., 2005). There is also survey and interview data spanning 40 years that indicates minority officers perceive discriminatory treatment in internal disciplinary processes

(Bannon &Wilt, 1973; Beard, 1977; Bolton, 2003; Bolton & Feagin, 2004), and that officers in general, particularly in large departments, have concerns about the fairness of discipline (Mac-Farlane & Crosby, 1976; McDevitt et al., 2011). More recently, there is literature on the need for guidelines-style discipline matrices (Shane, 2012; Stephens, 2011) as well as the effect of discipline on subsequent behavior (Harris & Worden, 2012). We identified four published empirical studies in the most recent decade that specifically analyzed police discipline case processing in the U.S. (Hickman et al., 2000b, 2001; Rojek & Decker, 2009; Hassell & Archbold, 2010) as well as one technical report (Fyfe et al., 1998). There may also be additional technical reports conducted by or for specific agencies that remain internal documents.

As a backdrop, Pate & Fridell's (1993) national use of force study (discussed earlier with regard to complaints) also provided basic information about disciplinary action for sustained use of force complaints and should be mentioned here. 194 city police departments provided data on disciplinary action following up from 1,430 sustained complaints. Overall, 32.6% of these sustained complaints resulted in a reprimand; 41.8% in suspension; 13.6% in termination; and 12% in other disciplinary outcomes. The distribution of disciplinary actions had slight variations by size of agency; for example, suspensions comprised a larger proportion of disciplinary actions among large agencies (those with 1,000 or more officers).

We would also note that the Christopher Commission (Independent Commission on the Los Angeles Police Department, 1991) examined LAPD statistics on disciplinary punishments for cases involving excessive force against handcuffed suspects, as there was widespread consensus that this was something that would not be tolerated by the department. Of 36 sustained complaints of this type during the period of study, two led to terminations, and the median suspension for the remaining cases was less than 10 days. Among 171 sustained complaints of excessive force or improper tactics, 13 resulted in termination and seven resulted in long terms of suspension (greater than 22 days). In a sample of 39 out-of-policy shootings, including four fatal shootings and 10 injured suspects, a 10-day suspension was the highest punishment imposed.

Below we review the available empirical case-processing studies from the United States, which are limited to just four departments: the New York City Police Department (Fyfe et al., 1998), the Philadelphia Police Department (Hickman et al., 2000b, 2001), the pseudonymous "Centerville" Police Department (Rojeck & Decker, 2009), and a "Midwestern" police department (Hassell & Archbold, 2010).

As part of a Disciplinary Review Task Force initiated by New York City Police Department (NYPD) Commissioner Howard Safir, Fyfe et al. (1998) were tasked with studying whether the disciplinary system was biased against black, Hispanic, and female officers. More specifically, the study focused on the higher of two tiers of discipline, "charges and specifications," which deals with serious and/or chronic matters, as compared with the less-formal command discipline system. In a sample of more than 4,700 cases over a 10-year period, including uniformed officers appearing for the first time, officer race was unrelated to the imposition of a penalty while controlling for a variety of other case characteristics. While there was an observed disproportionality (in that minority officers comprised 27% of all officers, but 38% of

© pryzmat/Shutterstock.com

The Christopher Commission examined cases of excessive force against handcuffed suspects and found disciplinary action lacking.

disciplinary actions, and the rate of disciplinary actions per 1,000 officers was 42.7 for minorities compared to 25.8 for whites), this was attributable to higher rates among minority officers for behaviors requiring mandatory charges, off-duty behavior, and to differences in the demographic composition of the rank structure.

Hickman et al. (2000b) examined the effect of gender on police disciplinary outcomes in the Philadelphia Police Department. They examined nearly 3,700 discipline cases handled by the Police Board of Inquiry (PBI) over an eight-year period. They reported an observed gender disproportionality, in that females comprised 19% of the full-time sworn personnel during the period of study, but female officers appearing for the first time before the PBI were 27% of those receiving punishments greater than a reprimand. However, the disproportionality was not attributable to post-charging discrimination in the disciplinary process, but rather to differential involvement in charging by police supervisors. When disaggregated by the type of offense, gender was found to be unrelated to disciplinary outcomes for "Disobedience of Orders" and "Neglect of Duty" charges, but the evidence suggested that the PBI may have worked to the slight benefit of female officers in "Conduct Unbecoming" cases (being more lenient with female than with male officers) and slightly against them in "Insubordination" cases (being more punitive with female than with male officers).

In a second study with the Philadelphia Police Department, as part of a larger study focused on police integrity and the development of Early Warning Systems, Hickman et al. (2001) surveyed a random sample of about 500 officers, and linked their survey data to official disciplinary data. About one-third of the sample had ever been charged with a disciplinary offense during their career. Race and gender were found to be unrelated to charging, hearing or waiver of hearing, and determination of guilt, while rank and years of service were related to both charging and the officer's decision whether to waive a hearing.

Rojek & Decker (2009) examined nearly 1,200 cases involving officers investigated for misconduct in the "Centerville" Police Department during a five-year period. They found that minority officers were disproportionately represented in complaints (in that minority officers comprised about 36% of the department, but 45% of all complaints), but that race was unrelated to guilt determination or the degree of punishment when controlling for other explanatory variables. The only variable that was related to sustained findings was the source of the complaint (internal complaints were more likely to be sustained than external complaints). In terms of differentiating between the receipt of minor discipline (reprimands and retraining) and major discipline (suspensions and demotions), officers with greater years of service and incidents involving multiple officers were less likely to receive major discipline. Officers with multiple allegations and internal complaints were more likely to receive major discipline.

Although officer race in the Rojeck & Decker (2009) study was not related to complaint dispositions nor to degree of punishment, it is important to note that minority officers were more likely to be the subject of an internal complaint (minority officers were 58% of all internal complaints, but just 37% of citizen complaints), and these complaints were more likely to be sustained and receive major discipline. As Rojek & Decker (2009) point out, it is unknown whether the disproportionality in internal complaints is a result of discretionary decisions to formally document a complaint, or the differential initiation of complaints. However, if it were attributable to behavioral differences, one would expect to see disproportional representation in both internal and external complaints.

As previously discussed, Hassell & Archbold (2010) examined complaints against patrol officers in a "Midwestern" municipal police department during 2002–2005; they also examined disciplinary action. They differentiated between serious discipline (written reprimand, suspension, resignation, termination) and minor discipline, but none of the study variables (officer gender, years of experience, education, productivity, number of officers on scene, and type of complaint) were significantly related to serious vs. minor disciplinary action.

Finally, with regard to research on disciplinary systems, it is important to note that the final disciplinary outcome at the agency level (for example, as imposed by the Chief) is not necessarily the final word. Appeals from discipline and arbitration are an important but understudied area in policing. For example, Iris (1999) examined all 328 disciplinary decisions taken by binding arbitration in the Chicago Police Department (CPD) during a four-year period. Iris (1999) reported that 135 (41%) of the disciplinary decisions were upheld in full, 133 (40%) were overturned in full, and the remaining 60 (19%) were upheld in part (for example, with reductions in the degree of penalty). The net effect was that arbitrators reduced punishments by almost exactly half: Collectively, the 328 cases imposed a total of 1,584 days of suspension, which were reduced by arbitrators to a total of 794 days of suspension. Iris (1999) speculates that one possibility is that arbitrators, out of their own self-interest, may have a desire to appear balanced in their decision-making; alternatively, that a more random process may be at play.

Similar to what we noted previously in discussing citizen complaints, it is challenging to synthesize what we know about disciplinary systems due to a limited amount of research and the idiosyncratic nature of these systems. Nevertheless, the available literature on police discipline systems indicates that:

- There is a perception among police officers of unfairness in police disciplinary processes, both along racial lines and in general terms, and this has persisted for at least 40 years;
- Racial disproportionality in police discipline has been observed in empirical studies conducted in at least three cities;
- An independent effect of officer race on disciplinary outcomes has not been established, with observed racial disproportionalities explained by other factors such as differential involvement in complaints, more serious allegations, off-duty behavior, and internal complaints;
- Appeals from discipline and arbitration are an important but understudied area, and any effect of officer race in these processes is not known.

Wherever discretion is exercised, the potential for implicit or explicit bias is a risk. In addition to guiding discretionary decision-making, discipline matrices have gained increased acceptance in law enforcement administration as a risk management tool, an asset to collective bargaining agreements, and a best practice for improving and maintaining morale (Shane, 2012; Stephens, 2011). A matrix does not limit the discretion of the Chief but rather is a living document which reflects, at a glance, what punishment has been imposed in the past and deemed proportional and just. Similar to sentencing guidelines, a discipline matrix might include a requirement to justify disciplinary decisions in writing when they "depart" from the guideline range. The goal is simply to improve rationality in decision-making, a goal that is difficult to argue against.

EXTERNAL MECHANISMS

While internal mechanisms—such as an internal affairs function tasked in part with the receipt and review of citizen complaints, and a disciplinary process for imposing punishments for poor officer behavior—are important elements of an accountability structure, it is natural in a democracy to ask whether the police are truly capable of effectively self-policing themselves, as well as whether it is appropriate to leave this essential task exclusively to the police. In this section, we discuss external mechanisms including citizen oversight systems, **officer decertification** processes, and federal intervention in the behavior of law enforcement agencies.

CITIZEN OVERSIGHT

Citizen oversight comes in many forms and names, but the growth of citizen oversight over the past 40 years has been substantial. Walker (2001) described the conceptual rise of citizen oversight from the 1920s through World War II as thoroughly controversial, with notable first steps in Washington, DC's Complaint Review Board (CRB) in 1948, New York City's Civilian Complaint Review Board (CCRB) in 1953, and particularly with the creation of the Philadelphia Police Advisory Board (PAB) in 1958, which operated for about a decade. But by the end of the 1960s these entities had all been disbanded, largely due to the political strength of police unions (Walker, 2001). During the 1970s citizen oversight picked up some steam and Walker describes the 1980s and 1990s as an era where citizen oversight had become a "national movement" as evidenced by the growth of oversight agencies from 13 in 1980, to 38 in 1990, and approximately 100 operating by the end of the 1990s (Walker, 2001: 40). Today, there is a major professional association for oversight professionals, the National Association for Civilian Oversight of Law Enforcement (NACOLE, www.nacole.org), which provides training, resources, and annual conferences at both a regional and national level.

As previously noted, Walker (2001: 5) defines *citizen oversight* as "a procedure for providing input into the complaint process by individuals who are not sworn officers." A key aspect of such an oversight system is the degree of independence enjoyed by the citizen oversight body. This independence can be examined along structural, process, and perceptual dimensions; Walker identifies four general structural models of oversight systems (Walker, 2001: 61-62):

Class I: Responsibility for investigating complaints is given to a separate agency external to the police department; persons who are not sworn officers conduct the initial fact finding; a recommendation is sent to the police chief regarding final disposition.

Class II: Complaints are received by an external agency, but are investigated by the police department, which then sends investigative reports back to the external agency for review and a recommendation to the police chief regarding final disposition.

Class III: These oversight agencies are the least independent and essentially serve in an appellate capacity. The police department receives, investigates, and determines final disposition for citizen complaints, but the complainant may appeal the results to the external oversight agency. The external agency can refer the case back to the police department for further investigation but cannot overturn the disposition.

Class IV: These oversight agencies are generally referred to as auditor systems. They do not receive and investigate individual complaints, but have the authority to audit the police department's complaint process.

There are hybrid systems that do not neatly fit within these general classifications. Seattle is such an example, where the Seattle Police Department's Office of Professional Accountability (OPA) is internal to the organization and uses sworn investigators, but is headed by a civilian director. Seattle also is somewhat different in that it also has an independent civilian auditor for the OPA; the rationale is that although OPA is headed by a civilian and is intended to be operationally independent of the police department, it is internal to the organization and all staff are employees of the police department. The OPA auditor, who is a contractual hire with legal expertise (presently staffed by a former Judge), serves as an additional independent layer of oversight to review OPA operations and enhance public trust in the process.

In addition to structural independence, there is concern over process independence; that is, although the oversight agency may be structurally independent, does it actually function in a truly independent manner? There is concern that members of review boards may either come to the table, or become sympathetic over time, to police officers; Walker (2001) provides examples of some oversight agencies where this appears to have been the case. Finally, there is the perceptual component of independence. Returning to the previous chapter, we had conceptualized police integrity as comprised of both behavioral and perceptual components, with the resulting dilemma that it really doesn't matter if your police are Boy Scouts—if the public doesn't see it that way, you have an integrity problem. The same can be said for the independence of civilian oversight: structural and process independence are effectively crippled by weak perceptual independence.

OFFICER DECERTIFICATION

Certification is the process by which a state authority determines that an individual has met the state's basic law enforcement training requirements and issues that individual a commission, certificate, license, or other documentation verifying their completion of basic training. This is the end result of the lengthy and demanding screening, selection, and training process for entry into the law enforcement profession. Once working in law enforcement, officers may commit misconduct that leads to their termination (or dismissal) from their department. However, dismissal isn't always the final word on the matter.[1] Officers may be rehired by another jurisdiction, in which case the new jurisdiction inherits another jurisdiction's problem. This can be a conscious decision by the hiring agency, especially in small jurisdictions where financial resources are limited and lateral officers are simply scarce (Goldman & Puro, 2001). Fortunately, most states have the authority to revoke an officer's peace officer certification (often referred to as decertification), essentially invalidating their training credentials and making them unemployable as a law enforcement officer. The reasons for decertification vary, but in all such cases a state authority determines that the subject officer(s) should not be allowed to continue exercising the duties and privileges of a law enforcement officer.

The goal of state decertification is to ensure integrity in law enforcement by preventing the *intrastate* rehire of problem officers. For example, if an officer separates from a law enforcement agency in Washington State, a notice of the separation is reported to the Criminal Justice Training Commission. The law enforcement agency reporting the separation must indicate whether they are aware of "disqualifying misconduct" that could lead to the subject officer's decertification. The Training Commission can investigate and decide whether to proceed against the officer, and if the officer is ultimately decertified, he/she is unemployable by other law enforcement agencies within Washington State.

The International Association of Directors of Law Enforcement Standards and Training (IADLEST) developed the National Decertification Index (NDI) as a means to further enhance integrity in law enforcement by preventing the *interstate* rehire of problem officers. Thus, the hypothetical officer decertified in Washington State cannot simply move to another state and gain employment as a law enforcement officer. The hiring agency can query the NDI to check whether the applicant has been decertified in another state, request relevant records from the other state, and make an informed decision about hiring the officer.

Atherley and Hickman (2013) recently reported the findings of a survey of all state POST directors with regard to decertification practices. POST agencies in 45 states had the authority to revoke officer certification in 2011. Hawaii, Massachusetts, New Jersey, New York, Rhode Island,

---

[1] Material in this section is taken from: Atherley, L., & Hickman, M. (2013). Officer decertification and the National Decertification Index. *Police Quarterly, 16*(4), 420–437.

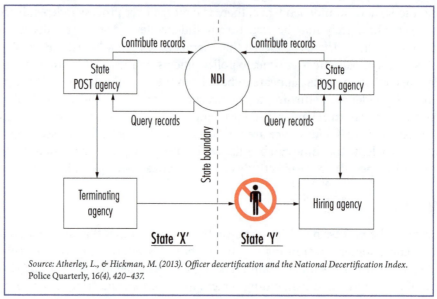

Source: Atherley, L., & Hickman, M. (2013). Officer decertification and the National Decertification Index. Police Quarterly, 16(4), 420–437.

Figure 14.1 How the National Decertification Index (NDI) Works to Prevent the Interstate Rehire of Problem Officers.

and the District of Columbia did not have this authority. It should also be noted that California's decertification authority was severely restricted by legislative changes in 2004, such that they may only decertify for fraud or administrative error in the application process.

They found that during calendar year 2011, more than 700 law enforcement officers were decertified in the United States (more than 1,350 if correctional officers and others certified by state POST agencies are included). The base rate of decertification for law enforcement officers was estimated to be 1.2 per 1,000 officers, varying from zero to 7.6 per 1,000 at the state level. One key finding was that the rate of decertification in a state may be related to the strength of state surveillance mechanisms for officer misconduct. In some states, law enforcement agencies are required to report all separations from employment to the state POST agency, and in some cases are also required to indicate any awareness of misconduct that could lead to decertification; in other states there is no such requirement, and the state POST agency may learn about officer misconduct from other sources (such as newspaper articles). At the time of the study, 18 states reported that the law enforcement agencies in their state were required to report all separations and indicate their awareness of any misconduct; the rate of decertification in these states was 1.8 per 1,000 officers, compared to 0.9 per 1,000 in states without such a requirement.

With regard to the NDI, 30 agencies reported that they contributed decertification records to the NDI during 2011. Twenty-two agencies reported "always" (15) or "frequently" (7) querying the NDI. Fourteen agencies reported "occasionally" (10) or rarely (4) querying the NDI, and 14 agencies reported "never" querying the database.

FEDERAL INTERVENTION

When the existing accountability structure has failed to adequately control officer behavior in a police department, a remaining mechanism is the so-called **pattern or practice investigation** carried out by the Special Litigation Section (SLS) of the US Department of Justice Civil Rights Division. The box below, from the SLS website, describes the work of the SLS on "Conduct of Law Enforcement Agencies."

SPECIAL LITIGATION SECTION—CONDUCT OF LAW ENFORCEMENT AGENCIES

OVERVIEW

The Section works to protect the rights of people who interact with state or local police or sheriffs' departments. If we find that one of these law enforcement agencies systematically deprives people of their rights, we can act.

We use information from a variety of sources to bring our cases, including information from community members. The voice of every member of the community is very important to us. We receive dozens of reports of potential violations each month. We collect this information and it informs our case selection. We may sometimes use it as evidence in an existing case. However, we cannot bring a case based on every report we receive. Nor do we have authority to investigate federal law enforcement agencies. We also cannot assist in individual criminal cases, including wrongful arrest or convictions, appeals or sentencing.

DESCRIPTION OF THE LAWS WE ENFORCE

The Violent Crime Control and Law Enforcement Act of 1994, 42 U.S.C. § 14141, allows us to review the practices of law enforcement agencies that may be violating people's federal rights. If a law enforcement agency receives federal funding, we can also use the anti-discrimination provisions of the Omnibus Crime Control and Safe Streets Act of 1968, and Title VI of the Civil Rights Act of 1964, which forbid discrimination on the basis of race, color, sex or national origin by agencies receiving federal funds. We may act if we find a pattern or practice by the law enforcement agency that systemically violates people's rights. Harm to a single person, or isolated action, is usually not enough to show a pattern or practice that violates these laws.

The Section has investigated dozens of law enforcement agencies nationwide. In our investigations, we typically meet with law enforcement officers and other members of the local community. We hire police practice experts to help us review incidents, documents, and agency policies and practices. These experts also help us to develop remedies, and to assess whether corrective steps have fixed the violations of law.

The problems addressed in our cases include use of excessive force; unlawful stops, searches, or arrests; and discriminatory policing. We have looked at bias based on race, ethnicity, national origin, gender, and sexual orientation. We have also addressed unlawful responses to individuals who observe, record, or object to police actions.

RESULTS OF OUR WORK

Our settlements and court orders frequently require:

- increased transparency and data collection
- community-police partnerships
- steps to prevent discriminatory policing
- independent oversight
- improved investigation and review of uses of force
- more effective training and supervision of officers

The reforms we obtain create models for effective and constitutional policing nationwide. They provide significant, systemic relief, increase community confidence in law enforcement, and improve officer and agency accountability.

The 1994 Violent Crime Control and Law Enforcement Act, also known as the "Clinton Crime Bill," created the authority for the Civil Rights Division to investigate police departments that they believe are engaging in unconstitutional "patterns or practices" of conduct. The underlying issues are often centered on the use of force, racially discriminatory policing, and procedural violations. When the Civil Rights Division completes their investigation, if they find evidence of a pattern or practice they typically issue a findings letter that clearly indicates that finding as well as a threat to file a civil lawsuit if the deficiencies are not corrected. In short, they threaten to sue and force reform if the agency/jurisdiction does not willfully engage in reform. Settlements are the norm and they may take the form of a **consent decree**, in which the parties agree to the required reforms and the appointment and role of a monitor who will oversee the reform process on behalf of the court. The DOJ Civil Rights Division has increased their activity in this area substantially under the Obama Administration (see the list of all 68 investigations since passage of the 1994 Crime Act listed in Table 1, below). Questions remain, however, about the effectiveness of these interventions. A recent *Washington Post/Frontline* investigation entitled, "Forced Reforms, Mixed Results" explored some of the costs and benefits of federal intervention. The full report can be found here: http://www.washingtonpost.com/sf/investigative/2015/11/13/forced-reforms-mixed-results/?hpid=hp_hp-more-top-stories_cop-reforms-615pm%3Ahomepage%2Fstory.

	Agency	State	Started	Agreement	Closed	Status	Primary Issues
1	NEW JERSEY STATE POLICE	NJ	12/1/1994	12/30/1999	10/26/2009	Consent Decree	Biased Policing; Search and Seizure
2	TORRANCE POLICE	CA	5/1/1995		9/14/1998	Closed without Agreement	Biased Policing
3	ADELANTO POLICE	CA	6/16/1995		9/14/1998	Closed without Agreement	Use of Force
4	STEUBENVILLE POLICE	OH	7/31/1995	9/3/1997	3/3/2005	Consent Decree	Use of Force; Search and Seizure; Accountability Structure
5	PITTSBURGH POLICE	PA	4/11/1996	4/16/1997	6/16/2005	Consent Decree	Use of Force; Arrest; Search and Seizure
6	ILLINOIS STATE POLICE	IL	4/15/1996		9/27/2002	Closed without Agreement	Biased Policing
7	NEW ORLEANS POLICE	LA	4/15/1996		3/23/2004	Closed without Agreement	Use of Force; Accountability Structure
8	MONTGOMERY COUNTY POLICE	MD	6/1/1996	2/1/2000	2/1/2005	MOA	Biased Policing; Accountability Structure
9	LOS ANGELES POLICE	CA	7/31/1996	6/15/2001	5/16/2013	Consent Decree	Use of Force; Arrest; Search and Seizure; Accountability Structure
10	BEVERLY HILLS POLICE	CA	8/12/1996		11/14/2000	Closed without Agreement	Biased Policing
11	NEW YORK CITY POLICE	NY	8/21/1997		12/23/2004	Closed without Agreement	Use of Force
12	ORANGE COUNTY SHERIFF'S OFFICE	CA	11/1/1997		5/11/2001	Closed without Agreement	Use of Force
13	BUFFALO POLICE	NY	12/9/1997	9/19/2002	7/8/2008	MOA	Use of Force; Accountability Structure

continued

TABLE 14.1   DOJ Civil Rights Division Investigations of State and Local Law Enforcement Agencies since Passage of the 1994 Crime Act (continued)

	Agency	State	Started	Agreement	Closed	Status	Primary Issues
14	COLUMBUS POLICE	OH	3/13/1998	9/1/2002	5/14/2004	MOA/LETTER AGREEMENT	Use of Force; Arrest; Search and Seizure
15	EASTPOINTE POLICE	MI	3/20/1998		1/12/2005	Closed without Agreement	Biased Policing
16	DC METROPOLITAN POLICE	DC	1/31/1999	6/13/2001	2/10/2012	MOA	Use of Force; Accountability Structure
17	NEW YORK CITY POLICE	NY	3/17/1999		3/31/2005	Closed without Agreement	Biased Policing; Stop and Frisks
18	CHARLESTON POLICE	WV	3/31/1999		11/12/2003	Closed without Agreement	Use of Force
19	RIVERSIDE POLICE	CA	6/29/1999		3/26/2007	Closed without Agreement	Use of Force; Biased Policing
20	PRINCE GEORGE'S COUNTY POLICE	MD	7/1/1999	3/1/2004	3/12/2007	Consent Decree	Use of Canines
21	CLEVELAND DIVISION OF POLICE	OH	10/1/1999	2/1/2004	3/15/2005	MOA/LETTER AGREEMENT	Use of Force; Detention Procedures
22	MT. PROSPECT POLICE	IL	1/1/2000	1/22/2003	12/28/2006	MOA	Biased Policing
23	HIGHLAND PARK POLICE	IL	5/8/2000	7/1/2001	12/7/2004	MOA	Biased Policing
24	PRINCE GEORGE'S COUNTY POLICE	MD	10/1/2000	1/22/2004	1/13/2009	MOA	Use of Force
25	DETROIT POLICE	MI	12/1/2000	6/12/2003		Consent Decree	Use of Force; Arrest, Detention and Confinement Procedures
26	TULSA POLICE	OK	2/8/2001		7/21/2008	Closed without Agreement	Biased Policing; Use of Force
27	CINCINNATI POLICE	OH	5/7/2001	4/12/2002	4/12/2007	MOA	Use of Force; Biased Policing; Accountability Structure

continued

	Agency	State	Started	Agreement	Closed	Status	Primary Issues
28	SCHENECTADY POLICE	NY	4/4/2002		1/9/2013	Closed without Agreement	Use of Force; Accountability Structure
29	PORTLAND POLICE	ME	5/6/2002		6/27/2005	Closed without Agreement	Use of Force; Search and Seizure; Accountability Structure
30	MIAMI POLICE	FL	5/31/2002		5/19/2006	Closed without Agreement	Use of Force; Vehicle Pursuits; Search and Seizure; Accountability Structure
31	PROVIDENCE POLICE	RI	12/11/2002		3/26/2008	Closed without Agreement	Use of Force; Search and Seizure; Accountability Structure
32	VILLA RICA POLICE	GA	1/27/2003	12/23/2003	12/23/2006	MOA	Biased Policing; Search and Seizure
33	ALABASTER POLICE	AL	3/4/2003		9/7/2005	Closed without Agreement	Use of Force; Accountability Structure
34	BAKERSFIELD POLICE	CA	6/24/2003		1/25/2008	Closed without Agreement	Use of Force; Accountability Structure
35	THE VIRGIN ISLANDS POLICE	VI	2/13/2004	3/23/2009		Consent Decree	Use of Force; Accountability Structure
36	BEACON POLICE	NY	8/3/2004	12/23/2010		MOA	Use of Force; Accountability Structure
37	WARREN POLICE	OH	11/29/2004	1/26/2012		Consent Decree	Use of Force; Accountability Structure
38	EASTON POLICE	PA	10/14/2005	9/8/2010		MOA	Use of Force
39	ORANGE COUNTY SHERIFF'S OFFICE	FL	1/10/2007	9/16/2010	4/4/2013	MOA	Use of Force
40	AUSTIN POLICE	TX	5/25/2007		5/27/2011	Closed without Agreement	Use of Force
41	YONKERS POLICE	NY	7/24/2007			TA Letter Issued/ Investigation	Use of Force; Accountability Structure

continued

TABLE 14.1 DOJ Civil Rights Division Division Investigations of State and Local Law Enforcement Agencies since Passage of the 1994 Crime Act *(continued)*

	Agency	State	Started	Agreement	Closed	Status	Primary Issues
42	PUERTO RICO POLICE	PR	4/3/2008	7/17/2013		Consent Decree	Use of Force; Search and Seizure; Biased Policing
43	HARVEY POLICE	IL	9/5/2008		1/24/2012	Closed without Agreement	Use of Force; Accountability Structure
44	LORAIN POLICE	OH	11/20/2008		5/22/2012	Closed without Agreement	Use of Force; Sexual Misconduct
45	ESCAMBIA COUNTY SHERIFF'S OFFICE	FL	1/9/2009		10/14/2012	Closed without Agreement	Use of Force
46	MARICOPA COUNTY SHERIFF'S	AZ	6/1/2008	7/17/2015		Settlement	Biased Policing
47	INGLEWOOD POLICE	CA	3/11/2009			TA Letter Issued	Use of Force; Accountability Structure
48	SUFFOLK COUNTY POLICE	NY	9/9/2009	1/13/2014		MOA	Biased Policing; Accountability Structure
49	EAST HAVEN POLICE	CT	9/30/2009	11/19/2012		Consent Decree	Biased Policing
50	NEW ORLEANS POLICE	LA	5/15/2010	1/11/2013		Consent Decree	Use of Force; Stops, Searches, Arrests
51	ALAMANCE COUNTY SHERIFF'S	NC	6/2/2010			Litigation	Biased Policing
52	SEATTLE POLICE	WA	3/31/2011	7/27/2012		Consent Decree/ MOA	Use of Force; Biased Policing
53	NEWARK POLICE	NJ	5/9/2011			Findings issued	Biased Policing; Use of Force; Accountability Structure
54	PORTLAND POLICE BUREAU	OR	6/7/2011	8/29/2014		Consent Decree	Use of Force
55	LOS ANGELES SHERIFF'S	CA	8/19/2011	4/28/2015		Settlement	Biased Policing; Stops and Arrests; Use of Force; Search and Seizure

continued

TABLE 14.1 DOJ Civil Rights Division Investigations of State and Local Law Enforcement Agencies since Passage of the 1994 Crime Act (continued)

	Agency	State	Started	Agreement	Closed	Status	Primary Issues
56	MIAMI POLICE	FL	11/16/2011			Findings issued	Use of Force
57	MERIDIAN POLICE	MS	11/29/2011	9/17/2015		Settlement	Arrests of Juveniles
58	UNIV. OF MONTANA OFFICE OF PUBLIC SAFETY	MT	4/25/2012	5/9/2013	7/10/2015	MOA	Gender discrimination
59	MISSOULA POLICE	MT	4/25/2012	5/15/2013	5/11/2015	MOA	Gender discrimination
60	MISSOULA COUNTY ATTORNEY'S OFFICE (see note)	MT	5/1/2012	6/10/2014		MOA	Gender discrimination
61	COLORADO CITY MARSHAL'S OFFICE	AZ	6/12/2012			Litigation	Biased Policing - Religious Affiliation
62	ALBUQUERQUE POLICE	NM	11/27/2012	11/14/2014		Consent Decree	Use of Force; Accountability Structure
63	CLEVELAND DIVISION OF POLICE	OH	3/1/2013	5/26/2015		Consent Decree	Use of Force; Search and Seizure
64	FERGUSON POLICE	MO	9/1/2014			Findings issued	Biased Policing
65	VILLE PLATTE POLICE	LA	4/21/2015				Seizures - Use of Investigative Holds; Accountability Structure
66	EVANGELINE PARISH SHERIFF'S OFFICE	LA	4/21/2015				Seizures - Use of Investigative Holds; Accountability Structure
67	BALTIMORE POLICE	MD	5/8/2015				Use of Force
68	CHICAGO POLICE	IL	12/7/2015				Use of Force

Note: The Missoula County Attorney's Office is included here for completeness; the investigation was launched under the same statutory authority as part of investigations into the University of Montana Office of Public Safety and the Missoula police department.

Source: Majority of information in table is from The Marshall Project (www.themarshallproject.org). Authors added detail about the nature of the investigation and updated as possible.

CONCLUSION

In this chapter, we discussed different internal and external mechanisms for holding the police accountable for poor behaviors. We highlighted the importance of citizen complaints, but also some of the many difficulties in understanding the utility of data about citizen complaints as well as variety in complaint processes. We explored internal affairs functions, disciplinary systems, civilian oversight structures, decertification processes, and the role of federal intervention. Hopefully, in evaluating the role and purpose of each of these individual mechanisms, you have come to appreciate the need for multiple layers of accountability. There are many examples of agencies with what appear to be perfectly adequate accountability mechanisms that may suggest structural independence, but they do not, in the words of Sam Walker, deliver on process and/or perception. In these cases, the very accountability mechanisms that are designed to help ensure public confidence in the police may completely fail to achieve that essential goal.

REVIEW QUESTIONS

1. Do you think that police departments are capable of policing themselves? Why or why not? Which general model of external civilian oversight do you think is best?
2. Draft your idea of a model accountability structure for police departments. What would it entail? Would you include internal, external, or both forms of oversight? Would you require the use of any innovative technologies?

GLOSSARY

Accountability a condition that exists when the police acknowledge behaviors that the public views as a violation of their trust, and the police seek to either explain or correct the identified problems in a timely manner.

Citizen oversight defined by Samuel Walker as a procedure for providing input into the complaint process by individuals who are not sworn officers; can take a variety of different structural forms.

Consent decree a type of settlement following a pattern or practice investigation in which the parties typically agree to a set of required reforms, as well as the appointment and role of a monitor who will oversee the reform process on behalf of the court.

Early warning systems a means used by police leadership to identify a potentially problematic officer before his or her behavior becomes very serious. Sometimes called Early Intervention Systems.

Federal pattern or practice investigation a civil rights investigation carried out by the Special Litigation Section of the Civil Rights Division of the US Department of Justice; these investigations focus on police departments that may be engaging in unconstitutional "patterns or practices" of conduct, typically centered on the use of force, racially discriminatory policing, and procedural violations.

Officer decertification the process by which a state authority determines that a law enforcement officer should not be allowed to continue exercising the duties and privileges of a law enforcement officer. Decertification essentially invalidates an individual's training credentials and makes them unemployable as a law enforcement officer in that state.

REFERENCES

Atherley, L., & Hickman, M. (2013). Officer decertification and the National Decertification Index. *Police Quarterly, 16*(4), 420–437.

Bannon, J., & Wilt, G. (1973). Black policemen: A study of self-images. *Journal of Police Science and Administration, 1*, 21–29.

Beard, E. (1977). The black police in Washington, DC. *Journal of Police Science and Administration, 5*, 48–52.

Bender, L., Jurkanin, T., Sergevnin, V., & Dowling, J. (2005). *Critical issues in police discipline: Case studies.* Springfield, IL: Charles C. Thomas.

Black, D., & Reiss, A. (1967). *Studies in crime and law enforcement in major metropolitan areas.* Report submitted to the president's commission on law enforcement and administration of justice. Washington, DC: Government Printing Office.

Bolton, K. (2003). Shared perceptions: Black officers discuss continuing barriers in policing. *Policing: An International Journal of Police Strategies and Management, 26*, 386–399.

Bolton, K., & Feagin, J. (2004). *Black in blue: African American police officers and racism.* New York: Routledge.

Brandl, S., Stroshine, M., & Frank, J. (2001). Who are the complaint-prone officers? An examination of the relationship between police officers' attributes, arrest activity, assignment, and citizens' complaints about excessive force. *Journal of Criminal Justice, 29*, 521–529.

Cao, L. (1999). *Curbing police brutality: What works? A reanalysis of citizen complaints at the organizational level.* Final report to the National Institute of Justice (Grant No. 98-IJ-CX-0064).

Cao, L., Deng, X., & Barton, S. (2000). A test of Lundman's organizational product thesis with data on citizen complaints. *Policing: An International Journal of Police Strategies and Management, 23*, 356–373.

Dugan, J., & Breda, D. (1991). Complaints about police officers: A comparison among types and agencies. *Journal of Criminal Justice, 19*, 165–171.

Fyfe, J., Kane, R., Grasso, G., & Ansbro, G. (1998). Gender, race and discipline in the New York City Police Department. Paper presented at the annual meeting of the American Society of Criminology, Washington DC, November.

Griswold, D. (1994). Complaints against the police: Predicting dispositions. *Journal of Criminal Justice, 22*, 215–221.

Harris, C., & Worden, R. (2012). The effect of sanctions on police misconduct. *Crime & Delinquency*, forthcoming.

Hassell, K., & Archbold, C. (2010). Widening the scope on complaints of police misconduct. *Policing: An International Journal of Police Strategies and Management, 33,* 473–489.

Hickman, M. (2006). *Citizen complaints about police use of force.* Washington, DC: Bureau of Justice Statistics.

Hickman, M., & Piquero, A. (2009). Organizational, administrative, and environmental correlates of complaints about police use of force: Does minority representation matter? *Crime & Delinquency, 55,* 3–27.

Hickman, M., & Poore, J. (2015). National data on citizen complaints about police use of force: Data quality concerns and the potential (mis)use of statistical evidence to address police agency conduct. *Criminal Justice Policy Review,* in press.

Hickman, M., Piquero, A., & Greene, J. (2000a). Does community policing generate greater numbers and different types of citizen complaints than traditional policing? *Police Quarterly, 3,* 70–84.

———. (2000b). Discretion and gender disproportionality in police disciplinary systems. *Policing: An International Journal of Police Strategies and Management, 23,* 105–116.

Hickman, M., Lawton, B., Piquero, A., & Greene, J. (2001). Does race influence police disciplinary processes? *Justice Research and Policy, 3,* 97–113.

Hudson, J. (1970). Police-citizen encounters that lead to citizen complaints. *Social Problems, 18,* 179–193.

Independent Commission on the Los Angeles Police Department. (1991). *Report of the independent commission on the Los Angeles police department.* Los Angeles, CA: International Creative Management.

Iris, M. (1999). Police discipline in Chicago: Arbitration or arbitrary? *Journal of Criminal Law & Criminology, 89,* 215–244.

Lawton, B., Hickman, M., Piquero, A., & Greene, J. (2001). Using GIS to analyze complaints against police: A research note. *Justice Research and Policy, 3,* 95–108.

Lersch, K. (1998). Police misconduct and malpractice: A critical analysis of citizens' complaints. *Policing: An International Journal of Police Strategies and Management, 21,* 80–96.

Lersch, K., & Mieczkowski, T. (1996). Who are the problem-prone officers? An analysis of citizen complaints. *American Journal of Police, 15,* 23–44.

———. (2000). An examination of the convergence and divergence of internal and external allegations of misconduct filed against police officers. *Policing: An International Journal of Police Strategies and Management, 23,* 54-68.

Liederbach, J., Boyd, L., Taylor, R., & Kawucha, S. (2007). Is it an inside job? An examination of internal affairs complaint investigation files and the production of nonsustained findings. *Criminal Justice Policy Review, 18,* 353–377.

Littlejohn, E. (1981). The civilian police commission: A deterrent of police misconduct. *Journal of Urban Law, 59,* 5–62.

MacFarlane, R., & Crosby, A. (1976). Police officer discipline: A study of experience and attitude. *Journal of Police Science and Administration, 4,* 331–339.

McDevitt, J., Posick, C., Zschoche, R., Rosenbaum, D., Buslik, M., & Fridell, L. (2011). *Police Integrity, Responsibility, and Discipline.* Topical Report from the National Police Research Platform. Accessible at: <www.nationalpoliceresearch.org/storage/updated-papers/Police%20Integrity%20Responsibility%20and%20Discipline.pdf>.

Pate, A., & Fridell, L. (1993). *Police use of force: Official reports, citizen complaints, and legal consequences* (Vol. 1). Washington, DC: Police Foundation.

Rojek, J., & Decker, S. (2009). Examining racial disparity in the police discipline process. *Police Quarterly, 12,* 388–407.

Shane, J. (2012). Police employee disciplinary matrix: An emerging concept. *Police Quarterly, 15,* 62–91.

Stephens, D. (2011). Police discipline: A case for change. Paper prepared for the Harvard Executive Session on Policing and Public Safety, Kennedy School of Government, Harvard University.

Terrill, W., & Ingram, J. (2015). Citizen complaints against the police: An eight city examination. *Police Quarterly,* in press.

Wagner, A. (1980a). Citizen complaints against the police: The complainant. *Journal of Police Science and Administration, 8,* 247–252.

———. (1980b). Citizen complaints against the police: the accused officer. *Journal of Police Science and Administration, 8,* 373–377.

Walker, S. (2001). *Police Accountability: The Role of Citizen Oversight.* California: Wadsworth.

Worrall, J. (2002). If you build it, they will come: Consequences of improved citizen complaint review procedures. *Crime & Delinquency, 48,* 355–379.

15 POLICING IN THE FUTURE

LEARNING OBJECTIVES

After reading this chapter, students should be able to:

1. List three themes that we suggest will guide the future of policing.

2. Explain three concrete steps that agencies can take to become more "democratic."

3. Describe four ways that technology is likely to improve policing in the near future.

4. Name three challenges of body-worn cameras for police agencies.

What will policing look like 10 years from now? 20 years? 50 years? While we do not have a crystal ball and cannot know for certain what the future holds, there are some current trends that we think will likely shape policing in the near and not-so-near future. For one, there is no doubt that technology will continue to play a significant role in the evolution of policing. Technological innovation is likely to touch almost every aspect of policing, from the uniforms that police officers wear and the tools that they carry to the way they communicate with members of the public and personnel in other agencies. Technology will improve how detectives investigate crimes and identify suspects, and it will help patrol officers to address community problems more efficiently and effectively.

Beyond technology, a renewed emphasis on democratic policing principles is likely to change the ways that officers are trained, how they interact with the public, and how we define, measure, and report police performance. Data will also continue to drive police operations and support. In this chapter, we describe some of these trends and envision what they might mean for police agencies, police officers, and the public. We center our discussions around four main themes: democratic policing, intelligence-led policing, partnerships, and technology. Students reading this chapter might consider how trends in these thematic areas may open new career paths not previously considered, as well as additional areas of study.

DEMOCRATIC POLICING—THE DEMAND FOR TRANSPARENCY AND ACCOUNTABILITY

As you learned in chapter 1, the principle concern of democratic policing is the behavior of police, not citizens. A number of recent high-profile incidents involving negative police–citizen interactions—particularly those in which officers killed citizens—have invigorated public debate about the need to scrutinize police behavior. These incidents, many of which were televised, have resulted in a public outcry for increased transparency and accountability. Police agencies must respond in a meaningful way or they risk (further) undermining their legitimacy in the eyes of the public. As we noted in Chapter 1, democratic policing is best viewed as a *process*—something that can never really be achieved, but something that we should constantly strive to demonstrate. We noted that democratic policing requires constant evaluation to determine whether policing is working toward the goals of transparency, accountability, and fairness. Thus, in a broader sense, when agencies are unresponsive to public concerns the process of democratic policing effectively becomes stalled, and we lose the ability to say that we are truly engaged in democratic policing.

One of the ways that agencies are responding is by equipping officers with wearable video cameras (body-worn cameras). A growing number of agencies have begun to test and deploy this relatively new technology. There are many significant challenges in drafting effective policies for the use of body cameras, ranging from general privacy concerns to technical concerns such as the storage and retention requirements for massive amounts of digital video. In response to the many high-profile incidents mentioned above, President Obama announced the availability of grants to law enforcement agencies to purchase body-worn cameras in 2015. And, while there are a growing number of studies examining the effects of body cameras on a variety of outcomes, the evidence remains somewhat mixed and we err on the side of caution by concluding that the impact of body cameras is really not yet known as this text goes to print. Yet body cameras have been a popular response, spurred in part by the availability of federal funding, public support for body cameras, and because it is relatively easily implemented, unlike some of the other changes discussed below.

In response to many high-profile incidents, many more officers are now wearing body cameras.

Another way that agencies are responding is by making more information available to the public, usually through the department's website. For example, Fullerton Police Department (CA) and Spokane Police Department (WA) have "accountability" pages on their department websites where they publish use-of-force investigation reports, policy manuals, and other items of interest (check it out here: http://fullertonpd.org/about/accountability.asp or https://my.spokanecity.org/police/accountability/). These agencies realize that there is little downside to making this already public information truly public, and it is likely that many more agencies will follow their lead in the future.

A few police leaders are starting to strategize the "long game" to proactively change the culture of policing rather than reactively addressing the consequences of past failures. As we mentioned in Chapter 1, a handful of forward-looking agencies have already begun to change how they train new police officers by emphasizing people skills in addition to tactical training. We expect more training academies will follow suit in the coming decade as citizens and politicians demand their police officers behave as guardians of democracy, rather than as warriors engaged in a battle with the citizens they serve. Agencies are also providing training on implicit bias and "soft" people skills to experienced officers as part of their in-service training requirements.

We are also starting to see a push toward developing new methods to measure police performance. Rather than continuing to rely on Uniform Crime Report data to compare cities on crime rates as an indicator of whether police are "doing a good job," a small number of agencies are starting to seek alternative methods to define and assess police performance. Currently, researchers affiliated with the National Police Research Platform are working with more than 100 local law enforcement agencies of various sizes to develop a new method of measuring police performance and public satisfaction with police. Among other things, this new measure aims to capture whether officers are practicing procedural justice principles (are fair, respectful, and unbiased) and providing appropriate victim support, as well as whether the public views the department as efficient, effective, and legitimate, and is willing to cooperate with police.

> **CHECK IT OUT!:**
>
> Want to know more. Check out the website: http://nationalpoliceresearch.org/

INTELLIGENCE-LED POLICING—INCORPORATING ILP THROUGHOUT THE AGENCY

In 2011, Jim Bueermann, President of the Police Foundation, made a bold prediction that every police department would have a resident criminologist by 2022 (Cohen McCullough & Spence, 2012). While we are still a few years away from that, your textbook authors and Bueermann all believe that intelligence-led policing will continue to grow and expand as technology becomes increasingly affordable for smaller departments. We expect that as analysts are able to provide useful information in near real-time, intelligence-led policing will become infused throughout local law enforcement agencies of all sizes. Bueermann proposes the next logical step is to co-locate crime analysts alongside dispatchers in police communication centers in order to provide real-time analysis as officers are en route to calls.

In the future, crime and intelligence analysis will become even more sophisticated and powerful as software programs are created to mine and extract data held in records management systems and other databases. As police budgets continue to shrink, analytics—the detection of trends and patterns in large datasets—will become increasingly important to police operations and responses. So will the people who can perform this type of analysis (this should be a cue for the reader—be sure not to rule out analytic careers in the justice sector, as this will likely be the largest area of employment growth in the very near future!). Similarly, predictive policing, which is now in its infancy, will grow as law enforcement agencies become familiar with the concept and build up their technological infrastructure to allow for such sophisticated approaches. These methods may not only improve crime prevention efforts, they may also have the potential to reshape personnel deployment and training.

FIELD PERSPECTIVES: THE FUTURE OF POLICING

Chief Jim Bueermann (Ret.)

INTRODUCTION

Our world is changing at an exponential rate. Almost everyone is aware of the social tension that exists today in many communities between the police and the people they are paid to "protect and serve." Smartphones, drones, and self-driving cars are all examples of disruptive technologies that have, and will continue to, change how we live and do business. As the economic divide between the "one percenters" and the rest of us increases there will be increasing pressure to level the economic playing field. Climate change and all it implies is the focus of most environmental debates. And finally, the political stalemate that results in little substantive action at the federal level—on almost any issue—has accentuated the importance of our political future.

Jim Bueermann

As our world changes, so too does policing. Policing is a complicated and nuanced activity that can produce—practically at once—both beneficial and tragically harmful outcomes. And the reality is that in the future, policing will be even more complicated. Effective policing in the future will require that police officers are more reflective of the communities they protect, are more highly educated, trained differently, use advanced technology and, with a clear intent, focus on building community trust and confidence in the police (and by association the rest of the criminal justice system).

While policing has perhaps never been more challenging than it is today, there are also more opportunities than ever to redefine policing's true purpose, leverage taxpayer investments in public safety, build a diverse society's trust and confidence in the police, leverage a wide breadth of technological advances to increase police effectiveness, and control crime and disorder in a scientifically based manner that is "smart on crime."

THE PURPOSE OF POLICING

The "spirituality of policing" is gaining increased attention among thoughtful police and community leaders. This spirituality refers to an agnostic, philosophical, perhaps even a metaphysical orientation to the "true" purpose of policing and encourages a move from traditional indicators of policing such as the number of arrests to a purpose-driven approach focused on reduced community harm and increased safety.

A policing organization intent on finding its true purpose will have to do so in conjunction with the community it serves. Asking community members what outcomes they want from their "perfect" police department, for example, forces police leaders to re-examine, and perhaps "re-position" the department's mission from a traditional one of "To Serve and Protect" to one that encompasses an outcome-driven approach such as "Controlling Crime Before it Occurs." This latter example requires the organization to learn and focus on preventative and interventive skills and strategies to accompany its traditional crime suppression approaches.

In the future, policing organizations will embrace the spirituality of policing and align their structure, policies, and practices with their "true" purpose and desired outcomes that are less about enforcing the law and more about facilitating a healthy, safe, and sustainable community where the police use respectful, constitutionally correct and equitable strategies—even when enforcing the law.

THE "NEW" BUSINESS OF POLICING: COST REDUCTION AND BUILDING COMMUNITY TRUST

In almost every municipality the policing function is the most expensive function of its general fund. As the cost of policing continues to rise, and the budgets for other tax-payer-funded governmental functions such as paving roads, trimming trees, and operating recreation programs are reduced to pay for public safety, community outcry and political sensitivity will increase. As such, there will be changes in the "business of policing" that mirror many of the strategies employed in the private sector to control costs and increase profits with increasing efficiency. And they will be required to develop a laser-like focus on outcomes (e.g., community harm reduction) rather than the production of outputs (e.g., number of arrests made, tickets written, etc.). This outcome-based approach will allow agencies to move away from the highly suspect officer-to-population staffing models that currently drive operating costs.

In the near future police organizations will be under increasing pressure to civilianize, regionalize, or privatize portions of their now-sworn-officer workforces. These include custodial responsibilities (jailer, not custodian), crime analysis, aviation support, minor crime and traffic accident report taking, and computer services. Police agencies will be forced to reduce their drain on the General Fund by utilizing civilian volunteers, "crowdsourcing," focusing on business analytics in the same way the private sector has to "measure what matters," and regionalize or consolidate many functions like SWAT, forensic services, narcotics task forces, and dispatch/call centers. The use of regional SWAT teams is especially pertinent given America's on-going discussion of police militarization.

To achieve all of their "new" desired outcomes, policing leaders will have to increasingly focus on organizational development. They will have to create agency cultures that are conducive to becoming a "learning organization" in which evidence-based policing becomes a primary operating principle. They will have to allow for greater workforce participation in framing organizational equity/fairness initiatives and moving their organization from a "warrior" to a "guardian" orientation.

In the future, communities will demand that a key metric for gauging police performance is the extent to which the police are viewed as trustworthy and whether their practices and behavior are considered legitimate. To do this, policing leaders will have to engage their communities at a much deeper level to "co-produce" public safety. They will need to consider public input on identifying the desired core competencies of "their" police officers and identifying the acceptable parameters for crime control strategies. In addition, they will have to dramatically increase the level of transparency and accountability measures they employ—especially as they relate to police use-of-force. Increased training in implicit bias, de-escalation of force, effective communication and multicultural sensitivity will soon carry as much emphasis in the development of police officers as traditional "officer safety" training does today.

Finally, as a way of developing trust and confidence in the police, the public will increasingly demand that the police are using the best available scientific evidence to drive their control of crime and disorder. In 1998, criminologist Lawrence Sherman put forth the notion of "Evidence Based Policing" to capture the movement toward the police use of science. This "smart on crime" approach has generated an increase in both the research about the methods the police use to control of crime and the police interest in that science. In the future, community leaders will increasingly demand that the police demonstrate that their strategies are evidence-based and not simply the result of political influence, tradition, or police bias.

TECHNOLOGY

There will be an increasing police reliance on a variety of technologies in the future. From data to body cameras, drones to less-lethal tools, police officers will increasingly be tied to technology to be more efficient, effective, and responsive to their communities' needs. Challenges police leaders will face as technology advances include understanding the "human side of technology," identifying and avoiding the unintended consequences of new technologies, addressing the increases in cost associated with new technologies, balancing public safety needs with privacy concerns (e.g., "just because we can do it, doesn't mean we should"), and maintaining the connection between their organizations and their communities to mention just a few.

In the future, information management, big data, open data, predictive analytics and all things social media will make police officers true "knowledge workers." The amount of data potentially available to policing agencies in the future is staggering. Public safety organizations will have to develop the capacity to acquire and manipulate the data and understand the ethical considerations in using it.

CONCLUSION

The future of policing will be increasingly more complicated and will demand policing organizations demonstrate a clear understanding of their local "purpose," are more reflective of the communities they protect, are more highly educated, train their officers differently, use advanced technology, and, with an articulated intent, focus on building community trust and confidence in the police.

Jim Bueermann is the president of the Police Foundation. He retired from the Redlands Police Department (CA) in 2011 after serving the department for 33 years, 13 as chief of police and director of Housing, Recreation and Senior Services. As chief, he developed a holistic approach to community policing and problem solving that was recognized as one of the country's 25 most innovative programs in the 2000 Innovations in American Government program sponsored by Harvard's Kennedy School. He currently sits on policing advisory boards at numerous universities and previously was an executive fellow with the US Department of Justice's National Institute of Justice and a senior fellow at George Mason University.

PARTNERSHIPS: NEW AND RE-ENVISIONED

Police partnerships can serve many purposes. In the future, tight budgets will push agencies to investigate and enter into partnerships that were once considered to be unconventional. In particular, we expect to see even more civilianization, especially in areas of the country that have been slow to embrace this trend, and in specialty assignments that require a specific set of skills or knowledge but do not require peace officer powers. There will be more regional partnerships between agencies of all sizes to address special problems and situations such as gangs, human trafficking, terrorism, and tactical operations units (SWAT). We may see more consolidation between multiple law enforcement agencies, as well as between law enforcement agencies and other public safety departments (such as fire and/or ambulance service), as municipalities strive to conserve limited tax revenue.

Both budgets and technology will aim to expand partnerships between law enforcement and community members. For example, we expect that many agencies will begin or renew efforts to recruit volunteers to serve in a variety of capacities, including as reserve police officers and on community safety patrols. Additionally, law enforcement agencies are increasingly reaching out to community members to provide information to identify suspects and solve crimes. While many police agencies have a long tradition of seeking the public's help when a crime has occurred, social media has made this easier than in the past, and personal security cameras have made residents and business owners more likely to have obtained useful evidence. This leads us to the role of technology in shaping the future of policing partnerships and practices.

TECHNOLOGY AND COMMUNITY POLICING: CHANGING THE CO-PRODUCTION OF CRIME CONTROL

The theme of community policing, and its emphasis on citizens as co-producers of crime control, is taking on new meaning with technology. How citizens interact with the police is changing, with more and more community members using their cell phones and tablets to keep tabs on and communicate with their local police officers. Although community policing has historically placed a high value on increasing face-to-face contact between police and members of the public, many community members now choose, and in some cases prefer, to interact with officers digitally. Police agencies are adapting to this new world and many have Facebook groups, Twitter feeds, Instagram, and even Snapchat. Some agencies even do "tweets by beat" whereby the neighborhood beat officer tweets activities during her shift.

Technology is also making it easier and more convenient for members of the general public to partner with police in the co-production of crime control. For example, some citizens are using their cell phones to record or take pictures of suspicious persons and activity. Others have home security systems that alert them to intruders or record all activity around the house. Recently we have seen victims take to social media with pictures of thieves stealing packages from their front door or entering their homes in hopes of retrieving their stolen items and finding the perpetrator. Some victims have watched thieves in their home and called police while the burglary was in progress. The 2013 Boston Marathon bombing is another example of the power of partnership. In this case investigators requested that members of the public provide any pictures or video they took of the surrounding area during the race. These public-provided photos proved invaluable in identifying the suspects and the destructive device.

Surveillance camera operating on city road

© Vasin Lee/Shutterstock.com

TECHNOLOGY: IMPROVING COMMUNICATION FOR FIRST RESPONDERS

NG-911 systems will allow dispatchers to receive texts as well as calls to better communicate in certain emergency situations.

In February 2012, President Obama signed a bill to establish and fund a Nationwide Public Safety Broadband Network (NPSBN). This will "provide a secure, reliable, and dedicated interoperable network for emergency responders to communicate during an emergency" (DHS, 2012). This encrypted set of interoperable radio frequencies share a platform that allows local, state, and federal law enforcement agencies and other first responders to communicate with each other during emergencies, or even routine events. It should dramatically improve communication and allow local agencies to forge new partnerships and collaborations with neighboring agencies.

Additionally, Next Generation 911 systems (NG-911) will be a big improvement for communicating with the public. Not only do these systems allow dispatchers to know, with more accuracy, where a caller is calling from, the newest systems that are currently being developed and tested will allow dispatchers to receive text messages from members of the public. This has many potential benefits. For example, it can enable the transmission of information in situations where a victim cannot speak near an offender. As another example, it can enable individuals with hearing or speech impediments to communicate quickly and effectively with dispatchers. The newest system has already saved at least two lives (PERF, 2014).

TECHNOLOGY AND INVESTIGATIONS: SPOTLIGHT ON EVIDENCE COLLECTION AND ANALYSIS

As more and more individuals are using their phones to record police encounters as well as suspicious persons and activity, police and prosecutors need to re-think what constitutes evidence. Instead of viewing evidence as something only collected by police, it is becoming more commonplace to recognize that citizens may have also collected useful evidence while witnessing an encounter or discovering a crime. During an investigation, police routinely request video footage from local businesses and sometimes review footage from traffic cameras; however, few police think to ask community members for evidence they might have collected pertaining to a crime at a specific location at a specific time (such as cellphone video/pictures or home security camera footage). Investigators also rely on victims to enable tracking apps on their digital devices and alert police when their stolen device appears "online."

Some agencies are already using shot-finder technology that identifies the time and location of gunshots and alerts police. In the future, more jurisdictions will begin to use this technology as the evidence of its utility accumulates. Investigators are (or were) using Sting Ray technology to identify potential criminals using digital devices (there is currently a case before the US Supreme Court that may prohibit the use of this device by police without a warrant).

TECHNOLOGY: NEW TOOLS FOR PATROL OFFICERS AND SUPERVISORS

In chapter 3, you were introduced to Retired Sergeants Bill Donogue and Joel Davis. Donogue started his career on foot patrol in St. Louis, MO in 1956 with a revolver, a set of handcuffs, a ticket book, and a pocket notepad. Neither he nor his partner carried a handheld radio—if they needed help, they had to get to a call box or rely on the public to phone the police. When they made an arrest they had to call for a wagon and wait. Fast forward almost 25 years to 1980 when Joel Davis began his career in Irvine, CA, much had changed. Davis, like Donogue, started his career with a pen and notepad, revolver, handcuffs, and a ticket book, as well as a few other tools including a map book. Unlike Donogue, however, Davis also had a radio in his patrol car and was sometimes able to carry a handheld radio with him when he left his vehicle. News outlets and private citizens routinely monitored the police radio for activity and sometimes showed up before he did. Officers starting their careers today have personally assigned portable radios for their use on duty and, in many parts of the country, have the luxury of using an 800 MHz encrypted radio frequency that cannot be heard by the public. But that's not all that changed.

After a few years the mounted notepad in Davis' patrol car was replaced with an MDT (Mobile Data Terminal) that displayed call information and allowed him to run a drivers' license and warrant check on subjects he encountered in the field. Eventually, the MDT was replaced with a laptop that could be used to write reports and much more (not all officers are lucky enough to have such fancy equipment—many agencies still use MDTs or MDCs [Mobile Data Computers] in patrol cars). Before long, those laptops are likely to be replaced with tablets that will allow officers greater mobility and functionality. While some agencies and states have already created apps that allow officers to access subject and call information, as well as other information, from their smartphones (for example, the Redlands, CA, police department was an early leader in this area), in the future we expect more agencies and states to do this and for the apps to become even more useful. There will even be apps that allow supervisors and others to manage tactical operations from their smartphones or tablets.

We also anticipate seeing officers in the near future wearing "smart body armor" that is capable of monitoring an officer's heart rate and other vital information, as well as compression vests that can detect a stab or gunshot wound and apply pressure until medical help arrives. We envision real-time personnel monitoring aimed at knowing when and where officers are experiencing physically and psychologically stressful situations, and possibly initiating backup response before it is even requested (and in cases where it can't be requested). Of course, a broad variety of other wearable technology outside of law enforcement is also on the horizon, which may have law enforcement applications.

THE PROMISE AND CHALLENGE OF VIDEO CAMERAS

As previously indicated, many police departments are embracing body-worn cameras as a tool for increasing accountability (and in some cases, transparency). Despite the expected benefits, the technology comes with its share of challenges, including data storage and retrieval. If you take digital videos you are aware that they require a lot of storage space. Consider for a moment the amount of space a department needs to store one week's worth of video for a 10 patrol officer department. Given that there are 168 hours in one week and there are at least two officers on patrol at all times, this agency would need storage space for up to 336 hours of video each week. If the agency chooses to store videos for six months to one year, that means this small department may need to store between 8,736 and 17,472 hours of video. That would require a server with many terabytes of storage capacity (imagine the needs of much larger departments!). Of course, police departments need to keep this data safe and secure, which means that they either need to store the video on a hard drive that is not connected to a network, employ a computer expert with the necessary skills and invest in the security technology that would minimize external intrusions, or they need to partner with a third-party vendor to provide those services. Cloud-based solutions, while logical, are still being viewed with some degree of skepticism as this book goes to print, but we anticipate that will change rapidly.

For many police departments it makes sense to partner with a third-party provider (such as evidence.com and Amazon) for security reasons. Thus, there will be a greater need for third-party evidence storage providers in the future. These repositories will take responsibility for storing and securing data. In addition, they will be the ones responding to FOIA (Freedom Of Information Act) requests (per each agency's specified policy). Since these requests can become very burdensome and resource-heavy for police departments, this is a logical and likely cost-effective solution.

Viewing footage is a time-consuming process that also needs to be addressed. There will be a need to augment video review techniques and increase automated processes. Developing computer algorithms to identify potential problem encounters will be a goal for technology companies and police departments and will lead to new jobs in video analytics. Footage could also provide valuable information for officer training. It is also plausible that the police-recorded video could provide a database of images for facial recognition software to find wanted persons or suspects. Video footage could eventually be streamed to real-time crime centers over the NPSBN. As you can see, this is likely to be a rapidly growing area, in need of some talented individuals with strong computer skills. Do you know anyone like that?

CONCLUSION

While we have to admit that we don't know what policing will really look like in 10, 20 or 50 years, we think the areas discussed above are pretty safe bets. For students thinking about post-graduate careers (or current career changes), rest assured, employment opportunities in law enforcement, and criminal justice generally, will continue to grow. For those interested in careers as law enforcement officers, history shows that over the long-term you can expect about 1.3% growth annually. Of course there will be "dry" years and "wet" years, but on balance, law enforcement employment has historically grown at that rate for the past few decades. Patience and a willingness to re-locate are the keys to success in landing a career as a law enforcement officer. .

We hope that this book has opened your eyes to some other opportunities as well. Don't rule out an analytic career if that interests you. Not only will there be future growth in crime analyst and intelligence analyst positions, but these jobs will likely experience greater civilianization in the near future. Law enforcement agencies are beginning to recognize that it is in general a far better use of resources to hire individuals with the requisite analytic skills and teach them about law enforcement on-the-job, than it is to take a trained and experienced law enforcement officer and turn them into an analyst. This is not to say that law enforcement officers-turned-analysts are not highly valued personnel—they certainly are, and that's the traditional way of staffing those positions—but the crime analyst position has changed dramatically in recent years and has become increasingly technical, requiring specialized skills in statistics, research methodology, crime mapping, database management, and so on. A mix of highly trained civilians and experienced officers is probably optimal, but there will undoubtedly be increased employment opportunities for direct-hire civilian analysts.

Finally, we hope that by now a central theme of the book has become crystal clear: The future of democratic policing depends on our willingness to engage in the process of democratic policing. This applies to law enforcement agencies and citizens alike: citizens must remain motivated to demand accountability, transparency, and fairness from law enforcement agencies and their personnel, and law enforcement agencies must accept that their own behavior is the central focus in a democracy. Don't rule out career opportunities in law enforcement oversight agencies, such as investigator positions or, if law school is on your horizon, legal positions. We realize that this is not a "traditional" career path in criminal justice, or one that students necessarily consider or aspire toward, but law enforcement oversight is absolutely essential—every bit as essential as law enforcement itself, and perhaps even more so.

REFERENCES

Cohen McCullough, D. & Spence, D. (2012, September). *American policing in 2022. Essays on the future of a profession.* Washington, DC. United States Department of Justice Community Oriented Policing Services. Retrieved from: http://www.cops.usdoj.gov/Default.asp?Item=2671

Department of Homeland Security (DHS) (2012, June). Office of Emergency Communications Fact Sheet: Nationwide Public Safety Broadband Network. Retrieved from. http://www.dhs.gov/sites/default/files/publications/Fact%20Sheet_Nationwide%20Public%20Safety%20Broadband%20Network.pdf

Police Executive Research Forum (PERF) (2014). *Future trends in policing.* Washington, DC: Office of Community Oriented Policing Services.

GLOSSARY

Abuse of authority misuse of power by an officer in the course of duty.

Accountability a condition that exists when the police acknowledge behaviors that the public views as a violation of their trust, and the police seek to either explain or correct the identified problems in a timely manner.

Accountability a condition that exists when the police acknowledge behaviors that the public views as a violation of their trust, and the police seek to either explain or correct the identified problems in a timely manner.

Ballistics the scientific identification of firearms and bullets.

Banishment orders orders that combine civil and criminal processes and penalties to reduce social disorder in defined places. Also known as civil orders.

Biased policing making a choice to stop, cite, or arrest a person based on the person's race, ethnicity, gender, sexual orientation, economic status, or other personal trait.

Bill of Rights the first 10 Amendments to the Constitution of the United States of America.

Biometrics a method of authenticating a person's identity through behavioral or physiological characteristics such as iris scanners and fingerprinting.

Bow Street Runners paid constables who investigated crimes, served warrants, and performed other tasks for the Bow Street magistrates.

Broken windows policing a method of policing based on the broken windows theory that focuses on reducing low level disorder and disorderly behavior in order to reduce serious crime.

Broken windows theory a theory proposed by James Q. Wilson and George Kelling in 1982 that proposes that unkempt areas invite additional disorder and serious crime.

Broken Windows theory a theory proposed by James Q. Wilson and George Kelling in 1982 that proposes that unkempt areas invite additional disorder and serious crime.

Centralization includes spatial centralization, but also refers to centralization of decision-making authority (and therefore, discretion) exercised at different units and supervisory levels of the organization.

Citizen oversight defined by Samuel Walker as a procedure for providing input into the complaint process by individuals who are not sworn officers; can take a variety of different structural forms.

Civil gang injunctions a police suppression program that involves getting a court order to prohibit gang members from being in particular places, with specifically named people, and/or engaging in specified prohibited activities.

Civil orders orders that combine civil and criminal processes and penalties to reduce social disorder in defined places. Also known as banishment orders.

Clearance rate the measure that is often used to assess the effectiveness of the police; it compares the number of cases closed by arrest or exception to the number of crimes reported.

Code of Hammurabi a set of laws written by the King of Babylon around 1750.

Coerced-compliant false confession a suspect who confesses to a crime in response to extreme interrogation methods; the suspect believes that confessing to the crime will result in a more positive outcome than continuing to tell the truth.

Coerced-internalized false confession a suspect who confesses to a crime because he/she has been convinced (incorrectly) of their guilt.

Community constable a man, appointed by a nobleman, who supervised the volunteer tythingsmen in a hundred.

Community Policing a policing philosophy that focuses on building community partnerships to reduce and prevent crime and improve police—community relations.

Community-Oriented Policing a policing philosophy that focuses on building community partnerships to reduce and prevent crime and improve police–community relations.

Compstat an intelligence-led approach developed by NYPD in the mid-1990s that entails holding middle managers accountable for crime and other performance indicators in their area.

Compstat an intelligence-led approach developed by NYPD in the mid-1990s that entails holding middle managers accountable for crime and other performance indicators in their area.

Computer-Aided Dispatch an automated computer system that assists police dispatchers receive calls for service, then assign and manage responding officers and information.

Computer-aided dispatch an automated computer system that assists police dispatchers receive calls for service, then assign and manage responding officers and information.

Consent decree a type of settlement following a pattern or practice investigation in which the parties typically agree to a set of required reforms, as well as the appointment and role of a monitor who will oversee the reform process on behalf of the court.

Constable a local law enforcement officer who was responsible for collecting taxes and enforcing ordinances in the colonial and post-colonial period United States, similar to sheriff; constables today are typically law enforcement officers in small towns.

Crackdowns short-term, intensive operations that target an unwanted behavior and usually include a lot of arrests and/or citations.

Crime analysis The analysis of crime data and other sources of information by police personnel for the purpose of targeting responses to reduce crime, catch a perpetrator, or otherwise improve the efficiency or effectiveness of police.

Crime mapping a process of using a geographic information system to conduct spatial analysis and investigation of crime.

Crime Prevention Through Environmental Design (CPTED) crime prevention strategy that attempts to reduce crime by altering the environmental conditions that present criminal opportunities.

Crime trend analysis A type of analysis that involves analyzing specific types of crime looking for patterns. it is often called crime pattern analysis.

Criminalistics using scientific methods to collect and analyze physical evidence in criminal cases.

Crisis intervention team (CIT) specially trained officers who responded to mental-health related calls.

Decentralized the idea that law enforcement authority is spread both within and across levels of government, as opposed to a single centralized law enforcement authority.

Democratic policing a model of policing that is consistent with, and supports, the basic tenets of a democratic government; recognizes that the police derive their authority from the people and are therefore accountable to the people for fulfilling the important role of protecting life, liberty, and property, and doing so by enforcing the laws while also obeying the laws; best viewed as an ongoing process (rather than an achievable end) in which law enforcement agencies constantly strive to demonstrate transparency, accountability, and fundamental fairness.

Department of Homeland Security an agency created by the Homeland Security Act of 2002 whose mission is to protect the homeland by preventing and reducing the country's vulnerability to terrorist attacks, as well as minimizing damage, assisting in recovery, and acting as a focal point for crises and emergency planning. (KH)

Department of Justice a department within the executive branch of the federal government designed to enforce the laws of the United States. (KH)

Differential response a method of triaging calls for service in which the most urgent calls are dispatched first.

Digital evidence items related to a criminal case that can be found in a computer, cell phone, tablet, or other electronic device such as a camera.

Directed patrol spending an allotted amount of time patrolling a specific area of the community that is considered to be a high-crime area.

Discovery crime crimes that are discovered by the victim after the suspect fled the scene.

Dispatcher a person who answers emergency and non-emergency calls for police services from the public and coordinates the movements of officers in the field.

Division of labor the idea that employees are organized into work units based upon specialized skills.

DNA Profiling a forensic science procedure that uses variations in the genetic code to identify individuals.

Documentary evidence items related to a criminal case that provide information about or document activities or transactions affiliated with a crime.

Early warning systems a means used by police leadership to identify a potentially problematic officer before his or her behavior becomes very serious. Sometimes called Early Intervention Systems.

Evidence-based policing policing strategies proven effective through social scientific research.

Evidence-based policing policing strategies proven effective through social scientific research.

Excessive force level of force used by an officer on an individual that is considered to be more than was appropriate or necessary.

Exclusion orders orders that ban a named person from a specific place within a jurisdiction for a defined period of time.

Exclusionary rule US Supreme Court ruling that any evidence seized by police in violation of the Constitution cannot be used in court against a defendant.

Fairness referring to fairness in the distribution of justice; policing that is objective, unbiased, and consistent.

Federal law enforcement agencies responsible for enforcing particular categories of federal law and/or providing law enforcement services (such as custody and security functions) for particular federal jurisdictions.

Federal pattern or practice investigation a civil rights investigation carried out by the Special Litigation Section of the Civil Rights Division of the US Department of Justice; these investigations focus on police departments that may be engaging in unconstitutional "patterns or practices" of conduct, typically centered on the use of force, racially discriminatory policing, and procedural violations.

Focused deterrence a proactive policing strategy that uses the legal system and available social services to encourage identified individuals to refrain from committing crime. Also known as pulling levers.

Force factor a single value describing the proportionality of officer force relative to suspect resistance.

Fragmented a consequence of our decentralized system of government, our tradition of local control, and our historical population growth and expansion; generally refers to the problems of overlapping physical and legal jurisdictions, duplication of effort, lack of standardized practice with regard to recruitment and selection, training, policy, and management, and inefficiency particularly with regard to the coordination of agencies.

Frankpledge a communitarian system of law enforcement in England between 1066 and 1285.

Fruit of the poisonous tree doctrine US Supreme Court ruling that any evidence obtained by law enforcement as a result of an illegal search or seizure is inadmissible in court, as is any additional evidence obtained after the illegal search; it is an extension of the exclusionary rule.

Functional differentiation describes the extent to which an organization has created subdivisions of specialized labor that are focused on a particular task.

Fusion Center an information sharing center that allows federal, state, and local law enforcement personnel to collaborate to assess potential terrorist threats and implement corrective action.

Gang graffiti words, numbers, and symbols that provide information on the gang claiming a given territory and their relationship with other gangs; considered to be the "newspaper of the streets."

Gideon v. Wainwright 1963 US Supreme Court case which established that indigent defendants accused of felonies in state courts have a right to counsel provided for them.

Good faith exception an exception to the exclusionary rule that allows evidence from an invalid search warrant to be presented in court, provided the police acted in good faith.

Grass eaters those police officers who engage in relatively passive forms of inappropriate behavior by accepting small favors or money for looking the other way when illegal activities are taking place.

Hierarchical differentiation refers to the levels of supervision in an organization.

Hierarchy of authority the idea that an organization is characterized by the vertically higher-level supervision of lower-level employees.

Hot spots policing a proactive approach that devotes police resources to reduce crime or other problems at small geographic places based on crime, calls for service, or other data.

Hundred a geographic grouping that consisted of ten tythings in ancient England.

Inevitability of discovery exception an exception to the exclusionary rule that allows illegally obtained evidence to be used if police can prove that it would have been discovered eventually as the result of legal investigative procedures.

Intelligence analysis A type of analysis that focuses on the relationships between persons and organizations involved in illegal activity. It is often referred to as network analysis or link analysis.

Intelligence-led policing a policing practice that uses crime intelligence and criminal intelligence to reduce and prevent crime.

Intelligence-led policing a policing practice that uses crime intelligence and criminal intelligence to reduce and prevent crime.

International Association of Police Chiefs an association of police chiefs, formed in 1893, to advance the police profession.

Interrogation a formal conversation between a police investigator and a crime suspect in which the purpose is to determine the suspect's involvement in the crime and elicit a confession; often takes an accusatory tone in the United States.

Interview a formal dialogue between a police officer or investigator and an individual who has knowledge of or is potentially associated with a crime (for example suspect, victim, or witness); the goal is to gather information about the individual's knowledge of and/or potential involvement in a crime under investigation.

Investigative analysis A type of analysis that provides insight in the type of criminal and his/her motivation for committing a crime. It is also known as criminal profiling.

Involvement crime crimes in which the victim is confronted by the suspect.

Kansas City Preventative Patrol Experiment the first study conducted on the effectiveness of random patrol in the early 1970s.

Kerner Commission presidential commission formed to investigate the causes of the urban riots in the 1960s. The commission, which published its official report in 1968, was officially known as the National Advisory Commission on Civil Disorders.

Kin policing practice in which a family, clan, or tribe enforces customary rules and socially defined norms of behavior.

Knapp Commission commission created to investigate allegations of widespread corruption in the NYPD in the early 1970s.

Law Enforcement Assistance Administration a body created by the 1968 Omnibus Crime Control and Safe Streets Act to serve as a federal resource for local law enforcement agencies.

Law enforcement activities performed by peace officers that are directly related to enforcing the law and controlling crime.

Legalistic style a police style, proposed by James Q. Wilson, in which the primary focus is on the law enforcement function of policing; interactions with citizens are regular and formal; the law is the primary determinant of whether and how officers respond to situations, and there is emphasis on issuing citations and making arrests.

Lexow Committee a committee formed to investigate allegations of corruption within the New York Police Department in the late 1890s.

Local Police Department operated by municipal or township governments (about 98% of all local departments), as well as those operated by county, city-county, and tribal governments, and regional or joint entities; these are generally the most visible law enforcement agencies and personnel, serving cities and towns and providing the primary response to calls for service in those communities.

Mapp v. Ohio 1961 US Supreme Court case that extended the exclusionary rule to the states and articulated the "fruit of the poisonous tree" doctrine.

Meat eaters police officers who are more aggressive in their illegal behavior and actively search for ways to make money illegally while on duty.

Medjay paramilitary police force in ancient Egypt that protected Egyptian towns and other valuable areas.

Mercy booking arresting an individual for the purpose of accessing services (for example, food, shelter, medical care, treatment).

Militarization the increasing use of military equipment, technology, and personnel in policing since the 1980s.

Minneapolis Hot Spot Study a study conducted during the mid-1980s which found that crime is not evenly distributed and that focusing patrol resources on the specific places that produce the most calls for service effectively reduces crime.

Miranda rights the obligation of police officers to inform suspects of their right to remain silent and their right to an attorney.

Miranda v. Arizona 1966 US Supreme Court case that established the Miranda rule which requires police officers to advise suspects of their constitutional rights.

Multi-jurisdictional task force an efficient way to pool agency resources to both provide a service to several agencies that could not otherwise be provided by any single agency, as well as to address crime and public safety issues that are multi-jurisdictional in nature (such as gangs, drugs, human trafficking, and other regional issues).

National Incident-Based Reporting System (NIBRS) a national crime data collection program created and implemented during the 1980s in an effort to enhance the methodology for collecting, analyzing, and publishing crime data.

Natural rights rights imbued to individuals as part of their personhood, generally life, liberty, and property.

Newark Foot Patrol Experiment a study conducted during the late 1970s that tested the effects of different levels of foot patrol on crime, arrest rates, citizen attitudes, and officer attitudes.

Next Generation Identification (NGI) a database of digitized fingerprints, palm prints, and photos held by the FBI; it is the largest fingerprint database in the world.

Occupational deviance criminal and non-criminal behavior committed under the guise of police authority or in the course of normal police activity, including corruption and misconduct.

Occupational differentiation describes the extent to which labor is subdivided among work tasks, some of which require very little specialized knowledge or skills, and those that require a higher degree of specialized knowledge or skills.

Occupational stress mental or emotional strain that results from circumstances that develop in or are related to a person's workplace or occupation.

Off-limits orders orders requiring an individual to stay away from a specified geographic area as a condition of probation or parole.

Officer decertification the process by which a state authority determines that a law enforcement officer should not be allowed to continue exercising the duties and privileges of a law enforcement officer. Decertification essentially invalidates an individual's training credentials and makes them unemployable as a law enforcement officer in that state.

Omnibus Safe Streets and Crime Control Act of 1968 a highly influential act passed by Congress that created the Law Enforcement Assistance Administration, provided grants for law enforcement personnel, education, training, equipment, and research.

Operational analysis The analysis of department data for the purpose of deploying department resources most effectively to reduce crime or achieve other operational goals

Operations analysis A type of analysis that examines how department resources are deployed. It is sometimes called administrative analysis.

Order maintenance activities performed by peace officers that promote and orderly and peaceful society.

Parish constable system system of English law enforcement created by the Statute of Winchester in 1285.

Peace Officer Standards and Training organizations (usually state-level) that set eligibility and training standards for peace officers.

Physical evidence any physical item that can be seen or felt and is related to a criminal case.

Police cynicism an attitude that develops among officers that they must be skeptical of all people and can trust no one.

Police discretion decision-making authority of officers to choose a course of action based on suspect, situational, and contextual factors.

Police Executive Research Foundation an independent research organization founded in 1976 devoted to critical issues in policing.

Police Foundation an organization established by a Ford Foundation grant in 1970 to advance policing through innovation and science.

Police integrity defined by Carl B. Klockars as the normative inclination among police to resist temptations to abuse the rights and privileges of their occupation.

Police legitimacy the extent to which we recognize and are willing to defer to the authority of the police to regulate behavior.

Police legitimacy the extent to which we recognize and are willing to defer to the authority of the police to regulate our behavior; can be conceptualized as falling along a continuum ranging from strong to weak, with the position along the continuum being determined by both police behavior and the public's perception of that behavior.

Police paramilitary unit a dedicated unit originally formed to deal with dangerous confrontations, but increasingly used in everyday policing. Also known as SWAT. (KH)

Police power the power to regulate behavior through the enactment and enforcement of laws.

Police subculture the accepted norms, values, attitudes, and practices shared by law enforcement offices.

Posse comitatus townsmen who were summoned by the sheriff to help regain order during the colonial period; in Latin, "power of the county."

Praefectus Urbi also known as urban cohorts, three cohorts of 500 men that patrolled the streets of Rome during the day to keep the peace starting in 13 BC.

Praetorian Guard nine cohorts of 500 men that protected the city of Rome and the emperor starting around 27 BC.

Predictive policing an emerging strategy that uses computer software to model historical crime data in order to predict future crime events.

Preliminary investigation evidence-gathering activities performed at the scene of a crime immediately after the crime was reported to or discovered by the police.

President's Commission on Law Enforcement presidential commission formed to investigate law enforcement practices and the effects on citizens. The commission published its report, titled The Challenge of Crime in a Free Society, in 1967.

President's Task Force on 21st Century Policing presidential task force appointed to address police-community relations concerns in the wake of questionable police shootings of suspects in 2014–2015.

Preventative patrol patrolling the community on an unpredictable and routine or random basis.

Primary prevention prevention programs that target an entire population without discerning which individuals are at elevated risk of committing criminal activity.

Private Police non-governmental entities that may provide services that public police in some jurisdictions are otherwise unable to provide, such as spending additional time and attention on specific community concerns, *addressing quality of life i*ssues, and perhaps even helping to build the sense of community.

Problem-oriented Policing a method of policing developed by Herman Goldstein in 1979 that broadens the role of police and involves identifying and addressing the root causes of problems.

Problem-Oriented Policing a method of policing developed by Herman Goldstein in 1979 that broadens the role of police and involves identifying and addressing the root causes of problems.

Procedural justice the idea that the process by which decisions are made should be fundamentally fair, which is very important to the formation of citizen's attitudes about both specific interactions and generally toward the police; four key aspects of procedural justice include: citizen participation (or "voice"); perceived neutrality on the part of the police; police treating all parties with dignity and respect during the interaction; and whether the police convey trustworthy motives.

Protective factor biological, psychological, family, social, and environment factors that decrease the risk that an individual will commit delinquent/criminal acts.

Public safety exception an exception to the exclusionary rule and the 5th Amendment protection against self-incrimination that allows officers to use information and evidence obtained by questioning a suspect prior to advisement of his/her Miranda rights if the concern for public safety is so great as to outweigh adherence to the rules.

Pulling levers a proactive policing strategy that uses the legal system and available social services to encourage identified individuals to refrain from committing crime. Also known as focused deterrence.

Pulling levers A suppression/intervention strategy that threatens gang members with heavy legal consequences if they engage in violence and simultaneously offers social services to gang members who refrain from violence.

Quality of life policing NYPD Chief Bratton's version of broken windows policing, first instituted in 1994. It later became known as zero tolerance policing.

Quasi-military organization refers to a military-like structure; a hierarchical rank structure with a unified chain of command.

Racial profiling selection of individuals based solely on the race or ethnicity of the person or group.

Random routine patrol the practice of police officers randomly driving around their beat, hoping to discourage criminal activity through visibility.

Real-time crime center centralized technology and analysis centers that use advanced data mining, analytic, and forecasting software and high-tech tools to provide near-real-time information to police personnel.

Reasonable force the acceptable amount of force that officers can use when subduing a suspect or making an arrest.

Reasonable suspicion a reasonable belief, based on objective factors and officer experience, that a crime has been or is about to be committed; it is the standard of proof that is necessary for officers to stop a suspect and/or conduct a search.

Records Management System a computer system that stores pertinent information on crimes, suspects, victims, and other incidents and can be searched and queried.

Regional intelligence center an information sharing center that allows federal, state, and local law enforcement personnel to collaborate to assess potential terrorist threats and implement corrective action. Also called Fusion Center.

Reid technique the most common interview and interrogation method in the United States.

Risk factor biological, psychological, family, social, and environmental factors that put an individual at increased risk of committing delinquent/criminal acts.

Rotten apple corruption theory that states that individual officers within an organization are corrupt, not the entire organization. Corrupt officers are referred to as "rotten apples."

Rotten orchard a large group of corrupt officers (such as a unit or station)

Rotten pockets small groups of corrupt officers within an organization.

Rule of law the idea that laws should govern behavior and decision-making; addresses the behavior of citizens as well as those in power.

SARA acronym for scan, analyze, respond, and assess—the four stages of the problem-oriented policing strategy.

Saturation patrol a dramatic and sudden increase in patrol officers in a specific area to increase police visibility and deter potential criminal behavior.

School resources officer (SRO) a sworn police officer assigned to a school or set of schools as part of his/her normal duties to act as a liaison and address student misbehavior and criminal behavior.

School-to-prison pipeline the term used to describe the trend of school officials referring student misbehavior to law enforcement officers for formal criminal justice system processing, rather than traditional school discipline.

Secondary investigation investigation conducted by detective to identify suspects and prepare a case file for prosecution.

Secondary prevention Prevention programs that target individuals deemed to be at an elevated risk of committing criminal activity.

Service style a police style, proposed by James Q. Wilson, in which *police interact with* citizens regularly and seek to provide a response to all citizen requests, but these interactions tend to be less formal and officers tend to avoid arrest.

Service activities performed by peace officers that are considered a public or community service.

Sheriff a local law enforcement officer who was responsible for collecting taxes and enforcing ordinances in the colonial and post-colonial period United States, similar to a constable; sheriffs today serve as law enforcement officers at the county level.

Sheriff's Office almost all traditional counties and parishes in the United States have a sheriff's office; typically provides traditional law enforcement functions, but also provides court-related services (such as process serving and court security), and about three-quarters of them also operate jails.

Shire reeve a man, appointed by the King of England, to maintain order, enforce laws, and collect taxes within a shire.

Shire geographic area roughly equivalent to a county in the United States.

Situational crime prevention crime prevention strategy based on routine activities theory that focuses on making it harder to commit a crime or reducing the rewards for committing a crime.

Slave patrols police-like groups in the South in the colonial era that focused on regulating the activities of slaves. Vigilante justice—the taking on of law enforcement responsibilities and the dispensing of punishment by private citizens; the precursor to modern policing in the south.

Span of control the number of subordinates a supervisor can effectively supervise.

Spatial differentiation refers to the extent to which the organization's territorial coverage is divided up into localized units.

Special Weapons and Tactics team (SWAT) a paramilitary policing unit originally formed to deal with dangerous confrontations, but increasingly used in everyday policing. (KH)

Specialization the idea that employees train in and specialize in a particular type of work or area of focus.

State police each state has a state law enforcement agency that provides general law enforcement services; often identified as the "State Police," "State Patrol," "Highway Patrol," or "Department of Public Safety," they may have very different specific responsibilities making comparisons difficult.

Stipendiary policing the early practice of private policing in England.

Stop and frisk The police practice of stopping and detaining a "suspicious" person for further investigation. It may include a superficial pat down of the suspicious person's body and clothing for contraband, weapons, or other items if an officer can articulate reasonable suspicion that the person committed a crime or is a threat to public safety. The term has also been associated with New York City's aggressive style of policing that focuses on conducting these stops in high crime areas.

Stop and frisk the police practice of stopping and detaining a "suspicious" person for further investigation. It may include a superficial pat down of the suspicious person's body and clothing for contraband, weapons, or other items if an officer can articulate reasonable suspicion that the person committed a crime or is a threat to public safety. The term has also been associated with New York City's aggressive style of policing that focuses on conducting these stops in high crime areas.

Strategic analysis The analysis of department data to inform department policies and strategies.

Suppression programs aimed at reducing the influence of gangs in a community.

Symbolic assailants an individual whose dress, behavior, and gestures indicate suspicion and possible danger to a police officer.

Tactical analysis The analysis of crime and other data to support officers working front-line assignments.

Tagging artistically painted pictures, words, and symbols generally considered to be vandalism but which are usually intended to be enjoyed as art by the "artist"; it is often confused with gang graffiti.

Team policing a method of policing developed in England during the 1970s that involved a team of officers assigned semi-permanently to a specific neighborhood; a pre-cursor of community-oriented policing.

Terry stop The standard for allowing police officers to stop and search suspicious persons as defined in Terry v. Ohio.

Terry v. Ohio 1968 US Supreme Court case that granted police officers the right to stop and question a person they reasonably suspected of being involved in criminal activity and also conduct a limited pat down of the detained person if the officer reasonably suspected the person to be in possession of a weapon.

Tertiary prevention intervention programs that target individuals already engaged in repeated or serious delinquency.

Testimonial evidence knowledge and memories provided by victims, witnesses, suspects, and key others about a crime or suspect.

Thief-takers men who were paid to recover stolen property, identify and capture criminals in the middle ages in England.

Transparency the idea that the police should be accessible and open to public scrutiny, and that they should make clear how decisions are made and with what results.

Trespass affidavit programs a program whereby private property owners sign a document authorizing a law enforcement agency to enforce trespass laws in the property owner's absence.

Trespass laws allow private property owners to limit access to their property.

Tything a volunteer group of men from 10 families living near each other who were sworn to uphold justice.

U.S. v. Davis 2014 11th Circuit Court of Appeals case that ruled that investigators need a search warrant to obtain cell phone location data for a suspect.

Uniform Crime Report (UCR) an official data-reporting tool created in 1930 to provide uniform definitions of crimes and annual summaries of crime and arrest data for the vast majority of local and state law enforcement agencies in the United States.

USA Patriot Act a Congressional act passed shortly after the September 11, 2011, terrorist attacks in the United States, focusing primarily on providing law enforcement with legal authority to support efforts to fight terrorism. (KH)

Vigilance committees groups of individual citizens who administered justice on their own during the colonial period.

Vigiles individuals who fought fires and kept watch during the night in Rome starting in 6 AD.

Violent Crime Control and Law Enforcement Act of 1994

Volstead Act of 1919 an act that amended the constitution of the United States and prohibited the sale and manufacture of alcohol. Also known as Prohibition. It was repealed in 1933.

Voluntary false confession a suspect who voluntarily confesses to a crime to gain fame or notoriety, protect another person, or because they (due to a mental or psychological condition) are unable to discern reality from fantasy.

Watchman style a police style, proposed by James Q. Wilson, in which police have relatively less frequent interaction with citizens, there is very little emphasis on arrests, and the primary focus is on the order maintenance function of policing; officers exercise great discretion in determining what should be done, if anything.

Weeks v. U.S. 1914 US Supreme Court case that established the exclusionary rule and prohibited illegally obtained evidence from being used in Federal trials.

Wickersham Commission a presidential commission that published the first national comprehensive report on the state of the American criminal justice system in 1931. It focused much attention on law enforcement's concerns about Prohibition.

Zero tolerance policing an aggressive style of policing focused on eliminating disorderly behavior through a high number of arrests and citations. Based upon the broken windows theory, it was first instituted in New York City in the late 1980s to early 1990s.

Zero tolerance policing an aggressive style of policing focused on eliminating low level disorder and disorderly behavior, based upon the broken windows theory. It was first instituted in New York City in the late 1980s to early 1990s.

INDEX

CPSIA information can be obtained
at www.ICGtesting.com
Printed in the USA
LVHW05s0854110718
583368LV00002B/2/P

9 781465 291